A
QUESTION
OF
MANHOOD

BLACKS IN THE DIASPORA
Darlene Clark Hine, John McCluskey, Jr.,
and David Barry Gaspar

GENERAL EDITORS

A
QUESTION
OF
MANHOOD

A Reader in U.S.

Black Men's

History and Masculinity

VOLUME 2

The 19th Century:
From Emancipation to Jim Crow

Edited by
Earnestine Jenkins and Darlene Clark Hine

INDIANA UNIVERSITY PRESS   BLOOMINGTON & INDIANAPOLIS

This book is a publication of

Indiana University Press
601 North Morton Street
Bloomington, IN 47404-3797 USA

http://iupress.indiana.edu

Telephone orders   800-842-6796
Fax orders   812-855-7931
Orders by e-mail   iuporder@indiana.edu

© 2001 by Indiana University Press

The paper used in this publication meets the minimum requirements
of American National Standard for Information Sciences—Perma-
nence of Paper for Printed Library Materials, ANSI Z39.48-1984.

Manufactured in the United States of America

Library of Congress Cataloging-in-Publication Data

A question of manhood : a reader in U.S. Black men's history and
masculinity / edited by Darlene Clark Hine and Earnestine Jenkins.
p.   cm. — (Blacks in the diaspora)
Includes bibliographical references and index.
Contents: v. 1. Manhood rights
v. 2. The 19th Century
ISBN 0-253-33639-2 (v. 1 : alk. paper). — ISBN 0-253-21343-6
(v. 1 : pbk. : alk. paper)
ISBN 0-253-33924-3 (v. 2 : alk. paper). — ISBN 0-253-21460-2
(v. 2 : pbk. : alk. paper)
1. Afro-American men—History. 2. Masculinity—United States—
History.   I. Hine, Darlene Clark.   II. Jenkins, Earnestine.
III. Series.
E185.86.Q46   2001
305.38'896073—dc21   99-24464

1 2 3 4 5 06 05 04 03 02 01

In memory of my father,
World War II veteran Levester Clark (1921–1983)
—Darlene Clark Hine

In memory of my grandfather,
World War I veteran Garvin Fouse Sr. (1893–1983)
—Earnestine Jenkins

CONTENTS

PART TWO: "TO OWN OUR OWN LABOR": BLACK MEN, ECONOMIC SELF-SUFFICIENCY, AND WORKING-CLASS CONSCIOUSNESS

PART THREE: BLACK MEN, THE PROFESSIONS, AND FRATERNAL ORGANIZATIONS

PART FOUR: PROVING BLACK MANHOOD: THE ALLURE OF SPORT AND THE MILITARY IN THE LATE NINETEENTH CENTURY

PART FIVE: END-OF-THE-CENTURY ARCHETYPES: SYMBOLIC CONSTRUCTIONS IN BLACK MANHOOD AND MASCULINITY

FOREWORD

BILL STRICKLAND

In 1897, a little more than a century ago, W. E. B. Du Bois, fresh from the Herculean task of sociological investigation that would result in *The Philadelphia Negro*, delivered a paper before the American Academy of Political and Social Science in which he urged a longitudinal study of "the group of social phenomena arising from the presence in this land of eight million persons of African descent." Du Bois justified this research on the grounds that "the phenomena of society are worth the most careful and systematic study and whether this study may eventually lead to a body of knowledge deserving the name of science, *it cannot in any case fail to give the world a mass of truth worth the knowing*" (my emphasis).

In the publication of this second volume of A *Question of Manhood*, Darlene Clark Hine and Earnestine Jenkins have taken up the cause espoused so eloquently by Du Bois so long ago. They have cast the historical net widely, and with care, bringing to the surface, as Du Bois predicted, some insights which may not as yet have attained the stature of established "truths," but are nevertheless suggestive of hypotheses "worth the knowing."

Using the lens of gender, this anthology takes us into a nineteenth-century world both old and new, triumphant and downtrodden; a world where Peter Jackson is not permitted to fight for the heavyweight championship of the world, and where the feats of other black champions of his time, such as jockey Isaac Murphy and cyclist Major Taylor are conveniently dropped down what George Orwell in his novel *1984* dubbed "the memory hole."

It is a world where a black baseball team may beat a white team only at its peril, and where black men newly mustered out of the Union Army may be killed for real, imaginary, or anticipated "effrontery." It is also a world where black women may be beaten and raped solely because of their real, imaginary, or suspected association with these military "sons" of "Father Abraham." This world of perpetual menace and perpetual threat circumscribed the lives, hopes, behavior, and world view of the black men whose fifteen decades of history are thematically portrayed in the two volumes of A *Ques-*

tion of Manhood. But there is also another world, another space that black men have inhabited, and the editors have guided us into this world as well.

In this more autonomous sphere, young black men like Calvin Lindsey Rhone successfully court their sweethearts, marry, raise a family, and educate themselves and their children. In this world, black lawyer James Milton Turner straddles the two political parties like a black mini-Colossus — securing, after a protracted legal and political struggle, the government subsidy due the black former bondsmen of the Cherokees.

Focusing on the impact of gender on the plight of nineteenth-century black men, Darlene Clark Hine and Earnestine Jenkins usher us into the brittle worlds of black men across time and space — men from different classes; men who live in different regions, represent different levels of educational attainment, and subscribe to different religions, or to no religion at all. They belong to different political parties and pursue different careers. They are doctors and lawyers and politicians, policemen, soldiers, musicians, and cowboys. They are unimaginably abused convict laborers, and routinely discriminated-against railroad workers. They are not a monolithic group. But they do share one overriding reality in common: They must contend against a system of racial privilege that is fluid, dynamic, and resilient in its ability to change the rules, rewrite the laws, disown the meaning of language (as in "freedom," "democracy," and "equality"), and alter the agenda in order to preserve and uphold racial advantage. The challenge, therefore, of — and to — their manhood was to try to survive and even, somehow, to prevail against the ever-present possibility of victimization.

This struggle may be interpreted from the point of view of gender, because white men have constructed a society that reflects their image, interests, and values. But in such a racially constructed society, race and gender are often, if not always, conflated: each signifying a reinforcing power that leaves those on the outside bereft of status, identity, potency, and rights. Thus the struggle of black men for self and gender cannot, in the final analysis, be meaningfully separated from the struggle of black people itself.

Nowhere is this dual identity/responsibility more clearly seen than in the famous 1863 Civil War recruitment call by Frederick Douglass and others:

> *Men of color. To arms!* in which black men were told it was, *now or never . . . fail now and our race is doomed. . . .* For generations we have suffered under the horror of slavery, outrage and wrong, *our manhood has been denied,* our citizenship blotted out, our souls seared and burned, our spirits cowed and crushed, *and in the hopes of the future of our race involved in doubt and darkness. . . .* (My emphasis)

Forty-three years later, in 1906, the Douglass appeal for black men to take up military arms was echoed at the second annual gathering of black men and women of the Niagara Movement, held at Harper's Ferry, Virginia, the site of John Brown's historic raid. Only this time black men were called upon to take up *political* arms, not against a slave-owning South, but against a rights-denying, vote-depriving, lynching-ignoring Republic.

Led by W. E. B. Du Bois, the men and women of Niagara II asked, "*In the name of ten million* the privilege of a hearing." They stated, "We will not be satisfied to take one jot or tittle less *than our full manhood rights. . . .* We claim for ourselves *every single right that belongs to a freeborn American,* political, civil, and social; and until we get these rights we will never cease to protest and assail the ears of America" (my emphasis).

Though the equality and citizenship claims of Niagara were framed in terms of "manhood rights," the intent—like the assemblage—was manifestly racially and gender-inclusive. That is why the history of black men, examined within the context of America's racial history, cannot fail to be mindful of its gender-inclusive political dimension. For only then can that history be accorded its full significance.

In the years from Douglass to Du Bois, an evolution of sorts occurred in the historic role of black men, which was symbolized by the Niagara Declaration. This bold racial manifesto went beyond the traditional boundary of race to appropriate the grandeur and moral authority of the American Democratic Ideal itself. But it also reached out to fair-minded white Americans—even as it condemned their morally negligent nation for its indifferent attitude toward the besieging of black people.

> The battle we wage, it is said, is *not for ourselves alone, but for all true Americans: it is a fight for ideals,* lest this, our common fatherland, false to its founding, become in truth the land of the Thief and the home of the Slave—a byword and hissing among the nations for its sounding pretensions and pitiful accomplishments. (My emphasis)

In the dawning twentieth century, black men thus expanded their salvatory role from race to nation. They reaffirmed their Americanness and propounded their claim to all the prerogatives associated with the American Heritage. At the same time, they demonstrated a new readiness to criticize America as their notions of how to attain "manhood rights" evolved from a quasi-innocent hope in America's willingness to truly embrace its darker native sons—and daughters—into a more radical critique of America's racial failings.

A decade before Marcus Garvey crossed the sea to America, and twenty years before Malcolm X was born in Omaha, Nebraska, we see the seeds of consciousness subsequently identified with the "New Negro" in the plowed ground of militancy out of which will come the next stage of black men's struggle—and, presumably, the next volume of *A Question of Manhood.*

PREFACE

DARLENE CLARK HINE AND EARNESTINE JENKINS

Class, race, and gender: These pivotal categories of analysis have come to permeate our view of the world in the second half of the twentieth century. Now, as the century comes to an end, the last of them is finally being applied to our view of the past. In the past few decades, the field of women's studies has caused a conceptual shift in scholarly thought, focusing for the first time on gender as a crucial category of historical analysis. Women's historians have shown that gender is as important as race and class in understanding the past and comprehending modern society, and historians in all fields have been forced to acknowledge that men not only are as influenced by their gender as women, but have actively participated in a history of gender construction, shaped by certain prevailing notions about what it means to be a man in American society and culture.

However, although there is no dearth of historical studies concerning individual "great" men—and/or the world viewed from a generic male perspective—few have examined men as gendered beings, whose lives and actions have been shaped by specific constructs of masculine identity and manhood. Historian Bruce Dorsey declares in the journal *Radical History Review* (1996) that the main task before historians of gender is the "intellectual quest to engender all of American history," and men's studies has only recently begun that task. Most of men's studies is situated in the present and, having been very much influenced by the feminist movement, is concerned with modern-day male behavior, in particular the ramifications of white male dominance and its legacy. It is necessary now for historians to demonstrate how concepts of manhood have been subject to change over time. Throughout American history, social, economic, and political changes—along with race, class, and even sexuality and region of birth—have all influenced the development of gender systems.

At present, there still exist only a few dozen monographs that have attempted to add a historical context to men's studies. Among the representative and innovative works are Peter Stearns's *Be a Man! Males in Modern*

Society (1979); *Him/Her/Self: Sex Roles in Modern America* by Peter Filene (1986); *The American Man*, edited by Joseph and Elizabeth Pleck (1980); and *Manhood in America* by Michael Kimmel (1996). Stearns deals with how the roles of middle- and lower-class men have changed since the eighteenth century, concluding that industrialization created more rigid gender roles for men and women. Filene analyzes masculine behavior from the late nineteenth century to the present in the context of the family, work, war, sexuality, and social reform movements. *The American Man* offers a new periodization, dividing men's history into Agrarian Patriarchy (1630–1820), the Commercial Age (1820–1860), the Strenuous Life (1861–1919), and Compassionate Providing (1920–1965). Kimmel's work examines the changing culture of masculinity, suggesting that being required to "prove" manhood eventually became a dominant theme in American history. He goes on to describe how this particular idea paralleled the rise of capitalism in U.S. society, leading to the construction of a hegemonic manhood bereft of a strong inner self and making manhood into a "possession" that males are forced to "acquire."

The methodologies and topics covered in these texts are indicative of the direction in which historical men's studies is headed, influenced significantly by social history. In the past, traditional historical scholarship focused on the public accomplishments of great men, a perspective that marginalized or even obscured certain groups of men and women. This view also negated the importance of collective identities and group action on the part of those who were considered minor players in American history. Contemporary men's studies has begun to investigate the experiences of working-class men, as well as the middle class and the elite. This social-historical approach has highlighted the role of gender in class formation and the politics of power. It has revealed the existence of hegemonic masculinities lying at the heart of social distinctions that are divisive within groups of men and groups of women, even as they divide men from women.

Social history has also focused our attention on race. As a result, the field of men's studies has begun serious research into the life experiences of African American men. Actually, few groups have received as much public scrutiny as black men. This is understandable, given that being black and male in America has always been, as social philosopher Kenneth Clatterbaugh says in *Contemporary Perspectives on Masculinity* (1997), a "sociopolitical issue." Unfortunately, however, past and present scholarship has been obsessed with black men as a sociological ill. Since the early twentieth century, academe has been influenced by schools of thought that portray black people as America's great social problem, drawing attention away from the real culprit, racial oppression. Within that theoretical framework, the few contemporary academic studies on black men have for the most part been written by those outside their experience, who see only the impact of historical oppression, drugs, imprisonment, fatherlessness, and unemployment. It is no surprise, then, that black manhood has been stereotyped as negative and dismal. In *Slim's Table: Race, Respectability, and Masculinity*, sociologist Mitchell Duneier admits that sociological research has produced invaluable insights into the lives of black men. But he describes how the discipline has also contributed to one-dimensional images of the black man as hustler and criminal, navigating his way through the mire of the urban ghetto. These contemporary images of a negative, self-destructive black masculinity tend to validate historical assumptions about black men as violent, oversexed, ignorant, and immoral. Certainly there should be serious concern about the status of all groups of black men and women in American society, but to present only the negative is simply not historically accurate. What it means to be a black man in America cannot be reduced to the sum total of negative experiences and stereotypes.

A Question of Manhood: A Reader in U.S. Black Men's History and Masculinity is a wide-ranging exploration of the history of African American men from a gendered perspective. We need to examine black male behavior in response to the dynamics of slavery and racial oppression across regions and centuries. The essays in this anthology analyze how black masculinities were constructed to resist the dominance of white middle-class male identity. However, it is well to underscore that the evolution of black manhood has been more than a history of public contests between white men and black men. Clearly, by the early National era black men were born into existing slave and free communities and cultures, where they first learned about manhood from other black men and women, family members, friends, and the community. The process of constructing a viable black manhood continued in the decades following emancipation. Just as the examination of black women's history and womanhood proved to be of transformative significance, the study of black men's history and manhood is enormously instructive and will greatly facilitate the ongoing project of reconstructing American history.

ACKNOWLEDGMENTS

The second volume of A *Question of Manhood* was as much a pleasure to complete as was the first volume of this project. We benefited enormously from the assistance and support of a special group of friends and colleagues.

We begin by recognizing the critically important contribution made by Linda Werbish, assistant to Darlene Clark Hine. Linda typed all the charts and graphs of the articles included and served as an overall manager for this two-volume reader. Joan Catapano remained fiercely committed to this project and provided just the right spark to keep us on schedule. We continue to derive inspiration and energy from the wonderful graduate students of the Comparative Black History Ph.D. program at Michigan State University who helped with the research, photocopying, and critical readings of our essay: Kenneth Marshall, Julia Robinson-Harmon, Jacqueline McLeod, Hilary Jones, Marshanda Smith, and Matthew Whitaker. We appreciate the insightful comments of William Strickland. We treasure the support of our families.

INTRODUCTION

> We are highly gratified by the appellation by
> which the colored soldiers are addressed by their
> officers, viz: *men*; and we urge the colored men in
> all places, at all times, and under all circum-
> stances to cease using that vulgar phrase, "nigger."
>
> —BLACK SOLDIERS STATIONED IN MEMPHIS, 1863

Black men and women irrefutably staked their claim for freedom during the
Civil War. However, black people did not experience freedom as an ideal. It
was a "lived" struggle. Everyday racism, political terrorism, the failure of
Reconstruction, and the onset of legal segregation toward the end of the
nineteenth century, all marred the era of emancipation.

This second volume of *A Question of Manhood: A Reader in Black Men's
History and Masculinity* continues to focus on gender, examining the tumultuous period following the Civil War through the end of the nineteenth
century from the perspective of African American men. The writings included in this volume touch on themes in the lives of black men such as
leadership, work and the professions, family and community, sports and the
military, and the image of black men in the larger society.

The essays in Part One are studies in the evolution of African American
political leadership. After emancipation, black men and women looked to
singular individuals for guidance as they faced the exhilarating, and often
inhospitable, challenges that freedom had wrought. Most of these essays
explore black men's political leadership in Reconstruction politics. However, black soldiers, having most recently fought on the front lines of battle,
occupied a deserving place in the minds of black Americans as natural
leaders. Kevin R. Hardwick therefore leads off this section with "'Your Old
Father Abe Lincoln Is Dead and Damned': Black Soldiers and the Memphis
Race Riot of 1866," a discussion of black soldiers as leaders in a black urban
community after the Civil War. Thousands of freed people migrated to

Memphis because of the presence of black troops in the city. Former slaves, with reason, saw uniformed, armed black men as their protectors. Hardwick argues that black soldiers seriously began to accept this view of themselves and to conduct themselves accordingly. They were not above drawing their arms in response to threats from white policemen, advising former slaves against unscrupulous white landowners, and protecting their women and children from the aggression of white people. Hardwick's emphasis on the manner in which one postwar black urban community began to construct grassroots leadership reminds us of the importance of scholarship from the inside out. Freedmen and -women were clearly developing some well-defined beliefs and values concerning leadership.

William C. Hine and Richard Lowe inquire into black Reconstruction politics. These case studies, based respectively in South Carolina and Virginia, are focused on the local level. One of the more insightful lines of thought in both essays is how class functions in the construction of leadership. In the past, scholarship assumed that black Reconstruction politicians were invariably of mixed heritage, and a class removed from the people they actually represented. To some extent, this may be an accurate appraisal of black political leadership on the national level, but it does not hold true for local politics.

In "Black Politicians in Reconstruction Charleston, South Carolina: A Collective Study," Hine illustrates that most black politicians in the state of South Carolina were identifiable as such (based upon census records), instead of as mulatto. More significant, though, is Hine's discovery that free status before the war played more of a role in the career success of black politicians than color consciousness among their black constituents.

Lowe's case study, "The Freedmen's Bureau and Local Black Leadership," investigates how white agents working for the Freedmen's Bureau in Richmond, Virginia, identified those whom they perceived as the state's local black leaders. Lowe also found that free status was a factor in the selection of leaders. White bureau agents overwhelmingly selected mixed-race black men who had been free before the war. However, their list of leaders did not correspond to the men that black Virginians identified as political leaders in their local communities. Former slaves predominated as leaders in Virginia's local towns and cities.

In "For Justice and a Fee: James Milton Turner and the Cherokee Freedmen," Gary R. Kremer investigates the activities of a black politician named James Milton Turner, who was a respected educator, orator, and lawyer in his community. Former slaves living with the Cherokee nation in Oklahoma asked Turner to lead the fight for their civil rights in Indian territory. This piece enlarges our understanding of relations, both friendly and acrimonious, between freed blacks and Native Americans, some of whom were former slave owners. While James Milton Turner engaged in some political maneuvering that caused his attackers to label him an "opportunist," such as aligning himself with the Democrats, he facilitated the passage of a bill that gained the Cherokee freedmen their full tribal rights.

The studies in Part Two address issues related to black men's labor history. The dominant theme here is black men's transition to wage-earning work. The Civil War exacerbated anxieties about American manhood and challenged white America's stereotypical notions about black people and work. It is a well-documented fact that most blacks ended up in the sharecropping system by the end of the 1870s. Sharecropping was yet another traumatic system of inequality. Still, emancipation marked black men's introduction into the American workplace as paid workers. African Americans gained their freedom as the country was poised to become a world economic power, and was experiencing the pains of urbanization, industrialization, and technological innovation. The family farm, with its independent male head, was beginning its slow, inexorable decline. The essays in this section examine black men in the labor force in contexts other than sharecropping. Moreover, they illuminate how black and white men interacted and competed for jobs that white men often claimed as theirs only.

In "Black Policemen in New Orleans during Reconstruction," Dennis C. Rousey focuses on post–Civil War New Orleans, where black men emerged as some of the country's first policemen of color. Rousey cites the influence of the Radical Republicans, but also analyzes the historical and class differences between whites, mulattos, and blacks in the city that affected the extent of freedom and opportunities for work available after the war. The New Orleans police department hired members of the city's free Creole or mulatto population, but not former slaves. It was the Creole population's long history of freedom and participation in military service that made it possible for this group to pressure the Republican party and the federal government to integrate the police force.

Kenneth W. Porter's essay, "Negro Labor in the Western Cattle Industry, 1866–1900," reintroduces us to the history of the African American cowboy. Its detailed attention to the everyday experiences of the black men who worked the cattle trails out west remains unique in the scholarship. Contemporary popular culture glamorized the cowboy as the romantic icon of the American West. In reality, cowboys performed extremely dirty, arduous, and dangerous work, the type of job that the average middle-class American male would not have chosen as a profession. Cowboying was work done by poor whites, former slaves, Mexicans, and immigrants.

Cowboys were men of diverse racial and ethnic backgrounds, who worked under the auspices of the Texas Trail Drivers Association, and as such formed the cornerstone of a major post–Civil War industry. During the height of the cattle industry, from 1866 to 1895, they were responsible for herding cattle over western trails, and for the daily maintenance of ranches. Approximately 9,000 of the estimated 35,000 American men who rode the western frontier were African American. In this early experiment in integrating the American workforce, the average outfit consisted of two black males, along with seven whites, one Mexican, and one white trail boss.

Porter points out that despite the relative equality, independence, and equal pay, racism and segregation affected black male workers in the cattle industry. Black men worked all positions, but white males sought to maintain their authority and leadership roles by relegating black males to the lower-ranked jobs. Blacks were rarely placed in the top-level position of trail boss, or foreman over a cattle ranch. White men claimed that black cowboys lacked the prerequisite intelligence and capabilities. Most important, they explained that even if black men possessed such skills, white men would not follow them as leaders, or respect them as authority figures.

The black farmer and landownership is the subject of Manning Marable's essay, "The Politics of Black Land Tenure, 1877–1900." Like most Americans, freedmen and -women associated the ownership of property with economic security and middle-class respectability. In spite of a great desire to obtain land, by the late 1870s black people were increasingly trapped in the exploitative and oppressive sharecropping system. Marable describes how a small group of black agricultural workers eventually began to acquire land. These landowning black farmers were the origins of what Marable defines as the southern, rural, black middle class. One of the most interesting aspects of this study is its connection of the emergence of this particular class to late-nineteenth-century developments in black community building. African American landownership was made possible by the black banks and other businesses that loaned black farmers money, and by the black agricultural institutions that trained them, so that they could compete with white farmers.

In "'Like Banquo's Ghost, It Will Not Down': The Race Question and the American Railroad Brotherhoods, 1880–1920," Eric Arnesen zeroes in on white racial attitudes and discrimination directed toward black male workers in the railroad industry. In presenting the other side of racism—why and how a certain group practices this type of social behavior—the author reveals the highly "functional" nature of racism. Arnesen shows that racism has historically provided white American workers with what he describes as a "non-quantifiable advantage," or "psychological wage." No matter how disadvantaged white workers might be, they possessed advantages over black workers. Arnesen identifies the psychological function of racism as an effective way in which white males were able to construct race, to emphasize difference, and to protect their identity.

The last essay in this section, Alex Lichtenstein's "'A Constant Struggle between Interest and Humanity': Convict Labor in the Coal Mines of the New South," explores yet another dimension of black men's labor history. Growing out of the iron industry in Tennessee, Alabama, and Georgia, the coal-mining industry was built by exploiting cheap prison labor. Between 1870 and 1928, thousands of black male convicts performed forced labor in southern coal mines. The whites in charge of this brutal system whipped black men like slaves with a leather strap they called the "negro regulator." Yet black men devised ways to resist, such as feigning illness and developing indifferent attitudes about work performance. Sometimes they loaded freight cars with slate instead of coal, and in more extreme instances they would strike, trigger mine collapses, and commit arson. Eventually this system was replaced by the infamous chain gangs, which were particularly well suited to the goals of social control and suppression associated with Jim Crow. Black men were forced to toil on the South's state infrastructure, or road and rail systems. Their labor was also leased out to other businesses. Chain gangs were an unsettling image because they were reminiscent of slavery.

Sam Cooke, one of the architects of soul music, immortalized this aspect of the black male experience in America with his song "Chain Gang" (1960). In the biography *You Send Me: The Life and Times of Sam Cooke* (1995), author Daniel Wolfe writes that Cooke was inspired to compose the song while he and singer Jackie Wilson were touring the "Chitlin Circuit" down south in the 1960s. While driving past the endless red dirt fields, they saw "a dozen coal-black men dressed in eye-stunning pure white uniforms." They thought it was a striking picture until they got close enough to see the mounted guards with their double-barreled shotguns, and realized that the men were prisoners, chained ankle to ankle. Sam Cooke started writing the song immediately. When he returned to the RCA recording studios in Manhattan, Cooke hammered out a classic that was social commentary, a message song, and a lively dance tune that reached number two on the pop and r&b charts. Lichtenstein's purpose in researching black men and the penal system was twofold: to bring attention to a neglected episode in American history, and to note that these events are not only in the past, but remain with us still.

Part Three looks at African American men in the professions, their personal relationships, and fraternal organizations. In "A High and Honorable Calling: Black Lawyers in South Carolina, 1868–1915," J. R. Oldfield examines the experiences of black lawyers, while in "Entering a White Profession: Black Physicians in the New South, 1880–1920," Todd L. Savitt presents the difficulties that black physicians encountered during emancipation, Reconstruction, and Jim Crow. Both lawyers and physicians struggled to find schools that would admit them for higher learning. Ultimately, most black professionals in the South would be trained at what we now call historically black colleges. In addition, black professionals had to overcome the initial distrust and lack of confidence frequently exhibited toward them in the black communities they served. Circumstances demanded that they create internal systems of professional support, and strong "group allegiance" as well, in order to surmount the racial barriers at local, state, and national levels.

In "The Courtship Letters of an African American Couple: Race, Gender, Class, and the Cult of True Womanhood," Vicki Howard provides a rare glimpse of romanticism in her examination of the courtship between a young middle-class African American couple living in rural Texas in the 1880s. The letters that Calvin Lindsey Rhone wrote to Lucia J. Knotts during their nineteen-month courtship form the basis of Howard's investigation into the ways a black couple negotiated their respective gender roles before marrying in 1887. The letters reveal values and beliefs about men's and women's roles that parallel the larger society, yet exhibit conflict and resistance to white middle-class American culture. Diaries and letters written by blacks are scarce documents. Hence Howard's work brings a much-needed personal dimension to African American gender studies and history.

Calvin and Lucia reached a crossroad in their relationship when they addressed Calvin's expectations that Lucia would adopt an entirely domestic role after the marriage. His position was in conflict with Lucia's desire to continue her college education and to work outside the home as a teacher. Calvin soon gave in to Lucia's wishes. According to Howard, their concerns and decisions were directly related to African American culture, community, and history.

She describes how economic necessity usually required that working-class and middle-class black women work outside the home after marriage. Among the middle classes, the ideology of racial uplift was a factor as well. Black men and women viewed the skills derived from a "career-oriented education" as a necessary means of survival for the black family and community. Black women's educational training was a recognized asset. It was an unaffordable luxury for a black woman to pursue an education, then abandon her hard-won skills, because of attempts to fit in with certain white, middle-class notions about class, work, and womanhood. Neither were black men in a position to demand black women's complete subordination to the "cult of true womanhood, " when women had performed the same fieldwork as males during slavery. Black women's educational work was viewed as a "mission," and of invaluable benefit to the race as a whole.

Betty M. Kuyk's "The African Derivation of Black Fraternal Orders in the United States" addresses similar ideas about community and benevolent work. Gender-based organizations have historically been an important expression of self-respect and identity, and an important opportunity for black men and women to provide leadership and community service. These associations fulfilled political, economic, and social functions in black communities. Members of the associations collectively built banks, founded businesses, started newspapers, created educational opportunities, and provided black politicians with a political base. In the past, scholars have attributed the origins of black male associations to white male organizations. Kuyk, however, searches for their origins closer to home, in West African brotherhoods.

Kuyk's research is especially interesting in its analysis of religious, class, and cultural similarities and differences. But her strongest argument may be her assertion that the functions of the chief, the priest, and the father are traditional African male gender roles, social patterns of behavior and cultural expression that remain deeply embedded in African American male organizations, particularly secret societies and fraternities.

Kuyk finds that rites and rituals in African and African American all-male organizations revolve around the expression of strong religious beliefs and practices, and place equal emphasis upon the election of elder and respected male figures, whose role is to provide experienced spiritual and moral leadership. No official meeting of a secret society or fraternity can take place without the presence of a priest in the African context or a minister in the American setting to lead the recitation of prayers and blessings or the singing of religious songs. The elder members elected to serve as father figures offer advice, counsel, and guidance to younger members of the group. It is no surprise that the highest-ranking officers in African and African American male associations tend to be priests and ministers.

Part Four looks at the influence of sports and the military on black men's perceptions about manhood in the second half of the nineteenth century. In "Peter Jackson and the Elusive Heavyweight Championship: A Black Athlete's Struggle against the Late Nineteenth Century Color-Line," David K. Wiggins relates the little-known story of a boxer who was probably the most internationally known black athlete of the late nineteenth century. Wiggins places Peter Jackson within the context of the other great black men of that century who struggled to participate in the sport on an equal playing field. Jackson followed in the footsteps of Bill Richmond and Tom Molineaux, ex-slaves whose boxing skills had gained them their freedom. Richmond migrated to England, which was then the center of the boxing world, where he became a notable pugilist. He was there to receive and train Molineaux, who left America for England in 1809. Molineaux became the first black man to have a shot at the heavyweight title when he fought Tom Crib, the British heavyweight champion. Molineaux lost the battle, but the 39-round fight is considered one of the most celebrated bouts in boxing history. It established Molineaux as the first in a long line of great black heavyweights.

By the time Peter Jackson arrived on the scene in the 1880s and '90s, he had to contend with America's growing intolerance for interracial sport. Boxing was just beginning to achieve popularity in the United States in the 1880s. The world heavyweight champion, John L. Sullivan, who fought bare-fisted in championship bouts, promoted the sport by touring the country and fighting all challengers. Sullivan, however, persistently refused to fight Jackson. Jackson's inability to arrange a championship fight for himself, according to Wiggins, makes for one of the most frustrating careers in the history of sports. While the other major black athletes of the late nineteenth century were able to compete and emerge victorious in their respective professions, Jackson was never allowed to fight for the greatest of prizes, the heavyweight championship of the world.

Wiggins suggests that increasing racism in American sports, segregation, and intolerance for interracial social contact all factored into America's unwillingness to see black and white fighters in the ring on equal terms.

Boxing became popular at a time when pseudo-scientific theories about race were strongly influencing social views. As a result, the sport emerged as a symbol of white Anglo-Saxon purity and racial superiority. In contrast to team sports, boxing pits an individual against his opponent in face-to-face, fist-to-fist, body-to-body combat. The man with superior skill and intelligence, strength, will, and bare-knuckle courage triumphs. When black men and race entered the arena in the nineteenth century, boxing became America's dominant metaphor for the racialized conflict between black and white men.

When Jack Johnson finally achieved the unimaginable by defeating Jim Jeffries in 1910 to become the world's first black heavyweight champion, he "took" something for men of color that white men had always believed to be theirs alone. Since then, the sports world has waited for a "great white hope" to appear on the horizon. Even the language used in boxing is reflective of the sport's racial and masculine symbolism.

Two recent events in the history of boxing have woven together the threads of American racism, championship boxing, and the icon of the heroic black male. When *USA Today* selected Muhammad Ali as "Athlete of the Century," many of the newspaper's readers found fault with the decision. They named other deserving candidates, among them Jim Thorpe, Babe Ruth, Jesse Owens, and Jackie Robinson. But none of those men seems to have possessed the combination of male virility, talent, and charisma, and the idea of the heroic individual male, that Ali's position as the fighter/boxer personified, as expressed in his public battles against racism and his refusal to participate in the Vietnam War.

In addition, Hollywood, which has produced several outstanding films about the theme of boxing in American culture, recently released *Hurricane*, the real-life story of Rubin "Hurricane" Carter, the middleweight champion who in 1967 was railroaded into prison on trumped-up murder charges. Carter spent twenty years in prison before he was freed. He, like Ali, was a black fighter whose outspoken behavior and bold racial male pride provoked white fear. Carter was able to endure his physical confinement in prison only through the development of an individual, austere inner strength, self-reliance, and the physical discipline that is most associated with the sport of boxing.

In their prime, Ali and Carter were feared and hated by many whites. Black fighters symbolized black men as conquerors. They beat white men at their own game with bare fists. In the double-faceted sport of American boxing, race pride and white racism are two sides of the same coin. It is interesting to note that when the ancient sport of boxing was revived in western Europe, specifically in England in the seventeenth century, it was popularized as a democratic sport, one that traversed acrimonious class divisions by attracting the avid interest of kings and paupers, elites and urban working poor. At the beginning of the second millennium, boxing's masculine mystique is associated with African American champions, and has become synonymous with the black heroic ideal.

"The Black Bicycle Corps" is an important contribution to the history of black men, sports, and the military. Marvin E. Fletcher writes of the history of the 25th Infantry, one of the four black regiments stationed west of the Mississippi after the Civil War. Better known as the Buffalo Soldiers, the 24th and 25th Infantries, along with the 9th and 10th Cavalries, guided and protected American settlers as they moved out west, and managed relations between the settlers and Native Americans as a peacekeeping force. The 25th was posted on the Texas frontier until the 1880s, when it was reassigned to Dakota Territory, and then to Montana eight years later. In the cold northern frontier, black soldiers assisted the homesteaders in relief operations, rescuing white settlers and domestic animals, who were often stranded in severe weather conditions. They delivered supplies to distant settlements, patrolled railroad mines during strikes, and even fought forest fires. One of their more unusual and little-known assignments was to test bicycles for military service. In the late 1880s, bicycling had become one of America's most popular pastimes, and the bicycle had been tested in Europe as a useful vehicle for transport services in the military. The U.S. Army's first experimentation with bicycles was carried out with black soldiers from the 25th Infantry.

Fletcher's essay recounts the range of racial difficulties that the bicycle squad encountered in the performance of their task. The corps' most challenging test occurred in 1897, when they rode 1,900 miles from Fort Missoula, Montana, to St. Louis. The trip lasted forty days, and took them through Montana, Wyoming, South Dakota, Nebraska, and Missouri. Although the military eventually decided that bicycles were of limited use, the experiment was considered a success: The 25th Infantry had more than demonstrated the feasibility of using bicycles in the field.

The Spanish-American War was the last major conflict of the nineteenth century. Piero Gleijeses's study "African Americans and the War against Spain" takes an innovative approach that focuses on the debate among black men about their participation in the war. Using black newspapers as his main source material, Gleijeses highlights the increase in segregation and racism during this period, especially the practice of lynching. The black press provided detailed coverage of the increased confrontations between black and white men during the last decade of the nineteenth century. Physical violence and confrontations escalated when black men appeared in uniform, a pattern witnessed in earlier periods. Not surprisingly, riots and accusations of rape against black men increased as well.

Black newspapermen who voiced their objections and resistance to military service were at the center of the controversy and turmoil. A. L. Manley, the founder and editor of Wilmington, North Carolina's, only black newspaper, *The Daily Record*, wrote an editorial that castigated white men for creating the myth of the black male rapist as an excuse for lynching. Like Ida B. Wells before him, he said that white women were usually the aggressors in relationships with black men. Manley boldly reminded white people of the "unpublicized crime of white men raping black women." In the riot that followed on November 10, 1898, white men burned the offices of Manley's paper.

In Part Five, aspects of late-nineteenth-century white terrorism provide a closer look at symbolic constructions of black manhood. "The Anatomy of Lynching," by Robin Wiegman, is pivotal research in this field. Scholars delving into the history of white terrorism have begun to unravel what Wiegman calls "the enduring power of the black male rapist mythos." This essay probes the psychological ramifications of black freedom and white terrorism. Weigman analyzes how the myth functioned to script the disturbing changes that occurred in racial relations in the United States during the late nineteenth century.

Brett Williams and George M. Eberhart search for the historical reality behind two of America's most enduring legends with black male protagonists. In "The Heroic Appeal of John Henry," Williams defines the character of the "steel drivin man" as exemplifying the heroic ideal. He attributes the story's steadfast appeal as well to its versatility. Ever since the legend's local beginnings in West Virginia and its close relationship to the country's railroad industry, John Henry has represented the American laborer, the railroad worker and history, the African American experience, American culture, and the family.

While the origins of John Henry remain unknown, Eberhart had more success in nailing down the origins of Stagger Lee. As he tells us in "Stack Lee: The Man, the Music, and the Myth," the American archetype for the "bad" black man can be traced back to an altercation between Lee Shelton, alias Stagger Lee, and Billy Lyons, which took place in St. Louis on December 25, 1895. Most of us are familiar with the ballad, but the facts surrounding the murder case are less widely known. Lee Shelton went to trial not once but twice for the murder of Billy Lyons. Why? Because the St. Louis community, familiar with the character of both men, believed that Shelton had acted in self-defense. The fascinating, little-known story of the trial connects the real-life events to political rivalries between black Republicans and black Democrats. Hence the shooting was viewed as a misunderstanding between two friends that escalated to murder, fueled by drink and political argument. Lee Shelton acted in self-defense. He was neither the murderer nor the "bad" black man that his metamorphosis into Stagger Lee made him out to be.

The last essay, "Where Honor Is Due: Frederick Douglass as Representative Black Man" by Wilson J. Moses, focuses on how that major American icon, Frederick Douglass, manipulated American ideals about "Anglo-Saxon manhood" in order to project his own image of the self-made man. Moses portrays Douglass as the ideal symbol of the black American male, because he was, in fact, quite typical of black men's experience. On one hand, Douglass was a slave who escaped, then became a member of a free class of black men who were literate and were guided by Christian principles in their thought and work. His ideas about manhood were influenced by other black males important in his life, including those who befriended him, those whose intellect and courage he admired, and those with whom he experienced conflict and disagreement.

This study's most important contribution, however, lies in Moses's perceptive analysis of Douglass's ambivalent actions and character. As much as he was admired, and unquestionably a man of courage, principle, and dignity, Douglass was equally self-serving and opportunistic, and made his way in the world by cultivating his own myth. Furthermore, he exhibited as much confusion and concern as any other black man about the explosive issues of his time. Among them, Moses identifies separation versus integration, Afrocentric ideology versus Eurocentrism, and the dynamics of male-female relationships. These same issues continue to confront black men and women today. In the final analysis, it appears that Frederick Douglass's very human, personal failings, as well as his triumphs, are the very things that make him a "Representative Black Man."

It is hoped that the two volumes of *A Question of Manhood: A Reader in Black Men's History and Masculinity* will contribute to the growing interest in African American masculinities. Much erroneous information about black men exists, and is widely circulated in the popular media. Most of it depicts black men as negligent, criminal, and genetically prone to violence. But we have chosen historical essays that tell a more complex reality. They convey some sense of the depth and complexity of black men's multifaceted experiences in the United States. Historically, the great struggle that has engaged black men and women since the first days of their sojourn in the western world has been the survival of all peoples of African descent in the diaspora. As Aldon D. Morris wrote in the foreword to the first volume, we embrace and place before you "the noble side of the notion of what it means to be a man."

EARNESTINE JENKINS
DARLENE CLARK HINE
JANUARY 2000

PART ONE

CONSTRUCTING CITIZENSHIP: THE EVOLUTION OF BLACK MALE LEADERSHIP

ONE

"Your Old Father Abe Lincoln Is Dead and Damned": Black Soldiers and the Memphis Race Riot of 1866

KEVIN R. HARDWICK

> Your old father Abe Lincoln is dead and damned.[1]
>
> —Statement made by an Irish police officer to black soldiers at the start of the Memphis Riot, Tuesday, May 1, 1866

Between May 1 and May 3, 1866, racial conflict erupted violently in Memphis, Tennessee. Irish policemen and firemen, together with white laborers and small businessmen, rioted in the southern part of the city. For three days they attacked the black residents living in the shanty settlement surrounding Fort Pickering, a Union military installation on the outskirts of the city. The rioters initially focused their attacks on the former soldiers of the Third United States Colored Heavy Artillery regiment, which had disbanded April 30—the last of three black regiments to be mustered out of United States service at Memphis. On May 2 and 3, however, the rioters increasingly targeted the civic institutions and property of the black community of south Memphis, including schools, churches, and black-owned houses. By May 4, when federal military authorities declared martial law and detachments of white troops enforced order in the city, two whites and at least forty-six blacks had been killed, between seventy and eighty others had been wounded, at least five black women raped, more than one hundred people (mostly black) robbed, and four churches, twelve schools, and ninety-one houses burned.[2]

Contemporary observers attributed the violence to the unruly conduct of black soldiers in Memphis and to the longstanding animosity between blacks and the Irish, who competed for work as manual laborers. The Memphis *Daily Avalanche*, for example, argued, "it is only with the negro soldiers that

trouble has ever existed. . . . With their departure, will come order, confidence, and the good will of old days. Had we had [white troops] instead of
negro troops, neither this riot, nor the many lawless acts preceding it during the past six months, would have occurred." The superintendent of the
Memphis Freedmen's Bureau, Major General Benjamin P. Runkle, stressed
that "there was also a conflict of labor between the Irish hack-drivers, dray-
drivers, porters, laborers, &c, and the negroes employed in the same occupations; there was a good deal of bitterness felt upon the part of the Irish, from
the fact that these southern gentlemen preferred to hire negro servants."
Another observer, Ewing O. Tade, a representative of the American Missionary Association, stated succinctly that "the late Memphis Riot was beyond a reasonable doubt instigated by the Irish Police of this city."[3]

The rioters, however, were a diverse lot, and their ethnic and occupational
background does not support such a narrow, socio-economic interpretation
of the violence. While the Irish overwhelmingly dominated the city's police
force and fire companies, they represented only 50 to 60 percent of the
identifiable rioters; at least 40 percent of the rioting mob, and quite likely
more, was American born. Most of the rioters were artisans, professionals,
and small shop keepers, not the "lower sort" and "rowdies" described by
contemporary accounts. Only 27 percent of the identifiable rioters came
from the occupational groups that observers considered most likely to be in
competition with blacks for employment.[4]

Nor was the riot a spontaneous eruption of racial hatred. The contempt
that many whites maintained for blacks, after all, was pervasive both before
and after the riot. Racism cannot in itself explain the violence. To understand what happened in Memphis during the first three days of May 1866,
the events of the riot must be placed within the local context of Memphis
and its particular history as a center for the recruitment and administration
of black military units.

Black soldiers, whose uniform conferred upon them the authority of the
victorious Union army, occupied a particularly strategic and powerful position within the larger community of black people living in Memphis, and
were prominent in the efforts of the former slaves to redefine their position
within southern society. The freedmen sought to repudiate the strictures of
the traditional order and to claim their independence. Many of the white
citizens of Memphis were committed to the enforcement of an altogether
different vision of racial relations, in which blacks, while legally no longer
slaves, remained subordinate to white authority. The violence of early May
culminated numerous lesser confrontations in the preceding months. Conflict over the appropriate deportment and behavior of black men and women
in Memphis had been festering for some time, as black soldiers insisted that
whites treat them in a more dignified and equalitarian fashion.

Black soldiers, prominent in the Memphis garrison since 1863, were
culturally significant both to blacks and whites. The experience of military
life in the victorious Union army empowered many black soldiers, and

thousands of blacks hastened to cities like Memphis to enlist in the Union army. Black non-commissioned officers exercised responsibility in active leadership roles in the military and figured prominently in the political leadership of black communities after the war. Black soldiers had access to firearms and training in their use, an inversion of social norms that, prior to the war, had reserved access to firearms almost exclusively to whites. Further, the social role of soldier, carrying with it the authority and prestige of the Union army, in itself enhanced the power and self-image of black soldiers. At a mass meeting in Memphis held on the first anniversary of the Emancipation Proclamation, participants expressed the sense of dignity that military service provided. "We are highly gratified by the appellation by which the colored soldiers are addressed by their officers, viz.: *men*; and we urge the colored men in all places, at all times, and under all circumstances, to cease using that vulgar phrase, 'nigger.'"[5]

When black men acted as provost guards in Memphis and other southern cities, they enforced a new order that, from the standpoint of many white Southerners, represented the world turned upside down. Thus, black soldiers were at once deeply threatening to those whites committed to the old order, and psychologically, as well as actively, liberating to blacks struggling to create the new. The presence of black soldiers in Memphis, and their relations with both black and white residents of the city, are central to understanding the riot. The riot was in part directed at stripping these men, in the most direct and brutal way possible, of the authority that federal service had provided them.[6]

I

The violence of the riot, and the social tension that underlay it, ultimately derived from the wartime migration of thousands of black men and women. Memphis, like most southern cities, experienced a vast influx of former slaves during and after the war. By March 1863, General Stephen A. Hurlbut was writing from Memphis requesting instructions on what to do with "the vast numbers of worthless negroes" that congregated around the city. Hurlbut reported the presence of almost 5,000 black men and women directly dependent on federal forces, as well as "a very large number . . . not supported by the Govt." In 1865, when a city census was taken, the population stood at 28,000 of whom 11,000 were blacks. Large numbers of black people lived in the suburbs of Memphis, however, and a Freedmen's Bureau report of September 1865, estimated the total black population "in and about" the city at 16,000. In less than five years the black population of Memphis had expanded more than four-fold.[7]

Throughout the war the status of Tennessee slaves remained ambiguous, and federal policy regulating their treatment evolved as the exigencies of fighting the war and occupying the region demanded. Federal troops invaded Tennessee in February 1862, occupying Memphis in June. General

William T. Sherman, who assumed command of Memphis in July 1862, hoped at first to avoid disputes about the status of fugitive slaves. However, he, like other Union commanders in Tennessee, quickly recognized the value of slave labor to the Confederate army, and took steps to deprive his opponents of its benefit. Sherman thus welcomed fugitive slaves and put them to work constructing fortifications around Memphis. In October 1862, assuming control of law enforcement in Memphis, Sherman ordered police to treat all blacks in the city as freedmen, until federal courts determined otherwise. A month later he issued orders declaring that "runaway slaves must be treated as free, and people encouraged to give them employment as such."[8]

Federal policy in Tennessee was complicated by the fact that many slaveowners, especially in the eastern part of the state, were unionist, and many army officers felt compelled to protect the slave property of such men. President Lincoln recognized the support of Tennessee unionists by exempting the state from the emancipation proclamation in January 1863. As a practical matter, however, slavery in west Tennessee was a dying institution following the passage in July 1862, of the Second Confiscation Act. That law confiscated and freed the slaves of secessionist slaveowners at the time that slaves came within Union lines, and complicated the efforts of unionist authorities throughout Tennessee to enforce local slave codes. In November 1862, Sherman declared the superiority of the Second Confiscation Act over local laws regulating slavery in Memphis, effectively ending the ability of local civil authority to enforce the slave codes. While the status of freedmen in Memphis remained ambiguous, by late 1862 they were no longer subject to the full repression of legal bondage.[9]

Memphis was an attractive destination for black men and women. While the war was in progress and the formal freedom of slaves belonging to unionist masters still unsure, the presence of Union military units, especially black military units, offered fugitive slaves some security from irate planters seeking to reclaim their property. Further, many black men were attracted to Memphis by the opportunity to enlist in the Union army. In fall 1863 Memphis became the military collection depot for black soldiers in west Tennessee, and a number of black regiments were raised there. By the end of the war, 39 percent of all Tennessee black men between the ages of 18 and 45 served in the Union army.[10]

After the war large numbers of former slaves migrated to Memphis to avoid difficult labor conditions on plantations. In the countryside, blacks were vulnerable to exploitation and violence when dealing with plantation owners and other whites. One Freedmen's Bureau official wrote from Memphis in April 1866 that "numerous outrages have been committed upon the Freedmen in this Sub-District and that Freedmen have, by reason of such outrages, been compelled to flee from the country and seek protection within the limits of the city. . . ." In late 1865 another Union officer in Memphis reported that "large numbers of negroes are arriving daily from

North Miss. many of the latter alleging that they have been driven out of Miss. by the militia organizations of that state who under the pretext of disarming them take all their property." For thousands of black men and women, the continued presence of U.S. troops, particularly black troops, and the Freedmen's Bureau offices in Memphis offered some protection from white aggression and greater power in asserting control over their own lives.[11]

Once large numbers of black soldiers came to be stationed at Memphis, members of their families began to settle there as well. Many Union officers, however, disapproved of the presence of the families of black soldiers. Colonel John Foley, commander of the 61st U.S. Colored Infantry Regiment, which was stationed at Fort Pickering, complained bitterly about the disruptive effect of the families settled near the fort. The "several hundred negro women living in Temporary huts, between the camp of this regiment and the city" he reported in January 1865, "are, for the most part, idle, lazy vagrants, committing depredations, and exercising a very pernicious influence over the colored soldiers of this Post." These women, he continued, "are generally in a destitute condition, and their wants are partially supplied by soldiers of colored regiments who claim them as wives." Foley was particularly incensed that family members "carry off rations from the companies in spite of the utmost vigilance of company commanders, and also carry off axes, shovels, spades, and picks . . . to use in building and maintaining these households."[12]

Union officers several times attempted to force the families of black soldiers to move to locations more isolated from the fort, but to small avail. Captain Thomas A. Walker commanded a detail to relocate the families of black soldiers to nearby President's Island, where they would work as field hands on neighboring plantations. He reported in a January 1865 letter that "the people are unwilling to be moved, and will give no assistance themselves, but lock their doors, and run to their husbands in the various military organizations for protection—the husbands swear their families shall not be moved to the Island and in some instances have come out in arms to prevent it." Earlier efforts to relocate the families of black soldiers to plantations around Helena, Arkansas, where "they can have daily communication by Boat with their husbands at Memphis," had been similarly unsuccessful.[13]

As the numbers of slaves and former slaves living in Memphis grew, connections between soldiers and the rest of the black community became increasingly complex. Many families depended on military wages to meet exorbitant rents and high food prices. Lieutenant Colonel Robert Cowden, commander of the 59th U.S. Colored Infantry Regiment, investigated the conditions in which the families of the men lived. "In the largest house which is probably 18 x 35 feet and two stories high and containing four or five rooms there are seven families of soldiers of this Regiment most if not all of whom pay Mr. Boyle $8 per month." Another officer observed in December 1865 that "probably three fourths of these [colored] troops have families depending upon them for support—they have not been paid during the last six months and cannot provide for their families who being destitute trespass upon the property of citizens and many of them resort to stealing." Tensions mounted when landlords threatened black tenants with eviction, and soldiers responded to protect their families. In August 1865, Colonel Cowden defended the actions of one of his men. A local property owner had "sent a number of colored men to tear down the house in which a sick woman the wife of a soldier in the fort lay lying and her husband stopped them with threats until he could move his wife which he has done. This is what [the landowner] reported as one of the 59th having a gun and threatening to shoot &c. . . ."[14]

Soldiers provided clothing for their families and perhaps for others in the black community as well. Colonel John Foley observed that "the soldiers of my regiment also steal each others clothes for their families to wear and dispose of. . . ." Colonel A. Von Schrader, a Freedmen's Bureau inspector, noted in January 1866, "that a great many [black] people are found to wear more or less parts of the Uniform prescribed by the U.S. Army. . . ." Such a widespread dispersal of federal military clothing had important implications for the black soldiers, since it linked them even more tightly to the rest of the black community and made it more difficult for the casual observer to distinguish between soldiers and black civilians. "Some of these People as instances have proved, have used the Uniform of the U.S. Soldiers as a garb under which to Commit Crimes in order that Persons belonging to the Army by Suspicioned of their foul deed," Von Schrader wrote. "If there can be no measures adopted to prohibit persons not belonging to the Army, to wear its Uniform, the best disciplined troops, will unjustly be charged with depredations which were not Committed by them."[15]

II

One important consequence of emancipation was a reduction in black labor. Since a planter's coercion could not match that possible under slavery, blacks did not work as hard or as long as they had before they became free. In addition, many withdrew entirely or partially from the labor force. Old people, children, and women removed themselves from plantation labor whenever possible. "Rather than work like slaves, the freedmen chose to offer an amount of labor comparable to the standard for free laborers of the time," two recent analysts of the postwar southern economy write.[16] The result was a massive shortfall in plantation labor that affected most parts of the black belt. In Memphis, as the magnitude of the labor shortage in the surrounding plantation districts became apparent, observers focussed on the growing population of freedmen living near Fort Pickering.

Early in the war many Union army officers wished that the problem of fugitive slaves would just go away. General Hurlbut, for example, rather naively remarked in March 1863 that "if the fugitives now lurking about

Memphis could return to their homes in the city & vicinity & their former owners would receive them & treat them kindly until the final determination of their status much of the misery and vice which infests the city & vicinage would be removed." By 1865, however, it was clear that large numbers of freedpeople would not voluntarily return to plantation labor. One officer reported "from my experience here I am entirely satisfied that the larger proportion of the freed persons will not hire out of their own choice but will rely on such a precarious living as they can make in the city."[17]

Efforts by blacks to escape plantation labor and to remove women and children from the labor force received scant sympathy, even from the officers of the Freedmen's Bureau. Planters and businessmen in Memphis complained constantly to federal officers about the "idleness" of former slaves. Many employers agreed with the Memphis attorney who remarked, "almost everybody is aware that the negro does not work as faithfully or as much as he did formerly while a slave, and persons who employ them are irritated a good deal by their shirking." Communications between officers in the army and the Freedmen's Bureau often echoed these concerns. John H. Grove, reporting in September 1865 on the conditions of black life in Memphis, asserted that while many blacks in Memphis lived comfortably and had jobs, "a large number are vagrants, who left the plantations upon which they were formerly employed . . . who are idle and destitute. . . ." General Nathan A. M. Dudley, Freedmen's Bureau superintendent for the Subdistrict of Memphis, wrote to his superiors in Nashville on September 30th, 1865. "There is a surplus population of at least six thousand colored persons women and children in and about Memphis who have no visible means of support who are, however, in a great measure induced to remain about the city by the employed colored people. Very many of this number are lazy, worthless vagrants who will never be induced to leave the life they are now leading except by use of force, as long as they can beg, steal, or obtain sufficiencies to sustain life." P. D. Beecher, a Freedmen's Bureau surgeon, offered an equally stern assessment of the situation of the black population, writing "I am satisfied, . . . great numbers lead a life of prostitution, . . . idleness or depending as means of support upon those who are more industrious." For onlookers like Dudley, Grove, and Beecher, the presence of black children, women, and old people who were capable of work but not actively working merely confirmed racist stereotypes of freedmen as lazy and indolent.[18]

As the summer of 1865 drew to a close, the Freedmen's Bureau in Memphis, headed by General Dudley, came under increasing pressure from military officers, planters, and white citizens to relocate the city's "surplus" black population to the plantations of the surrounding countryside. Major William Gray, one of Dudley's officers, remarked in September, that "I am daily urged by influential persons in the city" to compel freedmen and women to accept plantation jobs. Dudley's attitude regarding the status of the freedmen is apparent in a letter that same month, in which he wrote "worthless, idle, persons have no rights to claim the same benefits arising from their freedom that the industrious and honest are entitled to." In October he ordered that the streets be patrolled by soldiers from Fort Pickering to pick up "vagrants" and force them to accept labor contracts with rural planters.[19]

To some, and especially to blacks, this policy seemed akin to the reimposition of slavery. Warner Madison, a freedman, protested the Freedmen's Bureau policy of forcing blacks to accept labor contracts. "If you dont want to go with Mr. who every it may be they dont find out whether you want to go or not atall they make out the agreement sell you for the price that the man give them," he wrote. "It is positively a fact that they get one dollar a head from these worst secession Men. and i have seen one case where a boy was made to go by the point of a bayonet. . . ."[20]

Many whites in and around Memphis, however, approved of Dudley's use of coercion. The *Daily Appeal,* a conservative Memphis newspaper, supported the Freedmen's Bureau policy. "While jealously guarding the rights of freedmen," the *Appeal* opined, Dudley "inflexibly requires of them to labor for the support of themselves and their families, and to fulfill faithfully their contracts. If the Freedmen's Bureau, everywhere, was administered by such officers as Gen. Dudley, vagabondage would disappear, [and] labor would be reorganized harmoniously with the interest of both races. . . ." The Memphis *Daily Avalanche,* another of the city's conservative presses, described the inhabitants of the black shantytown about Fort Pickering. Living in "wretched, miserable huts and hovels, rudely constructed, with capacity of holding barely one person, and yet many of them crowded almost to suffocation," the people who lived in South Memphis were, in the eyes of the *Avalanche,* "the most drunken, blasphemous and licentious wretches that can be found among the negro race, in any city on this continent." Such people deserved no mercy or consideration, especially since their refusal to accept plantation work threatened starvation on themselves, and financial ruin on the planters.[21]

Northern republicans in Memphis were appalled by the Freedmen's Bureau policies. The Reverend T. E. Bliss, the white pastor of Union Church in Memphis, fired off a scathing letter to Dudley. "How is it that the colored children in Memphis even *with their spelling books in their hands* are caught up by your order & taken to the same place & there insolently told that they 'had better be picking cotton.' Is it for the purpose of 'conciliating' their old rebel masters & assisting them to get help to secure their Cotton Crop? Has it come to this that the most Common rights of these poor people are thus to be trampled upon for the benefit of those who have only wronged them all their days?" Bliss concluded indignantly "What a mockery to call those 'Freedmen' who are still subject to such things!" A subsequent investigation of the situation in Memphis revealed that Dudley and his officers had indeed been bribed to supply planters with the black laborers picked up by their patrols, and that many blacks were bound over to planters by force. Dudley was removed from charge of the Freedmen's Bureau in

Memphis in December 1865, but his successors continued to encourage the freedmen of Memphis to accept contracts to labor in the countryside.[22]

Union officers far more scrupulous than General Dudley were troubled by the large number of freedmen who appeared to have little to no regular work. General Davis Tillson, who served as head of the Freedmen's Bureau in Memphis in the summer of 1865, also attempted to induce the Memphis freedmen to accept labor contracts on the surrounding plantations. In a report of August 1865, he wrote, "we are proceeding cautiously but at the same time vigorously in removing the colored people who are without means of support from this city and vicinity. Precaution has been taken to have the freedpeople understand that the action of the Bureau is *not* in disregard of their rights or freedom but for their own good."[23]

Tillson's concern, at least in his view, was humanitarian. From his perspective (and many Union officers shared his view) the conquered South faced a massive food shortage if the former slaves refused to work. The large numbers of freedmen concentrated in places like Memphis, without jobs and therefore without the money to buy food, would be vulnerable to famine. Tillson justified his policy of relocating freedmen to the countryside, in some cases forcibly, by proclaiming that it was "to prevent inevitable suffering and dearth during the coming winter, among the large numbers of Freed people in and about this city." Major Arthur T. Reeve, superintendent of the Freedmen's Bureau for Shelby County (in which Memphis was located), likewise asserted in a December 1865 circular that unless the freedmen accepted contracts in the countryside they would find themselves destitute come winter. "If you neglect to enter into contracts . . . you will find yourselves at the close of the present contracts homeless and without means of support." Reeve concluded paternalistically: "To the colored people in this city I would say, unless you have a good business to support you, you had better leave the vice and strife of the Crowded City and return to the Country, where the fields are needing your labor, and where you can secure comfortable and healthy homes, and good wages for your work."[24]

The freedmen, however, were not receptive to efforts to remove them from the city and put them to work on the plantations. Neither Tillson and Dudley's use of force, nor Reeve's paternal rhetoric succeeded in reducing the large numbers of former slaves in and about Memphis. John H. Grove noted in September 1865, that, "it seems almost impossible to induce [freedmen] to accept an offer to give them work upon a plantation. There are daily a number of planters, mostly from the states of Mississippi and Tennessee, who call on the office of the Superintendent to employ these people . . . but in most cases they meet with no success." Indeed, black soldiers actively undermined the efforts of the Freedmen's Bureau to force freedmen to accept plantation work. General Tillson complained in August 1865 that "the [white] soldiers employed to visit the Freed people in and about Memphis and inform them that none but those having sufficient means or so permanently employed as to be able to take care of themselves will be allowed to remain" had reported that "colored soldiers interfere with their labors and tell the freed people that the statements made to them . . . are false, thereby embarrassing the operations of the Bureau." One black man, protesting Tillson's labor policy, noted "I know laborers were wanted in the Country Many thousand would have Remained in Country & worked for wages if they had been treated Right." For most blacks, the situation in Memphis, difficult as it was, remained preferable to a return to plantation labor.[25]

III

At public meetings, private parties, and informal interactions in taverns and on sidewalks, the freedmen, and especially the black soldiers, challenged traditional norms for black behavior and demeanor. Blacks held mass public meetings at least three times in Memphis in the summer of 1865, including a parade led by the Fort Pickering military band on May 30 that began at Main and Beale streets, on the edge of the Memphis business district. In each instance officers at Fort Pickering released off-duty soldiers to attend. Captain Woodruff, adjutant to the commander of the Defenses of Memphis, reported to the commander of the fort that "it is the desire of the managers [of the parade] to have as many soldiers present as possible." Two months later, the Sons of Ham, a black fraternal organization, organized a celebration for the first of August that gathered in the heart of central Memphis. Colonel Ignatz G. Kappner, commanding officer of a black regiment at Fort Pickering, detailed a squad of a dozen men and a white officer, "as *guards*, . . . to report at 7 o'clock A.M. tomorrow the 1st of August (in dress uniform) to the Managers of the Festival of the *Sons of Ham*," and announced in a circular "that as many of you men of this command as can be spared, be permitted to witness said celebration in charge of commissioned officers who will be responsible for their good behavior." Such mass displays, prominently attended by black soldiers, were disquieting for whites who remained committed to the cultural order of slavery.[26]

Union military officers routinely detailed black soldiers to police dances and other social events. In June 1865, for example, the commander of one black regiment received orders to "detail from your command (1) one non commissioned officer & two (2) men as guards for a colored ball."[27] Three months later the commander of the Third U.S. Colored Heavy Artillery Regiment at Fort Pickering reported to his superior "I have never received any orders to stop Negro dances, but have been ordered many times to furnish guards for such to prevent disturbances by citizens."[28]

Many white observers perceived dances (and other social events at which independent black community was prominent) as disorderly, and both the civil and military authorities attempted to regulate them. Dances were the occasions of violence and confrontation between blacks and the white community. In late September 1865, Brigadier General John E. Smith barred all further black dances. "The public entertainments, balls, and parties heretofore frequently given by the colored people of this City, having been the cause of much of the disorderly conduct, late of nightly occurrence, by which the peace and quiet of the city are disturbed, hereafter no more balls, or parties of the character mentioned, among the colored people, will be permitted." Smith's policy was apparently less than successful, since Brigadier General Benjamin P. Runkle, Freedmen's Bureau Superintendent for Shelby County, deemed it necessary to issue orders regulating the operation of dance houses for the use of freedmen in early 1866.[29]

When the city police attempted to enforce these orders, trouble resulted. At one ball in February 1866—held with the permission of the Mayor of Memphis—police broke in and arrested a number of soldiers' wives on charges of being prostitutes. "The husbands and brothers then interfered & prevented the arrest. The two policemen then went to the Engine house and returned with a force of some seven men armed with muskets & carbines and cocking their weapons demanded a surrender. They behaved in a very rough and boisterous manner crying 'Shoot the damned niggers.'" On several other occasions black soldiers responded violently when their dances were interrupted by the police. "I saw about twenty or thirty [black soldiers] going right by my house," stated one observer, "firing in every direction, and the policemen had to get out of the way. I understood there had been a ball or something broken up. They came firing and cursing, and everybody had to get out of the way."[30]

Tension often arose between black soldiers who patrolled the area immediately surrounding Fort Pickering (including most of the black shanty town of South Memphis) and the Irish police that enforced order in Memphis itself. In the southern part of the city, especially along South Street where there were numerous taverns and bars that sold liquor to off-duty troops, conflicts frequently arose between the Memphis police force and drunken soldiers. Such conflicts were further heightened by ill-defined jurisdictions, since military patrols shared responsibility with the city constables for policing off-duty soldiers, and since many soldiers worked in Memphis when not on active duty. "Occasional disturbances take place on South Street caused by soldiers furnished with whiskey by citizen store keepers there," reported the commander of Fort Pickering. "Frequent arrests are made by patrols sent out by the officers . . . at the first notice of a disturbance." Policemen attempting to maintain their perception of social order, particularly when they were heavy handed, provoked violent responses from the soldiers. "There have occurred on one or two occasions a conflict between parties of the colored soldiery and the city police," reported an officer in January 1866, "the police were in the first instance blameable for attempting the arrest of an innocent soldier and in the second place the colored troops for using arms and violence to effect the release of the prisoner." This kind of conflict

would more than likely have been endemic regardless of any other antagonism between the soldiers and the police, and indeed, occurred between the
constables and white troops as well.[31]

But conflict between the Irish police and black soldiers suggested a deeper
animosity. H. G. Dent, like other observers, noted "within the last four or
five months the negroes in South Memphis have been very annoying, firing
off pistols at all hours of the day and night." Henry Parker, a captain in the
Memphis militia, described the behavior of the black soldiers. "As a general
thing, when they've had whiskey in them, they've certainly been very boisterous. I've once been shoved, myself, off the sidewalk by a negro in United
States uniform, for the simple reason that he did not wish to get into the
mud. . . . I've seen them push citizens off the sidewalk, using language not fit
to be used by white or black." Such behavior on the part of black soldiers was
fundamentally challenging to the Memphis police, who prior to the war had
been charged with enforcing the local slave codes. The soldier's conduct was
disorderly, but it was flagrantly so by comparison with the expectations of
black public behavior under slavery.[32]

While the police could not systematically enforce black behavior appropriate to slavery, they took out their frustration on black soldiers whenever
they could. When black soldiers refused to get off the sidewalks for white
policemen, which blacks had normally been obliged to do before emancipation, the police responded forcefully on a number of occasions. First Sergeant Peter Robinson of the 88th U.S. Colored Infantry Regiment described
an incident involving a fellow noncommissioned officer in November of
1865. "A policeman came along with his hand in his bosom, and threw his
whole weight against Sergt Backner." Harry Brown, another witness, told a
commission investigating the incident, "he just walked along and shoved
him with his elbow as he passed hard enough to push sergt. Backner out of
his place up against the other wall." Likewise, black "insolence" on occasion
received violent retaliation from police. Joe Brown, a sergeant in a black
regiment stationed at Fort Pickering, testified about an encounter with a
policeman. The policeman, Brown related, "said to me I wish I could get a
chance to kill all the Damned Nigger Soldiers and I said you cant kill me—
he then stepped back a few paces and ran up and struck me with his *club*, on
the head—at that time another Policeman came up and he struck me several
times. And they thru me down and stomped me in the back while lying on
the ground."[33]

IV

Conflict between soldiers and policemen became routine in the weeks
before the riot exploded on May 1. Captain A. W. Allyn of the 16th Regiment of regulars stationed at Fort Pickering, whose men put a temporary halt
to the riot that evening, was accustomed to wild and disorderly behavior in

South Memphis. He did not intervene earlier, he claimed, because he did not realize that a riot was occurring. "Disturbances had been going on for a week, more or less; pistol firing and carousing." When asked who made these disturbances, Allyn replied, "I discovered it was a disturbance made by the negroes at a dance-hall where they were in the habit of going to dance. I heard several shots, but I thought the negroes were, as usual, discharging their pistols in the air."[34]

On Monday, April 30th a party of black soldiers, just mustered out of service, got into a fight with a number of city policemen. No one was killed, but one of the soldiers "was struck with a pistol [and] appeared to be considerably hurt; the blood ran from his nostrils and the side of his head." Many witnesses remembered the fight between the black soldiers and the police on April 30th as the real beginning of the riot.[35]

Certainly the mood of the city was tense at the end of April. The black veterans of the 3rd U.S. Colored Heavy Artillery, mustered out of service on the last day of the month, were not given their discharge pay at their final muster. Many of them, without duties to perform, wandered into Memphis while they waited to collect their pay. On the first of May at about three o'clock several policemen attempted to arrest a black man, charging him with disorderly conduct, and were prevented from doing so by some fifty uniformed black veterans. The police came back about an hour later with reinforcements and arrested two of the soldiers, who again resisted. Shooting broke out, apparently started by the soldiers, who fired into the air, but then returned by the outnumbered police. At the end of the first skirmish one of the policemen was dead, and the police retreated in disarray.[36]

The police withdrew into Memphis, where they collected reinforcements and raised a citizen posse to quell the disturbance. They quickly spread the word throughout the city that the soldiers were rioting. Ellen Dilts, a resident of east Memphis, just north of the shanty town, recalled, "the police went up and down and spread the alarm, and I should think there were a hundred policemen congregated." Large numbers of men throughout Memphis moved towards the neighborhoods around Fort Pickering. One businessman watched the crowd of citizens and police move past him. "I stopped one on the corner and asked what was the matter. They said if I'd go up there I'd see what was the matter; that the negroes were shooting everybody." U.S. Marshal Martin T. Ryder stopped an excited policeman and asked him if the trouble was over. "He said it was not; that the negroes were all armed with guns, and that they could not fight them with pistols, but were going back to get guns."[37]

As rumors of black insurrection spread, Memphis city officials appealed to the local Union military commander, General Stoneman, to suppress the riot, and then organized citizen posses to suppress it themselves. One witness recounted how J. C. Creighton, Memphis City Recorder, spoke to a crowd on Adams street later that evening. "He put his hand in his pocket and took out his revolver. 'By God,' he said, 'I am a brave man; we are not prepared now, but let us prepare to clear out every God damned son-of-a bitch out of town.'"[38]

A mixed crowd of policemen and local whites descended on South Memphis, and the soldiers fought a brief skirmish with them, and then retreated to Fort Pickering. There Captain Allyn's garrison disarmed them. Allyn dispatched two squads of Regulars to patrol South, Shelby, and Main Streets. These men dispersed the crowd (although they did not disarm the Memphis police), and ordered the black veterans that they met to return to the fort. About ten o'clock Allyn's troops left South Memphis, and some time thereafter a larger "posse" arrived in the area. Finding no organized resistance, this new group split up into small groups to look for black soldiers. Under the pretext of searching for arms, and led by policemen and local community leaders, these men entered the homes of many blacks, beating and killing the inhabitants, robbing them, and raping a number of black women.

The white crowd rampaged in South Memphis until early Wednesday morning before dispersing, but returned later on Wednesday and the riot continued for another day. Small groups of whites, many from the surrounding neighborhoods, attacked blacks in the streets, and burned black houses, churches, and businesses. General Stoneman declared martial law the next day, effectively ending the riot on Thursday, May 3.[39]

The violence of the riot was not random. It was targeted at those black individuals and institutions most symbolic of black empowerment—the soldiers themselves, and the institutions that their presence sheltered. It was no coincidence that the riot occurred the day after the last black troops in Memphis were mustered out of federal service. As soon as these men lost the protection, and the ability to protect others, that their status as Union soldiers afforded them, they became vulnerable to white repression.

From the beginning the rioters focused on black veterans. Horatio N. Rankin, a black schoolmaster at Memphis, testified that "the policemen commenced shooting at the negroes on South Street but seemed to fire principally at those dressed in uniform." Thomas Leonard, Judge of Shelby County, similarly remembered seeing a number of unarmed black men and women during the riot. "The crowd was not firing at these colored people, but seemed to be looking after and pursuing the colored soldiers." Shelby County Coroner Francis Erickson who examined the bodies of thirteen black men killed in the riot, reinforced this testimony. "The bodies of all the negroes were dressed in soldier's clothes," he reported.[40]

White posse members assaulted blacks under the pretext of looking for firearms. It is clear, however, that while the rioters were very much concerned with disarming blacks, they sought more fundamentally to subjugate the black community, and especially community members with Union military connections. Dr. S. J. Quimby, formerly the surgeon of a black regiment, witnessed an assault upon a black veteran. "There was one man by the name of Fayette Dickerson, who had formerly been a soldier in the fifteenth colored infantry; he was standing by his house; two men came up and struck him over the head with a stick; they then shot him in the head, a glancing shot; they then shot him in the abdomen." They "then asked him if he had any arms about himself or the house." Another veteran was killed under similar circumstances. The rioters "went into the house of one man and asked him if he had any arms; he said not. They then went into his house and searched it and took everything valuable in the shape of watches and jewelry. They asked him if he had been out that day. He told them no; that he was in government service; they then shot him through the head."[41]

White policemen or citizens interrogated many blacks to determine if they were former soldiers. "Six white men stopped me in front of the Gayoso house, and one of them asked me if I had been a soldier," one freedman testified. "I told him I had been on a gunboat. He then called me 'a damned smoked Yankee,' and struck me on the left arm with a club, and broke my arm between the wrist and the elbow. One of the other men struck me on the head with a club, and knocked me down." Taylor Hunt was attacked by a policeman under similar circumstances. "After he had shot me," Hunt remembered, "he asked me if I was a soldier. I said no. He said it was a good thing I was not, and he then went along." The men who broke into Obadiah Stockley's house gave him some timely advice. "They asked me if I had been a soldier; said I had better not own it if I had."[42]

The rioters targeted homes where they believed soldiers could be found. Phyllis Premier described the actions of the men who broke into her house. "They got twenty dollars out of one of the trunks belonging to my brother; said they wanted to kill him because he was a soldier." Primus Lane was asked why he thought the mob selected his house to burn. "I will tell you as near as I can. I had a son in the army and my son came here; there was a grocery right opposite. They came to that store, and they must have let them know about my boy, and they came after him, I think."[43]

Likewise, the rioting crowd assaulted people wearing blue or wearing parts of a Union uniform. Dr. Quimby described the death of one of the soldiers from his regiment. "This corporal was either going or coming from some work he was doing. He was unarmed, but he had on at that time blue pants." One black woman described how the mob had refused to let a neighbor out of her burning house. A man in the crowd recognized her: "He seemed to know this woman said 'That is a very good woman; it is a pity to burn her up, let her come out.' She came out with her little boy with her. The boy had blue clothes on. They pushed him back, and said 'Go back, you damned Son of a Bitch.'"[44]

Four of the five black women who were raped during the riot had clear ties to the Union army. Francis Thompson testified that seven men entered her house Tuesday afternoon. "They said they must have supper, and asked me what I had, and said they must have eggs, and ham, and biscuit." Lucy Smith, who was with Thompson and whom the rioters also raped, recounted how "we got up, and made a fire, and got them supper. . . . What was left of the sugar, and coffee, and ham they threw into the bayou." After the men forced the women to make them food, "they drew their pistols and said they would shoot us and fire the house if we did not let them have their way with us. All seven of the men violated us two. Four of them had do with me, and the rest with Lucy." The men then broke open a pair of trunks owned by Thompson and robbed her of the money that was stored there. "We had some quilts in the room that we had been quilting red, white, and blue," Smith recalled. "They asked us if we had made them before or after the Yankees came. We said after. They said, 'You niggers have a mighty liking for the damned Yankees, but we will kill you, and you will have no liking for anyone then.'" Smith explained at the end of her testimony: "There were some pictures in the room: we had General Hooker and some other Union officers, and they said they would not have hurt us so bad if it had not been for those pictures."[45]

Two other rape victims, Lucy Tibbs and Harriet Armour, were likewise associated with the army. The men who raped Tibbs robbed her of $300, which had belonged to her brother, a private in the 59th Colored Infantry. She testified of the men who broke into her house, "I think that there were folks that knew all about me, who knew that my brother had not been long out of the army and had money." Harriet Armour's husband was a soldier, and he was with the other soldiers in Fort Pickering while the riot was occurring. A neighbor described seeing men enter Armour's house. "I saw them going into the house and saw them coming out, and afterwards she came out and said they [had raped her]. She has sometimes been a little damaged since then, her husband left her after he found out what had been done, he said he would not have anything to do with her any more. They drew their pistols and made her submit."[46]

Much of the behavior of the mob served to emphasize and reinforce the powerless and dependent position of blacks. Thus, for example, the woman whose child was forced back into the burning building "fell on her knees and begged them to let the child out. . . . They let her little boy out afterwards." Another black woman who the crowd forced into a burning house got out by a back exit. "When I was running away with my babe," she recalled, "a man put a pistol to my breast, and said he 'what are you doing?' 'I am trying to save my babe.' 'Sit down,' said he, and I sat down, and they did not trouble me any more." For these women, supplication to white authority was sufficient to mollify the crowd. W. B. Greenlaw described the manner in which two black men were similarly intimidated. "At this time two white men spoke to the negroes and ordered them to get down on their knees, threatening to kill them." J. M. Randolph, a white witness, did not see any blacks killed, but he did see them "maltreated." "Maltreated in what way? Such as catching them by the head or throat and jerking them off the sidewalk. . . . Occasionally a policeman would catch a little darkey and jerk him across the sidewalk." Incidents like these created in actuality the white goal of black subordination. White Southerners could achieve this goal in Memphis only by destroying the most potent symbols of black power in the city—the soldiers themselves.[47]

V

The Memphis riot was a brutal episode in the ongoing struggle that continued well past the actual moment of emancipation to establish the boundaries around and possibilities for action by blacks. The rioters asserted dominance over blacks and attempted to establish limitations on black behavior. Where one cultural code had governed racial interaction under slavery, another, more appropriate to the new black status, had to be established after blacks claimed their freedom. The riot in Memphis was one of a series of similar incidents that occurred in urban centers throughout the south. "Whatever the precipitating incident," Leon Litwack has remarked, "nearly every race riot reflected that growing conflict between how ex-slaves and whites chose to define emancipation and the determination of whites to retain the essentials of the old discipline and etiquette."[48]

While the houses, schools, and churches of the black community in Memphis were repaired or rebuilt in the years following the riot, the three days of violence placed limits upon the ability of black men and women to assert their freedom. The riot was a graphic demonstration of white power and authority, a threatening manifestation of white determination to control and subordinate the black community. "The chief source of all our trouble being removed," the *Daily Avalanche* exclaimed, "we may confidently expect a restoration of the old order of things. The negro population will now do their duty. . . . Negro men and negro women are suddenly looking for work on country farms. . . . Thank heaven, the white race are once more the rulers in Memphis." Austin Cotton, a freedman, explained to the Congressional committee investigating the riot why he was not maltreated. "No one abused me," he said. "It was because I was humble as a slave, almost. I have heard them say to me, 'You are right, Uncle; you are humble, just like a slave.'"[49] Not every former slave chose to behave like Cotton. But the savage attacks on the former soldiers—those members of the black community most empowered to assert authority in post-emancipation Memphis—severely circumscribed the options of blacks who chose to behave differently.

NOTES

1. "Memphis Riots and Massacres," 39 Congress, First Session, *House of Representatives Report 101, 1865–1866* (1866), p. 7, henceforth cited as *Report*. This document has been reprinted. See United States Congress, House, Select Committee on the Memphis Riots, *Memphis Riots and Massacres* (reprint ed., New York, 1969).

2. *Report*, pp. 35–6; James Gilbert Ryan, "The Memphis Riots of 1866: Terror in a Black Community during Reconstruction," *Journal of Negro History* 62 (July 1977): 243. For other studies of the riot, see Jack D. Holmes, "The Effects of the Memphis Race

Riot of 1866," *West Tennessee Historical Society Papers* 12 (1958): 58–79; *Idem.*, "The Underlying Causes of the Memphis Race Riot of 1866," *Tennessee Historical Quarterly* 17 (Sept. 1959): 195–221; Altina L. Waller, "Community, Class and Race in the Memphis Riot of 1866," *Journal of Social History* 18 (Winter, 1984): 233–246.

3. Memphis *Daily Avalanche*, May 12, 1866, p. 3, as quoted in Holmes, "Effects of the Memphis Race Riot," pp. 73–74; *Report*, pp. 276–277; E. O. Tade to Rev. M[ichael] E. Strieby, 21 May 1866, in Joe M. Richardson, ed., "The Memphis Race Riot and its Aftermath: Report by a Northern Missionary," *Tennessee Historical Quarterly* 24 (Spring-Winter 1965): p. 64.

4. Waller, "Community, Class and Race in the Memphis Riot," pp. 234–237. See Table 1, "Occupation of Rioters," for Waller's analysis of the occupation of rioters. I derived the twenty-seven percent figure by assuming that *all* artisans, laborers, unemployed persons, and persons whose occupations was unknown were from groups that competed with blacks for employment. It is thus likely that the figure errs on the high side.

5. Philadelphia *Press*, July 18, 1863; Boston *Liberator*, January 29, 1864, as quoted by John Cimprich, *Slavery's End in Tennessee, 1861–1865* (University, Alabama, 1985), p. 104.

6. See *Freedom: A Documentary History of Emancipation*, ser. II, *The Black Military Experience*, ed. Ira Berlin, Joseph P. Reidy, and Leslie S. Rowland (Cambridge, U.K., 1982), pp. 733–737, 765–770. For further discussion of the military experience of black soldiers, see Leon F. Litwack, *Been in the Storm So Long: The Aftermath of Slavery* (New York, 1979), pp. 79–103, 267–274.

7. See Litwack, *Been in the Storm So Long*, pp. 310–22, on black migration to southern cities. Maj. Gen. S. A. Hurlbut to President Lincoln, Memphis, TN, 27 March 1863, Vol. 1/18, 16 AC, pp. 83–85 (#187), Letters and Telegrams Sent, Ser. 385, 16th Army Corps, U.S. Army Continental Commands, RG 393, pt. 2 [henceforth abbreviated RG 393], National Archives and Records Administration [henceforth abbreviated NARA] [C-4861 FSSP]; Major General S. A. Hurlbut to Lt. Col. Jno A. Rawlins, Vol. 1/18 16 A&C, p. 83 (#186), Letters and Telegrams Sent, Ser. 385, General records, 16th Army Corps, RG 393, pt. 2, NARA [C-4860 FSSP]; J. H. Grove to Capt. W. T. Clark, Nashville, TN, 21 Sept. 1865, Box 2, G-41 (1865), Letters Received, Ser. 3379, Headquarters, Office of the Assistant Commissioner, TN, Records of the Field Offices of the Bureau of Refugees, Freedmen, and Abandoned Lands, RG 105, TN and VA [henceforth abbreviated as RG 105], NARA [A-6130 FSSP]; on the 1865 city census, see Kathleen Berkeley, "Like a Plague of Locusts: Immigration and Social Change in Memphis, Tennessee, 1850–1880" (Ph.D. diss., University of California, Los Angeles, 1980), p. 168.

8. Order issued by D. C. Anthony, Provost Marshall of Memphis, Memphis, TN, 11 Nov. 1862, enclosed in F. A. Nitchy to Maj. Gen. Curtis, 19 Nov. 1862, in *Freedom: A Documentary History of Emancipation, 1861–1867*, ser. 1, Volume I, *The Destruction of Slavery*, ed. Ira Berlin, Barbara J. Fields, Thavolia Glymph, Joseph P. Reidy, and Leslie S. Rowland, (Cambridge, U.K., 1985), p. 439. See also Cimprich, *Slavery's End in Tennessee*, pp. 19–45.

9. See Ira Berlin, et al., *Destruction of Slavery*, pp. 251–268. See also Berlin et al., *Black Military Experience*, pp. 11–15, and the extended discussion of federal policy in Tennessee in Cimprich, *Slavery's End in Tennessee*, pp. 33–45, 81–97.

10. Holmes, "Underlying Causes," p. 216; Ryan, "The Memphis Riots of 1866," p. 244; Berlin et al., *Black Military Experience*, Table 1, p. 12.

11. Special Order No. 50, Bvt. Brig. Gen. [Benjamin P. Runkle], Memphis, TN, 7 April 1866, Vol. 151, p. 30, Special Orders and Circulars Issued, ser. 3523, Subassistant Commissioner for the Subdistrict of Memphis, RG 105, NARA [A-6497 FSSP]; Bvt. Maj. Gen. Jno E. Smith to Bvt. Brig. Gen. Wm. D. Whipple, Memphis, TN, 20 Dec. 1865, No. 183, vol. 1/2 DWT, pp. 192–93 (#402), Letters and Telegrams Sent, Ser. 2865, District of West TN, No. 183, RG 393, Pt. 2, NARA [C-2237].

12. On efforts to reestablish family ties after emancipation, see Berlin et al., *Destruc-*

tion of Slavery, pp. 1–56, 249–269; and Litwack, *Been in the Storm So Long*, pp. 229–247. Lt. Col. John Foley to Lt. Col. T. Harris, 11 Jan. 1865, filed with Capt. T. A. Walker to Capt. J. S. Lord, 24 Jan. 1865, in Berlin et al., *Black Military Experience*, p. 719.

13. Capt. T. A. Walker to Capt. J. S. Lord, 24 Jan. 1865, in Berlin et al., *Black Military Experience*, pp. 719–720; Circular issued by Lt. Col. John Phillips, 4 April 1864, in Berlin et al., *Black Military Experience*, note, p. 720.

14. Lt. Col. Robert Cowden to Bvt. Brig. Gen. W. W. Morgan, Memphis, TN, 17 Aug. 1865, Letters Received, Box 39, 59th USCI, Regimental Books and Papers USCT, Colored Troops Division, RG 94, NARA [G-215 FSSP]; Bvt. Maj. Gen. Jno E. Smith to Bvt. Brig. Gen. Wm. D. Whipple, Memphis, TN, 20 Dec. 1865, vol. 1/2 DWT, pp. 192–93 (#402), Letters and Telegrams Sent, Ser. 2865, District of West TN, No. 183, RG 393, pt. 2, NARA [C-2237 FSSP]; Lt. Col. Robert Cowden to Bvt. Brig. Gen. W. W. Morgan, Memphis, TN, 17 Aug. 1865, Letters Received, Box 39, 59th USCI, Colored Troops Division, RG 94, NARA [G-215 FSSP].

15. Lt. Col. John Foley to Lt. Col. T. Harris, 11 Jan. 1865, in Berlin et al., *Black Military Experience*, p. 719; Lt. Col. A. Von Schrader to Brig. Gen. Wm. D. Whipple, Mobile, AL, 31 Jan. 1866, Vol. 53/95, pp. 39–40, Reports Sent, Ser. 1056, Inspector, Records of Staff Officers, Department of the Cumberland and Division and Department of TN (P), RG 393, Pt. 1 NARA [C-89a FSSP].

16. See Roger Ransom and Richard Sutch, *One Kind of Freedom: The Economic Consequences of Emancipation*, (New York, 1977), pp. 44–47. Quotation is from p. 44.

17. Maj. Gen. S. A. Hurlbut to President Lincoln, Memphis, TN, 27 March 1863, Vol. 1/18, 16 AC, pp. 83–85 (#187), Letters and Telegrams Sent, Ser. 385, 16th Army Corps, RG 393, pt. 2 [C-4861 FSSP]; Major Wm. Gray to Capt. W. T. Clark, Memphis, TN, 13 Sept. 1865, Box 66, Unregistered Letters Received, Ser. 3522, Subassistant Commissioner for the Subdistrict of Memphis, RG 105, NARA [A-6501 FSSP].

18. Testimony of Henry G. Smith to Congressional Delegation, *Report*, p. 294; J. H. Grove to Capt. W. T. Clark, Nashville, TN, 21 Sept. 1865, Box 2, G-41 (1865), Registered Letters Received, Ser. 3379, RG 105, NARA [A-6130 FSSP]; Bvt. Brig. Gen. N. A. M. Dudley to Capt. Clark, Memphis, TN, 30 Sept. 1865, Box 1, D-66 (1865), Registered Letters Received, Ser. 3379, Headquarters, Office of the Assistant Commissioner, TN, RG 105, NARA [A-6108 FSSP]; P. D. Beecher to Gen. Runkle, Memphis, TN, 18 May 1866, Unregistered Letters Received, Ser. 3380, Headquarters, Office of the Assistant Commissioner, TN, RG 105, NARA [A-6057 FSSP].

19. Major Wm. Gray to Capt. W. T. Clark, Memphis, TN, 13 Sept. 1865, Box 66, Unregistered Letters Received, Ser. 3522, Subassistant Commissioner for the Subdistrict of Memphis, RG 105, NARA [A-6501 FSSP]; Bvt. Brig. Gen. N. A. M. Dudley to Capt. Clark, Memphis, TN, 30 Sept. 1865, Box 1, D-66 (1865), Registered Letters Received, Ser. 3379, Headquarters, Office of the Assistant Commissioner, TN, RG 105, NARA [A-6108 FSSP]. For a larger discussion of the policies of the Freedmen's Bureau, see Eric Foner, *Reconstruction: America's Unfinished Revolution, 1863–1877* (New York, 1988), pp. 153–170.

20. Warner Madison to Gen. Fisk, enclosed in Bvt. Brig. Gen. N. A. M. Dudley to Capt. Clark, Memphis, TN, 30 Sept. 1865, Box 1, D-66 (1865), Registered Letters Received, Ser. 3379, Headquarters, Office of the Assistant Commissioner, TN, RG 105, NARA [A-6108 FSSP].

21. Memphis *Daily Appeal*, 8 Nov. 1865; Memphis *Daily Avalanche*, 17 May 1866, quoted in Holmes, "Causes of the Memphis Race Riot," pp. 204, 209. See for a wider discussion, Litwack, *Been in the Storm So Long*, pp. 336–449.

22. Rev. T. E. Bliss to Gen. N. A. M. Dudley, Memphis, TN, 3 Nov. 1865, enclosed in W. T. Clark to Gen. Fisk, Memphis, TN, 18 Nov. 1865, Box 1, C-93 (1865), Registered Letters Received, Ser. 3379, Headquarters Office of the Assistant Commissioner, TN, RG 105, NARA [A-6100 FSSP].

23. Brig. Gen. Davis Tillson to Capt. W. T. Clark, Memphis, TN, 30 Aug. 1865, Unregistered Letters Received, Ser. 3380, Headquarters, Office of the Assistant Commissioner, TN, RG 105, NARA [A-6054 FSSP].

24. Circular No. 5., Office Supt. R. F. and A. L. Subdist. Memphis, TN, 28 Aug. 1865, Unregistered Letters Received, Ser. 3380, Headquarters, Office of the Assistant Commissioner, TN, RG 105, NARA [A-6054 FSSP]; Maj. A. T. Reeve, Circular, Memphis, TN, 19 Dec. 1865, Vol. 151, p. 19, Special Orders and Circulars Issued, Ser. 3523, Subassistant Commissioner for the Subdistrict of Memphis, RG 105, NARA [A-6494 FSSP].

25. J. H. Grove to Capt. W. T. Clark, Nashville, TN, 21 Sept. 1865, Box 2, G-41 (1865), Registered Letters Received, Ser. 3379, RG 105, NARA [A-6130 FSSP]; Brig. Gen. Davis Tillson to Bvt. Brig. Gen. Morgan, Memphis, TN, 26 Aug. 1865, Vol. 133, pp. 42–43 (#86), Letters Sent, Ser. 3517, Subassistant Commissioner for the Subdistrict of Memphis, RG 105, NARA [A-6577 FSSP]; Anthony Motley to Gen. Fisk, 28 Sept. 1865, M-84, Registered Letters Received, Ser. 3379, Headquarters, Office of the Assistant Commissioner, TN, RG 105, NARA [A-6501 FSSP].

26. See, for further discussion of mass public activity by blacks, Cimprich, *Slavery's End in Tennessee*, pp. 104–117. These large public gatherings are documented by several circulars issued by Col. Ignatz Kappner; see Circular; Col. I. G. Kappner [Commanding 59th USCI], Memphis, TN, 24 May 1865; Circular; Col. I. G. Kappner, Memphis, TN, 30 May 1865; Circular, Col. I. G. Kappner, Memphis, TN, 31 July 1865, Issuances, Box 40, Regimental Books and Papers USCT, 59th USCI, RG 94, NARA [G-217 FSSP]. Quotes are from Capt. J. G. Woodruff to Col. I. G. Kappner, Memphis, TN, 30 May 1865, CN 181, box 2, Letters and Reports Received, Ser. 2842, Headquarters, Post and Defenses of Memphis, No. 181, RG 393, Pt. 2, NARA [C-8517 FSSP]; Special Order No. 138: Col. I. G. Kappner; Circular: Col I. G. Kappner, Memphis, TN, 31 July 1865, Issuances, Box 40, Regimental Books and Papers, 59th USCI USCT, Colored Troops Division, RG 94, NARA [G-217 FSSP]. Emphasis is Kappner's.

27. Capt. Chas. P. Brown to Col. I. G. Kappner, Memphis, TN, 21 June 1865, C#179, Letters Received, Ser. 2821, Ft. Pickering, No. 179, RG 393, Pt. 2, NARA [C-1830 FSSP].

28. Col. I. G. Kappner to Bvt. Brig. Gen. W. H. Morgan, Ft. Pickering, TN, 13 Sept. 1865, Box 2, K E 110 DWT 1865, Letters Received, Ser. 2869, District of West TN, No. 183, RG 393, pt. 2, NARA [C-2218 FSSP].

29. Special Order No. 240, Bvt. Maj. Gen. J. E. Smith, Memphis, TN, 24 Sept. 1865, Issuances, Box 40, Regimental Books and Papers USCT, 59th USCI, RG 94, NARA [G-217 FSSP]; Bvt. Brig. Gen. Benjamin P. Runkle, Circular, n.p., n.d. [entered in vol. between orders of 28 Feb. and 21 Mar. 1866], vol. 151, p. 24, Special Orders and Circulars Issued, Ser. 3523, Subassistant Commissioner for the Subdistrict of Memphis, RG 105, NARA [A-6495 FSSP].

30. Affidavit of Charles Swear, Robt. R. Church, and John Green, in Lt. S. S. Garrett to Maj. Wm. L. Porter, Memphis, TN, 17 Feb. 1866, Box 72, Affidavits and Statements, Ser. 3545, Provost Marshal of Freedmen, Memphis TN, RG 105, NARA [A-6586 FSSP]; Testimony of H. G. Dent before Congressional Delegation, *Report*, p. 166.

31. One white regiment, the 11th Missouri, was sent to Memphis to allay fears of a black uprising rumored to be scheduled for Christmas of 1865. However, the soldiers proved to be so disruptive and uncontrollable that they were removed several days after they arrived. Indeed, compared to white troops, many observers thought the black soldiers were remarkably well behaved. See e.g., Bvt. Maj. Gen. Jno E. Smith to Bvt. Brig. Gen. Wm. D. Whipple, Memphis, TN, 9 Jan. 1865, Vol. 1/3 DWT, pp. 20–4, Letters and Telegrams Sent, Ser. 2865, District of West TN, RG 393, Pt. 2, NARA [C-2237 FSSP]; Lt. Col. A. Von Schrader to Brig. Gen. W. D. Whipple, Mobile, AL, 31 Jan. 1866, Vol. 53/95 DT, pp. 38–51, Reports Sent, Ser. 1056, Inspector, Records of Staff Officers, Department of the Cumberland and Division and Department of TN (P), RG 393, Pt. 1, NARA [C-89a FSSP]. Quotes are from Col. I. G. Kappner to Bvt. Brig. Gen. W. H. Morgan, Ft. Pickering, TN, 13 Sept. 1865, Box 2 K E 110 DWT 1865, Letters Received, Ser. 2869, District of West TN, No. 183, RG 393, pt. 2, NARA [C-2218 FSSP]; Bvt. Major Gen. Jno E. Smith to Bvt. Brig. Gen. Wm. D. Whipple, Memphis,

TN, 9 Jan. 1866, Vol. 1/3 DWT, pp. 20–4, Letters and Telegrams Sent, Ser. 2865, District of West TN, No. 183, RG 393, pt. 2, NARA, [C-2237 FSSP].

32. Testimony of H. G. Dent before Congressional Delegation, *Report*, p. 166; Testimony of Henry Taylor before Congressional Delegation, *Report*, p. 130. Col. I. G. Kappner of the 3rd USCHA at Fort Pickering reported that "the complaints of continued discharge of fire arms are certainly exaggerated, although hardly a night passes without some firing east of the fort." Kappner to Bvt. Brig. Gen. W. H. Morgan, Fort Pickering, TN, 13 Sept. 1865, K E DWT 1865, Box 2, Letters Received, Ser. 2869, District of West TN, No. 183, RG 393, NARA [C-2218 FSSP].

33. Testimony of Peter Robinson and Harry Brown before the Military Commission in the Case of John J. Magevney, Memphis, TN, 8–22 Dec. 1865, MM3338, Court Martial Case Files, ser. 15, RG 153, NARA [H-8 FSSP]; Statement by Sgt. Joe Brown, 11 Sept. 1865, in Berlin et al., *Black Military Experience*, pp. 743–744.

34. Testimony of Captain A. W. Allyn before Congressional Delegation, *Report*, p. 245.

35. Testimony of Ellen Dilts before Congressional Delegation, *Report*, p. 64.

36. See Ryan, "The Memphis Riots of 1866," for an excellent description of the events of the riot. See also Testimonies of Ellen and Rachel Dilts, Dr. S. J. Quimby, and William Brazier before Congressional Delegation, *Report*, pp. 63–8, 104, 119–21.

37. Testimony of Ellen Dilts, David T. Egbert, and Martin T. Ryder before Congressional Delegation, *Report*, pp. 64, 121, 252.

38. Testimony of George Todd before Congressional Delegation, *Report*, p. 256.

39. See Ryan, "Memphis Riots of 1866," and Waller, "Community, Class and Race," *passim*.

40. Testimony of H. N. Rankin and Thomas Leonard before Military Commission Organized by Order of General Stoneman, *Report*, pp. 313–314; testimony of Francis Erickson before Congressional Delegation, *Report*, p. 109.

41. Testimony of Dr. S. J. Quimby before Congressional Delegation, *Report*, pp. 104–105, 107.

42. Testimony of Louis Bennett before the Military Commission Organized by Order of Major General George Stoneman, *Report*, p. 330. Testimony of Taylor Hunt before Congressional Delegation, *Report*, p. 101. Testimony of Obadiah Stockley before the Commission Organized by the Freedmen's Bureau, *Report*, p. 336.

43. Testimony of Phillis Premier before the Commission Organized by the Freedmen's Bureau, *Report*, p. 338. Testimony of Primus Lane before Congressional Delegation, *Report*, p. 97.

44. Testimony of Dr. S. J. Quimby and Cynthia Townsend before Congressional Delegation, *Report*, pp. 107, 163.

45. The rapes of these women are discussed in Herbert G. Gutman, *The Black Family in Slavery and Freedom, 1750–1925* (New York, 1976), pp. 24–28. Testimony of Frances Thompson and Lucy Smith before Congressional Delegation, *Report*, pp. 196–197.

46. Testimony of Lucy Tibbs and Cynthia Townsend before Congressional Delegation, *Report*, pp. 161, 163; see also Testimony of Harriet Armour, pp. 176–177.

47. Testimony of Cynthia Townsend, Mary Jordan, and J. M. Randolph before Congressional Delegation, *Report*, pp. 125, 163, 234–235. Testimony of W. B. Greenlaw before the Military Commission Organized by Order of Major General Stoneman, *Report*, p. 316.

48. Litwack, *Been in the Storm So Long*, pp. 280–281.

49. Memphis *Daily Avalanche*, 5 May 1866, p. 2, as cited in Holmes, "Effects of the Memphis Race Riot," p. 71. Testimony of Austin Cotton before Congressional Delegation, *Report*, p. 102.

TWO

Black Politicians in Reconstruction
Charleston, South Carolina:
A Collective Study

WILLIAM C. HINE

Few groups in United States history have provoked greater controversy and inflamed passions more than the black men who rose to political prominence during Reconstruction. Reviled and vilified as ignorant and incompetent by more than one generation of historians,[1] their reputation in recent years has markedly improved as the racial attitudes of contemporary historians have moderated and as those scholars have intensified their study of black political leadership during that era.[2]

Yet, aside from David C. Rankin's pathbreaking inquiry into the backgrounds of black leaders in New Orleans, virtually nothing is known of the hundreds of men who participated in the lower echelons of politics in the urban South during Reconstruction.[3] This study represents an effort to rectify that situation by examining the origins and the patterns of life of the black men who were politically active in Charleston, South Carolina, from 1865 to 1877.

In the century prior to the secession crisis of 1860–1861 Charleston had achieved fame and notoriety as a bustling port and lively center of antebellum culture. The city was dominated by wealthy planter-aristocrats, who reigned magisterially over it and South Carolina's low country.[4] But the inception of Congressional Reconstruction in 1867 dramatically altered the political picture as dozens of black men both from within Charleston's sizeable black community as well as from other localities surged forward and grasped for the political reins of power in the decade after the Civil War.[5]

In order to identify these grass-roots black politicians and probe their backgrounds the names of more than five hundred political activists were culled from Charleston newspapers published between 1865 and 1875.[6] By methodically combing a variety of records, including the eighth and ninth United States censuses, registers of free Negroes in Charleston, city censuses of 1848 and 1861, city directories, military service records, and tax records, it was possible to isolate 234 black men (including 39 Democrats) who participated in politics in Charleston.[7] Every effort was made to ascertain accurately the race and residence of each individual to confirm that they were indeed black and lived in the city of Charleston.[8]

Not all these 234 men would be strictly defined as political leaders. Aside from depending on officeholding as the main criterion, it is difficult to determine with precision the attributes of political leadership. Men such as Jonathan C. Gibbs, Martin Robison Delany, Macon B. Allen, and Samuel Dickerson, for example, were important in Republican circles in Charleston, but none of them ever held elective office. Therefore, to include the broadest spectrum of black political involvement, minimum criteria were established for inclusion in this study: to have been nominated for political office by one of the parties (or a faction of one party), to have served as an officer with a party organization, or to have been elected at least as a ward delegate to a city or county convention for one of the parties or their factions at some time during Reconstruction. Those who were alternate delegates or merely served in an appointive governmental capacity were not included. The 234 men thus represent the most active black politicos down to the lowest levels of organized politics in Charleston during Reconstruction.

The overwhelming majority of these politicians had spent the pre-war years in Charleston and South Carolina (Table 1). Nearly half had resided in Charleston, and that figure was no doubt higher because the United States censuses in 1860 and 1870 listed origins only by state and not by city or county.[9] Altogether more than three-quarters of these men had lived in South Carolina before the war. Many of these men who entered politics had whatever advantages that accrued from living in Charleston in the antebellum era. They were molded and conditioned by the cosmopolitan environ-

TABLE 1

Prewar Residence of Charleston Black Politicians during Reconstruction

| | All Black Politicians (N = 234) | | Black Democrats Only (N = 39) | |
Locality	Number	% age	Number	% age
Charleston	110	47.0	20	51.3
South Carolina	70	29.9	7	17.9
Other States	16	6.8	1	2.6
Unknown	38	16.2	11	28.2

TABLE 2

Antebellum Legal Status of Black Politicians
in Charleston during Reconstruction

	All Black Politicians (N = 234)		Black Democrats Only (N = 39)	
Status	Number	% age	Number	% age
Free	115	49.1	19	48.7
Slave	34	14.5	9	23.1
Unknown	85	36.3	11	28.2

TABLE 3

Color of Black Politicians in Charleston during Reconstruction

	All Black Politicians (N = 234)		Black Democrats Only (N = 39)	
Color	Number	% age	Number	% age
Black	148	63.2	30	76.9
Mulatto	86	36.7	9	23.1

ment and diversity of life in the city. Fewer than 7 percent of the Reconstruction politicians came from other states, and only Ohio with three and New York with four contributed more than one.[10]

In a city where the free black population was less than one-fifth of the total black population in 1860, nearly one-half of the black politicians had been free prior to the Civil War (Table 2).[11] The advantages of having grown up free, perhaps with some degree of economic security and independence as well as limited educational opportunities, seem to have manifested themselves in the postwar world of politics. Remarkably, though freedmen were frequently attracted to politics and participated fairly extensively, not one of their number ever became a key political figure and/or major Republican officeholder in Charleston. The early and the complete dominance of free black men from Charleston and from the North effectively excluded the ex-slaves. It can be determined with certainty that only one ex-slave, Frank Brown, was elected alderman, and he served as a Democrat. Ex-slaves who served in the legislature from Charleston invariably represented the rural parishes of the county and not the city. Furthermore, just thirty-four men could be identified with a reasonable degree of certainty as having been slaves. That figure was undoubtedly higher, but there are few prewar records which identify individual slaves.

TABLE 4

Date of Birth of Black Politicians in Charleston during Reconstruction

	All Black Politicians (N = 234)		Black Democrats Only (N = 39)	
Dates	Number	% age	Number	% age
1794–1804	4	1.7	1	2.6
1805–1814	15	6.4	1	2.6
1815–1824	38	16.2	7	17.9
1825–1834	36	15.4	3	7.7
1835–1844	56	23.9	8	20.5
1845–1854	22	9.4	5	12.8
Unknown	63	26.9	14	35.8

Determining with accuracy the color of Afro-American politicians proved difficult (Table 3). Records were not carefully and consistently complied. Census marshals were too often imprecise in distinguishing between brown men and black men, or octoroons and quadroons. But if the records are only partially accurate, a substantial majority of the black men involved in politics had a dark complexion. Yet many, but by no means all, of the prominent Afro-American leaders and officeholders were light-skinned men. Francis Louis Cardozo, Robert C. De Large, William McKinlay, Benjamin A. Boseman, Edward P. Wall, and several others were brown men. Some of these politicians were related to prominent white families in Charleston. Francis Cardozo was the son of Isaac Nunez Cardozo, a prosperous Jewish merchant.[12] Benjamin Kinloch was a light-skinned Democrat, whose ancestors formed one of Charleston's well-known Scottish families.[13]

Though ex-slaves were virtually barred from the higher levels of political leadership, the same was not always true of dark-skinned men. There was generally, moreover, a high correlation between being free before the Civil War and light skin color, and yet there were a number of dark men who rose to major positions of leadership. Richard H. Cain became a state senator and later a congressman. Malcolm Brown was an alderman. Martin Delany ran on a reform ticket in 1874 for lieutenant governor. The evidence strongly suggests that prewar status as a slave was a greater hindrance to political mobility than a dark complexion.

Typically, the black Reconstruction politician was neither a particularly young or old man (Table 4). As of 1870 nearly 40 percent of them (39.6 percent) were over thirty-five years of age. Many older men, in their forties and fifties, took their first plunge into politics in the late 1860s and early 1870s. Yet there was a healthy infusion of younger blood as well. Seventy-eight black politicians, or one-third (33.3 percent), were under thirty-five

TABLE 5

Literacy of Black Politicians in Charleston during Reconstruction

| | All Black Politicians (N = 234) | | | Black Democrats Only (N = 39) | |
Literacy	Number	% age		Number	% age
Literate	105	44.9		15	38.5
Semiliterate	13	5.6		3	7.7
Illiterate	32	13.7		5	12.8
Unknown	84	35.9		16	41.0

TABLE 6

Charleston Population Age 21 and Over Unable to Write
1870

	Male	Female	Total	Total Population (All Ages)
Black	3,736	5,688	9,424	26,173
White	216	388	604	22,749
				48,922

years of age in 1870. Thus, the black Reconstruction politicians in Charleston combined age and experience with a substantial measure of youth and vitality.

At least half the Negro politicians were literate or semiliterate according to available records (Tables 5 and 6). Those who were semiliterate possessed the ability to read but not write.[14] Of the nearly 36 percent whose literacy was unknown, surely some were literate, though a substantial number of adult blacks were classified as unable to write in the 1870 census. A relatively small number totaling almost 14 percent of the politicians were categorized as illiterate. A number of black leaders were very well educated and had attended various institutions of higher learning. Benjamin A. Boseman spent a term at Dartmouth College and was a graduate of the Bowdoin Medical School.[15] Francis L. Cardozo had received a classical education at the University of Edinburgh.[16] Richard H. Cain had attended Wilberforce College in Ohio for at least a year.[17] Martin R. Delany completed one term at the Harvard Medical School in 1850–1851 before he was summarily dismissed with two other black students.[18] Others had gone as far as high school. Robert C. De Large claimed to have attended Wood High School.[19] George H.

TABLE 7

Occupations of Black Politicians in Charleston during Reconstruction

Occupation	All Black Politicians (N = 234)		Black Democrats Only (N = 39)	
	Number	% age	Number	% age
Agriculture	6	2.6	1	2.6
Business	6	2.6	3	7.7
Cotton Shipper	1			
Wood Factor	2			
Livery Stable	1			
Fish Factor	1			
Factor	1			
Professional	15	6.4	2	5.1
Minister	8			
Attorney	1			
Physician	2			
Teacher	4			
Skilled	97	41.5	13	33.3
Carpenter	21		4	
Tailor	16			
Butcher	13			
Bricklayer	8			
Barber	6		3	
Shoemaker	5			
Others	28		6	
Unskilled	46	19.7	8	20.5
Unknown	64	27.4	12	30.8

Lee, a transplant from Massachusetts, had attended Salem High School in his native state.[20]

Two-fifths of Charleston's black politicians were skilled workers, and more than half of these craftsmen were tailors, carpenters, and butchers (Table 7). The men in these particular occupations showed a greater proclivity for politics than did men with other skills. For example, in the 1848 city census there were the same number of black bricklayers as tailors—seventy-eight. Yet, during Reconstruction sixteen tailors were involved in politics and only eight bricklayers. There were thirty-seven bakers listed in 1848. Only one baker participated actively in politics. Of twenty-three shoemakers listed in the 1848 census five of that trade emerged in Reconstruction politics.

Almost 20 percent of the black politicians were unskilled laborers— porters, draymen, stevedores, and chimney sweeps. (No house servants were listed as politicians.) Thus, fully 60 percent of the black politicos in Charleston were laboring men. There were many who held more than one occupation over the years from the antebellum era through Reconstruction. Joseph J. Grant was a drayman and a carpenter. Peter Frost was a carpenter and a painter. Samuel Johnson was listed at various times as a butcher, carpenter, and minister. Malcolm Brown was a farmer before the war and a contractor during Reconstruction. Men like Francis Cardozo and H. H. Hunter combined careers in religion and education. The multiplicity of occupations may have been due in many instances to unstable economic conditions in Charleston after the war. Men searched about for work in the turbulent postwar world and were willing to try several jobs and occupations in hopes of achieving a modicum of economic security.

The absence of a substantial class of black professionals in Charleston was reflected in the small number of teachers, ministers and physicians involved in politics. Just eight ministers (some evidently part-time), four teachers, and two physicians were politically active. However, three of the ministers—Francis Cardozo, Richard Cain, and Benjamin F. Randolph—were among the most influential of South Carolina's leaders during Reconstruction. Nor were there many black businessmen deeply committed to politics. Some businessmen, like Joseph Dereef and Richmond Kinloch, avoided politics entirely. Perhaps they and others were too preoccupied with their businesses, or possibly they had no desire to take part in an activity that demanded so much public exposure. Those businessmen who were prosperous and did turn to politics like Robert Howard and Richard E. Dereef generally limited their involvement to the local level and showed no inclination to extend their political careers into Columbia or Washington. Conceivably, they were unwilling or unable to leave their businesses for extended periods. It is also likely that many black businessmen were not so classified but were instead categorized as skilled laborers in the censuses and city directories. Surely some of the tailors, carpenters, blacksmiths, and other craftsmen were prosperous, self-employed entrepreneurs and not merely skilled laborers.

Charleston's wealthiest black men did not assume a significant role in post-war politics. Though seven of those who had been among the city's fifteen wealthiest black men in 1859 were subsequently elected as aldermen during Reconstruction, only one—William McKinlay—played an active and continuous role in politics. He was the sole political leader of substantial financial means who was elected to the state legislature from the city. Each of the other six served one term as an alderman, and none were deeply involved in day-to-day political developments in Charleston.[21]

Available tax records for the Reconstruction years suggest that many of the black politicians were men of modest means (Table 8). And the absence of tax records for the postwar years for 152 (64.9 percent) of the men may be an indication that they had little or no taxable real estate or personal property. On the other hand, there were some politicians like Richard Cain who owned land outside of the city, and such information did not appear in local records.

TABLE 8

Total Taxable Wealth for 1870, 1871–1872, and 1874 of
Black Politicians in Charleston during Reconstruction
(N = 234)

Wealth	Number	Percentage
$1—500	11	4.7
501—1,000	19	8.1
1,001—2,500	29	12.4
2,501—5,000	9	3.8
5,001—10,000	8	3.4
10,001—25,000	5	2.1
25,001—50,000	1	0.4
Unknown	152	65.0

Many of these politicians not only joined political parties but were active in a variety of other social and service organizations where some of them achieved positions of leadership. At least twenty-one of Charleston's Reconstruction politicians were members of the Brown Fellowship Society. This was an elitist social and benevolent organization that had been founded in 1790 to provide insurance, education, and a cemetery for members and their families.[22] Among its prominent politicians and members were Robert De Large, William McKinlay, Whitefield J. McKinlay, (who became its president in 1876), Robert Howard and Malcolm Brown (who was treasurer in 1869). The society broke precedent and admitted a non-Charlestonian when Benjamin Boseman, a native of New York, joined the organization. The organization took no active role in politics, and its rules prohibited the discussion of political affairs.[23] If politics had been discussed, it might have caused some lively exchanges because some of its members, including Richard Dereef, George A. Glover, and Benjamin Kinloch, held decidedly Democratic and conservative views.

The Humane and Friendly Society, founded in 1802, was similar in purpose and membership to the Brown Fellowship Society. As a benevolent and elitist group it likewise provided mutual aid and operated a burial ground. Among its politician members were John W. Gordon, William T. Oliver, and Edward P. and Lafayette F. Wall. A number of members of the Brown Fellowship Society also belonged to the Humane and Friendly Society, including Richard Dereef and Robert Houston.[24]

In the years after the Civil War blacks in Charleston formed dozens of social, service, and religious organizations. The Freedman's Bank, where many of these groups deposited their funds, contained financial records of these organizations and the names of their officers.[25] Among the many politicians participating in these associations was Isaac Reed, who was secretary of the Veterans Republican Brotherhood.[26] Peter Miller was a captain in the Comet Light Infantry, a state militia unit.[27] William Dart was the president of the Baptist Teachers Association.[28] Some politicians rose to prominence in organizations that did not maintain Freedman's Bank accounts. William H. Mishaw was the president of the Union Star Fire Engine Company. Julius W. Lloyd was the president of the Sons and Daughters of Zion. Richard Birnie was the vice-president of the Brotherly Association. John B. Wright served as president of the Colored Young Men's Christian Association. Alonzo J. Ransier and Benjamin Boseman were president and vice-president respectively of the Amateur Literary and Fraternal Association. Most of the black politicians appear to have belonged to several black organizations. Such participation gave them the advantage of circulating with other members of the community, thereby permitting them to maintain contacts with their constituents and supporters.

A fascinating but tangential facet of black politics in Reconstruction Charleston was the seemingly incipient development of black political dynasties. A number of black families committed father and son to political involvement. Their participation was in keeping with a tradition long established by such prominent white families as the Pinckneys, the Middletons, and the Hayneses. The two most notable black families to plunge into politics were the McKinlays and the Walls. In each instance, father and son embarked upon political careers. The McKinlays were tailors. Both served in the constitutional convention, and both were elected to the state legislature in 1868 with the father, William, representing Charleston and the son, Whitefield J., serving Orangeburg County. Edward P. Wall and his son Lafayette F. were also tailors. Both were elected as Republican aldermen in November 1868. Both were later appointed to service with the United States Customhouse. There was also a case of a father-and-son team of freedmen, Primus Green, Sr., and Primus Green, Jr., but their political activity was confined to serving as delegates to Republican county conventions, limiting any higher political aspirations they might have had.

Surely the least recognized Reconstruction politician has been the black Democrat. But such political figures most certainly existed in Charleston (Tables 1–7). The thirty-nine men who were so identified defy simple explanation or categorization. They were neither conservative, elite, white-obsessed mulattoes nor poor, deluded, former slaves. They were both and more. Analyzed collectively, the black Democrats, like the black Republicans, represented a cross section of Charleston's diverse black community. Most had been free. Most were black, and the largest number were skilled workers. George A. Glover was a saddler who had been free. Thomas Brown had also been free and was a barber. Joseph A. Gaillard was a free mulatto carpenter, but Augustus Carroll, who was also a carpenter, had been a slave. A few were very rich, former slaveowners like Richard Dereef, a wood factor, and Elias Garden, a butcher. They had owned twelve and two slaves respectively in 1859. Some were apparently poor like Henry Holmes and Robert Madora, who were merely listed in the 1870 census as laborers. One of the unusual black Democrats was Sidney Eckhard. He had been arrested in the spring of 1867 as one of the leaders in the effort to desegregate Charleston's horsedrawn streetcars. But by 1874 Eckhard was the president of the Ward 5 Honest Government League, one of several Democratic "front" organizations formed for blacks during Reconstruction.[29] There were other black Democrats who switched political affiliations. L. J. Taylor was secretary of the South Carolina Democratic Conservative Club in 1868, but in 1872 he was a Republican delegate to the county convention.

Explaining motivation is perhaps the most important and yet the most elusive factor concerning black Reconstruction politicians. Why did these 234 men gravitate to politics? What pulled or pushed them into the political arena? There is understandably no simple, clear-cut answer. There were as many reasons for taking part in politics as there were men in politics, and unraveling those reasons is nearly impossible. But some men were almost certainly drawn to politics because it represented a fascinating segment of society previously closed to the black man. Others may have been captivated by the prestige and public admiration associated with political leadership. Still others sought political power, deriving gratification from making decisions and manipulating people and issues. Then there were those black men who sincerely believed that governmental service was the most effective way they could contribute to the progress of their race and community. They were guided by a commitment to public service and were political missionaries devoted, along with ministers and educators, to uplifting a race and a nation. However, another important factor—often overlooked—that may explain the attraction of political life was the desire to acquire a measure of economic security.

Many black men who had achieved modest economic standing as craftsmen and laborers before the war were staring at the harsh reality of deprivation and destitution in the ruins of postbellum Charleston. Politics may have meant hope for the race and advancement of the society, but is was also a new profession marked by economic opportunity. A political career may have appeared as a potentially rewarding opportunity for the middle-class black man who possessed little formal education but was self-confident and wise to the ways of his society and community.

There is some evidence to suggest that the quest for economic advancement was the most significant factor that impelled black men (and white men) to pursue politics in Reconstruction Charleston (Table 9). For example, there was a strong desire on the part of many politicians to hold more than one political or governmental position simultaneously. William McKinlay was a state legislator, alderman, register of mesne conveyances, and school commissioner in 1869 and 1870. Benjamin Boseman was a member of the state House of Representatives and physician to the Charleston jail prior to his appointment as postmaster of Charleston. Thomas Small

TABLE 9

Prewar and Postwar Records Indicating Assessed Value of Real Estate of Black Politicians in Charleston During Reconstruction*

Name	1859	1860	1862	1867	1870	1871	1872	1874	Increase or Decrease
Malcolm Brown	$9,100		7,600	3,000				1,800	Decrease
James Carroll	6,200			5,000		2,650			Decrease
Richard E. Dereef	25,400		27,000	11,500		9,590		6,920	Decrease
Paul B. Drayton			500	500		1,400			Increase
William Henry Francis	1,500					650			Decrease
Elias Garden	14,000		12,500	13,500		11,365			Decrease
George A. Glover	1,200		1,000	1,000		1,380		1,420	Increase
John W. Gordon		2,000		1,800		1,080		1,230	Decrease
R.H. Harney	6,650		9,000	4,800		1,600			Decrease
Richard Holloway	7,900		9,200	14,200		8,208		8,270	Decrease
Samuel Holloway	2,950		3,300	4,635					Increase
Robert Howard	33,900	37,100	31,300	31,500		26,255		16,035	Decrease
Benjamin Kinloch		3,500			1,500				Decrease
Charles C. Leslie						400		1,300	Increase
William McKinlay	23,820	24,000		25,000			22,800	19,935	Decrease
Paul Poinsett	1,200			1,000			1,700		Increase
Alonzo J. Ransier							7,857	3,200	Decrease
W.G. Rout	18,500						10,150		Decrease
Jacob Royall				300			2,640	3,237	Increase
Thomas Small	7,800		7,300	8,200			6,590	6,090	Decrease
Philip Thorn	2,000			1,500			1,600		Decrease
Edward P. Wall	1,800		1,500	1,500	1,800		2,785	5,115	Increase

*Purchases or sales of real estate as well as losses in slave property would skew these figures.

SOURCE: 1859: *List of Tax Payers of the City of Charleston for 1859* (Charleston, 1860); 1860: Manuscript, Eighth U. S. Census: 1862: Tax Ledgers, Free Persons of Color, City of Charleston; 1867: Tax Ledgers, City of Charleston; 1870: Manuscript, Ninth U. S. Census; 1871: (Letters A to K) Charleston County Auditor's Tax Duplicates; 1872: (Letters M to Z) Charleston County Auditor's Tax Duplicates; 1874: Charleston County Auditor's Duplicates.

was an alderman and school commissioner. Edward P. Wall was an alderman, county commissioner, and a customhouse inspector from 1868 to 1870. In 1869 Robert De Large was a state legislator, head of the state census in Charleston, a magistrate, and later land commissioner for South Carolina. These were the men who achieved the greatest success in politics; dozens of others were never able to win even one election or gain an appointive office.

Those politicians, out of office or in danger of losing an office and the economic benefits that it provided, showed an overwhelming desire to get or keep that political position. After the Democrats swept the municipal elections in 1871 Republicans faced a patronage crisis. Joseph P. Howard, a minor Republican functionary who was black and a bricklayer, wrote Governor Robert Kingston Scott in the summer of 1872 to explain his predicament and appeal for an appointment as a trial justice. "There is but very little business going on in our city, and what little is doing, the patronage are extended to those of different politic[s] from myself: this fact renders it compulsory on my part—always to ask favors from those only of the Republican Party."[30] Scott did not appoint Howard, and the bricklayer wrote a more heartrending letter seven months later to the new governor, Franklin James Moses, Jr. "I am forced through actual necessity again to respectfully ask your excellancy's [sic] attention to myself and family viz: (a dear, affectionate wife and five little ones) present a lamentable condition, having no business for some length of time, makes me feel despondent and almost broken-hearted. The prominent part I had always manifested together with my activity and energy towards the success of the Republican party has placed me in such a manner as to become obligated solely to that party for suste-nance and support."[31] Not long afterward he was appointed a trial justice in Charleston.[32]

In 1876 former Lieutenant-Governor Alonzo Jacob Ransier though that he was about to be removed as the collector of internal revenue for the Second Congressional District. He wrote Governor Daniel Henry Cham-berlain and begged the governor for aid in securing a nomination on the state Republican ticket in the upcoming Republican convention: "I have a large family and no means for their support and would be greatly obliged if my friends will take me into consideration in connection with such a position on the state ticket as they may think me qualified for."[33] Ransier's plea for patronage was not untypical of the Reconstruction politician, al-though it was a bit unusual that such a prominent leader was constrained to ask for support. Generally, it was the marginal political figures such as Joseph Howard who deluged the governor and other major officeholders with pleas for political appointments.

There is further evidence, though it should be emphasized that it is strictly tentative, that indicates that many black men were suffering eco-nomic reversals in the postwar years. Incomplete tax records in Table 9 show that a number of prosperous black men, including Richard Dereef, Elias Garden, William McKinlay, George Glover, and Edward P. Wall, had experienced financial losses in the aftermath of the war. But the table also shows that seven of the twenty-two politicians listed evidently gained wealth during the Reconstruction years. Though the evidence is anything but certain, it could be concluded that if wealthy blacks had suffered losses then blacks of modest means who had been free before the war also confronted serious economic difficulties in 1865, 1866 and after. Thus, it was middle-class carpenters, tailors, and butchers who were most inclined to get in-volved in politics. It may have been that those were the particular trades caught hardest in the economic squeeze in the immediate postwar years, while others, such as bakers and blacksmiths, were not as severely affected.

In any event, and in conclusion, the evidence does indicate that the black men who were involved in politics at the grass-roots level in Charleston's eight wards during Reconstruction were mainly skilled laborers who had grown up free in the city. Most seem to have been at least able to read. A sizable number of these men participated in social, service, and religious groups in the community in addition to their involvement in politics. As a whole, the group tended toward middle age, and nearly two-thirds were blacks, not mulattoes.

APPENDIX

The information on the origins and backgrounds of Charleston's black politicians was compiled from a variety of sources. The newspapers provided the names of the politicians by periodically listing (although frequently misspelling) the delegates to various party conventions and identifying members of different political factions that appeared and disappeared during Reconstruction. By then taking the compiled list of more than five hundred men active in politics and carefully examining demographic data on Charleston, it was possible to create a composite picture of 234 local black politicians. The main sources included the Eighth and Ninth Manuscript Federal Censuses for the City of Charleston. However, the 1870 census is notoriously unreliable. Also utilized were two censuses undertaken by the city of Charleston in 1848 and 1861 because city authorities were convinced the city had been underenumerated in the federal censuses. Charleston also maintained an annual register of free Negroes, the main purpose of which was to make certain blacks paid a capitation tax. The registers for 1824, 1827, 1832, 1833, 1834, 1838, 1840, 1842, 1843, 1844, 1845, 1846, 1848, 1849, 1850, 1851, 1855, and 1857 were examined. City directories for 1855, 1859, 1860, 1867 and 1876–1877 were used. The *List of Tax Payers of the City of Charleston for 1859* (Charleston, 1860) and the "City Tax Ledgers for Free Persons of Color for 1862" aided in the identification of free Negroes. The registers of signatures of depositors in the Freedman's Bank in Charleston also contain some biographical data as do the Service Records of Union Soldiers who served with the United States Colored Troops. Also providing occasional bits of personal information were the Charleston newspapers. Secondary sources of information were Lawrence C. Bryant, *Negro Lawmakers in South Carolina Legislature, 1868–1902* (Orangeburg, S. C. 1968); Emily B. Reynolds and Joan R. Faunt, comps., *Biographical Directory of the Senate of South Carolina* (Columbia, 1969); and the *Biographical Directory of Congress, 1774–1971* (Washington, 1971).

It should be pointed out that Charleston did not keep a register of births or deaths in the nineteenth century. And the Reconstruction government's 1869 census of the state has been either lost or destroyed.

In spite of the weighty volume of information, there were gaps and contradictions in the data. In many cases it was impossible to document prewar status as a slave. In a few instances newspaper reports and records of depositors in the Freedman's Bank identified former slaves. For the most part, however, there was no consistent means of determining conclusively those individuals who had been slaves. There were, fortunately, enough sources in most cases to confirm the status of free blacks. Where there were contradictions among the data regarding color, literacy, or other vital information local sources were usually given precedence over the federal census.

Democrats in the list are indicated by [D] following the name.

Black Politicians in Reconstruction Charleston

Name	Prewar Legal Status	Color	Prewar Residence	Occupation	Literate	Most Advanced Political Position
1. E. J. Adams	F	B	New Jersey	Minister	yes	Nominee for House, 1872
2. Thomas Aiken		B	South Carolina	Butcher	yes	Ward 3 delegate Rep. County Conv., 1872
3. H. Allen		B	South Carolina			Ward 5 delegate Rep. County Conv., 1867
4. John Allen		B	South Carolina			Ward 5 delegate Rep. County Conv., 1868
5. Macon B. Allen	F	M	Indiana	Attorney	yes	Judge, Inferior Court
6. Robert B. Artson	S	B	South Carolina	Tailor	yes	House, 1872–74
7. Peter Ash	S	M	South Carolina	Chimney Sweep		Delegate, State Rep., Conv., 1872
8. Albert A. Aspinall	F	M	Charleston	Mechanic	yes	Ward 5 Rep. nominee alderman, 1871
9. James Baxter		B	South Carolina	Cooper	yes	Ward 7 delegate Rep. County Conv., 1872
10. Samuel L. Bennett	F	M	Charleston	Shoemaker		Ward 3 School Comm., 1870
11. William H. Birney	F	M	Charleston	Bricklayer		Ward 6 School Comm., 1870
12. Richard Birnie [D]	F	B	South Carolina	Cotton shipper		Ward 4 Conservative nominee alderman, 1873
13. William Black [D]	F	B	Charleston	Carpenter	yes	Vice-Pres., Conservative Conv., 1870
14. John Bonum	S	B	Charleston	Street huckster	no	Ward 5 delegate Rep., Conv., 1867
15. Benjamin A. Boseman	F	M	Troy, N. Y.	Physician	yes	House, 1868–73/Postmaster
16. James A. Brawley		M	Charleston	Upholsterer	yes	Ward 2 Rep., nominee, School Comm., 1867
17. James A. Bright	S	B				Ward 3 delegate Rep. County Conv., 1867
18. William J. Brodie	F	M	Charleston	Carpenter		1868–70, 1876–77 House
19. Benjamin Brown [D]	S	B	South Carolina	Barber	no	Treasurer, South Carolina Colored Conv., 1869
20. Daniel Brown	S	M	South Carolina	Blacksmith	no	Ward 5 delegate Rep. City Conv., 1873
21. Frank Brown [D]	S	M	South Carolina	Preacher	yes	Ward 5 alderman, Reform Ticket, 1871
22. John Brown	S	B	South Carolina	Painter	semi	Ward 6 delegate Rep. County Conv., 1867
23. Malcolm Brown	F	B	Charleston	Farmer	yes	Ward 6 alderman, 1868
24. Peter Brown	F	B	Charleston	Barber		Ward 3 delegate Rep., County Conv., 1867

#	Name		Race	Place	Occupation		Positions
25	Robert C. Brown		B	South Carolina			Ward 4 delegate Rep. County Conv., 1873
26	Thomas Brown [D]	F	B	Charleston	Barber		President, Ward 1 Colored Dem. Assn., 1868
27	Dennis Bunch		M	South Carolina	Carpenter	yes	Ward 1 delegate Rep. County Conv., 1872
28	William Eden Burke	F	B	Charleston	Porter		Ward 8 delegate Rep. County Conv., 1873
29	Nelson Butler		B	South Carolina	Laborer	no	Ward 6 delegate Rep. City Conv., 1873
30	Jonas Byrd	F	B	Charleston	Fisherman	yes	Nominee for House, Reform, 1870
31	Richard H. Cain	F	B	Brooklyn, N.Y.	Minister	yes	State Senate, 1868–70
32	John N. Campbell		B				Ward 6 delegate Rep. County Conv., 1867
33	M. G. Camplin	F	B	South Carolina	Physician	yes	Ward 6 nominee alderman, Conservative, 1873
34	Francis Louis Cardozo	F	M	Connecticut	Teacher/minister	yes	Secretary of State/State Treasurer
35	Augustus Carroll [D]		B	South Carolina	Carpenter	yes	Vice-Pres., Ward 7 Democrat Club., 1868
36	James Carroll	F	B	Charleston	Shoemaker		Ward 5 delegate Rep. County Conv., 1868
37	John E. Clyde	F	M	Charleston			Nominee for the House, 1872
38	James W. Cochran		B	South Carolina	Laborer	yes	Ward 5 Rep. County Conv., 1867
39	Marlow Cochran [D]		B				Vice-Pres., Colored Conservatives
40	William Collins [D]		B				Vice-Pres., Ward 4 Dem. Club
41	Samuel R. Cox	F	M	Charleston	Fisherman	yes	Ward 8 Rep. Nominee, School Comm., 1873
42	George H. Dantzman		M	South Carolina	Butcher	yes	Ward 6 delegate Rep. County Conv., 1872
43	William Dart	F	M	Charleston		yes	Chaired Rep. Mass Meeting, 1868
44	Thomas A. Davis		B		Painter	yes	House, 1870–72, 1874–76
45	A. A. Deas [D]	F	B	Charleston	Teacher	yes	1st Vice-Pres., Colored Conservative Club, 1869
46	John M. Deas		M	Florida	Laborer	yes	Ward 5 delegate, Rep. County Conv., 1872
47	Martin Robison Delany	F	B	Ohio	Educator	yes	Nominee lieutenant governor Reform Ticket, 1874
48	Robert C. De Large	F	M	Charleston	Tailor	yes	U. S. House, 1870–72
49	Richard E. Dereff [D]	F	M	Charleston	Wood factor	yes	Ward 5 alderman, 1868
50	J. M. Devees		B				Ward 8 delegate Rep. County Conv., 1867
51	Richard Dickerson		B	South Carolina	Butcher	yes	Ward 6 delegate Rep. County Conv., 1875
52	Samuel Dickerson		B	South Carolina	Whitewasher	yes	Raconteur/Spokesman/Gadfly
53	Moses H. Dingle	F	M	Charleston	Carpenter	yes	Ward 2 delegate Rep. County Conv., 1872

Name	Prewar Legal Status	Color	Prewar Residence	Occupation	Literate	Most Advanced Political Position
54. Paul B. Drayton	F	B	Charleston	Carpenter	no	Delegate, Rep. State Conv., 1874
55. Sidney Eckhard [D]	F	M	Charleston	Cigar maker	yes	Ward 5 Pres., Honest Government League 1874
56. Samuel Elliott	F	B	Charleston	Fisherman	yes	Delegate, Rep County Conv., 1872
57. W. E. Elliott	S	B	Charleston	Fisherman	yes	Nominee, House, 1870
58. W. E. Evans		M			yes	Delegate, Rep State Conv., 1868
59. A. F. Farrar		B				Secretary, City Central Committee, 1871
60. Cyrus Fenwick	F	B	Charleston	Laborer	no	Nominee, House, 1870
61. William G. Fields	F	M	Charleston	Carpenter	yes	Ward 4 Rep. nominee alderman 1873
62. Adam Finley	S	B	Charleston	Laborer	semi	Ward 7 Rep. City Conv., 1873
63. Adam Pyatt Ford	S	B	Charleston	Pastor	yes	House, 1870–74, 1876–77
64. Richard Forrest	F	M	Charleston	Shoemaker		Ward 6 delegate, Rep. County Conv., 1867
65. Boston Fowler	F	M	Charleston	Drayman		Ward 3 delegate, Rep. County Conv., 1872
66. William Henry Francis [D]	F	M	Charleston	Bellhanger	semi	Ward 6 nominee, House, 1870
67. Paul Fraser		B	South Carolina	Laborer	no	Ward 2 delegate, Rep. County Conv., 1872
68. John M. Freeman, Jr. [D]	F	M	Charleston	Mechanic	yes	House, 1874–76
69. Peter B. Frost	F	M	Charleston	Carpenter/painter	yes	Ward 5 delegate, Rep. County Conv., 1872
70. Washington Gadsden		M	South Carolina	Laborer	yes	Ward 3 delegate, Rep. County Conv., 1872
71. Joseph A. Gaillard [D]	F	M	Charleston	Carpenter		President, Ward 3 Colored Dem. Club
72. Samuel E. Gaillard	F	B	South Carolina	Millwright	yes	State Senate, 1871–77
73. S. F. Ganett [D]		B				Nominee alderman, Citizens' Party, 1871
74. Elias Garden [D]	F	M	Charleston	Butcher	yes	Ward 6 alderman, 1871–73
75. Samuel B. Garrett		B		Minister	yes	Ward 3 alderman, 1871–77
76. Jonathan C. Gibbs	F	M	Philadelphia, Pa.	Minister	yes	Delegate, Rep. State Conv., 1867

77. Robert Given		B	Charleston	Saddler	yes	Ward 6 delegate, Rep. County Conv., 1867
78. George A. Glover [D]	F	M	South Carolina	Tailor	yes	Ward 4 alderman, 1871–73
79. Samuel Glover		B	Charleston	Butcher	yes	Ward 2 delegate, Rep. County Conv., 1872
80. John A. Godfrey	F	M	Charleston	Butcher	yes	Ward 5 nominee alderman, 1873
81. John W. Gordon	F	M	Charleston	Shoemaker	yes	Ward 7 nominee alderman, 1873
82. Robert Gordon	F	M	Charleston		yes	Vice-Pres., Independent Reps., 1874
83. W. L. Gourdin [D]		B				President, Ward 4 Colored Dem. Club, 1868
84. Joseph J. Grant	F	B	Charleston	Drayman/ carpenter	yes	House, 1872–76
85. Josiah Grant	F	B	Charleston	Ship carpenter		Ward 3 delegate, Rep. County Conv., 1872
86. William A. Grant	F	M	Charleston	Butcher	yes	House, 1872–74
87. William H. Grant		B		Bookkeeper		House, 1868–70
88. Joseph Green [D]		B	South Carolina		no	Delegate, State Rep. Conv., 1872
89. Primus Green, Jr.	S	B	South Carolina			Ward 2 delegate Rep. County Conv., 1872
90. Primus Green, Sr.	S	B	South Carolina			Ward 2 delegate Rep. County Conv., 1872
91. A. F. Gregorie	F	B	Charleston			Ward 5 delegate Rep. County Conv., 1872
92. Peter M. Gregory	F	M	Charleston	Carpenter/farmer		Ward 8 nominee alderman, 1873
93. W. R. H. Hampton	F	B	Charleston			Ward 4 alderman, 1869–71
94. James J. Hardy		M	South Carolina	Brickmason		House, 1870–72
95. S. H. Hare	F	B	Charleston	Tailor		Ward 6 delegate, Rep. County Conv., 1867
96. R. H. Harney	F	B	Charleston	Laborer		Ward 6 delegate, Rep. County Conv., 1867
97. July Hasel		B	South Carolina		no	Ward 7 delegate, Rep. County Conv., 1872
98. James N. Hayne		M	South Carolina	Tailor	yes	Ward 8 delegate, Rep. County Conv., 1867
99. Richard Holloway	F	M	Charleston	Carpenter	yes	Ward 4 alderman, 1868
100. Samuel Holloway	F	M	Charleston	Livery	yes	Nominated County Comm., 1870
101. Henry Holmes [D]	F	B	Charleston	Laborer	no	1st Vice-Pres., Ward 1 Colored Demo. Assn. 1868
102. Thomas M. Holmes	F	M	Charleston	Sexton	yes	Republican State Exec. Comm., 1868
103. William R. Holmes	F	M	Charleston	Tailor		Delegate, Rep. City Conv., 1868
104. Robert Houston	F	B	Charleston	Tailor	yes	Secretary, Rep. State Exec. Committee, 1868

Name	Prewar Legal Status	Color	Prewar Residence	Occupation	Literate	Most Advanced Political Position
105. Jacob Howard	F	B	Charleston	Factor		Ward 3 delegate, Rep. County Conv., 1867
106. Joseph P. Howard	F	B	Charleston	Bricklayer		Ward 3 delegate, Rep. County Conv., 1872
107. Robert Howard	F	M	Charleston	Wood factor	yes	Ward 3 alderman, 1868
108. Hezekiah H. Hunter	F	M	Brooklyn, N. Y.	Minister/teacher	yes	House, 1870–72
109. William R. Jervay	S	M	Berkeley, S. C.	Farmer	yes	Senate, 1872–76
110. Isaac Johnson	S	M	South Carolina		yes	Ward 5 delegate, Rep. County Conv., 1872
111. Samuel Johnson	F	M	Charleston	Butcher/carpenter minister	no	House, 1868–70
112. T. H. Jones	S	B	Charleston		yes	House nominee, 1872
113. Benjamin Kinloch [D]	F	B	Charleston	Millwright	yes	Ward 4 delegate, Dem. County Conv., 1872
114. Ralph Knight [D]		B				2nd Vice-Pres., Ward 1 Colored Dem. Assn., 1868
115. Henry Larcomb		B				Ward 3 delegate, Rep. County Conv., 1867
116. Joseph S. Lazarus [D]	F	B	Charleston	Carpenter	yes	President, Ward 7 Dem. Club, 1868
117. Edward Lee	F	M	Charleston	Sexton	yes	Ward 4 delegate Rep. County Conv., 1872
118. F. S. Lee		B	Charleston	Butcher		Nominee, House, 1872
119. George H. Lee	F	B	Salem, Mass			House, 1868–70
120. Joseph Lesesne		B	Charleston	Laborer	no	House, 1876–77
121. Charles C. Leslie [D]	F	M	Charleston	Fishfactor	yes	Conserv. nominee for alderman, Ward 5, 1873
122. S. J. Liston [D]		B				1st Vice-Pres., Ward 3 Dem. Club, 1868
123. Julius W. Lloyd	S	B	South Carolina	Laborer	semi	House, 1870–72
124. Aaron Logan		B	Charleston		yes	Vice-Pres., Union League, 1869
125. R. T. Lopez	S	B	South Carolina	Bricklayer		Delegate, Rep. State Conv., 1874
126. Aaron McCoy		B	South Carolina	Laborer	no	Ward 1 delegate, Rep. County Conv., 1873
127. Whitefield J. McKinlay	F	M	Charleston	Tailor	yes	Ward 2 delegate, Rep. County Conv., 1872
128. William McKinlay	F	M	Charleston	Tailor	yes	House, 1868–70

#	Name			Location	Occupation		Office/Position
129.	Thomas McPherson [D]	S	B	Charleston	Porter	semi	3rd Vice-Pres., Colored Dem. Club, 1868
130.	Robert Madora [D]	F	B	South Carolina	Laborer		Treasurer, 7th Ward Colored Dem. Club, 1868
131.	Edward P. L. Martin	F	B	South Carolina	Laborer	yes	Ward 4 delegate, Rep. County Conv., 1874
132.	George Martin	S	B	South Carolina	Blacksmith	no	Ward 8 delegate, Rep. County Conv., 1867
133.	Joseph N. Martin [D]	F	B	Charleston	Ricemill worker	no	Treasurer, 3rd Ward Colored Dem. Club, 1868
134.	David B. Mathews	S	B	South Carolina		yes	Ward 6 delegate, Rep. County Conv., 1872
135.	Edward Mathews	S	B	Charleston	Laborer	no	Ward 2 delegate, Rep. County Conv., 1872
136.	Stephen Maxwell	S	M	Charleston	Bricklayer/mechanic	yes	Vice-Pres., Mass Meeting, 1868
137.	Robert J. Meares		M	Charleston		yes	Nominee, House, 1872
138.	S. M. Mears [D]		B	Charleston			Recording secy., Ward 3 Colored Dem. Club, 1868
139.	Charles Michaels [D]		B	Charleston	Confectioner/fruiter		Ward 1 alderman, 1871–73
140.	Edward C. Mickey	F	B	Charleston	Tailor/minister	yes	House, 1868–72
141.	Peter Miller	F	B	Charleston	Wharf hand	yes	Ward 4 delegate, Rep. County Conv., 1872
142.	William Miller	F	M	Charleston		yes	Ward 5 delegate, Rep. County Conv., 1867
143.	Alexander F. Mills [D]	F	M	Charleston	Carpenter/painter	semi	Secretary, Ward 1 Colored Dem. Assn.
144.	Jacob Mills	S	B	South Carolina	Butcher/minister	no	Ward 8 nominee alderman, Conservative, 1873
145.	H. C. Minott		M				Nominee, House, 1872
146.	William H. Mishaw	F	M	Charleston	Barber	yes	Nominee, state senator, 1870
147.	Arthur B. Mitchell	F	B	Charleston	Cooper	yes	Ward 3 nominee alderman, 1873
148.	William J. Mitchell	F	B	Charleston	Bricklayer/butcher	yes	Vice-Pres., Mass Meeting, 1868
149.	Benjamin Moncreef	F	B	Charleston	Carpenter	semi	Ward 5 nominee alderman, 1873
150.	Norman Montgomery	S	M	South Carolina		yes	Treasurer, Central Exec. Comm., 1871
151.	J. D. Moore		B	South Carolina			Ward 5 delegate, Rep. County Conv., 1867
152.	John B. Morris	F	B	Charleston	Wheelwright	yes	Ward 8 delegate, Rep. County Conv., 1867
153.	J. Morrison		B	South Carolina	Laborer		Ward 2 delegate, Rep. County Conv., 1872
154.	William Mortimore	F	M	Charleston	Fisherman/carter	semi	Ward 3 delegate, Rep. County Conv., 1874
155.	W. J. Moultrie		B	South Carolina	Boatman	no	Ward 7 delegate, Rep. County Conv., 1872

Name	Prewar Legal Status	Color	Prewar Residence	Occupation	Literate	Most Advanced Political Position
156. W. F. Murray		M	South Carolina	Carpenter	yes	Ward 4 delegate, Rep. County Conv., 1868
157. John A. Mushington	F	M	South Carolina		yes	Secretary, Union League, 1875
158. J. B. Mushington	F	M				Nominated, County Comm., 1868
159. John Nesbit		B	Charleston	Mechanic	no	Ward 1 delegate, Rep. City Conv., 1874
160. Rebit Nesbit		B		Farmer	no	Delegate, Rep State Conv., 1874
161. Samuel Noisette	S	B	South Carolina	Bricklayer	yes	Ward 7 delegate, Rep. County Conv., 1872
162. Frank Oliver [D]		B	Charleston	Farmer		3rd Vice-Pres., Ward 1, Colored Dem. Assn.
163. William T. Oliver	F	M	Charleston	Shoemaker	yes	Ward 5 delegate, Rep., County Conv., 1872
164. Albert O'Neal		M	South Carolina	Tailor	yes	Ward 3 delegate, Rep. County Conv., 1867
165. Thomas Osborne	S	M	South Carolina		yes	Ward 4 delegate, Rep. County Conv., 1874
166. Joseph Parker [D]		B		Waiter		Ward 8 delegate, Tax Union, 1874
167. James Pawley		B				Ward 3 delegate, Rep. County Conv., 1867
168. Samuel Peronneau	F	M	South Carolina	Butcher		Ward 7 delegate, Rep. County Conv., 1872
169. John Perrineau	F	M	Charleston	Carpenter		Ward 5 delegate, Rep. County Conv., 1872
170. Edward Petty		B		Laborer	yes	House, 1872–74
171. H. B. Pickenpack	F	B	Charleston	Butcher		Ward 8 delegate, Rep. County Conv., 1867
172. J. Pinckney		B				Ward 5 delegate, Rep. County Conv., 1867
173. William G. Pickney	S	B	South Carolina	Laborer	yes	House, 1874–77
174. E. M. Pitray		M				Ward 3 delegate, Rep. County Conv., 1872
175. Paul McCall Poinsett	F	M	Charleston	Barber		Ward 6 delegate, Rep. County Conv., 1867
176. James Price	F	M	South Carolina	Saddler		Ward 6 delegate, Rep. County Conv., 1867
177. Isaac Prioleau		B	Charleston	Laborer	yes	House, 1872–74, 1876–77
178. Benjamin F. Randolph	F	M	Ohio	Minister	yes	Delegate, Rep. State Conv., 1868
179. Alonzo J. Ransier	F	M	Charleston	Shipping clerk	yes	Lieutenant governor, 1870–72
180. Isaac Reed	F	B	Charleston	Carpenter	semi	Ward 5 delegate, Rep. City Conv., 1868

Name			Birthplace	Occupation		Activity
181. Julius Reed	F	B	South Carolina		no	Ward 1 delegate Rep. County Conv., 1872
182. William Reed	S	M	Charleston		no	Ward 1 delegate Rep. County Conv., 1872
183. R. L. Richardson		B	South Carolina	Laborer		President, Mass Meeting, Ward 8, 1872
184. Elias W. Riley	F	B	Phelpston, N. Y.	Farmer		Ward 5 delegate, Rep. County Conv., 1872
185. Stepheny Riley	F	B	South Carolina	Stablekeeper		Nominee, Ward 4 alderman, 1875
186. Isaac B. Rivers		B	South Carolina	Laborer	no	Chaired, Rep. Meeting, 1874
187. P. Robinson		B	South Carolina		no	Ward 2 delegate, Rep. County Conv., 1872
188. W. G. Rout		B	South Carolina			Ward 5 delegate, Reform County Conv., 1871
189. Jacob Royall [D]		B				Democratic nominee, House 1872
190. James Russell		B	South Carolina		no	Vice-Pres., Union League Conv., 1869
191. P. Saulters, Jr.		M	South Carolina		yes	Ward 5 delegate, Rep. County Conv., 1872
192. Robert Savage		B	South Carolina		no	Ward 5 delegate, Rep. County Conv., 1872
193. Tobias Scott	F	B	Charleston	Porter		Delegate, Independent Rep. State Conv., 1874
194. George Shrewsberry	F	M	Charleston	Butcher	yes	Nominee, Ward 6 alderman, 1873
195. Thomas Small	F	B	Charleston	Carpenter		Ward 8 school comm., 1870
196. Christopher Smalls		B		Teacher		Nominee, Ward 5 school comm., 1873
197. Abraham Smith		B	South Carolina	Sexton	yes	House, 1868–72
198. Adam Smith	S	B	South Carolina	Brickmason	yes	Nominee, House, 1870
199. B. F. Smith		B			no	Ward 5 delegate, Rep. County Conv., 1874
200. S. L. Smith [D]		B				Corresponding Secy., Ward 7 Colored Dem Club, 1868
201. Nathaniel T. Spencer	S	M	Charleston	Tailor	yes	House, 1872–74
202. R. Stevens		B	South Carolina	Laborer	no	Ward 5 delegate, Rep. County Conv., 1867
203. James Stocker	F	B	Charleston	Laborer		Ward 7 delegate, Rep. County Conv., 1874
204. Abram Taylor	F	B	Charleston			Ward 7 delegate, Rep. County Conv., 1872
205. L. J. Taylor [D]		B	South Carolina	Laborer	semi	Secretary, Colored Conservative Club, 1869
206. H. G. Thomas		M	South Carolina		yes	Credentials Comm., Rep. City Conv., 1873
207. John Thomas [D]		B				2nd Vice-Pres., Colored Conservative Club, 1869
208. Phillip Thorn	F	M	Charleston	Carpenter/ undertaker		Ward 5 alderman, 1869–71

Name	Prewar Legal Status	Color	Prewar Residence	Occupation	Literate	Most Advanced Political Position
209. Julius C. Tingman		B	Charleston	Farmer	yes	House, 1872–74, 1876–77
210. Robert W. Turner		M	Virginia		yes	House, 1872–74
211. C. H. Vanderhorst, Jr.		B				Nominee, House, 1872
212. R. H. Vanderhorst	F	B	Charleston	Painter/carpenter	yes	Ward 8 delegate, Rep. County Conv., 1867
213. John Vanderpool	S	B		Field hand	yes	House, 1872–74
214. William Viney	F	M	Ohio		yes	Rep. delegate, County Con., 1874
215. Albel B. Walker [D]	F	B	North Carolina	Laborer	no	2nd Vice-Pres., Ward 3, Colored Dem. Club, 1868
216. James L. Walker	S	B	Charleston	Carpenter	no	Ward 4 delegate, Rep. County Conv., 1872
217. Edward P. Wall	F	M	Charleston	Tailor	yes	Secy.-Treas., Rep. State Executive Comm., 1868
218. Lafayette F. Wall	F	B	Charleston	Tailor	yes	Ward 3 alderman, 1868, 1869–71
219. R. M. Wallace		B	South Carolina			Ward 2 delegate, Rep. County Conv., 1872
220. April Washington		M	South Carolina			Ward 3 delegate, Rep. County Conv., 1867
221. S. L. Washington [D]	F	M	Charleston		yes	Recording Secy., Ward 7 Colored Dem. Club, 1868
222. H. L. Wayne	F	B	Charleston	Carpenter		Ward 5 delegate, Rep. County Conv., 1867
223. George Webb		B	South Carolina	Stevedore	no	Ward 5 delegate, Rep. City Conv., 1873
224. William Weston	F	B	Charleston	Tailor		Ward 4 alderman, 1868
225. Edward Wethers		B	South Carolina		no	Ward 2 delegate, Rep. County Conv., 1872
226. A. B. Williams	F	B	South Carolina	Watercart driver		Ward 8 delegate, Rep. County Conv., 1867
227. Alexander Williams	F	B	Charleston	Upholsterer	yes	Ward 4 delegate, Rep. County Conv., 1872
228. J. A. Williams		M	South Carolina			Nominee, House, 1872
229. Oliver Williams		B				Ward 3 delegate, Rep. County Conv., 1867
230. Paris Williams	F	B	Charleston	Barber	semi	Ward 1 delegate, Rep. County Conv., 1872
231. Thomas Williams		B	South Carolina			Ward 5 delegate, Rep. City Laborer Conv., 1868
232. William Wilson		B				Ward 4 delegate, Rep. City Conv., 1873
233. John B. Wright	F	B	Charleston	Tailor	yes	House, 1868–72
234. John J. Young	S	B			semi	Ward 4 delegate, Rep. County Conv., 1873

NOTES

1. Serving as benchmarks among traditional accounts of Reconstruction are John W. Burgess, *Reconstruction and the Constitution, 1866–1876* (New York, 1902); William A. Dunning, *Reconstruction, Political and Economic, 1865–1877* (New York, 1907); Claude G. Bowers, *The Tragic Era: The Revolution After Lincoln* (Cambridge, Mass., 1929); and E. Merton Coulter, *The South During Reconstruction, 1876–1877* ([Baton Rouge], 1947). Though more moderate on race, Francis B. Simkins and Robert H. Woody's *South Carolina During Reconstruction* (Chapel Hill, 1932) still belongs among the traditional studies.

2. The revisionist accounts begin with two black historians in the 1920s and 1930s. See Alrutheus A. Taylor, *The Negro in South Carolina During the Reconstruction* (Washington, 1924); and William E. B. Du Bois, *Black Reconstruction . . . in America, 1860–1880* (New York, 1935). For more recent studies see Kenneth M. Stampp, *The Era of Reconstruction, 1865–1877* (New York, 1965); John Hope Franklin, *Reconstruction: After the Civil War* (Chicago and London, 1961); Allen W. Trelease, *Reconstruction: The Great Experiment* (New York, 1971); and Joel Williamson, *After Slavery: The Negro in South Carolina During Reconstruction, 1861–1877* (Chapel Hill, 1965). Furthermore, the histographical pendulum has not swung back to the point that black leaders are now merely viewed sympathetically as heroes and/or tragic victims caught up in a confusing and stormy era. For critical revisionist accounts see Thomas Holt, *Black over White: Negro Political Leadership in South Carolina During Reconstruction,* (Urbana, Chicago, and London, 1977); Euline W. Brock, "Thomas W. Cardozo: Fallible Black Reconstruction Leader," *Journal of Southern History,* XLVII (May 1981), 183–206; Armstead L. Robinson, "Beyond the Realm of Social Consensus: New Meanings of Reconstruction for American History," *Journal of American History,* LXVIII (September 1981), 276–97; and Howard N. Rabinowitz, ed., *Southern Black Leaders of the Reconstruction Era* (Urbana, Chicago, and London, 1982).

3. Rankin, "The Origins of Black Leadership in New Orleans During Reconstruction," *Journal of Southern History,* XL (August 1974), 417–40. There also have been several full-length biographies of black men who held office during Reconstruction. See Okon Edet Uya, *From Slavery to Public Service: Robert Smalls, 1839–1915* (New York, London, and Toronto, 1972); James Haskins, *Pinckney Benton Stewart Pinchback* (New York, 1973); Peggy Lamson, *The Glorious Failure: Black Congressman Robert Brown Elliott and the Reconstruction in South Carolina* (New York, 1973); Peter D. Klingman, *Josiah Walls: Florida's Black Congressman of Reconstruction* (Gainesville, 1976); and Loren Schweninger, *James T. Rapier and Reconstruction* (Chicago and London, 1978).

4. Charleston's economic role in the nation declined fairly rapidly after the panic of 1819 as cotton prices fluctuated and competition from the Southwest increased. Exports from Charleston failed to keep pace with those of other southern ports, so that even Mobile exceeded Charleston in exports by 1840. Charleston's rank in population fell from sixth in the nation in 1820 to twelfth in 1850. Yet, in the minds of many northerners and southerners Charleston remained thoroughly identified with the southern way of life. By 1860 more than one-fifth of South Carolina's wealthiest planters maintained residence in the city. Julian J. Petty, *The Growth and Distribution of Population in South Carolina* (Columbia, S. C., 1943), 65, Table Six, 85–86; Charles S. Sydnor, *The Development of Southern Sectionalism, 1819–1848* ([Baton Rouge], 1948), 23, 251–52; Chalmers G. Davidson, *The Last Foray: The South Carolina Planters of 1860: A Sociological Study* (Columbia, S. C., 1971), 3, 170–267; John Radford, "The Charleston Planters in 1860," *South Carolina Historical Magazine,* LXXVII (October 1976), 228–29; George C. Rogers, Jr., *Charleston in the Age of the Pinckneys* (Norman, 1969), 52–53.

5. For more on antebellum black life in Charleston see Marina Wikramanayake, *A World in Shadow: The Free Negro in Antebellum South Carolina* (Columbia, S. C., 1973), 21–22, 52, 73–74, 77–92, 110–12, 116–17, 120, 124–31, 133–53, 175–81; Ira

Berlin, *Slaves Without Masters: The Free Negro in the Antebellum South* (New York, 1974), 36, 54, 65, 73–74, 214, 221, 230, 234, 236–38, 254–56, 344; Richard C. Wade, *Slavery in the Cities: The South, 1820–1860* (New York, 1964), *passim;* E. Horace Fitchett, "The Traditions of the Free Negro in Charleston, South Carolina," *Journal of Negro History*, XXV (April 1940), 139–52; and Fitchett, "The Origins and Growth of the Free Negro Population of Charleston, South Carolina," *ibid.*, XXVI (October 1941), 421–37.

6. The most useful newspapers were the Charleston *Mercury*, 1865–1868; the Charleston *Daily Courier*, 1865–1873; the Charleston *Daily News*, 1865–1873; the *News and Courier* merged in 1873 and formed the Charleston *News and Courier*, 1873–1875; the Charleston *Advocate*, 1867–1868; and the Charleston *Daily Republican*, 1869–1871.

7. See appendix for the list of politicians and a discussion of the sources.

8. Determining the color of Reconstruction politicians—white, black, or mulatto—proved to be especially difficult. There were seventy-nine men who were impossible to identify as either black or white, and thus they were not included in this study.

9. Consequently, a number of politicians whose nativity was listed in South Carolina were probably born and raised in Charleston.

10. Southern communities like Charleston attracted free blacks and runaway slaves alike during the antebellum period. Urban areas furnished opportunities for social intercourse, for economic improvement, and for acquiring some semblance of education. Though conditions could be desperately harsh and difficult in the cities, blacks continued to migrate to them both before and after the Civil War. For more information on urban life among slaves and free blacks, see Berlin, *Slaves Without Masters*, 159, 219; Wade, *Slavery in the Cities*, 50–54, 84–87, 114–15, 143–46, 214–20, 252–58; and Wikramanayake, *A World in Shadow*, 21–22, 100, 102–103.

11. The 1860 U. S. Census listed 17,146 blacks in Charleston, of whom 3,237 (18.8 percent) were free, and 13,909 (81.1 percent) were slaves. Blacks constituted 42.3 percent of the total population of 40,522, while 23,376 whites accounted for 57.7 percent. The 1861 city census listed 21,140 blacks, of whom 3,785 (17.7 percent) were free. In 1870 blacks numbered 26,173 (53.5 percent of the total population of 48,922), an increase of 52.6 percent over 1860. Whites numbered 22,749 (46.5 percent of the total), a decline of 2.7 percent. U.S. Bureau of the Census, *Population of the United States in 1860 . . . Eighth Census* (Washington, 1864), 452; Frederick A. Ford, comp., *Census of the City of Charleston, South Carolina, for the Year 1861* (Charleston, 1861); U. S. Bureau of the Census, *Ninth Census*; Volume I: *The Statistics of the Population of the United States . . .* (Washington, 1872), 258.

12. Simkins and Woody, *South Carolina During Reconstruction*, 116, and Wikramanayake, *A World in Shadow*, 15–16, incorrectly state that Francis L. Cardozo's father was Jacob Newton Cardozo, who was Isaac's older brother. See John F. Farley, "Francis L. Cardozo" (Senior thesis, Princeton University, 1949), 5–6.

13. Wikramanayake, *A World in Shadow*, 16.

14. In many instances census takers indicated the ability to read but not write. However, the definition of literacy involves the ability to read and write. "Persons of that age [10 years and over] who, as reported by the enumerators, were able to write, whether in English or in some foreign language, were classed as literate, while those who could not write, even though they could read, were classed as illiterate." *Negro Population, 1790–1915* (Washington, 1918), 403.

15. Charleston *Daily Republican*, September 21, 1869; Mary H. Hughes, Special Collections Librarian, Bowdoin College, letter to author, April 19, 1979.

16. Farley, "Francis L. Cardozo," 5–11.

17. Emily B. Reynolds and Joan R. Faunt, comps., *Biographical Directory of the Senate of the State of South Carolina* (Columbia, S. C., 1964), 191.

18. Victor Ullman, *Martin R. Delany: The Beginnings of Black Nationalism* (Boston, 1971), 115–17; Floyd J. Miller, *The Search for Black Nationality: Black Emigration and Colonization, 1787–1863* (Urbana, Chicago, and London, 1975), 124.

19. *Biographical Directory of Congress, 1774–1971* (Washington, 1971), 845. The location of Wood High School is unknown. De Large may have been exaggerating his educational accomplishments.

20. Charleston *News*, February 20, 1872.

21. Those six were Malcolm Brown, Richard Holloway, Elias Garden (a Democrat), Thomas Small, Robert Howard, and George Shrewsberry. Additionally, six wealthy blacks were appointed in 1868 by military authorities to serve as aldermen. They were Richard E. Dereef, Richard Holloway, Robert Howard, William McKinlay, and William Weston. They served for nearly a year. The published 1859 list of taxpayers provided information on and the taxable wealth of Charleston's black and white residents. *List of Tax Payers of the City of Charleston for 1859* (Charleston, 1860).

22. Compiled from the membership rolls, Brown Fellowship Society Minutes, January 8, 1869, to July 6, 1911, Xerox copy in Charleston County Public Library. The original minute books are in the rare book room of the Robert K. Smalls Library of the College of Charleston.

23. The rules were evidently adhered to because society minutes reveal no political discussions. Most meetings were brief and concerned such routine matters as care of the society's cemetery, election of new members, and the election of officers. *Ibid*. See also Robert L. Harris, Jr., "Charleston's Free Afro-American Elite: The Brown Fellowship Society and the Humane Brotherhood," *South Carolina Historical Magazine*, LXXXII (October 1981), 294.

24. Charleston *News and Courier*, January 15, 1874.

25. Registers of Signatures of Depositors in Branches of the Freedman's Savings Bank and Trust Co., 1865–1874. Records of the Office of the Comptroller of the Currency, Record Group 101 (National Archives, Washington, D. C.).

26. *Ibid.*, July 7, 1870.

27. *Ibid.*, June 8, 1870.

28. *Ibid.*, June 15, 1871.

29. For more on the streetcar episode see William C. Hine, "The 1867 Charleston Streetcar Sit-ins: A Case of Successful Black Protest," *South Carolina Historical Magazine*, LXXVII (April 1976), 110–14.

30. Howard to Scott, June 12, 1872, Box 21, Folder 5, Governor's Papers (South Carolina Department of Archives and History, Columbia, S. C.). See also Lawrence N. Powell, "The Politics of Livelihood: Carpetbaggers in the Deep South," in J. Morgan Kousser and James M. McPherson, eds., *Region, Race, and Reconstruction: Essays in Honor of C. Vann Woodward* (New York and Oxford, 1982), 315–47.

31. Howard to Moses, January 6, 1873, Box 1, Folder 30, *ibid*.

32. "Appointments," January 10, 1873, Box 1, Folder 34, *ibid*.

33. Ransier to Chamberlain, September 8, 1876, Box 14, Folder 27, *ibid*. Ransier's fear of losing the Internal Revenue collectorship was unfounded. He retained the position through the Hayes administration.

THREE

The Freedmen's Bureau and Local
Black Leadership

RICHARD LOWE

The Bureau of Refugees, and Abandoned Lands, a branch of the United States War Department commonly known as the Freedmen's Bureau, was designed to help former slaves make the transition from slavery to freedom after the Civil War. It was the federal agency most directly involved with the black folk of the old Confederacy; as such it has received close scrutiny from scholars, and it has been the object of considerable pulling and tugging by various historical schools of thought in the last several decades. Since the mid-1950s, the agency has been interpreted by many revisionist scholars as a kind-hearted and generally successful attempt to provide needed assistance to black Americans and to introduce them to the American political process; in the 1970s, postrevisionist writers began to reassess the bureau as reactionary, paternalistic, and too concerned with establishing and maintaining close ties to the white southern establishment to make a substantial difference in the lives of the freedmen.[1]

Many facets of the bureau's operations have been studied in the last four decades. Its dealings with the emerging class of black political leaders in the countryside and towns of the South, however, have not been examined as fully as some other aspects of its history, primarily because relatively little scholarly research has been devoted to group studies of African-American leaders on the local and county levels.[2] Among the mountains of Freedmen's Bureau records, one set of documents does provide a glimpse of the bureau's relationship with local- and county-level black leadership and shed further light on the Bureau's attitude toward the rise of an entirely new political class.[3]

Early in the spring of 1867 the bureau's assistant commissioner for the former Confederate state of Virginia, Brevet Brig. Gen. Orlando Brown, ordered bureau officers in the forty-one subdistricts of the state to provide headquarters with "the names of six of the most intelligent of the freedmen belonging to each county, in whom both races have confidence and who have the most influence over their own people."[4] The order was issued only six days after Congress passed the radical first Reconstruction Act, which called for a biracial martial-law regime. Within two weeks he ordered a bureau officer stationed in Lunenburg County in south-central Virginia to provide "the names of two citizens of Lunenburg County, of the first respectability, who are competent and willing to act on a Court to be organized under the authority of the Military bill" (the first Reconstruction Act). One day later he ordered bureau officials scattered around the state to send headquarters "a list of the Magisterial Districts in each County of your District, together with the boundaries of each Magisterial District as they were in 1860 . . . also a list of the voting precincts in each County as they were in 1860. . . . The information is required immediately." Whether Brown intended to provide the names to the military governor of the state for appointment to voter registration boards or to Freedman's Bureau courts or to various local offices — or to all of those — is not specified; the timing and the wording of the orders, however, make it clear that Brown was preparing lists of black Virginians who would be qualified to hold local and county office under the new military government of the Old Dominion.[5]

The lists of names began arriving at bureau headquarters in Richmond in spring 1867. Bureau officers had spent considerable time and effort identifying the men they considered to be the black leaders of the state's counties and towns; many supplied more than six names, and they supplied names for at least 93 of Virginia's 102 counties and cities. Of the 9 counties without surviving lists in the bureau records, 7 were located on the far western and southwestern fringes of the state, where the black population was very small.[6]

An examination of the 621 individuals named in the reports reveals the type of black man considered officeholding material by the bureau. Indeed, the list of men compiled by the white, northern-born federal officials reveals at least as much about the identifiers as it does about the identified.

In addition to the names, bureau officials sometimes provided other identifying information about black men — their occupations, their levels of literacy, and the locations of their homes. For example, the reports indicated that Ossian Johnson of Albemarle County in the central Piedmont region had "purchased own freedom." Nelson H. Clark of Amelia County was a "soldier in 1812." In the eastern Tidewater, Levi Henderson of New Kent County and William Geary of Princess Anne County were identified as Union army veterans, while Logan Waller of New Kent had "worked for QM [the Union army quartermaster] at Yorktown during the war." John Mautley of Matthews County on the western shore of Chesapeake Bay had established such a solid reputation that he "could get $100 credit at any store in the county before the war." At least some bureau officers consulted the black communities in their districts to ascertain the names of men considered to be leaders. In short, many of the Freedmen's Bureau agents took their responsibilities seriously, and they painstakingly identified those black men who, in their opinion, had demonstrated some ability and capacity for leadership in the two years since the end of slavery.[7]

Nearly half (49 percent) of the 621 men listed in the reports can be identified in the 1870 manuscript census.[8] A quantitative profile of those African Americans shows some characteristics considered important by the Freedmen's Bureau officials. The African Americans chosen were mature men in the prime of their adult lives (mean and median ages of 42.6 and 42.0); only about one in eight (12.4 percent) was younger than thirty. Virtually all of them (97.5 percent) had been born in Virginia. Compared to the average Virginia black adult male, they were considerably more likely to be literate (62.2 percent compared to 9.1 percent), a startlingly high figure, especially for a statewide selection of men at the grass-roots level who generally were not among the most elite leaders of the state. A man's ability to read and write was clearly an important consideration for bureau agents.[9]

About one-seventh (14.1 percent) of the total "colored" population of Virginia was of mixed black and white ancestry; roughly six-sevenths was entirely "black" in 1870. Among the men named by the bureau, however, more than one-third (34.6 percent) were of mixed percentage. Mulattoes, quadroons, and others of mixed heritage were greatly overrepresented on the bureau list. Furthermore, on the eve of the Civil War, only about one of every ten black Virginians (10.5 percent) was free. More than one in three (35.4 percent) of the men on the bureau list, however, had been born free or had secured their freedom before the Civil War.[10]

A comparison of the men selected as potential officeholders by the Virginia Freedmen's Bureau with the established black leaders in New Orleans and with elected black delegates to Reconstruction conventions in various states shows that the characteristics of literacy, mixed racial heritage, and prewar freedom were even more pronounced in the latter two groups. (See table 1.) The men identified by the bureau were much more likely to be literate than the average Virginia black adult male, but they were less likely to be literate than were those identified as black leaders in New Orleans, where there was a long tradition of a strong black urban elite (62.2 percent to 98.1 percent). Among the black delegates to the various state constitutional conventions, the literacy figure was 84.0 percent. Similarly, black convention delegates and black leaders in New Orleans were more likely to be of mixed blood (52.1 percent and 91.2 percent, respectively) than the men on the Virginia bureau list (34.6 percent). The same pattern emerges with respect to prewar legal status. In New Orleans nearly all African-American leaders (97.1 percent of all those identified) had been free prior to 1861. Among the black delegates to the Reconstruction constitutional con-

TABLE 1

Comparisons of Black Men Identified by the Virginia Freedmen's Bureau as Local Leaders with Other Groups of African-American Adult Males during Reconstruction

	Percent Literate	Percent with Mixed Racial Heritage	Percent Free before 1861	Mean Property Holdings[a]
Local Leaders in Virginia	62.2	34.6	35.4	$1,189.14
All Adult black males in Virginia	9.1	14.1	10.5	413.80
Black members of southern constitutional conventions	84.0	52.1	58.9	NA[b]
Black leaders in New Orleans	98.1	91.2	97.1	NA

SOURCES: The figures in lines 3 and 4 of the table are from Richard L. Hume, "Negro Delegates to the State Constitutional Conventions of 1867-1869," in *Southern Black Leaders of the Reconstruction Era*, ed. Howard N. Rabinowitz (Urbana, 1982), 137-38; and David C. Rankin, "The Origins of Black Leadership in New Orleans during Reconstruction," *Journal of Southern History*, 40 (August, 1974), 421, 427, 432.

[a] Among those who owned any property, real or personal.

[b] Not available.

ventions, nearly three-fifths (58.9 percent) had been free. The figure for local leaders identified by the Freedman's Bureau in Virginia was considerably lower: 35.4 percent.[11]

The men named by the bureau agents were considerably wealthier than the typical Virginia black male. Considering only those who held any real or personal property at all, the mean wealthholding for Virginia black adult males was $413.80; the figure for those with property on the bureau list, however, was nearly three times as large, $1,189.14. The property holdings of the latter group, on the other hand, were significantly lower than those for either black or white members of the 1867–1868 constitutional convention in Virginia. When all possible property holders are considered, those who owned real or personal property as well as those who owned none at all, the mean wealthholding for white delegates to the constitutional convention was $14,843.79; for black delegates, $786.87; for men on the bureau list, only $402.55. The median figures for these three groups ($7,000, $397, and $0, respectively) display the same pattern.[12]

Assistant Commissioner Brown's original order to provide the names included the stipulation that his subordinates identify men "in whom both races have confidence and who have the most influence over their people." This difficult combination may well have led some local bureau officers to exclude from the lists outspoken black men who had already established a reputation for alienating the native white community. For example, the bureau list named only 11 of the 87 African Americans who would serve in the Virginia General Assembly in the last third of the century. Similarly, only 3 of the 24 black delegates to the 1867–1868 constitutional convention—men who were elected by overwhelmingly black votes—had been identified as potential leaders by the bureau. Among the 21 black convention members not on the list were several who would emerge as the most outspoken and radical leaders of black Virginia: Thomas Bayne of Norfolk, a literate escaped slave whose demands for reform in the Underwood convention (the 1867–1868 state constitutional convention) earned him the ridicule of conservative white newspapers; Lewis Lindsay of Richmond, also a former slave and as outspoken as Bayne; Willis Augustus Hodges of Princess Anne County, a freeborn native Virginian, friend of abolitionists John Brown and Gerrit Smith, and a man who had lived in New York for several years before the war and edited his own newspaper in New York City; Daniel Norton of York County, the most prominent black leader of the lower Peninsula; and J. B. Baldwin, a freedman of Prince William County, who proposed in the Underwood convention the confiscation of large landed estates for sale to poor loyal men.[13]

It is possible that some bureau officials simply knew too little about the black community to come up with the names of men like Bayne and Lindsay, individuals who were obviously considered leaders by black Virginians in the election of delegates to the constitutional convention only a few months later. On the other hand, given Assistant Commissioner Brown's directive to include the names of those "in whom both races have confidence" and given the care obviously bestowed on the lists, it is likely that some bureau agents consciously excluded men most likely to alienate local whites. In either case, it is clear that the bureau's official vision of local black leadership did not correspond perfectly with that of black voters in the hinterlands.

Nevertheless, some African Americans who were or would become identified in conservative minds as dangerous radicals were included in the lists. For example, Robert Norton of York County worked closely in the politics of the lower Peninsula with his radical brother, Daniel Norton. George Seaton of Alexandria County and Cornelius Harris of Richmond had served on radical judge John C. Underwood's federal grand jury to indict Jefferson Davis. Harris and other prominent black men, according to historian Alrutheus Ambush Taylor, would become the objects of ridicule and derision in conservative Virginia newspapers. Joseph Gregory was one of the leading black men of Southampton County; his strong stands in favor of black rights would soon make him the target of white abuse and legal harassment.[14] It is not clear whether some bureau agents simply misunderstood the political stance of these men or ignored the guidelines set down by Assistant Commissioner Brown, but the names of some radical blacks who clearly would not "have the confidence" of white Virginians did appear on the bureau list. Thus, while the bureau's vision of the ideal black leader was not altogether congruent with that of local black voters, the two views did overlap to some extent. Conversely, despite Brown's guidelines, most white Virginians would have found none of the bureau's suggestions acceptable.

Did the African-American men identified by the bureau in fact hold office at the local and county levels, once the Reconstruction Acts allowed them to enter the political life of Virginia? Unfortunately, no centralized, systematic record of local and county officers during the Reconstruction period was compiled by Virginia's state or county governments. Most of what historians know about the identity of black local and county officials has been based on painstaking searches of some town and county archives. Recently discovered documents in the state archives, however, include the names of all men appointed by the military governors of Virginia from 1867 to 1869 to the county offices of sheriff, commissioner of revenue, and clerk of court.[15]

A comparison of these sources with the Freedmen's Bureau lists of potential officeholders indicates that very few of the men identified by bureau agents ever held public office. Three of the twenty-four members of the 1867–1868 constitutional convention, one overseer of the poor, one member of a county board of supervisors, one superintendent of the poor, two city council members, one customs inspector, and eleven of the eighty-seven black members of the General Assembly in the last third of the century came from the ranks of the bureau nominees. To the delight of most white Virginians, not a single freedman was among the 376 men appointed by the military governors of Virginia to the offices of sheriff, county commissioner of revenue, or clerk of court during the years of congressional Reconstruction. Thus, only 20 of the 621 men named by the bureau were among the 350 or so black Virginians known to have held some type of public office during and after Reconstruction.

This figure may be somewhat misleading, however, given the lack of a complete and systematic record of all local and county officers in postbellum Virginia. It is quite possible that many more than twenty held some type of public office. It is also certain that some of the men listed by the bureau provided leadership for the black community in ways other than holding office. Alexander Dunlop of James City County and William Thornton (or Thorton) of Elizabeth City County, both prominent in the political affairs of the lower Peninsula, had been among the seven African Americans who testified before the Joint Committee on Reconstruction. Robert P. Vickers, an unsuccessful candidate for the Underwood constitutional convention from Russell County, would win the votes of all but one of the black voters in his county. R. D. Beckley of Alexandria was an active political figure in his area even though he never held public office. Cornelius Harris of Richmond played a prominent role in the politics of the capital from the end of the war well into the 1880s. Tazewell Branch of Prince Edward County led the struggle for his county's public school system in the early 1870s. In addition, at least six, and possibly more, men on the bureau list participated in one or more of the numerous "colored conventions" held in various locations after the Civil War.[16] Finally, the generals who served as military governors of the Old Dominion apparently ignored the lists so carefully constructed by the bureau when they made appointments to the most important county offices. In summary, while bureau officials did identify more political leaders than raw numbers of officeholders alone would imply, it is also clear that the overwhelming majority of the men the bureau suggested were passed over by Union generals and black voters alike in favor of other leaders.

Freedman's Bureau agents in Virginia, ordered to identify potential local and county officeholders, selected from among the men in their counties those African Americans who were well into their mature years, who were wealthier, and who were more likely to be literate, lighter in skin, and free before the war than the average Virginia adult black male. The bureau officers did not provide complete satisfaction to either of the groups pulling at them from opposite directions. Most white Virginians, with the frequent cooperation of their military rulers, resisted the elevation of any black men to political office at any level. And newly enfranchised African Americans in many cases had their own ideas about who should lead them. Nonetheless, the bureau did identify some black men who were or would soon become prominent radical leaders; some of the men they named were certainly political leaders in their communities even if they held no elected offices; and incomplete records raise the possibility that many more of the bureau nominees may have held office than can be documented 130 years later. In addition, the refusal of generals John M. Schofield and George Stoneman to appoint blacks to important county offices hamstrung the bureau's efforts to indicate that the bureau was considerably more sympathetic to black political participation than were the state's military governors. Thus, the bureau fits neatly into neither the revisionist nor the postrevisionist model. It was neither as sensitive to the black community as some revisionist accounts imply nor as reactionary as postrevisionists insist.

NOTES

1. The first general, sympathetic account of the bureau was George R. Bentley, *A History of the Freedmen's Bureau* (Philadelphia, 1955). For postrevisionist critiques of that agency, see Louis S. Gerteis, *From Contraband to Freedmen: Federal Policy toward Southern Blacks, 1861–1865* (Westport, 1973); Leon F. Litwack, *Been in the Storm So*

Long: The Aftermath of Slavery (New York, 1979); and William S. McFeely, *Yankee Stepfather: General O. O. Howard and the Freedmen* (New Haven, 1968).

2. The best treatment of the general subject is Howard N. Rabinowitz, ed., *Southern Black Leaders of the Reconstruction Era* (Urbana, 1982). Only two of the sixteen essays in the book (those by David C. Rankin and Michael B. Chesson) provide collective portraits of local leaders, and both deal with large cities (New Orleans and Richmond) rather than with the towns and counties of the hinterlands. Moreover, the scores of books and articles cited in the notes to the various essays in the book deal primarily with black leadership on the national and state levels.

3. Reports on Prominent Whites and Freedmen, March-May 1867, Miscellaneous Records, Records of the Assistant Commissioner for the State of Virginia, Bureau of Refugees, Freedmen, and Abandoned Lands, 1865–1869, RG 105 (National Archives, Washington, D.C.).

4. O. Brown to G. R. Chandler et al., March 8, 1867, Letters and Telegrams Sent, *ibid.*

5. O. Brown to D. J. Connolly, March 22, 1867, *ibid.*; O. Brown to J. H. Remington, March 23, 1867, *ibid.* The requested reports on magisterial districts are in Reports on the Boundaries of Magisterial and Voting Precincts, March-April 1867, Miscellaneous Records, *ibid.*

6. See the reports (not separately titled, but arranged by county) in Reports on Prominent Whites and Freedmen, March-May 1867, Miscellaneous Records, *ibid.* The nine counties for which lists do not appear in the Freedmen's Bureau records are Bland, Buchanan, Carroll, Craig, Fluvanna, Gloucester, Highland, Lee, and Wise. Seven of the nine (all except Fluvanna and Gloucester) were in the western and southwestern mountainous region and had very small black populations in 1870 (ranging from 1.2 percent to 8.4 percent of the total county population). The African-American populations in Fluvanna (in central Virginia), Gloucester (bordering Chesapeake Bay), and the state as a whole were 51.6 percent, 53.2 percent, and 41.9 percent, respectively: United States, Bureau of the Census, *The Statistics of the Population of the United States; Complied from the Original Returns of the Ninth Census (June 1, 1870)* (Washington, 1872), 68–70.

7. See the reports of Albemarle, Amelia, New Kent, Princess Anne, and Matthews counties in Reports on Prominent Whites and Freedmen, March-May 1867, Miscellaneous Records, Records of the Assistant Commissioner for the State of Virginia, Bureau of Refugees, Freedmen, and Abandoned Lands, 1865–1869. The report for Montgomery County is a good example of the fuller, more detailed reports.

8. Given the obscure status of many of the men listed by the Freedmen's Bureau, the geographic mobility of many freedmen after the war, and the imperfect compilation of the 1870 federal census, it is not surprising that about half (318 of 621, or 51 percent) of the local figures named by the bureau could not be located in the manuscript census. Thus, composite figures and percentages given below do not include all local individuals identified as potential officeholders. For the manuscript records of the 1870 federal census in Virginia, see Ninth Census of the United States, 1870, Schedule 1 (Inhabitants), Records of the Bureau Census, RG 29 (National Archives). For other census-based studies of the Civil War era that have located about 50 percent of their target individuals, see Maris A. Vinovskis, "Have Social Historians Lost the Civil War? Some Preliminary Demographic Speculations," in *Toward a Social History of the Civil War: Exploratory Essays*, ed. Maris A. Vinovskis (New York, 1990), 1–30, esp. 14; Thomas R. Kemp, "Community and War: The Civil War Experience of Two New Hampshire Towns," *ibid.*, 31–77, esp. 59–60, n75; and W. J. Rorabaugh, "Who Fought for the North in the Civil War? Concord, Massachusetts, Enlistments," *Journal of American History*, 73 (Dec. 1986), 695–701. Vinovskis located 55 percent; Kemp 47 percent; and Rorabaugh, 48 percent.

9. Literacy figures are in Bureau of the Census, *Statistics of the Population of the United States . . . Ninth Census (June 1, 1870)*, 432–33, 618–19. Literacy status (anyone able to read or write or both was considered literate) for the men named by the Freed-

men's Bureau was determined by consulting the bureau reports and the 1870 manuscript federal census. In the few cases in which these two sources conflicted, the literacy status noted in the bureau report was accepted, since bureau officers were likely to learn more about the backgrounds of the men in question than census marshals normally knew. For the manuscript records of the 1870 federal census in Virginia, see Ninth Census of the United States, 1870, Schedule 1 (Inhabitants), Records of the Bureau of the Census.

10. Bureau of the Census, *Statistics of the Population of the United States . . . Ninth Census (June 1, 1870)*, 68–70, 608–9; United States, Bureau of the Census, *Population of the United States in 1860; Compiled from the Original Returns of the Eighth Census* (Washington, 1864), 516–18. The racial ancestry of individuals named by the Freedmen's Bureau was taken from the manuscript records of the 1870 United States census: Ninth Census of the United States, 1870, Schedule 1 (Inhabitants), Records of the Bureau of the Census. For individuals who could not be located in the 1870 census, racial type was taken from the bureau lists when such information was available.

11. David C. Rankin, "The Origins of Black Leadership in New Orleans during Reconstruction." *Journal of Southern History*, 40 (Aug. 1974), 421, 427, 432; Richard L. Hume, "Negro Delegates to the State Constitutional Conventions of 1867–1869," in *Southern Black Leaders of the Reconstruction Era*, ed. Rabinowitz, 137–38. All figures on literacy, racial heritage, and prewar legal status in these two articles are for men who could be reliably identified, not for the entire sets of leaders.

12. Loren Schweninger, *Black Property Owners in the South, 1790–1915* (Chicago, 1990), 292–94; Richard L. Hume, "The Membership of the Virginia Constitutional Convention of 1867–1868: A Study of the Beginnings of Congressional Reconstruction in the Upper South," *Virginia Magazine of History and Biography*, 86 (Oct. 1978), 472, 477.

13. For Thomas Bayne, Lewis Lindsay, Daniel Norton, and J. B. Baldwin, see Richard Lowe, *Republicans and Reconstruction in Virginia, 1856–70* (Charlottesville, 1991), 51, 78–81; for Willis Augustus Hodges, see Willis Augustus Hodges, *Free Man of Color: The Autobiography of Willis Augustus Hodges*, ed., Willard B. Gatewood, Jr. (Knoxville, 1982).

14. Lowe, *Republicans and Reconstruction in Virginia*, 51, 118, 174, 180; Alrutheus Ambush Taylor, *The Negro in the Reconstruction of Virginia* (Washington, 1926), 214, 286; Daniel W. Crofts, *Old Southampton: Politics and Society in a Virginia County, 1834–1869* (Charlottesville, 1992), 246, 270–76.

15. Luther P. Jackson, *Negro Office-Holders in Virginia, 1865–1895* (Norfolk, 1945), and various other sources include the names and sometimes descriptions of roughly 350 local, county, and state African-American officeholders. List of Local Officials Appointed by Authority of Brevet Major General George Stoneman, 1867–69, Registers and Lists, no. 72, Papers of the Auditor of Public Accounts, RG 48 (Virginia State Library and Archives, Richmond, Va.). This document also includes appointments by Stoneman's predecessor, Brevet Major General John M. Schofield.

16. *Report of the Joint Committee on Reconstruction*, in *The Reports of the Committees of the House of Representatives*, 39 Cong., 1 sess., vol. 2, pt. 1, pp. 52–53, 57–58; Robert Francis Engs, *Freedom's First Generation: Black Hampton, Virginia 1861–1890* (Philadelphia, 1979), 16, 52, 89, 92; Election Records, 1776–1946, Russell County, no. 427, box 108, Papers of the Secretary of the Commonwealth, RG 13 (Virginia State Library and Archives); Taylor, *Negro in the Reconstruction of Virginia*, 211; Lowe, *Republicans and Reconstruction in Virginia*, 86; Peter J. Rachleff, *Black Labor in the South: Richmond, Virginia, 1865–1890* (Philadelphia, 1984), 87, 93, 99, 103; *Richmond Dispatch*, Jan. 20, 1871, p. 3; Philip S. Foner and George E. Walker, eds., *Proceedings of the Black State Conventions, 1840–1865* (2 vols.; Philadelphia, 1979–1980), II, 256, 259, 264, 265–66; Philip S. Foner and George E. Walker, eds., *Proceedings of the Black National and State Conventions, 1865–1900* (Philadelphia, 1986), 210, 213, 338, 350, 352.

FOUR

*For Justice and a Fee: James Milton Turner
and the Cherokee Freedmen*

GARY R. KREMER

In mid-April of 1879, black Missourian James Milton Turner led a movement to create an organization that would meet the physical needs of black
exodusters fleeing the white racism of the South. His goal was to sustain the
migrants in their flight, as well as to help them establish settlements in
Kansas and Oklahoma, so that they would not become "paupers in the land
whither they journey."[1]

The Colored Immigration Aid Association was a colossal failure in its
avowed goal of providing relief and direction to black exodusters. It did,
however, have one long-range effect: it introduced James Milton Turner to
the Oklahoma Territory and to the former black slaves of Indians who
remained there after the Civil War. In the process of trying to help Southern
blacks find a place to move, Turner became aware of what he considered to
be gross violations of the Indian freedmen's civil rights. Consequently, in
1883 he set out to seek legislative and judicial remedies to their problems.
Ultimately he succeeded, but only after engaging in increasingly intense
political maneuvers which combined to sully his reputation and to earn him
the label of an unprincipled opportunist.

In September, 1883, the *Indian Chieftain*, a weekly newspaper published
in Vinita, Indian Territory, carried an announcement that "J. Milton Turner,
the colored orator and politician of St. Louis . . . " had been in Indian
Territory and was "working up a scheme to locate a colored colony on the
strip of country called Oklahoma." The *Chieftain* noted that Turner had
been a frequent visitor "to Vinita and other points in the territory within a
few months. . . ."[2]

Turner's continuing interest in a black colony in 1883, however, represented a change of focus away from Southern blacks, in favor of the former
slaves of Indians in the Oklahoma Territory.[3] As early as 1881 he had written
to the Commissioner of Indian Affairs in an attempt to ascertain the legal
status of freedmen within the Choctaw and Creek Nations. Unfortunately,
the original letter that Turner wrote has long since disappeared, making it
impossible to determine exactly what he asked.[4]

The September, 1883, edition of the *Chieftain*, which carried the announcement that Turner was in the territory, also begrudgingly acknowledged that there was unhappiness among black freedmen about the treatment they were receiving in Indian Territory, particularly in the Cherokee
Nation. The *Chieftain* took the position that insofar as the Cherokee Nation
was concerned, "the obligations she voluntarily assumed towards her colored citizens have been carried out in good faith and there is no portion of
the race . . . within the limits of the United States whose condition is so good
or privilege so extensive and valuable."[5]

The Cherokee freedmen took a different view of their condition, arguing
that the Cherokee Nation was systematically and illegally depriving them of
the full tribal and political rights to which they were entitled. This difference
in the perception of the status of freedmen cannot be understood without
reference to the previous twenty years or more of Cherokee-black relations.

The origins of the relationship date to the antebellum era of slavery, the
Civil War, and the Reconstruction Treaty of 1866. The Cherokee Nation
had been split into Northern and Southern factions since the 1830s. Most of
the slaves were found among the Southern Cherokees, who generally sided
with the Confederacy during the Civil War. The war was disastrous for both
sides. All of the bitter animosities displayed on the larger scene between
North and South were played out in microcosm with the Cherokee Nation.
Homes were burned, fences and farm implements destroyed, livestock
slaughtered, and, of course, human blood shed. So bitter was the hatred, in
fact, that the northern-aligned Cherokees confiscated the land of the Confederate members of the tribe.[6]

The federal government tried to restore order in the Cherokee Nation in
late 1865. On September 1 a meeting was called to draft a Reconstruction
Treaty. The Commissioner of Indian Affairs, unwittingly serving as a pro-
tagonist rather than a conciliator, began the first session by accusing all
Cherokees of being traitors to the United States during the Civil War. Thus,
he refused to distinguish between the minority Southern party which had
joined the Confederacy and the majority Northern party which had not.
That charge set the stage for a debate that lasted more than ten months,
until, on July 19, 1866, the Cherokee Nation became the last of the Five
Civilized Tribes to sign a Reconstruction Treaty.

While the major issue had been whether or not to divide permanently the
Cherokee nation into Northern and Southern factions, the question of what
to do with blacks within the Cherokee Territory was also important. South-

ern representatives Stand Watie and Elias C. Boudinot argued that the federal government should remove all blacks from Cherokee territory at government expense. The Northern faction, first headed by John Ross and then, after his death, by Lewis Downing, argued for a section of land to be set aside within Cherokee Territory for the exclusive use of black freedmen.

Ultimately, both sides agreed to the government's compromise offer. It included a provision allowing former slaves still living in the Cherokee Nation in 1866, as well as former slaves who had fled during the Civil War years but who returned within six months after the date of the Treaty, to enjoy thereafter all the rights and privileges of full-blooded Cherokees. The six-months provision and the confusion it created over who did and who did not have legal status within the nation posed problems for the Cherokees for nearly fifty years.[7]

The treaty provision granting a narrowly defined group of freedmen undefined equal political and civil rights was the focal point of controversy in which Milton Turner became involved in the 1880s. In 1883 the Congress of the United States ordered $300,000 to be paid to the Cherokee Nation in return for the cession of several millions of acres of land west of the Arkansas River. The money was to be distributed among members of the Cherokee Nation as the Cherokee Council saw fit. Problems arose, however, when the Cherokee Council voted to limit the distribution of the money to full-blooded Cherokees, thus excluding black freedmen. Chief Bushyhead vetoed the act, but it was subsequently passed over his objection.[8]

The Cherokees advanced a two-fold argument in defense of their action. They reasoned that the dispersal of the money was an internal matter in which no outside party had a right to interfere. Land, they maintained, was a commodity held in common by the Cherokee people. No individual had a right to buy or sell land within the nation, nor, for that matter, to derive any personal benefit from the sale of land by the nation. Money received in return for land cessions went into a common fund which the Cherokee Council distributed according to its own definitions of the needs of individual tribal members. There were, as far as the Cherokees were concerned, no inherent individual rights or claims to the material bounty of the nation. The Cherokee Council used money in the common fund to provide social services such as educational facilities and poor relief whenever it deemed those services to be necessary. The black freedmen, it argued, had not contributed toward the expansion of the common fund and, therefore, were not entitled to share in the 1883 appropriation. The council did not view that decision as discriminatory. The decision was simply one of distributing the money among the persons who had contributed to the common fund. Almost as an afterthought, the Cherokees added a second argument against sharing money with their former slaves. They pointed out that no other reconstructed state had been forced to share its financial resources with black freedmen.[9]

The freedmen, of course, viewed the situation differently. They immediately expressed their dissatisfaction with the council decision and agitated for its reversal. During the early summer of 1883, the annual "Emancipation Day" fair became a forum for the discussion of ways to force the Cherokees to share the $300,000. A decision was made to send two black members of the tribe to Washington to plead the freedmen's case. Consequently, on June 2, 1883, Lewis Daniels and Ike Rogers arrived in the capital city. On June 9 they met with the Secretary of the Interior, who listened to their story but declined to become involved in the matter. Ten days later Daniels and Rogers were back in Indian Territory planning to pursue the matter by means of a mass meeting of all freedmen in the Cherokee Nation.[10]

Two mass meetings were held in December of 1883. They were well attended, owing to the wide advertisement provided by local newspapers and messengers. The first of the meetings was held on December 6, 1883, at Lightning Creek in Indian Territory, and the second on December 11, at Fort Gibson.[11]

Out of these meetings came a committee empowered to select and employ an agent to represent the freedmen in their claims against the Cherokee Nation. Daniels' and Rogers' experience with the Secretary of the Interior convinced the freedmen that the success of their cause depended upon their ability to solicit the support of a prestigious spokesman to intervene on their behalf. Consequently, they approached J. Milton Turner, who had become a well-known person in Indian Territory, and, upon his acceptance of the mission, they granted him the power of attorney for the whole group.[12]

The choice of Turner was a reasonable one. He was a popular educator, orator, and lawyer who had spent most of the decade of the seventies as Minister Resident and Consul General to Liberia on the West Coast of Africa. That position gained national notoriety for him, just as the Radical Republicans had hoped it would. Indeed, they had facilitated his placement in that position in 1871 in the hope that "he can come back in '72 and take his place as the chosen leader of his race . . . whose claims to leadership will not be disputed."[13]

Turner's attempts at colonization had led him to a realization of the problems confronting freedmen in Indian Territory. By 1883 he had developed some rather negative views about the Indians. In June of that year he wrote to Missouri Republican Congressman James H. McLean about how "Indians discriminate against [blacks] on account of color." Blacks, he told McLean, were trying to become industrious and "to materially build up themselves and their children and obtain a substantial ownership of the soil. . . ." "While the Indian goes down showing no longevity to withstand civilization," he continued, "the Negro . . . shows a desire for the text books and takes to the ways of civilized life." He concluded: "Whatever else may be said upon this subject, it is true that the Negro is in no sense advanced or improved by contact with the Indians."[14]

Turner made it clear that not all of the blame should fall on the Indians.

The federal government, which of course had been dominated by Republicans since the Civil War, was also at fault for creating an atmosphere that was conducive to the violation of black rights. The government had been too mild toward all former slave states. The Cherokees had freed their slaves and made concessions to blacks in the 1866 Reconstruction Treaty only because they feared government reprisals. However, the Turner scenario went, as the federal government became more and more permissive of racist actions against blacks, the Cherokee Nation embarked upon a program of "debarring the black freedmen from their rights."[15]

To counter that trend, Turner accepted the position of attorney for the freedmen and launched a campaign in support of their rights. His motives, however, were not confined to the benefits he believed he could gain for his downtrodden black brethren. He clearly entered the case with the hope of personal gain, indicating, according to a man whose aid he solicited, that "there is a lot of money to be made in this thing."[16] When he signed the "Power of Attorney Agreement" drawn up on December 20, 1883, he also signed a contract that promised him twenty-five percent of the gross amount to be paid by the United States, in addition to a sum equal to "all necessary expenses in the prosecution of this claim."[17]

After signing the contract on December 20th, 1883, Turner left for Washington, "in company with Joseph Brown, a Cherokee freedman, and a regularly authorized representative of the Cherokee freedman [sic]. . . ." In either February or March, 1884, he and Brown presented their claim to the Commissioner of Indian Affairs, who according to Turner, "prepared a bill which was argued . . . before the Indian Committees of both the Senate and the House of Representatives." The Senate Committee on Indian Affairs subsequently recommended that money be appropriated to send a special subcommittee on a fact-finding trip to Indian Territory. Although the Senate endorsed that procedure, the subcommittee did not begin its work until May, 1885.[18]

In the meantime, Turner returned from Washington, where he had spent 273 days, to St. Louis. From there he traveled to Muskogee and Vinita in Indian Territory for a two months stay, came back to St. Louis late in 1884, and returned again to Washington in January, 1885.[19]

Prior to the special Senate subcommittee's May trip into Indian Territory, Turner was instructed by the chairman of the group, Senator Henry Dawes, to gather witnesses at Vinita, where their testimony would be taken about May 20, 1885. Turner complied with the chairman's request and had twenty-nine witnesses assembled at Vinita at the appointed time. Abruptly, however, the subcommittee changed its mind and decided instead to meet at Muskogee rather than Vinita. Consequently, Turner was forced to transport the freedmen to Muskogee at his own expense. The trip cost him $169.65, with an additional $50 being spent for food and lodging. Fifteen of the twenty-nine persons presented by Turner testified before the subcommittee.[20]

In addition to his work in Indian Territory, Turner had begun to lobby among congressmen in an effort to convince them to support the freedmen's claim to $75,000 as their share of the 1883 settlement. Realizing that he did not know many political leaders in Washington, he employed someone who was acquainted with the legislative process and who could introduce him to those persons whose friendship would be valuable in his attempt to get a freedmen's bill passed. Shortly after his arrival in Washington, then, the attorney for the freedmen contacted Henry Cuney, who agreed to assist him in the case. Subsequently, Turner and Cuney visited political notables such as Samuel West Peel, Democratic Representative from Arkansas and Chairman of the House Committee on Indian Affairs. They also met with, among others, David Browning Culberson, Democratic Representative from Texas; Constantine B. Kilgore, also a Democrat from Texas; Benjamin Butterworth, Republican from Ohio; Thomas M. Bayne, Republican from Pennsylvania; Charles Boutelle, Republican from Maine; and Dwight M. Sabine, Republican Senator from Minnesota.[21]

Turner returned to St. Louis from the May meeting with Dawes's subcommittee and remained there until January, 1886, when he again went to Washington. By that time he had become impatient with the slowness of the legislative machinery. In an attempt to speed up the process, he addressed an eighteen-page petition to President Grover Cleveland on February 8, 1886, in the hope that the President might make it possible for him to bypass the Congress. The petition was a cogent rehearsal of the narrative of events from the signing of the 1866 treaty to June, 1886. The treaty provisions, the black lawyer argued, were clear. The freedmen were entitled to "all the rights of native Cherokees," including an equal share to all tribal wealth; and, he continued, the federal Constitution clearly recognized the preeminence of treaty provisions over statutory enactments. Hence, he concluded his petition by asking the President to issue an executive order, forcing the Cherokee Nation to end its discrimination against blacks.[22]

While the President rejected the idea of an executive order, he did submit a letter of recommendation to the Commissioner of Indian Affairs, endorsing Turner's position, and employing much of Turner's language in a recommendation that remedial legislation be passed. A few days later Turner went with Missouri Democratic Congressman John J. O'Neill to the office of the Commissioner of Indian Affairs, J. D. C. Atkins. Atkins pronounced the freedmen's claim to be "manifestly just," and subsequently forwarded the President's correspondence to the Senate, along with a draft of a bill prepared by the commissioner that would grant the freedmen a share in the $300,000 payment. It was the bill drafted by the commissioner that became law.[23]

Within scarcely more than a month, the bill was introduced into the Senate, and Turner appeared before a special Senate Committee on its behalf.[24] The bill passed the Senate by mid-summer, but ran into trouble in the House, where it failed to be considered before the expiration of the term of the Forty-ninth Congress.[25]

That setback shattered Turner's hope of a speedy timetable for the passage of his bill. He had written in July that he expected the bill to be passed quickly by the House and signed by the President.[26] The legislative wheels ground slowly, however, and by November, 1886, Turner had temporarily despaired of seeing the freedmen's bill passed. He was so frustrated that he told a *St. Louis Post-Dispatcher* reporter that he intended to abandon politics. "I am satisfied," he said, "that the colored man will never achieve his rightful place in society through the door of politics. . . ."[27]

Black political agitation, he explained, was offensive to whites. Black powerlessness, then, dictated "that they try some other means of raising themselves than through politics." Alternatively, Turner turned to what was for him a familiar theme:

> What the negro wants to make him a valuable citizen is education and money, and he isn't going to get either as long as he remains rooted right where he was born. . . . Living right along in the same sections with their former masters, they have contracted and caused so many hatreds that they cannot live at peace with their white neighbors and have not advanced at all. They must be separated from the old influences, and in the redistribution they will get an impetus toward the improvement of themselves. They must also get an interest in the land they cultivate: they must become owners of property and have a real interest in the government. What business has a colored man who represents no property interests at all imposing taxes by legislation upon property. When the negro owns land and helps to make the wealth and worth of the country, he will have a right to say something, beside casting his vote, in the governing of the country.[28]

How did Turner plan to resolve this problem? He proposed that blacks separate themselves from white society in an effort to become economically self-sufficient. He had already picked a colony site, in Butler County, Missouri, about 180 miles south of St. Louis. In that spot, Turner maintained, blacks would "have an opportunity of getting both land and education under the most favorable circumstances. The race is hardy" he continued, "and under proper conditions industrious, the principal qualifications for their success in this colony."[29]

The southern Missouri colonization scheme was short lived, however, and Turner was back in politics in early 1887. By spring, with his legislation still unpassed, the attorney for the freedmen was devising other means to achieve his desired end. The first of these came in the form of an effort to influence an election in the Cherokee Nation in 1887. The freedmen's case had become one of the issues between the two major Cherokee political parties in that year and Turner entered the struggle, supporting and even agitating for the election of the National Party which, he believed, would grant the freedmen their claim to $75,000 and full tribal rights. Turner's presence in Indian Territory created a furor which culminated in a petition by fifty-four members of the Cherokee Nation (eight of whom were black) to the United States Indian Agent at Muskogee, to have him physically removed from the territory.[30]

The major point of contention was the petitioners' claim that Turner was being paid to deliver votes to the National Party. In support of their argument, they submitted to Indian Agent Robert L. Owen sworn testimony from two persons. Mr. Ilo Martin testified that "On or about the twentieth day of May, 1887, J. Milton Turner told me that he was to get two hundred dollars a District" for making political speeches throughout the nation. Likewise, Mr. Columbus McNair testified that Turner told him "he was employed to make a political canvas of this nation in the interests of the National Party for which he expected to be paid."[31]

Turner readily admitted his involvement in Cherokee politics, but he adamantly denied having received any money for the venture. In fact, he argued that the trip to Oklahoma, rather than profiting him, had cost him $120.[32] Whatever the truth of the charges, Turner stood to gain if the National Party won, both for himself and for the cause he represented.

The National Party lost the 1887 election. That, combined with Turner's growing disbelief in the ability of the Fiftieth Congress to pass the freedmen's bill, led to a new strategy on Turner's part. In July of 1888 he called for a convention of black Independent and Democratic voters to be held in Indianapolis. The purpose of the convention, as he expressed it, was to register a protest against the Republic Party and acknowledge the Democrats as the proper benefactors of blacks. Aware that both the Democratic President and the Democratic Commissioner of Indian Affairs had supported his proposed legislation, and that it still needed to pass through a Democratically controlled House, he asserted that the election of Cleveland to the Presidency had brought political emancipation to blacks. In return, he argued, blacks ought to support Cleveland's bid for re-election.[33]

Such a political reversal of his intense pro-Republican stands of the decade before did not occur overnight.[34] His increasingly ambivalent attitude toward the Republicans was given an impetus by the concrete benefits to be gained by catering to the Democratically controlled Congress. Turner's longtime friend, George B. Vashon, himself a black Democrat, wrote in 1901 that Turner became a Democrat in 1885 as part of a strategy for getting the Cherokee bill passed. He indicated that in that year Milton Turner made a "radical Democratic speech" at Union City, Tennessee, an event which marked the Missourian's desertion of the party of Grant.[35] Likewise, Henry Cuney later wrote that Turner had turned Democrat "in order to pass his Bill."[36] According to Cuney, Turner "decided to get up a convention of colored Democrats," in Indianapolis, Indiana, thereby ingratiating himself with the party hierarchy and ensuring the passage of his legislation.[37] The evidence overwhelmingly supports the statements of Vashon and Cuney.

While Turner was maneuvering overtly in Democratic circles, he had a colleague moving more quietly but with equal if not greater success among Republicans on behalf of the Cherokee bill. By January 1888, the bill had been floundering for nearly two years in the House, held up largely by the lobbying of Cherokee Elias C. Boudinot who sought to have the whole case referred to the courts as an alternative to trying to resolve the problem through the legislative process.[38]

The same desperation that led Turner to become involved in the Indianapolis convention, then, also led him to ask Washington attorney and businessman Garrett H. Ten Broeck for help. He told Ten Broeck in January, 1888, that up to that time he had been able to find work in Washington to cover his expenses but that he "was entirely out of funds, [with] no prospect of employment in Washington and that unless he could secure some outside assistance he would lose all that he had put into the case. . . ." Ten Broeck quietly lobbied for the bill among congressional leaders known to him through his business contacts. After a ten-month effort he was able, primarily with the help of Republican Congressman David B. Henderson of Iowa, to have the bill called up. The two-pronged attack of Turner courting the Democrats and Ten Broeck the Republicans, combined with the continued lobbying of Henry Cuney and others, resulted in a favorable vote on the bill in October, 1888.[39]

The new law provided for the distribution of $75,000 among the Cherokee freedmen and other "adopted citizens," specifically the Shawnee and Delaware Indians living under Cherokee rule.[40] The significance of that step for the Cherokee freedmen was best summed up by Turner in December when he wrote that "the passage of this act settled their condition, relieves their apprehension that they will be forced to leave, defines their status, confirms their title to an interest in the 11,035,000 acres of land held by the Cherokees, and in fine to all the rights of the native Cherokees as provided for under the Treaty of 1866."[41]

The 1888 Cherokee Act did not, by any means, solve the entire problem, but it was a start. Years of legal wrangling were to follow, with Turner and others of like mind trying to extend the logic of the Act to other freedmen living among the Five Civilized Tribes. The tribes meanwhile battled not only to keep that from happening but also trying to gain judicial sanction for their attempt to exclude blacks from per capita distributions.

Ultimately the freedmen won, and their victory was further legitimized by the United States Court of Claims and the Supreme Court. Monetarily, that meant that 3,524 freedmen would receive $903,365, or, as the Court of Claims put it, "more than $250 for each person — more than $1000 for every family of the freedmen."[42]

Turner stayed with the fight until the end. The slowness of governmental response to the wrongs done to the Cherokee freedmen, even after the Interior Department acknowledged the wrongs, was appallingly slow. Perhaps the *Indian Chieftain*, which had spoken so critically of his part in the 1887 tribal elections, was right when it wrote in 1890 "that Turner probably accomplished in their [the freedmen's] behalf what no other man in the country could. . . ."[43] To be sure, his motives were not selfless. Moreover, his political maneuvering and Machiavelian machinations made him many enemies en route to victory. He was never able to shake off the label of opportunist that his critics had assigned to him. Still, it is difficult to see how he could have accomplished what he did without resorting to such tactics. Perhaps that is the saddest fact of all about the Cherokee freedmen's case.

NOTES

1. U. S. Congress, Senate, *Report and Testimony of the Select Committee of the United States Senate to Investigate the Causes of the Removal of the Negroes from the Southern States to the Northern States.* Report No. 693, part 2, 46th Cong., 2nd Sess., 1880, pp. 120–121. The most recent work on the Exodus movement is Nell Irvin Painter, *Exodusters: Black Migration to Kansas after Reconstruction* (New York: Alfred A. Knopf, 1977).

2. *Indian Chieftain* (Vinita, Cherokee Nation), September 14, 1883. In the spring of 1883, Turner had attempted to get a federal appointment as a "special agent of the Department of the Interior . . . with the view of facilitating the investigation of fraudulent entries of portions of the public lands." John W. Hamilton to Secretary of the Interior H. M. Teller, April 27, 1883; J. Milton Turner to H. M. Teller, May 3, 1883; Department of the Interior, Appointment Division, File No. 784, December, 1883, National Archives.

3. Morris L. Wardell, *A Political History of the Cherokee Nation 1838–1907* (Norman, Oklahoma: University of Oklahoma Press, 1938), p. 231. Other accounts of Turner's work on behalf of the Cherokee freedmen include Lawrence O. Christensen, "J. Milton Turner: An Appraisal," *Missouri Historical Review*, Vol. 70 (October, 1975), pp. 1–19, and Tim Gammon, "Black Freedmen and the Cherokee Nation," *Journal of American Studies* Vol. 11 (December, 1977), pp. 357–364.

4. Only a brief abstract of the letter remains. The original letter was H. C. Carter and J. Milton Turner to the Justice Department, March 22, 1881, Letters Received, Land Division, Bureau of Indian Affairs, Record Group 76, National Archives (hereafter cited as L.D., BIA, R.G. 76, NA). Turner recalled in 1889 that in 1881 and 1882 "I was representing the Freedmen of the Choctaw Nation before the Department of the Interior." No specifics were given. Affidavit filed by J. Milton Turner, Enclosure, Turner to Secretary of the Interior, September 10, 1889, File 298, Special Files of the Office of Indian Affairs, 1807–1904, National Archives Microfilm Publication M574, roll 81, frame 0238 (hereafter cited as Special File 298).

5. *Indian Chieftain*, September 14, 1883.

6. Hanna R. Warren, "Reconstruction in the Cherokee Nation," *The Chronicles of Oklahoma*, Vol. LIV, No. 2 (Summer, 1976), p. 180; Walt Wilson, "Freedmen in Indian Territory," *The Chronicles of Oklahoma*, Vol. XLIX, No. 2 (Summer, 1971), p. 230.

7. Information in this and the preceding two paragraphs has been synthesized from the following sources: Warren, "Reconstruction in the Cherokee Nation," pp. 181–189; Wilson, "Freedmen in Indian Territory," p. 233; Paul F. Lambert, "The Reconstruction Treaty of 1866," *Journal of the West*, Vol XII, No. 3 (October, 1973), pp. 474, 488–489.

8. Wardell, *A Political History of the Cherokee Nation, 1838–1907*, p. 235. For a concise chronology of the case, see J. Milton Turner to President Grover Cleveland, June 11, 1886, Letter No. 15802, Letters Received, L.D., BIA, R.G. 75, NA.

9. United States Congress, House of Representatives, 48th Cong., 1st sess., 1884, House Resolution 1345, Special File 298, frames 664–672.

10. Lewis Daniels, Affidavit filed with the Commissioner of Indian Affairs, September 28, 1889, National Archives Special File 298, frames 299–303; David Martin and Andrew Norwood, Affidavits filed with the Commissioner of Indian Affairs, September 19, 1889, National Archives, Special File 298, frames 269–270.

11. Minutes of the Meeting of the Freedmen held at Lightning Creek, December 6, 1883, National Archives, Special File 298, frames 397–399; Letter from Lightning Creek Committee to Permanent Committee, December 14, 1883, National Archives, Special File 298, frames 414–417.

12. Minutes of the Meeting of the Permanent Committee held at Four Mile Creek, December 20, 21, 1883, National Archives, Special File 298, frames 409–413; Special Contract of J. Milton Turner, National Archives, Special File 298, frames 51–53.

13. Gary R. Kremer, "Background to Apostasy: James Milton Turner and the Republican Party," *Missouri Historical Review*, Vol. 71 (October, 1976); p. 67.

14. Turner to James H. McLean, June 2, 1883, Letter No. 10546, Letters Received Relating to Choctaw and Other Freedmen, BIA, R.G. 69, NA.

15. Enclosure No. 2, Turner to Commissioner of Indian Affairs, June 8, 1887, Letter No. 14942, Letters Received, L. D., BIA, R.G. 75, NA.

16. Henry M. Cuney to John M. Noble, Secretary of the Interior, August 16, 1889, National Archives, Special File 298, frame 146.

17. Special Contract, National Archives, Special File 298, frames 51–53.

18. Turner to William F. Vilas, Secretary of the Interior, undated, received in the Department of the Interior December 12, 1888, Special File 298, frames 0034–0042.

19. *Ibid.*

20. *Ibid.*

21. Henry M. Cuney to John M. Noble, Secretary of the Interior, August 16, 1889, National Archives, Special File 298, frames 145–152; Richard Harvey Cain to Henry M. Cuney, August 16, 1889, National Archives, Special File 298, frame 170; Henry M. Cuney to Senator Constantine B. Kilgore, August 18, 1889, National Archives, Special File 298, frame 174; Senator Dwight May Sabine to Henry M. Cuney, August 28, 1889, National Archives, Special File 298, frame 181. Turner later denied having hired Cuney, although the evidence is heavily weighted against Turner's contention. There never was a formal contract drawn up between the two men.

22. Turner to President Grover Cleveland, February 3, 1886, Letter No. 15802, Letters Received, L.D., BIA, R.G. 75, NA; *Indian Chieftain*, February 11, 1886.

23. United States Congress, Senate, "Messages From the President of the United States," *Senate Executive Document No. 82*, March 3, 1886, Special File 298, frames 604–614; *Indian Chieftain*, February 18, 1886.

24. *Indian Chieftain*, April 1, 1886.

25. *Indian Chieftain*, July 15, 1886; July 22, 1886. Henry L. Dawes wrote on September 4, 1886 that although Senate Bill 1800 had passed the Senate, "the condition of business in the House made it impossible to get action upon it"; H. L. Dawes to Joseph Bralay, National Archives, Special File 298, frame 727.

26. *Ibid.*; Turner to Editor of *Indian Chieftain*, July 15, 1886, *Indian Chieftain*, July 22, 1886.

27. *St. Louis Post-Dispatch*, November 19, 1886.

28. *Ibid.*

29. *Ibid.*

30. Petition to the Commissioner of Indian Affairs, undated, received June 7, 1887, Letter No. 14871, Letters Received, L.D., BIA, R.G. 75, NA; Aleck Hawk, Affidavit, September 19, 1889, National Archives, Special File 298, frames 277, 278. See, also, the *Indian Chieftain*, June 2, 1887. The *Chieftain* advised Turner "not to monkey with the politics of the country," and exclaimed that his actions had "the appearance of being that of one who is paid for what rumor says he is doing." See, also, Turner to the Reverend Laurence Ross, May 26, 1887, *Indian Chieftain*, June 26, 1887.

31. Petition to Commissioner of Indian Affairs, Letter No. 14871, Letters Received, L.D., BIA, R.G. 75, NA.

32. Turner to the Commissioner of Indian Affairs, June 8, 1887, Letter No. 14942, Letters Received, L.D., BIA, R.G. 75, NA.

33. "A Wrangling Convention," *New York Times*, July 26, 1888; Lawrence Grossman, *The Democratic Party and the Negro: Northern and National Politics, 1868–92*, Blacks in the New World Series, ed. (Chicago: University of Illinois Press, 1976), p. 145n3.

34. For Turner's pro-Republican stance of the 1870s, see Kremer, "Background to Apostasy."

35. George B. Vashon, "Progress of Negroes in Their Efforts to Free Themselves from Republicanism," *Republic* [St. Louis], August 4, 1901.

36. H. E. Cuney to Col. Robert Christy, January 20, 1890, National Archives, Special File 298, frames 0178–0187.

37. *Ibid.*

38. Henry M. Cuney to John M. Noble, Secretary of the Interior, August 16, 1889, National Archives, Special File 298, frame 147; Richard Harvey Cain to Henry M. Cuney, August 16, 1889, National Archives, Special File 298, frame 170; Elias C. Boudinot to Secretary of the Interior, July 6, 1889, National Archives, Special File 298, frames 0495–0502; *Indian Chieftain*, September 12, 1889.

39. Garrett H. Ten Broeck to Secretary of the Interior John W. Noble, January 11, 1890, National Archives, File 298, frames 0802–0805. Subsequent to the passage of this bill, there emerged a controversy over whether or not Turner was entitled to a $15,000 fee for his efforts on behalf of the freedmen. The Department of the Interior conducted an investigation into the matter, ruling more than one year later that Turner was the attorney of record, and that, although he had received help from Ten Broeck and others, he alone was entitled to receive the $15,000. It did not, however, absolve Turner from his responsibility to compensate those persons who had helped him. Final Decision of Secretary Noble in the Claim of J. Milton Turner, March 26, 1890, National Archives, Special File 298, frames 0895–0944.

40. Cherokee Freedmen Act. 25 Stat. 608 (1888). According to Turner's attorney, Congress learned from Turner's efforts that certain adopted Delawares and Shawnees were entitled to the same considerations as the former black slaves. Hence, they lumped them all together for the sake of uniform legislation. J. H. McGowan to John W. Noble, April 5, 1889, National Archives, Special File 298, frame 0474–0476.

41. Turner, affidavit filed with the Commissioner of Indian Affairs, Incomplete Date, 1888, National Archives, Special file 298, frame 40.

42. United States Court of.Claims, *Whitmire, Trustee v. Cherokee Nation and the United States, Cases Decided in the Court of Claims of the United States at the Term of 1894–1895*, 30: 138–159; United States Court of Claims, *Whitmire, Trustee v. Cherokee Nation and the United States, Cases Decided in the Court of Claims of the United States at the Term of 1908–1909*, 44: 453–468; United States Supreme Court, *Cherokee Nation and United States v. Whitmire, Trustee for Freedmen of the Cherokee Nation, United States Reports: Cases Adjudged in the Supreme Court at October Term, 1911*, 30: 115.

43. *Indian Chieftain*, November 20, 1890.

PART TWO

"TO OWN
OUR OWN
LABOR":
BLACK MEN,
ECONOMIC
SELF-SUFFICIENCY,
AND
WORKING-CLASS
CONSCIOUSNESS

FIVE

Black Policemen in New Orleans During Reconstruction

DENNIS C. ROUSEY

For southerners, both black and white, Reconstruction brought about many changes, raising sublime hopes for some and evoking nightmarish fears for others. Some of the changes became permanent fixtures in the firmament of southern society—others were mere ephemera. One of the new (though transitory) experiences for black men in some parts of the South was the opportunity to join the forces of "law and order," when some municipal governments, for the first time, hired black policemen. Of course, not all cities opened their police forces to black recruits, and some of those departments which hired blacks practiced a policy of internal segregation, confining black policemen to official activities within the black community.

New Orleans came as close to equalitarianism in policing as any other southern city, and probably closer. Though the conservative restoration of the late 1870s destroyed any prospect of permanent reform, during Reconstruction black officers in the Crescent City arrested whites, held important administrative and command posts, carried firearms, wore uniforms, and at times held a percentage of police jobs roughly equal to the black proportion of the city's total population. Such progress was possible during Reconstruction because New Orleans carried over a tradition of unusual race relations from the antebellum period, when the barriers of race were formidable but not impermeable. Admittedly not a utopia of color blindness, New Orleans entered the post-slavery period with an extraordinary heritage promising exceptional potential for building up black institutions and extending black participation in urban public life.

The Crescent City's antebellum tradition in race relations was probably unique — certainly, at least, it was a rarity in the United States.[1] Although the formal law imposed a considerable "web of restraints" (in Richard Wade's phrase) on both slaves and free blacks, in practice both groups found numerous ways to circumvent such laws. Many whites — including employers, policemen, grogshop keepers and professional criminals — had a vested interest in helping blacks flout the law.[2] The large number of northerners in the city may have contributed to white toleration of black freedoms, as most evidently were not much concerned about the institution of slavery.[3]

Free blacks probably made the most important contribution to the special racial mixture of New Orleans. Of all Deep South cities, New Orleans had been home to the largest prewar population of free people of color, second only to Baltimore. The free black community of the Crescent City had a rich and a dynamic tradition, especially distinctive because of the large number of mulattoes and the influence of French culture. Though separated from slaves by law (and often by culture), free blacks forged links with the slave community by many means. They played a major role in manumitting slaves,[4] and became increasingly conscious of a racial bond with the enslaved, thus experiencing an "awakening of liberal conscience" as a result of the Civil War.[5] Those blacks who had been free during the antebellum period expected to lead the black community after abolition,[6] and in fact most of the city's black leaders of the postwar period had been free before the war.[7]

And so the nouveau regime proved more genuinely reformist in New Orleans than in most of the South. During Reconstruction New Orleans became a center — perhaps *the* center — of black progress. More Afro-Americans lived there than in any other city in the country: 50,456 according to the 1870 census (followed by Baltimore with 39,558 and Washington, D.C. with 35,455). After the Civil War New Orleans made remarkable advances in civil rights for blacks. Racial integration afforded blacks access to the city's streetcars, the New Orleans Opera House, the Boys' House of Refuge, the City Insane Asylum, and some of the city's social clubs, churches, saloons, steamboats, theaters and public schools. Three colleges offered educational opportunities to blacks, including the academically esteemed and racially integrated Straight University. As the site of the state capitol, New Orleans served as headquarters for a state legislature with a substantial percentage of blacks, and for three black lieutenant governors. Despite widespread and persistent white resistance, black New Orleanians were pushing across the color line in to a new frontier.[8]

New Orleans, in 1867, appears to have been the first southern city to integrate its police force during Reconstruction. By 1870, racially integrated forces policed at least twelve southern cities. In the entire South, there were probably about 350 black city policemen in 1870, or perhaps somewhat less. New Orleans had by far the largest contingent of black officers, some 182 men (in a total force of 647). Thus, though the experiences of black policemen in New Orleans may not have been typical for all southern cities, this case study encompasses a majority of the black southern urban policemen. Moreover, if black policemen were ever to achieve equal status with their white counterparts, it would most likely happen first in the Crescent City.[9]

It was appropriate that New Orleans should have witnessed the debut of black policemen in the postwar South. Their appearance there revived an earlier practice, hearkening back to the first decades of the nineteenth century when New Orleans had inaugurated racially mixed civil policing. As early as 1804, the new urban center of the American Southwest displayed a willingness to consider the employment of black policemen. Mayor Etienne Boré suggested in that year the formation of a mounted patrol service, and called for a company of white men, "or in lieu thereof, of free mulattoes whose officers will be white men." When the following year the city government established a municipal police force known as the Gendarmerie, modeled along the contours of Mayor Boré's proposal of the previous year, there may have been a substantial number of free black men on that early force.[10]

Although the racial composition of the Gendarmerie is conjectural, black men certainly served on subsequent police forces in New Orleans. The city authorities abolished the Gendarmerie in 1806, but by 1809 a permanent municipal force called the city guard was operational. In a ten-man sample of that force in 1814, at least two city guardsmen (Charles Allegre and Constant Michel) were free men of color. Of a sample of 17 city guardsmen in 1820, at least one (Pierre Aubry) was black. Samples for 1828 and 1830 both show at least one black policeman on the city guard muster roll (August Bolen).[11]

Black participation in policing also involved the militia. Most students of Louisiana history are familiar with the role played by free black troops in the battle of New Orleans in 1815. Although state law deactivated the black militia in 1834, the black veterans of 1815 participated in public commemorations of the victory over the British until the outbreak of the Civil War. On many occasions in the first quarter century of American hegemony over New Orleans, state and city authorities deployed the militia as an auxiliary police force. In 1817, the city council explicitly ordered that both whites and free blacks render service in these militia patrols. In addition to the Gendarmerie, and its successor the city guard, several other officers of civil government exercised police functions, among them the rural/suburban syndic. At least one of the syndics in 1803 was a free quadroon (Delille Dupard).[12]

Black men thus played the roles of gendarme, city guardsman, militia man and syndic during the first third of the century. But those early black policemen found themselves in a tense and ambivalent relationship with the white establishment. If any part of the United States ever transcended the rigid dichotomy of black and white—with blackness understood by whites as a designation of slave status—it was Franco-Hispanic Louisiana. Free people of color stood apart in New Orleans, constituting a third category between free whites and enslaved blacks to a greater extent than anywhere else in the United States. Yet that peculiar and precarious status relegated its occupants to an ambiguous, marginal niche in society that racism eroded over time—reducing many of them, as Ira Berlin has suggested, to become virtual "slaves without masters."[13] Still, blacks in New Orleans enjoyed more freedom than in most other cities in the slave states.

The tension produced by this growing marginality affected the black role in policing. As early as 1804, Mayor Boré's proposal for a mounted police force showed a distinct preference for white men to serve as rank and file, and stipulated that its commanders be white. When in 1816, the city council sought to prevent looting in a flooded portion of the city by deploying a patrol boat, it insisted that all rowers be white. The double standard of the city council led to occasional ironies: it allowed free black militiamen to bear arms when they participated in police patrols, but prevented blacks from giving or receiving instruction in fencing.[14]

From 1830 to Reconstruction, no evidence exists of black policemen in New Orleans. The hardening of white southern attitudes on race and slavery evidently led to their exclusion from the police force, although this policy was never embodied in law or ordinance. Even though the 1860 census shows two Afro-Americans (one "black," one "mulatto") who gave their occupation as police officer, neither man's name appears in the personnel books of the police department. If there were Negro policemen, at that late date they must have been light-skinned mulattoes, probably Franco-Americans, passing for white. It would be difficult to imagine white toleration of revolver-carrying black policemen in the 1850s, given the intensity of white racial anxieties and antipathies in the late antebellum period.[15]

Not until 1867 did the Crescent City once again hire black men as police officers. In early May, the federal military commander in New Orleans, General Sheridan, ordered Mayor Edward Heath to "adjust the present police force so that at least one half of said force shall be composed of ex-Union soldiers." The black community immediately pressed for inclusion of Negroes on the force. The editor of the black-managed New Orleans Tribune pointed out that a large proportion of the population of New Orleans had African ancestry. His appeal for black policemen emphasized not only the justice of appointing black officers, but also the capacity for such service demonstrated by the many black men who had fought in the Civil War.[16]

Under pressure from the black community, the Republican party and the military government, Mayor Heath proceeded to integrate the force. On May 30, 1867, he appointed Dusseau Picou and Emile Farrar as policemen in the second district. They were the first black men—"newly enfranchised citizens," as the editor of the *New Orleans Tribune* called them—to serve as police officers in New Orleans in more than a generation. In the next week, the city appointed more than a dozen black officers, with additional appointments following later. Governor Wells also initiated the appointment of black men to the board of police commissioners with the selection of Charles J. Courcelle.[17]

Despite the appointment of white Unionists and black men to the police force, the department did not immediately become a preserve of racial equality and harmony. White resistance to black policemen was remarkably moderate at the outset, but in their position at the vanguard of social change, black officers held a precarious beachhead. Their position was especially vulnerable because they depended on unreliable local leadership and the federal government. When President Andrew Johnson ordered the enforcement of a state law excluding blacks from jury service, the *New Orleans Tribune* asserted that his example had triggered an open avowal of hostility to both the Republican Party and racial equality by white members of the police. The result for blacks and for white Republicans on the force was, the *Tribune* said, "every means is resorted to [to] make them abandon their position." The inconsistency of local leadership also placed black policemen in an anomalous situation. Mayor Heath, who had appointed the first black officers, also proclaimed the right of white businessmen to refuse service to Negroes.[18]

After reorganization of the police force in 1868 black police officers received more consistent long-term support. In that year the legislature abolished the old municipal police force and replaced it with a state-controlled, Republican-dominated metropolitan organization. This force was headed by a board of commissioners, fifty percent black, and police ranks were sixty-five percent black in October of 1868 when they went on duty for the first time. Their jurisdiction extended well beyond the bounds of the city, embracing the neighboring parishes of Jefferson and St. Bernard, and metropolitan officers were authorized to execute warrants throughout the state. In 1873, the police force was incorporated as a state militia brigade, subject to the governor's call for military service anywhere in Louisiana.[19]

The new organization faced serious opposition. From their institutional beginnings to their extinction as a policy agency, the metropolitans were engaged in a virtual war for individual and collective survival. Many whites refused to accept the legitimacy of this force and opposed it with physical violence, litigation and economic sanctions.

Even before the Civil War and Reconstruction brought so much bloodshed to the South, the job of policing had been filled with danger. New Orleans had long been a hotbed of violence. Its people fairly bristled with lethal weaponry: revolvers, pepperbox pistols, dirks, bowie knives and slungshots—a private arsenal concealed in the pockets and waistbands of respectable gentlemen and proletarian thugs alike. The murder rate in New Orleans was evidently the worst of any major city in America, far higher than in other large port cities like Philadelphia and Boston. At least eight New Orleans policemen were killed in the line of duty between 1854 and 1860 —surely a per capita record for American cities of the period—and many officers received non-fatal wounds.[20]

Policing grew even more dangerous during Reconstruction. The first appearance of the metropolitans on the job led to antipolice riots, and during their tenure of less than nine years, they fought several battles and quelled a number of riotous disorders. In May 1869, the metropolitans had to fight the Jefferson City police to secure jurisdiction over Jefferson Parish; in the struggle they suffered one fatality and eleven wounded. In November 1872 the metropolitans massed for an attack against a detachment of the state militia at the Carondelet Street armory, but the timely intervention of federal authorities brought about a peaceful resolution. The following year, in March, the police confronted several hundred armed opponents at Jackson Square by firing blank cartridges from a cannon. The confrontation ended with the accidental death of an unfortunate bystander. In the next two months, the metropolitans were called out of the district on militia service, arriving at an interracial battle in Colfax after the fighting had ceased. In May, the police found themselves trapped and besieged at St. Martinville. Two metropolitans suffered wounds there, but the arrival of federal troops spared them further casualties. But the most serious of all armed struggles for the metropolitans, the battle of Liberty Place, occurred in September 1874, when paramilitary units of the conservative White League drove the police from the streets, killing eleven and wounding sixty. Federal intervention once again saved the metropolitans, restoring the police to their duties until January 1877 when Reconstruction ended in Louisiana.[21]

Unable to win acceptance from most whites, the police had to adapt and endure. For safety, they often patrolled in pairs, which had not been the usual practice of the antebellum police when one man per beat had been the prewar norm. Opposition to their legal authority also drove them into adopting a military mode of organization. Uniformed in the style of Union soldiers and drilled in infantry formation, with a detachment of mounted men, they armed themselves with revolvers, repeating rifles, cannon and Gatling guns. They looked and sometimes acted like a small army. They paid a high price: from 1868 through 1874 the metropolitan police suffered an average of twenty-two gunshot wounds (not to mention other types of wounds).[22]

Conservative whites also endeavored to strangle the metropolitan force, choking off needed revenue by a strategy of massive tax delinquencies, aimed at subverting the entire Republican state government. Financial constraints compelled a reduction by more than fifty percent in the size of the force between 1870 and 1876; policemen meanwhile were usually paid in warrants whose real value rarely exceeded sixty percent of face value.[23]

White Democrats predictably castigated the metropolitans, likening them to a brutal and repressive army of occupation. The metropolitan police were caught in a severe bind, compelled to present as formidable a police presence as possible to defeat overtly illegal resistance from conservatives, yet damned for their every effort to exercise any authority at all.

As a racially integrated body, the metropolitans found the criticism from racist whites vitriolic. The racial composition of the force registered high among the explicit complaints. When the metropolitan force first went on duty in 1868 and encountered violent protest, the superintendent (a Union army officer) felt obliged to suspend all of the black policemen. In a city whose population was approximately 26 percent black, a police force 65 percent black—as it was at the outset—certainly overrepresented black people, just as the earlier all-white force had underrepresented them. But by 1870 the black percentage of the force had dropped to 28.1 percent, roughly proportional to their 26.4 percent of the whole population.[24]

Despite such avid opposition, the metropolitan police had a fair claim to distinction as the best force the city had fielded at any time during the nineteenth century. The metropolitan force was less abusive of civil liberties than either its predecessors or successors, and its officers were held to a strict accountability. Police delinquencies dropped from the 1850s, with about 2.0 complaints per officer annually, compared with 2.5 in the years 1854–56. A complaint against a metropolitan officer was also more likely to result in punishment (77.1 percent led to some form of punishment, in contrast to only 45.6 for the period 1854–56). The metropolitan police sharply reduced arrests on the vague and antilibertarian charges of vagrancy and suspicion, down from 17.8 percent of total arrests in the mid-fifties to 4.8 percent in the years 1868–74. Police commanders even sought to decriminalize prostitution, which had long been a lucrative source of graft for the police.[25]

The metropolitans were more productive in nearly every measurable and presumably desirable sense in which a police force may display activity. By 1874, the number of arrests per officer averaged sixty-two per year, compared with an annual rate of forty-seven during the 1850s. Their involvement in public health increased with the creation of a company of sanitary police in 1868. The social welfare function of the police also expanded, as they provided stationhouse lodging for nearly 15,000 people each year, an increase of fifteen times from the immediate antebellum era. Police absenteeism dropped with the establishment of stricter medical discipline, from the prewar range of 13 to 28 percent per year to just 1.7 percent annually. Opportunities for modest pensions, never before widely available, also gave stability to the metropolitan police.[26]

Of fundamental importance to any evaluation of their record was the hiring of black officers in numbers approximating the proportion of black people in the city's population. Although the police department in New Orleans formed the largest integrated force in the urban South, it was not

TABLE 1

Black Police in Southern Cities, 1870 and 1880

	1870		1880	
	Police Depts.	Total Pop.	Police Depts.	Total Pop.
New Orleans	28%	26%	7%	27%
Charleston	42%	54%	19%	55%
Mobile	37%	44%	0%	42%
Montgomery	50%	49%	0%	59%
Vicksburg	50%	55%	14%	49%
Petersburg	37%	54%	0%	54%
Portsmouth	29%	35%	0%	34%
Norfolk	3%	46%	0%	46%
Augusta	2%	42%	0%	46%
San Antonio	13%	16%	12%	15%
Galveston	8%	22%	13%	24%
Washington, D.C.	4%	33%	5%	33%
Savannah	0%	46%	0%	51%
Nashville	0%	38%	0%	38%
Richmond	0%	45%	0%	44%
Atlanta	0%	46%	0%	44%
Memphis	0%	39%	23%	44%
Louisville	0%	15%	0%	17%
St. Louis	0%	7%	–	–
Baltimore	0%	15%	–	–

SOURCES: Ninth Census (1870) and Tenth Census (1880), Population Schedules, U.S. Census Office, *Ninth Census—Volume I. The Statistics of the Population of the United States* (Washington, 1872). U.S. Census Office, *Statistics of the Population of the United States at the Tenth Census* (Washington, 1883).

the only one to include black officers. In 1870, at least twelve southern cities employed black policemen, most of them in proportions close to the percentage of blacks in the local population (see Table 1).

Local political considerations rather than any national or regional policy determined the employment of black policemen. A tradition of decentralization in the American criminal justice system thus persisted during Reconstruction. Savannah and Charleston, for example, were similar cities in roughly the same class in terms of population size (49,000 in Charleston in 1870 and 28,000 in Savannah). Both had a large proportion of blacks (54 percent in Charleston, 47 percent in Savannah), and almost the same proportion of immigrants (42 percent of the white adult male population in Charleston, 43 percent in Savannah). Situated near one another, they shared the same geography and climate, and each served as a commercial outlet for an agricultural hinterland. Yet Charleston had a racially integrated force, while Savannah had an all-white corps, dressed in Confederate gray and under the command of a former Confederate officer.[27]

Savannah and Charleston were separated by a state boundary, but even within the jurisdiction of a single state there could be great variation in the racial composition of urban police forces. In Virginia, the Petersburg force was integrated, while Richmond had no black policemen at all. Norfolk had only token integration on its force, yet the twin city of Portsmouth was almost fully integrated. The struggle for integration was thus largely localized. In some places, conditions and forces within the individual city determined the outcome; in other cases such as Tennessee and Louisiana, the involvement of the state government in municipal politics shaped the course of change.[28]

Winning jobs on the force did not end the struggle for black policemen. One historian, Howard Rabinowitz, has suggested that in some cities black officers were restricted from official interaction with whites by law, administrative order or custom. Rabinowitz observes an exception in Montgomery, where black policemen gained the authority to arrest whites but only after a struggle between the leading black and white Republicans in the city.[29]

Although the Rabinowitz hypothesis may apply to many southern towns during Reconstruction, New Orleans, with nearly half of all black policemen in the South, operated in a more equalitarian fashion. Evidence suggests that there were no invidious distinctions between black and white police officers in the Crescent City. Black men held positions on the board of police commissioners and commanded precincts. As ordinary cops on the beat, they wore uniforms, carried guns, and otherwise fully embodied the authority of police officers. No formal rules restrained black policemen from arresting whites, nor is there evidence to indicate any informal or covert efforts within the police force to apply any segregationist policy. Indeed, in a city only partially desegregated, the police were among the pioneers of integration. In one case, for example, a black policeman found himself assigned to duty at a ballroom catering to whites only—doubtless a considerable shock to the white patrons who found themselves under a black officer's scrutiny.[30]

Black officers did in fact have the power to arrest whites, and they exercised that power. Whether or not they arrested proportionately more blacks than whites must remain unknown, because for most arrests it is not possible to ascertain the race of both the policeman and the arrestee. However, at least some interracial arrests did occur. For example, during the months of June, July, and August 1870, black policemen arrested whites on at least sixteen occasions, and possibly on many more.[31]

The fact that blacks held important police leadership positions also indicates that black men were full-fledged police officers serving on an integrated force. The board of police commissioners which served as the governing body of the force included several black men. At the outset blacks held three of the six seats. Among the black commissioners were Charles J. Courcelle, J. B. Gaudette, James Lewis, J. W. Quinn, C. C. Antoine, Oscar J. Dunn and Thomas Isabelle.[32]

Although a black man never held the post of police superintendent, blacks did serve at the next level of command, as precinct commander. At least seven blacks commanded either a precinct or a precinct substation. Four of these men held the rank of captain: Octave Rey, James Lewis, Eugene Rapp and Peter Joseph. Three other precinct or substation commanders were sergeants: H. E. de Fuentes, J. B. Gaudette and Ernest Chaumette. Black officers headed at least two precincts during most years. In 1873, blacks commanded three of the ten precincts in the city plus an additional substation, while in the previous year, three of nine precincts were under black leadership.[33]

Black policemen participated fully in their work and this meant that they carried firearms on duty. During one of the early battles of the metropolitan police, the *New Orleans Times* mentioned the carrying of Enfield rifles—as well as the usual revolver—by black policemen. In more peaceful times, a traveler to New Orleans visited the state legislature and observed that at "the doors stand negro policemen, armed with clubs and revolvers."[34]

Integration of the police brought with it internal racial frictions. In December 1867, some white members of the force evidently expressed open hostility toward the Republicans, as "they prefer to be 'damned' rather than give their votes to a party which recognizes *negro equality*." In 1872, a white police captain argued with his white sergeant, and in the heat of the moment, called the sergeant a "nigger." The sergeant then shot the captain. The use of that racial epithet by a police captain, and the sergeant's reaction, suggest that prejudice must have persisted among many white policemen. Some black policemen evidenced prejudice, too. In 1869, a black secretary of the board of commissioners called a civilian, P.V.J. Kennedy, a "d--d Irish----," and stated that Kennedy had been "transported to this country, and every foreigner like him."[35]

Despite some continuing prejudice, the police force as a whole seems to have exercised the power of arrest without any pattern of racial discrimination. Arrest data classified by race are available only for one year, October 1, 1868 to September 30, 1869. In that year, 27.2 percent of persons arrested by the police were black, roughly equal to the black share of the population (26.4 percent). The absence of a discriminatory arrest policy can only be inferred. If the actual crime rate among blacks was higher or lower than for whites, then the rate of arrests should have reflected the difference. Unless blacks committed proportionately fewer crimes than whites, however, it is reasonable to assume that the police did not arrest black people more readily than others.[36]

Although almost all policemen lived with people of their own race, a few police officers maintained racially mixed households. Such cases constituted no more than one percent of all police households, but it is noteworthy that members of the metropolitan police could participate in interracial cohabitation without jeopardizing their position on the force. New Orleans had a tradition of interracial sexual relationships that was much stronger than elsewhere in the South, although the antebellum quadroon balls and the open resort to black women by white men had been an embarrassment to many of the city's residents.[37] The interracial police households of 1870 all involved men of French descent or immigrants from Europe. In three households, white officers—a German, an Italian and a Spaniard—lived with black or mulatto women. Two of these households included children, although the 1870 census does not indicate the familial relationship of the head of household to its other members. Perhaps more startling, the census revealed four households where mulatto policemen lived with white women. Three of these men were Louisianans with French surnames, and the fourth was a native of Spain. The white women were natives of Ireland, England, New York and Louisiana. Despite the long-standing toleration of relationships between white men and Negro women, white women who wanted respectability among whites would certainly have had to avoid open cohabitation with male Negroes.

The absolute number of interracial unions involving policemen in 1870 was not striking, but their relative number was. Historian John Blassingame has found a total of 205 interracial unions in New Orleans in the 1870 census, twenty-nine of them involving white women and Afro-American men. Policemen constituted only 1.3 percent of all employed males over the age of sixteen, yet 3.4 percent of all interracial couples included policemen. Although only .4 percent of the male work force was comprised of Negro policemen, 13.8 percent of all interracial unions with white women involved Afro-American police officers. Thus, in a rare form of interracial relationship, policemen could be regarded as leaders. It is likely officials of the metropolitan police knew of these unions, for policemen were public figures and usually got their jobs because they had some standing in their ward or neighborhood. This suggests that toleration of interracial cohabitation must have been the practice among police commissioners and supervisory officers.[38]

The census reveals still more about black policemen. Most were fairly young men. In fact, 77 percent of white officers were forty years or younger. But black policemen were younger still, with 92 percent no older than forty, and with a mean age three years below that of their white counterparts (32.4 compared with 35.5).[39]

Black officers were also more likely to have been native-born than their white counterparts. A large percentage of white policemen in New Orleans were immigrants, notably Irish; black policemen were mostly Louisianans. Of the 182 Afro-American policemen in the 1870 census, only three (1.6 percent) were foreign-born. Of the native Americans, 130 (71.4 percent) came from Louisiana, while forty-two (23.1 percent) were from former slave states. Only seven (3.8 percent) immigrated to Louisiana from the northern states.[40]

Though more often native than their white fellow officers, most of the black police shared the same socioeconomic niche with white officers. Most policemen of both races owned less than $100 of personal property and no real estate at all. About one-sixth of each racial group transcended the $100 barrier in personalty, and about one-tenth for realty. However, black policemen were considerably likelier to own $100 or more of property, either real or personal, than the general black adult male of New Orleans. Thus, black policemen did not represent only the bottom of the black class structure; instead they were spread over the middle and lower class.[41]

In one sense, black policemen fared better economically than white cops. Black police came from a relative range higher in the black class structure than the range in the white economic structure from which white officers were drawn. White policemen in 1870 were less likely to own either personal or real property than the white public. Yet black policemen were *more* likely than the black public to own both kinds of property.[42]

. Though most policemen came from fairly humble economic circumstances, a minority of them occupied a middling position in the class structure. For the black policemen of 1870, it is possible to trace about one-tenth back to earlier years through the city directories and determine their prior occupations. Of seventeen men, two had low white collar jobs, seven worked in skilled blue collar trades, six were semiskilled or service workers, and two were employed as unskilled laborers.[43]

The city directories provide another link to black officers' pasts, for about one-tenth of the 1870 black policemen can be traced backward to determine their status as free men before the Civil War. That would not, however, be an accurate measure of how many black policemen of the Reconstruction Era had been free or slave before the war. City directories would have included only a few free black laborers, thus underrepresenting free men of color. Moreover, blacks who migrated to New Orleans during and after the war cannot be traced through New Orleans city directories for the antebellum period.

It seems likely that the black policemen of 1870 came disproportionately from the ranks of antebellum free men of color rather than from the prewar slave population. A suggestive indication of this comes from the relative number of Negro policemen designated as "mulatto" by the census takers, as opposed to "black." Of the 1870 Afro-American policemen in New Orleans, the census marshals described 75.8 percent as mulatto, but in the adult Negro male population of the city, only 34.5 percent appear on the returns as mulatto. The antebellum free black community had been heavily mulatto (77.3 percent), but the slave population was distinctively black (75.2 percent). Thus, a majority of the Afro-American policemen in New Orleans probably had been free before the war.[44]

Some of the 1870 black policemen had served in the Civil War. Approximately one-tenth (eighteen men) of the 1870 black police contingent can be identified as Union soldiers from Louisiana units. Others may have served under different names or in units from other states. The Louisiana black veterans all served with one of two regiments, the Sixth and Seventh Louisiana Colored Infantry.

Perhaps the most distinguished of the black policemen to have Civil War service was Jordan B. Noble. Noble gained fame in antebellum New Orleans as a veteran of three wars. A free black from Georgia, Noble joined the Seventh U.S. Infantry in 1813 at the age of thirteen. He served as a drummer in the battle of New Orleans in January 1815, and later in the same capacity during the Seminole War in Florida in the 1830s and the Mexican War of the 1840s. In a parade in 1860 commemorating the victory over the British, Noble delivered a short speech to the crowd and received a special medal at the order of General Winfield Scott. During the Civil War, the former drummer held the rank of captain, commanding C Company, Seventh Louisiana Colored Infantry. The 1870 census described Noble as "mulatto" and noted that he held real estate valued at $1500. He had achieved a higher rank in the Union army than any of the other black police veterans.[45]

The next highest ranking black veteran on the police force was Octave Rey. Born in New Orleans in 1837, Rey was the youngest of three brothers and the son of Barthelemy Rey, a member of the first school board of an institution for indigent orphans. Octave Rey married Louise Belleme in 1859 at St. Augustine Catholic Church and the couple had at least six children. A cooper by profession, Rey joined the Union Army during the Civil War, serving as a lieutenant in E Co., Sixth Louisiana Colored Infantry, and sustaining a leg injury while on commission in 1863 because "concord does not exist among the officers of the army and . . . " the difference of race [was] the cause of it.[46]

Rey joined the metropolitan police and became a captain commanding the fourth precinct. After losing his position as a result of "Redemption," Rey remained a respected member of the community and property owner (he held $500 worth of personalty and $500 of realty in 1870). He served as chief of special election marshals for the first congressional district in the November election of 1882. When he was involved in a shooting incident in 1886, the *Daily Picayune* referred to his service on the force during Reconstruction and described him as a "tall, fine looking man." At 6'2½", Rey was described by a fellow black New Orleanian as a "tall man of herculean proportions—energetic, powerful, and dynamic in his thinking." Although not highly educated, Rey was reputed to have a "prodigious memory for names and people," a trait that must have served him well as a policeman. He received a federal pension for his military service, and died in 1908.[47]

The restoration of conservative white government in Louisiana severely undercut the position of black policemen like Octave Rey. The size of the police force was reduced, and the percentage of black officers dropped precipitously. Only twenty-two of the 333 policemen in the 1880 census were black (6.6 percent), considerably less than the black population proportion of 26.7 percent. Of the 182 black men on the force in 1870, only four remained in 1880. Police forces throughout the South were "bleached" by Redemption, as Table 1 indicates. The result of Redemption was not only the underrepresentation of black people on the police force, but also the reemergence of racially intolerant and discriminatory policing.[48]

Yet blacks continued to hang on to some police positions in New Orleans. In 1900, fifteen of 293 policemen (5.1 percent) in the census were black. These black officers were "solid citizens" even more so than their white counterparts: 93 percent were married (compared to 78 percent of whites); 93 percent were heads of family (79 percent for whites); and 36 percent of heads of family owned their homes (in contrast to 19 percent of white police heads of family). Moreover, the median age of black policemen was four years older than that of white officers, reversing the age relationship of the Reconstruction period. This suggests constricted opportunities for black policemen, and a lower accession rate of black men onto the force. One black cop, fifty-five-year-old Joseph Johnson, had been in service at least since 1870. Married 33 years, Johnson owned a mortgaged home, and had served in the army during the Civil War. Another black officer, George Doyle, subsequently became a deputy U.S. marshal during Taft's presidency. Doyle was active in the plasterers' union, and headed an organization dedicated to commemorating the battle of New Orleans of 1815.[49]

The Reconstruction Era offered far more opportunities for black policemen than could be found in turn-of-the-century New Orleans. During Reconstruction blacks had enjoyed a remarkable degree of success in gaining access to police positions. The absolute size of the black community—the largest in America in 1870—probably helped make this possible. Certainly the strength of the antebellum free black community was important, too. Free black militiamen from New Orleans had played an important role in the American victory over the British in 1815, and these black veterans participated in commemorative parades even as late as 1860, a major source of pride for free people of color. Even slaves had been able to win greater de facto control over their own lives in the relatively loose urban fabric of New Orleans, as Richard Wade has suggested. A tradition among Afro-Americans in the Crescent City of comparative prosperity, high self-esteem and leadership—nurtured by the fluidity of racial attitudes and relationships in the Caribbean and by the pervasive and often egalitarian effects of Catholicism—proved a relatively strong foundation for postbellum black achievement.[50]

Few black men found employment as police officers in late nineteenth-century America. Even where black policemen were employed, they usually found themselves restricted to patrolling black neighborhoods and arresting people of their own color. New Orleans had been a national leader, the first city to hire black policemen in the early 1800s and again during Reconstruction, and the first to allow black officers to operate on a basis of equality with white officers, something that most American communities would not attempt until the 1960s.

Even though the metropolitan police experiment in New Orleans can be classified a failure, the fault did not lie with the police. Though imperfect, the police during Reconstruction performed the normal police functions as well or better than any previous or subsequent police force in nineteenth-century New Orleans. The relationships between the police and white community, and between the state and federal governments were responsible for the failure. White conservatives did, at times, admit the competence of the metropolitan police, but would not accept the legitimacy of the Republican, racially integrated government that created the metropolitan organization. Thus, federal involvement was critical to the creation and survival of the metropolitan police. When the federal government withdrew that support in 1877, the metropolitans were adrift in a sea of implacable white hostility.[51]

Police officers have a highly public role, one especially sensitive in a society with democratic values and institutions. After all, the police can be dangerous to life and destructive of civil liberties. Americans have long been critical of their police, even as they have depended upon them to enforce the law. One consequence of this mixture of dependence and fear has been a persistent desire to see police forces manned by trustworthy friends and allies. During much of the nineteenth century (and even the twentieth) American urban policing was heavily politicized with police personnel usually recruited from the ranks of the party in power. Police forces operated in a very personal, rather than formal style (as historian Wilbur Miller has argued), often responsive to pressures and incentives from the political system.[52]

Yet, the abuses of the politicized and personalized American police led not so much to public sentiment for formal, impartial policing as to bids by each self-conscious ethnic or racial group to be allowed to share in the system of responsive favoritism. In such a pluralistic society it became important for the police force to become a microcosm of the whole society—or at least the whole community. Irish Americans thus found it easy to accept the legitimacy of police forces in whose ranks members of their own ethnic group were well represented. Black Americans have been just as reluctant to accept police forces with few or no black officers. The bar against blacks in policing meant the denial of job opportunities, role models, connections to political power, and aspirations to dignity and first-class citizenship.

Representation on the police force was thus important to many ethnic and racial groups. Of course, a police force was not a legislature, but the vital public role played by the police made representation symbolically as well as substantively important to excluded groups. This sense of sharing helped legitimize authority in a heterogeneous and democratic society. For most black New Orleanians, black policemen were a source of pride and dignity, a further proof of black manhood and courage, and testimony to the legitimacy of democratic government. As pioneers in a new frontier of race relationships, black policemen provided role models for their contemporaries and for future generations.

NOTES

1. For a realistic assessment of the city's distinctive qualities, see Joseph G. Tregle, "Early New Orleans Society: A Reappraisal," *Journal of Southern History* 28 (February 1952): 20–36.

2. Richard Wade, *Slavery in the Cities: The South, 1820–1860* (New York, 1964), 83–89, 92, 145–46, 150–52, 164–66, 178, 219–20, 223–25. Other evidence of the relative freedom of blacks in New Orleans can be found in Richard Tansey, "Out-of-State Free Blacks in Late Antebellum New Orleans," *Louisiana History* 22 (Fall 1981): 369–86; and in the experiences of James Thomas recounted in Loren Schweninger, "A Negro Sojourner in Antebellum New Orleans," *Louisiana History* 20 (Summer 1979): 305–14. See also Ira Berlin, *Slaves Without Masters: The Free Negro in the Antebellum South* (New York, 1974), 108–32, 172, 262, 278.

3. William W. Chenault and Robert C. Reinders have suggested that northerners in New Orleans were "largely indifferent to the question of slavery." See their article "The Northern-born Community of New Orleans in the 1850s," *Journal of American History* 51 (September 1964): 232–47.

4. Laurence J. Kotlikoff and Anton J. Rupert, "The Manumission of Slaves in New Orleans, 1827–1846," *Southern Studies* 19 (Summer 1980): 172–81.

5. Ted Tunnell, "Free Negroes and the Freedmen: Black Politics in New Orleans During the Civil War," *Southern Studies* 19 (Spring 1980): 28.

6. *Ibid.*, 24–25.

7. David C. Rankin, "The Origins of Black Leadership in New Orleans During Reconstruction," *Journal of Southern History* 40 (August 1974): 417–40. Rankin has also argued that demographic and economic conditions, more than "Latin heritage" created a unique version of slavery and race relations in New Orleans; see his "The Tannenbaum Thesis Reconsidered: Slavery and Race Relations in Antebellum Louisiana," *Southern Studies* 18 (Spring 1979): 5–31.

8. The best study of the black community in New Orleans is John W. Blassingame, *Black New Orleans, 1860–1880* (Chicago and London, 1973). His chapter on "Race Relations" (173–210) is particularly valuable. Although there is no substantial account of Reconstruction-Era police in New Orleans, some useful material can be found in Joe Gray Taylor, *Louisiana Reconstructed, 1863–1877* (Baton Rouge, 1974), which is also good for context. See also Roger A. Fischer, *The Segregation Struggle in Louisiana, 1862–1877* (Urbana, 1974). The population data are derived from U.S. Census Office, *Ninth Census-Volume 1. The Statistics of the Population of the United States* (Washington, 1872), 77–296, and U.S. Census Office, *Population of the United States in 1860* (Washington, 1864), lvii–lviii.

9. The numerical strengths are based on a count of policemen from the population schedules of the 1870 census.

10. Proceedings of City Council Meetings, March 17, 1804; documents and letters of Laussat, colonial prefect and commissioner of the French government, and of the commissioners of His Catholic Majesty, 30 November 1803, New Orleans Public Library [NOPL]. Herbery Asbury, *The French Quarter: An Informal History of the New Orleans Underworld* (1936; reprint, St. Simons Island, Georgia, 1964), 70.

11. Allegre and Michel are identifiable from the city guard payrolls, (January, March, April, June, July, and August 1814 in Historic New Orleans Collection and May 1814 in Louisiana Collection, Howard-Tilton Memorial Library, Tulane University); death records of the city of New Orleans (Allegre was identified as black, Michel had no designation of race — microfilm, NOPL); the census of 1820, in which Michel was listed as a free man of color (there were no other heads of family of the same name in the 1820 census, and the only Allegre family was composed of free persons of color); and military service records for the War of 1812 (Allegre served in Fortier's Battalion of free men of color). See M. J. B. Pierson, *Louisiana Soldiers in the War of 1812* (Baton Rouge, 1963).

For Pierre Aubry, see death records of New Orleans, vol. 10, p. 141. He served in Fortier's Battalion of free men of color in the War of 1812; see Pierson, *Louisiana Soldiers*. In the 1820 census, the household headed by Pierre Aubry included only one adult male, a free man of color between 26 and 45 years of age. See also Payroll of City Guard, December 1820, Louisiana Collection. For Augustus Bolen, see death records of New Orleans, vol. 32, p. 525.

12. Ira Berlin, *Slaves Without Masters*, 118–28. Ordinances and Resolutions of the City Council of New Orleans, 18 December 1817. Documents of Laussat, 9 and 16 December 1803, NOPL.

13. Ira Berlin, *Slaves Without Masters*.

14. Ordinances and Resolutions of the City Council of New Orleans, 21 May 1816; Proceedings of City Council Meetings, 9 July 1804 and 30 April 1808; Documents of Laussat, 30 November 1803, NOPL.

15. Eighth U.S. Census (1860), Population Schedules, New Orleans, M653, Reel 418, p. 113 shows black police officer Marie Ursin, and Reel 419, p. 309 shows mulatto police officer R. Palio. Reel 419, p. 157 shows L. Badey, a black man whose occupation, nearly illegible, might be watchman. Ursin, Palio and Badey do not appear anywhere in the personnel books of the police department for the years 1859–1861.

16. *New Orleans Times*, 3, 10, and 11 May and 4 June 1867. *New Orleans Tribune*, 10 May 1867.

17. *New Orleans Tribune*, 28 and 31 May and 1, 2, 4 and 6 June 1867.

18. *New Orleans Tribune*, 19 June and 18 December 1867.

19. *New Orleans Times*, 4 December 1868; *Acts of Louisiana* (1868), 85–98; (1873), 76.

20. The homicide rate for New Orleans in the years 1857–1859 was 30 per 100,000 population annually; for Philadelphia in the years 1853–1859, 3.6 per 100,000 annually; and although no exact figure exists for Boston in this period, it was undoubtedly quite low. New Orleans rate: *Annual Report of the Attorney General to the Legislature of the State of Louisiana* (New Orleans, 1860), 7. Boston rate: Roger Lane, *Policing the City: Boston, 1822–1885* (Cambridge, 1967), 149. Philadelphia rate: Lane, *Violent Death in the City: Suicide, Accident and Murder in Nineteenth-Century Philadelphia* (Cambridge, 1979), 71.

The figure for New Orleans policemen killed represents homicides only — accidental deaths are excluded. *Daily True Delta*, 28 March 1855; *Commercial Bulletin*, 26 and 27 March 1856; *Louisiana Courier*, 20 March 1856; *Messages of Mayors*, 26 December 1860, NOPL. *Daily Picayune*, 29 March 1854, 13 June 1855, 24 December 1859; *New Orleans Bee*, 19 March 1856, 24 December 1860, and 10 January and 4 and 25 March 1861.

A slungshot was a small lead or iron ball attached to a short wooden handle by a cable or cord — a sort of unspiked pocketsized version of the medieval morning star.

21. *New Orleans Times*, 27–31 October, 1 and 5 November 1868, 18–20 May 1869, 6–8 March, 7, 13, 16, 23, 27, and 30 April, and 1 and 6–11 May 1873; *Daily Picayune*,

6–8 March 1873, and 9–13 September 1874; *New Orleans Republican*, 6 and 7 March and 22 and 26 April 1873. Stuart Omer Landry, *The Battle of Liberty Place: The Overthrow of Carpet-Bag Rule in New Orleans—September 14, 1874* (New Orleans, 1955), 123, 129.

22. Calculated from data reported in *Annual Report of the Board of Metropolitan Police*, 1868/69–1873/74.

23. *Metropolitan Police Annual Report*, (1868/69), 7–9, 44–48; (1869/70), 10–16; (1870/71), 7–8; (1872/73), 8; (1873/74), 11–12. *Acts of Louisiana* (1867), 171–173; (1869), 42, 65 (1870 Extra Session), 213–14; (1874), 68–72; (1875), 35–39. *Report of the Attorney General* (1869), 7. *Daily Picayune*, 16 June 1869; *New Orleans Republican*, 15 June 1869; *New Orleans Times*, 16–18 September 1868 and 28 May 1870.

24. *New Orleans Times*, 4 December 1868, Ninth Census (1870), Population Schedules, New Orleans. Blacks did not fare so well in securing jobs in other forms of law enforcement or security; three of twenty-three constables (13.0 percent); two of fifteen marshals, and deputy marshals (13.3 percent); eight of 161 private watchmen (5.0 percent); and none of thirty-eight sheriff's officers.

25. *Metropolitan Police Annual Report*, 1868/69–1873/74; Police Board Records, 1854–56, NOPL.

26. *Metropolitan Police Annual Report*, (1868/69–1873/74); Police Board Records, 1854–1856; Reports of the Third District Police, 1852–1863, NOPL.

27. Ninth Census (1870), Population Schedules, Charleston and Savannah, U.S. Census Office, *Ninth Census*. Edward King, *The Great South* (Hartford, Conn., 1875), 369.

28. Ninth Census (1870), Population Schedules, Norfolk, Petersburg, Portsmouth and Richmond. Robert Thompson Mowrey, "The Evolution of the Nashville Police from Early Times to 1880" (Bachelor's thesis, Princeton University, 1974), 35, 47–48 (copy in Tennessee State Library).

29. Howard N. Rabinowitz, *Race Relations in the Urban South, 1865–1890* (New York, 1978), 41–43.

30. *New Orleans Tribune*, 19 June 1867.

31. No official arrest books from the period survive. The only useful records are the newspaper reports of the period, but these do not indicate the race of police and arrestees. Many of the published arrests did not even report the names of the persons involved. When the newspapers did report names, the police officers were often cited only by last name, and while the arrestees' full names were usually given, they were not often accompanied by a designation of race. No police rosters for the period are available, but one can be reconstructed for the summer of 1870 from the population schedules of the federal census, and this list includes the officers' racial identities. Some of the arrestees can be found in the city directories for 1870 and 1871, which showed blacks as "colored," but most of the arrestees did not appear in the directories (probably due to their transience or social marginality). One further complication was the sharing of surnames by some white and black officers.

Thus, while some positive identifications of black-on-white arrests can be made, an accurate estimate of frequency or proportionality by race is impossible.

For arrest reports, see the *Daily Picayune* 2 June to 31 August 1870. City directories: *Graham's Crescent City Directory* (New Orleans, 1870), and *Edward's Annual Directory* (New Orleans, 1871–1873). For the police roster see the Ninth Census (1870), Population Schedules, New Orleans.

32. Courcelle: *New Orleans Tribune*, 28 May 1867. Gaudette and Lewis: Ninth Census (1870), Population Schedules, New Orleans, Quinn: *New Orleans Times*, 9 May 1872. Isabelle: Blassingame, *Black New Orleans*, 157. C. C. Antoine and Oscar J. Dunn both served as lieutenant governor of Louisiana, and were ex-officio members of the board.

33. Ninth Census (1870), Population Schedules, New Orleans, *Gardner's New Orleans Directory* (New Orleans, 1866, 1868, 1869); *Graham's Crescent City Directory*

(New Orleans, 1867, 1870); *Edward's Annual Directory* (New Orleans, 1871–1873); *Soards' Directory* (New Orleans, 1874–1877).

34. *New Orleans Times,* 20 October 1868. King, *The Great South,* 95.

35. *New Orleans Tribune,* 18 December 1867. *Daily Picayune,* 3 October and 20 and 28 November 1872; *New Orleans Times,* 13 May 1869.

36. *Metropolitan Police Annual Report* (1868/69), 33. Blassingame suggests that blacks had a relatively high crime rate, citing their percentages of all arrests in October and November 1867 (38 and 35 percent). He also observes that 30 percent of the inmates in the parish prison in the 1870 census were Negroes, and 43 percent in September 1874. Although he acknowledges the problem of inferring crime rates from arrest reports he does not comment on the difficulty in inferring crime rates, or even arrest rates, from static jail population figures. Even if blacks and whites had identical arrest rates, it was quite possible that fewer black arrestees would have been able to make bail, secure release on their own recognizance, or win their case in court because of economic inequality or discrimination by judges or juries. Blassingame, *Black New Orleans,* 162.

37. Edward Sullivan, *Rambles and Scrambles in North and South America* (London, 1852), 223–25.

38. Blassingame, *Black New Orleans,* 206–207.

39. Calculations based on Ninth Census (1870), Population Schedules, New Orleans.

40. Ibid.

41. The property values for the white and black male populations of the city are based on systematic random samples consisting of 2,378 whites and 856 blacks. Calculations for police property values are based on complete enumerations of 465 white officers and 182 black officers.

Roughly the same fraction of white and black policemen owned over $100 personalty: 17.9 percent of black policemen, 16.3 percent of whites. But among the one-sixth of blacks and whites who exceeded $100 of personal property, whites held substantially more. The mean value of personalty for the 16.3 percent of white policemen was approximately $428, while for the 17.9 percent of blacks only $255. Few policemen owned real estate: 8.7 percent of blacks, 10.3 percent of whites. For this minority of police real property owners, the mean value was higher for whites than blacks: $1203 in contrast to $972 for blacks.

Only 5.7 percent of the black population owned personal property worth more than $100, while the figure for black policemen was 17.9 percent. The mean value for policemen who had such property was less, however, than for the black population: $255 (police), $487 (population). The same was true for real estate. More black policemen owned real estate than was true for the general population of black males (8.7 percent versus 6.8 percent), but their mean value was less ($972 for black policemen, $1879 for the black population).

Of the white adult male population, 31.9 percent owned $100 or more of personalty, and 17.6 percent held realty. Among white policemen, only 16.3 percent possessed $100 or more of personal property and just 10.3 percent owned real estate.

42. For information on real and personal property, see note 41.

43. The occupations are classified in this manner: low white collar—clerk, barkeeper; skilled blue collar—bricklayer (2), carpenter (2), cigar maker, painter, shoemaker; semiskilled and service workers—butcher, drayman, cook, barber(3); unskilled—laborer (2). The butcher may have owned his shop, in which case he ought to be reclassified as low white collar (proprietor).

44. Ninth Census (1870), Population Schedules, New Orleans, *Population of the United States in 1860,* 194.

45. Ninth Census (1870), Population Schedules, New Orleans. Roland C. McConnell, *Negro Troops of Antebellum Louisiana: A History of the Battalion of Free Men of Color* (Baton Rouge, 1968), 74, 85, 114–15.

46. Rodolphe Lucien Desdunes, *Our People and Our History* (Baton Rouge, 1973), 114–20. Military service and pension file of Octave Rey, Records of the Veterans Bureau, Record Group 15, National Archives.

47. Tenth Census (1880), Population Schedules, New Orleans. Desdunes, *Our People*, 114–20. *Daily Picayune*, 7 November 1882, 21 April 1886.

48. Tenth Census (1880), Population Schedules, New Orleans. Dennis C. Rousey, "The New Orleans Police, 1805–1889: A Social History," (Ph.D. diss., Cornell University, 1978), 269–90. Only Memphis was an exception to this trend. A series of yellow fever epidemics there in the 1870s encouraged the hiring of black police officers, because they were less vulnerable to the disease than the Irish immigrants who dominated the police force. See Rousey, "Yellow Fever and Black Policemen in Memphis: A Post-Reconstruction Anomaly," *Journal of Southern History* 51 (August 1985): 357–74.

49. Twelfth Census (1900), Population Schedules, New Orleans, *Times-Picayune*, 23 November 1937.

50. Richard C. Wade, *Slavery in the Cities*.

51. *New Orleans Times*, 7 April 1873, provides an example of conservative acknowledgment of metropolitan police competence.

52. Wilbur R. Miller, *Cops and Bobbies: Police Authority in New York and London, 1830–1870* (Chicago and London, 1977).

SIX

Negro Labor in the Western Cattle Industry, 1866–1900

KENNETH W. PORTER

INTRODUCTION

The range-cattle industry in its various aspects, and in its importance to the United States and particularly to the Great Plains for the post-Civil War generation, has been the subject of numerous studies. This industry was rendered possible by such factors as vast expanses of grazing land, projected railroad lines across the Missouri and onto the Great Plains, the rise of heavy industry and the consequent demand for beef of less-than-high quality by the meat-hungry industrial population. But like the steel, mining, packing, and other industries, it also needed a labor force—workers with special abilities and qualities—for although the cowhand or cowboy possibly was no more than a "hired man on horseback,"[1] he was a hired man with skills in riding, roping, and branding which could not easily be acquired. Most of his working hours were spent in such routine tasks as riding the range and turning back drifting steers; rounding up, branding, and castrating calves; selecting beeves for the market; and, even on the "long drive," jogging along and daily "eating dirt" on the flanks or in the rear of a few thousand "cow critters." But he also needed the inborn courage and quick thinking to use these skills effectively while confronting an enraged bull, swimming a milling herd across a flooded river, or trying to turn a stampede of fear-crazed steers.

But the general public, under the influence of decades of "Western" movies, and, more recently, television shows has come to regard the cowboy's workaday activities as altogether secondary to fighting off hostile Indians, pursing rustlers and holding "necktie parties" for them, saving the rancher's daughter from Mexican raiders, and engaging in quick-draw gunfights in dusty streets. From similar sources this same public has also learned that cowboys, with the exception of an occasional low-browed villain or exotic and comic-accented *vaquero*, were all of the purest and noblest Anglo-Saxon type, as in Owen Wister's *The Virginian*.

In reality, as George W. Saunders of the Texas Trail Drivers Association has authoritatively estimated, of the fully 35,000 men who went up the trail from Texas with herds during the heroic age of the cattle industry, 1866–1895, "about one-third were Negroes and Mexicans."[2] This estimate is closely confirmed by extant lists of trail-herd outfits which identify their members racially. These lists also demonstrate that Negroes out-numbered Mexicans by more than two to one—slightly more than 63 percent whites, 25 percent Negroes, and slightly under 12 percent Mexicans.

The racial breakdown of individual outfits, of course, varied widely. Some were nearly all of one race, such as the 1874 outfit which was all-Negro, except for a white boss, or the 1872 outfit which consisted of a white trail-boss, eight Mexicans, and a Negro; but more typical were the two 1877 outfits composed, respectively, of seven whites and two Negro cowboys, and a Negro cook; and seven whites, two Negroes, and a Mexican hostler. Many outfits had no Mexicans at all, but it was an exceptional outfit that did not have at least one Negro and enough outfits were nearly all Negro, or a third or more Negro, to bring the number up to the estimated twenty-five percent of the total.[3] A trail-herd outfit of about a dozen men would on the average consist of seven or eight whites, including the trail boss, three Negroes—one of whom was probably the cook, while another might be the horse wrangler, and the third would simply be a trail hand—and one or two Mexicans; if a Negro was not the wrangler, then a Mexican was. Needless to say, this is not the typical trail outfit of popular literature and drama.

The racial make-up of ranch outfits, with their seasonal and day-by-day fluctuations, was not so well recorded as that of the trail-herd outfits, but available information indicates that ranch hands, in Texas at least, were white, Negro, and Mexican in proportions varying according to locality and to ranchowner tastes; probably the overall proportions differed little from those of trail outfits. A ranch in the Indian Territory during the late 1890s, for example, was staffed by eight cowhands, two of whom were Negroes.[4] Negro cowhands were particularly numerous on the Texas Gulf Coast, in the coastal brush east of the Nueces and at the mouth of the Brazos and south of Houston, and parts of the Indian Territory; in some sections they were in the majority, and some ranches worked Negroes almost exclusively.[5]

Negro trail drivers swarmed west and north with herds from the Texas "hive" and, though most returned, a few remained as ranch hands as far north as Wyoming, the Dakotas, and even Canada and as far west as New Mexico, Arizona, and even California and Oregon.[6]

WRANGLERS

Negroes occupied all the positions among cattle-industry employees, from the usually lowly wrangler through ordinary hand to top hand and lofty cook. But they were almost never, except in the highly infrequent case of an all-Negro outfit, to be found as ranch or trail boss.

Negroes and also Mexicans were frequently wranglers, or *remuderos*[7] — in charge of the saddle horses not immediately in use — usually regarded as the lowliest job in the cattle industry, except for the boy who sometimes served as wrangler's assistant.[8] There were exceptions, however, including some Negro wranglers who became "second in authority to the foreman" in a few camps.[9] Such wranglers were "horse men" in the highest sense: capable of detecting and treating illness and injury, selecting the proper horse for each job, and taking the ginger out of unruly animals. Among these wranglers-extraordinary were Nigger Jim Kelly, the horsebreaker, horsetrainer, handyman, and gunman of the notorious Print Olive; and the famous John Chisum's "Nigger Frank," "who spent a lifetime wrangling Long I horses" and whom a white cattleman declared "the best line rider and horsewrangler I ever saw."[10]

COWBOYS

The majority of Negroes on the ranch or "long drive" were neither wranglers nor yet authoritative cooks (of whom more later). They were top hands or ordinary hands who, on the long drive, rode the point, the swing, the flank, or the drag, according to their experience and ability. The point — the position of honor — was at the front of the herd where the steers were strongest, most restless, and most likely to try to break away. There the most experienced top hands rode. Farther back, the cattle were somewhat less troublesome, while in the rear, where the tired beasts were comparatively easy to manage, could be found the fledgling cowboys of the drag, "eating the dust" of the entire herd. Negroes rode in all these positions.[11]

These Negro cowboys, whether on ranch or trail, were generally regarded as good workers, who got along well with others and who took pride in their work. A white Texan, a former cowboy and rancher, went so far as to write that "there was no better cowman on earth than the Negro."[12]

Old, experienced Negro cowhands frequently served as unofficial, one-man apprentice systems to white greenhorns. This was particularly true, of course, when the fledgling was the employer's son or relative. Will Rogers, for example, got his first lessons in riding and roping from a Cherokee Negro employee of his father.[13] Almost any young would-be cowboy who showed the proper spirit, however, might have the good fortune to be "adopted" and "showed the ropes" by one of these black veterans, who would sometimes take on the inexperienced boy as partner when white cowboys were unwilling to do so.[14] Charles Siringo, later famous as a cowboy-detective-author, recalled that Negro cowboys again and again came to his rescue when, in his reckless cowboy youth, his life was threatened by a mad steer, a wild bronc, and even a hired assassin.[15]

Negro cowhands confronted all the dangers and met all the tests of the long trail. One poorly clad cowboy froze to death in his saddle during a "Norther" rather than give up and go in to the chuckwagon.[16] Stampedes were an ever-present danger, and experienced Negroes were frequently prominent in attempting to prevent or control them. Indeed they were also often among the few cowboys who stayed with the herd when others threw in their hands.[17]

Crossing the wide, deep, frequently flooded rivers was even more dangerous than stampedes. According to a white ex-cowboy, "it was the Negro hand who usually tried out the swimming water when a trailing herd came to a swollen stream"[18]—either because of his superior ability or because he was regarded as expendable. But whether or not this statement is valid, it probably would not have been made had not Negroes frequently demonstrated their ability to cope with the problems of river crossings. Numerous anecdotes about such crossings tell of Negro cowhands saving themselves by their own efforts, being assisted to dry land by white cattlemen[19] and, on more than one occasion, saving their lives.

Negroes not only often showed courage and quick thinking in extricating themselves and others from the danger of swollen rivers, but in at least one case also displayed ingenuity superior to that of a great trail boss. In 1877 Ab Blocker, "the fastest driver on the trail," had reached the Platte River, which was spanned by a bridge of sorts, but the wild longhorns had never seen a bridge and refused to cross it. It looked as if, after all, they would have to swim the herd when a Negro hand suggested—and his suggestion was adopted—that they should drive the chuckwagon slowly across, followed by old Bully, an ox; the lead steers would follow Bully and the rest of the herd would trail them.[20]

RIDERS AND ROPERS

Although every top hand had to be a skillful rider and roper, some were so outstanding as to be considered "bronco busters" and/or ropers *par excellence* rather than as merely uncommonly able cowboys. Numerous references suggest that Negroes and Mexicans were widely regarded as particularly expert in both these capacities—the Mexicans especially noted for their prowess with the *reata* (or lasso). Mexicans were also, correctly or not, blamed for cruelty toward animals and consequently fell into disrepute as horsebreakers,[21] whereas the Negroes maintained and even advanced a reputation which went back to antebellum days.

A white ex-cowpuncher-writer states that Negroes were hired largely for their ability to cope with bad horses which the white cowhands did not want to tackle. "The Negro cow hands of the middle 1880s . . . were usually called on to do the hardest work around an outfit. . . . This most often took the form of 'topping' or taking the first pitch out of the rough horses of the outfit. . . . It was not unusual for one young Negro to 'top' a half dozen hard-pitching horses before breakfast." Andy Adams, the cowboy-author and a man who was far from being a Negrophile, declared that the "greatest bit of bad horse riding" he ever saw was performed by a dozen Negro cowboys who were assigned to ride a dozen horses which the white cowpunchers of their outfit were afraid to tackle. But each of the Negroes stayed on his horse till the animal was conquered.[22]

The list of Negro bronc riders—the comparatively few whose names have survived—is still a long one. A few of the better known, partly because they attracted the attention of published writers, were the following: Isam, Isom, or Isham Dart of Brown's Hole, "where Colorado, Wyoming, and Utah cornered," who, although now remembered principally as a reputed rustler, was also "numbered among the top bronc stompers of the Old West";[23] Nigger Jim Kelly, whom oldtime cowboys considered the peer of any rider they had seen in the United States, Canada, or the Argentine;[24] a mulatto named Williams in the Badlands of South Dakota, who was a horse-trainer rather than a horsebreaker and whose methods won the admiration of Theodore Roosevelt;[25] and Jim Perry, the famous XIT cook, who was even better known as "one of the best riders and ropers ever to hit the West."[26]

While most of the famous riders were bronco busters only as one aspect of their work as cowhands, some, including a number of Negroes, were officially recognized as ranch horsebreakers, and a few were full-time or nearly full-time professionals. Perhaps the most famous of the professionals was Matthew (Bones) Hooks of the Panhandle—remembered, after his retirement from horsebreaking to Pullman-portering, for having once taken off his jacket and cap and laid aside his clothes brush, to mount and break an outlaw which no one had been able to ride, while his train stood in the station.[27]

Other Negro cowhands were particularly renowned as ropers, such as Ab Blocker's Frank, who was, according to a white cowboy, "the best hand with a rope I ever saw," and whose roping skill once saved his employer from an angry steer;[28] Ike Wood, according to Charles Siringo, "the best roper" at a roundup near Beeville, Texas;[29] Jim Simpson, "about the best roper" on his part of the Wyoming range;[30] and, more recently, the Negro rancher Jess Pickett who, according to a white neighbor, was "the world's best roper."[31]

Naturally enough, many of the famous Negro riders, such as Isom Dart and Jim Perry, were almost or quite as renowned as ropers. One of the most spectacular at both riding and roping was "Nigger Add," "one of the best hands on the Pecos," who would as a matter of course "top off" several bad horses of a morning. Walking into a corral full of tough broncs, he would seize any one he chose by the ear and nose, lead him out of the bunch, and then show him who was boss. As a roper he was even more sensational, and had the unusual technique of roping on foot, a practice which would have killed an ordinary man. He would tie a rope around his hips, work up to a horse in the corral or in the open pasture, rope him around the neck as he dashed by at full speed, and then, by sheer strength and skill, flatten the horse out on the ground where a lesser man would have been dragged to death.[32] Indeed, the prowess of such Negro riders, horsebreakers, and horse-trainers was so outstanding as to contribute to the commonly held belief of the time that there was some natural affinity between Negroes and horses.[33]

SINGING TO THE CATTLE

Riding, roping and branding were not the only skills required of a top cowhand. Singing to the cattle, particularly on night herd but sometimes during the day's march, was not only a practical necessity for calming the animals and reducing the danger of a stampede, it also had recreational and esthetic values for the drivers. Negro trail hands were conspicuous in this practice, although Negro chuckwagon cooks were the most noted cow-country musicians, singers, and composers. "Nigger" Jim Kelly, the Olives' versatile horsebreaker and gunman, is also credited with composing a humorous song, "Willie the Cook," which he sang to accordion accompaniment furnished by a white trail hand. "Teddy Blue," a white cowhand whose autobiography is a cow-country classic, tells movingly of his first memory of the "Ogallaly song," which had a verse for every river on the trail, beginning with the Nueces and ending in 1881, when he first heard it, with Ogallala.

> There were [he recalled] thirteen herds camped on the Cimarron that night and you could count their fires. A Blocker herd was bedded close to ours; it was bright starlight, and John Henry was riding around the herd singing the Ogallaly song. John Henry was the Blocker's [sic] top nigger. . . .
>
> 'We left Nueces River in April eighty-one
>
> With three thousand horned cattle and all they knowed was run
>
> O-o-o-o-oh!'
>
> and so on.[34]

The special quality which these Negro cowhands gave to the cattle country is epitomized in an episode at Doan's store on the Red River, which was the last place where a trail herd hand could receive mail and purchase supplies before reaching the Kansas cattle towns. One night a crowd sitting around the little adobe store heard the strains of "a lively air on a French harp." The door opened and in sailed a hat, closely followed by a big Negro who began to dance to his own accompaniment. "It was one of Ab Blocker's niggers"—perhaps John Henry himself—"who had been sent up for the mail, giving first notice of the herd's arrival."[35] The ranch or cattle trail, without its many Negroes, would not only have suffered from a lack of expert riders, ropers, and cooks, but would also have lacked much of its vitality and vivacity and spontaneous gaiety, and ranching and trail-driving would have been duller occupations.

COWBOY COOKS — MEN OF PARTS

High in the hierarchy of cow-country employees was the ranch or trail cook,[36] who ranked next to the foreman or trail boss and, in camp, ruled supreme over an area of sixty feet around the chuckwagon. In addition to culinary skill—including the ability to prepare a meal in a blizzard, cloud-burst, or high wind—the cook also had to be an expert muleskinner or bullwhacker, capable of driving two or three yoke of oxen or a four-mule team attached to the chuckwagon over the most difficult terrain, including flooded rivers. He could do more than anyone else to make life pleasant and many a cowboy selected an outfit because of the reputation of its cook. In compensation for duties which few men could satisfactorily perform, the cook normally was paid from $5 per month more than the ordinary cowhand up to even twice as much.

The cowboy cook was also commonly credited with other qualities less essential and certainly less endearing than the ability to cook and drive the chuckwagon. He was frequently something of a despot; bad-tempered, hard-featured, and unlovely. "As tetchy as a cook" is still a ranch byword. He was often an old "stove-up" cowpuncher who resented having to "wait on" cowboys still in their prime, "just kids" in his opinion. He often was also a "hard character," and frequently had a drinking problem. Finally, as one authority has stated, cooks were seldom good riders.

The above description of the cowboy-cook is synthesized from the reports of numerous observers on cooks of all races and backgrounds in all parts of the cow-country. Some of these qualities doubtless applied to most of them, and all to some of them. But numerous accounts of Negro cow-country cooks suggest that the traditional "hard character" pattern fitted them much less than it did whites. The cow-country cook of the Texas and Texas-influenced range, if not typically a Negro, was at least very frequently one.[37] To be sure, the historian of the cowboy-cook writes: "Most bosses preferred a native white cook. . . . Some Negroes were good cooks, but were usually lazy, and, too, white cowboys refused to take orders from them." This state-ment, however, is not confirmed by the literature of the cattle country, which strongly suggests that many if not most cattlemen were in agreement with the trail boss who wrote: "For cooks I always preferred darkies."[38]

The primary reason of this preference is probably that Negroes simply were on the average better workers than the available whites. They could, of

course, occasionally be lazy, stupid, careless, dishonest, and many whites
were excellent cooks, but the cow-camp menus on record seem to have been
disproportionately the work of Negro cooks. Good cooks occasionally supplemented the filling but somewhat monotonous diet of biscuits, "sowbelly,"
beef, molasses, and coffee by carrying a gun in the wagon and, between
dishwashing and starting the next meal, hunted deer, turkey, and other
game. An extraordinary cook who took full advantage of such opportunities
was a thirty-year-old Negro named Sam, who, in 1878, prepared for an outfit
on Pease River what one of its members years later described as "about the
most luscious eating. . . . I have ever enjoyed . . . an oven of buffalo steaks,
another . . . of roast bear meat, better than pork, a frying pan full of the breast
of wild turkey in gravy of flour, water, and grease, . . . antelope ribs barbecued
on a stick over the coals." Sometimes he would roast a turkey in its feathers
in a pit. He also cooked wild plums, stewing them or making them into a
cobbler. Small wonder that the cowboys of his outfit always saw to it that he
had plenty of wood.[39] Sam was merely one of a galaxy of Negro cow-country
cooks, each with his specialty—Dutch oven-baked peach pies, "cathead
biscuits," "son-of-a-gun stew," etc.

The cook was frequently in sole charge not merely of the kitchen but of
the ranch house itself, and on the long drive was of course frequently left
alone to protect the chuckwagon and its contents in any emergency, whether
crossing a river or encountering Indians. A Negro cook distinguished himself in an episode of 1877 in which the other members of his outfit played no
very heroic roles. Four white men and three Negroes were working cattle in
Coleman County, Texas, when Indians suddenly swooped down upon them.
All took refuge in a cave except "old Negro Andy, the cook," who stayed by
the wagon, fought off the Indians, and saved the supplies.[40]

By and large, Negro cooks managed their kitchens or chuckwagon, dealt
with Indians, and accomplished their culinary feats without the "cranki-
ness" which was almost as much standard equipment for cow-country cooks
as was their "starter" for salt-rising bread. Some white cooks manifested such
behavior to an almost psychopathic extent, and some Negro cooks lived up
to the tradition, to be sure, but more typical were those remembered for
opposite qualities.[41] Jim Perry was not only a fine cook but also "the best
Negro who ever lived"; Sam "always had a cheerful word or a cheerful song";
etc. Frank Dobie believes that Negro and Mexican cooks were notably
above average in their tendency to be "providers by nature" and in their
readiness to go out of their way to furnish extra services, from medicinal
supplies to home-made remedies. When, for example, a young cowboy
drank alkali water, and "wasn't feeling too good," Jim Simpson, the Negro
cook, told him to roll a can of tomatoes in his slicker for both food and drink;
the acid from the tomatoes would help neutralize the alkali.[42]

The Negro cook often possessed other skills beyond the culinary. So many
Negro cooks, in fact, were noted riders and ropers that something of a
pattern emerges. The wild-game cook extraordinary, Black Sam, was such a

good rider that "frequently one of the boys would get him to 'top' a bad horse." Jim Perry of the XIT was not only the best cook that ever lived, according to a white hand, but he was also the best rider as well. Jim Simpson, roundup cook and fiddler, who had come up from Texas in the 1880s with a herd of longhorns, was at one time also "about the best roper" in that part of the Wyoming range.[43] When an associate of one of the famous Blockers expressed some doubt about his roping ability, Blocker told his Negro cook, "Goat," to wipe the dough off his hands and get a rope and a horse. Blocker swung a regular "Blocker loop" on the first cow, which picked up her front feet, and the cow pony did the rest. "Goat" similarly roped and threw the next cow, Blocker the third, and so on, until they had roped about twenty, never missing.[44]

Negro cooks often left the chuckwagon for the saddle in an emergency. "Doc" Little, who had risen from cowboy to volunteer cook's assistant to full-time cook, "always remained the good cowboy" and in the event of a stampede was usually the first on a horse. The same was said of the Slaughter cook, "Old Bat." When a drove of 500 horses stampeded, taking the *remuda* with them, including the *remudero's* own picketed horse, the Negro cook threw himself on the trailing rope and "went bumping along for about a hundred yards" before he could stop the animal. He then mounted and took the lead in rounding up the herd.[45]

All cowboys, we have noted, were expected to be able to "sing" in order to soothe the restless cattle. Just as they were expert riders and ropers, Negro cooks were frequently singers, musicians, and even composers. Although hard-worked, they were about the only men in an outfit with the opportunity to carry and play a musical instrument. "The Zebra Dun," a song about a supposed greenhorn who surprised everyone by riding an outlaw horse, is said to have been composed by Jake, who worked for a Pecos River ranch.[46] One chuckwagon cook who supplemented his menu with deer and turkey which he shot himself, also sang and played the guitar.[47] Another, Old Bat, the Slaughter cook, played both the fiddle and the fife. Jim Perry, the XIT cook, was not only the best cook, the best rider, and the best Negro in the world, but also the best fiddler. Jim Simpson, Negro cook and roper of the Wyoming range, was also the regular fiddler for the Saturday night dances. Big Sam, cook and rider, played the banjo and sang until someone stepped on the instrument, whereupon the bunch bought him a fiddle on which he would play such songs as "Green corn, green corn, bring along the demijohn."[48] But the Negro cook-musician who made the most spectacular appearance on the cow-country stage was Gordon Davis, who led Ab Blocker's trail herd through Dodge City while mounted on his left wheel ox, fiddle in hand, playing "Buffalo Gals."[49]

Negro cooks, in addition to riding and roping, singing and playing, sometimes possessed skills so various as to be unclassifiable. The Negro cook, "Old Lee," was "handy as a pocket shirt, ready to do anything, and with the 'know-how' for almost anything that showed up, from cooking to horse-

wrangling to mending saddle leathers and boots." One of the most versatile
of Negro cooks was John Battavia Hinnaut ("Old Bat"), probably the most
useful man on the Slaughter spread. Although primarily and officially a
roundup cook, he was a first-class ranch-hand, a musician, an expert teamster and coachman, an Indian fighter, a mighty hunter, and also served as the
boss's valet, practical nurse and bodyguard.[50]

That the Negro cow-country cook frequently possessed unusual abilities
was due in part to limitations imposed because of racial discrimination. He
was much more likely than the average white man to have been brought up
about the kitchen and stables of a plantation or ranch and there, at an early
age, to have become acquainted with cooking and horses. He was less likely
to regard kitchen chores as somehow beneath him. The unusually able and
ambitious white cowboy would look forward to possible promotion to foreman or trail boss; the Negro of equal ability knew he had little chance of
attaining such a position. To become a ranch or roundup cook was about as
much as could be expected. Age, inexperience, or physical handicap might
preclude a white man from any ranch job outside the kitchen; but for the
superior Negro cowboy to preside over a chuckwagon or ranch kitchen
meant an increase in pay and prestige.

FOREMEN AND TRAIL BOSSES

The Negro cowhand, however able, as we have seen, rarely rise to a position
higher than chuckwagon or ranch-house cook. The principal obstacle to his
becoming a ranch foreman or trail boss was a general belief that a Negro
simply did not possess the qualities necessary for such a position. But even if
a ranch owner or group of cattlemen were confident that a Negro had the
necessary intelligence, initiative, and general capacity, there was always the
practical consideration that such a man, even if in charge of an all-Negro
outfit, would on occasion have to deal with white foreman and trail bosses
who might refuse to recognize his authority, and that expensive trouble
might ensue. A Negro, however great his ability, thus had difficulty in
attaining greater authority than could be exercised over a chuchwagon or
kitchen. The phenomenal success of Ora Haley, who for three decades was
the dominant figure in the range-cattle business of Northwestern Colorado,
is said to have been partly due to his Negro top hand Thornton Biggs, who
although he "taught a whole generation of future range managers, wagon
bosses, and all-round cowpunchers the finer points of the range-cattle business," himself "never became a range manager or even a foreman." The
fairer-minded recognized the handicaps under which their Negro cowhands
labored. Jim Perry, redoubtable cook, rider, and fiddler of the XIT ranch,
once wryly remarked: "If it weren't for my damned old black face I'd have
been boss of one of these divisions long ago."[51] "And no doubt he would
have," a white employee commented.

And yet a very few Negroes of exceptional ability, and sometimes under unusual circumstances, did make the grade. There was the master West Texas rider and roper, "Nigger Add" or "Old Add" who, by 1889 if not earlier, was the LFD's range boss, working "South Texas colored hands almost entirely." One of his qualifications was that he was a "dictionary of earmarks and brands" but probably more important was his universal popularity among cattlemen from Toyah, Texas, to Las Vegas, New Mexico.[52] Nigger Add's outfit consisted "almost entirely" of Negroes—and one wonders who the exceptions were. Probably they were Mexicans.

But did any Negro break through the color line to direct outfits including at least some whites? A leading authority on the cow country doubts that it could have happened.[53] Nevertheless at least one Negro, it seems, through sheer ability and force of character was able to defy the tradition that the white man always gives the orders and the black man obeys. Al Jones was a six-footer with a proud carriage and finely chiseled features of a somewhat "Indian" type. He went up the trail no less than thirteen times, and four times—once was in 1885—he was trail boss, directing Negroes, Mexicans, and sometimes white men. As a trail boss he was resourceful and decisive, but probably needed an abundance of tact to get the job done.[54]

Paradoxically, the race prejudice which prevented more than a very few Negro cowhands from rising to the status of foreman or trail boss may have spurred able and ambitious Negroes into taking up land, acquiring cattle, and setting up as independent small ranchers, whereas, lacking the incentive such an obstacle provided, they might have remained satisfied with a position as ranch foreman. But the story of the Negro rancher belongs to the history of petty capitalism rather than to labor history.

HENCHMEN, BODYGUARDS, "BANKERS," AND FACTOTUMS

Some especially able and trustworthy cow-country Negroes fulfilled roles for which there was no equivalent among white cowhands; as confidential assistants, factotums and, when it was necessary to transport large sums of money, bodyguards and "bankers."

Colonel Charles Goodnight wrote of Bose Ikard, his right hand man: "I have trusted him farther than any living man. He was my detective, banker, and everything else." Bose would sometimes have on his person proceeds from his employer's cattle sales amounting to as much as $20,000, since it was reasoned that a thief would be unlikely to search a Negro's belongings.[55]

John Slaughter's "Old Bat" played a similar role. Officially a roundup cook, he could also do almost any ranch work, but his major importance was as a general factotum in anything connected with Slaughter's personal needs—valet, practical nurse, and, above all, bodyguard. When Slaughter was on a cattle-buying trip, Bat always went along to guard the approximately $10,000 in gold which Slaughter usually carried in his money belt, watching while his employer slept. When Slaughter went into Mexico, where silver was preferable, Bat had charge of a mule loaded with "dobe" dollars. His fitness as bodyguard was demonstrated in action against the Apache and when, with another Negro, he stood at Slaughter's side and helped beat off an attack by Mexican bandits.[56]

Print Olive's handyman and bodyguard was Nigger Jim Kelly—wrangler, horsebreaker, gunman—who in the fall of 1869 accompanied his boss back from Fort Kearney, Nebraska, their saddlebags stuffed with currency and gold, and who in 1872, with a quick well-aimed bullet, saved Print's life after he had been shot three times and was about to be killed.[57]

Still another formidable Negro henchman was Zeke, a giant "two-knife" Negro, who in 1879 accompanied Colonel Draper to Dodge City on a cattle-buying trip with a paper-wrapped bundle of $5,000 in currency.[58] Finally, there was "Old Nep." The famous "Shanghai" Pierce may have thought more of him, according to Frank Dobie, than of anyone else; for thirty five years Neptune Holmes used to accompany Shanghai on his cattle-buying expeditions, leading a mule loaded with saddlebags which bulged with gold and silver and on which he would pillow his head at night.[59]

Where large sums of money were involved, and courage and loyalty in protecting and defending it was needed, prominent cattlemen such as Goodnight, Slaughter, Olive, and Pierce, characteristically preferred to depend on Negro bodyguards.

WAGES

For a generation and more, cow-country Negroes distinguished themselves as riders and ropers, cooks and bodyguards, as well as in the more common and still highly necessary positions of wranglers, ordinary cowboys, and top hands. What compensation, financial and psychological, did they receive for their services? And how did their wages, working, and living conditions, and opportunities for advancement and a "good life," compare with those of white hands of corresponding abilities and of Negroes outside the cattle country?

In view of the racial situation which then prevailed throughout the United States, particularly in the South and West, it can be assumed that Negro cowmen encountered discrimination and segregation. The question therefore is not: Did discrimination and segregation exist? But rather: What was their extent and character? And how uniform were they? For although racism was general, it did vary from region to region, from state to state, and even from community to community. It also varied from period to period, probably increasing rather than diminishing during the years in question.

Racial discrimination in the cattle country falls into several categories: wages and working conditions on the job, personal and social relations on the ranch or on cattle trails; and in town or at the end of the cattle trail.

Discrimination was probably least evident on the job. As to wages, cow-punching was, of course, by no means a highly paid occupation, regardless of race. Wages of various categories of cowhands varied widely not only from year to year and from region to region, but even within the same year and region and sometimes within the same outfit as well. Wages were generally low, but increased somewhat from the 1860s into the 1890s and were higher on the Northern Range than in Texas and Kansas. An ordinary hand in the South received from a minimum $15 per month immediately after the Civil War, to $20–$30 through the late 1860s, 1870s, and into the 1880s, to as much as $45 in the 1890s. An experienced top hand would receive $5 or $10 per month more than a less experienced man, and trail hands were paid somewhat more than ordinary ranch hands. Especially experienced trail hands, below the rank of trail boss, occasionally drew double wages of as much as $60 or even $75; but a "green" boy would receive half-wages of $10–$15. The wages of trail bosses and foremen normally ranged during this period from $100 to $150. Cooks' salaries, as we have seen, might be as little as that of a top hand or as much as double an ordinary cowhand's, but customarily were $5 or $10 more than those of the best-paid cowhand in the outfit. In the North, cowhands usually got about $10 a month more than those in the South. In all cases compensation included food and, in the case of ranch hands, sleeping accommodations, such as they were.[60]

Strange though it may seem, there is not clear-cut evidence that Negro cowhands were generally or seriously discriminated against in the matter of wages, though this was obviously so with Mexicans, who sometimes received one half to one third that of white cowboys earning $20–25.[61] "Teddy Blue," to be sure, says of the Olive outfit, for which he worked in 1879, that they hated Mexicans and "niggers" but "hired them because they worked cheaper than white men." He gives no details, however, and the notoriously violent Olives may have been no more typical in their wage policy than in their conduct generally. On the other hand, one trail boss stated: "I have worked white Americans, Mexicans, and Negroes and they all got just the same salary."[62] Wages were so much under the control of the individual employer that no doubt Negroes were sometimes discriminated against; but such discrimination seems not to have been characteristic and, when it occurred, was never nearly as serious as that to which Mexicans were subjected.

COWBOY STRIKES

The question of wages naturally brings up the further question: Did cow-boys, through united action, ever endeavor to raise their low wages? The general impression is that the happy, carefree, independent-spirited cowboy could not have cared less about wages, so long as they were sufficient to keep him in smoking tobacco and to finance a spree on pay day at the trail's end. The late Stanley Vestal—a better authority on the Northern Plain Indians

KENNETH W. PORTER

than on the cattle industry—was writing in this spirit when he enquired, rhetorically and contemptuously, "What cowboy ever wished to join a union?"[63] The answer could have been supplied by anyone acquainted with the cattle industry of the Texas Panhandle and of the Powder River region of Wyoming during the 1880s.

In 1883, just before the spring roundup, cowboys on a number of big Panhandle ranches issued an ultimatum to their bosses demanding higher wages—$50 per month instead of the $25–35 they were then receiving. Better food, particularly more vegetables, is said to have been another objective, but there was apparently no demand for shorter hours than the usual 105 for a seven-day week—15 hours a day! According to the official record of the Federal Bureau of Labor Statistics, the strike was a prompt and unequivocal success, but all other evidence indicates that, though from five to seven large ranches and over 300 cowboys were involved, the strike dragged on for over a year and finally "petered out." Texas Rangers, hired gunmen, and dancehall girls, who soon consumed the strikers' savings, are all credited with responsibility for the failure of this first cowboy strike.[64]

The Panhandle cowboy strike, though the first, was not the last. The Wyoming cattle industry was largely in the hands of absentee ranch owners from Great Britain and the Eastern states, and early in 1886 they ordered a general cut of at least $5 in the prevailing monthly wage of $35–40. Just before the spring roundup the cowboys on the south fork of Powder River struck for $40 a month all around; the strike was led by men who were themselves getting $40, but who objected to working beside men who were getting only $35 and even $30. The strike, which spread to the Sweetwater-Platte area, was generally successful, though its leader was later black-balled.[65]

Negro cowboys could hardly have played any important part in these strikes, as there were not many in the Panhandle and very few in Wyoming. The only negro cow-country employee in the Panhandle strike about whom we have clear-cut evidence was loyal to his employer rather than to his fellow workers. When it was rumored that a delegation of strikers was descending on the T-Anchor ranch, its owner planted a black-powder mine in an out-building—in case strikers should attempt to use the structure as cover for an attack on the ranch house. He commissioned "Gus Lee, the faithful and later famous Negro cook," in the event of such an attack, to crawl out and light the fuse. But the strikers, after a few bullets had kicked up dirt about their horses, advanced no farther and thus relieved Lee of this responsibility.[66]

A Negro or two may, however, have been among the Panhandle strikers. Both in the Panhandle and on Powder River the cowboy strike against the big ranches was followed within a few years by a bloody feud between the big ranchers and the "nester ranchers and little men," with the big ranchers hiring cowboy-gunmen and their opponents drawing support from dis-gruntled and sometimes blackballed cowboys. The little town of Tascosa in the Panhandle was headquarters for both the striking cowboys in 1883, and for the "nester ranchers" and their supporters in 1886. Among the cowboy partisans of the "little men" was "Nigger Bob" who, when cowboy-gunmen about 2 A.M. on March 21 invaded Tascosa, was "sleepin' on a hot roll" between a woodpile and a small adobe. As the gunmen advanced, firing, rifle shots apparently from the woodpile, drilled one of them through the chest. "Nigger Bob" claimed that, when the bullets got too close, he prudently left the scene, but his "tough hombre" reputation raised the suspicion that he might have done more shooting than he was willing to admit. If "Nigger Bob" and others like him were around during the strike, they probably supported it.[67]

WORKING CONDITIONS

Negroes were not discriminated against in the work permitted them — below the rank of foreman and trail boss. An experienced Negro would not be told to help the wrangler or to "eat dust" on the drag while a white greenhorn rode at point. On the other hand, Negroes may have been worked harder and longer than whites. John M. Hendrix, a white former cowpuncher and rancher, writing in the middle 1930s, approvingly presented the most extreme picture of discrimination. Negroes, he says, "were usually called on to do the hardest work around the outfit," such as "taking the first pitch out of the rough horses," while the whites were eating breakfast. "It was the Negro hand who usually tried out the swimming water when a trailing herd came to a swollen stream, or if a fighting bull or steer was to be handled, he knew without being told that it was his job." On cold rainy nights, moreover, Negroes would stand "a double guard rather than call the white folks" and would even launder everyone's clothes when the opportunity offered. "These Negroes knew their place, and were careful to stay in it."[68]

Their "place," according to this white Texan, was to do the most dangerous and difficult work, and more of it than any white hand, and in addition to serve as *valets de chambre* to the white hands.

But such a picture cannot be accepted as generally valid. There may have been some outfits to which this description applied and some Negro hands who endeavored to win favor by such works of superogation, but firsthand accounts of the cattle industry in its heyday — Hendrix's own experiences belonged entirely to the twentieth century — hardly seem to confirm this picture. Negroes were frequently expert riders and did "top" horses for less able wranglers, but contemporaries indicate that such work was regarded as a favor, not as a duty, and its beneficiaries were grateful for it. That Negroes were usually sent to test a swollen stream or handle a dangerous animal cannot be confirmed. There is a similar lack of information about Negroes gratuitously acting as valets. The only Negro trail hand so described did it exclusively for the trail boss and even this was regarded as unprecedented.[69]

The Negro, to be sure, was occasionally given unpleasant chores, but due to individual unfairness rather than to accepted custom. They might be given jobs which no one else would do—such as killing the calves dropped during the night on a cattle drive.[70] They were sometimes tricked or bullied into doing more than their share of work.[71] But there is no evidence that Negroes were normally expected to do double night-herding duty or guard the cattle while the whites went on a spree—merely that some cowboys were cheats or bullies who were ready to take advantage of Negroes or, for that matter, of inexperienced white cowhands.

LIVING CONDITIONS

Discrimination and segregation off the job, whether on the ranch or the cattle trail, would have been difficult. Hendrix insists on at least partially segregated eating facilities when he describes the Negroes as "topping" the white hands' horses while the whites ate breakfast—presumably the Negroes ate at the "second table"—and he also states that the Negroes "had their own dishes"! But one can hardly imagine the independent and even cranky chuckwagon cook actually taking the trouble to segregate the dishes! Hendrix may have been reading back into the 1870s and 1880s the pattern of race relationships which he considered proper in his own times.[72]

Actually, firsthand accounts of ranch and cattle-trail life indicate about as much segregation as prevailed on Huckleberry Finn's and the "Nigger Jim's" raft before the appearance of "The King" and "The Duke." The sleeping arrangements were usually such as to defy any idea of racial segregation. Ranchowner, trail boss, Negro and white cowhands—particularly in bad weather—frequently not only slept in the same shack or tent but also shared the same blankets.[73] The one case of such segregation I have encountered occurred on a Wyoming ranch in 1885 when an Irish cook (sex not specified) refused to allow a Negro bronc buster to sleep in the bunkhouse.[74] But when white women began to appear, those extreme manifestations of racial "integration" belonging to the womanless world of the cattle trail and the wintering camp yielded to a more formal and conventional pattern of conduct. When a highly respected Negro cowboy, in the midst of a blizzard, was permitted to sleep on the kitchen floor of a shack in which a camp manager was living with his wife it was regarded by the Negro as an example of extreme condescension or of humanity or both.[75]

HAZING AND ILL TREATMENT

A good deal of hazing and practical joking is inevitable in a community made up largely of rough and uneducated men. Negro hands, particularly those who were young, inexperienced, or timid, probably were subjected to more than their share of such horseplay. But no one in the cattle country—Negro or white, tenderfoot or old timer—was entirely immune to such treatment.[76] In the case of rough treatment which went beyond hazing and became grossly insulting or physically injurious, the Negro cowhand—nearly always a minority member of an outfit composed principally of whites—was in a difficult position. He was almost never a gunslinger. If he were, and if he succeeded in shooting a white opponent in a quarrel, it might have had very serious consequences for him. Negro cowhands rarely used, or attempted to use, a gun in a quarrel within their own outfit. One exception occurred in 1872, when Jim Kelly got the drop on a white cowboy with whom he had had words; but the boss, Print Olive, finally intervened on behalf of the threatened man.[77] Kelly, however, was not only a gunman; he was Print Olive's gunman as well, so nothing happened to him. In 1880 a Negro cowhand, who also served as the trail boss's flunky, attempted to draw on a recently-hired white cowboy who had "cussed him out" for taking his horse's hobbles after repeated warnings, but fell dead with three bullets through the heart.[78] In both these cases the Negro had a special relationship with his employer which encouraged him to brook no nonsense from a white man.

Cowboys seldom engaged in fisticuffs and I have found only one case of a fist fight between a Negro cowhand and a white: this involved the later famous "80 John" Wallace, then a youthful wrangler, and a white boy from another outfit, during a roundup. Wallace claimed the victory. But both participants were mere boys, who were encouraged by the older cowhands;[79] an inter-racial fight between adults probably would not have been so favorably regarded.

Negro cowhands normally depended for protection against insult or injury—whether from members of their own outfits or outsiders—not on fists or weapons but on good conduct, tactful behavior, and their standing among the better element of whites. Negro cooks, though supported by their traditional prestige and real power, were always in danger of encountering violently prejudiced white cowhands who would challenge their authority. For the most part, Negro cooks avoided such a challenge (or insured that, should it materialize, they would have the support of other white cowhands) by a policy of tact and good management—by means of their excellent cookery and, when they were exceptionally good riders, as they often were, by occasionally "topping" a difficult horse. Black Sam of Pease River was particularly skillful in maintaining his prestige without causing ill-feelings. He was an exceptional cook and rider and a popular musician, as well as the biggest and most powerful man in camp. One day when a cowboy jokingly said that he was "too big for man but not big enough for a horse," he promptly replied that he *was* a horse and would give a dollar to many man who could ride him without spurs. Sam then stripped, with only a bandanna around his neck to hold on by, and one by one he hurled his would-be riders to the ground—thereby demonstrating, but in a friendly and tactful fashion, his ability to take care of himself. He never had any trouble.[80]

White cowhands repeatedly came to the support of Negro members of their outfits. When a drunken cowpuncher in Dodge City began to abuse a Negro cook, for no reason except that he was colored, a sixteen-year-old boy belonging to the Negro's outfit promptly sailed in—carrying guns was banned in Dodge at this time—and soon had the best of the fight. Potentially, a much more serious occasion arose in 1879. It involved the Olive brothers' trail boss, Ira Olive, who had killed a Mexican cowhand a year or so before and who for some reason now began to abuse Jim Kelly—with the aim, E. C. Abbott believed, of getting Kelly to go for his gun so that he could kill him. Kelly, himself a gunman, later claimed that he would have drawn and killed Ira except for the knowledge that he would have to reckon with his brother Print if he did; this he wished to avoid, since Print was his friend. So he took the abuse until Ira struck him in the mouth with his gun, knocking out two teeth. What might have happened next will never be known for at this point the nineteen-year-old Abbott brashly intervened. "If you hit that boy again," he warned ("that boy" was forty years old) "I'll shoot your damn eyes out."[81]

But such protection was not always available. In 1878 a Negro was hired to work on the 22 Ranch, but a member of the outfit—a "nigger killer" type—set out to run him off and one morning began shooting at him. In desperation, the Negro scrambled onto a horse and fled, with the white man in pursuit. Only the white man returned to camp and the Negro's horse showed up the next day with the saddle still on; a few years later a human skeleton, believed to be the Negro's, was found in the neighborhood. The Negro, during this fracas, apparently never attempted to defend himself nor did any member of the outfit lift a finger or even his voice on behalf of the man, or venture to question the white man's conduct. Possibly, had the Negro been with the outfit long enough to establish himself, someone would have intervened, but this is speculation: the outfit stands condemned, with not a single man of the calibre of young Abbott or the sixteen-year-old boy in Dodge City.[82]

RECREATION AND SOCIAL LIFE

The Negro cowboy engaged in the same amusements as the white—on a basis ranging from apparently complete integration to rigid separation. The extent of this segregation depended upon how well the parties knew one another and, more important, upon whether or not the whites included women.

To understand the character and degree of this segregation, and the way in which it was regarded by both whites and blacks, one must remember that the white men and women of the cow country were largely Southerners, or Westerners with a Southern exposure, while the Negroes, if not former slaves, were usually the children of ex-slaves. Both whites and Negroes were thus acquainted, by personal experience or recent tradition, with racial *discrimination* far more severe than anything practiced in the post-bellum cow country, even though racial *segregation* under slavery was less rigid than it became during the late nineteenth century.

When ranch work was slack, particularly in the winter, the hands sometimes held a dance, either a "bunkhouse 'shindig'" in which the participants were all males or a "regular dance" with girls from neighboring ranches or from town if one was close enough. On these occasions the Negro hands had the opportunity to shine, as musicians or dancers or both. Although serving as musicians at either type of dance, they were more conspicuous as dancers in the womanless bunkhouse affairs. Indeed, they might not appear on the dance floor with white women, though, singly or in groups, they might present dancing exhibitions as part of the entertainment.[83]

Segregation in a cattle town, where the Negro cowhand was more of a stranger and white women were present, was much more clearcut than on the familiar ranch. But even here the restrictions were not always as rigid as one might perhaps expect. On the town's streets and among members of the same outfit, segregation might be non-existent. A French baron, returning in 1883 from a visit to the Black Hills, was astonished to see a group of cowboys throwing the lasso and wrestling in front of the door to the hotel bar, with a Negro participating "on a footing of perfect equality." Consequently, he naively assumed that "race prejudice had disappeared,"[84] but had the cowboys *entered* the bar this illusion would probably have vanished, even though the region was the Northern Range, not Gulf Coast Texas.

Even in Texas, however, segregation in the saloons was apparently informal. Whites, it seems, were served at one end of the bar, Negroes at the other. But should a white man and a Negro choose to drink and converse together in the "neutral zone" between the two sections probably no objection would be raised. The gunman and gambler Ben Thompson once undertook to "integrate" a San Antonio saloon at the point of a revolver, forcing the bartender to permit the Negroes to "spread out" from their crowded corner into the vacant space at the "white" end of the bar. His friends charitably assumed that he was suffering from a nervous breakdown, but since, upon an earlier occasion, Thompson had shot a white bully who was trying to force a Cherokee-Negro cowboy to down a beer mug full of whiskey, he may actually have been in part influenced by a fleeting impulse to defend the underdog.[85]

If the Negro, however, moved from the saloon to a restaurant, he would encounter a completely segregated situation, partly because of the symbolic value attached to sitting down and eating together — as opposed to standing up at the same bar[86] — but principally because women might be guests in the dining room or cafe. In a town without a colored restaurant, the Negro might have food handed to him at the back door of the cafe — perhaps he might even be permitted to eat in the kitchen — but more probably would, like many white cowboys, prefer to purchase groceries and eat sitting on a hitching rail.[87]

Negroes, of course, were not lodged in "white" hotels — unless they were in attendance on prominent white cattlemen—but cowboys, black and white, usually felt that they had better use for their money than to spend it on hotel rooms. They preferred to spread out their "hot rolls" in a livery stable or some other sheltered spot.[88]

The most rigorously segregated cow-town establishments, at least so far as Negro cowhands were concerned, were brothels staffed with white prostitutes. However, the larger cow-towns at least, such as Dodge City, were also equipped with *bagnios* occupied by "soiled doves of color," while smaller communities usually had a few "public women" of color who operated independently. The rule that Negroes must not patronize white prostitutes did not of course bar relations between white cowhands and colored women.[89]

The cow-town gambling-house, on the other hand, was apparently entirely unsegregated. A gambler who intended to separate a Negro trail hand from his wages through the more than expert use of cards and dice could hardly do so without sitting down with him at the same card or crap table.[90]

The Negro cowhand was accustomed to a degree of segregation and apparently did not resent it—at least not to the extent of risking his life in defiance of the practice. Clashes between Negro cowhands and whites were exceedingly rare. When racial encounters occurred in cattle towns, the Negroes involved were almost always colored soldiers.

CONCLUSION

Without the services of the eight or nine thousand Negroes—a quarter of the total number of trail drivers—who during the generation after the Civil War helped to move herds up the cattle trails to shipping points, Indian reservations, and fattening grounds and who, between drives, worked on the ranches of Texas and the Indian Territory, the cattle industry would have been seriously handicapped. For apart from their considerable numbers, many of them were especially well-qualified top hands, riders, ropers, and cooks. Of the comparatively few Negroes on the Northern Range, a good many were also men of conspicuous abilities who notably contributed to the industry in that region. These cowhands, in their turn, benefitted from their participation in the industry, even if not to the extent that they deserved. That a degree of discrimination and segregation existed in the cattle country should not obscure the fact that, during the halcyon days of the cattle range, Negroes there frequently enjoyed greater opportunities for a dignified life than anywhere else in the United States. They worked, ate, slept, played, and on occasion fought, side by side with their white comrades, and their ability and courage won respect, even admiration. They were often paid the same wages as white cowboys and, in the case of certain horsebreakers, ropers, and cooks, occupied positions of considerable prestige. In a region and period characterized by violence, their lives were probably safer than they would have been in the Southern cotton regions where between 1,500 and 1,600

Negroes were lynched in the two decades after 1882.[91] The skilled and handy Negro probably had a more enjoyable, if a rougher, existence as a cowhand then he would have had as a sharecropper or laborer. Bose Ikard, for example, had a rich, full, and dignified life on the West Texas frontier — as trail driver, as Indian fighter, and as Colonel Goodnight's right-hand man — more so undoubtedly than he could ever have known on a plantation in his native Mississippi.

Negro cowhands, to be sure, were not treated as "equals," except in the rude quasi-equality of the round-up, roping-pen, stampede, and river-crossings — where they were sometimes tacitly recognized even as superiors — but where else in post-Civil War America, at a time of the Negro's nadir, did so many adult Negroes and whites attain even this degree of fraternity? The cow country was no utopia for Negroes, but it did demonstrate that under some circumstances and for at least a brief periods white and black in significant numbers could live and work together on more nearly equal terms than had been possible in the United States for two hundred years or would be possible again for nearly another century.

NOTES

1. May Davison Rhodes, *The Hired Man on Horseback: A Biography of Eugene Manloe* Rhodes (Boston, 1938), ix-xiii.

2. John Marvin Hunter (ed.), *The Trail Drivers of Texas* (Nashville, 1925), 453.

3. *Ibid.*, 987, 255, 717, 157, 505, 472, 817, 138–139, 805, 718–719; R. J. (Bob) Lauderdale and John M. Doak, *Life on the Range and on the Trail*, Lela Neal Pirtle, editor (San Antonio, 1936), 169.

4. John Hendrix, *If I Can Do It Horseback* (Austin, 1963), 205.

5. John M. Hendrix, "Tribute Paid to Negro Cowmen," *The Cattleman*, XXII (Feb., 1936), 24. See also J. Frank Dobie to KWP, Jan. 30, 1953, J. Frank Dobie, *The Longhorns* (Boston, 1941), 309.

6. William A. Keleher, *The Fabulous Frontier: Twelve New Mexico Items* (Albuquerque, 1962), 162–163, 245, 271; Theodore Roosevelt, *Ranch Life and the Hunting Trail* (N.Y., 1920; 1st ed., 1888), 10–11. See also Floyd C. Bard as told to Agnes Wright Spring, in *Horse Wrangler: Sixty Years in the Saddle in Wyoming and Montana* (Norman, 1960), 12–13; Sir Cecil E. Denny, *The Law Marches West* (Toronto, 1939), 187.

7. J. Frank Dobie, *A Vaquero of the Brush Country* (Dallas, 1929), 12–13; Lauderdale and Doak, *op. cit.*, 11; Hunter, *op. cit.*, 679, 204.

8. Douglas Branch, *The Cowboy and His Interpreters* (N. Y., 1926), 42–43; Ross Santee, *Men and Horses* (N.Y., 1926); Agnes Morley Cleaveland, *No Life for a Lady* (Boston, 1941), 111; William T. Hornaday, "The Cowboys of the Northwest," *Cosmopolitan*, II (Dec., 1886), 226; Edward Everett Dale, *Cow Country* (Norman, 1942), 46–47.

9. Branch, *op. cit.*, 42–43. "For my money he [the wrangler] was one of the most capable fellows around an outfit." Hendrix, *If I Can Do It Horseback*, 185–186.

10. Harry E. Chrisman, *The Ladder of Rivers: The Story of I. P. (Print) Olive* (Denver, 1962), 34–35, 77, 102, 147, 217, 378; Dane Coolidge, *Fighting Men of the West* (Bantam Books, 1952; 1st ed., 1932), 14, 32, 41; Frank Collinson, *Life in the Saddle*, Mary Whatley Clark, editor, (Norman, 1963), 145.

11. Charles A. Siringo, *Riata and Spurs: The Story of a Lifetime Spent in the Saddle as Cowboy and Ranger* (Boston, 1931; 1st ed., 1927), 27.

12. Ramon F. Adams to KWP, Feb. 6, 1953; Roosevelt, *op. cit.*, 10–11; Ellsworth Collings, "The Hook Nine Ranch in the Indian Territory," *Chronicles of Oklahoma*, XXXIII (Winter, 1955–56), 462; Angie Debo, editor, *The Cowman's Southwest, being the Reminiscences of Oliver Nelson, Freighter, Camp Cook, Frontiersman, in Kansas, Indian Territory, Texas, and Oklahoma, 1876–1893* (Glendale, 1963), 98–99, 107–108; Hendrix, *If I Can Do It Horseback*, 161, 205.

13. Homer Croy, *Our Will Rogers* (N. Y. and Boston, 1953), 19–20, 250, 334; Donald Day, *Will Rogers: A Biography* (N. Y., 1962), 11–16, Chrisman, 77; John Rolfe Burroughs, *Where the West Stayed Young: The Remarkable History of Brown's Park* . . . (N. Y., 1962), 109.

14. Collinson, *op. cit.*, 25–26; James Emmit McCauley, *A Stove-Up Cowboy's Story*, with an introduction by John A. Lomax (Dallas, 1956; 1st ed., 1943), 12.

15. Siringo, *A Texas Cowboy* (Signet Books, 1955; 1st ed., 1886), 38; Siringo, *Riata and Spurs*, 17, 18.

16. Dobie, *Vaquero*, 100–101.

17. Hunter, *op. cit.*, 112, 417–418; James C. Shaw, *North from Texas: Incidents in the Early Life of a Range Cowman in Texas, Dakota, and Wyoming 1852–1882*, Herbert O. Brayer, editor (Evanston, 1952), 46–47.

18. Hendrix, "Negro Cowmen," 24.

19. Hunter, *op. cit.*, 47–48, 987–988; A. J. Sowell, *Early Settlers and Indian Fighters of Southwest Texas* (Austin, 1900), 757–758; J. Frank Dobie, interview with Joe McCloud, Beeville, Texas, *ca.* 1928, in letter to KWP, Feb. 16, 1953.

20. Dobie, *Longhorns*, 246–247; E. C. Abbott ("Teddy Blue") and Helena Huntington Smith, *We Pointed Them North: Recollections of a Cowpuncher* (N. Y., 1939), 263.

21. Emerson Hough, *The Story of the Cowboy* (N. Y., 1934; 1st ed., 1897), 91; James W. Freeman (ed.), *Poetry and Prose of the Live Stock Industry* (Denver and Kansas City, 1905), I, 13; Louis Pelzer, *The Cattleman's Frontier* . . . *1850–1890* (Glendale, 1936), 48; Roosevelt, *op. cit.*, 10–11; Stanley Walker, "Decline and Fall of the Hired Man," *The New Yorker*, Sept. 12, 1953, p. 110; Clifford P. Westermeier, *Man, Beast, Dust: The Story of Rodeo* (n.p., 1947), 173.

22. Hendrix, "Negro Cowmen," 24; Elmo S. Watson, "Tales of the Trail," probably in a Colorado Springs newspaper in 1916, and Arthur Chapman, interview with Andy Adams, *Denver Times*, Aug. 18, 1915, p. 2. See also Wilson M. Hudson, *Andy Adams: His Life and Writings* (Dallas, 1964), 184, 251. To Professor Hudson's kindness I owe copies of the two newspaper items, *supra*.

23. Burroughs, *op. cit.*, 192–195; Coolidge, *op. cit.*, 79; Dean Krakel, *The Saga of Tom Horn: The Story of a Cattleman's War* (Laramie, 1954), 9–12.

24. Chrisman, *op. cit.*, 34–35, 77, 217, 378; Harry E. Chrisman, Denver, to KWP, Oct. 23, 1965.

25. Lincoln A. Lang, *Ranching with Roosevelt* (Philadelphia, 1926), 286.

26. Lewis Nordyke, *Cattle Empire: The Fabulous Story of the 3,000,000 Acre XIT* (N. Y., 1949), 138.

27. Jean Ehly, "'Bones' Hooks of the Panhandle," *Frontier Times*, XXXVI (June-July, 1963), 20–22, 54–55 (illustrated).

28. Edward Seymour Nichols, *Ed Nichols Rode a Horse*, as told to Ruby Nichols Cutbirth (Dallas, 1943), 8–9.

29. Siringo, *Texas Cowboy*, 82–83.

30. Bard, *op. cit.*, 67.

31. Fred Herring, Lometa, Texas, to KWP, July 20, 1965.

32. J. Evetts Haley, *George W. Littlefield, Texan* (Norman, 1943), 181–186.

33. Frederic Remington, "Vagabonding with the Tenth Horse," *The Cosmopolitan*, XXII (Feb., 1897), 352.

34. Abbott and Smith, *op. cit.*, 261–264.

35. Hunter, *op. cit.*, 778.

36. The standard work on the cow-country cook is, of course, Ramon F. Adams, *Come and Get It: The Story of the Old Cowboy Cook* (Norman, 1952). Almost every general work on the cowboy or the cattle country, and many reminiscences and special studies also contain useful information.

37. Rufus Rockwell Wilson, *Out of the West* (N. Y., 1933), 377; Hough, *op. cit.*, 138–139; J. Frank Dobie, *Cow People* (Boston, 1964), 132; Hunter, *op. cit.*, 485, 43, 307, 535, 295–303, 416–417, 981, 688, 231, 606–607, 81, 679.

38. R. F. Adams, *op. cit.*, 21–22; Lauderdale and Doak, *op. cit.*, 183–185.

39. Dobie, *Vaquero*, 137–139; Dobie, *Cow People*, 140.

40. J. S. Hart, "Jesse Hart, Callahan County Pioneer," *Frontier Times* (Jan., 1953), 86.

41. Cordia Sloan Duke and Joe B. Frantz, *6,000 Miles of Fence: Life on the XIT Ranch of Texas* (Austin, 1961), 172n.; Dobie, *Vaquero*, 137–139; Frazier Hunt, *The Long Trail from Texas: The Story of Ad Spaugh, Cattleman* (N. Y., 1940), 141–145; Bard, *op. cit.*, 145–146.

42. Dobie, *Cow People*, 139–140; Bard, *op. cit.*, 82.

43. Dobie, *Vaquero*, 137–139; Duke and Frantz, *op. cit.*, 172n, 84; Bard, *op. cit.*, 67.

44. J. Evetts Haley, *The XIT Ranch of Texas and the Early Days of the Llano Estacado* (Norman, 1953), 77–78.

45. Lauderdale and Doak, 183–185; Allen A. Erwin, *The Southwest of John H. Slaughter* (Glendale, 1965), 147–149; Hunter, *op. cit.*, 272.

46. John A. and Alan Lomax, *Cowboy Songs* (N. Y., 1938), 78–81; xvii-xix.

47. Max Krueger, *Pioneer Life in Texas* (San Antonio, 1930), 58–71.

48. Erwin, *op. cit.*, 147–149, 159; Dobie and Frantz, bet. 102 and 103; Bard, *op. cit.*, 102; Dobie, *Vaquero*, 137–139.

49. Colonel Jack Potter, *Cattle Trails of the Old West* (Clayton, N. M., 1939), 75.

50. Potter, *op. cit.*, 79–80; Erwin, *op. cit.*, 102, 147, 150, 159, 307–308, 317, 323.

51. Burroughs, *op. cit.*, 71; Duke and Frantz, *op. cit.*, 171–172.

52. N. Howard (Jack) Thorp, *Songs of the Cowboys* (Boston, 1921), 166–168; Thorp, "Banjo in the Cow Camps," *Atlantic*, CLXVI (Aug., 1940), 195–196; Thorp, *Pardner of the Wind* (Caldwell, Ida., 1945), 22, 285.

53. Ramon F. Adams, Dallas, to KWP, Feb. 6, 1953.

54. Frank Dobie, "Notes on Meeting of Trail Drivers of Texas, San Antonio, *ca.* October 1924"; Dobie, "The Old Trail Drivers," *Country Gentleman*, XC (Feb., 14 1925), 8, 28 (photograph); Dobie to KWP, Feb. 16, 1953; Dobie, *Cow People*, 222–223 (photograph); Hunter, *op. cit.*, 378.

55. J. Evetts Haley, *Charles Goodnight: Cowman & Plainsman* (Boston and N. Y., 1936), 166–167, 207, 215, 242–243; *The West Texas Historical Association Year Book* (Oct., 1942), 127.

56. Erwin, *op. cit.*, 102, 147–150, 159, 307–308, 317, 323.

57. Chrisman, *op. cit.*, 93, 124, 321, 358–359, 401.

58. George Bolds, *Across the Cimarron: The Adventures of "Cimarron" George Bolds, Last of the Frontiersmen*, as he related his life story to James D. Horan (N. Y., 1956), 48–49.

59. Dobie, *Cow People*, 47; Chris Emmett, *Shanghai Pierce: A Fair Likeness* (Norman, 1953), viii, 4, 10, 47, 51–52, 101, 127, 130, 133, 265–266.

60. All the general works on the cattle industry and most of the personal reminiscences give more or less attention to wages. Perhaps most generally useful is Louis Pelzer, *op. cit.*, 166, 246.

61. Freeman, I. *op. cit.*, 559; James Henry Cook, *Fifty Years on the Old Frontier as Cowboy, Hunter, Guide, Scout, and Ranchman* (New Haven, 1925; 1st ed., 1923), 8–9.

62. Abbott and Smith, *op. cit.*, 39; Lauderdale and Doak, *op. cit.*, 183–185.

63. Stanley Vestal, *The Missouri*, (N. Y., 1945), 163.

64. The only treatment of this strike in any detail is by Ruth Allen, *Chapters in the History of Organized Labor in Texas* (Austin, 1941), 33–42. Excellent as is this pioneer study, the "cowboy strike" deserves still further attention. Other accounts of, or references to, this strike—not mentioned in the Allen article—are in Charles A. Siringo, A

Lone Star Cowboy (Santa Fe, 1919), 268–269; and Lewis Nordyke, *Great Roundup: The Story of Texas and Southwestern Cowmen* (N. Y., 1955), 109–111.

65. Helena Huntington Smith, *The War on Powder River* (N. Y., 1966), 31–33, 289; John Clay, *My Life on the Range* (Chicago, 1924), 123, 125 (Clay mistakenly places this strike in 1884 rather than 1886; he also mentions another strike in the fall).

66. John L. McCarty, *Maverick Town: The Story of Old Tascosa* (Norman, 1946), 112–113; Boone McClure, "A Review of the T Anchor Ranch," *Panhandle Plains Historical Review*, III (1930), 68–69.

67. McCarty, *op. cit.*, 141–149, esp. 144 and 149.

68. Hendrix, "Negro Cowmen," 24.

69. Dobie, *Cow People*, 233.

70. Haley, *Goodnight*, 136.

71. Dobie, *Vaquero*, 97, 34–36, 46–47; Shaw, *op. cit.*, 34–36, 46–47.

72. C. Vann Woodward, *The Strange Career of Jim Crow* (N. Y., 1955), presents the thesis that segregation in the extreme form which it had assumed by the early 1900s was a comparatively recent development.

73. Siringo, *Riata and Spurs*, 27; Haley, *Littlefield*, 55, 90, 93, 100–101, 114, 134; J. Evetts Harley, *Jeff Milton: A Good Man with a Gun* (Norman, 1948), 19.

74. Amanda Wardin Brown, "A Pioneer in Colorado and Wyoming," *The Colorado Magazine*, XXXV (Oct., 1958), 274.

75. Duke and Frantz, *op. cit.*, 163–164.

76. Debo, *op. cit.*, 108; Dobie, *Longhorns*, 107–108; Hunter, *op. cit.*, 205; Ray M. Beauchamp, "The Town That Died Laughing," *Frontier Times* (Summer, 1960), 30–31, 50–52; Westermeier, *Trailing the Cowboy*, 202–203.

77. Chrisman, *op. cit.*, 104, 201; Harry E. Chrisman, Denver, to KWP, Oct. 23, 1965.

78. Dobie, *Cow People*, 233–237.

79. Hettye Wallace Branch, *The Story of "80 John": A Biography of the Most Respected Negro Ranchmen in the Old West* (N. Y., 1960), 17–18.

80. Dobie, *Vaquero*, 137–139.

81. Hendrix, "Negro Cowmen," 24; Ross Santee, *Lost Pony Tracks* (Bantam Books, 1956; 1st ed., 1953), 202–203; Abbott and Smith *op. cit.*, 38–40; Chrisman, 201.

82. William Joseph Alexander Elliot, *The Spurs* (Spur, Texas, 1939), 209–210.

83. Duke and Frantz, *op. cit.*, 102–103, 189–190; Santee, *op. cit.*, 158–159.

84. Edmond Mandat-Gracey, *Cow-Boys and Colonels: Narrative of a Journey across the Prairie and over the Black Hills of Dakota*, translated by William Conn (Philadelphia and N. Y., 1963), 325–326.

85. J. H. Plenn, *Texas Hellion: The True Story of Ben Thompson* (N. Y., 1955), 60, 142; Hendrix, "Negro Cowmen," 24; O. C. Fisher with J. C. Dykes, *King Fisher: His Life and Times* (Norman, 1966), 124–126.

86. Harry Golden, *Only in America* (Permabooks, 1959; 1st ed., 1958), 105–107, presenting his "Vertical Negro Plan" for abolishing segregation, advances the theory that no Southerner objected to mingling with Negroes so long as neither party sat down!

87. See Rhodes, *op. cit.*, 86–88, for the attempt of a Negro to eat in a white restaurant in a New Mexico cowtown.

88. Bolds, *op. cit.*, 48–49; McCarty, *op. cit.*, 149.

89. Nyle E. Miller and Joseph W. Snell, *Why the West Was Wild* (Topeka, 1963), 614–615, 127, 453; Burroughs, *op. cit.*, 71; William R. Cox, *Luke Short and His Era* (Garden City, N. Y., 1961), 54–55; Westermeier, *Trailing the Cowboy*, 209, 213; Walker D. Wyman and Bruce Silbert, *Nothing But Prairie and Sky: Life on the Dakota Range in the Early Days* (Norman, 1954), 142–143.

90. Lauderdale and Doak, *op. cit.*, 161; Haley, *Jeff Milton*, 95; Rhodes, *op. cit.*, 86–88; W. M. Hutchinson, editor, *A Bar Cross Man: The Life & Personal Writings of Eugene Manlove Rhodes* (Norman, 1956), 3–5.

91. Walter White, *Rope & Faggot: A Biography of Judge Lynch* (N.Y., 1929), *passim*; Jessie Parkhurst Guzman, editor, *Negro Year Book, 1941–1946* (Tuskegee, Ala., 1947), 306–307.

SEVEN

The Politics of Black Land Tenure, 1877–1915

MANNING MARABLE

A central chapter in the history of black America involves the evolution of black agriculture and land tenure in the Black Belt South. At the end of the Civil War, four million black people, about half of whom lived on the cotton-producing plantations of Georgia, Alabama, and Mississippi, owned almost nothing except their clothes, some agricultural tools, farm animals, and their own labor. Their immediate prospects for economic survival seemed bleak. But by 1910, a generation after Appomattox, black people had seemingly succeeded in achieving a minor economic miracle in the Deep South. The number of black owner-operated farms that year was 212,972, almost double the number of only twenty years earlier. With the financial support of black-owned banks, black farmers were purchasing land on credit, speculating on the cotton market, and successfully competing with most small white farmers and tenants. After World War I, the number of black owner-operators of farms gradually declined; a black exodus grew to major proportions as black families abandoned agriculture. The story of substantial black land acquisitions prior to World War I and of steady land losses after the war needs to receive more attention in the pages of black history.[1]

The historiographical emphasis placed upon black migrations from the Deep South and upon the ghetto experiences of subsequent generations obscures the fact that the vast majority of black people were farmers until the Great Depression of the 1930s. Most black people chose freely to live and work in the South after slavery. From the end of the Civil War through the 1870s, there was a moderate increase in black migration into urban centers, but the majority of black men, women, and children who left their homes moved into the Black Belt rather than into southern cities, the Upper South, or the northern states. Many Black Belt counties in Georgia and Alabama experienced an increase of up to 25 percent within ten years. The reason for the sudden relocation of blacks in the old cotton plantation region was primarily economic: almost all black men "expected the plantations of their ex-masters to be divided among them."[2] Unfortunately, the basic pattern of southern land tenure changed very little after 1865. The plantation system was severely shaken by the war and reconstruction, but it was hardly destroyed. Between 1850 and 1880 there was a significant increase in the number of farms in the Deep South and a decrease in the average number of acres per farming unit. Most of the new farms were purchased by poor whites or yeomen farmers. Some black men did acquire land, but the majority chose sharecropping as the best of possible alternatives.[3] As C. Vann Woodward noted, "The lives of the overwhelming majority of Negroes were still circumscribed by the farm and plantation. The same was true of the white people, but the Negroes, with few exceptions, were farmers without land."[4] Under a typical sharecropping agreement, the black farmer rented several acres of land and paid the owner a portion of the crop, usually about one-half. The major crop was cotton. Few farmers were overly concerned with the disastrous aspects and long-range problems involved with one-crop agriculture, but so permanently scarred was the Black Belt by its backward mode of agricultural production that patterns of life and labor well into the 1900s seemed timeless. As late as 1944, Gunnar Myrdal could write that "in the main, cotton is cultivated by a primitive labor-consuming agricultural technique which has not changed much since slavery."[5]

Reasons for this state of affairs were many. Black sharecroppers had little experience in scientific farming techniques. Crop rotation, so common in the North, was used infrequently in the Black Belt. Alternating cotton with corn retarded soil depletion and erosion but did little to stop either. Moreover, blacks who rented, sharecropped, or owned property planted a greater percentage of their land in cotton than did white farmers, so black-owned or operated lands declined in productivity and value at a faster rate. The domination of cotton also led to a decline in food production throughout the South. Black farmers were caught in a poverty cycle which was almost impossible to break. The entire cotton-producing South was overwhelmingly rural and existed, in effect, as a domestic colony for the remainder of the nation. Cities were few and towns were small and culturally backward. As a result of the general lack of banking facilities, local merchants controlled both the flow of trade and the relative accessibility of credit. Although storekeepers paid high interest rates to wholesalers and other suppliers, they made a good living by extending credit to sharecroppers and others at extraordinarily high rates. Moreover, they were in a position to demand that farmers in debt to them grow only cotton, since cotton could always be sold. The results were overproduction leading to low prices for that staple, further declines in productivity of the land, and reliance upon the merchant for most of the necessities of life, including food. Cotton's monopoly across the Black Belt made millions of dollars for white planters, local businessmen, and cotton speculators. It also degraded black and white labor, depleted the soil, and concentrated the bulk of the best farmland in the hands of a racist, class-conscious aristocracy. "For the South as a whole, cotton specialization was not more profitable than a diversified economy with a balance between agriculture and industry," Ransom and Sutch have asserted. "The curse of King Cotton was the lack of prosperity he imposed on the South."[6]

In spite of this complex of adverse factors, black farmers made remarkable progress toward landownership during the three or four decades that preceded the outbreak of World War I. In fact, by 1917 a distinct and flourishing black middle class was emerging in the rural South. The development of a number of small, black-owned banks and lending institutions helped to transform the poverty of black life. During the 1880s a small number of determined black ministers, entrepreneurs, and educators pooled their resources to begin savings banks. The Reverend W. R. Pettiford, pastor of the Sixteenth Street Colored Baptist Church, started the Alabama Penny Savings Bank in Birmingham and later created branch offices in Montgomery, Anniston, and Selma. Booker T. Washington initiated a savings department at Tuskegee Institute which functioned as a local bank. In the first decade of the twentieth century dozens of black banks were established which loaned thousands of dollars to poor farming families desperately attempting to compete within a demanding marketplace. By 1911 there were seven black-owned banks in Alabama and two in Georgia. Mississippi boasted eleven such banks located in Jackson (two), Vicksburg (two), Yazoo City, Columbus, Greenville, Mound Bayou, Indianola, Natchez, and Shaw. These black-owned banks and forty-two others throughout the country did an annual business of $20 million in 1910.[7]

The rise of literacy considerably brightened the prospects for black rural development. Immediately after slavery 90 percent of all black people over twenty years of age were unable to read and write. The creation of primary and secondary schools and agricultural colleges gradually lowered illiteracy rates, especially among younger black people. By 1890 about one-half of all blacks between ten and nineteen were literate. As illiteracy diminished below 50 percent after 1900, a greater number of black people were able to compete for jobs which required a minimal education. Black people across the Black Belt were aware that literacy and an aptitude in basic mathematics would make them more self-sufficient and ultimately more in command of their own lives.[8]

The development of a strong black land-base became an ideological imperative of black thought by the 1890s. Throughout the Black Belt, black farmers organized small agricultural fairs, exhibiting and selling swine, cows, sheep, and other livestock, vegetables and cotton. The Agricultural and Mechanical College for Negroes was established in Normal, Alabama, in 1875; there many black students learned the essentials of crop rotation,

proper fertilization techniques, and other skills needed to become progressive farmers. With the financial support of northern philanthropic agencies
and churches, dozens of black agricultural and teachers' training colleges
were established. The largest and most influential institutions included the
Georgia State Industrial College in Savannah, Knox Academy in Selma,
Tuskegee Institute, Haines Normal and Industrial School in Utica, Mississippi, and the State Normal School in Montgomery. William H. Holtzclaw,
the principal of Utica Institute, established a company which purchased
plantations for resale to black sharecroppers. Most of these schools held
yearly farmers' conferences, and many offered monthly training institutes on
advanced agricultural techniques. Within a single generation, thousands of
young black men were trained in the agricultural sciences. It was, of course,
only a beginning. But with the proper education and the gradually improving economic climate, young black graduates from these small institutes
could compete with whites on a more equal basis.[9]

Booker T. Washington was perhaps the most influential advocate of Black
Belt agricultural development. Known as the architect of the "Atlanta Compromise" of 1895, Washington was a complex and ambitious man. Always
the pragmatist, Washington sensed the shift in the political winds and
responded accordingly, issuing ambiguous statements which appeased white
racists while guaranteeing a continued flow of funds into his college and
other black educational institutions. From the founding of Tuskegee Institute in 1881, Washington was a strong advocate of scientific farming and
increased black land tenure.[10] Through Washington's subtle political initiatives and compromises, hundreds of black farmers became successful in
their efforts to buy land. In 1900, 157 black farmers in Macon County
owned land; by 1910 the number increased to 507. Tuskegee graduates
established "social settlements" in a sharecropping area of Lowndes County,
Alabama, purchasing old plantation property and reselling to black farmers.[11] Washington remained convinced that a rural black petty bourgeois
elite of farmers, small bankers, and merchants could form the basis for a
black economy inside American capitalism. In a lecture entitled "How to
Build a Race," given in 1898, Washington described in detail the problem of
black agricultural underdevelopment and possible solutions:

> We are living in a country where, if we are going to succeed at all we are going
> to do so by what we raise out of the soil. Without this no people can succeed.
> No race which fails to put brains into agriculture can succeed; and if you want
> to realize the truth of this statement go with me this month into the back
> districts of Georgia, Mississippi and Alabama and you will find these people
> almost in a starving condition, slowly starving to death and yet they are sur-
> rounded by a rich country. Are you going to stand still and see these people
> starve? Are you not willing to make any sacrifice in order to prepare yourself to
> help these people? I believe you will. Learn all you can about agriculture,
> about the use of improved machinery.

Washington warned his students that agricultural development was "our only [hope for] salvation as a race."[12]

A substantial petty bourgeoisie slowly began to take shape—black undertakers, grocery store owners, tailors, insurance men, and bankers. According to the statistics of the National Negro Business League, between 1900 and 1914 the number of black-owned drug stores increased from 250 to 695; black undertaking firms grew from 450 to 1,000; the number of black retail merchants increased from 10,000 to 25,000. Individual examples of black economic self-sufficiency and success existed in every major southern city and in many rural counties. R. R. Church of Memphis quietly accumulated real estate in that city and by the early 1900s he was worth approximately one million dollars. Charles Banks, a leading citizen of the all-black community of Mound Bayou, established a cotton seed oil mill, a loan and investment company, and a bank. Many of these black entrepreneurs shared Washington's philosophy of racial pride and his faith in the capitalist system.[13]

Increased industrialization of the South, combined with a rapid rise in cotton prices after 1898, made farming a profitable venture once more. Black farmers succeeded in buying millions of acres of land which had previously been unavailable to them. Between 1900 and 1910 Carolina blacks purchased over one million acres of farmland. Thousands of sharecroppers and tenant farmers in Mississippi, Alabama, and Georgia were able to purchase their own farms and compete with poorer white farmers. As Washington predicted boldly in 1898, "the vast unoccupied lands in the South . . . are simply waiting for those with capital, foresight and faith to step in and occupy."[14] Virtually all economists agree with the observation of Richard T. Ely and George S. Wehrwein that black land tenure in the South "reached its peak in 1910."[15] There were a total of 2,143,176 black farmers in 1911, a few of whom were as prosperous and efficient as white landlords. Deal Jackson of Albany, Georgia, a former slave, owned over 2,000 acres of rich farmland and held "forty [black] families as tenants on his plantation." Georgia blacks owned property worth $34 million and possessed 1,639,919 acres of land.[16] The thirst for land was so great within the black rural South that some blacks migrated directly to communities where there was a recent "history of lynchings and mob violence, so long as land could be purchased at low prices."[17] "For a decade the cotton belt had enjoyed a happy conjunction of rising production and rising prices," George B. Tindall wrote in *The Emergence of the New South.* "On the eve of [World War I] cotton fetched thirteen cents a pound; and a bumper crop of more than sixteen million bales, the largest yet known, was being laid to ripen."[18] In these flush times, black people acquired the largest amount of property they would ever own within the United States. In 1910 there were approximately 175,000 black full owners, 43,000 partial owners, and 670,000 sharecroppers. There were also 1,000 black managers and supervisors of farm property. Blacks operated 890,000 farms and had become the owners of more than 15 million acres of land. In the late summer of 1914, Washington's dream of a flourishing black economy in the South seemed on the verge of reality.[19]

The outbreak of World War I marked the beginning of a long and tragic decline of black agriculture and land tenure in the South. European nations which had been the largest consumers of cotton practically closed their doors to transatlantic commerce for a number of months. All farmers were forced to sell their cotton to speculators at five to eight cents per pound, well below current market value. Many struggling black farmers hauled their cotton into town and learned to their amazement that no one would buy it at any price. Southern politicians and regional capitalists realized that immediate steps had to be taken to help cotton producers, but most of the assistance went to white planters and merchants. Senator John H. Bankhead of Alabama proposed that his state extend $40 million worth of credit to farmers and store their cotton in state warehouses. Asa G. Candler, Atlanta millionaire and director of Coca Cola company, offered low interest loans to white planters and stored one-quarter million bales of cotton in his huge warehouses. Within two months southern farmers lost about $500 million. The 1913 average farm price for cotton was not reached again until June 1916.[20] The cotton disaster of 1914 ruined many thousands of black and white farmers and affected southern agriculture for years to come. As John Kenneth Galbraith observed, "unlike most industry, agriculture is peculiarly incapable of dealing with the problems of expanding output and comparatively inelastic demand."[21]

Black farmers who borrowed money to purchase their land suddenly had no way to pay annual mortgage payments. Sharecroppers who owned no property were not as threatened with sudden economic ruin as were small black owner-operators. But both groups had no experience in growing any money crop other than cotton, and many desperate county merchants refused to allow farmers credit to plant anything except cotton. In the summer of 1916, severe rainstorms destroyed much of that year's cotton crop throughout Alabama and Mississippi. Robert R. Morton, then principal of Tuskegee Institute, informed the U.S. Department of Agriculture and Alabama state officials in September that many black farmers "have grown discontented because of lack of the most ordinary necessities." He pleaded for seeds and agricultural supplies "so that they could have something growing, [and so] that many of them would be contented and not be inclined to leave the farm."[22] Making matters worse, many banks were forced out of business with the collapse of the cotton market. By 1918 only one black-owned bank remained in Alabama, the savings office of Tuskegee Institute. Only two black banks existed in Mississippi, in Mound Bayou and Indianola. With the failure of so many of these financial institutions, a significant source of credit disappeared.[23] Many thousands of farmers were forced to sell their land for only a fraction of its real value to pay off mounting debt. Black sharecroppers who might have planned to buy land and sell their own cotton crops on the open market were discouraged from doing so. My great-grandfather, Morris

Marable, was an independent farmer in Randolph County, Alabama, who operated his own cotton gin and marketed four or five bales of his cotton crop each year. With the fall in the price of cotton, he was forced out of the market. After several years he abandoned agriculture entirely, like thousands of other black farmers and small entrepreneurs.

More destructive than the impact of the war was the coming of the boll weevil. Entering from Mexico into southern Texas, the boll weevil spread across the state within ten years, destroying thousands of acres of cotton. By 1907 the boll weevil had crossed the Mississippi and was ruining cotton fields in the rich, black delta country. The weevil, unlike other insect pests, was difficult to detect until the damage was done. The adult female weevil lays her eggs in the fruit of the plant during the spring. When the eggs hatch in late summer, the young eat the cotton. By 1916 every county in Alabama was infested with boll weevils, and by 1920 every Georgia county reported the insects' damage. In each state in the Deep South, the boll weevil reduced the number of acres planted as well as the yield of cotton lint in pounds per acre. In the four years preceding the boll weevil infestation in Georgia, for example, an average of 4,953,000 acres of cotton was planted; four years after complete infestation, an average of 3,476,000 acres was planted with cotton, a reduction of almost 30 percent. The average yield of cotton lint per acre in Georgia was 230 pounds before infestation; after the boll weevil's appearance, an average yield was reduced to 117 pounds, a decline of 49 percent.[24] Black Belt farmers reduced their cotton acreage and because of the pests, they obtained approximately one-fifth to one-half less cotton lint than before per acre. Few sharecroppers and black owner-operators could afford expensive insecticides or poisons, and it was almost impossible to contain the spread of the insects. "Field after field of cotton was eaten away," Haystead and Fite wrote. Some farms were spontaneously "abandoned."[25]

Compounding the economic troubles of black farmers was a general worsening of race relations in the Black Belt. Those blacks who continued to vote after 1900 found that virtually every white political group in the Deep South opposed black suffrage. In northern Alabama, black Republicans published the *Huntsville Republican* and attempted to organize support for whites who sympathized with Negro rights. By 1902 the Republican Lily White faction succeeded in purging the integrated Black and Tan group from the state convention by placing armed guards at the doors to keep blacks out. Within the decade, Black and Tan Republicanism was also dead in Mississippi.[26] After World War I, Alabama blacks organized suffrage leagues and initiated court challenges of de jure segregation, but most cases failed at the local level. During the twenties neither the conservative nor progressive factions of the Democratic party sought to expand the slender black electorate. The number of black voters in Alabama declined from a statewide total of 3,742 in 1908 to 1,500 in 1930.[27] For all practical purposes, the Fifteenth Amendment to the Constitution no longer existed in the Black

Belt, and blacks found themselves increasingly vulnerable to racist violence. Georgia led the nation in lynchings between 1885 and 1918 with 398. Mississippi was a close second with 381 and Alabama was fifth with 246. In 1915 there were 18 lynchings in Georgia alone, twice as many as in any other state. Appropriately, Mississippi and Alabama were tied for second place with 9 illegal hangings of black people that year.[28] Carter G. Woodson, reviewing the economic chaos which had befallen black farmers throughout the South, refused to attribute the exodus of blacks into the North for any but political reasons. "It is highly probable that the Negroes would not be leaving the South today," the Negro historian wrote in 1918, "if they were treated as men."[29]

Facing economic disaster, most white farmers had sufficient resources to change the production habits of a century. Thousands of white farmers began to purchase and raise cattle. In Mississippi the number of cattle and calves rose from 873,356 in 1900 to 1,250,479 in 1920. Georgia cattle production went from 899,491 in 1900 to 1,156,738 in 1920. Farmers in the pine hills and wire grass country of southern Georgia and southeast Alabama discovered their red soil was excellent for peanuts, and peanut production increased during the 1920s and 1930s.[30] But whites borrowed heavily to maintain their land, and by crop diversification and decreased production of cotton, they were usually able to stay in business. Most black farmers, several years behind in debts, could do little except abandon their property and go into sharecropping, or leave their outstanding debts and flee to the North. Many chose the second option. From 1880 to 1910 only 79,400 blacks left the Black Belt for the North; between 1910 and 1920, the figure leaped to 226,900, and from 1920 to 1930 about 444,400 black migrants fled the Deep South. Most of these people were sharecroppers, small owner-operators, or worked in jobs connected with agriculture.[31]

There are many reasons which explain in part the demise of black land tenure in the Black Belt South, and the destruction of an authentic, black landowning class. We have isolated several causes—the emergence of white racism and Jim Crow legislation, the fall of cotton prices, the coming of the boll weevil, the lack of adequate credit at reasonable rates, and the general erosion and depletion of the soil. All of these reasons and others stem from a larger and as yet unanswered dilemma—the existence and survival of black people within the context of the American capitalist system. In theory, capitalism is characterized by a degree of labor mobility and a free movement of capital from disadvantageous enterprises to more profitable sectors. But under the economic conditions prevalent in the postbellum South, an elite group of white planters, bankers, investors, and merchants held a tight monopoly over the monetary supply, credit sources and rates, and the entire agricultural production of the region. This economic monopoly gradually promoted the collapse of the black economic miracle which black educators and entrepreneurs like Booker T. Washington dreamed of building. Given the structure of the domestic economy, it was inevitable that black farmers would be forced off the land and evicted from their homes to work at factory jobs in the cities of the New South and the urban ghettoes of the North.

As economist Paul Sweezy observed, "the very essence of monopoly is the existence of effective barriers to the [free] movement of capital."[32] Neither the South's social institutions, corrupted from the bottom up by violent racist ideology, nor its lily-white political institutions could provide fundamental solutions to the region's regressive economic order. History thus illustrates clearly that the goal of black economic self-sufficiency was a bitter illusion rather than a possibility; the collapse of black land tenure in the Black Belt South was not a failure of black people, but a direct result of the denial of equal economic opportunity for all members of the society.

NOTES

1. John Hope Franklin, *From Slavery to Freedom* (New York: A. A. Knopf, 1967), 398. This essay defines the Black Belt as those counties or districts in Georgia, Alabama, Mississippi, South Carolina, and Louisiana that contained a percentage of black people in excess of 50 percent of the county's total population. Blackbelt counties are also characterized by a high dependency upon cotton cultivation as the primary economic mode of production between the years 1865 through 1920. In 1880 about 5.5 million people lived in the Black Belt, including 3 million blacks. These counties produced 4.1 million bales of cotton in 1880, almost three fourths of the South's total production.

2. Peter Kolchin, *First Freedom: The Responses of Alabama's Blacks to Emancipation and Reconstruction* (Westport, Conn.: Greenwood Press, 1972), 4, 12, 19.

3. W. E. B. DuBois, *Black Reconstruction in America, 1860–1880* (New York: Harcourt, Brace, 1935), 508.

4. C. Vann Woodward, *Origins of the New South, 1877–1913* (Baton Rouge: Louisiana State University Press, 1951), 205.

5. Gunnar Myrdal, *An American Dilemma* (New York: Harper and Brothers, 1944), 233. Cotton's central place in the South's economy is reviewed in Gavin Wright's "Cotton Competition and the Post-Bellum Recovery of the American South," *Journal of Economic History* 34 (September 1974): 610–35.

6. Roger Ransom and Richard Sutch, *One Kind of Freedom: The Economic Consequences of Emancipation* (New York and London: Cambridge University Press, 1977), 182–85, 190–91, 300–305; 150–54; Stephen J. De Canio, "Cotton 'Overproduction' in Late Nineteenth Century Southern Agriculture," *Journal of Economic History* 33 (September 1973): 608–33; Glenn N. Sisk, "Rural Merchandising in the Alabama Black Belt, 1875–1917," *Journal of Farm Economics* 37 (November 1955): 705–15; Jack T. Kirby, *Darkness at the Dawning* (Philadelphia: Lippincott, 1972), 8.

7. Monroe Work, *Negro Year Book and Annual Encyclopedia of the Negro* (Tuskegee Institute, Ala.: Tuskegee Institute Press, 1912), 22, 168, 176, 177, 178. The emergence of the black entrepreneur within the southern political economy is documented skillfully by W. E. B. DuBois in his essay, "The Economic Revolution in the South," published in Booker T. Washington and W. E. B. DuBois, eds., *The Negro in the South* (Northbrook, Ill.: Metro Books, 1972).

8. Ransom and Sutch, *One Kind of Freedom*, 30.

9. Work, *Negro Year Book*, 17, 100, 114–18; Kilby, *Darkness at the Dawning*, 173.

10. Louis R. Harlan, *Booker T. Washington: The Making of a Black Leader* (New York: Oxford University Press, 1972), 130.

11. Kirby, *Darkness at the Dawning*, 171.

12. Booker T. Washington, "How to Build a Race," *Tuskegee Student* 12 (20 October 1898): 3–4. Copy in Tuskegee Institute Archives, Tuskegee Institute, Alabama.

13. August Meier, *Negro Thought in America, 1880–1915* (Ann Arbor: University of Michigan Press, 1963), 139–40, 148.

14. Booker T. Washington, "The Best Labor in the World," *Southern States Farm Magazine* 5 (January 1898): 496–98. Copy in the Booker T. Washington Papers, Container 864, Library of Congress, Washington.

15. Richard T. Ely and George S. Wehrwein, *Land Economics* (Ann Arbor, Mich.: Edwards Brothers, 1938), 205.

16. *Negro Year Book*, 163, 167, 180.

17. August Meier and Elliott Rudwick, *From Plantation to Ghetto* (New York: Hill and Wang, 1976), 233.

18. George Brown Tindall, *The Emergence of the New South* (Baton Rouge: Louisiana State University Press, 1967), 33.

19. Arthur M. Ford, *The Political Economics of Rural Poverty in the South* (Cambridge, Mass.: Harvard University Press, 1973), 20; Robert Browne, "Black Land Loss: The Plight of Black Ownership," *Southern Exposure* 2 (Autumn 1974): 11.

20. Tindall, *The Emergence of the New South*, 33; Clara Eliot, *The Farmer's Campaign for Credit* (New York: Laurence, 1927), 156–60.

21. John Kenneth Galbraith, "The Farm Problem and Policy Choices," in Edmund S. Phelps et al., eds., *Problems of the Modern Economy* (New York: W. W. Norton, 1966), 151; Arthur S. Link, "The Cotton Crisis, the South and Anglo-American Diplomacy," in J. Carlyle Sitterson, ed., *Studies in Southern History* (Chapel Hill: University of North Carolina Press, 1957), 122–38; Theordore Saloutos, *Farmer Movements in the South, 1865–1933* (Berkeley: University of California Press, 1960), 238–48.

22. Robert R. Moton to J. F. Duggar, 13 September 1916; Carl Vrodman to Robert R. Moton, 4 October 1916. Both letters are in the Robert R. Moton General Correspondence Collection, Container 7, Tuskegee Institute Archives.

23. Monroe Work, *Negro Year Book 1918–19* (Tuskegee Institute, Ala.: Tuskegee Institute Press, 1919), 368.

24. Ransom and Sutch, *One Kind of Freedom*, 172–74.

25. Ladd Haystead and Gilbert C. Fite, *The Agricultural Regions of the United States* (Norman: University of Oklahoma Press, 1955), 112.

26. Hanes Walton, Jr., *Black Republicans: The Politics of the Black and Tans* (Metuchen, N.J.: Scarecrow Press, 1975), 81–84.

27. On black Alabama politics between 1890 and World War I see Sheldon Hackney, *Populism to Progressivism in Alabama* (Princeton, N.J.: Princeton University Press, 1969) and Mary Tucker, "The Negro in the Populist Movement in Alabama, 1890–1896" (M. A. thesis, Atlanta University, 1957).

28. Work, *Negro Year Book, 1918–19*, 374.

29. Carter G. Woodson, *A Century of Negro Migration* (New York: Russell and Russell, 1969), 169.

30. Haystead and Fite, *The Agricultural Regions of the United States*, 116, 123, 128.

31. Ransom and Sutch, *One Kind of Freedom*, 196.

32. Paul M. Sweezy, *The Theory of Capitalist Development* (New York and London: Monthly Review Press, 1942), 272–73.

EIGHT

"Like Banquo's Ghost, It Will Not Down": The Race Question and the American Railroad Brotherhoods, 1880–1920

ERIC ARNESEN

Locomotive fireman W. H. Stover of Bristol, Virginia, appealed to the U.S. Railroad Administration in May 1918 to "correct a wrong and an injustice" that had been committed against him. Stover had worked on the Appalachia Division of the Southern Railway for the past eight years. As the fireman with the longest record of service, he felt entitled, under the railroad's seniority rule, to his first choice of runs. Such a change would have increased his monthly salary from $68 to $98. But because he was "a colored man," he maintained, the railroad had "disregarded" the rule.[1] Stover directed his plea to the federal government, which had assumed operating control over the nation's vast railroad system during World War I. This petition was his last resort.

The Southern Railway, in fact, was in compliance with its own seniority rules. What stood in the way of Stover's advancement was a carefully crafted system of racial quotas—known as percentage agreements—contained in the contract between the Southern Railway and the all-white Brotherhood of Locomotive Firemen and Enginemen. By World War I, the Southern Railway, like many other railroad companies in the American South, operated a dual seniority system based on race. Stover, though the most senior fireman on the division, technically was not entitled to his first choice of runs. Because "no discrimination is intentionally being made against colored firemen," Railroad Administration personnel rejected the complainant's request for intervention.[2]

Stover's plight illuminates the racial subordination that was a central feature in the experience of black railroad workers in the United States from the late nineteenth through the mid-twentieth century. A wide range of commentators—black railroadmen, contemporary black scholars, novelists, and activists, white liberals and radicals, and historians—have shared a blunt assessment of the railroad brotherhoods' stance toward African-American workers on the railroads: white unions staunchly opposed black advancement, and often the very presence of blacks, in their trades. The goal of the "Big Four" brotherhoods of firemen, trainmen, conductors, and engineers was, in the words of black civil rights attorney Charles Hamilton Houston in 1949, to "have the railroad train and engine service tied up tight for a white monopoly, for a 'Nordic closed shop.'"[3] Toward that end, white railroad brotherhoods devised a number of mechanisms to restrict or eliminate black competition. In Stover's case, the mechanism took the form of containment—the restriction of blacks through separate seniority lists and the maintenance of racial quotas on specific divisions of the railroad. At other times, white brotherhood men advocated the complete elimination of their black counterparts, relying on tactics that included strikes, selective violence, legislative lobbying, and contract negotiations. The racial beliefs and practices that were an integral part of the world of the members of two white railroad brotherhoods—the Brotherhood of Locomotive Firemen and Enginemen and the Brotherhood of Railroad Trainmen (which represented brakemen)—form the subject of this article.

In recent years, historians of labor and the African-American experience have begun to explore the racial dimension of white workers' identity, institutions, and strategies. During the 1980s, critics of the new labor history, such as Herbert Hill and Nell Irvin Painter, claimed that the field had a "race problem," that its practitioners were romanticizing white labor's struggles while ignoring its role in subordinating or excluding African-American and other non-white workers from both the trade union movement and the labor market.[4] If the first wave of the new labor history paid relatively little attention to the racial perspectives and programs of white workers, the second wave since the mid-1980s has actively embraced the subject. Even as Hill, Painter, and others were leveling their charges, numerous scholars were already at work on case studies documenting patterns of working-class relations and racial subordination. Today, such diverse occupations and industries as steel and auto manufacturing, coal mining, nursing, domestic service, longshoring, meat packing, and tobacco processing, in cities such as Atlanta, New Orleans, Mobile, Winston-Salem, Birmingham, Richmond, Pittsburgh, Detroit, and Seattle, have all received scholarly treatment that casts light on the racial attitudes and practices of white workers, in and out of unions. By 1990, Jacqueline Dowd Hall could characterize the field of southern labor history—in which issues of race and labor figure prominently—as "a cottage industry" and a "major trend"; in 1993, Robin D. G.

Kelly described the literature on organized labor, black urban workers, and southern working-class politics as "voluminous."[5]

The new works on race and labor follow no single model and share no consensus regarding the best questions to pose, methods to follow, or the answers offered. Most concur that racial egalitarianism was relatively uncommon, that biracial unions, where they existed, rested on pragmatic and often fragile foundations, and that there existed a diverse range of union racial practices.[6] A number of issues, however, continue to divide historians of race and labor: How, and to what extent, did the labor movement advance or undermine the position of black workers? What were the motivations of white unionists in adopting their policies toward non-whites? Did a consciousness of race generally undermine or overwhelm a consciousness of class? Are biracial coalitions, certainly imperfect by today's standards, to be appreciated for their deviation from a strict rule of racial exclusion, or should they be condemned for reproducing racial divisions? Historians also implicitly disagree on two additional questions. Given the white trade union movement's active role in the construction of working-class racism, could it have chosen differently? And were black workers primarily victims of white union racism or agents engaged in their own struggles against both employers and white labor?[7] Where historians differ most sharply is in the tone of their evaluations. For some, the glass is half full; for others, nine-tenths empty. Whatever answers historians offer, late twentieth-century political sensibilities continue to inform their accounts of the relationship between organized labor and non-white minorities.[8]

In recent analyses of the white working class and its relationship to non-white workers, some scholars have stressed racisms' economic role: it barred African Americans' access to higher paying skilled positions, thus ensuring a white monopoly for the best jobs. In an immediate sense, whites often benefited directly when blacks suffered racial discrimination, even if, in some accounts, racial divisions undermined the unity necessary to achieve benefits for both groups and, in Alexander Saxton's words, inhibited "working-class challenges to industrial capitalism."[9] In other studies, racism has operated simultaneously to provide whites with a non-quantifiable advantage—a psychological wage.[10] No matter how oppressed whites were, they nonetheless possessed advantages over black workers, who were even more oppressed. In both perspectives—which often overlap in the historiography—racism is highly functional. It not only served the interests of employers in keeping labor divided, but it offered advantages, real or imagined, to white labor. Recently, some have gone further in an effort to understand how class was constructed in racial (and gendered) terms. Assumptions about race and its corollary, American nationality, were constituent elements of white workers' collective identity, serving as a cultural lens through which whites defined themselves and distanced others.[11]

Drawing on the history of white locomotive firemen and brakemen, this article advances three basic propositions. First, the identification of the sources and content of white workers' racial thinking allows us to understand better the unfolding dynamics of class and race in specific labor markets and communities. While this is not a novel point, it deserves emphasis, for the sources and contours of white labor's racial beliefs have received considerably less attention in recent literature than the function and effect of race. Painting with a broad brush, historians have too often taken the existence and operation of race and racism for granted: white American workers, mired in racism, pursue a (short-sighted) strategy of maximizing their advantages over black labor for economic or psychological reasons. Racism, in many such accounts, becomes either the central fault line in American history, the raison d'être for white labor organizing, or the principal explanation for white labor's actions.[12] These treatments often abstract the notions of race and racism out of their historical context; these notions then serve as free-floating causes, invoked as explanations for why people act, organizations develop, or events unfold as they do. But when they are detached from their moorings in historical context, can race and racism bear the weight of historical causality historians place upon them? Judith Stein's critique of this approach, advanced two decades ago, holds considerable relevance today: when racism is put forth as an explanation "before the investigation is conducted," she maintained, it is "reified, divorced from the concrete and complex experiences of social groups in particular circumstances."[13]

Race—in this case, beliefs about the behavior, character, and capacity of whites, African Americans, and new immigrants—meant different things to different social groups in American society, as Barbara Fields has forcefully reminded us.[14] Not all social groups articulated identical racial beliefs or acted on them in the same way. The racial thinking and practices of white workers often differed from those of middle-class or elite whites, just as their actual experiences differed. While in agreement about the general idea of black subordination, white labor and capital expressed, were affected by, and acted on notions of race and racism in dissimilar ways. To be sure, white working-class racism drew heavily on the racial ideologies of the larger white society. Never isolated culturally, white workers were fully exposed to popular and scientific racism from journalists and scholarly authorities, entertainers' performances, politicians' speeches, party platforms, the pulpits of religious leaders, and the writings of educational authorities. But white labor's racial beliefs and practices were not merely imitations of larger cultural constructs, they were also shaped by specific historical and structural circumstances, firmly established in their workplaces and communities. Alexander Saxton is right to call attention to racism's class-specific character, whereby white workers' own organizations "independently generated racism." Yet the notion of "class specific" racism itself can be misleading, for it suggests that members of a class share a particular perspective reflective of a common interest. The white working class, geographically diverse and fragmented hierarchically along occupational and other lines, exhibited no monolithic approach toward African Americans. Some white southern coal miners, timber workers, and longshoremen, for example, developed racial practices very different from those of railroad workers, skilled shipbuilders, metal workers, and building tradesmen. As Dana Frank has argued in her study of Seattle labor in the 1920s, race was "no simple, ahistoric matter, nor was it negotiated and interpreted along a single axis."[15]

A second and closely related issue is the need to account for the strength and staying power of white labor's racial beliefs. Race, as numerous historians have argued, served many purposes. In addition to advancing economic interests and offering considerable psychological satisfaction, notions of race and nationality functioned as part of an interpretive framework that allowed white workers to understand the larger social and economic transformations of American society in the Gilded Age and Progressive Era. Employer assaults against white trade unions' power, the transformation of the labor process that produced considerable deskilling in some economic sectors, the prospect and reality of unemployment and underemployment, growing corporate concentration in the economy and influence in politics, increased immigration from Southern and Eastern Europe, Asia, and Mexico—all of these developments could be expressed, and partially comprehended, in terms of race and nationality. By conflating the causes and consequences of the ever-changing racial composition of the American work force with those of the conflict of social class, white workers framed their economic anxieties in a cultural mode that resonated deeply in their union halls and in their communities. At stake in the outcome was not just their economic position but their status as whites and as Americans as well.

Finally, this essay draws an analytic distinction between the categories of racial belief and racial practice. The racial beliefs of white locomotive firemen and brakemen changed relatively little over the four decades spanning the late nineteenth and early twentieth centuries covered in this article. In their union journals and organizers' reports, in speeches and resolutions at brotherhood conventions, in testimony before government bodies, and in statements to the press, union leaders and white rank-and-filers alike painted an overwhelmingly negative portrait of African Americans and the threat they posed not only to brotherhood members but also to the nation's very future. But white railroad men, like white labor generally, did not always act on their critique in the same way; their racism generated no uniform set of strategies to address their real or perceived problems. Knowing what white railroaders thought about African Americans reveals little about what course of action they ultimately pursued. How and why did white railroaders adopt the particular strategies that they did, when they did? Under what circumstances did their racial strategies succeed? Focusing on the sources, contours, and staying power of white racial ideology on the one hand and on white labor's organizational strategies for achieving its goals on the other, this article reconstructs the forces producing the widespread employment discrimination that denied locomotive fireman W. H. Stover and thousands of his fellow African-American railroad workers the opportunities they sought and deserved.

From its beginnings, the American railway labor force, with its multiple gradations of skill, prestige, and arduousness, was segmented along racial lines. In the unskilled construction and maintenance sectors of the industry, African Americans and immigrants from Europe, Asia, and Mexico dominated the crews that graded the road beds, laid the track, and ensured its upkeep over rail networks that extended tens of thousands of miles by the nineteenth century's end. The first two generations of railroad labor in the mid-nineteenth century drew on Irish and German immigrants in the Northeast, Mid-Atlantic, and Midwest. In the antebellum era, the relatively small railroad systems of the South depended almost exclusively on slave labor to lay and repair track; the spate of southern railroad building in the postbellum era required the labor of newly emancipated African-American men, who found wage labor on construction and track crews an attractive alternative to sharecropping on plantations. The construction of the transcontinental railroad utilized the physical energies—and often took the lives—of Chinese immigrants in the 1860s and 1870s; in the Northwest, the Great Northern and other railroads relied heavily on Japanese contract laborers in the last quarter of the century; and Mexican immigrants and Mexican Americans found employment as laborers on track crews of the Southwest and the Plains States, particularly after the turn of the century.[16]

A different relationship between skill and ethnicity prevailed in the more privileged positions in the operating department (also known as the running trades) on board the locomotive engines and on passenger and freight cars. Engineers and conductors, whose wages, authority, and autonomy rendered them something of a labor aristocracy, were the most highly paid and independent of railroad workers. Engineers had to possess considerable technical knowledge, experience, and strength to direct the physical operation of the train. The conductor was in charge of supervising other personnel, including brakemen and porters, as well as overseeing freight.[17] Working beneath engineers and conductors were lower-paid locomotive firemen and brakemen (also called trainmen). Firemen rode in the engine alongside the engineer and were responsible for feeding coal into the engine's boiler, while brakemen performed the dangerous work of setting hand brakes (before the introduction of air brakes in the 1890s) and the coupling of rail cars with a link and pin.[18]

Men employed in the running trades were far more ethnically and racially homogenous than were the laborers in the construction and maintenance-of-way departments. Throughout the nation until the 1950s and 1960s, only white men could work as conductors and locomotive engineers. Outside the South, the positions of fireman and brakeman were initially filled by native-born white Americans or immigrants from Northern Europe, and these jobs remained overwhelmingly white in subsequent decades. In the North and West, whites, who were well entrenched in these positions, insisted on a sharp color line, which railroad managers usually adhered to without much complaint. This effectively barred blacks from becoming engineers, conductors, firemen, and, to a lesser extent, brakemen (although blacks sometimes performed brakemen's work as "porter brakemen"—a distinct category that combined on-board service with brakemen's tasks). At the turn of the century, one critic noted, of "the thousands of miles of railway in the North, with its tens of thousands of manipulators, the only work, as a rule, . . . open to negroes is that of porters on trains—the most menial and ill-paid occupation within the gift of a railway corporation."[19]

A somewhat different racial division of labor prevailed below the Mason-Dixon line, where African-American men encountered a wider range of railroad employment options. In the antebellum era, slaves, either rented or owned by southern railroads, served not only as construction laborers and station helpers but as brakemen and firemen as well. After the Civil War, blacks retained a hold on a portion of those operating positions, despite an influx of whites into more skilled jobs. By the turn of the century, blacks constituted the vast majority of firemen and brakemen on the Gulf Coast lines; they made up some 90 percent of the firemen on the Seaboard Air line and the majority of such positions on some divisions of the Illinois Central, the Southern, and the Louisville & Nashville railroads in the South.[20] From the 1890s to roughly 1930, blacks outnumbered whites as locomotive firemen on Georgia's railroads, holding 60 percent or more of these positions. "It is an every-day occurrence in the South," one observer noted in 1900, "to see white locomotive engineers and colored firemen seated in the same cab."[21]

By the late nineteenth century, numerous trade unions represented white workers in a variety of the crafts and other occupational groupings on the nation's railroads. Known informally as the "Big Four," the largest white railroad brotherhoods—the Brotherhood of Locomotive Engineers, the Order of Railway Conductors of America, the Brotherhood of Locomotive Firemen and Enginemen, and the Brotherhood of Railroad Trainmen— were organized in the 1860s and 1870s. From their inception, race was written into the very definition of their union membership. The engineers' brotherhood officially restricted its membership to white men, as did the Locomotive Firemen and numerous other railway unions. Any applicant for membership had to be "white born, of good moral character, sober and industrious, sound in body and limb, and not less than eighteen years of age, and able to read and write the English language."[22]

The brotherhoods' achievement of improved conditions and their climb toward organizational recognition proved difficult and uneven in the late nineteenth century. Railroad work could be dangerous: accident and death rates in the operating service remained high, yet few corporate medical or welfare programs assumed responsibility for a victim's recovery or the financial plight of family survivors. The origins of the brotherhoods owed much to their members' need for benevolent and insurance programs, and, accordingly, the organizations provided medical and death benefits for members and their families.[23] Yet issues of power quickly commanded their attention. Railroad companies could be harsh employers, demanding long hours under poor conditions for low pay. Some of the most tumultuous labor conflicts of the late nineteenth century—in 1877, 1885–1886, and 1894—centered on the railroads. In many instances, bitterly fought railroad strikes collapsed in the face of massive corporate, state, and federal repression, and failed strikers often found themselves effectively blacklisted out of the industry.[24] Brotherhood leaders drew conservative lessons from these defeats, discouraging overt class conflict, decrying any sympathetic action on behalf of other aggrieved workers, and generally holding their organizations aloof from the affairs of other labor associations. In some cases, their caution paid dividends, for brotherhood members' skills, discipline, and organization, as well as their strategic position in a nationally vital industry, eventually enabled some to command impressive wages, impose elaborate work rules, and enforce adherence to strict seniority systems governing promotion and layoffs. By the early twentieth century, although the brotherhoods had adopted a more confrontational stance toward railroad employers, they retained their tendency to stand apart from the larger trade union movement.[25]

Drawing on a conservative vision common among late nineteenth-century skilled trade unionists, brotherhood members promoted an ideology of self-improvement and intense craft pride. The four cardinal principles were "Protection, Charity, Sobriety, and Industry." M. J. Boling, of Wilmington, North Carolina, proudly explained in 1893 that once, "the calling of the locomotive fireman was considered low, but to-day it is looked upon as being worthy and honorable," attributing this improvement to the brotherhood's success in raising "the standard of morality; no drunkard or person of dissipated habits can gain admission to the order." The growth of the firemen's association and the spread of its "conservative principles" in the South, one Nashville man reported in 1887, is "enabling every white born fireman to do justice to himself and family."[26] Brotherhood lodges not only provided insurance plans and entertainment but also encouraged moral and personal uplift, emphasizing the importance of both individual character and collective comportment. Workers in the operating trades expressed considerable pride in their mechanical competence and mastery of technological innovations. "Railroading is rapidly advancing into the dignity of a profession," noted veteran conductor Charles B. George in 1887, "requiring a knowledge of many branches of science, training of a high order, and careful application as well as unselfish devotion to public and corporate interests." Large sections of monthly union journals were devoted to explaining railroad technology and the latest innovations and to preparing workers to pass qualifying exams.[27] If the work of brakemen and firemen was dangerous, dirty, and arduous, some psychological compensation lay in the sense of skill and command of scientific knowledge the job required.

Self-improvement, sobriety, and technical education were not merely abstract virtues, they were also requirements for advancement up the railroads' occupational ladder. The possibility of social mobility was built into the structure of employment. A brakeman might eventually rise to become a conductor, while the locomotive fireman, as one nineteenth-century biographer explained, "was the engineer in embryo." The positions of conductor and engineer were more prestigious, often physically less strenuous, and substantially better paid. (Engineers, for example, earned roughly twice the firemen's wages.) But occupational mobility was not equally available to all railroad workers. Conductors' and engineers' jobs were off-limits to black workers at virtually all times and in all places. The prospective black worker "presents himself to the proper authorities as a person qualified for the work," complained the Reverend R. C. Ransom of the African Methodist Episcopal church in 1888, "but he is informed that he may not hope to enter there, that upon their engines white men hold the throttle, lift the tickets and manage the trains."[28] While the practice of excluding blacks from such jobs antedated the rise of trade unionism on the railroads, by the late nineteenth century the brotherhoods and railroad management shared responsibility for maintaining this exclusion. The conductors' and engineers' unions barred blacks as members and had never tolerated black competition in their fields. Railroad managers, for their part, would not propose placing blacks in positions of such authority, respect, and prestige, which required literacy, specialized technical knowledge, and a capacity to oversee the labor of the men beneath them. Even where unions were weak or nonexistent, managers kept the top positions an all-white preserve. Prevailing white notions about black workers' character, intelligence, and appropriate place in the economic hierarchy prevented African Americans from assuming such roles. The locomotive engineer had to possess "not only physical courage, but a moral stamina and mental quickness beyond the average man . . . He must be a man of iron will, able to withstand pressure and outside influence in the hour of danger," conductor Charles George concluded. In the mainstream of late nineteenth-century racial thinking, white workers, managers, and writers declared blacks wholly unqualified to fill any job requiring those moral and mental attitudes. Both "his color and mental capacity" rendered "'Mr. Nigger' . . . lacking in the qualifications requisite to the requirements demanded of an engineer," concluded Third Vice President A. P. Kelly, of the firemen's brotherhood in 1909. "Southern society would never tolerate the negro as locomotive engineers."[29]

African Americans were neither the only objects of white railroad workers' disdain nor the only group targeted for exclusion from the brotherhoods and the railroad labor force. From the 1880s through the 1920s, brotherhood members, like their skilled craft union counterparts in the American Federation of Labor (AFL), scorned new immigrants from Southern and Eastern Europe, from Mexico, and above all, from China and Japan. Drawing on a powerful nativist tradition, they assembled their evidence from popular and political culture, citing and reprinting in their own journals condemnations of new immigrants by U.S. and Canadian governmental commissions, investigative journalists, and academics. New immigrants, brotherhood members argued, were simply "birds of passage" with no commitment to the United States. "[A]bsolutely ignorant of American institutions" or "entirely oblivious as to the history of the country," these unassimilable men and women had neither "education, money nor knowledge of what constitutes decent living, as Americans understand it." The very words that white craft workers employed to describe the purported threat—"hordes," "vast surplus," "dregs," "beasts of burden," "flood," "deluge," and "tidal wave"—were steeped in the language of moral excess, social marginality, and natural disaster. On a more immediate level, these newcomers were pauper laborers who, content to live in "misery and squalor," transformed cities into congested wastelands, producing "death, disease, destitution."[30]

This language expressed an intense, deeply rooted fear of the intertwined consequences of capitalist industrialization, continued immigration, and the future of the nation. The brotherhoods' economic critique was straightforward. White male craft workers, maintaining what they believed to be (and what in fact often was) a precarious hold on their political and economic autonomy, linked the changing composition of the labor force to a corporate assault on their prerogatives. In their eyes, the new immigrants, blacks, and capital together posed a multifaceted challenge to their entire way of life. At the turn of the century, brotherhood men argued that they had entered a new era of economic concentration in which capital—alternatively described as "Big Business," the "Interests," the "Plutocracy," "the money gluttons," and the "aristocracy of wealth"—advocated unrestricted immigration and a use of black and new immigrant labor that was "violative of American ideals." It sought to "force upon the workers of the new world" —where labor had long been honorable—"the conditions and impositions of the old." That is, no longer would immigrant labor be raised to the level of American workers; rather, the converse would hold true if employers had their way. "Between cheap negro labor and the cheap foreign labor," one white fireman bitterly complained, "the intelligent American workingman is threatened in his desire to live and enjoy the benefits of our laws, to educate and raise up to some honorable calling the family about him without becoming a virtual slave himself, or permitting his family to sink into misery and squalor."[31] From the brotherhoods' perspective, the new immigrants and African Americans constituted a deadly threat to the wages and working and living conditions of true American workers.

New immigrants, they argued, also posed a dangerous challenge to the political health of the American Republic. Following a long tradition of working-class republican thinking, white railroad workers linked civic virtue to personal autonomy, economic independence, and manhood. Notions of gender and race were inscribed deeply into the concept of republican virtue. Since before the revolutionary era, virtue—that is, the willingness, essential to maintaining a viable and healthy republic, to transcend individual or parochial interests for the greater good of the community—was a gendered concept that excluded women on the basis of their dependent status and mental and physical character.[32] Only men could possess the attributes qualifying them to uphold the republic's interests—but not *all* men. A racialized concept of virtue similarly excluded large numbers of new male immigrants on account of their alleged character, behavior, and in some conceptualizations, race. Denouncing the changing "stock" of immigrants, whose fecundity and refusal to assimilate threatened "to absorb the institutions and traditions of the country and to create a chaotic social and political condition," one union official warned in 1902 that the United States was "rapidly undergoing a radical racial change."[33] Brotherhood terminology remained imprecise, however, and no official or members applied a coherent theory of race to European immigrants; their critical and exaggerated evaluations of immigrants most often centered on their behavior. But whatever the source of immigrant character—historical development, environment, or race—it was clear to brotherhood men that the new immigrants were different from earlier immigrants. The original men and women from Northern Europe and the "home makers and intelligent citizens" who had built up the United States; they easily achieved through hard work and moral demeanor the status of American citizens. The new immigrants, in contrast, were the worst that Europe and Asia had to offer, exhibiting little independence or inherent capacity for virtue. The terms brotherhood men employed to describe them left no room for negotiating their place in the American Republic: they represented a "lower grade of humanity," "the scum of the earth," and "human wreckage," who were collectively turning American into "a dumping ground, a human scrap heap."[34] Fears of multiple dangers to political liberty and economic independence were nothing new. In a period of rapid economic, demographic, and cultural transformation, however, the recycling and updating of these arguments proved useful both in focusing white railroad men's cultural disquietude and in rendering comprehensible the erosion of their social and economic status.

Brotherhood men set themselves apart from new immigrants and African Americans through a process of self-definition in which their notions of American nationality were linked explicitly to beliefs about character and behavior and implicitly to notions of racial difference. As Gwendolyn Mink has observed, with heightened racial and ethnic heterogeneity, the "overlapping characteristics of race, poverty, and dependency" among new immigrants and blacks bred "a moral politics aimed at reclaiming citizenship for old-stock white men only. This politics made race and nationality the new moral ratchets of citizenship."[35] Liberty, independence, and family life, so valued by brotherhood members, were core components in their version of

American nationality. Like civic virtue, they, too, were not attainable by all men; white railroad workers in the late nineteenth and early twentieth centuries reserved these concepts for themselves. "Shall America be a race of sturdy men," one union official asked rhetorically in 1919, "or shall we be merely a field of profitable exploitation . . . for the capitalists?" That race of sturdy men — "American white men" — deserved to "rear children and enjoy a white man's standard of living upon American farms" without having to confront the debilitating competition of cheap foreign labor.[36] As this statement suggests, white railroaders further equated "being American" with the attainment of a high standard of living. This was hardly unique to the railroad industry's labor force. As historian Lawrence Glickman has recently argued, skilled white labor often described the concept of the American standard of living as "an inherent trait" to be nurtured and protected, a "quality ingrained in white wage-earners through years of cultural habit." Their refusal to submit to low wages set white American workers apart from the new immigrants, whose lives of poverty and exploitation before and after their arrival in the United States allegedly demonstrated their inferiority. White Americans' very refusal "became understood as an act of national and cultural self-definition . . . [W]hite workers excluded others from the possibility of attaining the supposedly universal goal of the American Standard."[37] Thus brotherhood men articulated a definition of American national identity that possessed vaguely formulated racial criteria: only native-born white Americans or the descendants of old immigrants from Northern Europe — the social basis of the brotherhoods — qualified for true membership in the category "American," while just about all other groups were excluded.

The racial, ethnic, and national consciousness that white workers expressed did not derive from a "need" to stigmatize real or even potential economic competitors. Rather, it represented a cultural dimension of class identity and conflict. For all their fierce opposition to the new immigrants, the brotherhoods faced virtually no economic challenge from unskilled Asians or Europeans, who labored almost exclusively in the construction and maintenance-of-way departments. No rail managers proposed replacing white brotherhood firemen with Japanese firemen in the West, Mexican firemen in the Southwest or Italian, Hungarian, or Russian firemen in the East, even during periods of labor unrest. Viewing themselves as *American* workers, possessing a cherished and jealously guarded level of skill and political independence, white brotherhood men in the running trades had incorporated distinct racial beliefs into their consciousness of themselves as an occupational group and as a class. This perspective enabled them to identify and express solidarity with other white American workers who were threatened by the new arrivals. These racial views also gave a sharp moral edge to white workers' critique of capitalists' behavior in the labor-management conflicts of the era. Not only had capital encroached on the wages and autonomy of artisans and industrial workers but eroded the political independence of America's producing classes, but it had employed a specific weapon that went beyond economics and politics to threaten the demographic foundation of the nation. The battle against new immigrants and non-whites assumed a more exalted status than a simple fight against economic rivals, for it placed white organized labor at the forefront of a struggle not just to defend its members' security but to protect the nation from ultimate ruin. The brotherhoods' fixation on the racial threat posed by immigrants and African Americans reflected the profound cultural disquietude of a period of rapid social and economic change. It simultaneously allowed its members to claim what they saw as the high ground in the ideological battle against American business.

Like the new immigrants, black workers appeared to white brotherhood men as a real threat in the intensifying conflict between white labor and capital. Unlike those immigrants, however, black workers did not compete with white railroad labor. By the turn of the century, brotherhood leaders were portraying labor's struggle with business in life and death terms, not only for themselves but for the white American working class as a whole and the civilization it had built. Black strikebreakers, they argued, were a powerful weapon in the corporate war against the trade unions; they made possible the operators' "corporate greed" and the "Russianizing [of white] labor in America." For example, when miners in Pana, Illinois, struck in 1898 for "enough money to keep them from starving to death," mine operators simply "imported a lot of niggers from Alabama to take their places." Such a move—in which a white man, the operator, would "willingly take up with a nigger for the purpose of enslaving a white wage earner"—rendered the emancipation of the slaves a "questionable proposition."[38] The degradation of white labor at the hands of capital and its willing pawns, black strikebreakers, was already a reality in the coal fields and elsewhere; it was a problem, brotherhood men feared, that would only intensify over time. "It should be remembered that 'our colored brother' in the South is yet in his 'infancy' as a competition in the labor market," the *Locomotive Firemen's Magazine* concluded. "The vast element . . . has lain semi-dormant in lazy lassitude beneath the warm Southern sun." But a "movement is gradually making itself felt that will produce havoc and consternation in localities where white labor and Eastern capital now feel secure."[39] There was little doubt that an industrial awakening by blacks would lead to harder times for whites.

Not surprisingly, white railroaders subjected their black counterparts to denigration, repeatedly resorting to stock racial caricatures in articulating their case against black employment. M. E. Dowdy, a Springfield, Missouri, railroadman with much work experience in Georgia, Alabama, and the Carolinas, concluded that the black fireman was a "person almost devoid of ambition, energy, business ability, and manly qualities, who knows nothing but shovel coal, shine brass (and the engineer's shoes if necessary) . . . [H]is clouded intellect, degeneracy, and dormant perceptive powers are as unyielding to modern education as the tax is heavy on the white people who pay for negro schools."⁴⁰ The list of damning attributes was lengthy: the black fireman was "thick headed and non-progressive," "indolent, untrustworthy, shiftless," "without honor, principle, pride or fair intelligence," was "totally unfit, both socially and mentally," and "so illiterate and ignorant as to be unable to understand the first principles of law and justice."⁴¹

In addition to their low opinion of black intelligence and skill, white brotherhood men deeply resented African-American participation in the labor market, holding it responsible for their own organizational weakness—and for many of their other problems—in the South from the 1880s through the post-World War I era. Compared to their northern counterparts, southern white firemen and brakemen had considerable difficulty maintaining strong union locals. "The white firemen's organization has very little or no strength in the South, compared with the North," complained fireman C. S. Daniel in 1915.⁴² With few union checks on corporate power, wages were lower and conditions worse than those on northern railroads. In brotherhood reasoning, a direct causal chain linked black workers to harsh corporate practices, racially discriminatory hiring practices against whites (on certain railroads), and the brotherhoods' regional weakness. "Owing to the fact that so many locomotive engines" in North Carolina are "manned by negro firemen," white fireman Boling wrote in 1893, "the rich influence of the Brotherhood has never been felt by the corporations and the travelling public."⁴³ On a number of railroads in the southeastern states that employed a large majority of blacks, the handful of white members confronted "conditions not to be found in any other section of the country" on the eve of World War I. Widespread black employment in the South, a white organizer reluctantly concluded, meant that "no concerted movement" for wage increases or improvements could be conducted, for it was "next to impossible to 'standardize' the rates of pay and rules governing employment through concerted action." Only on railroads where white firemen were exclusively employed or where enough whites were employed to maintain a lodge did the union's Joint Protective Boards manage to negotiate wages and conditions comparable to those elsewhere in the nation.⁴⁴

The presence of black firemen on so many southern railroads lowered working standards in yet another way. The long tradition of black subservience and exploitation allowed whites—both managers and white workers in positions of authority—to insist on not just deference from blacks but a far greater range of labor that they usually could extract from whites. In the hierarchical division of labor on board the train, locomotive engineers oversaw the firemen's work. Their shared commitment to white supremacy and the connections between their memberships (over time, firemen often became engineers, and engineers often retained their membership in the firemen's brotherhood after joining the engineers' organization) made it logical that engineers would prefer and support their junior white assistants, but this was not always the case. "The truth of it is, a great many engineers like Negro firemen best," testified North Carolina's commissioner of labor before the U.S. Industrial Commission in 1900. "They treat them differently—make them wait on them. The white man does not do that." Racial conventions affected which tasks white and black firemen might reasonably be expected to carry out. One Florida engineer explained what he saw as the advantage of black firemen:

> The colored firemen will do a great amount of work that the white firemen would hesitate before doing. [He] will inspect the under portion of an engine, under the supervision of the engineer, looking for loose nuts, missing cotter keys, collar pins, etc. . . . [H]e will fill the headlight, signal lights, gage light, oil cans and lubricators, and although against the rules of some roads will fill the rod cups; he will take charge of the tool box, water bucket, cushion, feed cans, red light, etc., that must be carried from one engine to another running in the chain gang down here . . . [H]e will put away properly everything left in his charge, get the engineer a pail of water to wash in, and on being presented with a plug of tobacco or a dime he will take off his cap and say, "thank you, Cap'n."[45]

The subservience expected of blacks extended from the job to the performance of after-hours favors. The black fireman was "a sort of servant for the engineer," a white member noted with resentment in 1914. He "will carry products home" for the engineer that "he buys out on the road, run errands and otherwise serve him in a personal capacity."[46]

White engineers, who had already achieved the highest status attainable in the railroad labor hierarchy, encountered no direct competition from black workers. Given their authority over their train's operation, more than a few went further and exercised both a professional and personal mastery over their black subordinates. For blacks, white supremacy manifested itself less in the elimination of blacks than in whites' absolute control over them, a control that made engineers' lives considerably easier. They simply demanded of blacks subservience and the performance of extra labor as a condition of employment. Black firemen had little choice but to comply, given the desirability of railroad work and their restricted options outside the industry. (Their response changed abruptly during World War I, however, as they lodged angry complaints with the U.S. Railroad Administration, claiming that this tradition violated wartime regulations mandating equal treatment and pay for all workers, regardless of race, performing the same job.)[47] Predictably, numerous rank-and-file white firemen denounced the white engineers for their behavior. Engineers' preference for blacks not only undermined white firemen's ability to displace their black competition but constituted a direct challenge to their sense of themselves as skilled, dignified white workers. Blacks might bow and scrape before white authority, but white labor must not. It "is a hard matter to get a white fireman to crawl under one of these dirty old mills . . . to shine engineer's shoes and carry their grip home, and probably a watermelon or sack of potatoes, and at last cut some wood for 'de madam,'" a St. Augustine, Florida, fireman complained. And yet, where white firemen were few and the firemen's brotherhood was weak, managers often left their white employees little alternative but to perform at least the range of on-the-job tasks that blacks engaged in. According to a firemen's official, white workers were required to "clean engines, scour brass, place tools . . . and perform any service that may be required of them" on certain southern railroads. Only on the eve of World War I did previously resistant engineers conclude that "the great number of hours spent daily in the space so small as the cab of a locomotive should be be spent in the company of a fellow employee who is socially, morally and intellectually the equal of the engineer."[48]

The issue of wages proved particularly troublesome for southern white brotherhood men. A white brakeman formerly on the Louisville & Nashville Railroad complained that the "paltry salaries" of his southern compatriots could be traced to the fact that on "every crew in the South you will find the 'coon,' a man who is perfectly contented with one dollar a day." W. S. Carter testified in an arbitration hearing in 1913 that the "negro is the cause of wages being cheap in the south . . . There is no other cause."[49] Black firemen and trainmen did receive lower rates of compensation than white workers. Abundant evidence indicates that until 1918—when General Order 27 of the U.S. Railroad Administration equalized wages for blacks and whites performing comparable work—blacks were paid 10 to 20 percent below white rates.[50] If wage differentials were a badge of white superiority over blacks, they also prevented whites from receiving a proper "white man's wage," acting to restrain white wage advancement. As the firemen's magazine explained in 1896, "Railway officials on Southern roads frankly give as a reason for not advancing the wage of white [union] firemen . . . that they can get the same work done for but little more than half the present scale by resorting to colored labor." The payment of "'negro wages' are making paupers of white people" in the South.[51]

As much as white workers might deplore the use of blacks on southern railroads, the railroad companies had good reason to rely on black workers. African-American men were a source not simply of cheap labor but of efficient labor as well. In 1886, James C. Clarke, the president of the Illinois Central and a former slave holder, described his railroad's black firemen and brakemen in Kentucky, Mississippi, Tennessee, and Louisiana as "smart active men" who "show skill in learning quickly the duties they are to perform." Disavowing any prejudice on the part of his railroad, Clarke found black workers "generally amiable, docile and obedient . . . There is no better labor among any race in the world." Railroad companies could extract a greater amount and a wider range of labor out of their black work force, given the tradition of black subordination in the South and a harsher racial climate by the turn of the century. Blacks often worked longer hours than whites, putting in "more preparatory time before a train starts than white employees," the Eight-Hour Commission found. "In these ways an extra hour may be added to their shifts, for which they get no pay."[52]

Railroad managers found that they could use black labor to ensure control over their white labor force. Simply put, black labor could serve as a bulwark against white unionism and union power. Brotherhood members, often correctly, attributed their inability to organize whites to the deterrent effect of black competition and their loss of southern strikes to black strikebreakers. Following the defeat of white firemen and switchmen in the mid-1890s in strikes against the Louisville & Nashville Railroad, the company installed non-union blacks in most of the positions of brakemen, switchmen, and firemen on its Birmingham division to forestall renewed union agitation; subsequent efforts by the white brotherhoods to remove blacks from train crews failed.[53] Few railroads in the Southeast employed any new white firemen at all in the immediate aftermath of the failed 1909 strike by white Georgia firemen, perhaps as punishment but more likely as a form of insurance against future union trouble. Union officials contended that employers "want to be in a position to play negro labor against white labor, thus preventing labor troubles by the operation of a sort of alternating scheme."[54] Harvard economist and labor mediator William Z. Ripley, in 1918, attributed the Louisville & Nashville's success in crushing strikes to its financial strength, the "resolute antibrotherhood attitude of its president," and "its amply supply of negroes for firemen."[55]

It was this fear of employers' manipulation of the racial division of labor, far more than any actual threat, that lay behind a bitter strike of white firemen on the Cincinnati, New Orleans & Texas Pacific Railroad, also known as the Queen and Crescent (Q & C), in 1911. On January 3, management deliberately provoked a conflict with the brotherhood when it assigned three black firemen to preferred runs on passenger and freight trains on an 84-mile section of its third district connecting Chattanooga and Oakdale, Tennessee—a section previously staffed only by whites. Ignoring whites' objections, the railroad's general manager insisted that the company would retain these men, who were the most senior in the service, on their new routes. Outraged, white firemen quickly declared war. Backed by a unanimous vote of the brotherhood local's members, roughly 250 white firemen and as many as 100 white engineers struck on March 9. For the next three weeks, passenger service was halted, and freight service encountered numerous obstacles. The strikers' actions attracted considerable support from rural white mountain communities along the railroad's division in Tennessee and Kentucky. Along the route, sympathizers attacked trains staffed by black firemen, white strikebreakers, and railroad detectives; snipers and mountain marksmen fired at passing locomotive cabins, while crowds of masked supporters pulled crew members—white and black—off the trains to inflict severe beatings.[56]

A great deal appeared to be at stake to strikers and sympathizers alike. The company's action, in the words of a white Cincinnati newspaper, was but the "entering wedge to place negro firemen on practically every railroad south of the Ohio river and east of the Mississippi"; the firemen's magazine charged that the managers' "yielding to their instincts of greed and avarice" in "subordinating white firemen to negro firemen" would eventually displace white firemen. Company officials would increase the number of African Americans north of Oakdale until the Q & C had "so many negro firemen that the white men would be practically helpless in wage matters, as they were on all other parts of the Queen and Crescent Route," union officials charged.[57] In the end, neither the company nor its union emerged wholly victorious. The final agreement produced by federal mediation prohibited employing black firemen north of Oakdale but only so long as a sufficient number of competent whites were available—an extension of existing practice. Rail managers did accept two revisions dealing specifically with black seniority and advancement. First, in the future, the percentage of blacks in Q & C service would not exceed their percentage in service as of January 1, 1911. This had the practical effect of contractually limiting the number of black workers. Second, blacks, in order of seniority, would be assigned to no more than one half of passenger or preferred freight runs.[58] For their part, rank-and-file white firemen expressed dissatisfaction with a settlement that legitimized the use of contractual stipulations as a method for defining the racial boundaries of the labor force but that did not secure their complete white supremacist agenda. The real issue remained unresolved, the *Locomotive Firemen and Enginemen's Magazine* complained, for the "negro fireman question is one that must be settled sooner or later." An editorial in the Jackson, Tennessee, *Daily Sun* concurred: Americans are "unalterably determined that America shall be and remain a white man's country," it read. "The question of doing away with negro firemen has been mooted for several years and, like Banquo's ghost, it will not down . . . for Americans have determined that neither the negro, the Chinaman nor the Japanese will 'run' either this country or its railroads. If the 'cause' of the strike had been removed much bloodshed, suffering and sin would have been avoided, and it is incumbent upon the railroad managers to REMOVE IT before more trouble results."[59]

Given the real and imagined magnitude of the threat posed by African Americans to white job privileges, white firemen had two possible solutions to the so-called "Negro Fireman" problem. To borrow the concise formula proposed by Herbert Northrup in his testimony before the President's Committee on Fair Employment Practices in 1943, the brotherhoods could either "admit the Negro into their union and 'teach him and educate him' to present a solid front against the employer" or "force the railroads to eliminate the Negro from train and engine service."[60] This dilemma was one that repeatedly confronted white workers in a wide array of occupations; the choices outlined by Northrup were open to *all* white unionists, the only difference being that, in many places in the South, whites would neither have to "teach" nor "educate" their black counterparts, who had already organized or were familiar with trade unions.[61]

Not all groups of white workers responded in an identical way to the presence of African Americans in their trades. Although the tendency of most international unions in the AFL was to exclude or discourage black membership, some unions followed a dramatically different course. Important exceptions to the exclusionary rule included longshoremen (sometimes affiliated with the International Longshoremen's Association) in Galveston, Houston, Pensacola, Mobile, and New Orleans, bituminous coal miners (sometimes affiliated with the United Mine Workers of America) in Alabama's Birmingham district and in West Virginia, and timber workers in Louisiana and East Texas (affiliated in the 1910s with the Industrial Workers of the World). Beginning in the 1880s in longshoring and coal mining, industrial unions—which proved far more inclusive than exclusionary craft unions—multi-trade alliances of craft unions sometimes promoted collaborative relations between blacks and whites, who were organized into racially separate, or biracial unions. The biracial union tradition of the Gilded Age and Progressive Era emerged more from pragmatic accommodation to the exigencies of job market competition and the character of the work itself than from workers' ideological commitment to interracial solidarity. Performing relatively unskilled work, longshoremen and miners knew they could easily be replaced by determined employers who manipulated the racial composition of the labor force to unions' disadvantage. Where competition from unorganized black workers proved strong, or where black workers organized unions and sought to secure employment for themselves, whites found exclusion to be a dangerous and ineffectual policy. Moreover, these white workers' sense of themselves as workers was far less dependent on notions of craft, sobriety, mobility, and education than was the case in skilled trades such as the railroad's operating crafts. Although they might take considerable pride in their work and aggressively defend their work rules, they occupied a relatively low position in the occupational hierarchy of skill and power. Ideologically, they had less to lose and, practically, much to gain in making organizational accommodations with their African-American counterparts. Considerations of pragmatism and power, then, could prompt whites to enter into some form of structured relationship with blacks. While by no means all white longshoremen and miners followed this course, thousands discovered that success in regulating the labor supply or neutralizing the weapon of racial division in the employers' arsenal required an alliance with blacks.[62]

In contrast, the railroad brotherhoods, like numerous other unions of skilled white men, refused to experiment across racial lines. Without hesitation, firemen and brakemen embraced policies of black containment or exclusion. Most white locomotive firemen who participated in the public debate over the place of African Americans dismissed the very idea of accepting black workers into the organized labor movement. "Look at the Knights of Labor," a fireman from Birmingham argued in 1897. "What became of them after admitting negroes into their ranks? They collapsed, of course, just like the firemen or any other order who will recognize the negro will do."[63] Brotherhoods invoked racist caricatures to explain racial subordination and justify the policy of union exclusion. Ignoring the efforts of railroad managers and the brotherhoods to exclude blacks from top positions, deny them union membership, and force them to accept harsher conditions and lower wages, they instead insisted that African Americans were responsible for their own plight. Some whites contended that blacks, as a group, were unorganizable. The *Locomotive Firemen's Magazine* concluded in 1898 that "they are too shiftless to leave any hope that they can ever be successfully organized, and therefore they are a menace to organized labor." Extending membership to blacks was "repulsive to any working man in the South," one respondent put it, a "direct insult to the members in the South," another insisted. A white fireman from Denison, Texas, suggested that admitting blacks into the union might foster character traits that were incompatible with blacks' social position. Taking blacks under brotherhood care, he argued, would unleash dangerous forces, for equalizing wages would "urge the negro to ambition"; blacks would become "bold and hard to please."[64]

The brotherhoods of locomotive firemen and trainmen thus rejected black membership. Their very structure, social composition, and ideology, like those of many skilled unions, worked to reinforce their consistently anti-black (and anti-immigrant) stance. From their inception, the brotherhoods modeled themselves after older fraternal orders, drawing on a long history and the rituals of Freemasonry (and other fraternal bodies) in the United States. But the construction of fraternal solidarity, as Mary Ann Clawson has established, "was based as much upon a process of exclusion as it was a ritual of unification," for neither women nor African Americans qualified for membership. Since racial exclusion was a "hallmark of mainstream American fraternalism throughout its history," fraternal orders "may be seen as an active, albeit relatively small, part of a social structure organized to construct and maintain racial separation and inequality."[65] Representing the industry's overwhelmingly white, native-born male constituency outside the South, and that smaller constituency in the South itself, the brotherhoods adopted explicit provisions in their constitutions to ensure continued racial, ethnic, and gender homogeneity. Herbert Northrup concluded that the "social origins of the 'Big Four' made it almost inevitable" that they would exclude blacks, for most had been "founded as fraternal and beneficial societies," and they continued to place much emphasis on those "social features." "To admit Negroes, the Southern members declared, would be tantamount to admitting that the Negro is the 'social equal' of the white man," something "they refused to countenance."[66] Exclusionary provisions in brotherhood constitutions remained standard well into the 1950s and 1960s, when federal and state courts, responding to and helping to forge a gradual revolution in labor and civil rights law, declared such formal racial proscriptions unconstitutional.

The occupational dynamics of the railroads industry's job structure also led white craft unionists to advocate a strategy of exclusion or marginalization over one based on biracial unionism. Such an approach offered the advantage of designating certain jobs as for whites only. In the North and West, firemen and brakemen enforced a policy of segmentation, keeping African Americans out of railroad running trades and restricting them to unskilled positions. In the South, white firemen and brakemen looked approvingly on the success of their northern and western colleagues and apprehensively at their own problems of black competition, lower wages, and harsher working conditions. But everywhere, the highly desired positions of conductor and engineer remained a preserve of whites. White firemen's expectation of advancement over time generated a "throttle fever"—the desire to become an engineer—which tended to reduce turnover by providing an incentive for firemen to remain with their employer. Where the brotherhoods were powerful, promotions turned on seniority and competence (assessed by means of a qualifying exam). But labor-market and larger economic conditions always influenced the demand for conductors and engineers. When the economy was strong and labor was in short supply, a fireman might wait only a few years before advancing; conversely, during economic downturns or periods when labor markets were glutted, he might wait over a decade.[67] Admission of blacks into the brotherhoods or recognition of separate black unions might have necessitated according them equal access to coveted positions, a prospect that few brotherhood men could embrace. It would also have required them either to devalue their own work —to view it as less skilled and prestigious—or to evaluate African Americans' capacities more positively—to view blacks as capable and as qualified as whites. This would have entailed a virtually unthinkable break with prevailing southern racial beliefs. The dangers of a racially divided labor force did not lead white brotherhoods of firemen and brakemen to rethink their policy of exclusion. In essence, they accepted their vulnerability because the alternative—sharing the benefits of organization with blacks—appeared too unpalatable. "[W]e would rather be absolute slaves of capital," a Clarendon, Texas, fireman declared, "than to take the negro into our lodges as a equal and brother."[68] When it came to organizational efforts to build unions and extend working-class influence, the racial divide proved an insurmountable barrier separating white from black on the railroads.

Rejecting blacks as members was one thing, but achieving their elimination as labor market competitors was another. At a conference of the various brotherhoods in Norfolk in 1898, the Firemen's Grand Master, F. P. Sargent, looked forward to the day "when every locomotive in the country would be fired by a white man," and toward that end he promised an educational war, "a campaign in advocacy of white supremacy in the railway service."[69] More than education, however, was required to persuade or force railway managers to relinquish cherished managerial prerogatives, increase their labor costs, and abandon their insurance against white union demands. Strategy and tactics were the subjects of official union debate, and impatient rank-and-file railroaders would periodically experiment on their own when they felt they could not wait for negotiations to take their course. Over the next two decades and beyond, white railroaders would employ a variety of tactics, with varying degrees of success, to deny African Americans employment.

At one extreme were racial violence and terrorism. During strikes, strike-breakers regardless of race found themselves subject to verbal and physical abuse. But moments of overt class conflict were not the only occasion for white-on-black attacks, particularly in the South. In 1891, for instance, the introduction of a small number of black brakemen into the previously all white Mobile and Montgomery division of the Louisville & Nashville Railroad provoked violent opposition. The new black trainmen found themselves dodging bullets along their routes, and local whites punished a white brakeman, flogging him "in the bushes for consenting to make the run with the negro trainmen."[70] Far more serious violence occurred during the economic depression of 1921 and continued into the following year. Southern white brakemen and firemen on the Illinois Central's Yazoo Division intensified their campaign of terror against blacks, reportedly placing a $300 bounty on the head of every black railroader killed; at least a dozen blacks were shot at, injured, or killed in the ensuing attacks. White railroaders in the Deep South would launch a similar round of physical assaults in the early years of the Great Depression.[71]

Racial terrorism was generally a tactic of last resort, a desperate ploy in desperate times, not a staple of brotherhood tactics against black workers. Violence remained episodic, the product of local anger, racial beliefs and tensions, and fear of economic deprivation, receiving neither official sanction from brotherhood leaders nor general public approbation. Political officials and the white press found it too difficult to defend outright murder in the cause of white economic supremacy, for such violence infringed on employers' more important right to hire whomever they liked, contributed to the white South's reputation for lawlessness and chaos, and violated recognized legal norms. However effective in the short run, terrorism remained an unsanctioned technique resorted to only rarely—during economic hard times—in the decades-long campaign of white railroad workers against African Americans.

The strike, white railroad workers' most disruptive weapon, similarly carried risks. Before 1910, what "race strikes" there were encountered sharp employer opposition that thwarted white demands for the elimination of black labor. The Georgia "race strike" of 1909, which drew the widest national press attention of any labor-based racial conflict before the 1917 East St. Louis riot, is a case in point.[72] Blacks and whites exercised equal seniority on Georgia railroads, but because an employment bar against black engineers prevented black occupational mobility, many black firemen acquired considerable seniority, enabling them to claim a large number of preferred runs on passenger and freight trains. Newer white workers, often possessing less seniority than black co-workers, were compelled, in the words of the firemen's brotherhood vice president G. A. Ball, "To take what is left by the negro." This state of affairs, white strikers insisted, was unacceptable in a city and state that had disfranchised its black citizens and extended segregation statutes to cover public transportation and accommodations. White firemen pushed unsuccessfully for a dual seniority system that allowed the senior white fireman to "stand first for passenger engines or runs." Their three-week strike failed completely. In this as in many instances, railroad managers possessed sufficient power to resist white demands for black exclusion. This was a lesson that brotherhood leaders had undoubtedly understood. White railroad workers struck frequently over such issues as wages, conditions, union recognition, and work rules, yet relatively few of their walkouts centered on the removal of black workers.[73]

By the second decade of the twentieth century, the white brotherhoods' anti-black efforts began to produce modest success in the South. Ultimately, firemen's and trainmen's officials settled for contractual restrictions—percentage agreements—as an attainable substitute for the elusive goal of outright exclusion. Utilizing the threat of strikes (or, as in the case of Q & C firemen, the strike itself), they won formal restrictions on the numbers or placement of black workers in the labor force as well as the creation of racially separate seniority lines.[74] In 1918, the federal Eight-Hour Commission reported the use of contracts in limiting black employment to be widespread; in many cases, the brotherhoods and individual railroads had concluded agreements to "limit the proportion of colored workers in occupations under the jurisdiction of the union."[75] In the immediate aftermath of World War I, white trainmen and firemen successfully pressured the Railroad Administration into accepting rules that guaranteed to whites an even larger proportion of jobs. "Non-promotional" clauses, for example, effectively barred the employment of any man as firemen who did "not stand for promotion"—effectively ending new black hires,[76] while new percentage agreements sharply reduced the number of black workers on key railroad divisions. Unable to eliminate black workers, white unionists embraced contractual restrictions on blacks, advanced promotion bars, and manipulated seniority lines to ensure their numerical superiority. The new rules, which were adopted for their "freeze-out and eliminating effects," complained black labor activist Thomas Redd on behalf of some sixty-nine black Kentucky brakemen in 1928, constituted nothing less than a "negro elimination program."[77]

Black railroadmen lost ground steadily in the years following World War I, despite their vigorous protests. Reductions in the overall size of the nation's operating rail service, technological advances, and contractual and secret agreements between unions and rail managers all contributed to their displacement. By the late 1940s, Charles Houston could confirm to the NAACP's 40th Anniversary Conference that the Big Four brotherhoods, which had been "using every means in their power to drive the Negro train and engine service worker out of employment," had been largely successful in creating a "racially closed shop" among the firemen, brakemen, switchmen, flagmen, and yardmen.[78] After the World War I era, the brotherhoods, with the collusion of the federal government and railroad managers, ultimately accomplished much, if not all, of the brotherhoods' pre-war agenda.

A consciousness of race was an integral part of white workers' sense of themselves as workers, as Americans, and as citizens. For white railroad workers in the operating trades, the prospect or reality of racial competition and a desire to preserve their dominance of key jobs played important roles in the framing of racial beliefs and the forging of discriminatory practices toward non-whites. Undoubtedly, racial exclusion often entailed material and psychological benefits. But these perspectives by whites on race were grounded in more than function alone. Theirs was an elite craft structure, the access to which required the possession of highly valued skills, knowledge, and strength of character. Whether they were members of an aristocracy of labor (as in some northern and western states) or a weak, embattled, but aspiring elite (as in much of the South), brotherhood men in the "fraternity" on the railroads maintained an intense craft identity and pride. Rooted in their membership in a distinctive occupational group, their sense of collective identity also incorporated beliefs about race and nationality. To possess the requisite skill, knowledge, and character for the safe and effective operation of the nation's railroads, a railroad man had to be a white American. No matter how accomplished they proved themselves, African-American firemen and brakemen would not be included in the fraternity on wheels. White brotherhood members assumed that blacks simply could not possess the appropriate character traits.

Racial ideology also constituted part of a framework for interpreting the dramatic changes taking place in the United States in the late nineteenth and early twentieth centuries. The process of capitalist industrialization was nothing if not uneven, unstable, and unpredictable. Providing rising standards of living for some, it threatened impoverishment for others. The sheer level of class conflict in this era wove a perpetual insecurity into the fabric of working-class life. Not even skilled workers in the railroad operating trades could take their status for granted. In the struggle between capital and labor, employers drew on a vast supply of immigrants or black laborers whose reputedly squalid living standards, immoral behavior, and mental incapacity threatened to drag down the sturdy white working class and American civilization with it. Viewing themselves as embattled workers and as embattled citizens, white trade unionists occupied the front lines in a war in which class, race, and national identity were inextricably linked. Economic competition with non-whites—real or anticipated—became a high stakes moral contest with the American standard of living and republican liberty hanging in the balance.

African Americans in the operating service suffered from the evolving techniques of racial subordination and exclusion. By the World War I period, if not before, however, black railroaders, and most certainly their union leaders, had become good students of the political and economic circumstances out of which these mechanisms were forged and implemented. Possessing knowledge of their adversaries' precise tactics, the changing rules of the game, and their enemies' strength and motives did not, in the short run, enable them to preserve many of their jobs. W. H. Stover's quiet, personal protest, which opened this article, like that of the World War I—era black railroad unions, came to naught. But the outcome was somewhat different during the next war, when another generation of black railroad workers attempted to crack the white barriers of the brotherhoods and railroad managers. The judicial struggles of black railroaders such as Bester William Steele and Tom Tunstall were backed by legal teams employed by the National Association for the Advancement of Colored People, the Brotherhood of Sleeping Car Porters, and the Association of Colored Railway Trainmen and Locomotive Firemen, all extremely well-versed in the history of employment discrimination in the railroad industry. Knowledge of that history formed the basis for their challenges before federal bodies, the federal courts, and the public. While by no means achieving the full economic equality that they sought, this new generation of labor and legal activists managed to delegitimize the brotherhoods' racial barriers and establish the principle of fair employment as a national goal.

NOTES

1. W. H. Stover to W. G. McAdoo, May 1, 1918, in File No. 160, "Southern Railway v. W. H. Stover, Bristol, Va.," Records of the Division of Labor, Case Files of G. W. W. Hanger, Assistant Director, Division of Labor, 1918–1920, United States Railroad Administration, Record Group 14, National Archives, Washington, D.C.

2. W. S. Carter to W. H. Stover, May 22, 1918, in File No. 160, "Southern Railway v. W. H. Stover, Bristol, Va."

3. Charles H. Houston, "Foul Employment Practice on the Rails," *The Crisis*, 56 (October 1949): 270. In the late 1930s and 1940s, Houston was actively involved in judicial cases challenging the exclusionary policies of the white brotherhoods. See Genna Rae McNeil, *Groundwork: Charles Hamilton Houston and the Struggle for Civil Rights* (Philadelphia, 1983), 156–75. Also see Ira De A. Reid, Director, Department of Research and Investigations of the National Urban League, *Negro Membership in American Labor Unions* (New York, 1930), 54–58; "The Elimination of Negro Firemen on American Railways—A Study of the Evidence Adduced at the Hearing before the President's Committee on Fair Employment Practices," *Lawyers Guild Review*, 4 (March-April 1944): 32–37; Herbert P. Northrup, *Organized Labor and the Negro* (New York, 1944), 48–101; Abram L. Harris, *The Black Worker: The Negro and the Labor Movement* (1931; rpt. ed., New York, 1969), 284–315; Herbert Hill, *Black Labor and the American Legal System: Race, Work, and the Law* (Madison, Wis., 1985), 334–72; Howard W. Risher, Jr., *The Negro in the Railroad Industry* (Philadelphia, 1971); Malcolm Ross, *All*

Manner of Men (New York, 1948), 118–41; Lloyd Brown, *Iron City* (New York, 1952), 148–69.

4. Herbert Hill, "Myth-Making as Labor History: Herbert Gutman and the United Mine Workers of America," *International Journal of Politics, Culture, and Society* 2 (Winter 1988): 132–33; Nell Irvin Painter, "The New Labor History and the Historical Moment," *International Journal of Politics, Culture, and Society*, 2 (Spring 1989): 369; Painter, "Black Workers from Reconstruction to the Great Depression," in Paul Buhle and Alan Dawley, eds., *Working for Democracy: American Workers from the Revolution to the Present* (Urbana, Ill., 1985), 63–71; Noel Ignatiev, "The Paradox of the White Worker: Studies in Race Formation," *Labour/Le travail*, 30 (Fall 1992): 234. Also see David Roediger, "'Labor in White Skin': Race and Working-Class History," in Mike Davis and Michael Sprinkler, eds., *Reshaping the U.S. Left: Popular Struggles in the 1980s* (London, 1988), 289; Roediger, "Notes on Working Class Racism," *New Politics*, 2 (Summer 1989): 61–66.

5. Comments by Jacqueline Dowd Hall, "Prospects in Southern Studies: A Symposium," *University of North Carolina at Chapel Hill Southern Research Report*, No. 1 (Spring 1990): 32; Robin D. G. Kelly, "'We Are Not What We Seem': Rethinking Black Working-Class Opposition in the Jim Crow South," *Journal of American History*, 80 (June 1993): 89.

6. Michael Goldfield, "Race and the CIO: The Possibilities for Racial Egalitarianism during the 1930s and 1940s," *International Labor and Working-Class History*, 44 (Fall 1993): 3.

7. See Eric Arnesen, "Following the Color Line of Labor: Black Workers and the Labor Movement before 1930," *Radical History Review*, 55 (Winter 1993): 43–87.

8. For the case of the packinghouse and steel industries, the first approach that evaluates biracial union alliances more positively is exemplified by Rick Halpern, "Race, Ethnicity, and Union in the Chicago Stockyards, 1917–1922," *International Review of Social History*, 37 (1992): 25–48; James R. Barrett, *Life and Work in the Jungle: Chicago's Packinghouse Workers 1894–1922* (Urbana, Ill., 1987), 191–263; and Judith Stein, "Southern Workers in National Unions: Birmingham Steelworkers, 1936–1951," in Robert H. Zieger, ed., *Organized Labor in the Twentieth-Century South* (Knoxville, Tenn., 1991), 162–222. The second approach, far harsher toward organized white labor, is taken by James Grossman, *Land of Hope: Chicago, Black Southerners, and the Great Migration* (Chicago, 1989); William Tuttle, *Race Riot: Chicago in the Red Summer of 1919* (New York, 1970), 124–56; Robert J. Norrell, "Caste in Steel: Jim Crow Careers in Birmingham, Alabama," *Journal of American History*, 73 (December 1986): 669–94. Bruce Nelson adopts a stance midway between these two in his "Organized Labor and the Struggle for Black Equality in Mobile during World War II," *Journal of American History*, 80 (December 1993): 952–88.

9. Alexander Saxton, *The Rise and Fall of the White Republic: Class Politics and Mass Culture in Nineteenth-Century America* (New York, 1990), 293. Also see Michael Reich, *Racial Inequality: A Political-Economic Analysis* (Princeton, N.J., 1981); Robert Asher and Charles Stephenson, "American Capitalism, Labor Organization, and the Racial/Ethnic Factor," in Asher and Stephenson, eds., *Labor Divided: Race and Ethnicity in United States Labor Struggles, 1835–1960* (Albany, N.Y., 1990), 3–27; Alexander Saxton, "Historical Explanations of Racial Inequity," *Marxist Perspectives*, 2 (Summer 1979): 146–68.

10. For example, see David R. Roediger, *The Wages of Whiteness: Race and the Making of the American Working Class* (New York, 1991), 11–13; Michael Honey, *Southern Labor and Black Civil Rights: Organizing Memphis Workers* (Urbana, Ill., 1993), 20; W. E. B. Du Bois, *Black Reconstruction in America 1860–1880* (1935; rpt. edn., New York, 1985), 700.

11. On the construction of racialized and gendered identities, see Ava Baron, ed., *Work Engendered: Toward a New History of American Labor* (Ithaca, N.Y., 1991); Paul M. Taillon, "Trouble on the Southern Railroads: White Supremacy and the Georgia 'Race' Strike of 1909" (unpublished paper delivered at the 1994 meeting of the Organi-

zation of American Historians); Andrew Neather, "Popular Republicanism, American-ism, and the Roots of Anti-Communism, 1890–1925" (Ph.D. dissertation, Duke University, 1994); David Roediger, "Race and the Working-Class Past in the United States: Multiple Identities and the Future of Labor History," *International Review of Social History*, 38 (Supplement, 1993): 132–33.

12. Examples include William H. Harris, *The Harder We Run: Black Workers since the Civil War* (New York, 1982); Dennis C. Dickerson, *Out of the Crucible: Black Steelworkers in Western Pennsylvania, 1875–1980* (Albany, N.Y., 1986); Earl Lewis, *In Their Own Interests: Race, Class, and Power in Twentieth-Century Norfolk, Virginia* (Berkeley, Calif., 1991). A larger, more polemical literature similarly treats race and racism as unproblematic categories. See Hill, "Myth-Making as Labor History"; Herbert Hill, "Black Labor and Affirmative Action: An Historical Perspective," in Steven Shulman and William Darity, Jr., eds., *The Question of Discrimination: Racial Inequality in the U.S. Labor Market* (Middletown, Conn., 1989), 190–267; Steven Shulman, "Racism and the Making of the American Working Class," *International Journal of Politics, Culture, and Society*, 2 (Spring 1989): 361–65; Clarence Walker, "How Many Niggers Did Karl Marx Know? Or, A Peculiarity of the Americans," in Walker, *Deromanticizing Black History: Critical Essays and Reappraisals* (Knoxville, Tenn., 1991).

13. Judith Stein, "'Of Mr. Booker T. Washington and Others': The Political Economy of Racism in the United States," *Science and Society*, 38 (Winter 1974–75): 423–24. Similar arguments are found in Harold D. Woodman, "Economic Reconstruction and the Rise of the New South, 1865–1900," in John B. Boles and Evelyn Thomas Nolen, eds., *Interpreting Southern History: Historiographical Essays in Honor of Sanford W. Higginbotham* (Baton Rouge, La., 1987), 260; Daniel Letwin, "Race, Class, and Industrialization in the New South: Black and White Coal Miners in the Birmingham District of Alabama, 1878–1897" (Ph.D. dissertation, Yale University, 1991), 3; Barbara Fields, "Ideology and Race in American History," in J. Morgan Kousser and James M. McPherson, eds., *Region, Race and Reconstruction: Essays in Honor of C. Vann Woodward* (New York, 1982), 144, 155–57.

14. Fields, "Ideology and Race," 143–77; Barbara Fields, "Slavery, Race and Ideology in the United States of America," *New Left Review*, 181 (May-June 1990): 95–118. Also see Judith Stein, "Defining the Race, 1890–1930," in Werner Sollors, ed., *The Invention of Ethnicity* (New York, 1989), 77–80.

15. Dana Frank, *Purchasing Power: Consumer Organizing, Gender, and the Seattle Labor Movement, 1919–1929* (New York, 1994), 9.

16. Robert S. Starobin, *Industrial Slavery in the Old South* (New York, 1970), 28; Clarence L. Mohr, *On the Threshold of Freedom: Masters and Slaves in Civil War Georgia* (Athens, Ga., 1986), 136–42, 164–66, 182; Stephen Ray Henson, "Industrial Workers in the Mid Nineteenth-Century South: Atlanta Railwaymen, 1840–1870" (Ph.D. dissertation, Emory University, 1982), 24–25, 109–14; Jonathan W. McLeod, *Workers and Workplace Dynamics in Reconstruction Era Atlanta: A Case Study* (Los Angeles, 1989), 28–29, 33–34. A sample of the literature on Mexican, Mexican-American, and Asian immigrant railroad workers includes Victor S. Clark, "Mexican Labor in the United States," *Bulletin of the Bureau of Labor*, 78 (September 1908): 466, 477–82; Paul S. Taylor, "Mexican Labor in the United States: Chicago and the Calumet Region," *University of California Publications in Economics*, 7 (March 1932): 62–66, 82–86; Michael M. Smith, "Beyond the Borderlands: Mexican Labor in the Central Plains, 1900–1930," *Great Plains Quarterly*, 1 (Fall 1981): 240, 243–44; Michael M. Smith, "Mexicans in Kansas City: The First Generation, 1900–1920," *Perspectives in Mexican American Studies*, 2 (1989): 32, 34–36; Robert Oppenheimer, "Acculturation or Assimilation: Mexican Immigrants in Kansas, 1900 to World War II," *Western Historical Quarterly*, 16 (October 1985): 432–44; Mario T. Garcia, *Desert Immigrants: The Mexicans of El Paso, 1880–1920* (New Haven, Conn., 1981); Yuji Ichioka, *The Issei: The World of the First Generation Japanese Immigrants 1885–1924* (New York, 1988), 57–90; W. Thomas White, "Race, Ethnicity, and Gender in the Railroad Work Force: The Case of the Far Northwest, 1883–1918," *Western Historical Quarterly*, 16 (July 1985): 265–83;

William Thomas White, "A History of Railroad Workers in the Pacific Northwest, 1883–1934" (Ph.D. dissertation, University of Washington, 1981).

17. Shelton Stromquist, *A Generation of Boomers: The Pattern of Railroad Labor Conflict in Nineteenth-Century America* (Urbana, Ill., 1987), 105–06.

18. O. H. Kirkpatrick, *Working on the Railroad* (Philadelphia, 1949), 115, 120–25; "Fatality among Brakemen," *Seattle Sunday Star*, March 23, 1884. Also see Albro Martin, *Railroads Triumphant: The Growth, Rejection and Rebirth of a Vital American Force* (New York, 1992), 308.

19. Walter Licht, *Working for the Railroad: The Organization of Work in the Nineteenth Century* (Princeton, N.J., 1983); James Samuel Stemons, "Open Letters: The Industrial Color-Line in the North," *The Century Magazine*, 60 (1900): 477–78; David Montgomery, *The Fall of the House of Labor: The Workplace, the State, and American Labor Activism, 1865–1925* (New York, 1977), 365–66; Nick Salvatore, *Eugene V. Debs: Citizen and Socialist* (Urbana, Ill., 1982), 104–07; Joel Seidman, *The Brotherhood of Railroad Trainmen: The Internal Political Life of a National Union* (New York, 1962), 9–10. On African-American shop workers, see Colin J. Davis, "The 1922 Railroad Shopmen's Strike in the Southeast: A Study of Success and Failure," in Zieger, *Organized Labor in the Twentieth-Century South*, 113–43.

20. Starobin, *Industrial Slavery in the Old South*, 28; Licht, *Working for the Railroad*, 42, 65–69; Benn, Nashville, "The Sunny South," *Locomotive Firemen's Magazine*, 11 (September 1887): 546–47. Black railroad employment, both skilled and unskilled, remained heavily concentrated in the South, even after World War I. See "Negro Workers on Steam Railway Lines of the United States," *Savannah Tribune*, October 1, 1924; "Employment of Negroes on Railroads," *Monthly Labor Review* (November 1924): 16; Commission on Standard Workday of Railroad Employees, *Report of the Eight-Hour Commission* (Washington, D.C., 1918), 413; *The Colored American Magazine*, 11 (July 1906): 68; "Train Crews All White," *The Colored American Magazine*, 13 (October 1907): 254–55; Edward Aaron Gaston, Jr., "A History of the Negro Wage Earner in Georgia, 1890–1940" (Ph.D. dissertation, Emory University, 1957), 237–42.

21. Stemons, "Open Letters," 478; Unlucky, "St. Augustine, Florida," *Railroad Trainmen's Journal*, 18 (March 1901): 213–14.

22. *Constitution of Brotherhood of Locomotive Firemen* (September 1888), 40–41, at the Department of Labor Library, Washington, D.C. Also see Constitution (September 1892), Section 113, p. 40, quoted in Samuel McCune Lindsay, "Report on Railway Labor in the United States," in *Reports of the Industrial Commission on Labor Organizations, Labor Disputes, and Arbitration, and on Railway Labor*, No. 17 of the Commission's Reports (Washington, 1901), 823, 839; Pier Luigi Gregory DePaola, "Management and Organized Labor Relations of the Louisville and Nashville Railroad during the Depression Year 1893" (M.A. thesis, University of Louisville, 1968), 13; Reed C. Richardson, *The Locomotive Engineer 1863–1963: A Century of Labor Relations and Work Rules* (Ann Arbor, Mich., 1963), 189.

23. "Historical Sketch of the Brotherhood of Locomotive Firemen and Enginemen," *Locomotive Firemen and Enginemen's Magazine*, 54 (June 1913): 816. Also see Kurt Wetzel, "Railroad Management's Response to Operating Employees' Accidents, 1890–1913," *Labor History*, 21 (Summer 1980): 351–68. The Locomotive Engineers were organized in 1863, the Conductors in 1868, the Firemen in 1873, and the Trainmen in 1883. For an overview, see U.S. Department of Labor, "Handbook of American Trade-Unions," *Bulletin of the United States Bureau of Labor Statistics*, No. 420 (Washington, D.C., 1926).

24. On the hazards of railroading, see "Railroading More Deadly Than War," *Railroad Trainmen's Journal*, 17 (October 1900): 884–86; "Switchman Ground to Pieces in I.C. Yards," Louisville *Courier-Journal*, March 27, 1911. A selection of the extensive literature on late nineteenth-century conflict on the railroads includes Herbert G. Gutman, "Trouble on the Railroads in 1873–1874: Prelude to the 1877 Crisis?" *Labor History*, 2 (Spring 1961): 215–35; Stewart H. Holbrook, *The Story of American Railroads*

(New York, 1947), 244–59; O. D. Boyle, *History of Railroad Strikes* (Washington, D.C., 1935).

25. "Principles of the Brotherhood, Eloquent Address by Grand Master Sargent at the Opera House," in Harrisburg, Pennsylvania, *Daily Telegraph*, September 11, 1894, in *Terence Vincent Powderly Papers, 1864–1937, and John William Hayes Papers, 1880–1921, The Knights of Labor*, microfilm, Catholic University of America, Reel 69; Cloyd Herbert Finch, Jr., "Organized Labor in Louisville, Kentucky 1880–1914" (Ph.D. dissertation, University of Kentucky, 1965), 29–30; Kate Born, "Organized Labor in Memphis, Tennessee, 1826–1901," *Western Tennessee Historical Society Papers*, 21 (1967): 75. Uncritical histories of the brotherhoods and other railway unions include Richardson, *Locomotive Engineer*; Leonard Painter, *Through Fifty Years with the Brotherhood Railway Carmen of America* (Kansas City, 1941); Nixson Denton, *History of the Brotherhood of Railway and Steamship Clerks, Freight Handlers, Express and Station Employes* (Cincinnati, Ohio, 1965); D. W. Hertel, *History of the Brotherhood of Maintenance of Way Employes: Its Birth and Growth 1887–1955* (Washington, D.C., 1955). Also see Archibald M. McIsaac, *The Order of Railroad Telegraphers: A Study in Trade Unionism and Collective Bargaining* (Princeton, N.J., 1933); Selig Perlman, *A History of Trade Unionism in the United States* (New York, 1922), 184.

26. B. R. Lacy, Commissioner, *Seventh Annual Report of the Bureau of Labor Statistics of the State of North Carolina, For the Year 1893* (Raleigh, 1894), 103–05; James H. Ducker, *Men of the Steel Rails: Workers on the Atchison, Topeka & Santa Fe Railroad 1869–1900* (Lincoln, Neb., 1983), 53–56, 113; Samuel McCune Lindsay, "Report on Railway Labor in the United States," in *Reports of the Industrial Commission . . . on Railway Labor*, Report 17, 834; Benn, "Sunny South," 546. On the perspectives of elite craft workers, see Andrew Dawson, "The Parameters of Craft Consciousness: The Social Outlook of the Skilled Worker, 1890–1920," in Dirk Hoerder, ed., *American Labor and Immigration History, 1877–1920s: Recent European Research* (Urbana, Ill., 1983): 135–55.

27. Charles B. George, *Forty Years on the Rail: Reminiscences of a Veteran Conductor* (Chicago, 1887), 166; R. A. Bennett, "The Negro Question," *Locomotive Firemen and Enginemen's Magazine*, 48 (January 1910): 126–28; "Educational Training for Railroad Service," *Railroad Trainmen's Journal*, 18 (February 1901): 101–03.

28. Justin D. Fulton, *Sam Hobart, the Locomotive Engineer: A Workingman's Solution of the Labor Problem* (New York, 1883), 28; R. C. Ransom, "Closing the Doors of Various Trades against Colored People," *Christian Recorder*, June 28, 1888. On the requirements for occupational advancement, see W. Fred Cottrell, *The Railroader* (Stanford, Calif., 1940), 18–19; Henson, "Industrial Workers in the Mid Nineteenth-Century South," 74, 120–23.

29. George, *Forty Years on the Rail*, 175; "Southern Federated Board," in "President's Report to the Twelfth Biennial Convention," *Report of Grand Lodge Officers, Brotherhood of Locomotive Firemen and Enginemen, Twelfth Annual Convention, St. Paul, Minnesota, June 1910* (n.p., n.d.), 181; A. Philip Randolph, "The Crisis of Negro Railroad Workers," *American Federationist*, 46 (August 1939): 808; "Georgia Railroad Strike," *Seattle Union Record*, July 24, 1909. Also see *Railroad Trainmen's Journal*, 17 (June 1900): 499; Chicago Commission on Race Relations, *The Negro in Chicago: A Study of Race Relations and a Race Riot* (Chicago, 1922), 409; Testimony of Sidney S. Alderman, March 2, 1944, *Hearings before the Special Committee to Investigate Executive Agencies, House of Representatives*, 78th Congress, 1st and 2d Sessions, Part 2, 2133–34; "Discrimination in R.R. Employment," *Traffic World*, 72 (September 18 and December 18, 1943): 655 and 1535 respectively.

30. "Twenty-Sixth Convention — Important Resolutions Adopted: Immigration," *Locomotive Firemen and Enginemen's Magazine*, 55 (October 1913): 565; "Migratory Laborers and the Padrone System," *Locomotive Firemen's Magazine*, 20 (March 1896): 154; "Immigration Tidal Wave Threatens Welfare of American Workers," *Brotherhood of Locomotive Firemen and Enginemen's Magazine*, 69 (October 15, 1920): 8; "A Million New Workers Each Year," *Railroad Trainmen*, 27 (June 1910): 513; "Protection to

American Labor," *Locomotive Firemen's Magazine*, 20 (May 1896): 321; "Effects of Immigration," *Locomotive Firemen's Magazine* 23 (November 1897): 404. Fear of new immigrants diminished little over time, and brotherhood anti-immigrant and anti-black rhetoric remained remarkably consistent in these years. Only after the cut-off of European immigration during World War I did the rhetoric turn more toward Asians, the Japanese in particular. The mere prospect of a renewal of Asian immigration in the postwar era was enough to occasion fierce diatribes about the "yellow peril," the failures of the melting pot, and the hazards of "coolie" labor. "Immigration and Prosperity," *Railroad Trainmen*, 37 (November 1920): 677–79. In the *Brotherhood of Locomotive Firemen and Enginemen's Magazine*, see "The Japanese Immigration Problem," 70 (January 1, 1921): 12–14; "Plan to Market Coolie Labor Same as Steel, Coal, Etc.," 68 (March 15, 1920): 19–20; "They'll Swarm the United States with Chinese Coolies Yet," 63 (November 15, 1917): 5; "Industrial and Commercial Barons Determined to Flood United States with Chinese Coolies," 64 (March 1, 1918): 5.

31. "Industrial and Commerical Barons," 5. In the *Railroad Trainmen's Journal*, see "Wealth and Manhood," 16 (January 1899): 85–86; "The Slums," 15 (July 1898): 582; "Public Meeting of the Brotherhood of Railroad Trainmen, Fifth Annual Convention," 18 (June 1901): 495.

32. Ruth H. Bloch, "The Gendered Meanings of Virtue in Revolutionary America," *Signs*, 13 (Autumn 1987): 38; Christine Stansell, *City of Women: Sex and Class in New York, 1789–1860* (New York, 1986), 139–40; Thomas J. Whalen, "The Women God Gave Us," *Railroad Trainmen's Journal*, 18 (March 1901): 215–17; Neather, "Popular Republicanism, Americanism, and the Roots of Anti-Communism," 243–44, 265–71.

33. "Immigration and What It Means," *Railroad Trainmen's Journal*, 19 (June 1902): 477; also see "Plain Statement of Plain Questions," 18 (May 1901): 415–19.

34. Canuck, "Immigration," *Locomotive Firemen's Magazine*, 22 (April 1897): 221; "Aliens in the Majority in Basic Industries," *Railroad Trainman*, 37 (January 1920): 27; "A Million New Workers Each Year," *Railroad Trainmen*, 27 (June 1910): 513.

35. Gwendolyn Mink, "The Lady and the Tramp: Gender, Race, and the Origins of the American Welfare State," in Linda Gordon, ed., *Women, the State and Welfare* (Madison, Wis., 1990), 93–94. Also see Catherine Collomp, "Unions, Civics, and National Identity: Organized Labor's Reaction to Immigration, 1881–1897," *Labor History*, 29 (Fall 1988): 450–74.

36. "Must American Workers Compete with Chinese Labor in the U.S.?" *Brotherhood of Locomotive Firemen and Enginemen's Magazine* 64 (January 1, 1919): 14; "The Japanese Question," *Brotherhood of Locomotive Firemen and Enginemen's Magazine*, 70 (May 1, 1921): 4. On the question of nativism in the labor movement and in American society, key works include Gwendolyn Mink, *Old Labor and New Immigrants in American Political Development: Union, Party, and State, 1875–1920* (Ithaca, N.Y., 1986); John Higham, *Strangers in the Land: Patterns of American Nativism 1860–1925* (1955; rpt. edn., New York, 1963); Alexander Saxton, *The Indispensable Enemy: Labor and the Anti-Chinese Movement in California* (Berkeley, Calif., 1971). For a sample of contemporary discussions of the brotherhoods'—and the labor movement's—opposition to new immigrants, see "Immigration," *Locomotive Engineers' Monthly Journal*, 33 (June 1899): 421; in the *Locomotive Firemen's Magazine*, see "Immigration and the Labor Question," 20 (April 1896): 249–50; "Two Classes of Immigrants," 22 (January 1897); "Italian Standard of Wages," 24 (February 1898): 152–53; "Pauper Labor," 24 (January 1898): 61–62; "The White Man's Burden," 28 (April 1900): 282–93; in the *Brotherhood of Locomotive Firemen and Enginemen's Magazine*, see "They'll Swarm the United States with Chinese Coolies Yet," 5; "Industrial and Commercial Barons Determined to Flood United States with Chinese Coolies," 5–6; "Japanese Immigration Problem," 12–14; "Immigration Tidal Wave Threatens Welfare of American Workers," 8. In *Railroad Trainmen*, see "Aliens in the Majority in Basic Industry," 27–28; "The Melting Pot a Disappointment," 36 (September 1919): 627–29.

37. Lawrence Glickman, "Inventing the 'American Standard of Living': Gender,

Race and Working-Class Identity, 1880–1925," *Labor History*, 34 (Spring-Summer 1993): 226–27. Also see "The American Standard of Living," *Railroad Trainmen's Journal*, 19 (September 1902): 682–86; "Protection to American Labor," *Locomotive Firemen's Magazine*, 20 (May 1896): 321.

38. *Railroad Trainmen's Journal*, 15 (October 1898): 852; "The Crime of Competition," *Railroad Trainmen's Journal*, 15 (November 1898): 917; "Starving Miners," *Locomotive Firemen's Magazine*, 13 (August 1889): 707; "Omens of Strife," *Railroad Trainmen's Journal*, 19 (July 1902): 553. In the *Railroad Trainmen's Journal*, also see 15 (October 1898): 852; "Negro Domination," 16 (September 1899): 880; "Illinois Miners Win," 15 (December 1898): 1005–06. In *Locomotive Firemen's Magazine*, see "The Mining Situation," 23 (November 1897); 25 (November 1898): 541–42. On the mining conflicts, see Victor Hicken, "The Virden and Pana Mine Wars of 1898," *Journal of the Illinois State Historical Society*, 52 (Summer 1959): 263–78.

39. "The Negro and the Labor Question," *Locomotive Firemen's Magazine*, 21 (July 1896): 4.

40. M. E. Dowdy, "The Negro Fireman," *Locomotive Firemen's Magazine*, 30 (March 1901): 441.

41. In the *Locomotive Firemen's Magazine*, see Member of 522, Shreveport, La., "The Negro and Organized Labor in the South," 33 (September 1902): 426–27; Member of 76, Berkeley, Va., "The Negro Problem," 33 (September 1902): 427; Dilar, Mer Rouge, La., "The Negro and Organized Labor in the South," 33 (September 1902): 435–36; C. E. Pane, Augusta, Ga., "Negro vs. White Firemen," 27 (August 1899): 203–04; W. L. F., Missouri Valley, Ia., "Current Comment," 27 (November 1899): 593–95.

42. "Report on Committee on Welfare of the Order, Organizing Non-Union Men," *Proceedings of the Twelfth Biennial Conventions of the Brotherhood of Locomotive Firemen and Enginemen Beginning June 6, 1910, St. Paul, Minnesota* (St. Paul, 1910), 464, 466; W. W. Slaby, "Report of Special Organizer," *Proceedings of the Twelfth Biennial Convention of the Brotherhood of Locomotive Firemen . . . 1910*, 472, 478; also printed in "Special Organizer for Southeastern States," *President's Report to the Twelfth Biennial Convention, Brotherhood of Locomotive Firemen and Enginemen* (1910), 54–61; A. G. Walker, "McDonald, W.Va.," *Railroad Trainmen's Journal*, 20 (October 1903): 774–75.

43. Timothy Shea, "Conditions of the Brotherhood in the South," *Locomotive Firemen and Enginemen's Magazine*, 45 (September 1908): 406. Also see C.S. Daniel, Member of Lodge 80, "White Firemen Not Wanted," *Locomotive Firemen and Enginemen's Magazine*, 58 (May 1915): 609; Lacy, *Seventh Annual Report of the Bureau of Labor Statistics of . . . North Carolina . . . 1893*, 103–04; *Report of the Eight-Hour Commission*, 339.

44. C. J. Goff, "The Brotherhood in the South—The Negro Fireman Problem," *Locomotive Firemen and Enginemen's Magazine*, 60 (June 1916): 679–82; "Southern Region—Operating Conditions," *Railway Age*, 66 (March 14, 1919): 594.

45. J. C. Hall, Div. 309, "Colored Firemen," *Locomotive Engineers' Monthly Journal*, 33 (April 1899): 251–53; also see J. C. Hall, "The Negro Fireman and Promotion," *Locomotive Firemen's Magazine*, 27 (July 1899): 81–82.

46. Member of Lodge 201, "Employment Conditions in the South," *Locomotive Firemen and Enginemen's Magazine*, 57 (December 1914): 748. Also see "The Negro Fireman Question," *Locomotive Firemen and Enginemen's Magazine*, 59 (September 1915): 357–58; A. P. Kelly, "Southern Federated Board," in "President's Report to the Twelfth Biennial Convention," *Report of Grand Lodge Officers, Brotherhood of Locomotive Firemen and Enginemen, Twelfth Annual Convention, St. Paul, Minnesota, June 1910*, 182; "Argument of W. S. Carter," in *Proceedings, Arbitration between the Eastern Railroads and the Brotherhood of Locomotive Firemen and Enginemen at Waldorf Astoria Hotel, New York, March 26 to April 5, 1913* (New York, 1913), 3:2365; *Report of the Eight-Hour Commission*, 414–15.

47. Robert L. Mays to W. S. Carter, July 8, 1919, and the affidavits of Thomas C. Jefferson and Walter Jones, in File: Robert L. Mays, Atlantic Coast Line Railroad, in

Subject Classified General File of the Division of Labor, U.S. Railroad Administration, R.G. 14, in James Grossman, ed., *Black Workers in the Era of the Great Migration, 1916–1929* (Frederick, Md., 1985), Reel 9.

48. A White Fireman, St. Augustine, Florida, "Negro Firemen," *Locomotive Firemen's Magazine*, 27 (July 1899): 83; Goff, "Brotherhood in the South," 680–81.

49. Ex-L&N Brakeman, "From the South," *Railroad Trainmen's Journal*, 16 (April 1899): 346; "Argument of W. S. Carter on Behalf of the Brotherhood of Locomotive Firemen and Enginemen, April 4, 1913," in *Proceedings, Arbitraion between the Eastern Railroads and the Brotherhood of Locomotive Firemen and Enginemen*, 3: 2365–66. Also see New Orleans *Daily Picayune*, April 6, 1913; Samuel T. Graves, "The Negro No Good," *Railroad Trainmen's Journal*, 17 (June 1900): 505–06.

50. Goff, "Brotherhood in the South," 681; *Report of the Eight-Hour Commission*, 414; Jack, "The Negro Firemen," *Locomotive Firemen's Magazine*, 22 (January 1897): 58, 60; "Georgia Railroad Strike — The Negro as a Citizen," *Locomotive Firemen and Enginemen's Magazine*, 47 (December 1909): 893; *Atlanta Journal*, June 25, 1909; "Grand Fork," *Railroad Trainmen's Journal*, 17 (June 1900): 506–07; W. E. B. Du Bois, ed., *The Negro Artisan: Report of a Social Study Made under the Direction of Atlanta University* (Atlanta, 1902), 115–16; Gaston, "History of the Negro Wage Earner in Georgia," 238–39.

51. "The Negro Firemen Problem," *Locomotive Firemen's Magazine*, 26 (May 1899): 539–42; "The Negro and the Labor Question," *Locomotive Firemen's Magazine*, 21 (July 1896): 4–6; "Negro Wages Must Go," *Locomotive Firemen's Magazine*, 26 (January 1899): 109–10; Frank W. Trainman, "Another Problem," *Railroad Trainmen's Journal*, 20 (February 1903): 136.

52. J. C. Clarke to T. Morris Chester, April 29, 1886, President's In-Letters, J. C. Clarke, January 1–April 30, 1886, 1C5.2, Illinois Central Papers, Special Collections, Newberry Library, Chicago; *Report of the Eight-Hour Commission* 414. Also see David L. Lightner, *Labor on the Illinois Central Railroad 1852–1900: The Evolution of an Industrial Environment* (New York, 1977); C. M. Kittle, Federal Manager, to B. L. Winchell, January 18, 1919, in Records of the Division of Labor, Case Files of G. W. W. Hanger, Assistant Director, Division of Labor, 1918–1920, U.S. Railroad Administration, R.G. 14; *Report of the Industrial Commission*, Report 17, 217 (also cited in Du Bois, *Negro Artisan*, 169).

53. Paul Worthman, "Black Workers and Labor Unions in Birmingham, Alabama, 1897–1904," *Labor History*, 10 (Summer 1969): 375–407; Reid, *Negro Membership in American Labor Unions*, 57. The employer practice of recomposing the labor force along new racial and ethnic lines to forestall unionization was hardly unique to the South or the railroad industry. See White, "Race, Ethnicity, and Gender in the Railroad Work Force," 265–83; Yuju Ichioka, "Asian Immigrant Coal Miners and the United Mine Workers of America: Race and Class at Rock Springs, Wyoming, 1907," *Amerasia*, 6 (1970): 1–23; Ichioka, "Japanese Immigrant Labor Contractors and the Northern Pacific and the Great Northern Railroad Companies, 1898–1907," *Labor History*, 21 (Summer 1980): 325–50; Yuzo Murayama, "Contractors, Collusion, and Competition: Japanese Immigrant Railroad Laborers in the Pacific Northwest, 1898–1911," *Explorations in Economic History*, 21 (July 1984): 290–305.

54. Goff, "Brotherhood in the South," 680; "Negro and the Labor Question," 4–6; "Special Organizer for Southeastern States," *Proceedings of the Twelfth Biennial Convention of the Brotherhood of Locomotive Firemen . . . 1910*, 471.

55. William Z. Ripley, "Appendix VI: Railway Wage Schedules and Agreements," *Report of the Eight-Hour Commission*, 272; "Chesapeake and Ohio Railroad," in "President's Report to the Twelfth Biennial Convention Brotherhood of Locomotive Firemen and Enginemen," *Report of Grand Lodge Officers, Brotherhood of Locomotive Firemen and Enginemen, Twelfth Annual Convention, St. Paul, Minnesota, June 1910*, 222.

56. H. O. Teat, Acting Vice President, "Cincinnati, New Orleans & Texas Pacific Railway: 'Negro Question,' Resulting in Strike," in "Report of International President,"

Quarterly Report of the International Officers, Brotherhood of Locomotive Firemen and Enginemen, 4 (April 1, 1911): 84–85; "Firemen's Strike on the Queen & Crescent," *Railway Age Gazette,* 50 (March 24, 1911): 703–04; *Commercial Tribune,* March 17, 1911; Louisville *Courier-Journal,* March 18, 1911; "Strike on the Queen and Crescent," *Locomotive Firemen and Enginemen's Magazine,* 50 (April 1911): 519–20; *The Crisis,* 1 (April 1911): 7–8; "STRIKE: Statement of the Firemen's Position in the Strike Now on the C.N.O. & T.P. Ry," in File 42, Erdman Act Case Files, Records of the National Mediation Board, Record Group 13, Washington National Records Center, Suitland, Md.; Chattanooga *Daily Times,* March 24, 1911; March 10, 1911. On the Queen & Crescent Route, see "Southern Railway System—Historical Sketch," and "Queen & Crescent Route," in Richard E. Prince, *Steam Locomotives and Boats, Southern Railway System, Premier Carrier of the South* (Green River, Wy., 1965), 5, 35.

57. Cincinnati *Commercial Tribune,* March 7, 1911; "Strike on the Queen and Crescent," 520; Teat, "Cincinnati, New Orleans & Texas Pacific Railway," 94; Louisville *Courier-Journal,* March 15, 1911; "Firemen's Strike on the Queen & Crescent," 703. For contemporary accounts of the strike, see "General News Section," *Railway Age Gazette,* 50 (March 17, 1911); "Q. & C. Firemen's Strike Settled," *Railway Age Gazette,* 50 (March 31, 1911): 803; "Settlement of Queen and Crescent Strike," *Locomotive Firemen and Enginemen's Magazine,* 50 (May 1911): 655–57; Louisville *Courier-Journal,* March 10–16, 18–21, 23, 26, 27, 1911; *Louisville Times,* March 10, 11, 13–18, 21, 23–25, 1911; Chattanooga *Daily Times,* March 9–16, 18–21, 23, 26, 27, 1911; Cincinnati *Commercial Tribune,* March 7–18, 21–26, 28, 1911; Birmingham *Age-Herald,* March 10, 26, 1911; *Cleveland Press,* March 13, 1911; Spero and Harris, *Black Worker,* 291–92.

58. "The Firemen's Strike," *The Crisis,* 2 (May 1911): 16; "Settlement," and "Memorandum of Agreement, March 25, 1911," in File 42, Erdman Act Case Files, Records of the National Mediation Board, R.G. 13, Washington National Records Center.

59. "Settlement of Queen and Crescent Strike," 656; Jackson, Tennessee, *Daily Sun,* quoted in "Settlement of Queen and Crescent Strike," 657, and in Teat, "Cincinnati, New Orleans & Texas Pacific Railway," 101; "Firemen's Strike," 16.

60. Herbert R. Northrup, "The Negro in the Railway Unions," *Phylon,* 5 (1944): 160; C. Vann Woodward, *Origins of the New South 1877–1913* (1951; rpt. edn., Baton Rouge, La., 1971), 229. Classic and more recent works that have tended to emphasize discrimination and exclusion include Spero and Harris, *Black Worker;* Herman D. Bloch, "Craft Unions and the Negro in Historical Perspective," *Journal of Negro History,* 43 (1958): 10–33; Philip S. Foner, *Organized Labor and the Black Worker 1619–1981* (1974; rpt. edn., New York, 1981); Michael Honey, "The Labor Movement and Racism in the South: A Historical Overview," in Marvin J. Berlowitz and Ronald S. Edari, eds., *Racism and the Denial of Human Rights: Beyond Ethnicity* (Minneapolis, Minn., 1984), 77–94; Herbert Hill, "Race, Ethnicity and Organized Labor: The Opposition to Affirmative Action," *New Politics,* 1 (Winter 1987): 31–82; Harris, *The Harder We Run;* Joe William Trotter, Jr., *Coal, Class, and Color: Blacks in Southern West Virginia, 1915–32* (Urbana, Ill., 1990); Lewis, *In Their Own Interests;* Norrell, "Caste in Steel."

61. On the tradition of black unionism in the late nineteenth and early twentieth century, see Arnesen, "Following the Color Line of Labor," 43–87; Eric Arnesen, "'What's on the Black Worker's Mind'? African-American Workers and the Union Tradition," *Gulf Coast Historical Review,* 10 (Fall 1994): 7–30; Jeffrey Gould, "The Strike of 1887: Louisiana Sugar War," *Southern Exposure,* 12 (November-December 1984): 45–55; Melton Alonza McLaurin, *The Knights of Labor in the South* (Westport, Conn., 1978); Peter Rachleff, *Black Labor in Richmond, 1865–1890* (1984; rpt. edn., Urbana, Ill., 1989); Rachleff, "Black Richmond and the Knights of Labor," in Jerry Lembcke, ed., *Research in Urban Sociology,* 1 (1989): 23–52.

62. Eric Arnesen, *Waterfront Workers of New Orleans: Race, Class and Politics, 1863–1923* (New York, 1991); Letwin, "Race, Class, and Industrialization in the New South"; Herbert G. Gutman, "The Negro and the United Mine Workers of America: The Career and Letters of Richard L. Davis and Something of Their Meaning: 1890–1900," in Julius

Jacobson, ed., *The Negro and the American Labor Movement* (New York, 1968); Ronald L. Lewis, *Black Coal Miners in America: Race, Class, and Community Conflict 1780–1980* (Lexington, Ky., 1987); Worthman, "Black Workers and Labor Unions in Birmingham"; Stephen Brier, "Interracial Organizing in the West Virginia Coal Industry: The Participation of Black Mine Workers in the Knights of Labor and the United Mine Workers, 1880–1894," in Gary M. Fink and Merl E. Reed, eds., *Essays in Southern Labor History: Selected Papers, Southern Labor Conference, 1976* (Westport, Conn., 1976), 18–45; James Green, "The Brotherhood of Timber Workers 1910–1913: A Radical Response to Industrial Capitalism in the Southern U.S.A.," *Past and Present*, 60 (August 1973): 161–200; David R. Roediger, "Gaining a Hearing for Black-White Unity: Convington Hall and the Complexities of Race, Gender and Class," in Roediger, *Towards the Abolition of Whiteness: Essays on Race, Politics, and Working Class History* (New York, 1994), 127–80.

63. A Member of 426, Birmingham, Ala., "The Negro Question," *Locomotive Firemen's Magazine*, 22 (February 1897): 125–26.

64. "Current Comment," *Locomotive Firemen's Magazine*, 25 (August 1898): 214–15; S. H. LaLonde, Denison, Tex., "The Negro Fireman," *Locomotive Firemen's Magazine*, 30 (March 1901): 440–41; George H. Peters, "The Negro and Organized Labor in the South," *Locomotive Firemen's Magazine*, 33 (August 1902): 286. White brakemen engaged in a comparable discussion in the pages of the *Railroad Trainmen's Journal*; See "Colored Labor in Organizations," 16 (November 1898): 912–14.

65. Mary Ann Clawson, *Constructing Brotherhood: Class, Gender, and Fraternalism* (Princeton, N.J., 1989), 129–33. On masculinity and fraternal culture, also see Mark C. Carnes, *Secret Ritual and Manhood in Victorian America* (New Havens, Conn., 1989); Mark C. Carnes and Clyde Griffen, eds., *Meanings for Manhood: Constructions of Masculinity in Victorian America* (Chicago, 1990). On working class identity and "manhood," see Baron, *Work Engendered*.

66. Northrup, "Negro in the Railway Unions," 160.

67. "So wide are the local variations in time required for promotion that no average can be ascertained or would be significant," investigators found in 1918. *Report of the Eight-Hour Commission*, 390–91.

68. Southern Tallow Pot, "Organizing the Negro," *Locomotive Fireman's Magazine*, 33 (September 1902): 434.

69. "The Labor Factor in Race Troubles," *Literary Digest*, 17 (December 24, 1898): 740; "Union Meeting at Norfolk, Va.," *Locomotive Fireman's Magazine*, 26 (January 1899): 118–20.

70. Birmingham *Age-Herald*, August 14, 1891; *Mobile Register*, August 14, 1891.

71. "Memorandum" [c. 1930s] and "Narrative Statement Covering Negro Train and Engine Service Employes on Southern Lines—Illinois Central System, From the Recollection of Old Reliable Employees and from the Best Records Available on the Subject," in Folder: Discrimination of Colored Employees, Box 8, Records of the Illinois Central Gulf Railroad, Selected Personnel Department Files, Labor-Management Documentation Center, Martin P. Catherwood Library, Cornell University, Ithaca, N.Y. In the Papers of the National Association for the Advancement of Colored People, NAACP Administrative File, Subject File, Unions—Railroads—January 5–August 21, 1921, Box C414, Library of Congress, see Statement of Brakeman Bob Grant; Jesse Ficklin to J. H. Eiland, May 17, 1921; Walker James to *The Crisis*, March 8, 1921. Also see Norfolk *Journal and Guide*, September 24, 1921; *New York Age*, August 6, 20, 1921; *Birmingham Reporter*, December 3, 1921; Ross, *All Manner of Men*, 119. On earlier attacks, see "Blackhanders Drive Negroes from Train," *McDowell Times*, July 7, 1916. On the attacks of the 1930s, see Hilton Butler, "Murder for the Job," *The Nation*, 137 (July 12, 1933): 44–45; Ira De A. Reid, "Negro Firemen," *The Nation*, 137 (September 6, 1933): 272–73; T. Arnold Hill, "Railway Employees Rally to Save Their Jobs," *Opportunity*, 12 (November 1934): 346–47; Horace R. Cayton and George S. Mitchell, "Appendix B: Murders of Negro Firemen," *Black Workers and the New Unions* (Chapel Hill, N.C., 1939), 439–45.

72. For selected secondary treatments of the strike, see Taillon, "Trouble on the Southern Railroads"; Hugh B. Hammett, "Labor and Race: The Georgia Railroad Strike of 1909," *Labor History*, 16 (Fall 1975): 470–84; John Michael Matthews, "The Georgia 'Race Strike' of 1909," *Journal of Southern History*, 40 (November 1974): 613–30; John Dittmer, *Black Georgia in the Progressive Era 1900–1920* (Urbana, Ill., 1977), 33–34; Spero and Harris, *Black Worker*, 289–90. For a sample of primary accounts, see *The Nation*, May 27, June 3, July 1, 8, 1909; "The Race Strike of the Georgia Railroad," *Railway World*, 8 (June 4, 1909): 455; "The Georgia Railroad Strike," *The Outlook* (June 5, 1909): 310–12; "The Georgia Strike Arbitration," *Harper's Weekly*, 53 (July 3, 1909); "The Georgia Railroad Strike," *Locomotive Firemen and Enginemen's Magazine*, 47 (August 1909): 255–69; *Proceedings of the Eleventh Biennial Convention of the Brotherhood of Locomotive Firemen and Enginemen Beginning September 14th, 1908, Columbus, Ohio* (1908), 619–20, 865; "Georgia Railroad and Atlanta Terminal," *Report, President, Brotherhood of Locomotive Firemen and Enginemen, Twelfth Biennial Convention, St. Paul, Minnesota, June 1910*, 290–311. For a sample of the response of the black press to the strike, see *Atlanta Independent*, May 29, June 5, 12, 26, July 3, 1909; *Savannah Tribune*, June 5, 1909; "Significance of Atlanta Strike," *The Colored American Magazine*, 16 (June 1909): 382–83. On race relations and labor in Georgia, see Clifford M. Kuhn, Harlon E. Joye, and E. Bernard West, *Living Atlanta: An Oral History of the City, 1914–1948* (Atlanta, Ga., 1990); Mercer Griffin Evans, "The History of the Organized Labor Movement in Georgia" (Ph.D. dissertation, University of Chicago, 1929).

73. "The Georgia Railroad Strike," *Locomotive Firemen and Enginemen's Magazine*, 47 (August 1909): 261–62; "The Negro Fireman Situation," *Locomotive Firemen and Enginemen's Magazine*, 47 (August 1909): 284–85; F. S. Foster, "Georgia Railroad Strike—Mistaken Ideas of the Press," *Locomotive Firemen and Enginemen's Magazine*, 47 (November 1909): 740.

74. "Chesapeake and Ohio Railroad," in "President's Report to the Twelfth Biennial Convention," *Report of the Grand Lodge Officers, Brotherhood of Locomotive Firemen and Enginemen, Twelfth Biennial Convention, St. Paul, Minnesota, June 1910*, 222; "Southern Railway," *Quarterly Report of the International Officers, Brotherhood of Locomotive Firemen and Enginemen*, 6 (October 1, 1911): 160–77; "Discrimination against White Trainmen," *Railroad Trainman*, 36 (November 1919): 804; "Circular of Instructions," *Railroad Trainman*, 37 (May 1920): 304.

75. *Report of the Eight-Hour Commission*, 413; Reid, *Negro Membership in American Labor Unions*, 57.

76. U.S. Railroad Labor Board, November 4, 1921, Decision No. 307 (Docket 138), Association of Colored Railway Trainmen vs. Illinois Central Railroad Company, Yazoo & Mississippi Valley Railroad Company, Docket No. 138, Subject: "Association of Colored Railway Trainmen . . . Petition . . . ," in Records of the National Mediation Board, R.G. 13, Washington National Records Center.

77. Petition to the Illinois Central Railroad Company, May 18, 1928, Records of the Illinois Central Gulf Railroad, Selected Personnel Department Files, Box 8, Folder: Discrimination—Assoc. of Colored Railway Trainmen, Labor-Management Documentation Center, Martin P. Catherwood Library.

78. Houston, "Foul Employment Practice on the Rails," 269. See also Charles S. Johnson, "Negroes in the Railway Industry," *Phylon*, 3 (1942): 5–14; Charles S. Johnson, "Negroes in the Railway Industry, Part II," *Phylon*, 3 (1942): 196–205; "Preliminary Summary Statement on the Employment of Negroes on Railroads," Papers of the National Urban League, Series 6, Research Department, Early Surveys, Box 89, Folder: Labor Union Survey Reports—1933, Library of Congress; Willard S. Townsend, "One American Problem and a Possible Solution," in Rayford W. Logan, ed., *What the Negro Wants* (Chapel Hill, N.C., 1944), 177–81.

NINE

"A Constant Struggle Between Interest and Humanity": Convict Labor in the Coal Mines of the New South

ALEX LICHTENSTEIN

When he made a tour of the recently defeated Confederate States following the Civil War, William "Pig Iron" Kelley told the erstwhile slaveholders that "in your devotion to your peculiar system of labor you have forgotten that iron and coal are the most potent agents of civilization." Kelley, a Republican Senator from Pennsylvania, fervently believed that industrialization offered the best hope for the rejuvenation of the New South.[1] Many southerners agreed. In the decades after the South's defeat, the region's geologists, investors, politicians, and boosters sang the praises of the untapped resources lying under the southern tip of the Appalachian chain. Once made accessible by rail lines, its advocates claimed, the bituminous coal fields, iron ore deposits, and limestone "flux" would make the mountain districts of Tennessee, Alabama, and Georgia "a region of coke-made iron on a scale grander than has ever been witnessed on the habitable globe." They envisioned nothing less than "a chain of fiery [iron] furnaces . . . that will illumine the whole eastern margin of the Cumberland Table-land."[2] By the 1880s some local observers noted that the coal and iron resources of Tennessee, Alabama, and Georgia were "destined to revolutionize the iron manufacture of the country." They admitted, however, that "the important factor in the question of the cheap production of iron is prison labor."[3]

During the last three decades of the nineteenth century the convict-lease system, a new "peculiar system of labor" unique to the postbellum South, emerged to play an important part in the development of the coal and iron industry in the region. Instead of being confined in a penitentiary, southern convicts were leased to the highest bidder, who was then responsible for feeding, clothing, and restraining them. In exchange, the lessee acquired the right to put the convicts to work. Unlike northern penitentiaries, which might contract prison labor to private entrepreneurs, in the South the state completely relinquished control and care of the convict population to the contractor. Private enterprises replaced the penitentiary; southern coal mines became, in essence, prisons.[4]

By using this system to lease convicts from the state, mine operators in Georgia, Tennessee, and Alabama built an industrial complex that, by the 1890s, produced nearly 40% of the open-market pig iron in the U.S.[5] Although convicts never represented more than 15% of the mine labor force in these states, the most powerful corporations based their success on it. They used the predictable, steady output of fuel from their convict mines to build their industrial empires, as they rose to dominate the Deep South's coal and iron industry, absorbed competitors, and repelled the United Mine Workers' (UMW) attempts to organized the southern field. These successful vertically integrated enterprises that mined coal, produced coke, and then made pig iron, relied on the prison system for the core of their labor force. Convicts consistently predominated in the region's largest and most productive coal mines.

Three companies became especially notorious for the leasing of thousands of state and county convicts drawn from the penal systems of Alabama, Tennessee, and Georgia. First among equals was the Tennessee Coal and Iron Company (TCI), one of the nation's largest coal and iron producers, the dominant coal company in Tennessee, and by the 1890s the source of one-half of Alabama's output of coal and pig iron. In 1871, as a fledgling corporation, TCI became the first coal mining operation in the postwar South to use convict miners; by the close of the century the company became the first in the New South to produce steel. TCI's fiercest competitor for domination of Alabama's Birmingham District, the Deep South's industrial center, was the Sloss Iron and Steel Company, the state's second-largest pig iron producer. By the 1890s, 500 convicts worked in Sloss's Coalburg mines. Finally, Georgia's leading coal producer, the Dade Coal Company, supplied coal and coke to the iron furnaces of Chattanooga and the rolling mills of Atlanta, and was owned by that state's most powerful politician, Joseph E. Brown.[6] Few doubted the importance of these corporations to a region in desperate need of an economic jump-start. "The enforced employment of so many laborers in the mines," proclaimed one defender of the convict-lease, encouraged the growth of "branches of manufacturing, dependent on the coal mines for fuel" and stimulated basic industry in the South otherwise "impossible of development by free labor."[7]

Between 1870 and 1928, when Alabama finally abolished convict leasing, thousands of workers, most of them African-Americans, entered the South's coal mines "through the rugged gates of the penitentiary."[8] Convict labor attracted southern industrialists for several reasons. First, it was cheap. Joseph Brown's Dade Coal Company, for example, paid a fixed fee to Georgia for a twenty-year lease (1879–1899) of an undetermined number of convicts. By the mid-1890s the company worked over 600 long-term prisoners in its mines, at a daily cost of 3¢ a day per convict, at a time when free miners commanded $2.00 a day. The low cost of labor in convict mines also drove down wages in competitive free labor mines. The U. S. Bureau of Labor reported in 1886 that the "mine owners say that they could not work at a profit without the lowering effect in wages of convict-labor competition." The UMW, which objected strenuously to the employment of convicts in coal mines, complained that "miners working near the mines where convict labor is employed are working at lessor [sic] rates than they would if they had no convicts around them."[9]

The low cost of convict labor was complemented by what employers referred to euphemistically as its "reliability." Shelby Harrison, an investigator for *The Survey*, remarked that "in [Alabama's] Birmingham district most of the large companies have to keep from 50 to 75 per cent larger number of negroes on the pay roll than they expect to be working day to day" because of absenteeism. But in firms using convicts "300 men, for instance, go to sleep at night, and 300 men get up the next day and are ready for work." Harrison concluded: "[Convict labor] is regular. I was told by a number of employers that that was one of the greatest things they liked about it."[10]

Southerners contrasted the regularity of convict laborers to the alleged deficiencies of black workers, who in the prevailing racist view of the day, were believed to "work only long enough to get a little cash, whereupon they quit work and live in idleness upon their earnings."[11] "Without convicts," one Alabama coal superintendent complained in 1884, "we have to depend on free negroes to do the tramming, driving & dumping [of coal]. If the weather is cold, or if there is a funeral, a marriage or a circus in the neighborhood they are rarely in place." J. W. Sloss, owner of Sloss Iron and Steel in Birmingham, complained that to work his furnaces with free labor he needed 269 men but his monthly payroll averaged 569. He concluded: "That is one of our troubles [in the South]. The irregularity of labor." He had no such problems with the black convicts who supplied the coke and coal for the operation of his iron furnaces.[12]

Southern coal operators subscribed to the prevalent notion that in the mines "convict labor [was] more reliable and productive than free labor" and that "the convict accomplishes more work than the free laborer." Convicts were "forced to work steadily [and] their output may be depended upon."[13] Thus not only did convict labor end the problem of labor turnover and absenteeism, but compulsion replaced incentive as the mechanism of labor extraction. This was important during the "hand-loading era" of coal mining, when management exercised only weak control over the labor process inside the mines. The free miner worked without supervision at the mine face, blasting coal loose and loading it into a coal car which he sent to the head of the mine, and was paid by the ton. The notorious "miner's freedom" hewed from this system constrained management's ability to direct the pace of work and the conditions of mine labor. The South's convict mine operators, however, turned the tonnage system to their advantage. The piece-price system allowed free labor to contend for control over production; but in convict mines it became a task system that management used to push labor extraction to the limits of physical endurance.[14] "Having absolute control of the [convict] labor . . . [will] make it a certainty that the labor can be profitably used," was the chilling calculation made by Colonel Arthur S. Colyar, the man who initiated convict leasing for TCI in Tennessee.[15]

Prisoners in southern mines commonly had the task of mining four tons of coal a day or they would receive corporal punishment. Many convicts, however, failed to produce the prescribed amount of coal, due to factors such as their own physical limitations, poor conditions in the mines, or shortages of coal cars. An inspection of Alabama's Coalburg mines in 1894 revealed an "unprecedented amount of whipping" and concluded that "all of this whipping has been for failure of convicts to get their tasks." Of course, as another convict inspector informed the governor, "it is very natural for a man who expects to get his pay out of the labor of the convict to want him tasked to his upmost capacity."[16]

After beating a convict several times for coming up short, the "whipping boss" might reduce the allotted task. Yet, 40% of the convicts in one Georgia mine were unable to finish their task by nightfall. Those who finished early, on the other hand, got no respite. One ex-convict stated: "if they found a man could dig a task and get through with it by three or four o'clock in the evening they would increase it, and fix it so that he couldn't get out at that time."[17] Significantly, the leather strap used to punish convicts for failure to work at a pace set by the company was known colloquially as a "negro regulator." An Alabama convict inspector pointed to the brutal logic of the task system when he observed that "so long as the lease system is kept up, [whipping] will have to continue, for any other kind of punishment infringes the right to the labor of the convict, which the contractor has."[18]

Southern coal operators had additional reasons to depend on convict labor. As the UMW noted with disgust, convict labor could "prevent the spread of organization and [is] an 'effectual preventative' during a strike."[19] The most successful coal operators in the region never hid their knowledge of this fact. Arthur S. Colyar, the founder of TCI, remarked in 1872 that "to put on foot successful mining operations in Tennessee with two strikes a year was impossible. . . . This has been remedied by convict labor."[20] It gave a competitive advantage permitting Tennessee's coal industry to "avoid the conflict between labor and capital which has made the immense mines of Pennsylvania a boiling cauldron under the commerce of the nation," Colyar concluded melodramatically.[21] Northern visitors favorably contrasted southern coal mining with the industry in their region. "The condition of the coal trade in the North has been clearly portrayed by the almost constant strikes and disputes between employers and employed. . . . while here [in Alabama] there has been no interruption in the production of coal," remarked the editor of a Philadelphia paper during a trip to the South in the 1880s. He indicated that the use of convicts was a major cause of labor's inability to challenge the southern coal operators.[22]

The convict mines of Alabama proved instrumental in the defeat of the UMW during the massive strikes of the 1890s. "Free men cannot contend and strike in a state that the largest coal output is worked by convict labor," complained a UMW district organizer in Alabama in the wake of the failed strike of 1894, when 1,600 convicts continued to turn out coal while free miners stayed out of the mines. Mining companies readily agreed. Henry F. DeBardeleben told the Alabama General Assembly that "convict labor competing with free labor is advantageous to the mine owner. If all were free miners they could combine and strike and thereby put up the price of coal." As late as 1923, more than three decades after the UMW first attempted to organize the Alabama field, industrialist James Bowron predicted: "So long as coal is mined here by convicts the mine workers will never close this district." In Georgia, where virtually all coal miners were convicts, the UMW admitted that it was "questionable if ever a member of the United Mine Workers" was in the state.[23]

Faced with involuntary convict strikebreakers, free miners in Tennessee, however, took militant action to insure that "they would no longer be forced to compete . . . with men who had by their criminal acts forfeited the right to liberty."[24] The notorious "convict war" of east Tennessee in 1891 and 1892 was a direct result of attempts by mine operators to replace free workers with convicts.[25] Within the space of thirteen months, Tennessee's coal miners attacked five convict camps. When the legislature subsequently failed to abolish convict leasing, the miners planned and executed "the final attack on the convict camps and the release of the prisoners," burning TCI's largest convict camp to the ground, and freeing the prisoners. As the miners' paper pointed out, in Tennessee the convict question ultimately "resolved itself into a contest of labor against capital."[26]

The anti-convict labor insurrections in the Tennessee coal field reduced the state's coal output by 15% in 1892. In an internal report TCI noted that "we have sustained the most serious losses by reason of the 'Convict troubles' . . . which resulted in the actual destruction of much valuable property, the temporary stoppage of our works, the increased cost of the material produced by convict labor, and the general demoralization of all our labor."[27] Three years later Tennessee abolished convict leasing.

The Tennessee "convict war" was but the most dramatic illustration of the potential cost of convict labor to those who exploited it. Although this form of labor recruitment initially allowed the Deep South's most powerful corporations to overcome obstacles to industrial development and contributed to the region's economic growth, in the long run convict labor proved costly to the firms that relied upon it, and perhaps even to the economic health of the region as a whole. Convict leasing solved the problems of labor recruitment and turnover, but it also curtailed the capitalist's freedom to dismiss labor if coal sales dropped. Low labor costs aided the rapid development of weakly capitalized industries, but retarded the introduction of modern mining methods and machinery, and hurt the region's long-run ability to compete with northern mines. In addition, maintaining low labor costs required political monopolization of lease contracts to preclude the introduction of competitive bidding for convicts. Convict labor weakened the United Mine Workers, but it also generated violent opposition on the part of free miners. Coal operators could use the whip to enforce tasks in the mines, but the convicts' resistance to exploitation caused inefficiency and hurt the quality of the coal produced. While capitalists readily turned to the state to provide them with a bound labor force, the state in turn claimed the right to regulate the labor of convicts and protect them from the worst abuses of the lease system.

Even in the earliest days of convict mining, TCI came up against the potential dangers of the system's fixed labor costs. Arthur Colyar temporarily lost his control of the company in the Panic of 1873 because of indebtedness to the convict contractor who worked the labor. Similarly, in the depression year of 1894 TCI's director complained that "our company has a large number of convicts on their hands for which we have no profitable employment," and sought to transfer them from the mines to railroad construction work. "I think the convict system is injurious to employers of convicts, for in case of low price coal they are compelled to sell coal at any price to keep going, regardless of cost," testified an Alabama convict lessee during the depths of the depression of the 1890s.[28]

Nowhere did the economic pitfalls of over-reliance on convicts prove more disastrous than in Georgia, where almost the entire mine labor force consisted of prisoners. The Dade Coal Company went into receivership in the depression of the 1890s due to the cost of maintaining a convict labor force under a twenty-year lease that would not expire until 1899. For nearly two decades, the hundreds of convicts leased by Senator Joseph Brown and his partner and son Julius dug all the company's coal, stoked coke ovens, and mined iron ore; their labor was indispensable to the company's success and Georgia's growing industrial infrastructure.[29] But the tightly integrated operation left the Dade Coal Company extremely vulnerable to fluctuations in the price of pig iron, which dropped precipitously in the depression of the 1890s. Julius Brown insisted that it was the fixed costs of the convict-lease that proved fatal to the company.[30]

Brown, appointed receiver for the indebted corporation, had as part of his task "to provide means for the care and keeping of the convicts" leased to the Dade Coal mines. In attempting to reorganize the company, he desperately wrote to an investor in May 1895, pointing out that "we owe the State for nearly all the convict rental last year and the rental is due this year . . . and the State is pressing us for payment."[31] More damaging still to the company's financial prospects was that the convict force was a huge drain on resources during a period of receivership, since it could not be discharged like free labor, but had to be fed, clothed, housed, and cared for.[32] After Dade Coal's assets were reorganized and sold off, Julius Brown claimed that he and the other stockholders of the company had "sacrificed their own interest to take care of the convicts." He later argued that "if he had not been compelled to care for the convicts, the properties under his control could have been shut down when it was not profitable to operate them."[33]

Not only did the inelasticity of forced labor hamper a company's ability to respond to the market, lessees also found themselves in charge of workers who had no incentive to engage in productive labor. At the end of the day the "whipping boss" in a convict mine would measure each convict's output and mete out punishment to those who failed to achieve their appointed task. Convicts found ways, however, of cheating the whipping boss. One common method was to load worthless slate at the bottom of a car in order to appear to make the task while digging less coal. This practice proved especially irksome to the coal companies, since too much slate "injures the class of coal in every respect," as one whipping boss lamented.[34] In addition to frequent punishment for "shortage," and "idleness," "slate," and other designations referring to convict unwillingness or inability to complete their tasks, the "whipping reports" also show beatings for "feigning illness." This practice, known among prisoners as "betting the doctor," was a popular means of "beating the company out of a day's work." Finally, as a last resort to defend themselves against exploitation, convicts might even strike, knock out mine props to cause a cave-in, or set fires in the mine.[35]

Moreover, convicts were sloppy workers, mostly digging "slack," or broken, powdery coal, good only for coking. The poor quality "lump" coal produced by convicts proved difficult to market. This was one of the reasons the owners of convict mines quickly built their own coke ovens. One operator complained that "we have lost standing in various markets from the employment of this class of labor." Whether their poor work was due to lack of skill and experience, indifference, or outright sabotage, coal operators quickly discovered that "convict labor and clean mining do not go together."[36]

In the face of convict recalcitrance, some coal operators expressed dissatisfaction with the productive capabilities of their bound labor force. When Tennessee's Monitor mine replaced locked-out free miners with convicts in 1891, they found it required 170 prisoners to replace their 125 free workers; production levels still declined even with this larger labor force. A fellow mine operator accused TCI of sub-leasing him "a class of poor convicts, such as should never be sent to the mines," who could dig only two-and-one-half tons of coal a day, instead of the requisite four.[37] In Alabama, convict workers drawn from the cotton fields were understood to be limited by "the want of skill and adaptability to mine work." The Alabama House reported in 1897 that "a large number worked in the mines [are] wholly unfit for the work." The legislators estimated that only about one-sixth of the prisoners working in Alabama's mines were "first class convicts" who could meet a four ton daily task.[38] Georgia's mines, worked entirely by convicts, consistently produced only one-half the coal dug per man by free labor. Even the general manager of the Dade Coal Company admitted that the "amount of coal . . . was nothing in proportion to the amount of coal gotten out in other mines with the same number of men."[39]

Indeed, the effort to extract the task from the convicts and to get the state to "upgrade" the quality of their laborers continuously vexed Alabama's coal operators, while state inspectors tried to keep exploitation within limits. Reporting that 248 "darkies" had been punished in a single month at Sloss's Coalburg mines, a convict inspector urged that the company "should remove the difficulty of an unjust task which apparently made it necessary for [the warden] to punish them."[40] Similarly, in Georgia, task work came under scrutiny in the routine Grand Jury and legislative investigations of the convict camps which passed for oversight of the lease system.[41] In Georgia, the authority of a lessee to compel labor and maximize output was exercised through the whipping boss, who was solely authorized to administer corporal punishment in the mines. The state ostensibly regulated this punishment by approving the appointment of whipping bosses, and after 1897, by making the whipping boss a deputy warden paid by the state, not by the lessee.[42] In practice, however, the whipping boss remained a loyal employee chosen by the lessee, and might even be the general manager of the coal mine in which prisoners worked. Even while on the state payroll, many whipping bosses continued to receive a salary from the coal operator, to keep these wardens from "becoming cross wise with the Company."[43]

Nevertheless, lessees sometimes found their desire to wring as much labor as possible from the convicts checked by the state's feeble efforts to protect the prisoners' welfare. One Georgia coal operator complained to the prison commission that at the end of the day his convicts broke into song, and that "men ought to be worked so hard they couldn't sing." He demanded that the state officials at this mine get more work out of his labor force. The chairman of the commission, Judge Joseph S. Turner, responded that "the contractors only buy the labor," which the state had a right to regulate to ensure humane treatment. Yet the prison commission ultimately accepted the subordination of all penal functions to the single goal of labor extraction: "No punishment shall be administered to a convict except in cases where it is reasonably necessary to enforce discipline or *compel work or labor by the convicts*," the commission proclaimed.[44] This is precisely what made the convict-lease an especially cruel penal system.

Lagging productivity, convict resistance and increased state intervention to restrict the lessee's exploitation of prison labor gradually eroded the convict-lease system in Georgia. In addition to these factors, after 1900 Georgia's coal operators found themselves bidding competitively against the state's brickyards and turpentine farms for convicts. With the end of the twenty-year lease system, companies paid for convicts *per capita*. Competitive bidding quickly drove up the prices, with coal operators paying between $225 and $250 a year for each prisoner brought to the mines. As a result, "no [financial] advantage accrues to the contractor employing [convict] labor, except that his supply is more constant," concluded the Georgia prison commission in 1902.[45]

At the same time, without the mechanized coal picks that revolutionized mining in other coal fields, Georgia's mine productivity fell even further behind states where free miners predominated. By 1900, 25% of the nation's bituminous coal was mined by machine, and a decade later the figure was 41%. Mining machines were not used at all in Georgia until 1905 because reliance on forced labor inhibited the incentive to modernize. "As a large part of the work in [Georgia's] mines is done by convicts," the U. S. Geological Survey reported in 1905, "mining machines have not been introduced."[46]

Between 1895 and 1928 the combination of the inelastic and ever-increasing cost of convict labor, the convicts' indifferent work and persistent resistance to the task system, the state's encroachment on the lessee's control of labor and punishment, and the opposition of organized labor, ended the use of convicts in the coal mines of Tennessee (1895), Georgia (1908), and Alabama (1928). The convict-lease usually was replaced by public chain gangs working on the states' roads, a system whose brutality quickly came to symbolize the harshness and racial inequality of southern punishment.

Unfortunately, we have yet to learn the lessons of the convict coal mine and the chain gangs which supplanted it. In the 1990s, the idea of making prisoners work and the control of convicts by private firms both are increasingly popular "solutions" for America's penal crisis, as seen on the county roads of Alabama and at automobile plants in Ohio.[47] Before embracing these panaceas, however, Americans would do well to recall the words of the Alabama convict inspector who witnessed forced prison labor in that state's mines: "no system is a good one which allows the labor of a convict to be controlled by any one interested in its results. There is a constant struggle between interest and humanity."[48]

NOTES

1. William D. Kelley, *The Old South and the New: A Series of Letters* (New York, 1888), p. 3; American Iron and Steel Institute, *Bulletin* 20 (Dec. 29, 1886): 346–47.

2. John T. Milner, *Alabama: As It Was, As It Is, and As It Will Be* (Montgomery, 1876), p. 192; Tennessee Bureau of Agriculture, Statistics and Mines, *Tennessee: Its Agricultural and Mineral Wealth* (Nashville, 1876), pp. 129–30.

3. American Iron and Steel Association, *Bulletin* 20 (Dec. 29, 1886): 347.

4. The best description and summary of the various systems of nineteenth-century penal labor in the United States is found in U.S. Bureau of Labor, *Convict Labor,*

Second Annual Report of the Commissioner of Labor, 1886 (Washington, 1886), pp. 371–96. On the organization of convict labor in the North, see also Glen A. Gildemeister, *Prison Labor and Convict Competition With Free Workers in Industrializing America, 1840–1890* (New York, 1987).

5. U.S. Geological Survey (hereafter USGS), *Mineral Resources of the United States,* 1883–84, 1889–90, 1891, 1900; Emory Q. Hawk, *Economic History of the South* (New York, 1934), p. 482. On industrial growth in this region, see Gerald D. Jaynes, *Branches Without Roots: Genesis of the Black Working Class in the American South, 1862–1882* (New York, 1986), pp. 268–72; Gavin Wright, *Old South, New South: Revolutions in the Southern Economy Since the Civil War* (New York, 1986), chap. 6; Victor S. Clark, *History of Manufactures in the United States,* vol. 2 (New York, 1949 [1929]), pp. 211–20; and C. Vann Woodward, *Origins of the New South, 1877–1913* (Baton Rouge, 1951), chaps. 5 & 11.

6. Tennessee Division of Mines, *Second Annual Report of the Commissioner of Labor and Inspector of Mines* (Nashville, 1893), pp. 48, 50, 52, 62–63, 303 & 342; Tennessee Division of Mines, *Fourth Annual Report of the Bureau of Labor, Statistics and Mines* (Nashville, 1895), p. 283; USGS, *Mineral Resources,* 1891, p. 320; "Report on Tracy City Division of TCI, April 1, 1895," pp. 4 & 7, Erskine Ramsey papers, Birmingham Public Library (hereafter BPL); TCI *Annual Report for the Fiscal Year Ending January 31, 1892,* p. 3; Alabama, *Second Biennial Report of the Inspectors of Mines, 1898* (Birmingham, 1898), pp. 16, 19–20, chart; Alabama, *Second Biennial Report of the Board of Inspectors of Convicts, 1896–1898* (Montgomery, 1898), pp. 9–10 & 19; TCI, *Annual Report for the Fiscal Year Ending Dec. 31st, 1897* p. 6; Georgia, Principal Keeper of the Penitentiary, *Report,* 1880–1897, Georgia Department of Archives and History (hereafter GDAH), Atlanta, Georgia; Alex Lichtenstein, *Twice the Work of Free Labor: The Political Economy of Convict Labor in the New South* (Verso, 1995).

7. T. J. Hill, "Experience in Mining Coal With Convicts," in National Prison Association, *Proceedings of the Annual Congress, 1897* (Pittsburgh, 1898), p. 390.

8. *Ibid.*

9. Georgia General Assembly, *Acts and Resolutions,* 1876, pp. 40–43; Georgia Principal Keeper, *Report,* 1895–96, pp. 9 & 104; U.S. Bureau of Labor, *Convict Labor,* p. 301; *United Mine Workers Journal* (hereafter UMWJ), Sept. 15, 1892, p. 4 and Jan. 26, 1899, p. 4.

10. U.S. Congress, House of Representatives, *Hearings Before the Committee on Investigation of United States Steel Corporation* (Washington, 1912), testimony of Shelby Harrison, p. 2982; see also John A. Fitch, "Birmingham District: Labor Conservation," *The Survey* 27 (Jan. 6, 1912): 1527–40.

11. H. H. Campbell, *The Manufacture of Iron and Steel* (New York, 1903), pp. 674–75.

12. E.W. Tutwiler to J.W. Johnston, Feb. 7, 1884, Correspondence, Folder 2, Coalburg Coal and Coke Company Records, Southern Railway Collection, Virginia Polytechnic University, Blacksburg, Virginia, p. 18; U.S. Congress, Senate Committee on Education and Labor, *Report of the Committee of the Senate Upon the Relations Between Labor and Capital,* vol. 4 (Washington, 1886), pp. 286–90.

13. U.S. Bureau of Labor, *Convict Labor,* p. 301; U.S. Senate, Reports of the Immigration Commission, *Immigrants in Industries,* 61st Cong., 2nd sess., Doc. No. 633, pt. 1, vol. 2, *Bituminous Coal Mining* (Washington, 1911), p. 218.

14. Keith Dix, *Work Relations in the Coal Industry: The Hand-Loading Era, 1880–1930* (Morgantown, WV, 1977), intro. and pp. 12–16, 50–51, 105–06; Curtis Seltzer, *Fire in the Hole: Miners and Managers in the American Coal Industry* (Lexington, 1985), pp. 10–12; Carter Goodrich, *The Miner's Freedom: A Study of the Working Life in a Changing Industry* (Boston, 1925).

15. Nashville, *Republican Banner,* Aug. 14, 1870.

16. Reginald Heber Dawson to Governor Jones, Mar. 10, 1894, Box 28; W.D. Lee to Governor Seay, Aug. 26, 1887, Box 24, Governor's Papers, Alabama Department of Archives and History (hereafter ADAH), Montgomery, Alabama.

17. *Proceedings of the Joint Committee of the Senate and House to Investigate the*

Convict Lease System of Georgia, hereafter cited as *Proceedings* 1908, on microfilm, 5 vols., GDAH, vol. 1, p. 171.

18. *Proceedings,* vol. 1, pp. 156, 63; W.D. Lee to Reginald Heber Dawson, Mar. 19, 1890, "Reports from Inspectors and Other Officers," Incoming Correspondence, vol. 2, Department of Corrections Records, ADAH.

19. *UMWJ,* Apr. 30, 1891, p. 3.

20. Arthur Colyar, letter to the Nashville *Republican Banner,* Dec. 27, 1872.

21. Nashville *Republican Banner,* Dec. 17, 19, & 27, 1872.

22. Reprint of letter by A.K. McClure, *Philadelphia Times,* 28 Jan. 1885, in J.W. Burke, "The Coal Fields of Alabama," pamphlet, c. 1885, p. 39.

23. *UMWJ,* Mar. 28, 1895, p. 1; *The Tradesman* 30 (May 15, 1894): 61–62; *UMWJ,* Apr. 26, 1894, p. 4; Robert J. Norrell, *James Bowron: The Autobiography of a New South Industrialist* (Chapel Hill, 1991), p. 241; *UMWJ,* Nov. 29, 1894, p. 4.

24. *UMWJ,* Aug. 25, 1892, p. 4.

25. For contemporary descriptions of East Tennessee's "convict war" of 1891–92 see Tennessee Division of Mines, *Second Annual Report,* pp. 63, 142–43, 228–29 & 341; USGS, *Mineral Resources,* 1893, pp. 377–83; and Friedrich A. Sorge, *The Labor Movement in the United States: A History of the American Working Class from 1890 to 1896,* trans. Kai Schoenhals (Westport, 1987), pp. 13–24. Pete Daniel, "The Tennessee Convict War," *Tennessee Historical Quarterly* 34 (Fall 1975): 273–92; Archie Green, *Only a Miner: Studies In Recorded Coal-Mining Songs* (Urbana, 1972), pp. 155–91; and especially Karin Shapiro, "The Tennessee Convict Miner's Revolts of 1891–1892: Industrialization, Politics, and Convict Labor in the Late Nineteenth-Century South," (Ph.D. diss., Yale University, 1991), provide good secondary treatments.

26. "Hearing on receivership," Jan. 24, 1895, Fulton County Superior Court; Julius L. Brown (hereafter JLB) to A. Pluemer, Feb. 16, 1895; "Report of Receiver," Feb. 4, 1895, Fulton Superior Court; JLB to A. Pluemer, Feb. 15, 1895; JLB to F. H. Conner, Feb. 25, 1895, all letters in Julius L. Brown Letterbook, 1894–1895, Joseph Mackey Brown Papers II, Special Collections, University of Georgia (hereafter JLB Letterbook, JMB Papers II, UGA); other material from restricted collection, JMB Papers II, UGA.

27. Tennessee Division of Mines, *Fourth Annual Report of the Bureau of Labor, Statistics and Mines,* p. 282; USGS, *Mineral Resources,* 1892, p. 491–92; *UMWJ,* Aug. 25, 1892, p. 1; "Report of Assistant General Manager, Tennessee Divisions, TCI, Jan. 31st 1893," A. M. Shook Papers, BPL, pp. 1, 3, & 5.

28. Justin Fuller, "History of the Tennessee Coal, Iron and Railroad Company, 1852–1907," (Ph.D. diss., University of North Carolina, 1966), pp. 35–36; "First Annual Report of the Manager of the Coal Mines at Brushy Mountain, Tennessee," in Tennessee, *Report of the Board of Prison Commissioners, December 15, 1896,* p. 25; Alfred M. Shook to C. H. McGhee, Jan. 22, 1894, Shook Papers, BPL; Alabama, General Assembly, *Journal of the House of Representatives,* 1896–97, p. 640.

29. *Investigation of Charges Against Penitentiary Companies One, Two and Three,* Feb. 10–21, 1896, Julius L. Brown Papers, Atlanta Historical Society (hereafter JLB Papers, AHS), vol. 1, pp. 106–07; "Report of Receiver," Feb. 4, 1895, *Sibley Manufacturing Co. v. Georgia Mining & Manufacturing Co,* Fulton Superior Court; "Hearing on Receivership," Jan. 24, 1895, Fulton Superior Court, p. 5, both in restricted collection JMB Papers II, UGA.

30. JLB to Jacob W. Seaver, Jan. 10, 1895; JLB to O. P. Heath, Jan. 31, 1895, JLB Letterbook, JMB Papers II, UGA. On receivership see *Asheville Cigar Co. v. Brown,* 100 Ga. 171 (1896); *Brown v. Barnes,* 99 Ga. 1 (1896); *Dade Coal Company v. Penitentiary Co. No. 2,* 119 Ga. 824 (1904); "Petition for Receiver," Jan. 31, 1895 and "Report of Receiver," Feb. 4, 1895, *Sibley Manufacturing Co. v. Georgia Mining, Manufacturing and Investment Co.,* Fulton County Superior Court, Spring Term 1895; JLB to A. Pluemer, Feb. 16, 1895, JLB Letterbook, UGA.

31. Copy of minutes of Georgia Mining & Manufacturing Company meeting, Jan. 23, 1895, Fulton Superior Court, Jan. 24, 1895, p. 10; also "Petition for Receiver," Jan. 31, 1895; JLB to Jacob W. Seaver, May 8, 1894, all in JMB Papers II, UGA.

32. "Report of Receiver," Feb. 4, 1895, Fulton Superior Court, JMB Papers II, UGA; "Earnings and Expenses of the Georgia Mining, Manufacturing and Investment Company," Sept. 30, 1896, Folder 1, Box 1, JLB Papers, AHS; J. J. Ormsbee, "The Coal Interests of the South," *Tradesman* 36 (Jan. 1, 1897): 120–23; *Investigation*, 1896, JLB Papers, AHS, vol. 1, pp. 917 & 979.

33. *Investigation*, 1896, JLB Papers, AHS, vol. 1, pp. 917 & 925; *Asheville Cigar Co. v. Brown*, 100 Ga. 171 (1896), p. 174.

PHOTO—Raccoon Coal Mine

34. *Proceedings*, 1908, vol. 3, p. 783; *Investigation*, 1896, JLB Papers, AHS, vol. 2, p. 643.

35. Monthly Reports of Convicts Punished ("Whipping Reports"), vol. 1, Cole City Camp, 1901–1904, Records of the Prison Commission, GDAH; *Investigation*, 1896, JLB Papers, AHS, vol. 2, pp. 617–18; Reginald Heber Dawson Diaries, vol. 2, July 20, 1890, ADAH; Savannah *Tribune*, Nov. 21, 1908; *Proceedings*, 1908, vol. 4, p. 1556; *Investigation*, 1896, JLB Papers, AHS, vol. 2, pp. 693 & 788; see USGS, *Mineral Resources*, 1894, p. 189.

36. For slack and lump distinction, see for example, Tennessee Division of Mines, *Third Annual Report* (1893), p. 93; and Tennessee Division of Mines, *Fifth Annual Report* (1895), pp. 210–11. Tennessee Division of Mines, *Second Annual Report*, pp. 229–30; A.B. Johnston to J. W. Johnston, June 17, 1884, Correspondence, Folder 2, Coalburg Coal Company Records, Virginia Polytechnic University, p. 10; USGS, *Mineral Resources*, 1894, p. 189, Report by L.E. Bryant.

37. Tennessee Division of Mines, *Second Annual Report*, pp. 191, 146–47.

38. Alabama General Assembly, *Journal of the House of Representatives*, 1896–97, pp. 627–28 & 652–54; "Statement of Classification, Slope No. 2, Pratt Mines, Aug. 1890," Reports from Inspectors and Other Officers, Incoming Correspondence, vol. 2, Corrections Department Records, ADAH.

39. See the annual reports on coal production by the U.S. Geological Survey: USGS, *Mineral Resources of the United States*, 1883–1910. Report to Stockholders, May 3, 1893, Folder 1, Box 1, JLB Papers, AHS; *Investigation*, 1896, JLB Papers, AHS, vol. 1, p. 750.

40. A. T. Henley to R. H. Dawson, Apr. 11, 1889, Reports from Inspectors and Other Officers, Incoming Correspondence, vol. 3, Corrections Department Records, ADAH.

41. See for example, Dade County Grand Jury Presentments, March Term 1898, September Term 1901, on microfilm at GDAH; Georgia General Assembly, *Journal of the House*, 1890, pp. 722–23.

42. Georgia General Assembly, *Acts*, 1880–81, p. 107 and *Acts*, 1897, pp. 71–78.

43. The best evidence for this is found throughout the 1908 legislative investigation of Georgia's convict-lease, *Proceedings of the Joint Committee of the Senate and House to Investigate the Convict Lease System of Georgia*.

44. *Proceedings*, vol. 3, pp. 739–40, 1158–59, vol. 4, pp. 1298–301 & 1306; Hearing before the Georgia Prison Commission, Prison Commission Folder, Box 19 (Pratt, J.L.—Ransom, Richard), Hoke Smith Collection, Richard B. Russell Memorial Library, UGA.

45. Georgia Prison Commission, *Report*, 1897–98, pp. 12–14 & 44–45; 1900–01, p. 7; 1901–02, pp. 19–20; 1903–04, pp. 7–9; 1907–08, p. 4.

46. USGS, *Mineral Resources*, 1900, pp. 309, 372; 1905, p. 561; 1910, part 2, pp. 9–10, 113; 1907, part 2, pp. 50–52, 106.

47. Reese Erlich, "Prison Labor, Prison Blues: How Civilian Jobs are going to Jail," *Solidarity*, Mar. 1995, pp. 10–13; *New York Times*, Mar. 26, 1995.

48. *Daily Dispatch*, Apr. 9, 1889, James Bowron Scrapbooks, BPL.

PART THREE

BLACK
MEN,
THE
PROFESSIONS,
AND
FRATERNAL
ORGANIZATIONS

TEN

A High and Honorable Calling: Black Lawyers in South Carolina, 1868–1915

J. R. OLDFIELD

In recent years historians have begun to show considerable interest in the legal history of the South.[1] But while much of this interest has touched on Southern lawyers and notions of professionalization, scant attention has been paid to the scores of black lawyers who were admitted to the bar in the post-Civil War period. Who were these men? Where did they acquire their legal training and at what cost? What sort of practices did they run? How successful were they? What follows is an attempt to answer some of these questions, taking as a case study the state of South Carolina, cradle of secession, and, by any measure, one of the most conservative (and recalcitrant) Southern states during the Reconstruction and Redemption periods.

All estimates in a study of this nature are necessarily tentative, but the available evidence suggests that some fifty-six blacks were admitted to the South Carolina bar between 1868 and 1915.[2] The greatest surge came not, as one might expect, during Reconstruction, but between 1876 and the adoption of a new, white supremacist constitution in 1895. In all, thirty blacks were admitted to the bar during this period, compared to just sixteen between 1868 and the conservative victory of November 1876. After 1895 numbers fell dramatically. Nevertheless, the 1900 census reported that there were twenty-nine black lawyers in South Carolina.[3] How many of these men were full-time professionals for whom the law was their chief source of income is open to question. But the numbers were certainly large enough to suggest a significant black presence in South Carolina's courts, and, in Charleston at least, the makings of a black legal community.

The first blacks admitted to the South Carolina bar in 1868 were all Northerners attracted South after the Civil War. Jonathan J. Wright, a native of Pennsylvania, came to South Carolina as a legal adviser with the Freedmen's Bureau; William Whipper hailed from Michigan and had received his legal training in the office of a Detroit lawyer. The early life of Robert Brown Elliott is shrouded in mystery, but he too was a carpetbagger and, like Whipper, moved South with the Union army. This nucleus of Northern men was completed by Stephen A. Swails, also from Pennsylvania, Macon B. Allen, the first black admitted to the bar anywhere in the United States, and Richard T. Greener, who for five torrid years (1873–7) was the only black faculty member of the University of South Carolina.[4] Less easily pigeon-holed is Daniel A. Straker who was born and educated in Barbados. Straker arrived in Charleston in 1875 as an inspector in the customs service, having previously taught in a freedmen's school in Louisville, Kentucky, and spent two years at Howard University Law School. A brilliant and dynamic man, Straker was to have a profound and lasting effect on the black legal profession in South Carolina.[5]

Important as this group of men was, not least as a source of legal education, their ascendency was short-lived. By 1875 the black bar in South Carolina was already predominantly native-born, and by the end of the century almost exclusively so. Not surprisingly, most of these men came from the Low-country, where the bulk of the black population was concentrated. The incompleteness of the biographical data makes further analysis difficult, but it seems likely that mulattoes outnumbered blacks by perhaps as much as two to one, while a similar proportion could claim free-born ancestry stretching back several generations. A significant number came to the law through politics. Four were state senators during Reconstruction, and a further six served terms in the House of Representatives.[6] Some of these men, like Samuel J. Lee, subsequently used their political experience to launch successful legal careers, but for many of them admission to the bar was merely a way, as they saw it, of setting themselves on an equal footing with white legislators, past and present.

The unmistakable impression, therefore, is that most prospective black lawyers came from well-established, middle-class families which historically attached a great deal of importance to the professions and, more important, could afford to give their sons the right sort of training. Obtaining a legal education was not quite as problematic as one might imagine. A popular course was to read law with a practicing lawyer. While probably 40 per cent of native-born black lawyers acquired their training in this way, specific examples are tantalizing difficult to document. Whipper and Wright both trained young men in their offices, and Samuel J. Lee in Charleston trained his future partner, William J. Bowen, as well as Robert C. Browne and Thaddeus St. Mark Sasportas.[7] Others may well have worked with Northern white lawyers, and some, like George C. Clyde in Aiken, seem to have acquired all the knowledge they required while working as clerks of court.[8]

The alternative to such practical experience was to go to law school. Over 50 percent of black lawyers in South Carolina were educated in this way. A small number of young men were always sent out of state to colleges like Howard and Atlanta University. During Reconstruction a few were also lucky enough to be admitted to the University of South Carolina Law School.[9] But the most accessible college for blacks was Allen University in Columbia. Allen was established in 1880 by the African Methodist Episcopal Church and was unique among early black colleges in the South in having its own law school.[10] Modeled on neighbouring USC, Allen offered prospective students a two year course leading to the LL.B. degree and an excellent opportunity to familiarize themselves with the practices of the state and federal courts. In four terms the small faculty guided its charges through the intricacies of Robinson's *Elementary Law*, Blackstone's *Commentaries*, Kent's *Commentaries*, Greenleaf on evidence, Smith on contracts, Daniel on negotiable instruments, Bishop's *Criminal Law* and *Criminal Procedure*, constitutional law and the *General Statutes of South Carolina*. In addition, there were moot courts and lectures once a month from distinguished members of the Columbia bar.[11]

Overseeing this ambitious enterprise was Daniel A. Straker, who was dean from 1882 to 1887.[12] During his short term of office twelve students graduated from Allen University Law School, among them Straker's successor as dean, Thomas A. Saxon.[13] The school was apparently still open to students in 1912, but by this date the endeavor had been more or less abandoned, the last class graduating in 1898. The men who ran Allen University were understandably insistent on the importance of a legal training. "The profession of the lawyer is a necessity to our civilization," the prospectus informed students. "It is a high and honorable calling, and those who enter it have opportunities second to no class of professional men of being great benefactors to the human race."[14] Doubtless the thirty young men who graduated from Allen between 1884 and 1898, some of them from as far afield as Kansas and West Virginia, would have agreed. But for many the cost of a college education must have been prohibitively high. Allen charged its students $70 a year, exclusive of room and board, which could be anything from $3.50 to $6 a month.[15] Two hundred dollars was a lot of money for a black family to spend on education in the late-nineteenth century, and despite credit arrangements the surprise is that Allen managed to attract (and keep) as many students as it did.

The final hurdle for all prospective lawyers was an examination before the Supreme Court. Traditionally, this ordeal took the form of a sometimes perfunctory oral examination before several of the justices. In 1887, however, South Carolina introduced a written examination as part of a general effort to professionalize the bar.[16] If anything, this reform may have worked to the advantage of black applicants, but there were undoubtedly failures. As a result, some simply gave up. Even those who were successful did not always pursue a legal career. Of Allen's thirty graduates only seventeen were admitted to the bar and as few as eight (25 per cent) became professional lawyers. Many taught school or edited newspapers. Some worked as clerks for the state government or moved to Washington, D.C. to work for the federal government. A few, like Dock J. Jordan, ended their careers as presidents of black colleges.[17]

Of course, there was an element of free choice in all this, but the hazards involved in becoming a black lawyer were all too obvious. The main problem was the poverty of the black population itself. Typically, black lawyers in the South dealt with small property deals and criminal cases involving black clients who were usually too poor to be able to afford legal assistance. Opportunities to work for black business enterprises and, much later, organizations like the NAACP on the whole were limited. There were also local prejudices to contend with. Very few black lawyers attracted white clients, and by choice many blacks themselves preferred to employ the services of a white lawyer. As the *Charleston News and Courier* noted in 1895, "the colored people have not the same confidence in a colored man's abilities."[18] Clearly, for many such obstacles proved too daunting.

Prospects were particularly bleak in and about Columbia, the state capital. Despite the undoubted brilliance of at least two of the partners, the firm of Robert Elliott, Daniel A. Straker and T. McCants Stewart, based in Orangeburg, finally went bankrupt in 1879 owing to lack of business.[19] Straker subsequently moved to Columbia, but his decision to leave South Carolina in 1887 was influenced, in part, by the failure of his legal practice. As the *Columbia Daily Register* was at pains to point out, "while he [Straker] has been engaged in many important cases in which the personal and property rights of his colored clients have been faithfully and in most cases successfully represented, their poverty as a class has left his labor in their behalf unremunerated."[20] Meanwhile, W. T. Andrews complained that conditions in Sumter "are growing damned near intolerable and I am tired of it." Ever alert to the possibility of a move to Washington, D.C., Andrews survived only by teaching school and working part-time as an agent for the Pennsylvania Mutual Insurance Company.[21]

Given these difficulties, it is hardly surprising that many young men gravitated towards the Low-country where prospects were considerably brighter. Large black enclaves in Georgetown and Beaufort held out the promise of brisker business, while more alluring still was Charleston. As many as sixteen black lawyers had offices in Charleston between 1868 and 1915, although not all of them were active at the same time. The carpetbaggers had quickly grasped the potential of this area. Robert Elliott opened his first law office in Charleston, in partnership with William Whipper and Macon B. Allen, and Jonathan J. Wright worked there from the late 1870s until his death in 1885.[22] By 1895 the number of black lawyers in the city had risen to seven. This busy group of men was the nearest thing to a black legal community in South Carolina. Partnerships sprang up, and certain addresses were always instantly recognizable as the offices of black lawyers. For years 3–5

Chalmers Street was the office of John Gaillard and Martin A. Williams, while 104 Church Street was successively occupied by Robert C. Browne (1897–99), John B. Edwards (1901–13), and Thaddeus St. Mark Sasportas (1916–19).[23]

Easily the most influential figure in the black legal community in Charleston was Samuel J. Lee. Born a slave on the plantation of Samuel McGowan, an Up-country planter, Lee followed his master into the Civil War and was wounded at the second battle of Manassas and again near Hanover Junction on the retreat to Richmond. After the war Lee returned to Abbeville, where he took up farming, and later moved to Hamburg, then in Edgefield County. In 1868 he was elected a member of the House of Representatives for Edgefield and was subsequently twice elected representative for Aiken (1872–74). By the time he was admitted to the bar in 1872 Lee had emerged as one of the most able members of the House, and in recognition of the fact was elected Speaker in November of that year. Then in 1874 he dramatically resigned his seat and left politics to concentrate on his law practice in Aiken.[24]

Lee's meteoric rise undoubtedly had a great deal to do with McGowan, who was probably his natural father, and Senator Frank Arnim, with whom Lee worked in the late 1860s. But Lee was no fool. Poorly educated, he was nevertheless recognized as possessing a lively and inquiring mind. "Lee is certainly a remarkable man," wrote a correspondent in the *Charleston News and Courier* in 1873. "By dint of industry and application he has made himself one of the most creditable lawyers in the State for his age. I heard him argue a case at Chambers the other day, and he displayed a tact and ability that would have done credit to one longer engaged in the practice."[25] It was these same qualities that Lee brought to his responsibilities as Speaker. Edward King, touring the South in 1873–74, described him as "an elegant and accomplished man" who would have "creditably presided over any commonwealth's legislative assembly."[26] The Republican *Aiken Tribune* echoed these sentiments. "Even the opposition party and press have repeatedly expressed admiration at Speaker Lee's graceful and yet firm discharge of his duties," the newspaper noted. "His record is a proud one, and his people may well indulge in pride at the devotion to their interests he has evinced, and the prominent position among his fellows which he has assumed and so gracefully fills."[27]

Returning to Aiken in 1874, Lee went into partnership with George C. Clyde and set about building up a busy law practice.[28] The end of Reconstruction, however, found Lee a deeply troubled man. In 1875 he had already been convicted of fraudulently issuing cheques while a county commissioner, and in 1877 he was again charged with misconduct, this time in a larger scandal involving some of the key black office holders in the state.[29] Wisely, Lee chose this moment to escape to Alabama where he worked as a special federal agent for the detection of fraudulent entries of public lands. By 1878 he was back in South Carolina and trying to make his way as a lawyer in Charleston. Very much the outsider, Lee started out by taking cases for a white lawyer, R. W. Seymour, for which he appears to have received a percentage of the fees.[30] By 1882 he was the leading black lawyer in the state with a young partner and an office of his own in Court House Square.[31]

Fortunately, we know a great deal about Lee's Charleston practice. Most of his work was in the busy municipal and county courts. Lee was particularly active in the Court of General Sessions, which became something of a black preserve during the 1880s.[32] Within four years of his arrival in Charleston he had ousted many of his rivals and was involved in nearly two thirds of all criminal litigation handled by black lawyers. By 1885 his ascendency was complete. Of twenty-eight cases defended by black lawyers in the Court of General Sessions that year, Lee and his partner, William J. Bowen, were involved in twenty-one, while Lee was personally involved in a further two.[33] Lee's case load split almost evenly between crimes against property (larceny, grand larceny, burglary, receiving stolen goods) and crimes against the person (assault, murder, assault and battery). He showed considerable skill in defending accused murderers, and between 1882 and 1893 was involved in five rape cases, all of them attacks by blacks on blacks.[34] By contrast, Lee acted in only a handful of cases a year in Charleston's Court of Common Pleas, not merely because of fierce competition from white lawyers, but because very few blacks were in a position to contest wills or make claims for damages.[35] Black crime was of an altogether more desperate and violent character.

Lee was also active outside Charleston. He was a familiar figure in neighbouring Berkeley County, where there was a paucity of black legal talent, although in Beaufort Lee seems to have been willing to give way to William Whipper, by then well established again in the Low-country.[36] Then there were his appearances before the Supreme Court in Columbia, twenty-seven between 1880 and 1894 and far in excess of any other black lawyer in the state.[37] By and large these appearances were connected with criminal cases that Lee had personally brought up from the lower courts in Charleston, but there were notable exceptions. It was Lee, for instance, who acted for William Whipper in *Whipper v. Talbird* (1889), a civil action arising out of a contested election for the position of probate judge in Beaufort County.[38] Lee clearly relished these occasions. The sessions of the Supreme Court were widely reported, and they provided the ideal forum in which to display his wit and know-how.

Lee's reputation as a lawyer rested upon his success in the courtroom. To judge from the Charleston records, his clients always stood a better than even chance of being acquitted or, more likely, of having their cases dismissed. Lee was admittedly less successful before the Supreme Court, but very few lawyers, either black or white, could lay claim to such a record. James W. Polite and Robert C. Browne, two of Lee's closet black rivals, won only about a third of the cases they handled in the Court of General

Sessions, for instance.[39] Yet Lee was never a wealthy man. What little property he managed to buy in Charleston was heavily mortgaged, sometimes two or three times over, and on at least one occasion he was forced to sell in order to repay his creditors.[40] For all that we can gather, Lee was not a particularly extravagant man. On the contrary, his home life was described as being "quiet and unpretentious." Lee was rather the victim of a debt-ridden clientele and his own generosity of spirit. "He no doubt would have been well-to-do if his clients had all been able to pay him," the *Charleston News and Courier* concluded in 1895, "but he was not of a nature to refuse to do a poor man service and much of his time was given with no expectation of a fee."[41]

Remarkable as it was, Lee's pre-eminence in Charleston undoubtedly made life difficult for his competitors, and it is no accident that his sudden death in 1895 coincided with an influx of new talent into the city. One of these men was John B. Edwards, an Allen University graduate who moved to the Low-country in 1895 after nine frustrating years in the Sumter area. Edwards subsequently went into partnership with one of Lee's clerks, Thaddeus St. Mark Sasportas, and by 1913 was one of the leading black lawyers in the state.[42] In the meantime, a new generation of black lawyers was emerging; among them John Gaillard and Mark A. Williams, both admitted in 1897, and Edward F. Smith, admitted in 1900.[43] But these young men grew up in a harsher climate and some, like Williams and Eugene Hayne, soon went North to seek their fortunes in New York. The Wilson years witnessed further decline. In 1910 Charleston could still boast five black lawyers; in 1916 there were just two.[44]

Paradoxically, in Columbia prospects began to improve after 1900. Despite being the state capital, Columbia had never been a promising area for black lawyers and even talented men like Daniel A. Straker had struggled. But black migration and the work of organizations like the NAACP opened up new possibilities. By 1918 there were three black lawyers listed in the Columbia city directory: Nathaniel J. Frederick, Principal of Howard School; Butler W. Nance, an Allen graduate and former railway postal clerk; and another Allen graduate, Green Jackson.[45] Nevertheless, only Nance and Jackson were full-time professionals and after a brief flurry of activity stagnation quickly set it. The 1920s generally were a testing period for black lawyers. Admissions to the bar slowed down to a trickle, while opportunities to gain a legal training, particularly with a practicing lawyer, grew fewer and fewer. By 1930 there were only two black lawyers of any note in the whole state; Nathaniel J. Frederick in Columbia and Thaddeus St. Mark Sasportas in Charleston.

Throughout this period black lawyers constituted a very small elite among South Carolina's black population. Probably as few as 50 per cent of those admitted to the bar between 1868 and 1915, that is, twenty-eight out of fifty-six, went on to become practicing lawyers and fewer still enjoyed any measure of professional success. Despite a spirit of healthy competition, the size and vulnerability of the black bar encouraged familiarity and close co-operation. This was particularly true in Charleston where at different times John B. Edwards, Thaddeus St. Mark Sasportas, Robert C. Browne and Edward F. Smith were all business partners.[46] Understandably, ties with colleagues working elsewhere in the state became more and more important as time went on. When Butler W. Nance died in 1923, for instance, his pallbearers included Nathaniel J. Frederick, Green Jackson, and Thaddeus St. Mark Sasportas.[47]

Small in numbers, black lawyers in South Carolina also did not enjoy the same professional freedom as their white colleagues. Specialization, by 1900 increasingly common in larger white firms, was almost unheard of. Most black lawyers could not afford to specialize and, in any case, would have found the notion absurd. Relations with white lawyers on the whole were distant. There were unquestionably initial teething problems, and during Reconstruction some white lawyers left the state rather than suffer the ignominy of appearing in court against a black opponent.[48] Resistance eventually gave way to grudging acceptance. Many white lawyers found they had little cause to get involved with their black colleagues, particularly if they specialized in civil litigation, while others undoubtedly saw them as a necessary evil. Nevertheless, a certain degree of professional contact was inevitable; Samuel J. Lee worked with and against white lawyers all through his career. But there was never any question who held the upper hand. Black lawyers were never admitted to the South Carolina Bar Association, for instance, and to this extent they remained very much a race apart.

Survival as a black lawyer demanded intelligence and tact. Most were quick to assess the power and influence of the white legal community and act accordingly. In Lee's case, surely instructive, his success undeniably owed something to his willingness to accept the status quo. His obituary in the Charleston News and Courier pointedly drew attention to his manners in the court room, which it applauded as being "beyond criticism, extremely courteous and never presuming."[49] Lee's public stance was equally accommodating. Eschewing politics after an unsuccessful attempt to win the seat for the First Congressional District in 1880, he settled back into a life of middle-class respectability.[50] Never one to seek confrontations, Lee's courtesy and "good sense" won him the confidence of white Charlestonians and the respect and good-will of his colleagues, black and white. Significant, too, was the stance black lawyers took when it came to blacks and the law. None of these men could be described as activists or crusaders for black civil rights. Indeed, by and large they remained silent on the subject. Such reticence was perhaps well-advised, given conditions in South Carolina for most of this period, but it also reflected the background, status and aspirations of most black lawyers.

Not surprisingly, few black lawyers in South Carolina enjoyed financial security. When he died in 1895 Samuel J. Lee's estate consisted of a small law library valued at $230.25 and $115 in cash. His partner, William J.

Bowen, was more successful. On his death in 1937 Bowen left property valued at over $8,000. But such wealth was unusual, to say the least. Edward F. Smith died possessed of a personal estate of $500; Jonathan J. Wright, who for seven years served as a justice of the Supreme Court, left $1,130.[51] Estimates of average yearly income are almost impossible to arrive at. W. T. Andrews was reputably earning $1,000 a year in 1903, but without further data there is no way of knowing whether this was an unusually high or low figure.[52] Certainly, house ownership was rare even among the elite. In Charleston, for instance, John B. Edwards lived in rented property for most of his career, as did Robert C. Browne and Edward F. Smith.[53]

Only further state studies will help to put the South Carolina experience into proper context. However, it is clear that here, at least, black lawyers were an integral if subordinate part of the legal profession until well into the twentieth century. Expansion was particularly rapid during the 1880s and, as we have seen, the black legal community in Charleston was at its peak in the 1890s. What undermined the position of black lawyers in South Carolina was not so much Jim Crow, although this undoubtedly played its part, but economic recession, the First World War and the narrow, coercive mood of the 1920s. Only with the increase in federal activity in the field of social security and the rise of workmen's laws during the New Deal would the situation show any signs of marked improvement, and even then progress was often slow and halting. Black lawyers in South Carolina were consistently frustrated by impoverished clients, local prejudice and, except for a fortunate few, lack of business. Nevertheless, their efforts represent an important chapter in the legal history of the South and the history of black Americans.

NOTES

1. David J. Bodenhamer and James W. Ely, Jr., eds., *Ambivalent Legacy: A Legal History of the South* (Mississippi: University Press of Mississippi, 1984); W. Hamilton Bryson and E. Lee Shepard, "The Virginia Bar, 1870–1900," in Gerard W. Gawalt, ed., *The New High Priests: Lawyers in Post-Civil War America* (Connecticut: Greenwood Press, 1984), 171–86.

2. This figure is based on the following sources: *Charleston News and Courier; Columbia Daily Register;* Emily Reynolds and Joan Faunt, eds., *Biographical Directory of the Senate of South Carolina, 1776–1964* (Columbia: South Carolina Archives Department, 1964); Thomas Holt, *Black over White: Negro Political Leadership in South Carolina during Reconstruction* (Urbana: University of Illinois Press, 1977), 229–41; *Catalogue of Allen University, 1911–1912* (Columbia, 1912), 56–59. The Supreme Court's records of admission do not identify lawyers by race. See Solicitors' Roll, Supreme Court, Columbia.

3. George B. Tindall, *South Carolina Negroes, 1877–1900* (Columbia: University of South Carolina Press, 1952), 144.

4. Holt, 76–77, 82–83, 90; Peggy Lamson, *The Glorious Failure: Black Congressman Robert Brown Elliott and the Reconstruction in South Carolina* (New York: W. W.

Norton, 1973), 21–23, 76; Joel Williamson, *After Slavery: The Negro in South Carolina During Reconstruction, 1861–1877* (New York: W. W. Norton, 1975), 233, 330–33, 349.

5. Louis Harlan, ed., *The Booker T. Washington Papers*, Vol. 4, 1895–1898 (Urbana: University of Illinois Press, 1975), 236–37. Straker later went on to become one of Detroit's leading black lawyers.

6. Holt, 229–41.

7. Tindall, 145; Reynolds and Faunt, *Biographical Directory of the Senate of South Carolina* (entry for Thomas J. Reynolds); *Charleston News and Courier*, 14 December 1881; *Charleston City Directory*, 1886 and 1895.

8. *Aiken Tribune*, 6 December 1873. I am most grateful to John Hammond Moore for drawing this reference to my attention.

9. Williamson, 223, 233; Holt, 299–41.

10. Asa H. Gordon, *Sketches of Negro Life and History in South Carolina*, (1929; rept. Columbia: University of South Carolina Press, 1971), 94–95.

11. *Catalogue of Allen University, 1890 and 1891* (Columbia, 1891), 31–32.

12. Gordon, 95.

13. *Catalogue of Allen University, 1890 and 1891*, 40.

14. Ibid.

15. Ibid., 31–32.

16. *Charleston News and Courier*, 14 May 1887.

17. *Catalogue of Allen University, 1911–1912*, 59–69.

18. *Charleston News and Courier*, 2 April 1895.

19. Lamson, *The Glorious Failure*, 271, 273.

20. *Columbia Daily Register*, 24 July 1887.

21. W. T. Andrews to Whitfield McKinlay, 9 March, 13 and 27 September 1903, Carter G. Woodson Papers, Library of Congress, Washington, D.C.

22. Lamson, 75–76; Tindall, *South Carolina Negroes*, 145.

23. *Charleston City Directory*, 1879–1920.

24. *Aiken Tribune*, 6 December 1873; Solicitors' Roll, 6 March 1872; Lawrence C. Bryant, *Negro Legislators in South Carolina* (Orangeburg: South Carolina State College, 1967), 7–12.

25. Quoted in *Aiken Tribune*, 26 July 1873.

26. Edward King, *The Southern States of North America* (London, 1875), 460.

27. *Aiken Tribune*, 6 December 1873.

28. Ibid., 19, 26 June, 3, 10 July, 4 September 1875; 2, 16 October 1876. Clyde was admitted to the bar in November 1873.

29. *Aiken Courier Journal*, 13 December 1875; *Report of the Joint Investigating Committee on Public Frauds* (Columbia, 1878), 21, 31; Alrutheus Ambush Taylor, *The Negro in South Carolina During the Reconstruction* (Washington, D.C.: Association for the Study of Negro Life and History, 1924), 278, 284.

30. Copybook of Matthew Buswell and R. W. Seymour, 1867–83, South Carolina Historical Society, Charleston.

31. *Charleston City Directory*, 1882.

32. In 1882 black lawyers were handling 33 per cent of all cases in the Court of General Sessions. By 1886 this figure had fallen to 28 per cent. Over the same period, however, the number of cases where there was no lawyer involved at all increased from 30 per cent to 63 per cent. These figures are based on an analysis of the Bar Dockets, Court of General Sessions, Charleston County, 1882–93, State Archives, Columbia.

33. Bar Dockets, Court of General Sessions, Charleston County, 1882, 1885.

34. Session Rolls, Court of General Sessions, Charleston County, 1882–1893, State Archives, Columbia.

35. Bar Calendar Number 1 (1881–85), Number 2 (1881–88, 1892–99), Number 3 (1876–85, 1892–1900), Number 4 (1878–82), Court of Common Pleas, Charleston County, State Archives, Columbia.

36. *Reports of the Cases Argued and Determined in the Supreme Court of South Carolina* (hereafter *Supreme Court Reports*), Vol. 22 (November 1884), 298–301; Vol. 23

(April 1885), 209–12; Vol. 26 (November 1886), 296–300; Vol. 41 (April 1894), 526–31. For Whipper see the Leigh Whipper Papers, 114–1 (folders 45–60), Moorland-Spingarn Research Center, Howard University, Washington, D.C.

37. *Supreme Court Law Reports*, Vols. 14–43 (1880–94).

38. *Supreme Court Law Reports*, Vol. 32 (November 1889), 1–5. See also the companion case *Ex Parte Whipper*, 5–13.

39. All these figures are compiled from the Bar Dockets, Court of General Sessions, 1882–93.

40. Charleston County Court House, Charleston, Register of Mesne Conveyance, B22 169; D20 757; E22 150; F23 30; G19 319; H19 163; J19 21, M20 33, 355; Q20 46, 185, 207; U18 631; Y18 235, 236.

41. *Charleston News and Courier*, 2 April 1895.

42. *Catalogue of Allen University, 1890 and 1891*, p. 40; *Columbia Daily Register*, 24 February 1887; *Charleston City Directory*, 1895–1913.

43. Solicitors' Roll, 12 May 1897 and 19 December 1900.

44. *Charleston City Directory*, 1910–15.

45. *Columbia City Directory*, 1918; *Catalogue of Allen University, 1911–1912*, 59–69; "Butler W. Nance," vertical file, South Caroliniana Library, Columbia.

46. *Charleston City Directory*, 1895–1912.

47. "Butler W. Nance," vertical file, South Caroliniana Library.

48. Williamson, *After Slavery*, 255, 288.

49. *Charleston News and Courier*, 2 April 1895.

50. *Report of the Inquiry into the Contested-Election Case of (Samuel J.) Lee vs (John S.) Richardson*, n.d., Special Collections, University Library, College of Charleston, Charleston.

51. Charleston County Court House, Charleston, Probate Records, 298-0011 (Wright), 397-27 (Lee), 586-0024 (Smith), 784-0014 (Bowen).

52. W. T. Andrews to Whitfield McKinlay, 9 March 1903, Carter G. Woodson Papers.

53. Bureau of the Census, Manuscript Census Schedules, Population, 1900, Charleston, South Carolina, Vol. 13, E.D., 110, Sheet 12 and E.D. 113, Sheet 19; Vol. 14, E.D. 114, Sheet 6.

ELEVEN

Entering a White Profession: Black Physicians in the New South, 1880–1920

TODD L. SAVITT

In the late 1890s a young Kentucky physician wrote optimistically to black sociologist W. E. B. DuBois:

> I am located in a town of 12,000 inhabitants, one-third of whom are colored, and am thoroughly convinced that there is a great field here in the South for the educated colored man. As a physician I am well received by my white professional brother. We ride in the same buggy, consult together, and read each other's books. I have a few white patients, but most of them are colored. I have purchased property on one of our best residence streets and also a business house on the main street of our town.[1]

A few years later, a national monthly medical journal sandwiched between correspondence on treatments for hysteria and the prevention of dog bites the following letter, written, the editor announced, by a Southerner, and printed exactly as received, though without the writer's name:

WANTS TO KEEP NEGRO PHYSICIANS DOWN!

Dr. C. F. Taylor, Ed. of the Med. World

Dear Sir:—What is the negro physician doing as a whole through out the country as a physician and surgeon? What are they doing financialy? How do they compare with the white aplicants in State examinations through out the country? I notice in some places they seams to be makeing more money then the white physicians. What is the best thing we can do to keep them down? Please let me here from you in the nex No. of the WORLD.[2]

These two letters, contradictory in one regard, do agree that black physicians in the highly race-conscious New South were gaining recognition and achieving a measure of success according to the standards of the time. They also point to two major concerns of the first generation of post-Civil War black practitioners: reputation and rewards.

Like other physicians, black practitioners faced the problems of gaining their patients' confidence and establishing collegial relationships with other local doctors. They had to *earn* their status among patients and practitioners. Measures of achievement included the number, social standing, financial position, and loyalty of patients; the willingness of already established practitioners to share knowledge, books, and instruments, and to call or be called for consultation; and, finally, the acquisition of such material displays of wealth as home, office, and "rig" (horse and buggy) or automobile.

These were important matters to black physicians, but, they soon learned, competence, patient acceptance, and material gain were not enough. They also needed to develop group allegiance in order to surmount barriers the local, state, and national white medical profession had erected to keep them out. Black doctors had to build their own parallel professional structures by establishing hospitals, medical societies, pharmacies, medical journals, postgraduate educational institutions, and clinics, as a means of maintaining their standards in medical practice.

In concentrating their efforts on individual career growth and on improving collegial relations, black physicians of this period subordinated another concern: the overall improvement of black health and health conditions. As black doctors they expected and were expected to improve the health of fellow blacks both by providing medical care and by educating the ignorant regarding good health practices. Though it was an important force, one that inspired black physicians of the late nineteenth and early twentieth centuries to enter medicine, this broad ideal of racial betterment did not receive as much attention as other goals once doctors actually entered practice.[3]

In addition to these concerns, black practitioners in the turn-of-the-century South lived always with another issue that affected their careers and personal lives—race. For example, they had to overcome black patients' reluctance to use their services, low remuneration from a generally poorer, predominantly black clientele, and an unfriendly reception and professional exclusion from many white physicians. Furthermore, having gained a level of education superior to that of most other blacks, these doctors became representatives of their race to the white world, and community leaders in the black. So they found it difficult to escape matters of race in their daily lives. The sorts of situations Southern black physicians encountered and the ways they coped with them in their dealings with black patients, white physicians, white patients, and fellow black doctors as they entered the previously white medical profession are the subjects of this paper.

As Table 1 indicates, the number of black physicians in the United States increased markedly between 1890 and 1920 as medical schools devoted to educating blacks opened their doors.[4] Most graduates remained in the South, where they had grown up and learned medicine (there were no black

TABLE 1

Black and White Physicians in Southern States and Selected Southern and Northern Cities, 1890 and 1920

Location	1890 Black Physicians* (no.)	1890 White Physicians (no.)	1890 Black Physicians (% of all physicians)	1920 Black Physicians* (no.)	1920 White Physicians (no.)	1920 Black Physicians (% of all physicians)
United States	909 †‡	103,482 †	0.9 †‡	3,495 †	125,666 †	2.7 †
Southern States						
Alabama	28	1,798	1.5	106	2,137	4.7
Arkansas	40	2,224	1.8	150	2,183	6.4
Delaware	2	231	0.9	7	253	2.7
Florida	12	620	1.9	118	1,261	8.6
Georgia	40	2,343	1.7	228	3,027	7.0
Kentucky	42	3,214	1.3	155	2,844	5.2
Louisiana	38	1,212	3.0	94	1,816	4.9
Maryland	37	1,663	2.2	66	2,186	2.9
Mississippi	34	1,624	2.1	66	1,576	4.0
Missouri	28	5,225	0.5	200	5,614	3.4
North Carolina	46	1,488	3.0	125	1,983	5.9
Oklahoma	0	217	0	122	2,424	4.8
South Carolina	30	1,099	2.7	85	1,257	6.3
Tennessee	102	3,283	3.0	327	2,851	10.3
Texas	54	4,286	1.2	217	5,738	3.6
Virginia	39	1,892	2.0	178	2,179	7.6
West Virginia	4	1,022	0.4	56	1,635	3.3
Southern Cities						
Atlanta	6 †	205 †	2.8 †	41	456	8.2
Baltimore	28	764	3.5	53	1,381	3.7
Kansas City	10	473	2.1	52	891	5.5
Louisville	12	400	2.9	47	484	8.9
Memphis	14 †	140 †	9.1 †	83	329	20.1
Nashville	24	187	11.4	68	218	23.8
New Orleans	18	281	6.0	30	598	4.8
Richmond	6	144	4.0	28	317	8.1
St. Louis	2	787	0.3	106	1,607	6.2
Washington, D.C.	87	642	11.9	130	998	11.5
Northern Cities						
Boston	8 †	1,156 †	0.7 †	31	1,681 †	1.8 †
Chicago	11	1,783	0.6	209 †	5,143 †	+3.9 †
Cleveland	6	482	1.2	27	854	3.1
Detroit	3	372	0.8	28	1,291	2.1
Indianapolis	8 †	307 †	2.5 †	29	612	4.7
New York (Manhattan)	14	3,192	0.4	78 †	5,517 †	1.4 †
Philadelphia	15	2,095	0.7	95 †	3,309 †	2.8 †
Pittsburgh	4	340	1.2	27	976	2.7

SOURCE: U.S. Census, 1890 and 1920

NOTE: Unless otherwise indicated, figures are for males only. In only a few states and cities did the published census data provide statistics for female physicians by race. In 1890, 4.3 percent of white and 12.7 percent of "colored" physicians were female. In 1920, 2.7 percent of white and 1.9 percent of black physicians were female.

*The occupations listings of the 1890 census grouped blacks, Indians, and persons of Chinese and Japanese descent into one racial category labeled "Colored." (California alone listed 160 "colored" physicians, most of whom must have been of Oriental descent. Most "colored" physicians in the South were of Negro descent.)

† Includes both males and females

‡ The 1890 Census distinguished "Negroes" and "Colored" in this instance.

TABLE 2

Black and White Citizens per Black and White Physician in Southern States and Selected Southern and Northern Cities, 1890 and 1920

Location	per Black Physician 1890*	per Black Physician 1920	Change In Ratio (%)	per White Physician 1890	per White Physician 1920	Change In Ratio (%)
United States	8,403†‡	2,994†	-64.4	531†	755†	+42.2
Southern States						
Alabama	24,232	8,497	-64.9	464	677	+45.9
Arkansas	7,728	3,148	-59.3	368	586	+59.2
Delaware	14,193	4,334	-69.5	606	761	+25.6
Florida	13,848	2,792	-79.8	363	506	+39.4
Georgia	21,470	5,291	-75.4	418	558	+33.5
Kentucky	6,383	1,522	-76.2	495	767	+54.9
Louisiana	14,716	7,450	-49.4	461	604	+31.0
Maryland	5,829	3,704	-36.5	497	551	+10.9
Mississippi	21,840	14,169	-35.1	335	542	+61.8
Missouri	5,364	891	-83.4	484	574	+18.6
North Carolina	12,196	6,107	-49.9	709	900	+26.9
Oklahoma		1,225		271	751	+177.1
South Carolina	22,964	10,173	-55.7	420	651	+55.0
Tennessee	4,222	1,382	-67.3	407	662	+62.7
Texas	9,040	3,418	-62.2	407	683	+67.8
Virginia	16,293	3,877	-76.2	539	743	+37.8
West Virginia	8,173	1,542	-81.1	714	842	+17.9
Southern Cities						
Atlanta	4,683†	1,532	-67.3	183†	302	+65.0
Baltimore	2,397	2,044	-14.7	481	453	-5.8
Kansas City (Mo.)	1,370	591	-56.9	251	329	+31.1
Louisville	2,388	853	-64.3	331	402	+21.5
Memphis	2,050†	737	-64.0	255†	307	+20.4
Nashville	1,224	524	-57.2	250	379	+51.6
New Orleans	3,583	3,364	-6.1	631	478	-24.2
Richmond	5,388	1,930	-64.2	341	371	+8.8
St. Louis1	13,433	659	-95.1	540	437	-19.1
Washington, DC	869†	846	-2.6	241†	328	+36.1
Northern Cities						
Boston	1,016†	527†	-48.1	381†	435†	-14.2
Chicago	1,297	524†	-59.6	609	503†	-17.4
Cleveland	498	1,276	+156.2	536	892	+66.4
Detroit	1,144	1,459	+27.5	544	737	+35.5
Indianapolis	1,142†	1,196	+4.7	314†	457	+45.5
New York (Manhattan)	1,686	1,399	-17.0	467	393	-15.8
Philadelphia	2,625	1,413	-46.2	480	510	+6.3
Pittsburgh	1,963	1,397	-28.8	678	564	-16.8

SOURCE: U.S. Census, 1890 and 1920
NOTE: Unless otherwise indicated, figures are for males only. (See note, table 1)
*The occupation listings of the 1890 census grouped blacks, Indians, and persons of Chinese and Japanese descent into one racial category labeled "Colored."
† Includes both males and females
‡ The 1890 Census distinguished "Negroes" and "Colored" in this instance.

TABLE 3

Black Medical Colleges, 1865–1923

	City	Year Organized	Year Discontinued	Affiliation
Howard University	Washington, DC	1869		
Lincoln University	Oxford, Pennsylvania	1870	1874	Presbyterian (local)
Straight University	New Orleans	1873	1874	Congregationalist
Meharry Medical College	Nashville	1876		Methodist Episcopal
Leonard Medical School of Shaw University	Raleigh	1882	1918	Baptist
Louisville National Medical College	Louisville	1888	1912	Proprietary
Hannibal Medical College	Memphis	1889	1896	Proprietary
Flint Medical College of New Orleans University	New Orleans	1889	1911	Methodist Episcopal
Knoxville College Medical Department	Knoxville	1895	1900	Presbyterian
Chattanooga National Medical College	Chattanooga	1899	1908	Proprietary
State University Medical Department	Louisville	1899	1903 (Merged with LNMC)	Baptist (Ky.)
Knoxville Medical College	Knoxville	1900	1910	Proprietary
University of West Tennessee College of Medicine and Surgery	Jackson (1st location)	1900	1907	Proprietary
	Memphis (2d location)	1907	1923	
Medico-Chirurgical and Theological College of Christ's Institution	Baltimore	1900	?	?

medical schools in the North), but as the rest of the black population began to migrate northward in the early decades of the twentieth century, so did black physicians. Though their ranks grew in all parts of the country, black doctors generally constituted only a tiny proportion of the medical profession between 1890 and 1920. Similarly, the ratio of black citizens to black doctors in each state and in the nation as a whole improved greatly during that time period, but, with a few exceptions in cities with black medical schools, remained much poorer than for whites (see table 2).

Most black physicians in practice before 1920 had attended one of the dozen missionary or proprietary medical schools established in the South for former slaves after emancipation (see table 3). Through every phase of their educational career, beginning with the reading of medical college catalogues and ending with commencement addresses at degree-granting ceremonies, black medical students learned how black people needed them, how they could help raise up the race, and how personally rewarding the profession of medicine was. Never did they hear complaints—increasingly common in the white medical community before 1920—about an overcrowded medical field.[5] Black physicians were in demand.

The New Orleans University Medical Department (later renamed Flint Medical College), for instance, announced in its 1895–96 catalogue, "The school supplies a wide felt need in the far South."[6] That need, a graduating student at Leonard Medical School in Raleigh, North Carolina, explained to his classmates in 1886, extended beyond the mere provision of medical care to educating the ignorant about proper health practices. Lawton A. Scruggs, caught up in the excitement of Leonard's first graduation in 1886, enthusiastically titled his valedictory address "Medical Education as a Factor in the Elevation of the Colored Race." Discussing the need of black citizens to hear about recent advances in disease prevention, sanitation, and hygiene, Scruggs asserted, "No one can better teach them these practical and important truths than the educated colored physician who is one of their number." The challenges of medicine, he continued, would spur black physicians to help their fellow citizens "with the same self-sacrifice, courage and devotion as has ever characterized the profession. . . . We who stand before you tonight, are pioneers of the medical profession of our race."[7] Needed pioneers, as Booker T. Washington told eager Howard University medical students on the opening day of classes in October 1909:

> There is great demand for negro doctors. I think we have about 3,500 negro physicians in America. We need at least 7,000 in America. The white doctor has to seek [his] location, then hang out his shingle, but the location seeks the negro doctor. Everybody knows him. So our apparent disadvantages become our advantages.[8]

President Charles F. Meserve of Leonard Medical School had made similar claims in his 1906 commencement address: "This institution and others of similar character cannot begin to meet the calls that are coming constantly for trained physicians and pharmacists."[9] Letters in his files demonstrated this point. Citizens of one South Carolina town had communicated with Meserve several times over two years and even offered to send a representative to Leonard's commencement exercises in hopes of convincing one of the young graduates to set up practice there.[10] Meserve had to inform a citizen of this town that he thought all graduating seniors had "decided upon where they [would] locate."[11] At black medical schools across the South, prominent residents of large cities like Montgomery, Alabama, and small ones like Hertford, North Carolina, courted new graduates.[12] Competition was keen to win the services of these young men and women.

For the young black doctor, all of this attention[13] meant instant prestige and status in the black community. As the biographer of the early twentieth-century Memphis physician Joseph E. Walker described the situation (in exaggerated terms):

> In that age and time a Negro doctor was as popular in Negro life as money is in business. With Dr. before a man's name, he immediately became the community leader, the outstanding figure that received the honor, respect, and admiration of the entire populace. Everybody looked up to him and felt complimented to pay homage to him. Negro men accepted the ideas and thoughts of the colored doctor in all things as right and final, and Negro women worshiped them. In another field it would take time to build up—in medicine it was seemingly an over-night affair. The doctor lived in the best home, wore the best clothes, rode the best horse and was the unrivaled suitor of the fairest of the community's fair sex.[14]

But instant status did not mean a problem- and struggle-free transition from poor medical student to well-heeled local physician. Black doctors often encountered a disparity between the status accorded them as educated leaders in the community and the level of acceptance given them as professional healers. Just after graduation, however, with applause and words of praise still echoing in their minds, with confidence in their abilities and success on state licensing exams buoying their egos, and with expectations of developing a thriving practice and of helping their people urging them on, newly minted black physicians knew little of these other matters as they set out into the world. Deep within, though, some must have wondered, as did John Edward Perry on his graduation day in Nashville in 1895, "What does the future hold in store?"[15]

These black citizens, many just one, two, or three generations removed from bondage, had reached this position because of their drive and determination to succeed. They became some of the first blacks to gain not just literacy or even basic learning, but a higher education and a profession. Their letters of application to medical schools, their correspondence with school authorities about scholarships, summer jobs, and money matters, and the writings of contemporary observers about their situations indicate that few came from "monied" backgrounds. Most had limited funds and outstanding debts until several years after opening practices. They (and their families) had struggled and sacrificed to get through medical school and continued doing so as they entered medical practice.[16]

Most, then, arrived in their first towns poor, with no horse and buggy or automobile, no office or home, and few material possessions other than some medical books and instruments. They were on their own now to prove themselves capable of earning a living practicing medicine. Courtship with towns anxious for a physician was over, letters of reference from former professors were useless.[17] Black physicians now faced the realities of an impoverished patient population, competition with local established white practitioners, and black patients wary, not just of a new physician, but of a black physician. Success was not guaranteed. These new black physicians hopefully hung their shingles outside their rented offices, arranged their medical books on a shelf, readied their few instruments, and waited for patients to call.

It could be a lonely and trying time. A few months after graduating from Leonard Medical School, Dr. William E. Atkins wrote to his former advisor, "I am now in Hampton, Virginia, my future home. I like Hampton very much and consider the outlook very fair but of course it will take time and patience. I can do both if I just don't get too hungry."[18] Another recent Leonard graduate, John H.G. Williams, moved to Columbus, Georgia, in the spring of 1904 and wrote a more confident letter to President Meserve, though financial prospects also dominated his thoughts:

> I have arranged about my license and now have my office opened and also have my horse and buggy. I started last Sat. P.M. . . . got my turnout [buggy] then. I had my first call Sunday P.M. and several since. I am getting along nicely to be at an entirely new place. I think my chances are good here, anyway I am satisfied so far.[19]

Frederick Douglass Sessoms, Leonard class of 1906, had little spare cash upon his arrival in Herford, North Carolina, shortly after graduation. The Reverend G.D. Griffin had invited Sessoms to practice there well before commencement exercises. The young physician had visited the town, talked to its residents, and decided to settle in Hertford. He used some of his limited funds to rent a one-room office, but he did not have enough extra for a horse. So Sessoms visited his local patients on foot and asked plantations owners to provide him rides to and from their land.[20] And J. Edward Perry recalled years later his actions and feelings shortly after arriving in Mexico, Missouri, in 1893:

> With no funds with which to purchase office equipment or the payment for [office] space, the idea suggested itself to begin practice from my residence [rented rooms]. A sign was secured and tacked against the outside wall, cards were printed and I was ready for the first call. . . . There were only three lonely days before a request was made for me to see a [patient]. . . . [That first Sunday] a shadow of gloom hovered over me as I thought of friends, mother and father far away, while I struggled among strangers.[21]

Under such circumstances, pursuit of humanitarian ideals of racial health improvement and patient education must have seemed remote and easy to postpone.

Sometimes the local church provided comfort for lonely black physicians in new towns, and also some needed publicity to help start a practice. Upon arriving in Frankfort, Kentucky, for example, Edward Ellsworth Underwood, an 1891 graduate of Western Reserve Medical School, received from the townspeople "a rousing and hearty public welcome at the Corinthian Baptist Church."[22] And even Perry, on that first solitary Sunday in Mexico, Missouri, ultimately found warmth and company at the Methodist Church:

> At the conclusion of the services the presiding elder said, "For many years we have been planting an orchard in Nashville, Tennessee, that has been bearing fruit. All of these years I have not seen until the other day a single apple in this section from our orchard. If you were to spend money and time in growing an orchard, surely you would not be so silly as to say I will not use the fruit from my own trees. I have something to show you this morning that you have never seen before, a colored doctor, an apple from your own orchard."
>
> Those were the words of the solemn minister in the way of introduction. To me this was all a surprise, but I perchanced to have a bountiful supply of cards, which were generously distributed as the crowd surged forth to shake my hand at the conclusion of my remarks.[23]

Any new physician, white or black, arriving in town, would have experienced the same variety of feelings as those described here, their intensity depending on previous training, knowledge of the town, state of personal finances, and personality. But race added an extra measure of uncertainty to the arrival of a black practitioner. As the Mexico, Missouri, minister indicated, in the late nineteenth and early twentieth centuries few blacks and even fewer white lay people or physicians had ever met and dealt with, personally or professionally, a black with an M.D. So the same black citizens who accorded black physicians high status in the community because of educational superiority, professional position, and earning potential also treated warily someone so different from themselves who took on a role ("doctoring") usually reserved for whites.

Biographical and autobiographical sketches of black physicians during this period indicate that they assumed high posts in their churches, service organizations, and social clubs, and acted as liaisons with white community and civil authorities.[24] Blacks, wrote one graduate of Leonard Medical School practicing in Maxton, North Carolina, "generally seem to appreciate their people and yet the [black] doctor is such a strange man to a great many, they have to hesitate and 'look him up and down.'"[25] That is exactly what Perry encountered after Mexico's daily newspaper announced his presence: For "the first few days," he wrote in his autobiography, "as I passed on the streets, one person would call another and the two, a third one, and say, 'He's him.'"[26] Though they appreciated the attention, new black physicians also wanted the chance to prove themselves able practitioners, a sentiment well articulated by John H. Tompkins, newly arrived in Cumberland, Maryland, in a letter to President Meserve back at his alma mater: "In every avenue possible I am striving to do my best, and feel that if I get a start here and have a fair trial for a start I'll do well."[27]

But black citizens did not always find it easy to give their professional brothers and sisters a fair trial. They were distrustful of black physicians after years of conditioning with white practitioners. Dr. Robert F. Boyd, an

1882 Meharry graduate, reported to 1890 readers of the *Christian Educator*, a magazine of the Freedmen's Aid Society of the Methodist Episcopal Church, that as of three years earlier "very few good [black Nashville] families had ever given colored doctors their practice," because "they did not believe them competent."[28] Worse still was the attitude Dr. Thaddeus A. Walker, another Meharry graduate, encountered upon his arrival in 1887 in Baton Rouge, Louisiana: "I started my practice here with considerable opposition from my own people."[29] Other physicians reported similar problems.[30]

Two sociological studies performed in the early twentieth century confirmed the validity of these physician's claims. Thomas Jackson Woofter, Jr., used a Phelps-Stokes fellowship at the University of Georgia in 1913 to investigate various aspects of black life in Athens, seat of the university. He noted the same disparity between status and attitude that black physicians had observed in their speeches and letters: "All negroes in professions occupy a high position in the negro community. The negro preacher is possibly the most influential. [But] the negro doctors of Athens [Woofter counted five] [still] meet with some little prejudice and suspicion among the masses of the negroes."[31] James W. Martin, a graduate student at the George Peabody College in Nashville, applied his Phelps-Stokes fellowship particularly to observe the practices of black physicians in central and western Tennessee in 1920. He found a number of blacks who "were personally friendly [with black physicians], but of the opinion that a physician should be a white man."[32] Commenting on this seemingly contradictory attitude of black patients, a *Washington Post* reporter wrote in 1909:

> Now, nobody disputes the right of a Negro to practice medicine. . . . However, there is room for doubt that . . . [additional] Negro doctors would find the demand and reward for their labors considerable enough to pay expenses to keep themselves alive. An indefinable something resides in the breed that disinclines the Negro to give countenance and patronage to members of his own race.[33]

That "indefinable something" keeping black patients from using black physicians' services resulted in part from a reluctance to give up traditional reliance on white doctors and from a sense of uncertainty about black physicians' abilities. For years slaves had heard white racist assumptions about black incompetence and seen only white healers when sick, leaving many former bondsmen and their descendants presuming that only whites were capable of learning and practicing regular medicine. In addition, self-dosing in times of sickness was common among blacks. For rural dwellers without ready access to physicians' services, self-reliance in medical matters was a necessity. Such independence from professionals, born of necessity, became habit, except in severe situations. And medical intervention, even in the early twentieth century, did not mean certain cure. Medical knowledge was increasing, but primarily in the area of diagnosis rather than treatment.

Blacks, even in slavery times, when they were supposed to report ailments to masters or overseers, often first used treatments they had brought with them from Africa and the West Indies or had developed in the American South and had shared with others in the slave quarters.[34] They continued to apply these remedies and try out others after the Civil War, especially now that freedom had turned the watchful eyes of their former owners to other matters.

Freedom also allowed the more open practice and flourishing of another activity that interfered with blacks' acceptance and use of regularly trained black practitioners—rootwork. Based on a belief in the supernatural and on the magical powers of "conjurers" to control events in people's lives, this system, brought with slaves from Africa to the West Indies and then to the United States, had a large following among late nineteenth-century Southern blacks. Conjurers, adherents believed, could, through hexes and voodoo, bring on or relieve people of diseases and physical disorders at will, when asked (and paid) to do so.[35] Regular physicians and lay observers, black and white alike, denounced these beliefs as superstition. One white writer in the *Christian Educator* worried mightily about the problem and tied its solution to the black race's future: "So great and so common is superstition among the Negroes, especially in the South, that fears, doubts, and follies embarrass any effort to make him self-reliant." He believed that "the cultured Christian [black] physician, more than any other man" might, through his influence in the black community, "scatter these oppressive superstitions."[36] But even black doctors could not completely wrest voodoo from the popular place it held in the black mind. Rootwork successfully competed with allopathic medicine and kept some blacks (the number is difficult to determine) from gaining regular medical attention.[37]

Midwifery, common in the rural South through the early twentieth century, also kept black households from employing trained black physicians. Tradition and cost made the midwife's presence at deliveries a more attractive though not necessarily safer alternative to the physician's.[38]

Cost, of course, played a major role in discouraging blacks from calling on a physician in time of illness. But that reluctance would presumably have worked equally against physicians of both races, or even have encouraged black patients to try first the local black doctor, who might not charge as much or press for payment as quickly or firmly as the white practitioner. The problem of obtaining payment for services loomed large for the black physician.

Some black healers, professionally trained or not, created, by their actions, distrust for black physicians among local residents. A white visitor to Beaufort, South Carolina, shortly after the Civil War learned, for example, of a "Northern colored man" who had opened a medical practice there but soon left because fellow blacks found him "extortionate" and not to be trusted.[39] Incidents like that created difficulties not just for the practitioner involved but also for his colleagues in the area and for his successors. J.

Edward Perry encountered such a situation in 1895 on the Mexico, Missouri, train platform where he had just disembarked to begin his medical career. When the man whom he had asked for directions to the Baptist minister's house learned Perry was a physician, he responded: "A doctor! Lawd! Man, you curtanly made a mistake even stoppen in dis town; de folks here are fighten mad at nigger doctors and I know dey will run you out o' town soon as dey know you are heer." Perry discovered that a black "corn doctor" had recently spent a few days in town selling a patent or homemade remedy the efficacy of which he had guaranteed, and then skipped out with his "wild promises" unfulfilled.[40]

Less obvious but more insidious than the disliked or lying black healer who came and went in a short time was the well-entrenched but incompetent physician who undermined the standing of fellow doctors. Walter F. White, executive secretary of the National Association for the Advancement of Colored People from 1931 to 1955, described such a man in his 1924 novel, *Fire in the Flint*, about the return of Dr. Kenneth B. Harper, trained in the North, to practice in his hometown of Central City, Georgia:

> Perhaps the greatest factor contributing to the coloured folks' lack of confidence in physicians of their own race was the inefficiency of Dr. Williams, the only coloured doctor in Central City prior to Kenneth's return. Dr. Williams belonged to the old school and moved on the theory that when he graduated [from medical school] some eighteen years before . . . the development of medical knowledge had stopped. He fondly pictured himself as being the most prominent personage of Central City's Negro colony, was pompous, bulbous-eyed, and exceedingly fond of long words, especially of Latin derivation. . . . Through his fraternal [society] and church connections and lack of competition, he had made a little money, much of it through his position as medical examiner for the lodges to which he belonged. As long as he treated minor ailments—cuts, colic, childbirths, and the like—he had little trouble. But when more serious maladies attacked them, the coloured population sent for the old white physician, Dr. Bennett, instead of for Dr. Williams.[41]

White makes it clear that Bennett was only somewhat more competent than Williams but that even so, it took young Dr. Harper some time to overcome the prejudice against black physicians that Williams had engendered in Central City's "Negro colony." Only perseverance and successful medical outcomes could win over blacks who had had bad experiences with other black practitioners. White physicians as a group did not encounter this type of problem because its basis was racial; black doctors had a harder time proving themselves to their potential patients because they were black and doctors. A mistaken diagnosis or treatment, a high charge or perceived insult, a charlatan or unqualified physician, cost black physicians a much higher price than it did white physicians.

Drumming up business among reluctant black patients was only one difficulty the black doctor faced upon moving to a new town. His or her presence did more than cause some black patients to consider using a physician of their own race; it often stirred up racial tensions between blacks and whites. Exclaimed one black woman when, in May 1906, Joseph E. Walker announced himself as the new doctor in town (Indianola, Mississippi): "My God, what is dis here town coming to—dese white folks just now getting ober habing 'er nigger Postmaster and now here comes 'er nigger Doctor—Did Ros'velt send 'm 'ere too?"[42]

Black patients did not worry alone about the effect black doctors might have on local race relations; the physicians themselves had similar concerns. Sometimes they shied away from a particular state or region, as Leonard's President Meserve explained to the citizens of a South Carolina town: "I appreciate what you say about the need of a Colored physician in your locality. The fact is, Colored physicians do not desire to settle in South Carolina. You, of course, understand why without my saying anything further. I wish it were not so."[43] (See the citizen-to-physician ratios in table 2.) And generally black physicians knew that their arrival would upset the balance of patients and income that had previously existed among practitioners. Though some whites may have extended a helping hand to their black medical brethren, others held underlying or overt negative feelings as well.

The letter to the *Medical World* quoted at the beginning of this article illustrates the nature of the problem black physicians faced. Dr. Taylor's editorial response which was printed immediately beneath the letter, ventured "the opinion that [the letter] does not voice the sentiment of southern medical men," and remarked critically on its "literary attainments." Taylor also commented favorably on the good work he knew black physicians were performing in the South and invited their reactions to the letter.[44] Over the next two months Taylor published replies from black and a few white physicians, all attacking the provocative letter's author, denying the existence of his negative, racist attitude among the general population of Southern white doctors, and supporting the efforts of black practitioners.[45] But racism did exist, as this excerpt from a Clifton Forge, Virginia, physician's response inadvertently demonstrates: "The Southern doctor in question represents a very small minority of the Southern white physicians. . . . Simply regard [the letter] as one of the many obstacles which are constantly being thrown in the way of the man of color when he attempts to rise."[46]

For away from the limelight, in offices and patients' homes, incidents did occur that revealed some of these other beliefs and feelings of white physicians. A white Southern doctor could write an open letter to the *Medical World* looking for ways to limit competition from his black colleagues and receive open rebuffs for his views and denials of their representativeness from members of the medical profession; but back home this same man (and others like him) could (and did) act "to keep Negro physicians down." Dr. J. Edward Perry, for example, met with a less than cordial response from a white Columbia, Missouri, physician to his proposed move to that town in 1895. In reply to the young black doctor's request for "the acquaintance, goodwill and assistance of the [local] representatives of the profession," this man informed Perry that "the practice among your people is done by white brethren in the profession and it would be a mighty hard thing for a man of your age and most especially your color to wring it from their hands."[47] Corroboration of that competitive concern comes from James Martin's 1920 Tennessee physicians study. He found it "generally [though] not uniformly the case" that white physicians "regarded the negro physician as an economic competitor,"[48] so much so in a portion of west Tennessee that "negroes are forced [by their white colleagues] to charge the same as whites do."[49] Similarly, an Oklahoma physician in 1914 described white Southern doctors as "wont" to be "craving for [patients of] the opposite race as an [economic] asset to their practice."[50]

Some of these fears about competition from black doctors can be explained by the state of medicine and the national economy in the late nineteenth and early twentieth centuries. Black physicians were attempting to enter medicine at a time of professional overcrowding, when even in small towns too many physicians were competing for too few patients, and when economic conditions were at best only fair. But in addition to these professional and economic issues in the South were racial ones. White doctors in Tennessee could still say frankly to a white sociologist in 1920, "Mr. Martin, you will find that the negro mind is incapable of any considerable development, and Dr. A., being a colored man, is not to be seriously regarded as a real physician. He is a good negro, but still a negro."[51] And the NAACP executive Walter White, well acquainted with black physicians and their experiences, could, in *Fire in the Flint*, accurately reflect reality by having an inept white Georgia practitioner say of a black practitioner who had corrected his diagnosis and successfully treated his former patient that he "wa'n't goin' to let no young nigger doctor tell him his bus'ness."[52] Black physicians in the South, despite glowing reports to medical journals, alumni and religious missionary magazines, and former teachers, did encounter racial problems in their practices.

A severe one was white physician refusal to consult with or assist black colleagues in the treatment of patients in extremis. Written descriptions of such incidents are rare, but their very occurrence indicates the depth of white antagonism and strength of tradition that some black physicians had to overcome. One encounter took place in the vicinity of Washington, Georgia, in about 1908. Frederick Douglass Sessoms, recently relocated from Hertford, North Carolina, raced his horse and buggy eighteen miles to Barnett, where one of his patients had an abdominal wall abscess that urgently required surgery. Sessoms needed another physician to assist during the operation. The family had seen a white physician pass by shortly before, so Sessoms had the patient's son, Claude Davis, flag Dr. Beasley down on his return from visiting a patient. Dr. Beasley entered the Davis home, examined the patient, and agreed surgery was needed. Neither physician had the necessary instruments on hand, so they agreed to postpone surgery until seven the next morning, assuming the patient survived the night. Sessoms went home and returned at the appointed hour, this time by train, only to find that Beasley had informed the family he could not perform surgery with a Negro doctor. After determining that an operation might still help his patient, Sessoms acquired a horse and buggy, hurried four miles to the nearest telephone, and called Dr. Thomas J. Wills, an elderly white physician of Sessom's acquaintance who lived twenty miles away. Will's initial response to the black physician's request was, "I am very busy," to which Sessoms replied, "But I am no longer urging you, Dr. Wills, I am now begging and beseeching that you help me to save a life—a life that will otherwise be lost." "How can I get there?" answered Wills. He caught a train twenty minutes later, and arrived at the depot in an hour, where Sessoms and Claude Davis met him. They performed the procedure and saved the patient.[53]

Not surprisingly, Walter White's stereotypical fictional white Georgia doctor behaved just like the real-life Dr. Beasley. When the young black physician in Central City sought out a colleague to help perform an emergency appendectomy, "he realized his absolute dependence on Dr. Williams [the old black physician in town,] for he knew no white doctor would assist a Negro surgeon or even operate with a coloured assistant."[54]

Such openly racist behavior not only endangered patients' lives, it also undercut the position of black physicians before their patients. If black doctors could not obtain assistance from white colleagues when urgently needed, how could black doctors be relied upon to treat their patients' medical and surgical problems? The black physician Luther Burbridge, in his 1895 Emancipation Day speech, "The Colored Man in Medicine," in New Iberia, Louisiana, cited just this type of situation to exemplify the difficulties facing him and his colleagues: "A surgical operation of importance is to be performed, and the case falls into the hands of the colored doctor. He knows that there is little hope of any professional assistance from the neighboring physicians and his future reputation and success depend, perhaps, upon the issue of the case."[55] Burbridge described those circumstances to illustrate the loneliness of Southern black medical practice and the way these physicians were forced to rely on their own skills. Southern white doctors took advantage of black practitioners' vulnerable positions to isolate them professionally. For, in addition to refusing to consult with or assist blacks, they barred their black colleagues from joining local and state medical societies, refusing them admitting privileges to local hospitals, and overtly and subtly tried to reduce their competitiveness for patients who could afford to pay.[56]

As physicians accepted and incorporated more and more of the scientific discoveries and diagnostic methodologies of the late nineteenth and early twentieth centuries into their medical practices, communication of new ideas and approaches to patient problems became increasingly important. To practice good medicine, physicians had to keep up with the latest developments and learn how to apply them to patient care situations. Regularly reading medical journals and occasionally attending postgraduate courses at large medical centers helped practitioners keep abreast of current work in the field. Black physicians, if their response to the 1914 *Medical World* letter is any indication, did the former, and some, based on contemporary and later biographical sketches, also the latter, when time, money, and the lowering of racial barriers in the North permitted.[57]

Collegial face-to-face discussions and demonstrations of newly learned techniques and treatments or exchanges of opinion about difficult cases also taught physicians and improved their skills. Such communication occurred not only informally, at chance encounters or social occasions, but also at more formal county and state medical society meetings. From any of these potentially important and useful learning situations the black physician was usually, and in some areas always, excluded solely on the basis of race and social custom. J. Edward Perry, reflecting on his early career in small-town Missouri in the 1890s, considered that this professional, racially motivated isolation was most detrimental to young black physicians like himself:

> There is scarcely a day that the busy doctor is not confronted with some clinical enigma that taxes his scientific resources to the utmost. This is more true of the novice or inexperienced physician than of the one more seasoned in the dispensation of the healing art. At this period, it was my misfortune possibly to be meeting daily more and more cases that produced an anxious mind and sleepless nights. There were three reasons for these restless moments and disturbed emotions. First, a deficiency of knowledge; second, a lack of contact and clinical advice; third, destitute facilities.[58]

As Burbridge eloquently described it:

> Isolated, as many of them are, from intercourse with colored men of their own profession and despairing of any assistance from the opposite race, often their only recourse is their books and journals. Under such circumstances the Negro physician sometimes finds himself confronted with a deep and seemingly impassable gulf over which it seems impossible to leap and around which he can see no way.[59]

This gulf of isolation based on race appeared almost immediately after blacks entered the medical profession in the 1860s. Alexander T. Augusta encountered it during and just after the Civil War in Alexandria, Virginia, and Savannah, Georgia, in his dealings with white physicians,[60] and then again in 1869 and 1870, when he and two other black physicians applied for admission to the all-white Medical Society of the District of Columbia, and in 1870 to the American Medical Association.[61] It continued into 1882, when Dr. Whitfield Winsey, a Harvard-trained black physician, received seven blackballs from members of the Baltimore Medical and Surgical Society (five were needed for rejection from membership). All voted negatively on account of Winsey's race, one member stating "that his Southern

birth prevented him from recognizing a negro practitioner."[62] And the exclusionary policies extended to all other Southern medical societies through
the 1940s.[63]

The gulf that kept black physicians from professional intercourse with
white colleagues and medical societies also extended to hospitals. White
physicians simply denied admitting privileges to blacks, forcing them to
leave patients who required hospitalization (usually for surgery) at the entrance door, entrusted to the care of these same white doctors. This was a
particularly difficult problem because it affected the doctors' pocketbooks,
professional competency, and standing with patients. John W. Walker of
Asheville, North Carolina, speaking for his state's black doctors at the 1910
National Medical Association (NMA, the black counterpart to the AMA)
annual meeting, described the situation to a group already quite familiar
with the problem: "We realize that we are put to a great disadvantage when
we have cases to operate upon and have no hospital. We are obliged to
turn [patients] over to white physicians and when we do this it is hard for
our people to have the proper interest and confidence in us."[64] Dr. Albert
W. Dumas of Natchez, Mississippi, echoed Walker's sentiments, adding:
"[White surgeons] carry the patient[s] to the hospital and often you never see
[the patients] again until they die or recover."[65] Blacks thus had little opportunity to learn and refine surgical techniques once out of medical school, or
to provide continuity of care for their patients. Few blacks became surgical
specialists, and many lost income because of their actual or presumed
inability to perform surgery or because they could not provide needed
hospital medical care.[66] In several ways, then, white physicians in the South
isolated black pracitioners and so reduced blacks' effectiveness as doctors.

Income was another matter that caused tension between black and white
physicians in this era of economic stagnation (especially in the rural South).
At times, the entry of black physicians into an already crowded profession
worsened existing racial stress. White practitioners appear generally to have
surrendered their nonpaying and indigent black and white patients to the
new black doctors without strong protest. But black physicians, like white
physicians, had to feed their families. And some, perhaps most, had ambi-
tions besides healing and teaching better health practices to the poor. They
were professionals who wanted to make names for themselves and at least
live in comfortable homes like their white colleagues. This meant competing for patients with white physicians. Walter White's fictional (though
representative) Kenneth Harper explained one day to his brother why he
returned to Georgia after completing training at Bellevue in New York City:

> "Why did I come back? That's easy. I came back because I can make more
> money here than anywhere else. . . . I came back here where the bulk of
> coloured people live and where they make money off their crops and where
> there won't be much trouble for me to build up a big practice. . . . Oh, I
> suppose I could've made money [in the North] . . . , but I wanted to come back
> home. I can do more good here, both for myself and for the coloured people,

than I could up there. And I don't think I'll have any trouble down here. Papa got along all right here in this town for more than fifty years, and I reckon I can do it too. . . . Why, I'll have a cinch around this part of Georgia! There aren't more than half a dozen coloured doctors in all this part of the country who've had a decent medical education and training. . . . In a few years I'll be able to give up general practicing and give all my time to major surgery. I'll handle pretty nearly everything in this part of the State."[67]

Harper may have been more naive than most about the ease with which he would succeed in practice, but his attitude probably reflected that of many young black physicians setting out. They may have meant no harm to their white and black colleagues already in practice, but to earn a living they had to step on a few toes.

John H. Tompkins discovered this when he moved to Cumberland, Maryland, in 1896. He introduced himself to "many of the prominent whites" in town, "including several of the medical profession" and "got their general views of things personally, in regard to having a colored Dr. settle here." "Few of the latter," he reported to President Charles Meserve, "were incourging [sic]."[68] That response might have been expected from physicians concerned about losing patients to competitors. In general, ailing whites who patronized black physicians came from the poorer classes, but some white paying patients also turned to black physicians for their medical care, thereby confirming the fears of certain white doctors. The author of a 1903 study of "The Negroes of St. Louis" found, for instance, that one of the fourteen black practitioners in the city,

> who has been here ten years and has an excellent reputation, has a few white patients. They came to him at first by accident, but then continued to patronize him. Two others, whose offices are in districts inhabited by poor whites as well as Negroes, report that they have both white and colored patients.[69]

Luther Burbridge noted a similar trend in Louisiana, and described it in more political terms:

> We feel proud to state that the practice of a colored doctor is by no means confined solely to his own race. For even here in the historic old State of Louisiana, whose fertile vales have often echoed to the cry of the oppressed, the negro physician enjoys in many instances a small, but growing white patronage. This in itself is a confession of a recognition of skill and ability, wrung as it were from the lips of the oppressor.[70]

A number of black physicians pointedly mentioned in letters about their success the racial mixture of their patients. Wrote a Columbia, South Carolina, man, "I have an extensive and paying practice among my own people and a considerable practice among the poorer classes of the white people." And a Macon, Mississippi, physician bragged to W. E. B. DuBois, "My practice here is very large among both colored and white. . . . I have had white people come here from a distance and board here to get my treatment." The impact of such success on collegial relations, an Arkansas physician admitted, was not always positive: "I have experienced some prejudice among my white friends. We do not have much to do with each other as physicians."[71]

Evidence indicates that, though black physicians attracted some of their white clientele because of professional reputations, they also won white patronage for two less glamorous reasons. Perhaps in recognition of the generally low incomes of their patients, or perhaps in order to draw patients to their practices, some black physicians charged less than the usual fees for medical services. These doctors do not appear to have written to their colleagues, former classmates, or instructors about the practice, nor did newspaper, medical journal, or popular magazine accounts mention it. But James Martin, studying Tennessee black physicians in 1920, discusses its silent but pervasive presence in two very different regions of that state, and documents its persistence even when forbidden by white practitioners. Martin reported that the case charges of fourteen black physicians in five middle Tennessee counties (Lincoln, Giles, Marshall, Maury and William-son) and eleven in two western Tennessee counties (Haywood and Fayette) were "from 25 percent to 60 percent less than white doctors receive[d] for the same kind of work."[72] Several of the black practitioners told Martin they had "built up a considerable general practice among white people," a prac-tice Martin discovered upon further investigation "to be for the poorer white people, who called [on] the colored physician because his fees were lower."[73] Their clientele among white professional and business classes he found to be "very limited," with the exception noted below.[74]

Concerned about losing patients to black physicians, the white doctors of Tennessee's economically poor and predominantly agricultural "black belt" counties tried actively to compete for Negro patients. Martin described the situation and black physicians' answer to it: "The general custom in the Western counties seems to be that the white physicians give directions as to those matters [of fees charged] which the colored must obey. As a matter of course, these are often evaded, but secretly."[75] The experience of white and black practitioners in seven Tennessee counties does not necessarily repre-sent a situation that prevailed in the South. But the poverty of most late nineteenth- and early twentieth-century Southern blacks—the group that constituted the majority of black physicians' patients in the region—surely dictated that black physicians establish a lower fee schedule than that of their white colleagues.[76] And these cheaper prices must have induced some poorer whites to call on black doctors when sick. Whether these practitio-ners were also more lenient in their collection schedules is not well docu-mented. Lower fees, however, if they cut into the practice of local white physicians, would understandably have upset the white physicians.

If a difference in fee scales between physicians of the two races is difficult to document, the other reason some whites preferred black doctors to those of their own racial group is even more difficult to document because of its delicacy. This aspect of Southern black physicians' practice white doctors could not control, as it took place secretly. One fictional account of black medical practice in the South does confront the subject of venereal disease treatment directly. The author Walter White describes how Dr. Kenneth Harper began treating certain affluent, respected white males of Central City, Georgia, in the early 1920s:

> A new source of practice and revenue began gradually to grow. The main entrance to his office was on Lee Street. This door was some fifty feet back from Lee Street, and the overhanging branches of the elms cut off completely the light from the street lamp at the corner. One night, as he sat reading in his office, there came a knock at his door. Opening it, he found standing there Roy Ewing. Ewing had inherited the general merchandise store bearing his name from his father, was a deacon in the largest Baptist Church in Central City, was the president of the Central City Chamber of Commerce, and was regarded as a leading citizen.
> Kenneth gazed at his caller in some surprise.
> "Hello, Ken. Anybody around?"
> On being assured that he was alone, Ewing entered, brushing by Kenneth to get out of the glare of the light. Kenneth followed him into the office, meanwhile, asking his caller what he could do for him.
> "Ken, I've got a little job I want you to do for me. I'm in a little trouble. Went up to Macon last month with Bill Jackson, and we had a little fun. I guess I took too much liquor. We went by a place Bill knew about where there were some girls. I took a fancy to a little girl from Atlanta who told me she had slipped away from home and her folks though she was visiting her cousins at Forsyth. Anyhow, I thought everything was all right, but I'm in a bad way and I want you to treat me. I can't go to Dr. Bennett 'cause I don't want him to know about it. I'll take care of you all right, and if you get me fixed up I'll pay you well."[77]

"That," concludes the narrator, "was Kenneth's introduction to one part of the work of a coloured physician in the South."[78]

James Martin found evidence of this work in Tennessee. One pharmacist he interviewed said: "When a young fellow of the aristocratic class, and this is an aristocratic town, gets siphilis [sic] or gonorrhea, he usually goes to this negro [physician] and so avoids the embarrassment of submitting such a case to a friend of the family."[79] A few black doctors there developed a reputation for curing venereal diseases and attracted a large black and white clientele.[80] So black physicians did, in certain instances and for various reasons, compete successfully with their white counterparts for patients of both races.

But success in gaining patients did not necessarily mean financial ease. As a Thomasville, Georgia, physician wrote to President Meserve in 1904, "My practice is as good as I could wish. Collections keeps [sic] off the wolf."[81] Smaller fees and a generally poorer clientele must have taken their toll on black physicians' income, though actual numbers are not readily available, making comparisons with white physicians' income impossible.[82] Collection of fees for all physicians naturally varied depending on clientele, physician personality, local financial conditions, and other variables. An Oklahoma physician summed up the situation in his state in a 1914 letter to the editor of the *Medical World:* "In the state of Oklahoma there are over 100 Negro physicians, some doing well; others are not. They average from $600 to over $3,000 per annum."[83] Turn-of-the-century black medical graduates, often in debt for their education and fiscally overextended in order to open their practices, expressed concern when payments for services did not arrive in a timely fashion. J. Edward Ashburn, a Bowers Hill, Virginia, physician, contrasted for President Meserve the number of patients he saw and the amount actually collected: "In my practice I am doing very well; my field is very large. . . . [Actual income] is a little scarce, yet I am pushing perseveringly to the front."[84] Jeremiah M. Lloyd of Elizabethtown, North Carolina, echoed Ashburn's story: "I have a large practice in this town and surroundings. But I have not collected much money as the people are poor having lost all of their crops by a large freshet."[85]

So black physicians faced all of the problems any doctor encountered in opening a medical practice, and also met with difficulties due to their race as they entered this formerly white-dominated profession. Yet some of them succeeded quite well in the South. In 1890, for example, Dr. Albert L. Thompson, a Meharry graduate, offered readers of the *Christian Educator* a capsule account of his rise to local prominence and fortune:

> I began active work in this city [Dennison, Texas] two years ago, and for awhile the way appeared dark. I was treated kindly by the [medical] fraternity, and assured that the time would come when I would meet with the success hoped for. So the time moved on, and my practice became larger, and my collections better, until I have been enabled to secure a passable office outfit, a good buggy and horse, and real estate valued at fifteen hundred dollars in a fine portion of the city, within four blocks of Main Street, the business center of the city.[86]

Several available reports announce strikingly positive white physician responses to black practitioners' arrivals, responses that conveyed the promise of friendship and collegiality among potential rivals. Thaddeus A. Walker of Baton Rouge told readers of the *Christian Educator* in January 1887, "I was given the hand of fellowship by a leading white physician, Dr. J. W. Dupree, who welcomed me in these words: 'You are my colored medical brother, and I will go with you at any time.'"[87] And Robert F. Boyd of Nashville, a graduate and future faculty member of Meharry wrote, "All the physicians of the city treat me white."[88] "I have, when needed," wrote Green J. Starnes from San Antonio at this time, "counsel from the leading physicians of the city."[89] Another black doctor in Texas had "the respect of all the physicians of this city, one of whom made me a present of one hundred dollars' worth of good medical books."[90] President Meserve, who received numerous letters from graduates in practice, most living in the South, bragged in his 1903–4 annual report to a philanthropic fund that his school's alumni "are respected by the white physicians wherever they go, and have no difficulty in getting the white physicians to consult with them when critical cases demand it."[91] Such was the skill and reputation of a Columbia, South Carolina, practitioner that he reported to W. E. B. DuBois being often "called upon by white physicians to consult with them in medical cases and assist in surgical cases in their practice."[92] Race seemed not to interfere with professional matters for these physicians.[93] One North Carolina doctor summed it up by stating: "My intercourse with the white members of my profession is cordial along professional lines. I seek no others."[94]

Acceptance by white colleagues represented one measure of success for the black physician. Patronage by patients and the financial rewards that accompanied it represented another. Young black doctors happily reported their progress, though, as DuBois cautioned readers of his study of "the college-bred Negro," there were many failures. But people tended to discuss the good and ignore the bad. So letters to DuBois, Meserve, George W. Hubbard (dean of Meharry), and others emphasized accomplishments. "I have a fine practice, went in over 500 different families last year and I am doing [even] better this year. I drive my own turn out, and have purchased a home, and married," wrote (on letterhead stationary) a recent Leonard graduate practicing in Portsmouth, Virginia, to Charles Meserve.[95] J. Benton Dickson, an earlier Leonard alumnus, told Meserve he was "succeeding splendidly" in Jackson, Tennessee, and could now afford to purchase his printed diploma. "I should have sent for my diploma earlier," he explained, "but had a large number of debts to pay off and could not take money to pay for things I could do without awhile, when my other bills were past due." (Dickson's letterhead no doubt helped Meserve understand the source of Dickson's new financial status. In addition to giving his telephone number and morning, afternoon, and evening office hours, it also proclaimed that the young doctor was "in office all night.")[96] "When I came here I was owing three hundred and fifty dollars, all of which is now paid," a Gulf States practitioner wrote to Hubbard. "I have supported my family; equipped a fine office, which compares favorably with the best in the city; bought and paid for a horse, buggy, and road-cart, and household furniture amounting to two hundred dollars."[97] And so they wrote about the size of their practices, the mixture of white and black patients, and the financial rewards.[98]

Clearly, the major concern of these new black doctors was survival. They may have wished to fulfill the ideals of race betterment set out by and for them in medical school, for a few mentioned improvement of black health in their reports and letters (e.g., "I am doing all the good I can to all the people I can in every way possible.").[99] But these pioneering black physicians believed they first had to establish themselves professionally in their communities.

Their positive reports to alma mater and to public print media tended to minimize racial problems and a poor clientele in order to promote good will, a favorable public image, increased black attendance at medical schools, and cordial relations between whites and blacks. Even the fictional Kenneth Harper tried to ignore racial tensions in Central City, Georgia, in hopes of

TABLE 4

Black Medical Societies in the United States, 1914–15

National
  National Medical Association
State and Regional
  Alabama Medical, Dental, and Pharmaceutical Association
  Arkansas Medical Association
  Florida Medical, Dental, and Pharmaceutical Association
  Tri-State Medical, Dental, and Pharmaceutical Association of Florida,
  Georgia, and Alabama
  Georgia State Medical society
  Indiana Association of Physicians, Dentists, and Pharmacists
  Tri-State Medical Association of Indiana, Kentucky, and Ohio
  Kentucky Medical, Dental, and Pharmaceutical Association
  Louisiana Medical, Dental, and Pharmaceutical Association
  Maryland Medical, Dental, and Pharmaceutical Association
  Massachusetts, Medical, Dental, and Pharmaceutical Association
  Mississippi Medical, Dental, Pharmaceutical, and Surgical Association
  Pan-Missouri Medical Association
  North Jersey Medical Society of New Jersey
  North Carolina Medical, Pharmaceutical, and Dental Association
  Ohio Medical Association
  Central Pennsylvania Medial society
  Palmetto Medical Association (South Carolina)
  Tennessee Medical Association
  The Lone Star Medical, Dental, and Pharmaceutical Association (Texas)
  Tidewater Medical Society of Virginia
  Flat Top Medical Association of West Virginia
  West Virginia State Medical Society
City
  Freedman's Hospital Medical Society, Washington, D.C.
  Medico-Chirurgical Society of the District of Columbia
  South Atlantic Medical Society, Savannah, Ga.
  The Atlanta Association of Negro Physicians, Dentists, and Pharmacists
  The Aesculapian Society of Indianapolis, Ind.
  The Physicians, Dentists, and Pharmacists Club of Chicago
  The Falls City Medical Association, Louisville, Ky.
  Mound City Medical Association, St. Louis, Mo.
  Aesculapian Society of New York City
  Medico-Chirurgical Society of Greater New York
  Raleigh Medical Association, Raleigh N.C.
  Philadelphia Academy of Medicine and the Allied Sciences
  Charleston County Medical Association, Charleston, S.C.
  Bluff City Medical, Dental, and Pharmaceutical Society, Memphis, Tenn.
  Rock City Academy of Medicine and Surgery, Nashville, Tenn.
  Dallas Negro Medical, Dental, and Pharmaceutical Association
  The Richmond Medical Society of Richmond, Va.

SOURCE: Monroe Work, ed., *The Negro Year Book, 1914-15*, pp. 335-38

gaining acceptance and easing whites and blacks through a transitional period of increasing status for Southern blacks. But race did get in the way of success, for Harper and real-life physicians like J. Edward Perry, who described it in his autobiography, and for many who did not mention it in letters and reports. Those white physicians who made the effort to welcome and assist their black colleagues as they might have taken a newly graduated doctor of their own race under their wing contributed to the cause of harmony between black and white professionals. But they did not change the mores of Southern society. Whites still dominated; prejudice and segregation still existed. So the success of black physicians depended not only on their passively receiving welcomes from a few sympathetic white physicians and some local black patients. These doctors had actively to overcome negative white *and* black racial attitudes toward black medical professionals. They did this by practicing good medicine, by proving themselves competent, by becoming leaders in their communities, and by, as will now be shown, addressing directly some of the obstacles others put in their path.

Black physicians fought against professional isolation in several ways. Personal contact with white physicians sometimes helped.[100] More fruitful were activities that sought to circumvent the formal racial isolation imposed by whites. Though these methods simply established parallel segregated institutions for black physicians, they did provide professional opportunities that were otherwise unavailable. These practitioners acted to improve their situations not only at the local level, but also regionally and nationally. A key to all these endeavors was good communication among local black doctors. This, of course, was easier to do in urban areas than out in the country. A glance at city or medical directories of the period reveals the presence of more than one black practitioner in most towns of any size in the South.[101] Numbers allowed them to discuss ways of protecting their interests and to band together in formal and informal ways. Occasionally blacks in a city established a local medical society and met regularly for professional or social purposes (see table 4). In May 1911, for example, the physician members of the Falls City (Louisville) Medical Association met and established a fee schedule "in order to secure uniform prices and insure reasonable rates of service to the public."[102] Other physicians simply recognized common needs and acted to assist one another. A black physician in Columbus, Georgia, for instance, helped a recently arrived Leonard Medical School graduate establish his practice in town.[103] In turn-of-the-century Kansas City, Missouri, J. Edward Perry reported in his autobiography, the need for a united front was great:

> Those were tough days and lean pickings for the Negro doctor of Kansas City. We soon learned that the interest of one was the welfare of the other. The objective was to gain a reputation for the efficiency of the brother of color.
>
> Our greatest difficulty was continuing in the service of a patient after having been called. If a patient were stricken in his "tummy" and was not entirely relieved by noon the following day, a white physician was frequently called if

per chance the individual had the cash in hand. Ethics were of no significance at all to the white brother. It appeared to be the "survival of the fittest."

Often when an individual became seriously ill with pneumonia or typhoid fever, and one of the group perchanced to be in the neighborhood, a call would invariably be made upon the patient of a brother physician to see what was "going on" and to evidence interest. If a patient became abruptly, seriously ill and his regular physician was around town on calls, the visit was made by a brother physician, and in case of a collection the amount was readily "turned over," with a note as to findings or impressions of the malady, also information of the remedies administered. We were all for one and one for all.

With sincere service, honesty of opinion and a manifestation of interest in the general welfare of the people, gradually there was observed a broadening of our reputations, a multiplicity of friends and an increase in our practice and income.[104]

Cooperation among black physicians even extended to poor rural areas of the South, if for no other reason than to exchange information about fees and patients. Though perhaps not as well organized or successful as urban groups, these networks appear to have been useful. James Martin's brief statement about the physicians of middle and western Tennessee indicates that such arrangements existed elsewhere, as well: "Agreements among negro physicians as to case charges seem to be not very precise; but, in most places where there are two or more practicing, there are such agreements, indefinite and poorly kept as they are."[105]

Forming local societies, arranging fee structures, and providing mutual patient coverage were only some of the actions black doctors took to bolster their professional positions and combat isolation. Another major problem they faced was gaining access to hospitals. So black practitioners established their own, either individually or in groups, where they could care for their patients and perform surgery.[106] When, for example, Cornelius and Alice Woodby McKane arrived in Savannah and found no hospital, they made it a priority of theirs to open one. In 1893 the McKane Hospital began accepting patients and continued to care for blacks using black physicians long after its founders had left for Africa in 1895 as medical missionaries.[107] The pioneering South Carolina physician Matilda Evans opened hospitals in Columbia three times between her arrival in 1898, fresh from Women's Medical College in Philadelphia, and 1916.[108] Alonzo McClennan, a Howard graduate, gathered enough black community support to open a hospital and nurse training school in Charleston in 1897. All but one of the local black physicians joined with McClennan in the project, which gave them their only chance to obtain hospital-operating privileges.[109] An enterprising 1891 Meharry graduate, George S. Burruss, moved to Augusta, Georgia, and in 1901 established a hospital there. Five years later a reporter for a national black magazine described the Burruss Sanitarium for his readers:

It consists of a large three-story frame building, which contains twenty-seven rooms and one ward. The rooms are well ventilated, handsomely furnished and are provided with electric bells and electric lighting apparatus. The operating room is equipped with all the requisites of modern and aseptic [*sic*] surgery, including the operating table, instrument table, two wheel stretcher, a microscope for examining blood, sputum, etc., and an amphitheater for the convenience of doctors, nurses, and others who are privileged to be present during an operation. Not far from the operating room is the X-ray Department, in which there is an X-ray machine which was installed at a cost of more than $500. The first floor is taken up largely with a drug store, of which Dr. Burruss is sole proprietor, with his private offices and a large public reception room. The Sanitarium, building and equipment, I valued at $10,000 and is free from debt.[110]

The other eleven black physicians in Augusta, according to the writer, offered their "services and active hearty cooperation" to the enterprise.[111]

Of course not all or even most black physician-run hospitals succeeded like Burruss's. Little towns and rural areas required such facilities on a smaller scale. Nor were there always patients to occupy the beds or make use of the equipment. In the seven Tennessee counties he studied, James Martin found three hospitals, only one of which still functioned. In stark contrast to the Burruss Sanitarium, this facility comprised "a large, almost bare house in which there were a number of beds. There were, at the time of this visit, no patients and hence no nurse or caretaker other than the physician whose office was next door."[112] The other two hospitals Martin investigated were cooperative ventures among two or more black physicians.[113] Whether owned individually or by groups, these private hospitals sprang up across the South as black physicians encountered racial restrictions on their practices.

Like Kenneth Harper of Central City, Georgia, some black physicians had aspirations of becoming experts in surgery in their regions and founded hospitals as the only available means to achieve that goal. Robert C. Burt (Meharry 1897) of Clarksville, Tennessee, was such a man. According to biographical sketches in his personal papers, he nourished a "long cherished dream of operating a small hospital and to do surgery on a large scale." So in 1904 he bought some land and by 1906 had converted a house on it into a hospital equipped for surgery. With the support and assistance of black physicians and dentists in the area; Home Infirmary grew over the next few years into a regional hospital caring for hundreds of patients.[114] To help spur on people like Burt, successful black surgeons like Daniel Hale Williams and George Cleveland Hall, both of Chicago, traveled through the South in the early twentieth century, holding surgical clinics for fellow practitioners. These men would perform procedures on local patients in order to demonstrate surgical techniques and innovations to blacks barred from or unable to attend postgraduate courses and white hospital clinics.[115] Attesting to the influence of surgical clinics and to the felt need for and determination of Southern black practitioners to establish hospitals is Monroe Work's inventory of such institutions in his *Negro Year Book*. In the 1914–15 edition, for example, he listed seventy-seven hospitals in the region, almost all operated by blacks.[116]

Though expensive for practitioners both in direct costs and in lost patient revenues, taking postgraduate courses in the growing speciality areas offered isolated black physicians a chance to improve knowledge and skills, meet new colleagues, and visit large Northern cities like Chicago, Boston, New York, Washington, and Philadelphia. These courses were initially held at traditionally white medical schools and were closed to blacks, but most institutions had begun to accept blacks, and some black educational facilities had established postgraduate programs, by the decade following 1910.[117] (No Southern black institutions developed postgraduate facilities before 1920).

These sorts of individual initiatives and cooperative ventures, aimed at overcoming professional isolation, encouraged some black physicians to link colleagues on an even broader basis. In 1895, enough physicians expressed interest in founding a nationwide medical society that a group met in Atlanta at the Cotton States and International Exposition, the same exposition at which Booker T. Washington gained notice for his famous accommodationist speech, to establish the National Medical Association, with goals similar to those of local groups.[118] And by 1920, virtually every Southern state had a black medical society that sometimes included dentists and pharmacists along with doctors (see table 4).[119] Such groups met regularly to present medical papers, to exchange information and ideas about racial matters, and simply to socialize and become (re)acquainted with colleagues. The fifth annual meeting of the Mississippi Medical and Surgical Association in April 1905 was typical. The Jackson gathering offered those attending case presentations, medical papers, and discussions, and a presidential address that stressed, according to a local newspaper report, "promoting friendly co-operation with the white physicians of the state, and spoke in the highest terms of the white physicians generally." In an obvious reference to these remarks, the white newspaper approvingly included in its headlines for the story the words: "President May Makes a Good Talk in Which He Gives Association Sensible Advice."[120] All these organizations experienced difficult times when membership or attendance at meetings dwindled, but most survived until integration.

Black-oriented medical journals also provided a means not only of keeping physicians' knowledge current, but also of learning about colleagues' and institutions' activities and of contributing information of one's own. Miles Vandahurst Lynk of Jackson, Tennessee, published the first of these journals, the *Medical and Surgical Observer*, in 1892, just one year after his graduation from Meharry. A forceful and outspoken man on many subjects,[121] Lynk promoted his periodical with advertisements such as this:

> Say, Doctor, have you read the MEDICAL AND SURGICAL OBSER-VER, the Organ of the Colored Medical Profession of North America? It recognizes the necessity of a higher standard of medical education in this country, and will put forth its best efforts to raise and maintain the same. It contains all the progressive ideas of the professions—minus the chaff.

> Read and endorsed by the profession from the Atlantic to the Pacific and
> from the Arctic Ocean to Mexico.[122]

In the days before black physicians had organized a national professional
association, Lynk's advertisement smacked of hyperbole, but if the letters he
published from readers around the country indicate the journal's general
reception, then the *Observer* certainly filled a gap. One such letter from
Waco, Texas, read:

> I have before my gaze the pride and boast of every Negro doctor—a journal
> of our own—a counterpart of ourselves—a real living proof of capacity in
> science and art. In a brief way, allow me to congratulate you for pluck, energy
> and forethought. The accomplishment of a century in twenty-seven years
> [since Emancipation]! Who can say (but to be laughed at) that we are not
> coming once hundred thousand strong? God bless your efforts, provide for the
> permanence of such a literature and endow the editor with wisdom. My name,
> accompanied with subscription price of your valuable journal will be forth-
> coming in a few days.[123]

Though lively and interesting, the *Observer* could not (nor could its editor)
induce enough black physicians to part with one dollar for a subscription to
sustain the publication beyond 1893. Lynk, however, remained active in the
profession, calling for the establishment of a nationwide professional society
in 1892, and operating the University of West Tennessee School of Medicine almost single-handedly, first in Jackson, then in Memphis, from 1900
to 1922.[124]

Not until 1909 did a second national medical journal by and for black
physicians appear. (Alonzo McClennan had published the *Hospital Gazette*
in Charleston for a few years in the late 1890s, but its audience remained
local and oriented toward nursing.)[125] At that time the officers of the National Medical Association began issuing an official *Journal*. It, too, struggled
for survival, but endured hard times, strongly promoting the interests of
black physicians. It published papers presented at annual meetings, minutes
of NMA and state society meetings, and advertisements of upcoming black-
sponsored medical meetings and events. Individual physicians reading the
JNMA could feel part of a larger group and learn how and where to participate, if desired.

The *JNMA* published editorials as well, offering opinions on important
aspects of black medicine. In 1920 the death of a prominent practitioner, Dr.
George W. Cabaniss, provided the editors with an opportunity to look back
at the growth of the black medical profession and at the measures of success
black physicians had been using. They found their colleagues wanting:

> Too many men in the practice of medicine feel that when they have made
> money and established their economic independence, they have discharged
> their whole responsibility to their day and generation. . . . Let such a physician
> stop for a moment and consider how he has made his money,—from whence
> he has made it. . . . We venture to say that about ninety-nine per cent of [his]

practice is among Negroes; and we venture to say further that ninety-five per cent of that ninety-nine per cent is among the hard-working class of Negroes, the poor, the lowly, the ignorant—that mass of helpless dependents, many of them absolutely poverty stricken, living from hand to mouth. Doctor, when you drive through the slums in your high-powered, fast-going automobile and look upon this seething mass of disease-ridden, poverty stricken [people], ignorance personified, out of whom you have gained influence and opulence, do you stop for a minute to think that you owe them anything in return?[126]

The editors raised difficult questions for successful practitioners, questions these doctors had avoided or pushed aside in their pursuit of other goals, but which they would eventually have to confront.[127]

By 1920, Southern black physicians had come a long way in establishing themselves. Though they could never escape the race issue, in their dealings with both patients and colleagues, many had earned a good reputation and a good living. As a group they had developed an increasingly strong, active, and accepted body of medical professionals. Their commitment to the general improvement of black health may have suffered in their zeal to establish themselves and provide an enduring presence in a previously white profession. But they had made a good start in accomplishing their other goals.

NOTES

1. W.E.B. DuBois, ed., *The College-Bred Negro* (Atlanta, Georgia: Atlanta University Press, 1900), p. 83.
2. *Med. World*, 1914, 32: 65 (Charles Fremont Taylor, ed.).
3. On some black physicians' continued lack of concern for black health in the early twentieth century, see Edward H. Beardsley, "Making separate, equal: black physicians and the problems of medical segregation in the pre-World War II South," *Bull. Hist. Med.*, 1983, 57: 382–96.
4. On the pre-1920 black medical schools, see Herbert M. Morais, *The History of the Negro in Medicine* (New York: Publishers Co., 1967), pp. 40–67; Todd L. Savitt, "Lincoln University Medical Department—a forgotten nineteenth-century black medical school," *J. Hist. Med.*, 1985, 40: 42–65; *idem*, "The Education of Black Physicians at Shaw University, 1882–1918," in *Black Americans in North Carolina and the South*, ed. Jeffrey J. Crow and Flora J. Hatley (Chapel Hill: University of North Carolina Press, 1984), pp. 160–88; Darlene Clark Hine, "The anatomy of failure: medical education reform and the Leonard Medical School of Shaw University, 1882–1920," *J. Negro Educ.*, 1985, 54: 512–25; Walter Dyson, *Founding the School of Medicine of Howard University, 1868–1873*, Howard University Studies in History no. 10 (Washington, D.C.: Howard University Press, 1929); *idem, Howard University, the Capstone of Negro Education: A History, 1867–1940* (Washington, D.C.: The Graduate School, Howard University, 1941); James Summerville, *Educating Black Doctors: A History of Meharry Medical College* (University: University of Alabama Press, 1983); Darlene Clark Hine, "The Pursuit of Professional Equality: Meharry Medical College, 1921–1938, A Case Study," in *New Perspectives on Black Educational History*, ed. Vincent P. Franklin and James D. Anderson (Boston: G. K. Hall, 1978), pp. 173–92; Leslie A. Falk, "Meharry Medical College: a century of service," *Southern Exposure*, Summer 1978, 6: 14–17; Leslie A.

Falk and N. A. Quaynor-Malm, "Early Afro-American Medical Education in the United States: The Origins of Meharry Medical College in the Nineteenth Century," *Proceedings of the Twenty-Third Congress of the History of Medicine, London, 2–9 September 1972* (London: Wellcome Institute of the History of Medicine, 1974), pp. 346–56.

5. Examples of such complaints may be found in Gerald E. Markowitz and David Rosner, "Doctors in Crisis: Medical Education and Medical Reform During the Progressive Era, 1895–1915," in *Health Care in America: Essays in Social History*, ed. Susan Reverby and David Rosner (Philadelphia: Temple University Press, 1979), pp. 189–91.

6. New Orleans University, Department of Medicine and Surgery, *Catalogue of 1895–96*, p. 47. Similar pronouncements may be found in catalogues of the other black medical schools.

7. *African Expositor*, April 1886, p. 3. This issue of Shaw University's newspaper may be found in the North Carolina Collection, Wilson Library, University of North Carolina, Chapel Hill.

8. *Howard Univ. J.*, 8 October 1909, 7: 2.

9. The *Workers*, June-July 1906, 2: 2. Issues of this college magazine are located at the Shaw University Archives, Raleigh, North Carolina.

10. W. R. Brown to Meserve, 26 April 1897, Charles F. Meserve Letterbook 2, p. 287; P. H. Koon to Meserve, 12 March 1898, Meserve Letterbook 3, p. 262, Shaw Archives. For other examples, see Meserve to A. D. Wimbs, 23 September 1895, Meserve Letterbook 1, p. 704; C. G. Robinson to Meserve, 5 December 1896, Letter File 1, Shaw Archives.

11. Meserve to W. B. [*sic*] Brown, 20 February 1897, Meserve Letterbook 2, p. 70, Shaw Archives.

12. Booker T. Washington to Cornelius N. Dorsette, 28 February 1883, in *The Booker T. Washington Papers*, ed. Louis R. Harlan et al., 13 vols. (Urbana: University of Illinois Press, 1972–), 2: 219–20; Edward L. Wilkerson, *Struggling to Climb: A Biography* [of Frederick D. Sessoms, M.D.] (Cleveland, Ohio: n.p., 1958), p. 41.

13. See accounts of black medical school commencements in the *Christian Educator*, 1891–92, 3: 363; 1897, 8, 85–88; 1900–1901, 12: 77–78; the *Workers*, June-July 1906, 2: 1–4; *Daily American* (Nashville), 23 February 1883, p. 6; *New National Era* (Washington, D.C.), 9 March 1871, p. 2; 7 March 1872, p. 3.

14. T. J. Johnson, *From the Driftwood of Bayou Pierre* (Louisville, Kentucky: Dunne, 1949), p. 28.

15. John Edward Perry, *Forty Cords of Wood: Memoirs of a Medical Doctor* (Jefferson City, Missouri: Lincoln University Press, 1947), p. 134. For more information on Dr. Perry, an important Kansas City physician, see Martin Kaufman, Stuart Galishoff, and Todd L. Savitt, eds., *Dictionary of American Medical Biography*, 2 vols. (Westport, Connecticut: Greenwood Press, 1985), 2: 592.

16. On debts, see, for example, Caesar Bassette to Meserve, 1 September 1905, Letter File 3, William A. Mapp to Meserve, 30 December 1896, Letter File 1, Jeremiah M. Lloyd to Meserve, 23 November 1896, Letter File 1; and John W. Jones to Meserve, 1 April 1898, Meserve Letterbook 3, p. 402, all at Shaw Archives; Wilkerson, *Struggling to Climb*, p. 39; *Christian Educator*, 1889–90, 1: 108.

17. See, for example, Meserve to To Whom It May Concern, 6 May 1895, Meserve Letterbook 1, p. 485, Shaw Archives.

18. Aktins to Meserve, 8 October 1896, Letter File 1, Shaw Archives.

19. Williams to Meserve, 12 May 1904, Letter File 2, Shaw Archives.

20. Wilkerson, *Struggling to Climb*, p. 39.

21. Perry, *Forty Cords*, pp. 144–45.

22. William D. Johnson, *Biographical Sketches of Prominent Negro Men and Women of Kentucky* (Lexington, Kentucky: n.p., 1897), p. 62.

23. Perry, *Forty Cords*, p. 145.

24. A. B. Caldwell, ed., *History of the American Negro and His Institutions*, 7 vols. (Atlanta, Georgia: A. B. Caldwell, 1917–23); John A. Kennedy, *The Negro in Medicine* (Tuskegee, Alabama: Tuskegee Institute Press, 1912); J. W. Gibson and W. H. Crogman,

Progress of a Race or the Remarkable Advancement of the American Negro (Napierville, Illinois: J. L. Nichols, 1912).

25. William A. Mapp to Meserve, 30 December 1896, Letter File 1, Shaw Archives.

26. Perry, *Forty Cords*, p. 144. See also John H. Tompkins to Meserve, 7 December 1896, Letter File 1, Shaw Archives.

27. Tompkins to Meserve, 7 December 1896, Letter File 1, Shaw Archives.

28. *Christian Educator*, 1889–90, 1: 163.

29. *Ibid.*

30. See, for example, Luther T. Burbridge, "The Colored Man in Medicine," in *The Afro-American Encyclopedia*, comp. James T. Haley (Nashville, Tennessee: Haley and Florida, 1895), pp. 72–73.

31. Thomas Jackson Woofter, Jr., "The negroes of Athens, Georgia," Phelps-Stokes Fellowship Studies no. 1, *Bull. Univ. Georgia*, December 1913, *14*: 40. Phelps-Stokes Fund fellowships, established in 1912, provided money for Southern white graduate students at major Southern universities to study race issues using social science methodology.

32. James W. Martin, "A Study of the Negro Physician with Particular Reference to Certain Tennessee Counties" (Master's thesis, George Peabody College for Teachers [Nashville, Tennessee], 1921), p. 16. My thanks to James Summerville of Nashville for locating, obtaining, and sending me a copy of this thesis.

33. Unidentified article in the *Washington Post* reprinted in *JNMA*, 1910, 2: 46–47.

34. Todd L. Savitt, *Medicine and Slavery: The Diseases and Health Care of Blacks in Antebellum Virginia* (Urbana: University of Illinois Press, 1978), pp. 171–80.

35. Leonora Herron, "Conjuring and conjure-doctors," *Southern Workman*, 1895, *24*: 117–18; A. M. Bacon, "Conjuring and conjure-doctors," *ibid.*, 193–94; Wilbert C. Jordan, "Voodoo Medicine," in *Textbook of Black-Related Diseases*, ed. Richard Allen Williams (New York: McGraw-Hill, 1975), pp. 716–25. A comprehensive discussion and bibliography on the subject may be found in Elliott J. Gorn, "Black Magic: Folk Beliefs of Afro-American Slaves," in *Science and Medicine in the Old South*, ed. Ronald L. Numbers and Todd L. Savitt (Baton Rouge: Louisiana State University Press, forthcoming).

36. J. A. Kumler, "Importance of medical schools for colored people," *Christian Educator*, 1889–90, 1: 22. See also F. Tipton, "The Negro problem from a medical standpoint," *New York Med. J.*, 1886, *43*: 571; Ambrose McCoy, "Voodooism in the South," *Louisville Med. News*, 1884, *18*: 380–81; Lawton A. Scruggs, "Medical education as a factor," *African Expositor*, April 1886, p. 3.

37. See references in n. 35.

38. See, for example, I. A. Newby, *Black Carolinians: A History of Blacks in South Carolina from 1895 to 1968* (Columbia: University of South Carolina Press, 1973), p. 115.

39. George Campbell, *White and Black: The Outcome of a Visit to the United States* (London: Chatto and Windus, 1879), p. 339, quoted in George B. Tindall, *South Carolina Negroes, 1877–1900* (Columbia: University of South Carolina Press, 1952), p. 147.

40. Perry, *Forty Cords*, p. 141.

41. Walter F. White, *The Fire in the Flint* (New York: Alfred A. Knopf, 1924), pp. 48–49, 50.

42. Johnson, *From the Driftwood*, pp. 30–31.

43. Meserve to Koon, 8 May 1897, Meserve Letterbook 2, p. 408, Shaw Archives.

44. *Med. World*, 1914, 32: 65.

45. *Ibid.*, pp. 111–13, 147–49.

46. Edward T. Conner, M.D., to the Editor, *ibid.*, p. 148.

47. Perry, *Forty Cords*, pp. 159–60.

48. Martin, "Study of the Negro Physician," pp. 14–15.

49. *Ibid.*, p. 59.

50. Carl R. Williams to the Editor, *Med. World*, 1914, 32: 112.

51. Martin, "Study of the Negro Physician," p. 15.

52. White, *Fire in the Flint*, p. 56. The distinguished black physician Louis T. Wright wrote, in 1929, that *Fire in the Flint* "accurately depicted the life of the Negro doctor in the rural parts of the South" ("The Negro physician," *Crisis*, 1929, 36: 306).

53. Wilkerson, *Struggling to Climb*, pp. 46–50.

54. White, *Fire in the Flint*, p. 57.

55. Burbridge, "Colored Man in Medicine," p. 72.

56. Beardsley, "Making separate, equal," pp. 382–87. The daughter of an early twentieth-century black physician later recalled that her father, upon arriving in Bennettsville, South Carolina, in 1908, had to practice under the supervision of a white physician because the white doctors did not want him to have an independent practice. See Suzanne C. Linder, *Medicine in Marlboro County* [South Carolina], *1736–1980* (Baltimore: Gateway Press, 1980), pp. 62, 186.

57. See sources in n. 23 and entries for black physicians in Kaufman et al., eds., *Dictionary of American Medical Biography*. For a description of racial prejudice at postgraduate schools, see Perry, *Forty Cords*, pp. 193–200; Martin, "Study of the Negro Physician," p. 32; Wright, "Negro physician," p. 305.

58. Perry, *Forty Cords*, p. 248.

59. Burbridge, "Colored Man in Medicine," p. 72.

60. W. Montague Cobb, "Alexander Thomas Augusta," *JNMA*, 1952, 44: 327–29; Kaufman et al., eds., *Dictionary of American Medical Biography*, 1: 23.

61. W. Montague Cobb, *The First Negro Medical Society: A History of the Medico-Chirurgical Society of the District of Columbia, 1884 to 1939* (Washington, D.C.: Associated Publishers, 1939), pp. 6–39; Morais, *History of the Negro in Medicine*, pp. 52–58, 303; Herbert W. Nickens, "A case of professional exclusion in 1870: the formation of the first black medical society," *JAMA*, 1985, 253: 2549–52.

62. *Med. Rec.*, 1882, 21: 390.

63. Morais, *History of the Negro in Medicine*, pp. 58, 133.

64. *JNMA*, 1910, 2: 323.

65. *Ibid.*, p. 325.

66. *Ibid.*, p. 324; W. E. B. DuBois, *The Philadelphia Negro: A Social Study* (Philadelphia: University of Pennsylvania, 1899), pp. 117–18.

67. White, *Fire in the Flint*, pp. 24, 25, 27.

68. Tompkins to Meserve, 7 December 1896, Letter File 1, Shaw Archives.

69. Lilian Brandt, "The negroes of St. Louis," *Publication Amer. Stat. Assoc.*, 1903, 8: 234–35.

70. Burbridge, "Colored Man in Medicine," pp. 71–72.

71. DuBois, *College-Bred Negro*, p. 83.

72. Martin, "Study of Negro Physician," p. 59.

73. *Ibid.*, p. 42.

74. *Ibid.*, p. 43.

75. *Ibid.*, p. 60.

76. Some black physicians in the North encountered similar problems and acted in a similar manner. *Rochester (New York) Times-Union*, 12 February 1980, p. 1B, article on Dr. Charles T. Lunsford.

77. White, *Fire in the Flint*, pp. 63–64.

78. *Ibid.*, pp. 64–65.

79. Martin, "Study of the Negro Physician," pp. 41–42.

80. *Ibid.* For an example from the North, see *Rochester Times-Union*, 12 February 1980, p. 1B.

81. S. H. Wilson to Meserve, 14 April 1904, Letter File 2, Shaw Archives.

82. Martin, "Study of the Negro Physician," p. 54, calculated the average black rural Tennessee physician's worth at about $7,700, compared with the average American black family's worth of about $500.

83. Carl R. Williams to the Editor, *Med. World*, 1914, 32: 112.

84. Ashburn to Meserve, 8 October 1896, Letter File 1, Shaw Archives.

85. Lloyd to Meserve, 23 November 1896, Letter File 1, Shaw Archives. See also the *Freeman* (Indianapolis), 24 December 1910.

86. *Christian Educator,* 1889–90, *1:* 162.

87. *Ibid.,* p. 163.

88. *Ibid.*

89. *Ibid.*

90. *Ibid.,* p. 108.

91. "Slater Fund School Reports, 1903–4," in John F. Slater Fund, New York, *Proceedings and Reports, 1904* (New York, 1904), p. 22.

92. DuBois, *College-Bred Negro,* p. 83.

93. *Med. World,* 1914, *32:* 111–13, 148–49; the *Workers,* December 1906–January 1907, *3:* 12, Harlan, ed., *Booker T. Washington Papers,* 2: 257; *Med. Surg. Obser.,* 1892, *1:* 46.

94. DuBois, *College-Bred Negro,* p. 83.

95. Benjamin F. Hutchins to Meserve, 26 April 1904, Letter File 2, Shaw Archives.

96. Dickson to Meserve, 2 October 1896, Letter File 1, Shaw Archives.

97. *Christian Educator,* 1889–90; *1:* 108.

98. *Ibid.,* 162–63; DuBois, *College-Bred Negro,* p. 83; the *Workers,* January 1905, *1:* 15; February–April 1905, *1:* 5; February–March 1906, *2:* 23; December 1905–January 1906, *2:* 10; December 1906–January 1907, *3:* 11–12; *Augusta (Georgia) Chronicle,* 30 September 1919, front page of "Colored Section." See also references in n. 23 herein.

99. Dr. Robert F. Boyd in *Christian Educator,* 1889–90, *1:* 163.

100. See for example, Perry, *Forty Cords,* pp. 159–60; John H. Tompkins to Meserve, 7 December 1896, Letter File 1, Shaw Archives.

101. See city and medical directories of the period, and John M. Matthews, "Studies in Race Relations in Georgia, 1880–1935" (Ph.D. diss., Duke University, 1970), p. 270.

102. James Summerville, "Formation of a black medical profession in Tennessee, 1880–1920," *J. Tenn. Med. Assoc.,* 1983, *10:* 646; the *Freeman* (Indianapolis), 13 May 1911, p. 4.

103. J. H. G. Williams to Meserve, 12 May 1904, Letter File 2, Shaw Archives.

104. Perry, *Forty Cords,* pp. 280–81.

105. Martin, "Study of the Negro Physician," p. 60.

106. *Ibid.,* p. 31; Perry, *Forty Cords,* pp. 276, 279 ff.

107. Robert E. Perdue, *The Negro in Savannah, 1865–1900* (New York: Exposition Press, 1973), pp. 126–28; Sara W. Brown, "Colored women physicians," *Southern Workman,* 1923, *52:* 582–83.

108. *Palmetto Leader* (Columbia), 23 November 1935.

109. Report of W. T. B. Williams on Hospital and Training School for Nurses, 28 November 1905, pp. 6–7, 11, in General Education Board Papers, box 200, folder 1899, Rockefeller Archive Center, Tarrytown, New York. The Waring Historical Library, Medical University of South Carolina, Charleston, also has a file of materials on this school.

110. S. P. Wadsworth, "The Burruss Sanitarium [*sic*]," *Voice of the Negro,* 1906, *3:* 339. See also *Augusta Chronicle,* 3 November 1907.

111. Wadsworth, "Burruss Sanitarium," p. 339.

112. Martin, "Study of the Negro Physician," p. 31.

113. *Ibid.*

114. Robert C. Burt Papers, Fisk University, Nashville, Tennessee.

115. John W. Lawlah, "George Cleveland Hall, 1864–1930, profile," *JNMA,* 1954, *46:* 207–10; Daniel Hale Williams to Booker T. Washington, 7 September 1898, Booker T. Washington Papers, Library of Congress, Washington, D.C.; Martin, "Study of the Negro Physician," pp. 31–32.

116. Annual editions of Monroe Work, ed., *The Negro Year Book* (Tuskegee, Alabama: Negro Year Book Company, 1912–52).

117. See, for example, Martin, "Study of the Negro Physician," p. 32; certificates of

postgraduate education in Burt Papers, Fisk University; Wadsworth, "Burruss Sanitarium," p. 341.

118. Morais, *History of the Negro in Medicine*, p. 68; W. Montague Cobb, "The black American in medicine," *JNMA* suppl., December 1981, 73: 1225–26.

119. See list in each issue of Work's *Negro Year Book*; see also Summerville, "Formation of a black medical profession in Tennessee," p. 646; Morais, *History of the Negro in Medicine*, p. 67; Cobb, "Black American in medicine," p. 1225.

120. Jackson *Daily Clarion-Ledger*, 27 April 1905, p. 8. (I thank Mr. Thomas N. Boschert of Duncan, Mississippi, for this reference.) See also Summerville, "Formation of a black medical profession in Tennessee," pp. 644–46.

121. Miles V. Lynk, *Sixty Years of Medicine: Or the Life and Times of Dr. Miles V. Lynk* (Memphis, Tennessee: Twentieth Century Press, 1951); Morais, *History of the Negro in Medicine*, p. 64.

122. *Med. Surg. Obser.*, 1893, 1: cover.

123. Monroe A. Majors to the Editor, 29 November 1892, *ibid.*, 1892, 1: 47.

124. *JNMA*, 1952, 44: 475–76; Kaufman et al., eds., *Dictionary of American Medical Biography*, 1: 466; Morais, *History of the Negro in Medicine*, pp. 64–65, 67.

125. Cobb, "Black American in medicine," pp. 1230–32, 1235–36.

126. *JNMA*, 1920, 12: 32–33.

127. See Beardsley, "Making separate, equal."

TWELVE

The Courtship Letters of an African American Couple: Race, Gender, Class, and the Cult of True Womanhood

VICKI HOWARD

On May 31, 1886, Calvin Lindley Rhone wrote to Lucia J. Knotts in Round Top, Texas, asking "Do you ever think of me? Miss Lucia, it is unnecessary to say, I love you with all my heart."[1] This first declaration of love began a nineteen-month correspondence during which Calvin Rhone, an African American schoolteacher in Brenham, Texas, persuaded Lucia Knotts to marry him. Their courtship letters document Lucia's resistance to Calvin's proposal, his attempt to prove his devotion and love for her, and the couple's slow negotiation of the future conditions of their married life. In some ways, Calvin's love letters reflect both the courtship customs and the romantic rhetoric of urban white middle-class Victorian Americans, a tradition that has been well documented by scholars such as Ellen Rothman and Karen Lystra.[2] At the same time, however, the conflicts Calvin and Lucia faced and the solutions they found were uniquely theirs, arising out of their own personal experiences in the African American community.

A shortage of comparable critical work on rural middle-class African Americans necessitates a cross-cultural contextualization. Past studies of rural black family history in the nineteenth century lack a personal dimension. Due to the paucity of extant historical sources such as diaries and letters by African Americans, the study of rural African American family history has depended largely on census statistics.[3] The courtship letters of Calvin Rhone and Lucia Knotts thus provide a rare opportunity to see how one African American couple negotiated their gender roles before marriage, and how these roles both confirmed and challenged white society's feminine ideal. Although their correspondence does not provide enough evidence to generalize about black rural middle-class courtship patterns and customs, their letters serve as a case study of how one African American couple loved and courted in 1880s rural Texas.

Recently, critics have begun to look more closely at nineteenth-century black middle-class culture. For example, in her book *The Coupling Convention: Sex, Text, and Tradition in Black Women's Fiction*, Anne duCille examines nineteenth-century African American authors who adopted popular middle-class forms, such as the marriage-plot novel. Willard Gatewood studies the upper- and middle-class African American communities in his book, *Aristocrats of Color: The Black Elite 1880–1920*.[4] Both works reveal the unique dichotomy of race and class that middle-class African Americans faced in the nineteenth century in their quest for race uplift. Gatewood shows how blacks created a community that resisted white cultural domination by remaking white American middle-class customs. DuCille demonstrates how African American writers subverted Anglo literary forms to make a literature of their own.

An exploration of the complex ways that race, class, and gender intersect in the courtship correspondence of Calvin Rhone and Lucia Knotts demonstrates a similar type of resistance. Their words and actions can be seen as both reflections of and resistance to the larger society's conception of gender. This essay will place Lucia Knotts and Calvin Rhone's conflict over gender roles in the context of white middle-class culture's ongoing discussion of the division between private and public spheres in the nineteenth century, and it will demonstrate how a cultural conception of gender, such as the "cult of true womanhood," crossed race lines and transformed itself in the process.

Like most nineteenth-century African Americans, Calvin Rhone and Lucia Knotts both came from rural southern families. Lucia Knotts was born in Texas in 1866, although her parents came from Georgia. There were ten children in her family, all of whom were born in Texas after the Civil War except the eldest daughter, who was born in 1862 in Georgia.[5] This indicates that the family probably migrated to Texas sometime after the Civil War ended in 1865. Interestingly, the Knotts family was listed as mulatto in the 1880 census, but Lucia was recorded as black, as was Calvin, in the 1900 census. Both Lucia's father, Benjamin, who was a farmer, and her mother, Bafette, whose occupation was "keeping house," were listed as illiterate; however, all their school-aged children attended school and could read and write.[6] Little information about Calvin Rhone's early life could be found, other than the fact that he was born in Mississippi in 1861.[7]

A more personal narrative than is told by the census records unfolds within the Rhone family papers. Although the courtship correspondence ended with a letter from Calvin that set the date of their wedding for December 27, 1887, the rest of the family papers flesh out the story of their long married life together.[8] Later letters between Calvin and Lucia Rhone, and between other family members, reveal the prominent place this middle-class family held in the black community of Fayette County in Texas. Both Calvin and Lucia were schoolteachers, and thus would have been leaders in their community.[9] Calvin was a member of the La Grange District Association of the Baptist Church, and he also belonged to various fraternal organizations. He was known as "Professor Rhone," a title that indicated the respect others held for him. Lucia was a women's club member, and she also was active in the Baptist Church. During their long marriage, they had twelve children, eight of whom survived. At least five of their children attended Prairie View A&M College. One daughter, Urissa Brown Rhone, whose papers are among the collection, had a long teaching career and eventually became principal of Round Top-Carmine High School.

Among the thirty-seven courtship letters saved in the Rhone Family Papers, thirty-five were Calvin's and only two were written by Lucia. The preponderance of Calvin's letters in the collection indicates that Lucia must have been the one who actively saved the courtship correspondence. The reason for the presence of two of her letters to Calvin in the collection is unknown. The act of saving Calvin's letters underlines the values they had for Lucia; saved as keepsakes by her, Calvin's letters become part of her story. She preserved a record of his courtship of her for posterity, whereas the bulk of her letters to him can only be presumed lost.

One consequence of this imbalance is that Calvin's voice is louder than Lucia's. A study of their correspondence could easily become dominated by his story. Lucia's point of view, however, can be detected in Calvin's letters. His letters to her only provide one-half of their story, but as with many overheard conversations, her side of the conversation can be reconstructed from his. Her thoughts and actions can be read into his letters, which are, of course, partly a response to her words and letters. In addition, Calvin employed a rhetorical style that allows for some reconstruction of Lucia's letters to him. For example, he frequently repeated her questions in his letter before answering, and he rephrased her words. In these ways, the courtship correspondence becomes her story.

His letters to her provide little factual detail about their own community, or the world at large. What does come through, however, is the busy pace of their life. Their days appeared to have followed a fast tempo, indicated by their sporadic letter-writing. With their frequent train trips around Fayette, Washington, and Austin Counties, each appears to have had little leisure time for writing, revealed by the many complaints Calvin made about Lucia's neglect of him, and by his response to her request that he write longer letters.[10] Although Calvin seems to have written more than Lucia— if his complaints can be taken at face value—he often wrote short letters, usually two or three small pages.[11] His school in Brenham, which he stated was "in a flourishing condition," kept him very busy.[12] Lucia appeared to be equally occupied in Round Top with her plans for attending Prairie View, then a black teacher's college in Hempstead, Texas. She revealed the fullness of her daily life in one of her letters to him, when she stopped mid-sentence, writing, "I do not believe, — Allow me to pause" and signed off as if interrupted by some business at hand.[13] Their busy schedules also seemed to limit the time they could spend together. During school holidays Calvin would visit Round Top, where Lucia lived on her father's farm, but otherwise they seemed to see each other infrequently. Although obviously solid members of the middle class, each of them apparently had little time for the luxury of courting long distance.[14] In these ways, their correspondence inadvertently reflected their active public lives.

On the surface, the correspondence gives little indication of the volatile racial atmosphere of 1880s Texas.[15] The letters themselves never deal overtly with issues of race or racism. Without the presence of a collection of photographs in the Rhone Family Papers, the reader of the courtship correspondence would never know the racial identity of the two lovers. The letters contain little information about the public sphere of work, politics, and the everyday business of the outside world. Over nineteen months, there are only two references to public events. In one letter, Calvin reassured Lucia, denying a rumor about a hanging: "In regards to that speaker being hanged it is all false, he was in Brenham last Friday, and Saturday, left here today one week ago." Mentioning the hanging only briefly, with no identifying details, Calvin seemed to be unwilling to discuss such things with her and immediately returned to the topic of his health. He had been sick, and closes the letter stating that "my nerves are weak and my brain is in a mental state of debility."[16] The second and final public reference is a brief mention of the election on state prohibition.[17] Calvin provided no commentary on this highly contested event, stating only that "Election on State Prohibition today is the only topic of interest I know of at present."[18] Politics and the racist world of post-Reconstruction Texas had no place in the world of love Calvin constructed in his letters.

For the most part, the Rhone-Knotts correspondence belongs to the private sphere of romance and love, or home and family. Calvin's non-discussion of news topics suggests an unwillingness to move beyond or outside of the romantic rhetoric of the love-letter tradition. He used the letters to discuss feelings and emotions, which traditionally belong to the private sphere, as opposed to the public sphere dominated by reason and rationality. Calvin's letters demonstrate that he excluded Lucia from his public life and instead placed her within an inner personal world of romance.

The middle-class status of the Rhone-Knotts courtship allows for a comparison with the white Victorian tradition of courtship and romantic love. Their letters demonstrate many of the rituals and themes typical of middle-class nineteenth-century courtship in America. Around 1880, courting couples began to use "little girl" and "little boy" as terms of endearment.[19] In his letters, Calvin used the closing form "your dear boy," and he referred to Lucia as "my dear little wife" and "Darling Pet."[20] Lucia's letters take a less romantic stance than Calvin's, which may be explained by the early stage of

their courtship when she wrote the letters, and by the fact that she is the pursued one, not the pursuer. She called him "Mr. Rhone" and, more famil-
iarly, "Dearest Calvin."[21] The two also exchanged photographs, and Calvin
quoted poetry to her, thus creating at least a superficial common ground
with the courtship tradition of white native-born Americans of this era.

Calvin and Lucia also appear to be engaged in what Karen Lystra describes as a "courtship testing ritual."[22] After the loss of parental control over
marriage, white middle class couples created their own crises to test the love
of the other and to prove the strength of the romantic bonds needed for
marriage. Calvin and Lucia tested each other's loyalty by measuring the
frequency and length of the other's letters. The postal service was often the
source of this conflict, causing miscommunication as letters were delivered
late or crossed one another in transit.

In earlier generations, couples had difficulty expressing their feelings, but
by the end of the nineteenth century lovers placed a new value on frankness.[23] Whether each lover was true or false was a central concern to both
Calvin and Lucia. In a letter to Calvin excusing her delay in responding to
his letter, Lucia wrote:

> Dearest Calvin,
> For this I hope you will pardon me, and believe me not to be faulse I did not
> believe you were writing flattery in your letter when I rec'd it nor now. And of
> course we are not strangers.[24]

Her words indicate that she valued sincerity and forthrightness over fine-
sounding words.

Lucia and Calvin adhered to the "ideal of openness" that Ellen Rothman
states was prominent in the courtship of white middle-class couples during
the 1880s and 1890s.[25] Calvin's letters reveal the couple's interest in one
another's state of mind. Calvin described one of Lucia's letters as "most heart
searching."[26] He wrote, "Darling, do not think I am doubting your love in
the least for I believe you are as firm as the rocks of Gibraltar."[27] In another
letter he asserted that he did not doubt her "constancy."[28] He also thought
that she doubted him, and asserted he was "true."[29] In still another letter he
closed with the words, "I will be true to you until time shall be no more."[30]

A study of courtship letters cannot ignore one of their implicit subjects:
sex. Toward the end of the nineteenth century, courting couples treated sex
as a "serious spiritualized sacrament of romantic love."[31] Scholars such as
Lystra have challenged the stereotype of Victorian prudery, seeing instead a
"symbolic equation of sex and romantic love."[32] The Victorians thought sex
could be an expression of the spirit, or inner self.[33] The way in which
sexuality was treated varied among individual letter writers, as the studies by
Lystra and Rothman have shown. The prohibition against premarital sex
remained, however, although it was often handled in varying ways in courtship correspondence.

Calvin Rhone broached the subject of sex by narrating his dreams about Lucia to her. He alluded to the sexual element in his dreams but never discussed it explicitly, thus preserving Victorian decorum and at the same time revealing that he harbored such feelings for her. As in the letters Lystra has studied, his correspondence offers a glimpse of both the physical and psychological tensions created by the traditional Victorian prohibition of premarital sex.[34] He wrote to Lucia:

> I will tell you my whole dream of you that night, yet if you insist I will have to tell you all; but I deem it utterly unnecessary to state it all. I dreamed I was at your home, had gone there that night with you; and was very much surprised when I awoke and found myself [back] in Brenham. The remainder of my dream was concerning our future union and you guess the balance. I dream of you every night.[35]

Lucia must have written back to pursue the topic, for in his next letter Calvin firmly insisted: "I'll tell you the remainder of my dream after we marry."[36] On the surface, the restraint he demonstrated in telling Lucia about his dreams of her reflects the stereotypical conception of Victorian prudery. Dreams provided a way for him to transfer the liability for his thoughts to a realm over which he had no control and, therefore, no responsibility. In fact, the telling of his dreams allowed him to express his sexual feelings for her within the confines of what was socially acceptable, without violating Victorian society's ideal of womanhood.

Calvin's ritualistic use of romantic diction of poetry created a very personal dream-like world in which professional ambition, money affairs, current events, and even racial problems had no place. In his letters, all that mattered is that Lucia return his love:

> With out you or when away from you life seems at times to be in the yellow leaf. One thought of your sweet smile cheer me in my lonely hours. I get up and imagine you at my side and your bright eyes smiling in mine, and your sweetest voice of all voices ring continually in my ear.[37]

In true romantic form, Calvin quoted poetry to express his unhappiness. Without naming the poet, he borrowed a few lines from Robert Burn's *Man Was Made to Mourn:* "As the poet says, 'Man's inhumanity to man / Makes countless thousands mourn / . . . And every time add clearer proof / That man was made to mourn.'"[38]

Calvin seems to cast himself in the role of the romantic lover whose happiness depends on the return of his love. His language reveals his vulnerable position as the pursuer, and Lucia's power as the pursued. At one point, having been hurt by her refusal of his proposal of marriage, Calvin chastises her, and writes:

> But, however, you said you would rather hear from lips my proposal, and when you did hear it you turned me off almost as a beggar from your door. Which caused the heart within me to sob with sorrow[39]

Two months later, when their plans for the future were still tenuous, he continued to express his unhappiness in a dramatic mode, asking her,

> "How will it be with you some day maybe I will have to bid you Goodbye?— maybe never see you anymore—turn my back with a sigh on the many pleasant hours we've passed together; step out in to the wide world to roam, unfriended and alone.

His optimistic, practical outlook soon returns in the letter, in a characteristic shifting of mood and tone:

> Our way may look dark and gloomy now, but by and by the clouds will roll by . . . It is very seldom do people love and have no bother, I am going to La Grange Saturday. I hope to meet you on second Sunday in [illegible]. It is now 11 o'clock. Good-night. I am Yours until death. . . .[40]

Even after Lucia agreed to marry him, Calvin continued to express his sadness at her absence with the rhetoric of the romantic tradition: "Sometimes I feel sad and forlorn. The heart within me mourn like the dove mourning for her absent one's quick return."[41] These words reveal the power she had over him, even if it was only the power to make him happy within the private sphere of their personal relationship.[42]

This romantic tradition of courtship sees its fullest demonstration in the letters of the middle class, where education allows, first, for literacy, and, second, for knowledge of the elements of romantic rhetoric and style. Of course, this tradition was not solely the possession of the middle class. In the Rhone Family Papers is a letter to Lucia from James le Renisan, a farmer whose writing style was neither as literary nor as polished as that seen in the letters in the Rhone-Knotts correspondence. Yet this particular letter still demonstrates elements of the middle-class courtship tradition. Le Renisan's letter, without punctuation, reads as a stream of consciousness in which he attempts to express his feelings openly:

> you told me that there was a chance for me i would like to no what it means to gain or to lose . . . dear i am unable to lay open to you the present state of my feelings to wart you is stronger than those of friendship you says that you ony regards me as a frin if your love is very hard my love is so hard that i cant hardly rest saterfide . . . dont rite nothing that you dont mean if you love me enofe to marry let me no[43]

Although the studied romantic rhetoric used by Calvin is absent here, le Renisan's words create the same image of a consuming romantic love that alters the writer's state of being. James le Renisan's letter reveals that he, too, valued frankness and sincerity. He used the courtship letter form as a means of privately ascertaining Lucia's feelings for him, and of demonstrating his own feelings for her. Both James le Renisan and Calvin Rhone elevated Lucia, granting her power over their happiness, at least for the duration of the courtship. Le Renisan the farmer, however, probably did not stand a chance against Professor Rhone. Le Renisan's letter may have even hastened

Calvin and Lucia's marriage by forcing Calvin to agree to her terms. Lucia's receipt of a letter from a second suitor only two months before her marriage indicates that Calvin may have realized he might lose her if they delayed any further.

Lucia perhaps had the power to chose her suitors, and to play with their affections, but Calvin held the power to re-create her as his ideal, through his use of romantic rhetoric. Calvin's language reinvented Lucia by placing her within the white tradition of the "cult of true womanhood." In accordance with this popularly held ideal of gender, Calvin upheld the notion of separate spheres, which worked to preserve the true woman's natural attributes of innocence, piety, purity, submissiveness, and domesticity.[44] Calvin's adherence to this ideal of womanhood, and Lucia's rejection of it, created one of the central conflicts of their courtship. By resisting Lucia's wish to continue her teacher training after marriage, Calvin reflected the values of the dominant white culture.

Behind Calvin's rhetoric, however, is Lucia's counter attempt to regain the power of self-definition. Lucia's two letters to Calvin made explicit her wish to have some say in determining her future. This conflict over gender roles delayed their marriage but, significantly, did not prevent it. An examination of how Calvin and Lucia resolved this conflict reveals a different, more empowering version of the white gender construction popularly known as "true womanhood." At a time when work and marriage were considered incompatible for women, Lucia's wish to continue her teacher training, and by implication to teach after marriage, was at least contrary to prevailing white middle-class standards.[45]

Although the "cult of true womanhood" had its heyday in the first half of the nineteenth century, it was still very much a part of society at the time of Lucia and Calvin's courtship.[46] As many scholars have suggested, by the 1870s, 1880s, and 1890s the "new woman" began to supplant the "cult of true womanhood" in the public mind.[47] Old habits, however, die hard. Elements of "true womanhood" arguably can be seen even in the 1950s glorification of the housewife.[48] Scholars such as Shirley Carlson have recently taken "true womanhood" out of its white, early-nineteenth-century context and used it as a descriptive gender role for African American women in the late-Victorian era. In her study of black women in Illinois from about 1880 to 1910, Carlson successfully demonstrates that "Black Victoria" embodied the qualities of "true womanhood" valued by the larger white society. At the same time, however, she shows how "Black Victoria" exhibited qualities that made her successful in the public sphere.[49]

At the time Lucia and Calvin were courting, gender roles in white middle-class culture were still divided into separate spheres, based on the traditional division of labor. "True womanhood" limited women's economic opportunities by making them seemingly unsuited to the coarseness of public life.[50] The female role was "bounded by the kitchen and nursery."[51] Experiences or achievements outside of this private sphere could not interfere with a wom-

an's devotion to her home and family.[52] Even toward the end of the nineteenth century, when white middle-class women were increasingly working
outside of the home and when women's education was steadily improving,
marriage *still* entailed a cessation of public life, except in rare instances.[53]

Initially, in keeping with white society's definition of "true womanhood,"
Calvin expected Lucia to be domestic after marriage, and to discontinue her
studies. He encouraged and supported her wish to attend school before
marriage but expected her education to end when they married. Traveling to
Hempstead with Lucia, where she attended Prairie View, Calvin proposed
that she quit school in order for them to marry. After Lucia had apparently
asked him what his reasons were for her not to continue in school, he
referred to her responsibility as a mother, and her role as his wife: "You know
there is something [that] follows marriage, of course you can draw your own
ideas. Secondly, I think you would not be satisfied after leaving me nor
would I."[54] Justifying his views on marriage, he had written earlier:

> My reasoning for making such a proposition were as follows: I did not want
> to marry and you continue in school. 2nd. I didnt want to marry and board
> where I am. I can assure you, you are not as anxious as I am. But I think it
> behooves us to look to the future, and as you had not written anything con-
> cerning our nuptial, I took it for granted that you had consented to my
> proposal.[55]

Calvin's shifting position on the proper role for his future wife is symptom-
atic of the larger conflict over gender roles within the African American
community. Whereas some African American leaders objected to women's
participation in the public sphere, others vigorously supported it. Some
disapproved of women's education that went beyond training them for their
roles as wives and mothers.[56] Prominent leaders of the African American
community, however, such as W. E. B. Du Bois and Anna Julia Cooper,
believed that work outside of the home and the notion of "true womanhood"
were not mutually exclusive.[57] They embraced the "cult of true womanhood" as a value, but they also felt it was necessary for black women to extend
themselves beyond the home and to work for the improvement of the race in
the public sphere.[58]

The education of both black women and white women had served to
mold and reinforce each community's differing ideals of "true womanhood."
Earlier in the nineteenth century, a white woman's education emphasized
the female's role as mother and wife.[59] The ideal "companion wife" required
education, but her intellectual sphere was confined to the home.[60] Similarly, black colleges such as Spelman and Tuskegee trained their female
students to be good wives and mothers with courses in housekeeping and
domestic science; female students, however, were also given an industrial
education for work outside the home.[61] Booker T. Washington, a "propo-
nent of the domestic ideology," also believed that working outside the home
contributed to the improvement of the race.[62]

Perhaps in support of this gender value, the African American community began to use the word "ladies" to describe black women toward the end of the nineteenth century.[63] The term "ladies," though, did not refer to women of leisure who stayed at home as it did in white communities. A "lady" in the African American community was someone who assumed a responsibility for the problems of the society at large, not just for her own family's needs.[64] Thus, Lucia's act of seeking to continue teacher training at Prairie View after her marriage defied white culture's conception of the "cult of true womanhood" at the same time that it affirmed that she was truly a "lady" within her own community.

Calvin and Lucia's letters reveal the value each placed on education for women. Both of Lucia's letters in the collection refer to the teacher's college, Prairie View, which indicates that education was important to her. She wrote: "If I could possably get off to P.V. in September I would do so with all my heart."[65] Calvin also supported her education. He frequently asked her how her studies were going, and at one point he congratulated her on her "success."[66] He eventually even agreed to postpone their marriage to accommodate her wish to continue her schooling:

> Contrary to all signs I postpone the 16th of Dec. to a future day at your own suggestion. First I do so because, I believe you sincerely mean that I should answer you favorable. Seconds, I know I love you and know you love me and have my interest at heart, that is this having a desire to cultivate your brain in which I bid you God's speed and Third: You have always told me my fate was yours and with me you intend to spend your future days. Then to want to marry before you left would seem if I had not want to trust you.[67]

Although Calvin Rhone's initial resistance to Lucia's wish appeared to be based on white culture's ideal of womanhood, his eventual compliance in fact conforms to the ideal as it found expression in the African American community. Toward the end of their courtship he appeared to give Lucia his full support: "I am very glad you are anxious to continue in school." He finally conceded to her wish to marry and continue with her schooling, saying, "Well as you will not agree with me I will with you."[68] Beneath his words lie the historical circumstances that shaped his conception of African American gender roles. The values African Americans placed on education and woman's role in the community perhaps allowed him to accede to her wish to continue her schooling after their marriage and, presumably, allowed her to put her teacher's training to good use. In black society, Calvin's respect for Lucia's wish was not unusual.

Black women have historically had a tradition of working outside the home, even among the middle classes. Their ideal of womanhood included and even required work within the public sphere. Black women were encouraged by their community to educate themselves, but with the purpose of assisting in uplifting their race.[69] Pioneering African American educators such as Lucy Craft Laney encouraged this higher goal:

> The educated Negro woman, the woman of character and culture, is
> needed in the schoolroom not only in the kindergarten, and in the primary
> and the secondary school; but she is needed in high school, the academy, and
> the college. Only those of character and culture can do the successful lifting,
> for she who would mould character must herself possess it.[70]

Economic factors spurred this blurring of the private and public spheres
in the African American community. In the historical context of a segregated
South, black women's attempts to move out of the private sphere of the
home and into the public sphere of career-oriented education can be seen
more in terms of the survival of her family than as an attempt to find the
personal autonomy and self-fulfillment that Charlotte Perkins Gilman described in *Women and Economics*. Racism reduced opportunities and kept
wages low for African Americans, perhaps making it an economic necessity
for even middle-class black women to contribute to the support of their
families.[71]

White racism made it difficult for black couples to uphold a separation of
private and public spheres and conform to the white ideal of womanhood.
The traditional division of labor that developed into the idea of separate
spheres by the end of the eighteenth century of course did not apply to slave
women, who worked in the fields alongside men. Neither did the "cult of
true womanhood's" mandate that a woman's husband should be her whole
interest and focus apply to black women during slavery.[72] The idea of separate spheres of home and work continued to be an illusion for many African
American women after slavery.[73] Not surprisingly, white nineteenth-century
society did not see black women as the embodiment of "true womanhood."
Separate spheres entail two inviolable realms, and black women's experience has shown that their "sphere" was not inviolable, their homes and
families not considered sacred by white society. Similarly, black men's ventures into the public sphere of the white community were constricted and
thwarted. Perhaps for these reasons, a unique interpretation of the "true
womanhood" ideal developed in the African American community.

The Rhone-Knotts courtship letters reflect the romantic tradition in their
form and rhetoric, suggesting an internalization of the values of the dominant culture that produced the courtship tradition. At the same time, however, the letters become a venue for self-determination: the correspondence
serves as a negotiating place for Calvin and Lucia to define their own lives,
and create their own ways of respecting and admiring the other. The letters
have preserved a dialogue in which the white "cult of true womanhood,"
itself a limiting construction of gender, can be seen transforming itself into
something new. In these ways, the courtship letters of Calvin and Lucia both
reflect and contradict aspects of white culture's "cult of womanhood." Just as
literary conventions can be subverted in order to send the opposite message
from what was intended, the seemingly conventional form of the courtship
letter can also be manipulated to achieve different ends. The Rhone-Knotts
correspondence documents an African American woman's attempt to create

a marriage on her own terms. As a black woman, Lucia still had to balance the responsibilities of both work and home, which eventually grew to include eight children and a farm. By not creating a dichotomy of work and home, however, black women like Lucia Knotts were at least pointing in the direction of modern emancipation for all women.

NOTES

1. Calvin L. Rhone to Lucia Knotts, May 31, 1886, Rhone Family Papers (Center for American History, University of Texas at Austin; all letters cited below are from this collection).

2. Ellen K. Rothman, *Hands and Hearts: A History of Courtship in America* (New York: Basic Books, 1984); Karen Lystra, *Searching the Heart: Women, Men and Romantic Love in Nineteenth-Century America* (New York: Oxford University Press, 1989). See also Steven M. Stowe, *Intimacy and Power in the Old South: Ritual in the Lives of the Planters* (Baltimore: Johns Hopkins University Press, 1987). Although Stowe's work focuses on planter-class culture during the period 1820–1860, his analysis of courtship rituals provides an interesting counterpoint to that of Rothman and Lystra. Unlike Rothman and Lystra, who examine courtship in terms of gender roles, Stowe looks at courtship as "an emotional experience tied to considerations of social class" that reinforced the Southern "sense of legitimate mastery." Stowe, *Intimacy and Power in the Old South*, 105.

3. Herbert G. Gutman, *The Black Family in Slavery and Freedom, 1750–1925* (New York: Pantheon Books, 1976).

4. Ann duCille, *The Coupling Convention: Sex, Text, and Tradition in Black Women's Fiction* (New York: Oxford University Press, 1993); Willard B. Gatewood, *Aristocrats of Color: The Black Elite, 1880–1920* (Bloomington: Indiana University Press, 1990).

5. United States Tenth Census (1880), Fayette County, Texas, Population Schedules (microfilm, Texas State Archives, Austin).

6. Ibid. There is a letter from Benjamin Knotts to Calvin Rhone in the Rhone Family Papers, perhaps suggesting that the census taker was in error or that someone wrote the letter for him.

7. United States Twelfth Census (1900), Fayette County, Texas, Population Schedules (microfilm; Texas State Archives, Austin). According to the 1900 Census, Calvin Rhone was born in 1864, although the Rhone Family Papers collection finding aid lists his date of birth as after emancipation, in 1867; Julia Payne and Lawrence A. Landis, "Finding Aid," ([n.p.], 1984). Earlier census records for the Rhone family were not found.

8. Calvin Rhone to Lucia Knotts, Dec. 12, 1887.

9. Scholars have documented the prominent and respected role black schoolteachers held within African American communities. See Shirley J. Carlson, "Black Ideals of Womanhood in the Late Victorian Era," *Journal of Negro History*, LXXVII (Spring, 1992), 65–66; Lucy Craft Laney, "To Get An Education and Teach My People," in Ruth Bogin and Bert James Loewenberg (eds.), *Black Women in Nineteenth-Century American Life: Their Words, Their Thoughts, Their Feelings* (University Park: Pennsylvania State University Press, 1976), 300.

10. Calvin Rhone to Lucia Knotts, July 21, 1887. In response to her complaint that his letters were too short, he wrote a longer, newsier letter than usual, and then, seeming to tease her, stated that she should "look in the Galveston News for the remainder."

11. In general, courtship by letter in the 1880s and 1890s was less common than it had been earlier in the century, when white middle-class couples regularly wrote long letters to each other even when separated for only a few hours. In the last quarter of the century,

improvements in transportation and the busier schedules of both men and women
contributed to the decline of letter writing. During the Gilded Age, courtship by letter
occurred primarily when the couple lived far apart; see Rothman, *Hands and Hearts*,
10–12. For a discussion of antebellum courtship letter-writing customs, see Stowe,
Intimacy and Power in the Old South, 89–93.

12. Calvin Rhone to Lucia Knotts, Oct. 31, 1887.

13. Lucia Knotts to Calvin Rhone, July 27, 1886.

14. Even Lucia's other suitor, James le Renisan, complained of having too little time
to write, as indicated in his letter to her dated October 17, 1887. Their lack of leisure
time runs counter to the experiences of whites that Rothman details. Toward the end of
the nineteenth century, courtship was characterized by an increase in spare time and in
public forms of entertainment available to courting couples. Rothman, *Hands and
Hearts*, 204–205.

15. A standard work covering this era of Texas history is Alwyn Barr's *Reconstruction to
Reform: Texas Politics 1876–1906* (Austin: University of Texas Press, 1971).

16. Calvin Rhone to Lucia Knotts, Aug. 19, 1887.

17. Calvin Rhone to Lucia Knotts, Aug. 4, 1887.

18. Ibid. A large majority of African Americans voted against Prohibition, although
Calvin Rhone's position on this issue is unknown. For background on this election, see
Gregg Cantrell's "'Dark Tactics': Black Politics in the 1887 Texas Prohibition Cam-
paign," *Journal of American Studies*, XXV (Apr., 1991), 85–93.

19. Rothman suggests that this trend was a result of men and women associating intimacy with the parent-child relationship, having been raised in the increasingly child-
centered, emotionally dependent family typical of the late-Victorian middle classes.
Rothman, *Hands and Hearts*, 206.

20. Calvin Rhone to Lucia Knotts, Sept. 20, Nov. 29, 1886; and Oct. 15, 1887.

21. Lucia Knotts to Calvin Rhone, June 7, 1886.

22. Lystra, *Searching the Heart*, 166.

23. Rothman, *Hands and Hearts*, 226.

24. Lucia Knotts to Calvin Rhone, June 7, 1886.

25. Rothman, *Hands and Hearts*, 226.

26. Calvin Rhone to Lucia Knotts, Nov. 17, 1886.

27. Calvin Rhone to Lucia Knotts, Sept. 20, 1886.

28. Calvin Rhone to Lucia Knotts, Sept. 7, 1887.

29. Calvin Rhone to Lucia Knotts, Sept. 20, 1886.

30. Calvin Rhone to Lucia Knotts, Oct. 31, 1887.

31. Lystra, *Searching the Heart*, 66. Lystra shows how romantic love was rooted in the
concept of an ideal self. The essential act of romantic love was the free and open
communication of this ideal to another; *Searching the Heart*, 7.

32. Ibid., 71.

33. Ibid., 84.

34. Ibid., 64.

35. Calvin Rhone to Lucia Knotts, Aug. 4, 1887.

36. Calvin Rhone to Lucia Knotts, Aug. 19, 1887.

37. Calvin Rhone to Lucia Knotts, July 21, 1887.

38. Calvin Rhone to Lucia Knotts, Sept. 20, 1886.

39. Ibid.

40. Calvin Rhone to Lucia Knotts, Nov. 3, 1886.

41. Calvin Rhone to Lucia Knotts, Oct. 31, 1887.

42. The relationship between romantic love and women's power in the black Victorian household needs further exploration. If generalizations can be made from experiences of white Victorian women, Karen Lystra's *Searching the Heart* provides a good
starting point. She argues that the belief in romantic love allowed for the sharing of the
self and resulted in an intimate understanding of one another while in love. This
understanding between men and women created bridges between some sex-role divisions. Romantic love also gave women emotional power over men, and vice versa,

although Lystra argues that this type of power was more important to the women, considering their limited economic power, than it was to men. Lystra, *Searching the Heart*, 9.

43. James le Renisan to Miss Lucious Knotts, Oct. 17, 1887.

44. Barbara Welter, "The Cult of True Womanhood: 1820–1860," in *The American Family in Social-Historical Perspective*, ed. Michael Gordon (New York: St. Martin's Press, 1973), 224–250.

45. In her study of nineteenth century courtship, Rothman contrasts the feelings of antebellum and late nineteenth-century white women teachers on marriage and their careers. Before the Civil War, these teachers viewed marriage as a means of escaping isolation and financial insecurity. After the Civil War, however, marriage regretfully ended an occupation they enjoyed. Rothman, *Hands and Hearts*, 249.

46. Welter's seminal essay "The Cult of True Womanhood: 1820–1860" has seemingly set the antebellum period in stone as the time of this idea's primacy, although more recent work has used true womanhood as a descriptive gender role for later periods. See Carlson, "Black Ideals of Womanhood in the Late Victorian Era."

47. Charlotte Perkins Gilman, *Women and Economics: A Study of Economic Relations between Men and Women as a Factor in Social Evolution*, ed. Carl N. Degler (New York: Harper and Row, 1966), 148; Carroll Smith-Rosenberg, *Disorderly Conduct: Visions of Gender in Victorian America* (New York: Alfred A. Knopf, 1985), 46.

48. Betty Friedan, *The Feminine Mystique* (New York: W. W. Norton, 1963).

49. Carlson, "Black Ideals of Womanhood in the Late Victorian Era," 61–62.

50. Welter, "The Cult of True Womanhood: 1820–1860," 224–250.

51. Smith-Rosenberg, *Disorderly Conduct*, 13.

52. Rothman, *Hands and Hearts*, 250.

53. Welter, "The Cult of True Womanhood: 1820–1860," 225; Linda M. Perkins, "The Impact of the 'Cult of True Womanhood' on the Education of Black Women," in Darlene Clark Hine (ed.), *Black Women in United States History* (16 vols.; Brooklyn, N.Y.: Carlson Publishing Co., 1990), III, 1066.

54. Calvin Rhone to Lucia Knotts, Dec. 12, 1887.

55. Calvin Rhone to Lucia Knotts, Nov. 30, 1887.

56. Beverly Guy-Sheftall, *Daughters of Sorrow: Attitudes Toward Black Women, 1890–1920*, vol. II of Hine (ed.), *Black Women in United States History*, 97, 151.

57. W. E. B. Du Bois, "The Damnation of Women," in Du Bois, *Darkwater: Voices from Within the Veil*, intro. Herbert Aptheker (Millwood, N.Y.: Kraus-Thomson Organization, 1975), 163–186; Anna Julia Cooper, *A Voice from the South, by A Black Woman of the South* (New York: Oxford University Press, 1988).

58. Guy-Sheftall, *Daughters of Sorrow*, 95–96, 164.

59. Catherine Esther Beecher, *A Treatise on Domestic Economy* (New York: Source Book Press, 1970).

60. Lystra, *Searching the Heart*, 127; Carl N. Degler, *At Odds: Women and the Family in America from the Revolution to the Present* (New York: Oxford University Press, 1980), 307.

61. Guy-Sheftall, *Daughters of Sorrow*, 142–150.

62. Ibid., 150.

63. Ibid.

64. Ibid., 92–95, 164–166.

65. Lucia Knotts to Calvin Rhone, July 27, 1886.

66. Calvin Rhone to Lucia Knotts, Dec. 12, 1887.

67. Calvin Rhone to Lucia Knotts, Sept. 7, 1887.

68. Calvin Rhone to Lucia Knotts, Nov. 30, 1887.

69. Linda Perkins studied the applications to missionary societies sponsoring teachers to the South. She found that the "cult of true womanhood" was in fact an impetus for New England white women to come teach in the South after the Civil War. These women felt the need to do something to escape the idleness and boredom of their role. This contrasts with the black women she studied who applied to teach for reasons of duty

and race uplift. Perkins, "The Impact of the 'Cult of True Womanhood' on the Education of Black Women," 1065–1075.

70. Laney, "To Get An Education and Teach My People," 300.

71. Perkins, "The Impact of the 'Cult of True Womanhood' on the Education of Black Women," 1069.

72. Rothman, *Hands and Hearts*, 74; Welter, "The Cult of True Womanhood: 1820–1860," 233–239.

73. Perkins,"The Impact of the 'Cult of True Womanhood' on the Education of Black Women," 1065–1066.

THIRTEEN

The African Derivation of Black Fraternal Orders in the United States

BETTY M. KUYK

At the turn of the century, when lynching, Jim Crow laws, and disfranchisement were at their worst, black fraternal organizations offered Afro-Americans a place to preserve their self-respect. Scholars have studied these organizations little and understood them less. One early study dismissed them as
merely parodying white organizations, but hardly resembling them, while
the blacks, it claimed, exaggerated both regalia and ritual. When Noel Gist
published his *Study of Fraternalism in the United States,* Carter Woodson
charged that Gist failed to understand the importance of fraternal orders to
blacks and that, indeed, Gist barely mentioned the black orders. After a detailed analysis, W. E. B. DuBois found that even black and white orders that
shared a name might not resemble one another. He found similarities only
in Pythians, Odd Fellows, and Masons. He thought the other black societies were "Negro inventions" and "curious and instructive" organizations.[1]
"Invention," "curious," "exaggeration," "parody," "importance to blacks"—
these are the key phrases. All attempt to describe an amorphous quality of
black fraternal orders that make them unique. Yet while failing to define that
quality, its would-be describers avoid the issue.

Perhaps the failure to understand the black beneficial society stems from
a cultural compulsion to find roots in our European heritage. Historical
tradition adamantly states that the orders originated in ancient Greek and
Egyptian custom. Ignoring the African quotient in Egyptian, that tradition
translates ancient custom to mean European heritage. Organizational and
functional similarities buttress tradition in this "heritage" argument. Both
white and black orders organize themselves into stages of degrees, and since

the content of degrees is secret, the superficial judgment of similarity came to be based on the observable trait. Both white and black fraternal orders perform functions ascribed to secret organizations: to provide life or health insurance; to provide outlets for social, religious, national, or occupational interests; or to promote abstinence.[2]

Differences between white and black orders elude superficial examination. However, if we set aside the notion of European heritage and look instead at our African background, we find that the organizational structure noted in white and black American societies also appears in African societies. This appearance in Africa destroys the logic of a purely Europe-to-America transmission process. Moreover, in the African organization we also discover a functional structure that has a closer relationship to the black American order than either of these has to the white.

We cannot discover these similarities through narrative history, the usual method for tracing cultural transmissions from one society to another. In laying out documentation chronologically, narrative history would be unlikely to compare sociological functions at all. DuBois, who was one of the first historians to suspect that black American institutions have African origins, encountered the limitations of narrative history when he studied the growth of black economic cooperation.[3] He lacked the documentation that narrative history requires, and structural analysis had not yet evolved. Although we still lack enough data for a standard chronological documentation, we can search for the origins of beneficial societies by examining and evaluating similarities and identities within the organizational and functional structures of American and African institutions. The evidence should help us to decide whether Africans injected a concept of social organization into American society.

In pursuing the origins of beneficial societies, I will draw primarily on the Independent Order of St. Luke, which typifies the roughly thirty beneficials formed in Richmond, Virginia, by 1866.[4] The order had codified its ritual by 1877. Because the ritual was codified so early, we can compare it with African forms and have our comparisons relatively unsullied by American white society's impact later in the nineteenth century. For African forms I will draw primarily on the Efik and segments of the Igbo of West Africa,[5] who had similar concepts of social organization. Two categories of their organizations—title associations and secret society—had parallel features in black American fraternal orders. A title association was made up of a group of prominent men whose status depended more on wealth than on lineage. Its function varied, depending upon the community's governmental system. Most communities had secret societies serving a number of purposes. Since title associations often had secret aspects and often were closely tied to secret societies, they are sometimes categorized as secret societies, although not every secret society was a title association or vice versa. These two forms of organization supply particularly pertinent comparisons because their prevalence throughout the West African slave area increases the likelihood that their influence was present in the United States. The Efik and Igbo forms serve as examples applicable to Virginia.

Long before many white institutions were open to blacks, they formed their own beneficial societies. As early as 1815, the Free People of Color of the City of Richmond reportedly bought a lot for a cemetery. By 1852 the Beneficial Society of Free Men of Color of the City of Petersburg and the State of Virginia was developed to provide sickness and death insurance and "to promote social group spirit." Many of these societies existed among free blacks, especially in the North.[6]

Oral tradition has transmitted accounts of beneficial societies among slaves. A Hampton Negro Conference recorded the tradition. Societies to take care of the sick and provide acceptable funerals existed in Virginia's cities. Most of these societies were secret. They had secretaries who kept records with number codes. Members would drift in, state their numbers, and make payment without telling their names. Societies usually had a "privileged" slave as president. This slave could move freely and so keep in current communication with members. In the case of a funeral, members of the Richmond society surreptitiously sat together during the service. Afterwards, once they were far enough away from white surveillance, they formed a column of march. The conference reported that members reputedly "were faithful to each other and . . . every obligation was faithfully carried out." The system had developed to this rather complex stage by the early nineteenth century.[7]

Because beneficial societies multiplied in and radiated from Richmond after 1865, we must examine when and how African cultural patterns could have reached Virginia. In Virginia, we have not yet found institutions pure to any African tribal segment. The amalgamation of peoples obviously was too great. However, recent scholarship fairly well establishes a predominance of peoples in Virginia from the Bight of Biafra. After 1718, more slaves came to Virginia directly from Africa than from the West Indies or from other American colonies. This tendency increased rapidly and dominated through the 1760s. Virginia was a major destination for African slaves during this period. Concurrently, slaving along the Bight of Biafra increased, and that area produced higher percentages of the slaves going into Virginia than did other regions of Africa. People from a complex interior slave-trade system passed through the Biafra ports. They included Ibibio, Cross River peoples, Tiv, and a few Efik; but by far the largest number were Igbo.[8] The Efik controlled the slave trade through Old Calabar to British ships in the Bight of Biafra.

In Virginia, major landing places for delivering slaves imported directly from Africa included Bermuda Hundred on the upper James River, and Yorktown and West Point on the upper York. Both areas had access to Richmond across a network of common and stage roads. A logical conclusion, then, is that the amalgamation of Africans in and around Richmond included large numbers with Biafran, especially Igbo, heritage. Furthermore, Virginia acquired large numbers of Igbo from South Carolina, the second major destination for Biafran slaves. South Carolinian planters avoided buying Igbo and shipped them on to Virginia when possible.[9] Thus, cultural attitudes of the Igbo, who were sold to Virginia in great numbers, and of the Efik, whose control of slave trade assured their contact with Igbo, were the attitudes of large numbers of Virginia's African slaves. These attitudes would have been passed on to their Afro-American children in the natural course of upbringing and would have influenced developing institutions.

With the possibility for transmission from Africa to Virginia established chronologically, we can move on to an examination of structural similarities between the African and Afro-American associations. The organizational structure of title associations was similar to that of fraternal orders. Each contained some number of degrees, or levels, of membership; each degree had a set of symbols; and each required an initiation to change the candidate's status. Exhibits 1 and 2 show these similarities as they appear in the structure of the Independent Order of St. Luke and in the Agbalanze, which was the Onitsha division of Ozo, a title association prevalent among the Igbo.

Within the organizational structures, many small points appear similar. Taken singly, each would be meaningless, whereas taken as a whole, they suggest possible transmissions. The similarity in stage structure is obvious, and variation in numbers of stages is of no importance. For example, Ekpe, the Efik title association, had from seven to twelve stages.[10] Within the stages of both African and of Afro-American associations, however, comparable acts occur in similar order. This signifies that the two cultures had comparable concepts of how to arrange action. Examine the structure of fee payment in Exhibits 1 and 2. At stage two of Agbalanze, the process of haggling, paying money, re-evaluating the candidate, and demanding more money is repeated over several years; at each degree in the Independent Order of St. Luke, the candidate pays a fee to the Degree Chief. In Agbalanze, fee payment precedes an evaluation of the candidate in which he is found lacking but is allowed to continue if he pays more money; in the Independent Order of St. Luke, fee payment precedes ordeals and instruction, after which the candidate pays another fee to go on to the next stage. In both organizations, then, candidates pay fees, endure ritual ordeals, and pay fees to continue. Thus both arrange action in the same order.

We find several parallels among the symbols. The first set of symbols the Agbalanze initiate deals with are his "god emblems." Among these are five "sticks."[11] Four are *okposi*, representing his ancestors. One is *ikenga*, representing his father's fortune, whether good or bad. *Ikenga* has associations with wealth and with the age-grade groups, which is a formally constituted peer group. The initiate has a wooden bowl, his *okwachi*, to hold the god sticks, and an altar, a sacred place, where the emblems remain. In the Council Chamber of the Independent Order of St. Luke we also find "god

EXHIBIT 1

Independent Order of St. Luke

Degree Council Chamber contained: desk with three candles
altar with Bible, cross, five candles

Stages	*Symbols*	*Initiation*
Basic	White satin collars, white aprons Emblem of the order Men: red cross: women: white cross on red ribbon	
1	White satin rosette Silver star	Fee payment to Degree Chief Oath at altar Degree Chief's address to initiate Signs and passwords taught
2	White and purple rosette Silver star	Fee payment to Degree Chief Alarm play; wandering pilgrim play Oath Ceremonial bread and water: fellowship Signs and password taught
3	White, purple, red and blue rosette Silver star	Fee payment to Degree Chief Alarm; continue pilgrimage to cross Oath at altar Instructions on history of degree, financial card, and travel certificate Signs and password taught
4	Black and scarlet rosette Silver star	Fee payment to Degree Chief Alarm; commitment to principles of the order with oath at altar Ordeal: seizure in semidarkness; moral lesson Signs and password taught
5	Purple and pink rosette Silver star Purple collar Purple apron	Fee payment to Degree Chief Alarm; oath at altar Explanation of emblems Signs and password taught

6	Purple, black, scarlet rosette
	Silver star; purple collar with
	  yellow trim: white or gold cross
	Degree Chief: crown, robe with
	  scarlet and yellow trim
	Past Worthy chiefs: purple rosette,
	  gold star, gold cross on purple ribbon
		Fee payment to Degree Chief
		Ordeal: an intruder play; initiates sent out,
		  alarm to re-enter
		Oath: explanation of principles
		Sign and password taught

Goal	Love, charity, purity: to be worthy of the brotherhood	

SOURCE: William M. T. Forrester, comp., *Degree Ritual of the Independent Order of Saint Luke* (Richmond, Virginia, 1894).

EXHIBIT 2

Agbalanze

Stages	Symbols	Initiation
1A		
	Altar	Consecration of symbols
Inyedo mmuo—	4 okposi sticks	
"Bringing in	1 ikenga stick	
the father"	(= 5 carved emblems of gods)	
	Okwachi (wooden bowl)	
1B		
"Rubbing the		Notification: of whole siblings (the
ears of the		"kitchen"), of patrilineal siblings
kinsmen"		(the "ancestral house"), the
		extended patrilineage, the clan's
		senior Agbalanze member
		Meetings; reparations; prayers
2		
Igo mmuo—	Money	Haggling over price of fee payment;
"Carrying money		pressure on relatives to donate;
for ghosts"		money given to Ozo; candidate
		reevaluated and found lacking;
		more money demanded; process
		repeated for several years
	Palm wine	Ozo receive 100 or more pots of wine
3		
Mkpalo—	Okposi sticks	Fee payment to Ozo
"Consorting	Goat skin	Ordination
with the	Corn wine	Oath at altar; goat sacrifice; sitting on
ghosts"	Father's ofo stick	goat skin: too pure to sit on earth
	Crown	Ceremonial corn wine: priestliness
4		
Mmacha	Treasure box	Fee payment to Ozo
	2 osisi	Notification of kin
	White chalk	Isolation from women
	White clothing	Ceremonial purification and dedica-
	2 eagle feathers:	tion to nze; oath at treasure box
	truth	"Has money" procession
	Ivory trumpet	Fee payment
	Money	Ceremonies of reunion with wives
		Mock market
Goal	Purification: to be worthy of the brotherhood.	

SOURCES: Richard N. Henderson, *The King in Every Man* (New Haven, 1972), 111–13, 249–64; Onuora Nzekwu, "Initiation into the Agbalanze Society," *Nigeria Magazine*, 82 (September 1964), 173–87; Adebiyi Tepowa, "The Tiles of Ozor and Ndichie at Onitsha," *Journal of the African Society*, 9:34 (1910), 189–92; and Tony Amugbanite, "Iboland's Sleeping Customs," *West African Review*, 30 (October 1959), 659–51.

emblems": a Bible and a cross placed on an altar are the obvious ones. We also find five "sticks" — candles — representing Matthew, Mark, Luke, John, and Peter. While these men are not ancestral blood relatives of the St. Luke initiate, both the candles, for the St. Luke, and the *okposi* sticks, for the Agbalanze initiate, represent distant, historical donors of the candidate's religion. The St. Lukes' hall also contained three other candles, which represented the Worthy Chief, Vice-Chief, and Secretary of the order.[12] These three candles are comparable to the Igbo's *ikenga* stick in that they symbolize the group of peers most immediately responsible for the St. Luke's initiate's induction into the order, just as the Agbalanze initiate's father, or peer group as embodied in the *ikenga* representation, was most immediately responsible for his candidacy: in the eighteenth century, the Agbalanze father's death precipitated initiation of his senior son.

Color symbolism permeated both organizations. White symbolized purity to both Igbo and St. Luke. The Agbalanze initiate proceeded through stages of increasing purification until in the final ceremonies he was bathed in white chalk, dressed in white clothing, and had earned the right to "bathe" his god emblems in white chalk. In the Independent Order of St. Luke, purity was a basic goal; the regulation for basic regalia specified white collars and white aprons. The rosette for the first degree was entirely white; those for the second and third degrees contained white. The order's regalia designating degrees also contained a color pattern prevalent in West Africa: the trio white-red-black. Interpretations of these colors are fairly common and might seem meaningless. As Exhibit 3 shows, however, there was a vertical progression in their use and a horizontal coincidence between symbol and rite. The Independent Order of St. Luke followed an African pattern, progressing from white to black, whereas the usual pattern in European color symbolism progresses from black to white. The white-red-black triad appears in the sixth degree in a powerful combination of color symbolism and emblems. While red and black occur in the rosette, white occurs in two ways. One is in the water used as a symbol of the principle of purity. For the African, white, water, and purity were in a sense equivalent. As the Onitsha Igbo "bathed" his emblems in white chalk, he also called his clothes white if they were washed, no matter what their color. In parts of central Africa, clear water is called white water. The Independent Order of St. Luke represented purity with a "flowing fountain gushing forth its crystal streams." The second occurrence of white is in a white cross worn with regalia. A pattern thus appears here which Victor Turner notes time and again among African peoples: the conjunction of the white-red-black triad with water and with a cross motif. Further, he notes, "the critical situation in which these appear together is initiation."[13]

Structural parallels occurring within initiation rituals of both American and African groups include patterns of notification, of payment, and of ceremonies of oath-taking, self-improvement, "having money," and dedica-

EXHIBIT 3

Color	Meanings of color symbols[a]	Degrees	Corresponding rosette color symbols	Ritual traits paralleling color symbolism
White	Purity, cleanliness, harmony, peace Light: daylight Widespread knowledge	1	White	Most public degree Lecture: no fear of danger
		2	White Purple (a red variant)	Pilgrimage begins: possibility of danger implied
Red	Blood: therefore some-times dangerous power Power	3	White Purple, red Blue (a black variant)	Pilgrimage continues; warning of danger
	Sometimes, wealth			Wealth introduced via financial card
Black	Darkness, danger	4	Black Scarlet	Seizure ordeal in semidarkness
		5	Purple Pink	Wealth; promise to employ brothers
	Secret knowledge			Symbols of power taught
	Ritual death: regeneration	6	Purple Black Scarlet	Intruder ordeal: ininitate ousted, then allowed to re-inter

[a]Meanings derived by Victor Turner from the Ndembu and observed by others elsewhere in Africa. *See* Turner, "Colour Classification," 72-74, 77-79.

SOURCES: Victory W. Turner, "Colour Classification in Ndembu Ritual," in *Anthropological Approaches to the Study of Religion*, Michael Banton, ed., (London, 1966), 64-67, 58-61; and Forrester, *Degree Ritual* (1894).

tion. Looking at the Agbalanze ritual in Exhibit 2, we see much of stage 1B devoted to notification.[14] At the beginning of stage 4, before the ceremonies of ultimate purification can begin, ritual notification of the kin occurs again. In the Independent Order of St. Luke, as Exhibit 1 shows, "alarm" recurs at the beginning of degree initiation meetings. Alarm signals the notification ritual. The Senior Conductor officiates: He informs the Degree Chief and membership that there is a candidate, queries the candidate about his willingness to conform, and, when satisfied, knocks on the chamber door. "Alarm" ritually notifies the assembly that an initiation will begin. This pattern of notification occurs at every degree stage except the first, which appears in this respect, as in the use of color symbolism, to be the most public degree. The parallel structure of the pattern of fee payment, which occurs within initiation ritual in both forms of societies, has been discussed with reference to its delineation of stage structure.

Since ceremonies of oath-taking occur in all societies, they are not especially significant here except for a consistency in their pattern: both St. Luke and Agbalanze initiates took oaths in kneeling positions at a revered spot, usually an altar. In the Independent Order of St. Luke, the ceremony of self-improvement instructed the candidate, first in degree history, then increasingly in fellowship and morality as he was taught the significance of emblems and principles. Instruction was always linked to the candidate's promises to "become a better man (or woman)."[15] In Agbalanze the ceremony of self-improvement occurred in each purification ritual as the candidate moved toward becoming pure enough to assume a full priestly role in his community.

Patterns of fee payment were followed by ceremonies of "having money" at the higher stages in both organizations. They are more obvious in Agbalanze: having paid huge sums of money and come through his most secret purification rite, the candidate walked from the *nze* shrine to the village, accompanied by the Agbalanze members repeating, "has money, has money." Later, at the end of all the ceremonies, the village held a mock market, which closed when the newly titled Agbalanze member threw a shower of coins for children to gather. Ceremonies of having money were more subtle in the Independent Order of St. Luke. The first occurred in the third degree concurrently with a stepping up of the danger motif in the initiation ritual: the candidate was cautioned, adamantly, that any member in distress to whom he wished to give aid must be in good financial standing with the order. The distressed member must produce a "financial card" and back it up with the "travelling password and certificate" and addresses of the Worthy Chief and Recording Secretary of his council before he could be helped. In other words, he must "have money" to receive help from his brotherhood. The second ceremony of "having money" occurred in the fifth degree. Within the oath-taking ceremony, while promising to help and shelter fellow members, the candidate said, "I also promise to give him or her employment and employ him or her in preference to all other males and females. . . ." In order to give employment, one must "have money." Appearing in the midst of about fifty pages of instructions devoted to high moral principles—love, purity, justice, and so on—these two economic references seem almost blatantly materialistic. A third ceremony was couched in more moral terms: in the sixth-degree oath, having promised to be charitable, the candidate further promised to use his "influence for the promotion of the members of this Order, both morally and socially." And a fourth, more subtle, ceremony occurred in the same degree when the Degree Chief, ritually explaining the purity principle, linked purity with benevolent deeds: "So let our acts of benevolence be actuated by the purest motives, . . . setting an example for our brothers and sisters of lesser degrees and the uninitiated to gaze on our good works with admiration. . . ."[16] To perform good works, one must "have money." When we discuss the functional structure of these organizations, we shall see that this seemingly materialistic attribute is a deeply African conception.

Ceremonies in the highest stages of initiation in both organizations follow parallel patterns of dedication to symbols that stand for concepts. Having sworn to maintain secrecy, the St. Luke candidate for the fifth degree learned the meaning of the symbols of power in the order; an all-seeing eye, a figure of Justice with scales, a St. Luke monument, a cross with clasped hands below its base. In Agbalanze, this ceremony of dedication happened at the climax of the *mmacha* stage. At night the initiate was led to a shrine where the *nze* objects were kept. These symbols of the clan's "sacred mystery" were relics associated with its founding patrilineal ancestor. Kneeling there, the initiate took his final oaths to purity and began his final ritual. There he acquired his title, *agbala-nze*. He had achieved the ultimate purification necessary to serve *nze*.[17]

The final element in organizational structure of both the Agbalanze and the Independent Order of St. Luke was a social gathering, a relaxed and secular event. On the day after the *nze* ceremony, the new priest's oldest son and daughter and his senior wife rejoined him by participating in a public ritual dance. After that his entire community celebrated into the night. In the Virginia environment celebrations following ritual services were more subdued, possibly because of Baptist influence, but members shared refreshments, and, as noted by Richmond's black newspaper, "all highly enjoyed themselves."[18]

Turning to the functional structures of West African and American associations, we might at first think them less similar than the organizational. The trouble is merely complexity. Within single West African communities several title associations could exist and have overlapping functions. Ozo, for example, was an association of wealthy men who acted as councillors influencing political decisions and keeping order when people broke religious and social rules. Among the Onitsha Igbo, another title association, the Ndichie, held still tighter political control, with two groups of Ndichie representing the people while a third supported the chief. The Ndichie thus formed a check-and-balance system. Any men who wanted to join Ndichie must first belong to the Ozo. In addition, Ozo members also belonged to a secret mortuary society, the Mmuo, which performed both rites to satisfy ancestral spirits by ensuring proper burials and rites to enforce Ndichie laws.[19] In this simple illustration, we see the complex intertwining of functions. From legislating to enforcing laws, from conferring status to forming priesthoods, title associations combined political, social, religious, and psychological functions that operated to stabilize the community.

More striking to the Western mind, however, is the inclusion of an economic function. A clear example occurred among the Efik, who controlled trade at Old Calabar in the eighteenth century. Ekpe, a title association with a secret ritual, apparently became prominent when a credit system evolved to accommodate the slave trade. The economic function of Ekpe evolved through an association between a forest spirit, *Epke*, and the Efik's original fishing economy. By standing between the spirit and the community, by interpreting and enforcing the spirit's will, the members of Epke filled administrative, executive, and judicial as well as religious functions. Ekpe ultimately gained complete control over the Efik economic structure.[20]

Membership in Ekpe obviously conferred status. Ekpe also formed a sociable organization. The diary of an Efik chief, Antera Duke, frequently mentions feasting, drinking, and "playing" in conjunction with Ekpe activities. In addition, the Ekpe society was closely related to two other secret societies. One met for singing and gossip. The other, a mortuary society, was so closely tied to Ekpe as to be called a "brother."[21] All facets of community organization thus combined in Ekpe.

The unifying force in this highly complex set of associations is the lack of boundaries, or categories, delineating functions. To these Africans, all aspects of life—governmental, social, psychological, economic, and spiritual—were bound together so tightly that one could not be set apart without causing society's structure to collapse.[22] The same unifying force appeared in Virginia, where the African concept of the interrelatedness of all facets of life became embodied in the functional structure of the beneficial-fraternal society. Within the bounds of that institution, Afro-Americans acted out the unified complexity of life's aspects and did it with emphases that prove more characteristic of African thinking than of European.

In the process of transmission, changes within functions occurred as the new environment demanded. A shift in governmental functions is the most obvious. We have seen Ozo, Ndichie, and Ekpe as dominant law-making and law-enforcing title associations. The Virginia environment normally precluded political participation. Slaves obviously could have no dominant political role. Nor could free blacks. And in the half century after emancipation, Virginia blacks moved from political participation to political repression until 1902, when a WASP-dominated political system disfranchised virtually all of them.

Although the benevolent society's governmental impetus could not flow into politics in Virginia, it maintained its importance to the black community's social order by flowing in two other law-making channels. One channel created a complex body of procedural rules for the society. The Independent Order of St. Luke gives these examples: regulations that govern the order of business and the opening and closing of council meetings, that give the initiation forms for six stages of membership, that set forms for installing officers in subordinate councils, for installing a Past Worthy Chief, and for the opening, organizing, and consecrating of a new council. Rules for the "Burial Ceremony" prescribed dress, mode of transportation, order of march, a council service to be held before and after the church service and burial, and the form for behavior at the grave.[23]

In the second law-making channel, the impulse to govern flowed into legislating moral standards, delineating values through ritual, rules, and peer-group behavior. The Independent Order of St. Luke's basic goals were love, purity, and charity. The ritual ode[24] sung while consecrating a new council emphasized them:

> All hail the power of Love divine!
>   Our motto first, and sweetest link,
>
> . . . .
> All hail the power of Charity —
>   Hail her kind voice and tender deeds,
> Hail her angel of purity,
>   A friend that every brother* needs.

The fourth verse raises the three goals to the highest level of value by implying a comparison with the Holy Trinity:

> All hail our glorious trinity,
>   Our battle cry and our creed,
> Our potent three in unity,
>   They must and will succeed.

These three values appear throughout the ceremonies of initiation into the six stages of membership, and they are embellished by others. In the primary initiation rite, the Recording Secretary instructed new candidates for membership: "Strangers, allow me to inform you that the virtues which should characterize a true St. Luke, are honor, temperance, faithfulness, obedience, meekness, charity, and brotherly and sisterly kindness. . . ."[25] The first instruction of the first stage explained the symbols of St. Luke's principles — flowers for love, water for purity, and alms for charity. In the second stage, the candidate swore "to administer aid and relief to the sick and distressed wherever I may find them, but particularly to a brother or sister of this Order." After the oath he or she ceremoniously ate a piece of bread and drank from a cup of water. The Degree Chief explained that this ceremony commemorated the difficulties and persecutions suffered by Christians travelling to the Holy Land and that it should remind the candidate of his oath of charity to those in trouble and especially to his brothers and sisters of the order.[26]

Instructions for initiation into the third through the sixth degrees emphasized obedience and faithfulness to the laws of the order. At the fourth level, the initiate underwent a ritual ordeal to impress him with the need for charity: "The lights are all lowered, and as the candidate attempts to re-enter he is seized by several members and charged with being an enemy; his hands are chained or tied, and he is carried before the Degree Chief as an intruder, who has gained admission without the pass-word. Some will attempt to order him out. . . ." The Degree Chief then taught him the moral of the ordeal: "This should be a lesson to you. The scene of this occasion is a representation of what often follows misunderstanding or the want of proper instruction or training. How many of our fellow-men perish as victims for the want of some friendly advice and hand in the time of danger and distress. . . . Remember in future never be harsh to the unfortunate, the poor, or to those afflicted with the trials of life." In the fifth degree, the vocabulary of the oath to charity became more vigorous: "I solemnly swear to be in no plots or conspiracies against a brother or sister of this Council, or against the Order in general. . . . In case of any sad accident, I will fly to his or her relief."[27]

Peer-group pressure to conform to the moral laws established by the order emerged forcefully in the initiation ordeal of the sixth degree: "The members will form two lines, faces inward, and through this line the Assistant Degree Chief and the candidates must pass. On their way through, the members must seize the candidates, some charging them with intrusion, some with being an enemy, some with being a traitor, while others will express themselves as to the punishment such action deserves." The initiate there endured confrontation and bodily threats from every member of the sixth degree. Next he was charged with intruding into the council without proper signs and passwords. The Degree Chief admonished the Senior Conductor to "please see that the laws of this Council are enforced and that the penalty for the offense is inflicted." The candidate was then expelled from the council chamber. After a time he asked to be readmitted and was brought back by the Senior Conductor, who said, "Respected Degree Chief, I present you this pilgrim, who was a short while ago charged with being an intruder. In attempting to carry out our laws, I found that his . . . motives were pure, and that he comes to enlist with this Council for the promotion of love, purity, and charity." The candidate having been found worthy, the Degree Chief then accepted him, but only conditionally, for as long as he would conform to the group's standards: "Senior Conductor, if [these persons] are really pilgrims, and their desires true and their motives sincere, we shall be pleased to enlist [them as] our members. We want only true and faithful followers; those who are not afraid to face the hardships and the scorns of the world."[28]

Apart from these two channels—the body of regulations and the legislation of moral standards—a symbol appeared which seems almost a vestige of the African title association's original purpose of assuring law and order. It is the figure of "Justice," placed on the right side of the St. Luke emblem. Its presence reminded the member to be objective and rational in a dispute, to leave punishment to the "office of Justice."[29] Though the society could not control how Justice performed her offices in Virginia or the nation, this brief instruction directed members to obey her and so buttressed the preservation of law and order.

While governmental functions in the organizations shifted toward subtle fulfillment, religious and psychological functions continued to be dominant values which were expressed openly. In our examination of symbols and initiation rituals in organizational structures we have already seen some evidence that religious traits permeated both the Independent Order of St. Luke and the African title association. We shall now examine parallel religious functions in leadership, in purposes of rites, and in attitudes toward death.

First, the organizations have parallel components in their leadership—in chief, priest, and father roles. The Igbo initiation ceremony ordained a priest. All of the extended family's Agbalanze members gathered in the home of the candidate's family's chief priest for a major part of the ceremony. All of the chief priests of his extended family officiated. The priests made offerings to the candidate's personal god, asking blessings on their candidate; they held prayers among themselves and for the whole family. The "chief priest" concept has several interpretations. One refers to achievement, especially to earning the Ozo title. Achieving the title meant achieving the ultimate purification, becoming priestly. Another interpretation refers to the ancestors. Through his purity, the priest gained access to the ancestors. He therefore linked the living with the dead. Another interpretation, found at Onitsha, included a kingship institution with "chieftaincy" concepts. Nine clans founded Onitsha. Kings of eight of them were chief priests of the lineage. Their title included *eze*, which designated them as custodians of their clan's *nze*. The kings were also called "*ńnà-ányi*," meaning "our father."[30] Thus they linked paternal with priestly roles.

These religious functions were also present in the Independent Order of St. Luke, although the order was not an organization of priests and although priests, as such, did not officiate at its rites. The functions of top-ranking officers—prayer, oath-giving, teaching morality, leading hymns—were priestly, however, and repetition of the word "chief" in their title is notable: Past Worthy Chief, Right Worthy Grand Chief, Right Worthy Grand Vice-Chief, Worthy Chief, Degree Chief. Moreover, founders and high-ranking officers of fraternal orders were often also ministers, as was the Reverend Z. D. Lewis of the Independent Order of St. Luke.

The Virginia society also contained a paternal role along with this "chief priest" role. In Virginia, however, the two roles were not embodied in one person, but separated. An officer with the title "Worthy Father" filled the paternal role: "Brother (or sister) _____, you have been elected Worthy Father of this Council. . . . You are called upon to exercise a parental care over this Council. . . ."[31] Armistead Walker, Jr., husband of Right Worthy Grand Secretary Maggie L. Walker, served as Worthy Father of Heliotrope Council, No. 160. In March 1899, the council gave him a payment of ten dollars "as a mark of appreciation . . . for his service since March 1897."[32] Mrs. Dorothy Turner, the present Right Worthy Grand Secretary of the Independent Order of St. Luke, described the Worthy Father as an "older, respected person," one who would fill a "fatherly, advisory role."[33] We therefore have the religious functions of chief, priest, and father combined in the leaders of the American society as they were in the African.

Parallel religious functions also appear in purposes of rites. While initiation in the Independent Order of St. Luke was not an ordination rite as it was in the Agbalanze, the St. Luke rite was a ceremony of spiritual regeneration. The Ozo gained purity in order to be ordained; the St. Luke initiate learned purity to gain regeneration. Religious traits repeatedly buttressed the St. Luke member's progress through degrees, just as they did the Ozo initiate's. In each of the St. Luke's first- through fourth-degree rituals, the initiate swore an oath on the Bible, in the first and fourth he promised to be true to the Christian religion, and in the first to study the Scriptures. In the third through sixth degrees, he took the oath "in the presence of Almighty God," and in the third degree he added the presence of the apostles Peter, Matthew, Mark, and John. At the end of the oath for every degree, he kissed the Bible. Hymn singing began with the second degree. Many of the hymns came from the Baptist service. Just as the Igbo priests asked the god's blessings on their initiate, the St. Lukes' hymn for their sixth degree called for God's blessing on the order and His help in fulfilling its purpose:

> Almighty Jehovah,
>   Descend now and fill
> This Council with thy glory,
>   Our hearts with good-will.
>
> Preside at our meetings,
>   Assist us to find
> True pleasure in teaching
>   Good-will to mankind.[34]

The final instruction for the highest degree explained the order's three guiding principles in terms of Christian principles. Love derived from God's love, which inspired humans to do good works in compliance with His order to "'love thy neighbor as thyself.'" Purity must underlie benevolence so that members might deserve the sixth Beatitude: "'Blessed are the pure in heart for they shall see God.'" Charity derived from St. Paul's order: "'Above all these things put on charity, which is the bond of perfectedness.'"[35] Thus the order's three basic principles also filled a religious function.

In making this comparison between the Independent Order of St. Luke and the Ozo of Onitsha, we have noted that both include purity as a basic goal. Onitsha Ozo did not incorporate love and charity as basic principles. There is, however, evidence that all three were components of the Ozo title association in Awka. A titled man has reported that the organization there once had ten stages. The ninth, called *ozo*, is now the final stage, but in earlier generations the tenth was called *whum*. The titled man defined its quality: "This is asking for general love, between man and the gods, because this is measured in the amount of alms and good turns you can do to humanity. It is the final sacrifice of life. . . ."[36] Here is the relationship between love, charity, and purity clearly at work in the Igbo title association.

The relationship, with the religious force of its love and caring for mankind built on a foundation of purity, is the same as that described of the Independent Order of St. Luke by Mrs. Turner.[37] Could it be that sixth-degree St. Luke members have achieved *whum?* The question must be asked even if it can never be answered. With the vast choice of virtues available as guiding principles, and the even greater choice of combinations of them, the occurrence of the same triad — the St. Luke's "glorious trinity" — in both societies seems more than coincidental.

The third set of religious parallels occurs in concepts of dealing with death, both in basic attitudes toward death and in rituals surrounding it. The African mortuary society, constituted separately but related to the title association, expressed attitudes toward death and burial which are identifiable in slave behavior. Death was not a finality to the African. It was merely an interruption in the stages of life. The good dead went into worlds beyond this one; the bad dead stayed in this one, wandering restlessly and causing trouble. The good dead were buried with elaborate funerals which helped settle them properly in the worlds beyond. From there they would help with the upbringing of future generations. They could contribute good fortune, judgment, longevity, and physical and behavioral characteristics. It was therefore of paramount importance to send the dead into other worlds with correct observance of the ritual of passage.[38]

Slaves could perform only limited rituals for their dead. Shortly after emancipation, however, burial ritual became intricately complex. Merely twelve years after the Civil War, the Independent Order of St. Luke published its prescribed burial form. It was part of the church service for the dead, and it contained religious elements. The Hampton Conference recorded that slaves surreptitiously formed a funeral march; the St. Luke ritual prescribed a highly elaborated march. The St. Luke burial form included a council service within the procession. This pattern of behavior appears to revert from the simplified version, which was an adaptation to slavery's limitations, to the format of an African burial society. Efik Ekpe members belonged to a secret burial society, the Obon. Like the Independent Order of St. Luke's council service, Obon held its own ritual within the larger scope of the funeral observances.[39]

A number of traits of the St. Luke procession with service had parallel traits in traditional Igbo funerals. Parts of the march were similar. Once the Independent Order of St. Luke had formed its procession, it marched to the deceased's home before going to church or cemetery. Ozo members went to the gate of the deceased's home, then inside to his shrine and to the door of his house, shouting his name through their ivory Ozo trumpets. When an Igbo woman died, her relatives took her body home. Awka Igbo carried the body first to the front door of her father's house before taking it out to the farm for burial.[40]

Positioning of mourners at the grave was also similar in St. Luke and Igbo funerals. At the St. Luke grave, the council formed "a circle around the grave, as near as possible." The ritual placed officers at the head and sides of the grave: "the Senior P. W. Chief, Worthy Chief, Chaplain, and Clergyman at the head of the grave, the Vice Chief at the left hand side, the Worthy Father and P. W. Chiefs at the right hand side." Mourners were directed to stand at the foot. Members took these positions before the body was lowered into the grave. In Asaba, Okpala title members walked clockwise around the grave, also before lowering the body. Mourners in an Awka town gathered at one end, apparently at the foot, to wail before burial.[41]

Behavior initiating participation of the organizations in funerals shows two sets of characteristics in common. The St. Luke ritual began:

> At the death of any member of this Order, who is at the time financial and in good standing in his (or her) Council, the Worthy Chief, after being satisfied that all necessary arrangements have been made for the interment of the deceased member, shall appoint an hour agreeable with the time appointed for the funeral, for the members to meet at their Council chamber to attend the funeral of the deceased member.

First, wealth and standing were required in both Afro-American and African forms. As a deceased St. Luke must have been "financial," so members of title associations had to be well-to-do. When an Igbo Ozo member from Ogwashi died, women relatives threw cowry-shell money in their market. Okpala title members of Ubuluku Igbo received cowries at the death of a fellow member before his grave was dug. In Asaba, cowries were placed on the wrists of a deceased Eze title holder. As the St. Luke must also have been "in good standing," so an Igbo Eze from Asaba was dressed in his title association regalia—his red cap with two eagle feathers—to show his "good standing." While his body remained in his home, any stranger who came in paid respect to his "good standing" by saluting him.[42]

Second, the organizations began to join funeral rites only after initial preparations for acceptable burial were made. Among the Igbo, the body was prepared before title association members convened. At Amo-Imo village, elders consulted a diviner about burial to satisfy themselves that the method was proper.[43] For the St. Luke, the *Ritual* specified that the Worthy Chief must ascertain that "all necessary arrangements" for burial had been completed before he convened the council members.

Ritual gestures of St. Luke and Igbo mourners bore striking resemblances. Dress regulation specified that both St. Luke brothers and sisters would wear "a sprig of evergreen" on the left breast. In Awka, Igbo women who belonged to the Ekwe title association carried "branches of a strong smelling tree" in their procession for a fellow member. This parallel might be even closer: the Independent Order of St. Luke was primarily a women's organization and Ekwe was entirely so. St. Luke mourners wore the evergreen throughout the procession until near the end of the service read by the Senior Past Worthy Chief. All St. Luke members together threw their branches into the grave at the end of the lines:

> As St. Luke's, we now deposit this sprig of evergreen in the grave of our
> deceased brother (or sister) as a token, that while we bury his (or her) foibles in
> the grave with his (or her) body, that his (or her) virtues shall dwell green in
> our memory.

Ozo title members of the Isu village gathered before the burial; the senior
Ozo held a piece of vine to his neck while he said a prayer that the deceased
might prosper "in the spirit world"; the vine was then passed to each Ozo,
who repeated the prayer; then the vine was buried in the ground. Awka Igbo
frequently used palm leaves ceremoniously. They were placed in the grave,
cut up and planted in the ground by the body, or laid under the body. If the
body of a family member could not be brought home for burial, a palm leaf
might be buried as a substitute. The act of hitting the ground with the palm
leaf occurred repeatedly among Awka Igbo. The act seems to find an echo in
the St. Luke members' throwing a branch into the ground at burial. A
variation of the act occurred among Asaba Igbo. When a man of Nkpalo title
died at Okpanam, his associates came to his house. Each held an *isikeli* leaf
between his left thumb and forefinger, then clapped his right hand on it and
dropped it on the ground. The next gestures in the St. Luke ceremony also
reflected parallel attitudes. After casting the evergreen into the grave, the
Past Worthy Chief noted that members would "depart and shake from our
feet the dust of this City of the Dead." In the same spirit, the Nkpalo turned
away immediately after dropping his *isikeli* leaf and went home "without
turning to look back."[44] Both, in the ceremony of dropping the green,
separated themselves from death.

However, death was not the final for either the Igbo or the member of St.
Luke. The dead were buried with a piece of green plant, a symbol of life. For
the African, the spirit of the dead lived as long as the person was remembered. The St. Luke's "virtues" were to continue "green in our memory."
Continuity of life through the spirit was expressed forcefully with a comment on Christ's resurrection:

> *Worthy Chief.* — Shall my brother (or sister) rise again?
> *Response.* — If the dead rise not, then is not Christ raised.[45]

This apparently innocent Christian response reveals the African origin of
this Afro-American thought pattern. Christianity holds that since Christ rose
from the dead, mankind shall therefore rise. The St. Luke response reversed
the logic. It stated that Christ rose because all the dead rise to the spirit
world: "If the dead rise not, then is not Christ raised." It is clearly an example
of imposing Christian belief on an African religious system.

The final gesture of the St. Luke's council ceremony also echoed Igbo
burials. At the end of the litany led by the Worthy Chief, as members
answered, "Amen, even so, amen," they

> 1. Smite their left breast with right hand. 2. Then raise their right hands towards
> Heaven. 3. Then let them fall to the side three times.

Igbo of Okpala title in an Asaba village held up sand in the right hand, then the left, and passed it around their heads repeating, "'Don't let us die, don't let us fall sick.'" Igbo of Nsukka also raised hands, circling them around their heads. These gestures—like saying "even so, amen" with raised hands—expressed agreement that the dead member should join the spirits and leave the living behind. The life bond with the person was broken.[46] Thus we see that, as in the African association, the religious function so permeated the Order of St. Luke's ritual that it cannot be extracted.

The psychological function—to provide belonging and status—received the same kind of emphasis. An Igbo scholar stated that "Igbo are status seekers." He explained that this concern is more than material; it involved basic religious creed. Parents believed they knew what their children's roles and status in life would be and that parents must provide the "social and sociocultural environment" for fulfillment. In traditional society, taking titles in several title associations conferred great status. Through generations, parents established the title association environment into which children could grow to assume status.[47] We have seen this function in Ozo and Ekpe. Ozo titles translate as "I am among the aristocracy," "my father gave me good feathers," and "the title is in my village."[48] Title holders had political and economic power. Symbols of membership pointed out their importance.

In the United States, membership in the benevolent society filled exactly the same psychological function for the black American. Slavery's system did not allow belonging to a settled community. Any "community" of slaves could be disrupted at any moment by sale, by work, or simply at the master's whim. Yet slaves fulfilled their drive to belong by maintaining extended family connections.[49] Identification with secret burial societies during slavery also satisfied that drive. As the Civil War neared its end and as freedom's victory approached, benevolent societies proliferated. While the black was no longer owned, he was still an outcast. Where he could not join the white community, he built social institutions into a black community. Like the Igbo, black Virginians soon provided for their children's roles and status in children's divisions of their fraternals. The benevolent society became an institution for belonging and a badge of status. It served the black American psyche through the trauma of Reconstruction and through the disillusionment of disfranchisement and Jim-Crowism, and continues to serve through the tedious, slow acquisition of political, economic, and social rights in the twentieth century.

We see an example in William Johnson, whose life spanned these periods. He was born a slave in 1840. At the end of he war he settled in Richmond, where he learned brick laying and contracting. By 1907 he had established his own business, which became quite successful during the very period that Jim-Crowism was most vicious. When interviewed for the WPA study, however, it was not his success as a businessman that Mr. Johnson discussed, but his success as a lodge member. As early as 1872 he became a charter member of the Good Samaritans. Sixty-five years later he noted that he would attend a Petersburg conference as an elected delegate. By then he was ninety-seven years old. In 1874 he had joined the Forrester Council of the Independent Order of St. Luke and in 1879 had joined the Masons and Odd Fellows. In 1921 he had joined the National Ideals.[50] Altogether, then, Johnson's membership in five organizations represented 264 years of belonging. The sheer time and energy he spent testify to his pride and satisfaction in the status he achieved.

A more public example appeared in Richmond's black newspaper, *The Planet*, concerning the activities of the Knights of Pythias. An announcement of a convention to be held in Pittsburgh specified how many representatives a state could send and announced those from Virginia: John Mitchell, Jr., Dr. E. R. Jefferson, Thomas M. Crump, and N. A. Twitty, with W. M. Reid as an alternate. It then stated: "All of these Supreme Representatives have received the Supreme Lodge degree and are accordingly eligible to membership. No member of the Order who has not received this degree and is not entitled thereto can represent a state."[51] With the code for belonging thus rigidly laid out, status was conferred on the representatives. Moreover, it was conferred publicly, in print, where even their friends who were not Pythians could learn of it.

Johnson and the Pythians exemplify the communal psychological function—that is, to satisfy the need for status by forming an elite in the community. In studying fraternal orders in Mississippi, Howard Odum noted that "lay members as a rule put absolute confidence" in their leaders. "Their claims are enormous," he reported, "but they are rarely doubted. Field leaders and grand secretaries are usually presented with a 'purse' at each lodge and they are entertained royally. Gifts of more value are presented to higher officers": a council of the Independent Order of the Sons and Daughters of Jacob voted to give a diamond worth $150 to their Supreme Grand Master for wise and honest leadership.[52]

These "enormous claims" gave rise to the descriptions "curious," "exaggeration," and "parody" and have been applied to the visible symbols of status and membership—to regalia, titles and parade dress. Because whites thought of these symbols as mere parodies of their own customs, they misunderstood the symbols and ridiculed them:

> The Negro Shriners . . . have been a dark-town strutters ball since they started. The Imperial Potentate's Report to the Thirteenth Annual Convention of the Imperial Council, held in Atlantic City, the Desert of New Jersey, Ramdam 12th, 13th, and 14th, Hegira 1329, announces that the Imperial Divan traveled by airplane from Chicago to Fort Worth and "dispensated Ruby Temple there." Hither and yon, the Imperial Potentate and his Divan go, dispensating.[53]

A key to the African parallel in custom, however, lies in these "exaggerations." For they symbolize the importance of status in Afro-American thinking: they show that the degree of emphasis on belonging to the community and on having high status in it parallels the degree of emphasis in West African societies.

Furthermore, the fraternal orders' custom of having leaders visit chapters in various states—the custom myopically mocked in the quotation above—had important uses and is itself linked to West African customs. Fraternal orders grew to have branches in many states, and leaders visited as many branches as possible—an obvious way to unify and strengthen the order. Beyond this, however, travelling freely was a deeply imbedded status symbol of West African title associations. Ozo membership transcended the boundaries of family or village hostilities. Wherever a man of Ozo or Ekpe title travelled, his "brothers" extended respect and welcomed him into their homes. An Ozo could stop war. Because of his purity, he was also free from attack, for molesting him would invite anger from the spirits, and anyone who killed him must make payment equal to his worth, as the titled men said:

> The man who takes up his weapon,
> And strikes here and there,
> If striking he strikes Ògbu ēhi,
> If striking he strikes Ezè Nwaànyi,
> That man is finished![54]

In the United States, Afro-American fraternals issued travel cards and taught handshakes and passwords through which members could identify each other and get help when away from home.

Parade dress indeed assumed a "curious" form. Besides the usual marching groups with bands that we see in all parades, black fraternals sometimes had "military" divisions, and these divisions paraded as such. To anyone with experience of Jim-Crowism in the South in the first half of this century, the notion of a black military organization's being allowed to exist is not merely "curious," it is incredible. That the black military persisted despite the whites' terrorism and suppression of blacks testifies to the military's extreme importance to those who maintained it. As we see in these excerpts of an account of a Pythian military parade in 1906, the form fulfilled to an extreme degree its function of exhibiting, emphasizing, and giving status: the "Twenty-first Annual/Session of the Grand Lodge" began in Staunton, Virginia, with a parade led by "Brigadier General John Mitchell, Jr., on his grey charger," followed by "Colonel Casper Rowlett of Newport News, mounted on a magnificent black horse; Colonel John R. Chiles, Chief of Staff, on a bay; Colonel D. A. Ferguson, Assistant Adjutant General on a black horse, Major Robert S. Nelson on a bay charger." Maj. William A. Robinson commanded "the first Battalion of the First Regiment, Uniform Rank. . . ." The whole parade "passed in review before General John Mitchell and Staff."[55] Here are the symbols of status: titles of rank, uniforms, impressive mounts, and legitimate domination of Staunton's streets by masses of black men.

Where did this custom come from? One student suggested that it originated from Reconstruction, when black men belonged to state militias "with resplendent uniforms and rank and position."[56] This is possible, but not likely. Negro militias seems to have been more a product of the southern conservatives' propaganda of fear than of actual fact. State militia units, dubbed "Negro," contained whites. Only a part of the southern states had militias at all, and they were very active only in Arkansas, Texas, and South Carolina. Satisfaction in "resplendent uniforms, rank, and position" appears to have been possible only in the beginning. In the face of action, shortage of supplies quickly destroyed morale, and the violence of conservative reaction disposed of the institution.[57]

There is, however, another possible source for the militia custom. During the slavery period, Igbo Ndichie title holders paid their title fees in slaves. To capture these slaves, the title holders needed small private armies and would thus have had enviable military power. While these armies disappeared after the slavery era, the emphasis on military ceremonial remained. Military ceremony was not unique to Igbo. The Akan people of Ghana participate in *asafo*, an organization of military companies with captains. The men march in military order carrying guns and flags and wearing "colourful uniforms." *Asafo* is believed to have existed by the mid-seventeenth century, and possibly also evolved from the necessity for armed retainers during slavery.[58] Clearly, West Africans used military ceremonial to emphasize status, and this concept could have been transmitted to the United States by slaves.

Moreover, black reaction to militia service during Reconstruction indicates a value with a stronger cultural reference than a spontaneous reaction to a new situation: black churches expelled men who did not want to join the militia; black women used whatever domestic pressure they controlled.[59] Within the black community, there could hardly be any stronger punishment for refusal to comply with the value system. Since the outlet for military ceremonial collapsed with state militias, this impulse, too, was transferred into the black fraternal.

These "exaggerations," then, are precise indicators. They tell us that status was a value of utmost importance to American blacks as they emerged from the environment of slavery. The fraternal order was the medium for status; the ability to pay entrance fees was its hallmark. Members formed an elite in the new black community. The structure formed by these combined traits — the order, with its status, fees, and elite — absolutely parallels that of the African title association.

The link between status and fee payment is the key to understanding a relationship between the fraternal and its economic function that both parallels the African title association structure and diverges radically from the functions of white fraternal organizations. Although white fraternals developed life insurance and some homes for the elderly and made some donations to charities, they did not elaborate the economic function either in the same pattern or to the great extent that the black fraternal did. Just as the fraternal order was the medium for status, it also was the medium for "race progress"—i.e., for raising blacks' living standards through black economic enterprise. Writing in *Crisis* magazine, James A. Jackson noted the link between the fraternal organization's scope of influence on blacks and its significance as an economic vehicle when he said, "If I were obliged to select a medium for reaching the minds of the whole Negro race, to develop mass interest, to reach the high and mighty, or the lowly but faithful among us, I would make my path easy by approaching the colored American through his lodge, certain that here is a road that has long been trod by those who have had race progress consistently . . . in mind."[60] Here Jackson shows the fraternal society as an instrument purely of black culture, having no class or regional barriers. An instrument both individual and communal, it expresses the African belief that to be whole, life must be both individual and communal. By entwining economic functions into its structure, the fraternal society manifests the African belief in a vitally integral relationship between property and being human, as described by the African philosopher, Vincent Mulago: the "totality of being includes all that belongs to it: inheritance, family or group capital, etc. Indeed, for the *Muntu*, the human personality cannot be thought of without its belongings."[61]

A concrete example illustrates the absolute nature of this relationship between man's spiritual and material facets: Ogotemmêli, a Dogon elder, told an anthropologist that "'Trade began with twins,'" who were among the founders of the Dogon people. Ogotemmêli explained that since twins are alike in all respects, they have equal value. Trade is the exchange of goods of equal value. It is, he explained, exchanging twins. The seventh ancestor brought speech from God to mankind and therefore progress to the world and established cowries as currency. But currency is the mere representation of speech—the symbol of the words spoken between buyer and seller. An object which is sold takes with it a bit of its owner's life-force. An agreement to sell produces a harmony involving life-forces of buyer, seller, and of each object traded. And so, in Ogotemmêli's phrase, "'To have cowries is to have words.'" Just as words must be exchanged, cowries must be exchanged.[62] Igbo titled men voiced a similar philosophy in their prayer:

> We brought a goat with us!
> . . . .
> To trade with you, by barter!
> We shall get the yam in exchange!
> . . . .
> We shall get life in exchange!
> We shall get fruitfulness in exchange!
> We beg and beg and beg of you!
> The elders of the land
> Spoke in proverb,
> When they said:
> "The spirit that accepts man's property
> Must give man life in recompense."[63]

An Igbo myth further explains how God founded the Igbo marketing system by sending four strangers to establish and name the four market days in the Igbo week.[64] For the African, then, property was, in both a religious-philosophical sense and a practical-material sense, a life-support system. For the American black, also, property was a life-support system. He worked out the practicalities through his own religious-philosophical institution, his fraternal order.

As we have seen from the Hampton Conference report of slavery time, the process began with sickness and death insurance. This function directly parallels a function of the Igbo title association. If a titled man died leaving an orphan, this child collected shares from his father's title regularly. If a titled man had no children to support him when he could not work any more, the shares from his titles supported him. This custom was so ingrained that Christian converts, who thought of the title association systems as a pagan threat, could not wipe it out in about one hundred years of missionary effort.[65]

With political emancipation, American blacks gained freedom to develop other economic institutions. Richmond became the home of many blacks who were no more than one or two generations removed from those Africans who knew Igbo and Efik trade systems. Contrary to the myth of the ignorant savage, slaves exported to the United States came from an intricately developed interior trade system which used concepts of capital, currency, credit, and debt collection. Africans traded metal and fabric products of high quality along routes from the Sahara, India, and possibly Venice. Already established for somewhere between four and ten centuries, by the nineteenth century this network included imported European products.[66] In no sense was this a "primitive" barter system. The first Afro-American blacks thus brought with them concepts of economic structures—of systems of trade, credit, capital, and debt collection as well as of pooling funds for mutual benefit.

Having inherited these concepts, later generations of Afro-Americans built their new economic systems on an African pattern. When the slave trade expanded in the Bight of Biafra, the Efik established a vertical monopoly dominated by their Ekpe title association. Ekpe members kept inland peoples away from coastal trade at Old Calabar. They negotiated with Europeans for credit on imported copper, iron, cloth, and tools, often leaving one of their own sons as security for the loan. They controlled the shipping of imported goods to the interior and controlled their sale in return for slaves, ivory, barwood, and palm oil. They controlled the return transport to the coast, and they negotiated sales of export goods to the European shippers. Then they pocketed the profits of trade. Ekpe thus monopolized Old Calabar trade from source to consumer. Some title associations regulated economic production thoroughly. The Poro society, in Sierra Leone, organized and controlled production industries—weaving, smithing, etcetera—and regulated labor, prohibiting fishing, for example, if farms needed workers. At the Vonjama market, the Poro ran a "bank" to issue currency.[67]

Title association funds served as capital, a savings fund against which members could draw in cases of infirmity or death. New members' fees were divided and paid to older members as interest on the capital they had invested to join the association. Some associations allowed their members to use their titles as security for loans, and Ekpe members invested in "shares" in entrance fees, increasing profit according to the number of shares owned. People of Igboland discouraged hoarding while they encouraged lending any money saved—another version, perhaps, of the Dogon maxim that "cowries must circulate." As late as 1947, E. P. Oyeoka Offodile, an Awka Igbo, commented that investment by "modern means" was "purely selfish," while investing in a title helped the whole society "by the communal works which are performed."[68]

When emancipation came, Virginia's newly freed blacks built an economic system based on their inherited economic, social, and philosophical concepts and adapted to the environment of the United States in the second half of the nineteenth century. A pattern similar to the Ekpe vertical monopoly emerged. Its most complete form occurred in the Grand United Order of True Reformers. With the Reverend W. W. Browne as its leader, the True Reformers opened the first bank owned by blacks in the United States on 3 April 1889. In the depression of 1893, this bank paid in dollars while other Richmond banks issued scrip, and this bank advanced the money that enabled Richmond's school system to make its payroll. Its assets were estimated at over $500,000. The order bought Westham Farm, an area of about 635 acres, where it established a black community with its own railroad station. The farms there produced goods to be sold in stores run by the Reformers' Mercantile and Industrial Association in Washington, D.C., and in Richmond, Manchester, Roanoke, and Portsmouth, Virginia. The Association was also established to manufacture products and to run a newspaper, hotels, a building and loan company, and any other necessary business. The order began a system of housing for the elderly, and in 1901 it paid death claims in twenty-three states and the capital.[69] With these institutions, the True Reformers built a structure for a self-sufficient and far-flung community. Like the Dogon and the Igbo, they linked spiritual with material facets: the True Reformer bank held a prayer meeting before beginning business every day.[70]

Other orders repeated the pattern, though less completely. In 1900, the Independent Order of St. Luke also seemed headed toward a vertical monopoly. Reaching beyond the order's original concern with sickness and burial payments,[71] by 1901 Right Worthy Grand Secretary Maggie Walker called for a bank, a factory, and a newspaper. In an address to the thirty-fourth annual session of the Right Worthy Grand Council of Virginia, she made her appeal in religious terms: "First we need a savings bank. . . . Let us put our money out at usury among ourselves, and reap the benefit ourselves. Shall we continue to bury our talent, which the Lord has given us, wrapped in a napkin and hidden away, where it ought to be gaining us still other talents?" Here is yet another version—an Afro-American one—of the Dogon maxim that "cowries must circulate." The St. Luke Penny Savings Bank opened on 2 November 1903. Mrs. Walker continued: "We need . . . a newspaper, a trumpet to sound the orders, so that the St. Luke upon the mountain top, and the St. Luke dwelling by the side of the sea, can hear the same order, keep step to the same music, march in union to the same command, although miles and miles intervene."[72] Between 1900 and 1910 the St. Luke Association was established to acquire and manage real estate, and the order founded the St. Luke Emporium, a department store soon acknowledged as the most "advanced" in the South. The order got its "trumpet to sound the orders," the *St. Luke Herald*, and bought its own printing plant. A Regalia and Supply Department sold the necessary collars, aprons, and rosettes embroidered and trimmed with insignia and colors proper for the degrees of the order. This, too, was a profitable business. James Weldon Johnson noted that his Uncle William's regalia business enabled him to buy a two-story brick house that seemed like a palace to his young nephew.[73]

In the Grand United Order of Galilean Fishermen, which was organized as early as 1854, we also see traits conforming to this vertical structure. This order bought a farm in Nottoway County, Virginia, where it established homes for disabled and elderly members and for orphans. It bought land in Alabama, where it planned to build industries necessary to become self-sufficient: brickyards, cotton gins, dairies, sawmills, etcetera. Its newspaper, *The Ship*, was based in Bristol, Virginia, and the order ran a regalia business. It, too, had its own bank, as did the People's Relief Association and the Knights of Pythias in Richmond, the Gideons in Norfolk, and the Sons and Daughters of Peace in Newport News.[74] While these orders did not completely effect a self-sufficient black community, the extent to which they established economic enterprises broadens the model set by the True Reformers. Taken together, a structure emerges which presents a characteristically Afro-American institution indigenous to Virginia. While the orders adapted this economic structure to the realities of the early twentieth-century environment, the underlying concept of the African title association remained.

We therefore find that Afro-Americans in the United States built a social structure which, in both its organization and its function, directly parallels a social structure that their forebears knew in Africa. Although we normally do not find control groups against which to measure theories of how societies function, two social situations developed which show that these parallels between African and Afro-American social structures were not merely fortuitous. Both situations show that Africans who left traditional backgrounds and found themselves in new environments established social structures similar to the Afro-American fraternal structure.

One situation involved recaptives in Sierra Leone. After Britain outlawed slave trade, her navy captured slaves and returned the slaves to Africa. People of many different origins were resettled in Sierra Leone. These Africans quickly organized title societies. First, they joined a "Big Company" which furnished mutual help for whatever basic needs arose. Then they organized a "Little Company" composed of countrymen. The Companies contained most elements of title associations, or of fraternal orders. They made laws defining criminal and moral behavior; they kept peace; they provided burial and fire insurance; and they regulated economy, requiring that each member establish a farm and keep his fence mended. Punishment for refusing to farm was extreme: beatings and ostracism. As titles, the societies adopted names of prominent men of the colony—Macaulay, Savage, Dougan—thus adding a label of status.[75] Through this structure, mixed groups of immigrants organized their society and developed a settled community. This process was contemporary to slaves' secret societies and free blacks' beneficial societies in the United States.

The second situation shows the same concept of social order at work in twentieth-century Africa. Cities have grown rapidly, sometimes from village to city in a scant twenty-five years. Their institutions—rules governing education, marriage, inheritance, and so on—have not been able to cope with the sudden large mixture of people with different customs. New organizations have grown spontaneously. Now called "voluntary associations," they fill familiar functions: religious, social, beneficial, and, through savings plans and occupational groups, economic. They provide a medium for settling quarrels, and they teach standards of cleanliness and dress. Some grant titles—as Doctor, Lawyer, Overseer—which are more honorary than descriptive.[76]

Perhaps the basic social structure apparent in title associations, fraternal orders, the Big and Little Companies, and voluntary associations, arises to perform a harmonic function such as Robin Horton describes in West African secret societies as they occurred in "stateless societies." Horton's theory may well explain why transmissions of the basic concept happened. He defines a stateless society as having "little concentration of authority," with what little there is affecting only a small part of the people's lives. There would be no full-time leadership job in this society, and its members would form small groups in which they agreed to follow a set of rules. Horton says that secret societies appeared most often in what he defines as the "large compact village." Spatial relationships in this kind of village produced social relationships which engendered secret societies. Members of the village lived close together and distant from people outside the village. Defense against outsiders was the basic raison d'être of the village. Consequently members felt bound to each other and "on guard against all the outside." As a result, social distance did not grow between sub-units within the village while it did grow between the village and the outside; and institutions that crossed sub-unit lines within the village multiplied. They provided avenues to higher status for village members, eliminating a need for power struggles.[77]

It seems possible to read "Afro-American" for "African" in this description. As we have seen in the case of Virginia, "concentration of authority" became closed to members of the black community. "Members of the village" can be read as "black community" and "those outside" as "white." Although open violence between outside and inside was not the issue, members of the black community certainly were bound to each other against attack—whether physical, social, economic, or psychological—from the white. They did remain close to each other as the distance between their community and white society increased. Proliferation of fraternal orders did coincide with this trend. The orders cut across groups which might conflict with one another in the community, and the orders avoided conflict with each other because people in the community belonged to several orders at once. Thus fraternal membership overlapped as membership of title associations and secret societies had overlapped, forming complex cross-cutting structures within communities. Horton's harmonic function therefore seems a universal characteristic, explaining a link between African and Afro-American, between past and present.

Thus we have evidence of the transmission of a pattern of thought, a concept of how society should be organized to accommodate its value system. Perhaps the difficulty in uncovering African culture traits in the United States has been looking for the small detail rather than for the larger structure. The survival of artifacts—the rare grave marker or walking stick —immediately confirms the obvious principle that a person yanked from his own culture and placed in another does not forget his own. To fully understand our African heritage, though, we must understand that Africans brought their systems of values from their homes. And, once given a chance to organize their own communities, they did so according to patterns of behavior they had learned as infants and as children. We can only understand Afro-American values if we take a transcultural view. The "American" scholar must see the African comparisons; the "African" scholar must see the American. Only then can we begin to answer the crucial question: what African concepts and values have permeated our culture.

NOTES

    1. Charles W. Ferguson, *Fifty Million Brothers* (New York, 1937), 184–202; Carter G. Woodson, review of *Secret Societies: A Cultural Study of Fraternalism in the United States*, by Noel P. Gist, *Journal of Negro History*, 26:2 (1941), 268; and W. E. B. DuBois, "Some Efforts of American Negroes for Their Own Social Betterment," in *Atlanta University Publications*, 2 vols. (1898; reprint ed., New York, 1968), I, 13.
    2. William J. Whalen, *Handbook of Secret Organizations* (Milwaukee, 1966), 2–4.

3. W. E. B. DuBois, *Economic Cooperation among Negro Americans*, Atlanta University Publication No. 12 (Atlanta, 1908), 55. DuBois thought that elements of beneficial societies grew from "Obeah worship," but did not see that the societies' form as a whole could have an African origin.

4. W. J. Trent, Jr. "Development of Negro Life Insurance Enterprises" (M.B.A. thesis, University of Pennsylvania, 1932), 20. Trent adds that secret orders became "legion" in a short time, but he gives no source for his information. Carter Woodson stated that black fraternal orders originated in Richmond. He, too, gave no source. See Carter Woodson, "Insurance Business among Negroes," *Journal of Negro History*, 14:2 (1929), 205–6. These are two examples of many indications in black sources that much black history has been transmitted orally. American historians will have to learn quickly to follow the example set by Jan Vansina in using African oral tradition. Otherwise, a large body of information will be lost.

5. Americans generally know these people as Ibo. "Igbo" is linguistically more correct, and the Igbo themselves now prefer it.

6. Thomas E. Watson, "The Negro in Richmond, 1880–1890" (M.A. thesis, Howard University, 1950), 51; Luther Porter Jackson, "Free Negroes of Petersburg, Virginia," *Journal of Negro History*, 12:3 (1927), 386; and Trent, "Development of Negro Life Insurance," 6–12.

7. W. P. Burrell, "The Negro in Insurance," *Proceedings of the Hampton Negro Conference*, 8 (July 1904), 13–14.

8. Herbet S. Klein, "Slaves and Shipping in Eighteenth-Century Virginia," *Journal of Interdisciplinary History*, 5:3 (1975), 383–412; and Philip D. Curtin, *The Atlantic Slave Trade: A Census* (Madison, Wisconsin, 1969), 150. Although figures showing total numbers of slaves exported from Africa have been revised, the trend still shows that the high volume of Biafra export coincided with Virginia's import. For discussions of revisions, see Roger Anstey, "The Volume and Profitability of the British Slave Trade, 1761–1807," in *Race and Slavery in the Western Hemisphere: Quantitative Studies*, Stanley L. Engerman and Eugene D. Genovese, eds. (Princeton, 1975), 3–31; Philip D. Curtin, "Measuring the Atlantic Slave Trade," in *Race and Slavery*, Engerman and Genovese, eds., 107–28; and Philip D. Curtin, Roger Anstey, and J. E. Inikori, "Discussion: Measuring the Atlantic Slave Trade," *Journal of African History*, 17:4 (1976), 595–627.

9. Klein, "Slaves and Shipping," 396; Allan Kulikoff, "The Origins of Afro-American Society in Tidewater Maryland and Virginia, 1700 to 1790," *William and Mary Quarterly*, 35:2 (1978), 231–33; Curtin, *Atlantic Slave Trade*, 144, 156–58; and Darold D. Wax, "Preferences for Slaves in Colonial America," *Journal of Negro History*, 58:4 (1973), 394–98.

10. Ado N'Idu, "Ekpe—Cross River Cult," *West African Review*, 30 (November 1959), 749; and A. J. Udo Ema, "The Ekpe Society," *Nigeria*, 16 (1938), 314.

11. *Stick* is a word from pidgin English, referring to a length of wood. Simon Ottenberg, *Masked Rituals of Afikpo* (Seattle, 1975), 11. Here the "sticks" are carved symbols. The degree of carving may vary.

12. Onuora Nzekwu, "Initiation into the Agbalanze Society," *Nigeria Magazine*, 82 (September 1964), 173; and William M. T. Forrester, comp., *Degree Ritual of the Independent Order of Saint Luke* (Richmond, Virginia, 1894), 11.

13. Nzekwu, "Initiation," 174–75; Richard N. Henderson, *The King in Every Man* (New Haven, 1972), 251; John M. Janzen, "The Tradition of Renewal in Kongo Religion," in *African Religions: A Symposium*, Newell S. Booth, Jr., ed. (New York, 1977), 90; Forrester, *Degree Ritual* (1894), 47, 41; and Turner, "Colour Classification," 47–83, 79.

14. A tantalizing coincidence with this Igbo use of "rubbing" to mean gaining knowledge appeared in the following comment in a speech by one W. L. Taylor of Richmond: "I heard an elder say, 'I have never rubbed my head on a college wall'; but he knew more than some of the boys that had rubbed their heads against the wall." W. P. Burrell, *Twenty-Five Years History of the Grand Foundation of the United Order of True Reformers, 1881–1905* (Richmond, Virginia, 1909), 129.

15. Forrester, *Degree Ritual* (1894), 30.

16. Henderson, *King in Every Man*, 259–60; Nzekwu, "Initiation," 183; and Forrester, *Degree Ritual* (1894), 27, 36, 45–47.

17. Forrester, *Degree Ritual* (1894), 37–39; Henderson, *King in Every Man*, 259–60.

18. *Richmond Planet*, 28 October 1905.

19. Daryll Forde and Gwillym I. Jones, *The Ibo and Ibibio-Speaking Peoples of South-Eastern Nigeria* (1950; reprint ed., London, 1967), 20, 32, 37; and Ikenna Nzimiro, *Studies in Ibo Political Systems* (Berkeley, 1972), 46–50.

20. A. J. H. Latham, *Old Calabar: 1600–1891* (Oxford, 1973), 24–40.

21. Udo Ema, "Ekpe Society," 314; "The Diary (1785–88) of Antera Duke," translated into modern English by A. W. Wilkie and Donald C. Simmons, in *Efik Traders of Old Calabar*, Daryll Forde, ed. (1956; reprint ed., London, 1968), 27–65; and Donald C. Simmons, "An Ethnographic Sketch of the Efik People," in *Efik Traders*, Forde, ed., 18.

22. The danger of generalizing "African" is fairly universally recognized. Using the term is a pothole; we have to bump our way through to get on down the road. Here, it refers to philosophical characteristics prevalent enough in West African thinking to have been transmitted. Seminal works on African philosophy include Placid Temples, *Bantu Philosophy* (Paris, 1959); Jahnheinz Jahn, *Muntu* (New York, 1961); John Mbiti, *African Religions and Philosophy* (New York, 1969); and Dominique Zahan, *The Religion, Spiritually, and Thought of Traditional Africa* (Chicago, 1979). Help in understanding the concept of unity in social structure also come from Vincent Mulago, "Vital Participation," in *Biblical Revelation and African Beliefs*, Kwesi A. Dickson and Paul Ellingworth, eds. (Maryknoll, New York, 1969). Henderson's *The King in Every Man* helps with Onitsha Igbo thought, but more study of Igbo beliefs is needed.

23. Forrester, *Degree Ritual* (1894); and William M. T. Forrester, comp., *Ritual of the Independent Order of Saint Luke* (Richmond, Virginia, 1877). Both documents are in the Virginia State Library collection.

24. Forrester, *Ritual* (1877), 39. The asterisk in the sixth line reprinted here refers to a footnote in the original text which carefully specifies that "sister" be substituted for "brother" when applicable.

25. Forrester, *Ritual* (1877), 15.

26. Forrester, *Degree Ritual* (1894), 10, 16–18.

27. *Ibid.*, 32–33, 36–37.

28. *Ibid.*, 42–44.

29. *Ibid.*, 38.

30. Nzekwu, "Initiation," 173; and Henderson, *King in Every Man*, 315, 267. Nzekwu refers to ancestral spirits rather than "personal god." Henderson (see pp. 111–25) clarifies the distinctions between gods, ghosts, and spirits, and I have used his term, "personal god."

31. Forrester, *Ritual* (1877), 35–36.

32. *Richmond Planet*, 18 March 1899.

33. Personal interview, Richmond, Virginia, 16 December 1977.

34. Forrester, *Degree Ritual* (1894), 41.

35. *Ibid.*, 47–48.

36. Mr. F. A. Onwuemelie of Umuenechi, Awka, as recorded by Elizabeth Isichei, "An Ozo Title Holder Analyses the Title Structure in Awka," in her *Igbo Worlds* (Philadelphia, 1978), 67.

37. Personal interview with Dorothy V. Turner, Right Worthy Grand Secretary, Independent Order of St. Luke, Richmond, Virginia, 16 December 1977.

38. Mbiti, *African Religions and Philosophy*, 157–63; Tempels, *Bantu Philosophy*, 44–65, 100–101; Henderson, *King in Every Man*, 109–12; and Victor Chikezie Uchendu, *The Igbo of Southeast Nigeria* (New York, 1965), 12.

39. Simmons, "Ethnographic Sketch," 18.

40. Forrester, *Ritual* (1877), 46; C. K. Meek, *Law and Authority in a Nigerian Tribe* (1937; reprint ed., New York, 1970), 180; and Northcote Thomas, "Some Ibo Burial Customs," *Journal of the Royal Anthropological Institute*, 47 (1917), 176.

41. Forrester, *Ritual* (1877), 47; and Thomas, "Some Ibo Burial Customs," 204, 180, Plate V(1).

42. Forrester, *Ritual* (1877), 43; and Thomas, "Some Ibo Burial Customs," 198–99, 182.

43. Thomas, "Some Ibo Burial Customs," 160–212; and Meek, *Law and Authority*, 304.

44. Forrester, *Ritual* (1877), 43, 48; Thomas, "Some Ibo Burial Customs," 165–80, 185; and Meek, *Law and Authority*, 179.

45. Forrester, *Ritual* (1877), 49.

46. *Ibid.*; Thomas, "Some Ibo Burial Customs," 204; and Meek, *Law and Authority*, 309.

47. Victor C. Uchendu, "The Status Implications of Igbo Religious Beliefs," *Nigerian Field*, 29:1 (1964), 27–37.

48. Adebiyi Tepowa, "The Titles of Ozor and Ndichie at Onitsha," *Journal of African Society*, 9:34 (1910), 191.

49. See Herbert G. Gutman, *The Black Family in Slavery and Freedom, 1750–1925* (New York, 1976).

50. Charles L. Perdue, Jr., T. E. Barden, and R. K. Phillips, eds., *Weevils in the Wheat* (Charlottesville, Virginia, 1976), 169–70.

51. *Richmond Planet*, 12 August 1905. John Mitchell, Jr., was editor of the *Planet* and was also Grand Chancellor of the Knights of Pythias and Grand Worthy Counsellor of the Grand Court of Virginia, Knights of Pythias.

52. Howard W. Odum, "Fraternal Organizations and Benevolent Societies," in *Social and Mental Traits of the Negro*, Columbia University Studies in History, Economics, and Public Law 37:3 (1910), 129–30.

53. Ferguson, *Fifty Million Brothers*, 189.

54. Elizabeth Isichei, *A History of the Igbo People* (New York, 1976), 65; Udo Ema, "Ekpe Society," 314; Uchendu, *Igbo of Southeast Nigeria*, 82–83; and R. C. Arazu, "The Prayer of Titled Men," in Isichei, *Igbo Worlds*, 167. E. E. Metuh describes the origin in myth of the customary freedom to travel in "The Religious Dimension of African Cosmogonies: A Case Study of the Igbo of Nigeria," *West African Review*, 17:2 (1978), 9–21.

55. *Richmond Planet*, 23 June 1906.

56. Trent, "Development of Negro Life Insurance," 21.

57. Otis A. Singletary, *Negro Militia and Reconstruction* (1957; reprint ed., New York, 1963), 5–15, 100–11.

58. Nzimiro, *Ibo Political Systems*, 49; Ansu K. Datta and R. Porter, "The Asafo System in Historical Perspective," *Journal of African History*, 12:2 (1971), 279–97; Madeline Manoukian, *Akan and Ga-Adangme Peoples* (London, 1964), 46; and I. Chukwukere, "Perspectives on the *Asafo* Institution in Southern Ghana," *Journal of African Studies*, 7:1 (1980), 39–47.

59. Singletary, *Negro Militia*, 25.

60. James A. Jackson, "Fraternal Societies Aid Race Progress," *Crisis*, 45:7 (1938), 244.

61. Mulago, "Vital Participation," 138–39.

62. Marcel Griaule, *Conversations with Ogotemmêli: An Introduction to Dogon Religious Ideas* (London, 1965), 27, 199–205.

63. Arazu, "Prayer of Titled Men," 168.

64. Metuh, "Religious Dimension," 12.

65. E. P. Oyeoka Offodile, "Title Taking in Awka," *West African Review*, 18 (January 1947), 16.

66. Because this myth is so firmly fixed, the scholarship to destroy it is important. It is still recent and scattered. See David Northrup, "The Growth of Trade among the Igbo before 1800," *Journal of African History*, 13:2 (1972), 217–30; *idem, Trade without Rulers* (Oxford, 1978); Thurstan Shaw, "Excavations at Igbu-Ukwu, Eastern Nigeria: An Interim Report," *Man*, 60 (November 1960), 164; *idem, Igbo-Ukwu* (Evanston, Illinois,

1970), 237–39, 260–66, 284–85; idem, "Those Igbo-Ukwu Radiocarbon Dates: Facts, Fictions and Probabilities," Journal of African History, 16:4 (1975), 503–17; Babatunde Lawal, "Dating Problems at Igbo-Ukwu," Journal of African History, 14:1 (1973), 1–8; Gwillym I. Jones, "Native and Trade Currencies in Southern Nigeria during the Eighteenth and Nineteenth Centuries," Africa, 28:1 (1958), 46; idem, The Trading States of the Oil Rivers (London, 1963), 89; and A. J. H. Latham, "Currency, Credit and Capitalism on the Cross River in the Pre-Colonial Era," Journal of African History, 12:4 (1971), 601–2.

67. Simmons, "Ethnographic Sketch," 4–6; Latham, Old Calabar, 27–28; James Barbot, "An Abstract of a Voyage to New Calabar River or Rio Real, in the Year 1699," in A Collection of Voyages and Travels, Awnsham Churchill, comp. (London, 1744–47), V: 460; Merran McCulloch, Peoples of Sierra Leone, Part II of Ethnographic Survey of Africa: Western Africa, Daryll Forde, ed. (1950; reprint ed., London, 1964), 33; and K. L. Little, "The Role of the Secret Society in Cultural Specialization," in Cultures and Societies of Africa, Simon and Phoebe Ottenberg, eds. (1949; reprint ed., New York, 1960), 199–213.

68. Meek, Law and Authority, 174–75; Gwillym I. Jones, "The Political Organization of Old Calabar," in Efik Traders, Forde, ed., 140; Jones, Trading States, 96; and Offodile, "Title Taking in Awka," 16.

69. W. E. B. DuBois, "Economic Cooperation," 138; Abram L. Harris, The Negro as Capitalist (1936; reprint ed., Gloucester, Mass., 1968), 62–63; W. P. Burrell, "The True Reformers," Colored American Magazine, 7 (April 1904), 267–69; idem, Twenty-Five Years History, 83–84, 108, 147–58, 194, 267–68, 295–96.

70. Voice of the Negro, 2 (October 1905), 723. The National Negro Business League also held such prayer meetings. The Voice called them "peculiar" and commented, "This . . . is purely and originally Negro."

71. Dr. Bessie B. Tharps, "Rewards for Service," in Wendell P. Dabney, Maggie L. Walker and the I. O. of St. Luke (Cincinnati, 1927), 102.

72. Maggie L. Walker, "An Address to the 34th Annual Session of the R. W. G. Council of Virginia, I. O. of St. Luke," given at the Third Street African Methodist Episcopal Church, Richmond, Virginia, 20 August 1901, typescript in archive of Independent Order of St. Luke, Richmond. Virginia law forced the St. Luke Penny Savings Bank to separate from the order. The bank ultimately merged into the Consolidated Bank and Trust Company, which still operates in fine condition. Jesse E. Fleming, "A History of Consolidated Bank and Trust Company: A Minority Bank" (M.B.A. thesis, Rutgers University, 1972), 21–32.

73. Colored American Magazine, 10 (June 1906), 429; Dabney, Maggie L. Walker, 38–40; Trent, "Development of Negro Life Insurance," 23; and James Weldon Johnson, Along This Way (1933, reprint, ed., New York, 1968), 47.

74. Colored American Magazine, 4 (April 1902), 387–88; Fleming, "History of Consolidated Bank," 17.

75. Enclosures in Governor Campbell's confidential despatch, 30 July 1827 (CO 267/82), reprinted in Christopher Fyfe, Sierra Leone Inheritance (London, 1964), 140–41; and W. Hamilton, "Sierra Leone and the Liberated Africans," in The Colonial Magazine and Commercial-Maritime Journal, 7 (1841), 34–36, reprinted in Fyfe, Sierra Leone Inheritance, 142–45.

76. Kenneth Little, "The Organisation of Voluntary Association in West Africa," Civilisations, 9:3 (1959), 283–97.

77. Robin Horton, "Stateless Societies in the History of West Africa," in History of West Africa, J. F. A. Ajayi and Michael Crowder, eds. (New York, 1972), I, 78–104.

PART FOUR

PROVING
BLACK
MANHOOD:
THE ALLURE
OF SPORT
AND THE
MILITARY
IN THE
LATE
NINETEENTH
CENTURY

FOURTEEN

Peter Jackson and the Elusive Heavyweight Championship: A Black Athlete's Struggle Against the Late Nineteenth Century Color-Line

DAVID K. WIGGINS

Peter Jackson was full of optimism when he arrived in San Francisco in the Spring of 1888. At the urging of local sportswriter W. W. (Bill) Naughton, Jackson had made the nearly 9,000 mile trek from Australia in hopes of securing matches with America's leading boxers and ultimately wresting the world's heavyweight championship from the Boston Strong Boy, John L. Sullivan. Jackson's arrival was anxiously looked forward to by the West Coast sports who had read nothing but glowing reports about the boxing exploits of the man Australians admiringly referred to as the "Black Prince." Jackson had ascended swiftly to the top of the pugilistic ladder in Australia by defeating the country's top fighters, including Tom Lees for the heavyweight championship in 1886. The word out of Australia was that Jackson was a world beater. No one could stay in the ring very long with the talented black boxer and expect to survive. His enormous size, superior reach, and lightning quick hands had proven to much for even the best of the Australian fighters.

Unfortunately, Jackson's stay in America did not bring about the unconditional success he and his ardent admirers had hoped for. Instead it was a period in Jackson's career that coupled great triumphs with personal frustrations and disillusionments. Although he would establish himself as perhaps late nineteenth century's most famous black athlete, he would be denied the one thing he coveted most in life—fighting for the world heavyweight title.

Like most black athletes of the period, Jackson could not transcend the increasing American intolerance of interracial sport.[1] Despite several lucrative offers, Sullivan repeatedly refused to cross the color-line and fight Jackson. Sullivan's successor to the crown, James J. Corbett, cleverly avoided giving Jackson a match after he became champion in 1892. Corbett's conqueror, Bob Fitzsimmons, was the same—adamantly refusing to enter the ring with the talented black boxer. The fact that Jackson was never given the opportunity to fight for the world's title raises several questions. How did Jackson respond to having the color-line drawn against him? Was the racial discrimination faced by Jackson any different than that endured by other black athletes during the latter half of the nineteenth century? Was Jackson treated differently in America than he was in Australia and England?

Jackson's early years differed from those of most children. Born in the village of Fredieriksted on the island of St. Croix, Virgin Islands on July 3, 1861, Jackson emigrated to Australia with his parents when he was twelve. His father had become disenchanted with sailing the waters of the Caribbean as a fisherman and decided to seek employment elsewhere. But by the time Jackson was fifteen, his parents had tired of Australia and returned to their native land. The adventurous young Jackson stayed behind and became a sailor for American ship owner, Clay Callahan. He never saw his parents again. When he finally returned to St. Croix, some twenty-one years later, his parents had already passed away. The only remaining members of his family were a brother and two sisters who he never met.[2] Nonetheless, staying in Australia helped Jackson's career; because it was while under the employ of Callahan that he got his first taste of boxing. Both a highly successful businessman and boxer of some note in Sydney and its environs, Callahan took an immediate liking to Jackson. He was enamored of the skills Jackson exhibited in several of their informal boxing matches and in bouts Jackson had arranged with other crew members. In Jackson, Callahan saw a quiet and unassuming young man who possessed everything necessary to someday become world champion. Besides extraordinary athletic ability, Jackson possessed those character traits normally though to be lacking amongst members of his race. He was bright, hard working, ambitious, and perhaps more than anything else, a man with a great heart.

Callahan proved his respect for Jackson's talents by taking the fledgling black fighter to Sydney and introducing him to Larry Foley, the most famous man in Australian boxing. A smallish but rugged man, Foley was perhaps the person most responsible for the enormous popularity of boxing in Australia during the late nineteenth and early twentieth centuries. Shortly after defeating Abe Hicken for the Australian championship in 1879, Foley retired from the prize ring and became a distinguished boxing instructor at his White Horse Saloon in Sydney. Foley's saloon was one of the first great centers of prize fighting in Australia, only to be surpassed in popularity by the Sydney Amateur Athletic Club and the Melbourne Athletic Club in the early 1890s. Boxers, young and old, famous and not so famous, came from the most distant parts of the country to seek his advice and train under Foley's watchful eye. To many fighters, training under his tutelage was indispensable to their future success in the ring.[3]

Jackson's life changed dramatically the day he and Callahan arrived in Foley's saloon. His days as a sailor were over. Foley took one look at Jackson and decided to take him on as a pupil. Other than a couple of fighters he had seen as a young boy growing up in New South Wales, Foley had never laid eyes on someone so perfectly built to be a boxer. Though still in his late teens, Jackson was already a superb figure of a man, molded on such perfect lines that it was difficult to believe that so slender-looking a body actually tipped the scales at close to 200 pounds. His wide shoulders, deep chest, slim waist, and long arms and legs were so beautifully balanced on his six foot quarter inch frame, that his appearance suggested, in the words of English boxing authority W.S. Doherty, "an idea of some splendid glossy-coated thoroughbred racehorse."[4]

Jackson was brought along very slowly. He spent upwards of two years in Foley's saloon learning everything he possibly could about the sport. His training proved particularly beneficial because he had the luxury of going head-to-head with some of boxing's future stars, many of whom would figure prominently in Jackson's career. Also receiving their boxing education in Foley's saloon at the time were eventual world champion Bob Fitzsimmons and such outstanding performers as Frank Slavin, "Young Griffo" (Albert Griffiths), and Jim Hall. Like all good trainers, Foley was careful to teach the standard techniques and fundamentals of the noble science to Jackson without insisting that his black protege adopt a precise style. Foley, who had learned some of the finer points of the sport from famed English fighter Jim Mace during the latter's visit to Australia in 1877, stressed a defensive style of fighting that placed a premium on the short left jab and punches emanating straight from the shoulder. Jackson, for his part, took to the prize ring like a duck to water. He was a natural. During his sparring sessions, the rest of the boxers in Foley's basement gymnasium would invariably stop in the middle of what they were doing and gather around the ring to gape at Jackson's graceful moves and magnificent style. His arrow-like straightness of figure while fighting, his lightness of foot for so big a man, and the precision of his left hand were beautiful to watch. The feints, cross-counters, and side-stepping which were marked features of his coming fights, were already in evidence.[5]

By 1882 Foley began to match Jackson in a series of fights that would ultimately result in his becoming Australia's heavyweight champion. In the summer of that year, Jackson fought a four round draw in Sydney against Jack Hayes, a good but forgettable local fighter. In a return match two months later, Jackson overwhelmed Hayes in a seven round knockout. Just a few weeks after the second Hayes fight, Jackson kayoed Sam Britten, a bullish heavyweight from New South Wales, in the sixth round. In December Jackson scored his biggest triumph yet, a three round victory over Mick

Dooley, the doughty and herculean young New South Welshman who had devoured his previous opponents. In 1884, Jackson fought two intensely physical bouts with Bill Farnan, the hard hitting blacksmith from Victoria whose slugging style of fighting was reminiscent of the former English champion Tom Sayers. Unfortunately for Jackson, he was knocked out by Farnan in the third round of their first bout in Melbourne and had to settle for a draw with Farnan in a return match in the same city just one month later. Devastated by his lack of success against Farnan, Jackson spent the next two years in Foley's saloon honing his skills and occasionally fighting in exhibition matches. He was thoroughly determined to become his adopted country's recognized champion. Finally, on the evening of September 25, 1886, his dream of capturing the Australian championship became a reality when he defeated the spirited Victorian boxer Tom Lees in a gruelling thirty round fight in Foley's saloon. Certainly one of the more written about fights in Australian history, the victory over Lees was the culmination of four years of intense training by Jackson and convincingly proved that he was one of boxing's brightest stars.[6]

Jackson's elation after his victory over Lees was short-lived. Despite his willingness to fight all comers, Jackson quickly found out that it was, indeed, lonely at the top. He simply could find no one to fight. Why? First of all, there were only a handful of fighters in Australia at the time who stood a chance in the ring with Jackson. Former opponents such as Hayes, Britten, Dooley, and even Farnan, would have been outclassed by the Jackson of 1886. Secondly, Jackson and Frank Slavin, perhaps the most legitimate contender for the crown, could never come up with a mutually agreeable location in which to fight. Slavin would consent to a match with Jackson only if it were held in Melbourne, while Jackson was just as adamant that the fight be held at Foley's saloon in Sydney. The two boxers would not get together until some five years later when they fought a much celebrated match at the National Sporting Club in London. Lastly, Jack Burke, a popular boxer known as the "Irish Lad," repeatedly refused to cross the color-line and fight Jackson. He asserted that he did not want to injure his reputation by fighting a black boxer. Burke's decision was just one small example, of course, of the kind of racism that had been operating in Australia for years.[7] Jackson handled his first taste of discrimination in much the same way he did similar situations later on in his career. Instead of hiding his true feelings behind a facade of passive acquiescence, Jackson denounced Burke for his actions and repeatedly challenged him to fight. He pursued Burke with an aggressiveness that belied his basically easy-going and cheerful nature. His assailing tactics were probably best illustrated by the challenge he hurled at Burke immediately after the latter's exhibition match with Larry Foley in 1887. Prior to Burke's leaving the arena and before the crowd began to disperse, Jackson stepped to the side of the ring and angrily challenged Burke: "He says he [Burke] draws the color-line. Well, John L. Sullivan, who also draws the color-line, says he has no objection to meeting a colored fighter in private. If Mr. Burke is of the same way of thinking, I will gladly meet him tonight, tomorrow or any day he might select in a cellar barn or any private room he chooses to name, and will wager him 1,000 pounds on the result."[8] Jackson's little speech did nothing to change Burke's mind. The veteran white fighter simply glared at Jackson, said nothing, and quickly found his way out of the arena.

While Burke's unwillingness to fight frustrated Jackson, it made his decision to leave Australia that much easier. With no one to fight in his adopted homeland, Jackson set sail for America aboard the steamship Alameda arriving in San Francisco in April, 1888. Accompanying him on the trip were Australian lightweight boxers, Paddy Gorman and Tom Meadows.[9] The arrival of the three boxers in San Francisco was significant because they represented the initial wave of Australian fighters that invaded America in hordes during the last decade of the nineteenth century. Following closely behind the Jackson contingent, many of them settling in San Francisco, were such prominent Australian fighters as Bob Fitzsimmons, George Dawson, Jim Hall, Abe Willis, Joe Goddard, Jim Barron, Steve O'Donnell, Tom Tracy, Billy Smith, Jim Ryan, "Young Griffo," Billy Murphy, Jack Hall, George McKinzie, and George Mulholland.

Jackson was lured to America by the opportunity of financial gain and the chance to fight the world heavyweight champion, John L. Sullivan. Like the Eastern European athletes who have recently immigrated to this country, Jackson viewed America as the place where his potential could be fully realized and his fortunes made. He was encouraged to make the move by W. W. Naughton, the noted San Francisco sportswriter. Not that he needed a great deal of prodding, but Jackson had some mixed emotions about leaving Australia. He was treated quite well in Australia having become a darling of the sporting crowd. He also realized that American blacks were not treated much better than their counterparts in Australia and sometimes even worse. Ultimately the chance to gain wealth and prestige overshadowed Jackson's fears.

Jackson's first two months in San Francisco were taken up primarily by visits to some of the city's famous sporting establishments. He called upon the sporting men from such noted organizations as the Olympic Club, the Golden Gate Athletic Club, and the California Athletic Club (CAC). He soon became closely associated with the CAC, becoming its professor of boxing almost immediately after his arrival in the city. The club sponsored four of Jackson's most important fights and became one of America's most influential boxing organizations during its relatively brief seven year history. Organized in 1886 by Southern California native Sam Mathews and Jack Seymour, an Englishman who had been closely identified with pedestrian sports in Australia, the CAC was perhaps the first organization in America where the Queensberry glove contests were regularly staged. With a membership that exceeded 1,700 by 1890, the CAC was comprised of some of the most influential men in San Francisco.[10]

Jackson had difficulty in arranging matches during his initial days in San Francisco. No one dared to get into the ring with him until Con Riordan, boxing instructor at the Golden Gate Athletic Club, finally agreed to an exhibition match on June 4. Held at Jack Hallinan's Cremorne Garden, the fight with Riordan was Jackson's coming out party. This was the first opportunity for San Francisco's sporting element to see the much ballyhooed black boxer in action and Jackson did not disappoint them. In front of a crowd of about 1,500, Jackson flashed the skills that had made him one of Australia's most famous fighters. Those in attendance had nothing but praise for his abilities. It was the general consensus following the bout that Jackson was the cleverest boxer ever seen in the city. "Fear alone," said one of the spectators, "will prevent Sullivan from meeting Jackson."[11]

The local sporting press was so impressed with Jackson's efforts against Riordan that they immediately began clamoring for a fight between him and Joe McAuliffe, the San Francisco fighter considered one of the finest heavyweights on the West Coast. McAuliffe was a logical choice to fight Jackson. He had amassed an impressive ring record, defeating in succession such noted boxers as Dick Matthews, Mike Brannan, Paddy Ryan, and Frank Glover. Unfortunately, McAuliffe refused to cross the color-line and fight Jackson. Despite repeated efforts to induce him to fight, Mcauliffe steadfastly stuck to his decision not to fight Jackson. He had never fought a black man before and he was not about to start now.[12]

Unable to arrange a bout with McAuliffe, Jackson was forced to fight George Godfrey, the well-known black boxer from Boston. Jackson was not overly enthusiastic about the match. He understood that a victory over a good but non-contending boxer like Godfrey would not bring him any closer to a championship fight. In spite of this, Jackson agreed to the match with Godfrey for a purse of $2,000 and the "colored heavyweight championship of the world." He had been in America for nearly five months without fighting a major bout and desperately needed a match to hone skills already grown rusty from inactivity. Perhaps most importantly, Jackson needed the money. He had to recover some of the expenses he incurred on his trip from Australia and the money he had freely spent in San Francisco.[13]

The Jackson-Godfrey match came about through the efforts of the California Athletic Club and took place on August 24. None of the experts gave Godfrey much of a chance against Jackson. He was simply not as good as the black Australian. Clearly approaching the end of his career at the age of thirty-six, Godfrey owned a respectable but less than spectacular fight record. Similar to Sam Langford and other black boxers of the early twentieth century, Godfrey was compelled, because of economic reasons, to fight some of the same black boxers over and over again. His most recent opponent had been McHenry Johnson, a little known black boxer he had fought three times previously. Perhaps Godfrey's most famous fight was one he never fought. Legend has it that John L. Sullivan, just prior to capturing the world's heavyweight title from Paddy Ryan, once entered the ring with Godfrey in Boston, only to have the match interrupted by the police.[14]

It was apparent from the moment the two boxers entered the ring on the night of the fight that Jackson outclassed Godfrey. Wearing his customary blue stockings, soft-leather heelless shoes, and white tights, Jackson towered over his opponent and Godfrey was never able to overcome Jackson's reach advantage. There were moments when Godfrey landed some forceful punches, but most of his blows fell far short. Jackson hit his opponent with alarming regularity in the first ten rounds, sending Godfrey to the floor with an uppercut in the second round. By the beginning of the fourteenth round, Godfrey probably wished he was anywhere but in the ring with Jackson. Jackson relentlessly followed him around the ring, raining him with blows that caused blood to flow freely from his nose and mouth. Godfrey tried to prolong the inevitable by clinging to Jackson, but to no avail. Jackson simply held him up with his right hand and hit him with repeated lefts. Finally, in the middle of the nineteenth round, Godfrey murmured, "I give in," saying later that he had "no desire to be killed."[15]

Jackson's defeat of Godfrey was significant because it caused Joe McAuliffe to have a change of heart. Initially refusing to meet Jackson on account of his color, McAuliffe was now doing everything he could to get Jackson into the ring. His sudden decision to drop the color-line did not stem from any altruistic reasons, but was strictly a career move. McAuliffe was pragmatic enough to know that despite his hatred for blacks he would have to fight Jackson if he was ever to be considered a legitimate contender for the heavyweight title. There was a little bit of irony in all of this of course. While Jackson continued to be denied the opportunity to take part in a championship bout, boxers like McAuliffe often improved their chances of actually earned the right to fight for the title based on their performances against the black Australian.[16]

Jackson was obviously delighted that McAuliffe finally decided to drop the color-line. It would be the first time since his arrival in America that his abilities would truly be tested. As it turned out, Jackson passed his first test with flying colors. Though a 2 to 1 underdog, Jackson convincingly defeated McAuliffe at the California Athletic Club on December 28. At no point in the contest was Jackson in serious trouble. In fact, he simply toyed with McAuliffe for most of the fight. He had no difficulty in ducking McAuliffe's powerful right and administering counter punches to the face and body of the well-built white boxer. The fight ended about half-way through the twenty-fourth round, when Jackson delivered a left hook to McAuliffe's stomach and immediately followed it up with a straight right between the eyes. The badly beaten McAuliffe fell with his knees doubled under him near the ropes and was counted out amid cheers from many of those in attendance.[17]

The American public reacted to Jackson's victory over McAuliffe as it would throughout most of his career. His triumph almost immediately earned him hero status among this country's black community. Blacks from all over the country showered Jackson with unabridged admiration for what he had accomplished in the ring with McAuliffe. Perhaps more than any other athlete of his day, Jackson symbolized unbridled aggression for the black man in American society. While most black men of the period were taught to hold back and camouflage their normal masculine assertiveness, Jackson was openly expressing his aggressive impulses against white boxers. To be sure, Jackson typically assumed a defensive style in his fighting and was careful not to dole out undue punishment to white fighters. But he fought with a kind of fury that let blacks vicariously share uninhibited masculine drives.[18]

Perhaps no black community reacted more enthusiastically to Jackson's triumph than the one in San Francisco. One local newspaper noted that the city's black population had "not had such a jubilee since Mr. Lincoln signed the Emancipation Proclamation." Every black man who had been waiting outside the clubroom rushed back home immediately after the conclusion of the fight and unfurled the "glad tidings." The word around town following the bout was that anyone who employed a black man "got mighty little work out of him." Those blacks who had placed bets on the fight "jingled coins in their pockets," and for "once were disposed to dispute the superiority of any race other than their own." The black waiters in the restaurant of the luxurious Palace Hotel neglected their customers, supposedly doing nothing but discuss the fight. Groups of them "stood about chuckling" and "letting the hungry men sit and curse the hotel and all in it." Easily the most demonstrative and revealing reaction occurred in the early morning hours after the fight when some hundred blacks gathered on Market Street and began parading up and down the well-known thoroughfare singing the praises of Jackson's victory.[19]

Interestingly, some whites praised Jackson's victory over McAuliffe as heartily as blacks did. The defeat of McAuliffe provided one of the first real opportunities to discover how whites felt about Jackson and generally their reactions were quite favorable. Tellingly, much of the post-fight comments of the white press centered around Jackson's positive character traits as much as it did his boxing abilities. Jackson possessed those personal qualities deemed suitable for members of his race. While never explicitly stating it, the white community believed that other blacks would do well to emulate him. In public, Jackson often assumed a deferential mask and shaped his feelings in the direction he thought whites wanted them to be. He ordinarily adopted an ingratiating and compliant manner with members of the majority race. Even in his dress, Jackson was rather conservative in comparison to other prominent blacks of the period. He always dressed in the latest fashions, but never wore the "freak clothes or favored the big cigar and scintillating diamond which some Negroes run to as soon as they are successful."[20]

The irony in all of this was that Jackson was anything but submissive. It took an aggressive, driving, determined man to make it as far in the fight game as he had. Jackson was an expert at thoroughly concealing his ambition. Depending on the situation, Jackson could either be cleverly docile, verbally persuasive, or extremely forceful. One of his greatest gifts was versatility. Jackson was prepared to be passive if in a vulnerable position or when it assisted him in maintaining status. On the other hand, he could become combative when encountering discrimination, even though it might temporarily negate the quiet reticence on which he most relied. On more than one instance he got into street fights after whites hurled racial slurs at him. In the end, Jackson was prepared to stand on his dignity as a West Indian and protest American discrimination on his own behalf. Accustomed from infancy to standing up for his rights, Jackson did not hesitant to be forceful and more enterprising than many contemporary native black American athletes.

Jackson wandered aimlessly for nearly three months after the McAuliffe match, having no immediate fight plans and repeatedly refusing to grant McAuliffe a rematch. He divided most of his time equally among the California Athletic Club, Joe Dieve's Road House, and the various entertainment districts of San Francisco. Jackson established a well-deserved reputation as someone who enjoyed a night on the town partying with friends and, occasionally, a bevy of beautiful, if not altogether virtuous females. Like many others in his profession, he was a big spender and heavy drinker, and during the evenings, haunted the many saloons located on Morton Street near Union Square. In the end he squandered his winnings on booze and women. Jackson's generous nature and love of a good time did not allow him to do otherwise.[21]

Jackson nearly three month layoff came to an end when he agreed to fight Patsy Cardiff, the Peoria Giant, at the California Athletic Club on April 26, 1889. The West Coast sportsmen did not expect the bout to be a particularly difficult one for Jackson and they were right. Cardiff, who had gained a degree of notoriety for a match he fought against John L. Sullivan some two years earlier in Minnesota, was able to withstand Jackson's onslaught for ten rounds before finally admitting defeat. Jackson was never in serious trouble during the fight, repeatedly scoring with combination punches that left the tall and muscular Cardiff badly battered.[22]

Jackson decided to leave San Francisco shortly after his fight with Cardiff and traveled East seeking matches with legitimate title contenders. Increasingly frustrated in San Francisco, Jackson hoped for better luck in such boxing rich metropolitan areas as Chicago and New York. He embarked on his trip sometime in May, 1889. Traveling with him were some of the most prominent men in boxing. Sam Fitzpatrick, the former Australian boxer who guided the careers of several outstanding fighters including Jack Johnson, went along as Jackson's trainer. Jackson's sparring partner was Tom

Lees, the man he defeated for the Australian Championship in 1886. W. W. Naughton was along covering the trip for his newspaper. The final member of the contingent was Charles "Parson" Davies, a Chicago sporting man who had recently become Jackson's personal manager. Davies was widely known both as a promoter of pedestrian races and a manager of fighters. A shrewd and resourceful businessman, Davies recognized Jackson's money-making potential. He believed Jackson could be as big a drawing card as one of his former fighters from Boston, John L. Sullivan.[23]

Jackson and his friends arrived in New York City after approximately a three month long trip that was marked by an occasional exhibition match and an endless round of partying. Jackson was in New York for barely two weeks before he decided to leave the country at the urging of Parson Davies. Jackson's journey to London in the latter part of August 1889 came as no big surprise to insiders in the fight game. Almost everyone knew that Jackson had his sights set on Jem Smith, the former champion of England, probably best known for his 106 round bout against Jake Kilrain in 1887. Talk of a fight between Jackson and Smith had been brewing for some time, even before the match with George Godfrey. Negotiations between the two men resurfaced almost immediately after Jackson's victory over Joe McAuliffe. But on both occasions, Jackson and Smith had prior commitments that precluded them from making a match.[24]

Almost immediately upon his arrival in London Jackson arranged a bout with Smith at the famous Pelican Club.[25] It was one of his shortest but finest fights and he may never again have been so impressive a boxer. Standing some four inches taller than his opponent, Jackson moved effortlessly around the ring from the initial moments of the bout. Smith, on the other hand, looked like "a cart horse beside a thoroughbred." In the opening round Jackson avoided most of Smith's blows and landed his own punches whenever and wherever he pleased. In the second round Smith found things even more difficult. Jackson began to force the fight, battering Smith from one end of the ring to the other. Smith spent most of his time covering up and clinging to the ropes with his right hand for support. Finally, with about one minute left in the round, Smith caught Jackson around the waist, threw him heavily to the ground and used his left, as one Australian tabloid described it, "to smite Jackson in a part of the body which may be hinted at but not named in newspaper phraseology." Not surprisingly, Jackson got up rather slowly. But it did not matter. The officials, Lord Clifford and the legendary Marquis of Queensberry, immediately jumped into the ring and awarded the fight to Jackson amidst the cheering of the wildly partisan crowd.[26] The fight that had received so much advance publicity was over after just two rounds.

Jackson's victory over Smith was important because the sporting public began clamoring louder than ever for a contest between Jackson and Sullivan. There were a considerable number of organizations throughout America that offered to stage a fight between the two celebrated heavyweights.

Some of the offers were not worth the paper they were written on, but many were legitimate proposals that involved great sums of prize money. The California Athletic Club, for instance, offered to host a Jackson and Sullivan match sometime in the spring of 1890 for a purse of $15,000. The Santa Cruz Athletic Club did even better than that, offering a purse of $30,000 for the fight. Both the Erie County Athletic Club in Pennsylvania and the Seattle Athletic Club matched the $30,000 offer of the Santa Cruz Athletic Club. Perhaps the most intriguing proposal was received from a group of men from San Francisco and Nevada who offered to stage the fight in the middle of Lake Tahoe. The proposal called for a fight to the finish without gloves and was to take place, so as to insure that the authorities would not interfere, on a specially constructed barge anchored on the state line.[27]

Jackson was so encouraged by the various proposals that he decided to discontinue the exhibition tour he was currently making through Europe and return to the United States in the latter part of January, 1890. He should not have altered his plans. His hasty return to America only left him open to more frustration and disillusionment at the hands of Sullivan. The champion, in his own bratish way, refused to accept any of the offers. While experiencing great delight in dangling the carrot in front of Jackson by occasionally expressing his willingness to fight, Sullivan never had any real intentions of getting into the ring with the black Australian. As he would throughout the remainder of his career, Sullivan declined to meet Jackson on account of his color. If Sullivan could have arranged a fight with a less talented black boxer for the same kind if prize money that was being offered, then perhaps he would not have drawn the color-line quite so tightly. In fact, William Muldoon, Sullivan's manager, told boxing historian Nat Fleischer years later that he had kept Sullivan from making a match with Jackson because he wanted to "save [Sullivan] the humiliation of being defeated by a Negro."[28]

The failure to arrange a bout with Sullivan did not exactly shatter Jackson's career. If anything, he was more in demand than before he had left for England. The defeat of Smith had enhanced his reputation as one of the world's great boxers. One of the most visible indications of Jackson's enormous appeal was the many accolades and tributes that were handed out to him by the black community in the months immediately following his return to this country. Black Americans were absolutely ecstatic over Jackson's most recent accomplishments. The black press could not say enough about him. Such influential newspapers as the *New York Age, Indianapolis Freeman, Cleveland Gazette,* and *St. Paul Western Appeal* praised Jackson as a race hero of unparalleled proportions. His performances in the ring were reminiscent of those given by Tom Molineaux, Bill Richmond, and other great black boxers of the past.[29] In virtually every city Jackson visited the local black community went wild with excitement over his presence and would honor him with a testimonial dinner. New York's Harlem Unique Club, for instance, honored Jackson with a banquet in January, 1890 and similar dinners were organized for him in Baltimore, Washington, D.C., Philadelphia, Chicago, St. Louis, Boston and Indianapolis.[30]

Ironically, this attention was being lavished on Jackson during one of the most emotionally distressing periods of his career. Sullivan's continuing refusal to fight for the championship was beginning to exact its toll on Jackson. While he valiantly tried to maintain an air of confidence during his public appearances, Jackson was obviously dejected about the way he was treated by Sullivan. He was developing a sadness and intimacy with misery which was to become so much a part of Isaac Murphy, Sam Langford, and other outstanding black athletes who confronted racial discrimination around the turn of the century. Melancholy rather than happy-go-lucky was now a more accurate way to describe Jackson.

Jackson's frustrations could easily be seen in his boxing performances during 1890. He was rather listless in a five round victory over Gus Lambert in Troy, N.Y. in March, and only slightly more impressive in his triumph over "Denver" Ed Smith in Chicago a couple months later. Neither was a vintage Jackson performance. In October, Jackson fought one of the worst fights of his career against Joe Goddard in Melbourne, Australia. Although the bout was officially recorded as an eight round draw, Jackson probably deserved to lose the fight. A native of New South Wales who had just begun his professional boxing career, Goddard battered the black Australian as no other fighter ever had. Jackson's heart was simply not in the bout. He almost appeared to welcome the punishment doled out by Goddard, repeatedly dropping his hands and sticking out his chin as if to dare Goddard to hit him.[31]

Jackson's spirits were temporarily revitalized when he was able to arrange a fight with James J. Corbett in San Francisco for May, 1891. The fight was held at the California Athletic Club, the winner to receive an unprecedented $10,000 purse. Jackson's match with Corbett was one of the most thoroughly discussed fights in the last half of the nineteenth century. The fascination that many people had with the bout stemmed from several different reasons. First of all, Jackson and Corbett were both local fighters with enormous popular appeal. Corbett was born and raised in the city and had already shown unlimited potential. Jackson had spent most of his time in America in San Francisco, and had cultivated a loyal following among the city's black and white residents. Second, the fight took on added significance because it matched the most gentlemanly and scientific white fighter of the age with his black counterpart. Corbett and Jackson represented a new breed of fighter. They both fashioned themselves as men of honor who relied on ring generalship rather than the mauling tactics of old time fighters like Sullivan. Last, and perhaps most important, it was assumed by most people in boxing that the winner of the bout would be the logical choice to fight Sullivan for the heavyweight championship. To get at Sullivan, Corbett was willing to overcome his own abhorrence of blacks and fight Jackson this one time because victory over the black Australian would almost guarantee him a title shot. A triumph over Jackson combined with his previous wins over such boxers as Joe Choynski, Jake Kilrain, and Dominick McGaffrey would just about seal a championship fight for Corbett.[32]

The fight did not live up to its advanced billing. It was a painfully slow affair, with both men cleverly feinting, ducking, and jabbing each other for some sixty-one rounds before the referee, Hiriam Cook, decided that no useful purpose would be served by allowing the fight to continue. It was apparent from the outset that Jackson and Corbett had great respect for each other's boxing abilities and were content laying back and letting the other man be the aggressor. Round after round was fought without one solid punch being landed on either side. At moments during the bout, the two fighters livened things up a bit, but for most part they moved around the ring like two dancers performing the waltz. W. W. Naughton noted that about mid-way through the bout people began leaving the arena and the remaining spectators "stretched themselves out on the vacated benches and went to sleep."[33]

The fight between Jackson and Corbett had different effects on the careers of the two participants. For Corbett, simply staying in the ring with his celebrated opponent for sixty-one rounds greatly enhanced his reputation as a boxer and gave him immediate credibility among influential people in the fight game. His rather lackluster performance against Jackson was conveniently forgotten, and he now became most everyone's choice to fight Sullivan for the heavyweight championship. As for Jackson, it was the consensus of most sporting men that the black fighter had just about reached the end of his boxing career. Jackson was simply not the same man who had so handily defeated such fighters as George Godfrey, Patsy Cardiff, Joe McAuliffe and Jem Smith. At no time during the fight did he exhibit the physical skills he had become famous for.[34]

No one was more frustrated over the outcome of the fight than Jackson. Friends said they never seen him so despondent after a bout. His frustrations, interestingly enough, were not directed at Corbett, or Hiriam Cook for his decision to call the fight a draw, but at himself. Always critical of his performances in the ring, Jackson was particularly chagrined of the way he had fought Corbett. Outweighing his much less experienced opponent by some thirty pounds, Jackson knew it was a fight he should have won. [35]

In truth, Jackson was blinded to the reality of the situation. Corbett was just as responsible for the poor fight as he was. Even more unusual, however, was that Jackson never voiced any complaint about Corbett's sudden emergence as the number one contender for the heavyweight crown following their fight. Surely he must have been upset by the fact that Corbett was now being touted as the top challenger to Sullivan's title based on some impressive but limited number of fights. Corbett obviously had great talent, yet there was nothing in his boxing record to indicate that he was more worthy of a shot at the championship than himself. Like a host of other boxers, Corbett had gained a big reputation by limited fighting. In the words of San

Francisco's Daily Examiner, "it is not what he [Corbett] has done but what people believe he can do that makes him a famous fighter."[36]

Perhaps one of the reasons for Jackson's uncustomary silence was that he simply felt that no good purpose would be served voicing his complaints at this time since a fight between Corbett and Sullivan was inevitable. He would simply bide his time and challenge the winner of that particular contest. More likely, though, Jackson may have been reluctant to acknowledge that the boxing establishment had exerted any negative discriminatory influence over his life. While on one level Jackson was always painfully aware of the insensitivity and discriminatory practices of the boxing profession, on another level there was the opposite tendency—a determination not to see. Jackson sometimes acted as if the boxing establishment had done nothing to curtail his career, even in the face of such realities as Sullivan's continuing refusal to fight him and the fact that he was constantly being passed over for title shots for less deserving boxers like Corbett. The apparent reason for Jackson's blindness was that he desperately wanted to believe that the men in boxing were immune from racism and that advancement in the profession was based strictly on merit. By deluding himself into thinking such nonsense, Jackson could be assured that his efforts would be duly rewarded and that it was just a matter of time before he was given a chance at the title. In other words, he could feel as if he had some control over his own destiny and that his future did not hinge on discrimination and the personal whims of individuals in the fight game.[37]

Jackson remained in San Francisco for some nine months following his fight with Corbett, passing his time in the usual fashion. If he was not drinking and playing cards with the boys at Joe Dieve's Road House, he was out combing the streets looking for female companionship. To supplement his always depleted pocketbook, Jackson became an entrepreneur of sorts and opened a saloon that catered to the city's sporting fraternity. He was anything but a businessman, however, and after a short time sold the saloon to two acquaintances. Occasionally Jackson would drag himself into the gymnasium for some exercise. But as during most interludes between his fights, Jackson paid very little attention to those activities that contributed to physical fitness.[38]

Jackson left San Francisco in February, 1892 for a return trip to England. No one had to persuade him to go back. Most of the arrangements had already been made for a fight between himself and his old nemesis, Frank Slavin, for some time in the early spring. From a personal standpoint, this was perhaps the most important fight of Jackson's career. He and Slavin had been bitter rivals ever since their early days in Australia when they were both students of Larry Foley. The two fighters never got along, and for good reason. Their lifestyles differed and each resented the other's relationship with Foley. The two men were constantly competing for the affections of their former mentor, and it led to several heated confrontations through the years. Also contributing to the bad blood between the two Australian heavy-weights was the fact that Slavin was an unabashed racist who rivaled Corbett and Sullivan in his hatred of blacks. He had proudly stated on several occasions that he would never let a black man beat him. If all this were not enough, Jackson and Slavin had made the mistake of falling in love with the same girl. At one time or another, both fighters were involved with Josie Leon, the beautiful niece of a wealthy Jamaican planter. Jackson and Slavin had come to blows over the girl at least three times during their careers, the most famous a twenty minute brawl at Foley's White Horse Saloon in 1883. Neither one of them had anything to show for their efforts because Miss Leon eventually ran off and married someone else.[39]

There were obviously a great deal at stake, then, when Jackson and Slavin met at London's National Sporting Club[40] on the night of May 30, 1892. Boxing promoters, journalists, and various members of London's ruling class jammed the club's recently constructed 1,300 seat gymnasium in Covent Garden to witness the fight between the two bitter antagonists. It was imme-diately apparent upon their entry into the ring that Jackson and Slavin were a study in contrasts. Slavin, who was dressed in dark blue knee breeches, light blue stockings and russet shoes was a formidably built man whose rough-hewn figure bespoke of strength rather than grace. He had a large hairy chest and arms, smoldering, deep sunken eyes, and a black handle-bar mustache that covered up his always truculent frown. Jackson, on the other hand, wore white drawers, white socks, and dark leather shoes. His beauti-fully proportioned bronzed body bespoke more of balance and style than brute strength. His smiling face could easily be seen under the still not too familiar glare of the club's new electric chandeliers and through the dense cigar smoke that began to hang in a haze under the panelled ceiling.

The fight was everything that boxing fans had expected and more. Chroni-clers of the sport have repeatedly ranked it as one of the most viciously contested fights ever held in England.[41] From the moment they first emerged from their perspective corners, Jackson and Slavin went after each other like two ravenous alley cats grappling over a leftover piece of food. The fight was virtually even through the first three rounds with each boxer landing a number of telling blows on his opponent. In the fourth round, however, the tide began to shift in Jackson's favor. Jackson kept throwing stinging jabs until Slavin's left eye was nearly closed, his right cheek was marked with a gash three to four inches in length, and his lips looked like "two big lumps of bladder." Slavin was able to regroup somewhat and landed several meaning-ful punches over the next few rounds, but Jackson continued to batter him so severely that his face became nearly unrecognizable. Finally, in the tenth round Jackson settled the question as to who was the superior boxer. Taking advantage of every possible opening, Jackson rained blow after blow on Slavin's damaged face and eye. The white boxer became a pathetic figure, his head loosely flopping about as he wandered aimlessly around the ring.

The fight ended with about one minute left in the round when the courageous Slavin fell helplessly to the floor. He had let the unthinkable happen—he had lost to a black man.[42]

Jackson's victory over Slavin greatly increased his already enormous popularity among the English public. He mingled freely with a broad segment
of English society, treated more like a prince than a black boxer. He was
welcomed into the charmed circle of the finest men's clubs and learned
associations, and became a well-known figure in London's most fashionable
public places. Members of some of England's most famous families vied
with one another for Jackson's friendship and displayed no sign of aversion
to his presence. The fifth Earl of Lonsdale, for instance, President of the
National Sporting Club and one of Victorian society's most celebrated
sportsmen, was a friend and supporter of Jackson. Famous for his gray side-
whiskers, nine inch cigars, and gardenia buttonhole, the intensely individu-
alistic Lonsdale was perhaps the man most responsible for arranging the
bout between Jackson and Slavin.[43]

Jackson was obviously delighted with and appreciative of the kind treatment he received from polite society in England. In fact, ever since his bout
with Jem Smith in the latter part of 1889, Jackson had repeatedly compli-
mented the English on their hospitality and contrasted his freedom from
insult in that country with his experience of discrimination in supposedly
democratic America. Why Jackson was treated differently in England is a
difficult question to answer with any certainty. Not expectedly, many Englishmen took a rather patronizing attitude towards Jackson. He was their
pet. He was someone to pat on the back and play with. Coupled with this
sense of patronizing, however, was that the English seemed to react more
sharply to class than racial differences. Late nineteenth century Englishmen
were certainly color conscious but were unlike Americans since they were
more inclined to treat a black gentleman like Jackson as a gentleman.
Through his social connections and ability as a boxer, Jackson had both the
position to command respect and the money to pay his way. He gained
friends, influence, and training in the social graces to make him an acceptable visitor in distinguished circles. His success rested upon his ability to
conform to conventions of appropriate behavior. In manner, speech, dress,
confidence, and in his own social ease, Jackson was eminently qualified and
therefore accepted in the finest circles of English society. Jackson had been
raised in a West Indian home where English customs, notions of etiquette,
and social behavior had been adopted and followed for more than a century.
He had not only been taught to regard himself as a member of one of the
oldest British colonies, but was proud to think of himself as a British subject.[44]

After spending some five months socializing with England's privileged
classes and fighting an occasional exhibition match, Jackson suddenly decided to return to America in the latter part of October, 1892. The reason for
his unexpected departure was to seek a rematch with Corbett who just one

month earlier had defeated Sullivan for the heavyweight championship.[45] Shortly after his arrival back in the United States, Jackson, through manager "Parson" Davies, challenged the newly crowned champion to fight. His proposal was simple enough. He wanted to fight Corbett for a side wager of $20,000, the contest to take place at a "mutually agreed upon club no sooner than six to ten months from the date [February 10, 1893] of this challenge. Corbett agreed to Jackson's offer but with the stipulation that his acceptance would be void if he was first able to arrange a match with Charlie Mitchell, a full-time crook and part-time boxer from England. Corbett, and his manager, William Brady, desired a match with Mitchell above all others. Corbett felt obligated to give Mitchell first shot at the title since the Englishman was the first boxer to lay down a challenge, a representative of Mitchell having approached him with an offer immediately after his victory over Sullivan. Corbett also noted that a fight with Mitchell would be financially more rewarding and generate a great deal more interest among the sporting public. The majority of Americans, said Corbett, would rather see Mitchell "thrashed than any man living." Tellingly, Corbett was quick to point out that his decision to give Jackson second billing was not based on the latter's race. He told a group of reporters in Minnesota "that he had no objection to fighting Peter Jackson because he is colored. I think he is a credit to his profession."[46]

Corbett's choice of an opponent did not sit well with Jackson and "Parson" Davies. They were appalled by the champion's actions and let the sporting public know exactly how they felt. Jackson said he had no intention of being Corbett's "lackey," and refused to travel around the country begging for a fight. Davies was even more pointed than Jackson in his assessment of Corbett. In several scathing newspaper editorials Davies admonished Corbett for avoiding a match with his boxer. The only reason Corbett wished to fight Mitchell was to get back at the Englishman for some unkind remarks he had made about him at the Bowery Theatre in New York City the previous spring. Unlike Jackson, Mitchell had never won any kind of championship nor distinguished himself as a legitimate contender for the crown.[47]

By the latter part of February, 1893, Jackson had temporarily given up on Corbett and, like his antagonist, went on the stage. After much persuasion Jackson agreed to join L. R. Stockwell's Theatrical Company in San Francisco and play the role of Tom in *Uncle Tom's Cabin*. Jackson entered into this project rather reluctantly, agreeing to take part only after being convinced by Davies that a great deal of money could be made if the play was successful. His apprehension stemmed from the fact that he knew absolutely nothing about acting and was not eager to learn. While quite worldly in many ways, Jackson was like most members of his profession in that his total commitment to boxing had failed to prepare him for other kinds of work. As it turned out, Jackson's fears were well founded. He was totally inept as an actor, and, after about a three month long trip through such principal American cities as Portland, Seattle, Salt Lake City, Chicago, and Milwaukee, the play closed amidst less than enthusiastic reviews. It was an experience Jackson would like to have forgotten.[48]

Jackson's dreadful stage experience was soon blotted out because in April, 1894 he and Corbett had finally arranged a bout. The two boxers placed a $20,000 stake wager with Will J. Davies of Chicago, agreeing to meet sometime during the last week in June at a "responsible club north of Mason and Dixon's Line."[49] As might be expected, however, no sooner had Jackson and Corbett made their stake wager with Davies than a bitter argument broke out between the two fighters over the exact location of their proposed bout. Two clubs made legitimate offers for the fight, but for various reasons Jackson and Corbett could never come to an agreement. In May the National Sporting Club of London offered a purse of $15,000 for the fight. While Jackson was willing to accept the offer, Corbett refused it. Corbett believed, among other things, that he would not be treated fairly by the club since some of its most influential members were friends of Jackson. He insisted that the fight be held at the Duval Athletic Club in Jacksonville, Florida, but Jackson was adamantly opposed to the Florida club's offer having always made it clear that he would never fight in the South where he could not expect fair treatment.[50]

The verbal sparring match between Jackson and Corbett finally came to a conclusion on August 13, 1894 when the two fighters came face to face for the first time to discuss their differences at the Grand Union Hotel in New York City. Until then, Jackson and Corbett had communicated almost completely through the press, and each boxer welcomed the opportunity to personally present his side of the story. Corbett instigated the meeting through William Brady, contacting Jackson in July while on a theatrical tour of Europe, and asked for a conference upon his return to America. Jackson willingly accepted Corbett's overture and hurriedly made his way east from San Francisco. The meeting between the two boxers was not pleasant. In a cramped hotel room some twelve feet long and ten feet wide, Jackson and Corbett stood so close at times that their noses were not more than six inches apart and spoke to each other in the most combative way. Corbett reiterated that he would not fight in England under any circumstances. He insisted that the bout be held in America and that it be a fight to the finish. Jackson angrily responded by calling Corbett a bluffer. To show his sincerity, Jackson offered to give Corbett an American referee if the latter would go to England. But Corbett stubbornly refused the proposition. Finally, after about twenty minutes of wrangling, the two boxers decided further discussion was fruitless and angrily stalked out of the room. The much talked about rematch between Jackson and Corbett would never materialize.[51]

Some of the most influential people in boxing criticized Corbett for the way he treated Jackson. W. W. Naughton argued—and perhaps correctly so—that Corbett was avoiding the match until Jackson had physically deteriorated to the point where he would no longer be a serious challenger. The Referee, Australia's foremost sporting tabloid, castigated Corbett for his "underhanded" dealings with Jackson.[52] The fact remains, however, that Corbett made an offer that Jackson refused to accept. As badly as Jackson yearned to be heavyweight champion he was no different than Corbett in wanting the bout to be fought on his terms. He was simply unwilling to swallow his pride and consent to the various stipulations set down by Corbett. The champion had already passed him over to fight the less deserving boxer Charlie Mitchell and made him wait an unreasonable amount of time before seriously discussing a match. Considering such things, Jackson was not going to let Corbett dictate to him where and when the fight should take place.

Jackson certainly had good reason to be unhappy with Corbett, but was probably acting against his better judgement in not agreeing to fight in the South. He was not exactly in an ideal bargaining position. Corbett was, after all, heavyweight champion of the world and therefore had the upper hand in any dealings with prospective opponents. Jackson was at Corbett's mercy, not the other way around. Equally disadvantageous to Jackson was the fact that other than the Jacksonville Athletic Club and the National Sporting Club, virtually no organization was willing to sponsor a title fight between a black and a white fighter. For instance, the Olympic Club of New Orleans, one of America's most renowned boxing organizations, made no attempt to arrange a match between the two fighters. The sportsmen in that city had decided shortly after the featherweight championship bout between George "Little Chocolate" Dixon, a black, and Jack Skelly on September 6, 1892 that they would never sponsor another interracial bout. Unfortunately for Jackson, the idea of an interracial bout, particularly one for the heavyweight title, was becoming increasingly repugnant to the majority of white Americans. The world heavyweight championship had come to symbolize the Anglo-Saxon belief in racial superiority, and to allow Jackson to fight for the exalted title would have jeopardized the basic scientific underpinnings of American society. A black man might be allowed to fight for a title in the lower divisions, but not in the heavier divisions because these were, in the words of Randy Roberts, "the championships that mattered."[53] The bigger the fighters, the more important the contest, and the more crucial it was that a black and white boxer would not be allowed in the ring on terms of equality.

The inability to arrange a fight for the heavyweight championship was a stultifying experience for Jackson. In some ways, he was less fortunate than many of the other well-known black athletes of the late nineteenth century because he was unable to reach the pinnacle of his profession. Such star athletes as Isaac Murphy, Moses "Fleetwood" Walker and Marshall "Major" Taylor, were able, however temporarily, to reach the top of their particular sports. Murphy captured the Kentucky Derby three times, Walker played Major League baseball with the Toledo Mudhens and Taylor captured the National Cycling Championship twice. Similar to these athletes, Jackson was caught between two worlds, in neither of which he really belonged.

Since he relied on the boxing establishment for his position and material awards, he was separated somewhat from his origins. Yet no matter how great his achievements, he was still black. Even when he did triumph in the ring, he often received halfhearted praise from the American public, not the glory he might expect. Jackson lived in a continual state of agonizing ambiguity, a condition he found progressively difficult to deal with.

Following his meeting with Corbett at the Grand Union Hotel, Jackson decided to return to England where he stayed for most of the next three years. Shortly after his arrival Jackson began to fight a series of exhibition matches with David St. John, the mammoth heavyweight boxer from Ireland. Despite challenges from such fighters as Frank Slavin, Peter Maher, Frank Craig, and Charlie Mitchell, Jackson was content to travel through Europe sparring with St. John. When not on tour, Jackson was either conducting boxing classes at the Harmony Club in London or more likely partying with friends until all hours of the night. He was drinking more than ever now, and word out of London was that "almost any afternoon between 4 and 5 o'clock" he could be seen staggering down the Strand. Physically he was not the same man who had so convincingly thrashed Frank Slavin at London's National Sporting Club just a few years earlier. Alcohol had swollen his face and clouded his eyes. His body was marked by a certain flabbiness and laxity of movement that were uncharacteristic of him in his earlier days. Friends of Jackson's remarked that his hands shook when lifting a glass and there was a curious "halt now and then in his speech."[54]

In September, 1897 a thoroughly worn-out and restless Jackson grew weary of England and once more returned to San Francisco. Unfortunately, he did not receive a particularly cordial welcome in the city he considered his American home. Jackson quickly found out how fleeting fame is and how America's racial lines had hardened when denied a room at the well-known Baldwin Hotel, an establishment he had frequently stayed in during his previous sojourns in San Francisco. When Jackson arrived in the city, he went directly to the Baldwin, registered, and was assigned a room. However, after visiting with some friends that evening, Jackson found out that his registration and baggage had been moved to a room in the hotel annex across the street. He was absolutely livid and vehemently complained to the hotel management, but to no avail. The proprietor denied that the color-line had been drawn, explaining that the room in the annex was the only one available. Jackson was obliged to accept the room in the annex, and subsequently secured alternate accommodations across the bay in Oakland where there was a much larger black population. The man who had "dined with Earls, hobnobbed with Dukes and shaken hands with royalty," felt the pangs of discrimination in a city whose racial climate was generally considered to be mild in comparison to other parts of the country.[55]

Jackson was in the bay area for some six months when he arranged the last major fight of his career against Jim Jeffries, the burly Southern California native who would later become world champion. He made the match only after Tom Sharkey, the Whilom pride of the American Navy and future challenger for the heavyweight championship, drew the color-line and refused to fight him. At this point in his career, Jackson would have been better off if Jeffries had also drawn the color-line. He was humiliated by the heavy hitting white boxer in a three round bout on March 22, 1898 at San Francisco's Woodward Pavilion. Jackson gave a terrible performance; the few blows he landed had no effect on Jeffries. The hardest punch he threw all night was when he accidentally tripped over his own feet at the end of the first round and inadvertently struck Jeffries on top of the head. Jeffries, for his part, seemingly tried not to inflict undue punishment on Jackson. He had too much respect for the veteran to treat him in any other way. The three knockdowns Jeffries scored were caused more by Jackson's ineptness than by any punches he had thrown. The sight of Jackson moving helplessly around the ring was particularly sad for the legion of fans who had followed him faithfully throughout his career. They preferred to remember the lightning quick black boxer who had so effortlessly defeated such men as Joe McAuliffe rather than the sluggish and overweight fighter who was too helpless to answer the bell for the fourth round.[56]

Jackson stayed in San Francisco following his fight with Jeffries just long enough to say goodbye to old friends and then traveled north to Victoria, British Columbia. He hoped a change of residence would alter his luck, but was wrong. After five months in Victoria, Jackson came down with a viral pneumonia that brought him close to death.[57] To recuperate from the near fatal illness, Jackson decided to return home to Sydney, Australia in March, 1900 and take advantage of that country's warmer climate. Jackson received a hero's welcome in a country generally considered one of the most racist in the world. While never completely able to escape his homeland's abhorrent discriminatory practices, Jackson was almost universally admired by Australians for his boxing triumphs and his embodiment of qualities Australians found so worthy in their sport heroes. Jackson symbolized the very essence of English sportsmanship that was adopted and so rigorously applied in Australia. He was modest, unselfish, and above all else, an athlete who played by the rules. He never threw a fight, never made excuses for a poor performance, and never took advantage of an inferior opponent. In short, he was a hero to many Australians precisely because he never infringed the Victorian rules of good sportsmanship.[58]

During his initial days back in Australia Jackson appeared on the road to full recovery. He regained enough strength to travel throughout different parts of Australia with the Fitzgerald Brothers Circus.[59] He had gotten to the point where he was capable of giving an occasional boxing exhibition. Towards the end of the year, however, Jackson was stricken with sciatica, a debilitating disease that caused severe pain in his lower back and hips. No sooner had Jackson recovered from the sciatica when he was stricken with tuberculosis. At his doctor's request, Jackson traveled to the small town of Roma and entered the local sanitarium. He probably would have been better off staying in Sydney. Despite the close care he received Jackson grew steadily worse and died quietly in the arms of his close friend, the black comedian Ernest Hogan, on the evening of July 13, 1901. He was only 40 years old.[60]

The cause of Jackson's death was officially listed as tuberculosis. It was a broken heart, however, that was probably most responsible for bringing on his premature aging and early death. Jackson's failure to reach the pinnacle of his profession and fight for the heavyweight championship was a saddening experience. It was apparent that certain whites in the fight game had locked arms against him and that he lived not in a benign community but in a society that often viewed his success with hostility. The reality of being alternately assaulted, then singled out for some undue punishment had extracted its toll on Jackson. Ironically, Jackson sometimes appeared to be held back by an inner command to be anonymous. Despite his numerous ring triumphs, he was never completely comfortable with success and never liked to draw attention to himself. He continually shied away from—even while pursuing Corbett—the publicity and notoriety that inevitably came to an athlete of his stature. While he was highly skilled in the social graces and liked to enjoy himself, Jackson was always quick to guard his privacy. He liked to be alone much of the time, away from fans and the hangers-on of the boxing world.

In the final analysis, Jackson cannot be considered simply an innocent victim. He made some choices in his career that contributed to his inability to arrange a title fight. His decision not to fight Corbett in the South and the fact that he chose to stay in England for long periods of time cannot be passed off as inconsequential. If the heavyweight championship was his primary goal, and undoubtedly it was, then Jackson committed some tactical mistakes that a black man in late nineteenth century America simply could not afford to make. Nevertheless, Jackson's failure to arrange a title fight did not stop him from becoming the nineteenth century's most internationally renowned black athlete. In varying degrees, he was a hero to both blacks and whites in Australia, America, and England. Jackson was frequently ignored and sometimes discriminated against, but he was always deep in the consciousness of Sullivan, Corbett, other members of the boxing profession, and the sporting public.

NOTES

1. A number of scholars have examined the racial discrimination faced by the black athletes during the latter half of the nineteenth century. See for example: David K. Wiggins, "Isaac Murphy: Black Hero in Nineteenth Century American Sport 1861–

1896." *Canadian Journal of History of Sport and Physical Education,* 10 (May, 1979): 15–32, Jack W. Berryman, "Early Black Leadership in Collegiate Football: Massachusetts as a Pioneer, " *Historical Journal of Massachusetts,* 9 (June, 1981): 17–28; G.B. McKinney, "Negro Professional Baseball Players in the Upper South in the Gilded Age," *Journal of Sport History,* 3 (Winter, 1976): 273–280.

2. Jackson's early childhood is chronicled in Tom Langley, *The Life of Peter Jackson: Champion of Australia* (Leicaster: Vance Harvey, 1974); A. G. Hales, *Black Prince Peter: The Romantic Career of Peter Jackson* (London: Wright and Brown, 1931); Nathaniel S. Fleisher, *Black Dynamite: The Story of the Negro in the Prize Ring from 1782 to 1938,* 3 vols. (New York: The Ring Book Shop, 1938), 1: 123–130.

3. For details on Foley's career see, Alec Chrisholm, ed., The Australian Encyclopedia, 10 vols. (East Lansing: Michigan State University Press, 1971), 2: 81–84; 4: 127–128; 6: 86–87; Frank Gerald, *Millionaire in Memories* (London: George Routledge and Sons, 1936), pp. 193–213. Foley's saloon was frequented not only by boxers but also by many of Australia's most famous track men, scullers, horsemen, footballers, and cricketers. See Gerald, *Millionaire in Memories,* pp. 193–213.

4. W. J. Doherty, *In The Days of the Giants; Memories of a Champion of the Prize Ring* (London: George G. Harrap & Co., 1931), p. 49.

5. Chisholm, ed., *The Australian Encyclopedia,* 2: 81–84; 4: 127–128; 6: 86–87; Gerald *Millionaire in Memories,* pp. 193–213.

6. See *San Francisco Daily Examiner,* March 3, 1889; *National Police Gazette,* June 9, 1888; Langley, *Life of Peter Jackson,* pp. 16–17; Fleischer, *Black Dynamite,* 1: 131–136; *Sydney Morning Herald,* September 22, 25, 27, 30, October 4, 1886.

7. W. W. Naughton, *Kings of the Queensberry Realm* (Chicago: The Continental Publishing Company, 1902), pp. 187–188; Fleischer, *Black Dynamite,* 1: 138. To gain insight into the racial realities of Australian culture, see F.S. Stevens, ed., *Racism: The Australian Experience,* 2 vols. (Sydney: Australian and New Zealand Book Company, 1971); Humphrey McQueen, *Aborigines, Race and Racism* (Victoria: Dominion Press, 1974); Janine Roberts, *From Massacres to Mining: The Colonization of Aboriginal Australia* (London: War and Want, 1978); C.D. Rowley, *The Destruction of Aboriginal Society* (Harmonsworth: Penguin Press, 1970); David Davies, *The Last of the Tasmanians* (New York: Harper and Row Publishers, 1974).

8. Naughton, *Kings of the Queensberry Realm,* pp. 157–158.

9. *San Francisco Daily Examiner,* May 13, 1888; *San Francisco Call,* May 13, 1888; *National Police Gazette,* June 9, 1888.

10. For information on the California Athletic Club see DeWitt C. VanCourt, *The Making of Champions in California* (Los Angeles; Premier Printing Company, 1926), p. 11; Naughton, *Kings of the Queensberry Realm,* pp. 55–59. See also Nathaniel S. Fleischer, *The Heavyweight Championship: An Informal History of Heavyweight Boxing from 1719 to the Present Day* (New York: G.P. Putnam's Sons, 1949), p. 119.

11. *San Francisco Daily Examiner,* June 4, 5, 1888; *National Police Gazette,* July 14, 1888.

12. *San Francisco Daily Examiner,* June 11, 12, July 2, September 10, 1888. For information on the plight of black Americans during the latter part of the nineteenth century, see George M. Fredrickson, *The Black Image in the White Mind: The Debate on Afro-American Character and Destiny,* 1817–1914 (New York: Harper & Row, 1971); August Meier and Elliot M. Redwick, *From Plantation to Ghetto* (New York: Hill and Wang, 1963); C. Vann Woodward, *The Strange Career of Jim Crow* (New York: Oxford University Press, 1966); Rayford W. Logan, *The Betrayal of the Negro from Rutherford B. Hayes to Woodrow Wilson* (New York: Collier Books, 1965).

13. *San Francisco Daily Examiner,* July 9, 30, 1888; August 6, 1888; *National Police Gazette,* July 21, 23, 28, August 4, 18, 1888; *Cleveland Gazette,* August 4, 1888.

14. See Bill Edwards, *Gladiators of the Prize Ring or Pugilists of America, and Their Contemporaries from Tom Hyer to James J. Corbett* (Chicago: The Athletic Publishing Co., 1895): *San Francisco Daily Examiner,* July 2, 1888; William A. Brady, *The Fighting Man* (Indianapolis: The Bobbs-Merrill Company, 1916), p. 61; Donald Barr Chidsey,

John the Great: The Times of a Remarkable American John L. Sullivan (New York: Doubleday, Doran, 1942), pp. 108–109.

15. *San Francisco Daily Examiner*, August 25, 1888. See also, *San Francisco Daily Examiner*, August 26, 27, 1888; *National Police Gazette*, September 8, 22, 1888.

16. *San Francisco Daily Examiner*, August 26, September 10, 11, 1888. James Corbett would secure a championship fight with Sullivan in 1892 based partly on his performance in the ring against Jackson in 1891. Jim Jeffries would fight Bob Fitzsimmons for the crown in 1899 just one year after defeating Jackson in a three round fight in San Francisco.

17. *San Francisco Daily Examiner*, December 29–31, 1888; *National Police Gazette*, January 12, 1889; *Cleveland Gazette*, January 5, 1889.

18. *San Francisco Daily Examiner*, December 29–31, January 5, April 21, 1889; *National Police Gazette*, February 2, 1889; *Cleveland Gazette*, January 12, 1889. Randy Roberts has recently noted that black boxers, including Jackson, normally assumed a defensive style in their fighting. "Black Fighters," says Roberts, "viewed both the ring and the object differently. The ring, like the world, was assumed to be the white man's territory, and the black fighter's object was to yield it without suffering physical punishment, allowing his opponent to defeat himself." See Randy Roberts, *Papa Jack: Jack Johnson and the Era of White Hopes* (New York: Free Press, 1983), p. 26.

19. *San Francisco Daily Examiner*, December 29–31, 1888.

20. Almost everyone who wrote about Jackson mentioned his gentlemanly qualities, unassuming nature, and positive character traits. See for example: *Sydney Morning Herald*, October 4, 1886; *San Francisco Daily Examiner*, June 25, 1888; *Indianapolis Freeman*, May 17, 1890; *National Police Gazette*, September 30, 1896; Alexander Johnston, *Ten and Out! The Complete Story of the Prize Ring in America* (New York: Washburn Publisher, 1945), p. 90; Fred Dartnell, *"Seconds Out!" Chats About Boxers, Their Trainers and Patrons* (London: T. Werner Caurie, n.d.), p. 170; James Butler, *Kings of the Ring* (London: Stanley Paul and Co., 1936), p. 139.

21. Jackson always seemed to live from day to day, with no real faith in the future. His reckless squandering of money could apparently give him a temporary illusion of plenty.

22. *San Francisco Daily Examiner*, April 27, 1889; *Milwaukee Evening Wisconsin*, April 27, 1889; *Cleveland Gazette*, May 4, 11, 1889; *St. Paul Western Appeal*, May 4, 1889.

23. Davies was born in Ireland in 1853. He eventually traveled to America and settled in Chicago where he became a manager of wrestlers with his star attraction being Japanese grappler Matsada Sorokichi. At the time he wore a black beard and high collars and was frequently mistaken for a preacher, thus his nickname. See *National Police Gazette*, November 11, 1882; *London Evening News and Post*, August 31, 1889.

24. See *St. Paul Western Appeal*, June 9, 1888, *Cleveland Gazette*, June 2, 1888, January 19, 1889; *National Police Gazette*, January 26, February 2, 1889.

25. The Pelican Club was essentially the informal club of England's sporting aristocracy during its brief five year history. Information about the club can be gleaned from the histories written about another famous sporting organization, The National Sporting Club. See Guy Deghy, *Noble and Manly: The History of the National Sporting Club* (London: Hutchinson, 1956); A.F. Bettinson and W. Outram Tirstram, *The National Sporting Club: Past and Present* (London: Sands & Co., 1901).

26. *Boston Herald*, November 10, 1889; *Referee*, January 15, 1890. For descriptions of the Jackson and Smith fight, see also *Cleveland Gazette*, January 19, 1889; *San Francisco Chronicle*, November 11, 1889; *San Francisco Daily Examiner*, November 11, 12, 1889; *National Police Gazette*, November 23, 1889.

27. Examples of the various offers can be found in the *Milwaukee Evening Wisconsin*, December 4, 5, 10, 1889; *Referee*, March 19, 1890; *San Francisco Daily Examiner*, November 23, 24, 30, December 9, 14, 16, 1889; April 21, 22, 24, 1890; *National Police Gazette*, May 17, 1890; *Cleveland Gazette*, November 30, 1889.

28. Letter from William Muldoon to Nat S. Fleischer, April 11, 1931. Private collection of Bill Schutte, University of Wisconsin, Whitewater.

29. *Cleveland Gazette*, May 31, 1890; *New York Age*, December 20, January 4, 1890, *Indianapolis Freeman*, February 15, April 5, 26, May 10, 17, July 19, September 13, December 6, 1890; *St. Paul Western Appeal*, May 24, 1890.

30. *Cleveland Gazette*, March 15, 1890; *New York Age*, February 8, May 3, 1890; *Indianapolis Freeman*, July 19, 1890; *St. Paul Western Appeal*, April 26, 1890.

31. *San Francisco Daily Examiner*, March 6, 8, May 20, 1890; *National Police Gazette*, March 22, June 7, December 6, 13, 20, 1890; *Cleveland Gazette*, March 15, May 31, 1890; *Referee*, April 23, 1890; *Indianapolis Freeman*, December 6, 1890.

32. There was a great deal of discussion prior to the fight about the relative merits of Jackson and Corbett. See *San Francisco Daily Examiner*, May 21, 1891; *Milwaukee Evening Wisconsin*, May 21, 1891; *Referee*, May 27, 1891; *Cleveland Gazette*, April 4, May 16, 1891; *New York Age*, March 21, April 18, 1891.

33. *Referee*, June 24, 1891. For various descriptions of the fight, see *San Francisco Daily Examiner*, May 22, 23, 1891; *Referee*, May 27, June 24, 1891; *Milwaukee Evening Wisconsin*, May 22, 1891; *New York Clipper*, May 30, 1891; *Cleveland Gazette*, May 30, June 6, 1891; *Indianapolis Freeman*, May 23, 1891; Richard Kyle Fox, *Life and Battles of James J. Corbett, The Champion Pugilist of the World* (New York: R.K. Fox, 1892); James J. Corbett, *The Roar of the Crowd: The True Tale of the Rise and Fall of a Champion* (New York: G.P. Putnam's Sons, 1925).

34. See *San Francisco Daily Examiner*, June 14, 1891; *Boston Herald*, May 22, 1891; *New York Clipper*, June 6, 1891; *Referee*, June 24, 1891.

35. *San Francisco Daily Examiner*, June 14, 1891; *Referee*, June 24, 1891; *Boston Herald*, May 22, 1891.

36. *San Francisco Daily Examiner*, May 21, 1891.

37. *San Francisco Daily Examiner*, June 14, 1891; *Referee*, June 24, 1891.

38. See *Referee*, June 24, August 12, 1891; *Cleveland Gazette*, June 6, 1891.

39. The relationship between Jackson, Slavin, and Leon is most fully described in Hales, *Black Prince Peter*, pp. 134–48.

40. The National Sporting Club was organized in the spring of 1891 by John Fleming and A.F. Bettinson. Originally founded as a middle-class substitute for the aristocratic and bohemian Pelican Club, it would eventually become one of the world's great centers of boxing. The club went public in 1928 and the next year was forced to close. See Deghy, *Noble and Manly*; Bettinson and Tristram, *The National Sporting Club*; John Arlott, ed., *The Oxford Companion to World Sports and Games* (New York: Oxford University Press, 1975), p. 710.

41. See, for example: Butler, *Kings of the Ring*, pp. 140–145; Gene Corri, *Fifty Years in the Ring* (London: Hutchinson & Co., 1933), pp. 68–74; Jeffrey Farnol, *Epics of the Fancy* (London: Sampson Low, Marston & Co., n.d.), pp. 213–220; John Gilbert Bohun Lynch, *Knuckles and Gloves* (New York: Henry Holt & Co., 1923), pp. 121–126; Henry Sayers, *Fights Forgotten: A History of Some of the Chief English and American Prize Fights Since the Year 1788* (London: T. Werner Laurie, 1909), pp. 199–205; Trevor C. Wignall, *The Story of Boxing* (New York: Brentano's, 1924), pp. 253–256.

42. *San Francisco Examiner*, May 31, June 1, 1892; *Milwaukee Evening Wisconsin*, May 31, 1892; *New York Times*, June 1, 1892; *Cleveland Gazette*, June 4, 11, 1892; *Referee*, June 1, 8, 1892.

43. For information on Lonsdale see L. G. Wickham Legg, and E. T. Williams, eds., *Dictionary of National Biography*, 1941–1950 (New York: Oxford, 1959), pp. 529–530.

44. The status of blacks in Great Britain has been well chronicled. See, for example: Dougas A. Lorimar, *Color, Class, and the Victorians: English Attitudes to the Negro in the Mid-Nineteenth Century* (New York: Holmes and Meier Publishers, 1978); Edward Scobie, *Black Britannia: A History of Blacks in Britain* (Chicago: Johnson Publishing Co., 1972); Kenneth Little, *Negroes in Britain: A Study of Racial Relations in English Society* (Boston: Routledge and Kegan Paul, 1972); James Walvin, *The Black Presence: A Documentary History of the Negro in England, 1555–1860* (New York: Schocken Books, 1972).

45. The Corbett and Sullivan fight was certainly one of the most famous bouts in

boxing history. For a discussion of the fight see *New York Times*, September 8, 1892; *New Orleans Daily Picayune*, September 8, 1892; *Chicago Tribune*, September 8, 1892; *National Police Gazette*, October 1, 1892.

46. *San Francisco Daily Examiner*, February 12, 16, 14, 1893.

47. *Cleveland Gazette*, February 18, 1893; *San Francisco Daily Examiner*, February 12–14, 16, 1893.

48. *San Francisco Daily Examiner*, February 21, March 15, 19, 1893; *National Police Gazette*, March 4, 1893; *Indianapolis Freeman*, February 24, 1893.

49. *San Francisco Daily Examiner*, April 10, 1894; see also, *Milwaukee Evening Wisconsin*, May 1, 2, 18, 1894; *National Police Gazette*, April 28, 1894; *Referee*, May 23, 1894.

50. See, for example, *San Francisco Daily Examiner*, May 26, June 1, July 19, 28, August 4, 6, 1894; *Milwaukee Evening Wisconsin*, June 1, 7, 1894; *National Police Gazette*, May 12, 19, June 9, 16, 23, July 21, 1894; *Referee*, June 27, August 8, 1894; *Cleveland Gazette*, March 24, 1894; *Indianapolis Freeman*, April 21, 28, June 9, 1894.

51. See *San Francisco Daily Examiner*, July 19, 28, August 4, 6, 14, 1894; *Milwaukee Evening Wisconsin*, August 14, 1894; *National Police Gazette*, August 25, September 1, 1894; *Cleveland Gazette*, September 1, 1894. The real intentions of both Jackson and Corbett in this affair will never be known. It is quite possible, however, that Corbett would have found another excuse not to fight if Jackson had agreed to the bout at the Duval Athletic Club. That being the case why did Jackson not call Corbett's bluff and say yes to the proposition? Perhaps Jackson believed he no longer stood a chance with Corbett and that he would be courting disaster if he accepted the champion's offer. Jackson was, after all, 33 years old, and had been drinking quite heavily since his bout with Slavin, Corbett, on the other hand, had gained some twenty pounds since his fight with Jackson in 1891 and was still in reasonably good condition.

52. *Referee*, June 27, August 8, 1894.

53. Ibid.; August 22, 1894; Dale A. Somers, *The Rise of Sports in New Orleans 1850–1900* (Baton Rouge: Louisiana State University Press, 1972), pp. 181–183; Roberts, *Papa Jack*, p. 18.

54. *San Francisco Chronicle*, March 1, 2, 1897; *Philadelphia Record*, April 25, March 1, 6, 28, 1897; *Referee*, October 3, 1894; January 30, February 20, September 18, 1895; April 1, 1896 (quotes); May 12, 1897; *Cleveland Gazette*, December 1, 1894; February 9, 1895.

55. *Referee*, December 29, 1897; *San Francisco Call*, September 28, 29, 1897; *Cleveland Gazette*, October 16, 1897.

56. *San Francisco Call*, September 28, 1897, March 23, 24, 1898; *Referee*, April 27, May 4, 1898; *Cleveland Gazette*, April 2, 1898.

57. *Referee*, August 9, September 27, 29, 1899; *National Police Gazette*, September 16, 1899; *Indianapolis Freeman*, November 4, 18, December 30, 1899.

58. W. F. Mandle, "Cricket and Australian Nationalism in the Nineteenth Century," *Journal of the Royal Australian Historical Society*, 59 (December, 1973): 225–246.

59. *Sacramento Union*, March 22, 1900; *San Francisco Call*, April 17, 1901; *Referee*, March 14, April 11, 18, May 16, 23, April 11,18, May 16, 23, June 13, 20, July 25, August 1, September 12, October 17, November 28, December 12, 26, 1900; *Indianapolis Freeman*, March 20, 31, April 14, August 4, 1900.

60. *Sydney Morning Herald*, July 15, 1901; *Referee*, July 31, September 18, October 9, 1901; *Cleveland Gazette*, August 24, 1901.

FIFTEEN

The Black Bicycle Corps

MARVIN E. FLETCHER

Fort Missoula, Montana, in the late 1890s, was the starting point for a series of unusual experiments involving black soldiers and bicycles. These experiments came at the height of the bicycle craze in America, when developments in pneumatic tires and sprocket chain drives had made the vehicle relatively safe and easy to operate, especially in the cities. Across the country, bicycle-related activities, such as six-day races and cycling clubs, became common. In army circles, a wide-spread discussion arose over the bicycle's military applications, and an adventurous young officer, Lieutenant James A. Moss, decided to harness this technological innovation and test its usefulness. Drawing on volunteers from the all-black Twenty-fifth Infantry at Fort Missoula, Moss conducted four long rides during 1896–1897 over some of the most rugged terrain in the United States. These expeditions not only tested the adaptability of the bicycle for military purposes, but also explored its possible uses in the field.[1]

Military leaders in Europe were the first to investigate the possibilities of using bicycles in their armies. Germany, for example, began experiments in January of 1886, trying out bicycles for carrying messages to detached outposts. Later the Germans employed cyclists in various capacities during field maneuvers, using them as mounted orderlies, scouts, and shock troops. By the mid-1890s the Germans had decided that bicycles could be a valuable aid to the cavalry and they began supplying bicycles to battalion orderlies. On the other hand, experience demonstrated that cyclists could not adequately act as combat troops. Great Britain also experimented with bicycles during these years, but found different uses for them than the Germans had. The British assigned bicyclists to the infantry, where vehicles were developed to carry weapons and wounded soldiers.[2]

In the United States experimentation lagged. The first use of the bicycle by a military organization occurred in 1891, when a group of cyclists appeared at the Connecticut National Guard maneuvers. The following year Major General Nelson A. Miles exhibited some soldier cyclists at the army exercises at Fort Sheridan, Illinois, and predicted that during the next great war the bicycle would "become a most important machine for military purposes." When he became Commanding General of the Army several years later, Miles continued to push for experimentation with bicycles for the military. In his annual report for 1895, he noted how the European nations used cycles and suggested that the United States follow their example. To achieve this end, he recommended that a regiment of twelve companies be equipped with bicycles "and their utility thoroughly demonstrated by actual service." Several officers responded to his suggestion. One of them, Captain William R. Abercrombie, Second Infantry, sent a group of soldier-cyclists on a round-trip ride from Omaha, Nebraska, to Chicago, a distance of 1,100 miles. However, Abercrombie's experiment, and others in the mid-1890s, proved to be only a prelude to more extensive testing. Lieutenant Edward P. Lawton, Nineteenth Infantry, who was well versed in the subject of military cycling, urged that additional trials be made "to test the wheel in this country for other than mere courier service."[3]

As interest in military cycling increased, so did the discussion of its capabilities and utility. Several cycle drill manuals were published which included a series of exercises. These manuals contained tables of organization, bugle calls and whistle signals for maneuvering, and a description of the duties that the soldiers should perform. The last point came in for extended debate. Lieutenant Will T. May, who wrote a cycle manual in 1892, stressed that the cyclists' duties should involve "the rapid conveyance of orders and dispatches, scouting or patrolling, signaling . . . [and acting] in considerable bodies in support of advanced cavalry, or independently of it."[4]

Most writers, however, believed that the use of the bicyclist as a combatant was very limited. Lieutenant Rowland G. Hill, Twentieth Infantry, doubted that a cycle corps could replace light cavalry "in its duties of security and information" and in providing a screen for regular cavalry. On the other hand, bicycle advocates stressed that a group of cyclists had a certain advantage over cavalry: they could move quietly, conceal themselves easily, and travel without leaving tracks to indicate a direction to pursuers. But critics quickly retorted that cavalry had greater shock power. Most importantly, the army high command preferred the old ways. As a result, most of the experiments with bicycles revolved around their uses in staff, courier, and orderly services.

In the mid-1890s, at Fort Missoula, Montana, Second Lieutenant James A. Moss, a white officer assigned to the all-black Twenty-fifth Infantry, decided to test the bicycle in the mountainous terrain around his post. Moss was at the beginning of his military career. He had been born in Lafayette, Louisiana, graduated from West Point in 1894 at the bottom of his class, and was appointed to the Twenty-fifth Infantry. An infantry appointment at this time was a typical assignment for low ranking graduates of the Military Academy. In the years that followed, Moss showed great drive. He wrote a number of books on army recordkeeping and organization—for example, *Army Orders* (1914)—devised simplified muster roll and payroll forms, and originated American Flag Week.[5]

While in Montana, Moss became keenly interested in military cycling. After reading Will T. May's *Cyclists' Drill Regulations,* he decided to form a bicycle corps. In July of 1896 he asked for volunteers from among the four companies of the Twenty-fifth Infantry stationed at Fort Missoula. The regiment was one of four black regiments in the regular army (the others were the Ninth and Tenth Cavalry and the Twenty-fourth Infantry). When Congress authorized the creation of black regiments in 1866, many officers regarded them as an experiment, and viewed a commission in the new units as an undesirable assignment. The celebrated George A. Custer turned down a position as colonel of the Ninth Cavalry to take a lower rank with the Seventh Cavalry. During the Indian Wars, however, the black regiments all performed well and won many accolades. In the early 1890s, the black soldiers were participating in the usual peacetime routines of drill, practice marches, and fatigue duty that characterized life at army posts in the West. It must have been with enthusiasm that some of the enlisted men of the Twenty-fifth Infantry volunteered for Lieutenant Moss' bicycle corps. The young officer selected eight for his experiment.

For three weeks, Moss put his corps through a strenuous training program in the use and management of the machines. Each volunteer was picked because he had previous riding experience and one man, Private John Findley, F Company, was an experienced bicycle rider and a good mechanic. Findley was made the cycle mechanic of the outfit. Moss followed closely the drill regulations in May's manual. For example, in executing the command, "Prepare to Mount," the cyclist put his left foot six inches in front of the right, pushed the cycle forward, then grasped "the right handle with the right hand, place[d] the left foot on the step, and incline[d] the body slightly forward." After the black soldiers learned the skills of mounting and dismounting in the approved style, and riding together in a squad, Moss took them on daily trips averaging from fifteen to forty miles. They practiced dealing with problems they might encounter in the field, such as fording streams and climbing fences. Getting over fences began with the command, "Jump Fence." Working in pairs, one soldier rested his bicycle again the fence and went over as quickly as he could. The second soldier would hand over his own bicycle to the first, pick up and pass over the first soldier's bicycle, and then climb over himself. By late July the corps was ready to try something more difficult.[6]

The bicycle corps' first field exercise was a trip in August to Lake McDonald in northern Montana. The terrain to be covered would help Moss demonstrate the suitability of the bicycle in areas where roads were poor or nonexistent. It would also help his corps gain cohesion and experience. For this training practice, he required the soldiers to carry thirty to forty pounds of food and military equipment in knapsacks attached to their backs, as well as rifles, and ammunition.[7]

Shortly after leaving Fort Missoula, Moss' corps ran into a section of road covered with clay mud. After passing through it, the men had to stop to clean the wheels and fix the accumulated punctures in their tires. Bad roads plagued them constantly. During the first day, Moss and his soldiers had to dismount and walk their bikes some twenty times in the course of six miles on account of mud puddles and fallen trees. They reached Ravalli, forty-four miles from the post, late in the afternoon, rested a short time, and then continued to their overnight camp at Mission. The next day they pedaled on and reached Lake McDonald in the early afternoon. That night at the lake the soldiers cooked dinner from a combination of their own supplies and trout they caught.[8]

On the third day they started pedaling home over the same route. Between Mission and Ravalli, Moss tried to avoid some troublesome hills by using a railroad right-of-way. Unfortunately, the ties were unevenly ballasted. "It was impossible to ride our wheels except in a few places and rolling them along such a track was very hard work," he wrote later. "Had the devil himself conspired against us we would have had but little more to contend with." Later in the trip, the black cyclists demonstrated to some civilian spectators how they forded a stream. The soldiers split into pairs, placed a bicycle on a stick carried on their soldiers, transported the bicycle across the river, and then returned across the stream for the other machine. Surprisingly, the approach of the cyclists scared many of the domestic animals along the route. In other instances Moss reported that the "inhabitants would stop their work and gazed at us in astonishment." The corps arrived back at Fort Missoula at 1:30 P.M. on August 9, "having ridden and walked 126 miles in about 24 hours of actual traveling, under most adverse circumstances."

Moss quickly prepared for the next phase of his bicycle experiment, a much longer trip over more rugged roads. He planned an expedition to Yellowstone National Park and return, a distance he estimated to be about 1,000 miles. For this trip, the cyclists strapped their rifles horizontally on the left side of the bicycle frames, packed their ammunition in cartridge belts, and tied their knapsacks (with rations, clothing and shelter tent halves) in front of the handle bars. Bicycle repair kits and other equipment also were attached to the bicycle frame. All of this weighed about forty pounds. The greater diversity of equipment and the repair kits reflected the experiences of the Lake McDonald trip.[9]

The bicycle corps left Fort Missoula on August 19 and headed east. They averaged about six miles per hour going over the Rocky Mountains to Fort Harrison, a post located near Helena, Montana. Despite the different direction, the question of a proper route again proved to be a constant problem. The soldiers often found it difficult to pedal over roads churned to mud by recent summer rains. Little relief came when Moss ordered them to try an alternate highway: the railroad roadbed. As on the previous trip, it was hard going, but the lieutenant wanted to avoid tollkeepers and steep grades. Many times the soldiers would have preferred the mud to the jolting they experienced on the railroad ties. The cyclists had to repair their machines constantly. For example, on the second day of the trip, they had five punctures and two previously repaired had again sprung leaks. The corps also had to cope with broken chains, worn and damaged bearings, and tires that required recementing to the rims. Major repairs were done by handymen along the route, but for a high price. Near Fort Harrison Moss went to a blacksmith to have two seat springs made. The smith knew that Moss needed his help and tried to overcharge him. Moss haggled with him and brought the price down to $1.50 for a job he considered to be worth 25¢.[10]

At Fort Harrison the bicycle corps began traveling along the Missouri River toward Fort Yellowstone and Yellowstone National Park. The corps reached its destination in eight days. Moss' report on the soldiers reflected the "Sambo" stereotype that most whites held of blacks at that time. One story he related had to do with crossing the Continental Divide. As soon as Moss ordered the command to fall out, the men split into two groups, one on either side of the imaginary line. They shook each other's hands and, according to Moss, had the following conversation: "Well, ole man, how's eberyting wid you way down dah on de Pacific slope?" The reply was: "Oh, eberyting is fine wid us! How's tings getting along wid you fellers way down dah on de Atlantic slope." On another occasion the corps ran into a rainstorm which quickly turned the road into a quagmire. At this juncture, one soldier exclaimed: "A mule! A mule! My kingdom for a mule!" The corps spent five days in Yellowstone Park and visited all the sights. They were amazed by the geysers and sulphuric fumes. "I think the sulphuric fumes and the roaring from some of the geysers had a good moral effect on them," the lieutenant noted.[11]

On September 1 Moss and the black bicyclists departed for home, retracing their original route. Outside of Bozeman, a soldier's front wheel crumpled completely when the rim splintered. Forced to stop for the night, the corps searched for a place to sleep and ended up in a barn. The next day Moss got a civilian cyclist to take the wheel into Bozeman and get it repaired. This cost $3.50. Several days later, upon leaving Fort Harrison, the corps came to a divide in the road. Moss recorded that evening: "Took wrong road—after rolling our wheels about two miles up grade, over stones and ruts, the road disappeared amid grass and timber, and we realized our mistake." The corps pedaled into Fort Missoula on September 8. They had traveled 790 miles in 126 hours of riding time (sixteen days of elapsed time) and averaged 6.25 m.p.h.

As a result of his trip to Yellowstone Park, Moss believed that he had tested fully the capabilities of the bicycles and men for cross-country traveling. He was sure that the concept had proven itself. But others were not so sure. His department commander, Brigadier General John R. Brooke, observed that "it would be impossible to take a bicycle corps of any size from place to place in a mountainous country without its being scattered and liable to be cut to pieces, or else there would be so many delays for the whole corps that it would take a long time for it to get to its destination." However, Brooke was well aware that his superior, General Miles, was interested in bicycles, and tempered his criticism with the note that the bicycle probably could be used "in some sections to good advantage for courier service and reconnoitering."

Moss turned next to testing the bicycle for reconnaissance purposes. In mid-September of 1896, the bicycle corps went on a small scale maneuver with the Twenty-fifth Infantry out from Fort Missoula. The corps not only scouted ahead of the line of march, but also set up a courier service for the unit commander, Colonel Andrew S. Burt. Black cyclists stationed themselves at intervals along a line that stretched for a distance of fifteen miles, and relayed messages on road conditions, the availability of water, and possible camp sites. This information aided the company officers in deciding how far their men would march each day. The cyclists also provided Colonel Burt with information on the condition of the wagon train, located at the rear of his column of troops. This service proved very useful when company wagons sank deep into the mud and extra men were needed to get them out. Cross-country riding involved in this type of practice march was hard on the cyclists. Artist Frederic Remington watched the corps in action and noted: "It is heavy wheeling and pretty bumpy on the grass, where they are compelled to ride, but they manage far better than one would anticipate."[12]

Despite the fact that he had successfully organized and demonstrated the cross-country and scouting abilities of the bicycle soldier, Moss felt that more should be done. He saw the comments of General Brooke as indicative of the resistance by some army officers to change. He also knew that the bicycles had exhibited certain weaknesses in construction, especially in the rugged terrain of the west. During the winter Moss outlined the cycle problems to his superiors, and General Miles placed him on special duty to visit the leading bicycle and tire factories in the East and study the manufacture of "bicycles, tires, and bicycle sundries." Upon completing his tour, the lieutenant made plans to undertake another field exercise in the summer of 1897.[13]

To test the bicycle and his men more thoroughly, Moss projected a trip over a longer route and across terrain with all possible obstacles. He proposed a 1,900-mile expedition from Fort Missoula to Saint Louis. This included high and low altitudes, moist and dry climates, and up and down grades. It would involve, he wrote, "the mountainous and stony roads of Montana; the hummock earth roads of South Dakota; the sandy roads of Nebraska and the clay roads of Missouri."[14]

Although the earlier expeditions had been rigorous, Moss had no trouble filling his manpower needs. In June 1897 he asked for volunteers for a larger version of the bicycle corps. Forty black soldiers volunteered, and he chose twenty. His squad of twenty included five of the eight men from his first squad. The men were generally cyclists of experience and in good physical condition.[15]

Moss spent two weeks in June preparing the corps. He instructed the black soldiers in the use of the bicycle, conducted special walking exercises to make them limber, and took the men on short practice rides. These rides lengthened as the departure date neared. Moss also gave close attention to equipment and supplies. The corps would use new Spalding bicycles with steel rims and special gear cases. Eight brands of tires would be tested for endurance in the field. The men were to pack their cooking utensils and provisions into diamond-shaped pouches and attach these to the bicycle frames. Special pans were ordered to fit into the pouches. Individual rations included hard bread, biscuit, canned beef, sugar, coffee, and flour. Every soldier carried the standard Krag-Jorgenson rifle, which weighed about ten pounds, a cartridge belt, and fifty rounds of ammunition. Spare bicycle parts, such as pedal cranks, front spokes, and steel rims, went along also. Every second soldier received an oil can for use on the machines. Finally, Moss established nineteen ration stations between Missoula and Saint Louis, the Quartermaster's Department placing supplies in each. With these preparations proceeding smoothly, the corps soon was ready to depart.[16]

On June 14 the bicycle corps (Lieutenant Moss, a white surgeon, and twenty black soldiers) pedaled out of Fort Missoula and headed toward Helena. The citizens of Missoula turned out in large numbers to see the riders off. From the beginning Moss maintained a regular schedule. The group rose before dawn, cooked breakfast, and was on its way at daybreak. The men rode until 10 A.M., rested until 5 P.M., and then pedaled until dark. When the moon was full, Moss had them ride even later. The elements were not always favorable. Shortly after leaving Missoula, the cyclists ran into a cloudburst, which slowed them down to a walk. They crossed the Continental Divide in a sleet storm, with two inches of snow on the ground. It was so cold that the men stopped frequently, clapped their hands, and rubbed their ears. On June 23 they reached Billings, one of their ration depots. Between Gillette, Wyoming, and the South Dakota state line their food ran out and they had to travel forty-two miles without sustenance. On the twenty-fifth, the corps arrived at Fort Custer, South Dakota, located near the scene of the Battle of the Little Big Horn. Here, the soldiers took a day off and went sightseeing on Custer's old battlefield.[17]

Between Alliance and Grand Island, Nebraska, the corps encountered its greatest challenge. Here, the roads were barely adequate, and some of them were simply shifting masses of sand. Here also the summer temperatures soared above 100 degrees which slowed the progress of the corps. The group covered this distance of 170 miles in four and a half days, traveling generally over railroad roadbeds and battling alkali water and the heat most of the way. Moss and over half of the corps became sick, and two soldiers had their feet badly blistered from the burning sand. Bystanders were astonished at seeing black soldiers on bicycles and asked innumerable questions. Asked where the corps was going, one black soldier, according to Moss, replied: "De Lawd only knows, we're follin' de lutenant."[18]

On July 24 the riders finally reached Saint Louis. They were met on the outskirts by a large crowd of cyclists and escorted into the city. The local citizens gave them a royal welcome. The soldiers made quite a sight: faded blue coats, rifles slung across shoulders, bayonet scabbards clanking against wheel frames. The corps camped in the city park where it became an immediate attraction for both black and white townsfolk. Moss and his group stayed in Saint Louis for one week, then took a train back to Fort Missoula.[19]

The bicycle corps had traversed about 1,900 miles in forty days, thirty-five of which were actually spent in travel. This meant that the men averaged fifty-two miles a day. During the course of the trip their major problem was with punctures, and many of the cyclists became experts at patching tires. The extended riding had an impact on the physique of the riders. A number of the men gained in chest and arm measurements, and fourteen gained weight. Moss spoke enthusiastically about the black riders. "Some of our experiences, especially while in the sand hills of Nebraska," he reported, "tested to the utmost not only their physical endurance but also their moral courage and disposition; and I wish to commend them for the spirit, pluck and fine soldierly qualities they displayed."[20]

From this cross-country ride, Moss drew a number of conclusions. He noted, for example, that many of the roads in the section of the country they traversed seemed to be an index of the quality of people of the area. Where there were good roads, the inhabitants appeared "well informed, [and] used modern farming implements." The people in areas with poor roads were "narrow-minded, devoid of any knowledge of the topography of the country, and behind the times in everything." Moss also observed that the bicyclists with previous experience held up the best on the trip, and recommended that future corpsmen have "at least three years' experience in cycling before undertaking such use of the bicycle." The lieutenant found it impossible to keep the corps in military formation; in this he echoed the earlier comments of General Brooke. He also commented on the tires. If military cycling were to progress, Moss said, it was necessary to develop "a resilient, puncture-proof tire." None of the eight tires tested had proved completely satisfactory.[21]

Moss felt that further testing of the bicycle for military transportation was definitely needed. "Should not a modern, up-to-date army have both [bicycles and cavalry], [so] that it might avail itself of the advantages of the one or the other, as the proper conditions present themselves?" he asked. The lieutenant saw his experiments as furthering the knowledge of the bicycle's capabilities and improving it for use in reconnaissance, courier work, and road patrolling.[22]

Moss spent the winter of 1897 studying French and British books on military cycling and reviewing his own experiences. In February of 1898 he submitted a proposal to the Adjutant General of the Army requesting permission to conduct another test of military cycling. He specifically wanted to take a group of twenty cyclists from Fort Missoula to San Francisco and return. Such an undertaking would provide an "excellent and economic way" of determining further "the practicability and the durability of the bicycle as a machine for military purposes." He had established connections with Eastern bicycle manufacturers during his previous experiments, and was confident that they would furnish the equipment for the 1898 test march without cost to the government. He would promote no particular bicycle or tire company, but would field test many different brands. General Miles endorsed the project.

To give weight to his request, Moss secured letters supporting his proposal. Representative Robert F. Broussard of Louisiana wrote to Secretary of War Russell A. Alger, asking that if the army conducted further bicycle experiments, that Moss be placed in charge. "He is very much wrapped up in bicycle experiments," Broussard added. The young lieutenant also received an endorsement from his regimental commander, Colonel Burt, who characterized Moss as "a man of unusual energy and ability, full of enthusiasm and determination to get at the bottom facts connected with the bicycle in the Army." Despite these approving letters, the War Department turned down Moss' request. "Sufficient experiments, to meet all knowledge of its merits, have been made with the bicycle, at present," was the reply. A key factor in this decision probably was the rush of events after the sinking of the U.S.S. *Maine* on February 15, 1898. With war imminent, it did not seem wise to spend time and money on sending twenty black soldiers from Fort Missoula to San Francisco. The ensuing war with Spain that summer brought an end to the bicycle corps exercises.

Lieutenant Moss' bicycle corps experiment was an interesting episode in the development of military technology. It occurred during a period when the United States lagged behind in military developments and there was resistance in army circles to experimentation. Organizing an informal bicycle corps at Fort Missoula, Moss in 1896–1897 conducted strenuous marches (over 2,800 miles in 451 hours of travel) that clearly showed the capabilities of the bicycle as a military vehicle. In the end Moss concluded, as did the Germans, that the bicycle was most suited as an aid to couriers and to the staff. However, Moss' experiments had broader implications. From the beginning, bicycle frame and equipment manufacturers supported his tests and he, in turn, gave them the benefit of his experience and recommended improvements in bicycle design. Moss' use of black soldiers in the bicycle corps also was an interesting commentary on army thinking in the 1890s. While discrimination was increasing in civilian society, the military was willing, at least in this case, to grant blacks equal treatment and to allow them to advance on their own merits. Although a brief chapter in the history

of the United States Army, the bicycle corps experiment provides insight
into the growing military-industrial complex in the 1890s and the semi-
tolerant attitude in the army toward the black minority.

NOTES

1. A sketch of the bicycle corps is in John H. Nankivell (comp.), *The History of the
Twenty-fifth Regiment, United States Infantry, 1869–1926* (New edition, Fort Collins,
Colorado: Old Army Press, 1972), 60–62. See also Marvin E. Fletcher, "The Negro
Soldier and the United States Army, 1891–1917" (Ph.D. dissertation, University of
Wisconsin, 1968), 64–68.
2. Henry H. Whitney, "The Adaptation of the Bicycle to Military Uses," *Journal of
the Military Service Institution of the United States [JMSI]* XVII (December 1895), 545–
47, 550.
3. James Wagenvoord, *Bikes and Riders* (New York, 1972), 95–96. Report of the
Secretary of War, November 26, 1895, *House Document 2*, 54 Congress, 1 Session
(Serial 3370), 69. Edward P. Lawton, "The Bicycle in Military Use," *JMSI*, XXI (December 1897), 459–60.
4. Will T. May, *Cyclists' Drill Regulations, United States Army* (Boston: Pope Manufacturing Company, 1892), 33. Rowland G. Hill, "The Capabilities and Limitations of
the Bicycle as a Military Machine," *JMSI*, XVII (October 1895), 314.
5. Moss retired in 1922 from the army with the rank of colonel. James A. Moss,
Military Cycling in the Rocky Mountains (New York: The Spalding Company, 1897), 7.
For more information on the black soldiers, see William H. Leckie, *The Buffalo Soldiers:
A Narrative of the Negro Cavalry in the West* (U. of Oklahoma Press, 1967); and Arlen
Fowler, *The Black Infantry in the West, 1869–1891* (Westport, Connecticut: Greenwood
Publishing Company, 1971).
6. James A. Moss to Adjutant, Fort Missoula, October 10, 1896, No. 46408, Document File, 1890–1917, Records of the Adjutant General's Office [RAGO], Record
Group 94, National Archives. May, *Regulations*, 9; Moss, *Military Cycling*, 7.
7. "The Bicycle for Military Purposes," *Army and Navy Register [ANR]*, August 29,
1896, 130–31.
8. *Ibid.* Moss to Adjutant, October 10, 1896, No. 46408, RAGO.
9. "Fort Harrison Mont.," *Army and Navy Journal [ANJ]*, September 5, 1896, 5.
10. Moss, *Military Cycling*, 34. Moss to Adjutant, October 10, 1896, No. 46408,
RAGO.
11. Moss, *Military Cycling*, 38–39. Moss to Adjutant, October 10, 1896, No. 46408,
RAGO.
12. "The Bike for Military Purposes," ANR, November 14, 1896, 315. Moss to
Adjutant, October 10, 1896, No. 46408, RAGO. Frederic Remington, "Vagabonding
with the Tenth Horse," *Cosmopolitan*, XXII (February 1897), 350.
13. Moss to Adjutant General, February 7, 1898, No. 70545, RAGO.
14. Moss to AG, September 1, 1897, No. 60178, RAGO.
15. *Ibid.* Two members of the bicycle corps were among the 167 men of the Twenty-
fifth Infantry discharged without honor by President Theodore Roosevelt because of
their connection with a raid in August of 1906 on the town of Brownsville, Texas, in
which one white was killed. One of the bicyclists, Sergeant Mingo Sanders, was the man
most affected by the discharge order, since by that time he had earned over twenty-five
years of service credit, all of which was wiped out when he was discharged.
16. "25th U.S. Infantry Bicycle Corps," ANJ, August 7, 1897, 903. Moss to AG,
September 1, 1897, No. 60178, RAGO.
17. "History of Fort Missoula," unpublished manuscript, 23–24, Montana Historical

Society [MHS], Helena. "25th U.S. Infantry Bicycle Corps," *ANJ*, August 7, 1897, 903. Moss to AG, September 1, 1897, No. 60178, RAGO.

18. "History of Fort Missoula," 24–25, MHS. Moss to AG, September 1, 1897, No. 60178, RAGO.

19. "History of Fort Missoula," 24–25, MHS. *St. Louis Post-Dispatch* (Missouri), July 25, 1897.

20. "25th U.S. Infantry Bicycle Corps," *ANJ*, July 31, 1897, 887. Moss to AG, September 1, 1897, No. 60178, RAGO.

21. "25th U.S. Infantry Bicycle Corps," *ANJ*, August 7, 1897, 903; *ibid.*, October 2, 1897, 72. Moss to AG, September 1, 1897, No. 60178, RAGO.

22. Moss to AG, February 7, 1898, No. 70545, RAGO.

SIXTEEN

African Americans and the War Against Spain

PIERO GLEIJESES

Following the sinking of the Maine on February 15, 1898, war fever gripped the United States. For white Americans it was a time of great excitement, a patriotic upsurge while the country recovered from the harsh depression of the mid-1890s. For black Americans the prospect of war against Spain offered hope in a time of despair. Their willingness to sacrifice for their country might lessen white racism and help reverse the deterioration of their situation in the South.

To look at the reaction of black Americans to the war is to look at the ever recurring question of how oppressed people deal with their oppression, torn as they are between the desire to lash out and the need to court the goodwill of their tormentors. At no moment in addressing the issues raised by the Spanish-American War did black Americans lose sight of what was, for them, the overriding question of how the war would affect their situation at home. Should they push themselves forward, offering their services to their white rulers, or should they hold back in proud and dignified protest? In the *Colored American*, a popular African American newspaper in Washington, D.C., one writer asked, "While the air is filled with war clouds and sanguinary talk . . . the colored man is in a quandary. Why should he desire to take up arms against any foreign government, when the United States, his adopted country, offers him such little protection?"[1]

The most important documentary evidence of African American views of the political events in the 1890s is found in the more than one hundred and fifty black newspapers that were then published in the United States. Most of the papers supported the Republican Party, "the defender of a free ballot."[2] Although the Republicans may have been a weak and unreliable champion for black Americans after the Civil War, the Democrats were spearheading the onslaught against black rights in the South during the post-Reconstruction period.

Thanks largely to the excellent work of historian Willard Gatewood, the general reaction of these newspapers to the issues raised by the war—whether the United States should enter, whether blacks could enlist and fight in integrated units, whether the United Sates should annex the Philippines—is known.[3] It is nevertheless useful to go beyond the broad outline to get a closer look, a more intimate picture, of the way the African American press grappled on a day-to-day basis with the questions. To this end, a representative sample of eight African American newspapers has been examined from 1898 through 1899—the *Colored American* (Washington, D.C.), the *Washington Bee* (Washington, D.C.), the *Broad Ax* (Salt Lake City), the *Gazette* (Cleveland), the *Richmond Planet*, the *Parsons Weekly Blade* (Parson, Kans.), the *Freeman* (Indianapolis), and the *State Ledger* (Topeka). All of these were Republican papers except the *Broad Ax*, which was Democratic.

The *Colored American* and the *Washington Bee* were the most eloquent, and their views are representative of the opinions of the other papers. Of the two, the *Colored American* was the better written.[4] The *Washington Bee* was more racy, witty, and entertaining. An in-depth, week-by-week analysis of these two black papers of Washington, D.C., home of one of the largest concentrations of African Americans in the country, reveals the agonizing twists and turns along the road to accommodation and demonstrates the pathos of the choice oppressed blacks had to make between dignity and pragmatism. The survey also reveals the artificiality of the distinction between foreign policy and domestic policy. For the editors of the *Colored American* and the *Washington Bee*, the struggle to find a principled and politically astute response to the wars in Cuba and the Philippines was indistinguishable from their struggle to deal with the tightening vice of oppression at home. Thus the debate in 1898 was as much about encroaching disfranchisement at home and the escalating terror of lynching as it was about the war.

There are poignant moments in the history of dependent peoples, when the terms of their oppression have not yet been—or are no longer—fixed, when there is movement, be it forward or backward. Black Americans had been sliding backwards since the heady days of Reconstruction. Violence, fraud, and restrictive electoral laws were used by the Democrats to reduce and control the black vote in the South. "There are minor elections in which it is not thought needful to interfere," a British essayist observed in 1891. "But, speaking generally, the fact is too well known to need either proof or illustration that . . . the colored people are not suffered to use the rights which the amendments to the constitution were intended to secure."[5] By the time those words appeared, the South was already embarking on what one southern editor described as "a new method of dealing with that White Man's Burden which she has borne for more than thirty years-a method that, in spite of appearances of injustice, promises . . . more generous treatment of the negro."[6] The South would no longer seek to curtail and control the black vote, but to eliminate it altogether. In 1890 the Mississippi constitution established literacy requirements that were intended only for blacks, and South Carolina followed suit with similar amendments in its constitution of 1895.[7]

Although segregation had existed during Reconstruction and had intensified in the following years, the 1890s witnessed a sustained effort to codify segregation in every aspect of life. One southern state after the other passed laws against vagrancy and contract evasion, while new forms of bound labor — the convict lease system, the chain gangs, peonage — flourished.

Lynching, an old American tradition that had long flourished on the frontier, gained new importance in the South. According to historian Edward L. Ayers, "The visibility and ferocity of lynching seemed to assume new proportions in the 1880s and 1890s."[8] One British observer wrote that "In many instances deliberate arrangements for the 'execution' are made, special trains bring throngs of male and female visitors, and the event forms an interesting public holiday."[9] Lynchings were also educational events as "young black men learned early in their lives that they could at any time be grabbed by a white mob — whether for murder, looking at a white woman the wrong way, or merely being 'smart' — and dragged into the woods or a public street to be tortured, burned, mutilated."[10] The complicity and approval of southern whites were matched by the indifference of northern whites and the federal government. "It was a revealing reflection on the times that so few congressmen showed any concerns about the lynchings," notes one scholar.[11] Americans "are a nation of lynchers," distinguished African American journalist Ida B. Wells cried out to a British audience in 1898.[12]

As war with Spain beckoned neither disfranchisement nor segregation was yet complete, and conditions for southern blacks had not reached their lowest point. The emergence of the Populist Party in the early 1890s had given hope to African Americans, and for a brief time their condition did improve. Nowhere was this improvement more evident than in North Carolina, where the black vote proved decisive in the 1896 election of Republican governor Daniel L. Russell.

On November 3, 1896, William McKinley was elected president of the United States with the massive support of those blacks who were still free to vote.[13] Mindful of African American assistance in his election, McKinley condemned lynching in his inaugural address. He also appointed a number of blacks to minor positions in the federal government, including a few in the South (mainly as postmasters). The major objective of McKinley's Republican administration was to reconcile the North and the South: "It will be my constant aim to do nothing, and permit nothing to be done, that will arrest or disturb this growing sentiment of unity and cooperation, this revival of esteem and affiliation . . . but I shall cheerfully do everything possible to promote and increase it."[14] The president's goal of reconciliation augured poorly for African Americans. Within a year of McKinley's inauguration two events sent shock waves through the black community.

The first was the brutal murder of Fraser Baker, a black schoolteacher in Lake City, South Carolina. "Men are dying every day," noted the *Freeman*, "but they are not dying for such reasons as Baker of Lake City died. His death is as momentous as the death of the ill-fated seamen of the Maine."[15] Lake City's white citizens and the state legislature had howled in outrage at Baker's appointment as postmaster in late 1897. Although a mob burned the post office, Baker refused to resign, "assured that he was standing for the rights of his race." On the night of February 22, 1898, another mob set fire to the shanty that was Baker's home and temporary post office. "When the negro, followed by his wife and children, opened the door, a volley of bullets greeted him." Seriously wounded, his wife and three children were saved from the flames by other blacks living nearby. "The father and the youngest child were burnt to a crisp, and some parts of their bodies were found among the charred remains of the cabin."[16] From the comparative safety of Salt Lake City, an African American newspaper thundered, "if the negroes of South Carolina do not avenge the death of Baker and his children then they are unworthy of the name of freemen."[17] On the other hand, the white press in South Carolina, denouncing those "disreputable political prostitutes" who foisted black officials on southern communities, sent a clear message that "the placing of a negro in an official position over white men of the South is a criminal outrage of the most flagrant type. . . . It is an insult vicious and brutal."[18]

One month later, on March 24, 1898, a constitutional convention in Louisiana approved the "grandfather clause," which exempted male citizens who had been entitled to vote on or prior to January 1, 1867, their sons, grandsons, and all people of foreign birth who had been naturalized prior to January 1, 1898, from educational and property qualifications on suffrage. "Now it is known," the *Freeman* explained, "that the Negro was not a legal voter until 1870, when the famous Fifteenth Amendment was made a part of the country's constitution." Thus all but a small number of African Americans were disfranchised. "While a great wave of sympathy is sweeping across the entire geographic confines of the Republic for 'Cuba Libre,'" lamented the *Washington Bee*, "political chains are being forged [in Louisiana] for the black man, the like of which have caused even South Carolina and Mississippi to blush with envy."[19]

Concerned about the worsening conditions of southern blacks, Representative George Henry White of North Carolina, a Republican and the lone African American member of the U.S. Congress, had addressed the House of Representatives on March 7, 1898. He expressed the grievances of his people and pledged their loyalty:

> The nation has not at all times given us that protection to which our loyalty has entitled us. This is painfully evidenced by the almost daily outrages chronicled, showing lynchings, murders, assassinations, and even cremations of our people all over the Southland. . . . But, regardless of the faults of this grand old Union of ours, we love her still, and if the nation should find it necessary to resort to arms and our present strained relations with Spain should develop

into a war, I pledge you that the black phalanx is ready to be mustered in, one-half million strong.[20]

The *Colored American* supported Congressman White's position and did not argue whether the nation should or should not go to war. It left this decision "to the wisdom and patriotism of our representatives at the White House and Capitol."[21] What the *Colored American* desperately sought was to impress on the dominant race how eager the black man was to do his duty, to be "foremost among those who contended for the preservation of the nation's dignity and honor at any cost." In this way African Americans would benefit, whether in peace or war. "If no necessity for war arises, the colored man is a better American by reason of this test of his loyalty. If war should come, he will be the more strongly entwined in the warp and woof of the nation by reason of sacrifice and danger willingly endured."[22] When war finally beckoned in early April, the *Colored American* warmly endorsed it: "we fight as brethren of one blood, and under one flag. We are all American citizens, bound inseparably by a common cause."[23]

The *Washington Bee* reached the same conclusion but by a more tortuous path that reveals an understandable resistance to show allegiance to a flag that symbolized the oppression of the black race. In March, as the *Colored American* proclaimed its loyalty, the *Washington Bee* held its peace, declaring that "while we may be loyal and patriotic . . . severe silence becomes us. When we shall have been treated as men and accorded the rights for which we voted and fought . . . then we can make haste to prove that we possess our full share of patriotism. . . . Wisdom dictates silence in this case."[24] Less than two weeks later, the *Washington Bee* reversed its position and simply stated that "the crime of the Maine must be avenged."[25] The *Washington Bee* might have preferred silence instead of proclaiming that "thousands of valiant colored men are only waiting for Uncle Sam to say 'come on boys,' and a howling response will be forthcoming."[26] Reason, however, pointed to the direction already taken by the *Colored American*.

War with Spain meant that Congress would have to enlarge the regular army and the president would have to call on the states to supply tens of thousands of volunteers. On the eve of the Spanish-American War, the U.S. Army had 26,040 enlisted men. Of these, some two thousand were African Americans, and they were restricted to serving in four segregated regiments stationed on the western frontier.[27] The impending war would bring African American men the opportunity to serve their country—or so they hoped.

The career of Lt. Charles Young demonstrates the difficulties that blacks confronted in the military. In the spring of 1898, Lieutenant Young was the only African American among the U.S. Army's 2,143 officers. After graduating from West Point in 1889, where he had been a social outcast, Young served briefly as a 2d lieutenant in the Tenth Cavalry and later, at the same rank, in the Twenty-fifth Infantry. He was then assigned as a 2d lieutenant to the Ninth Cavalry, a black regiment. The officers of that regiment objected to the appointment; and Young, although retaining his rank and assignment in the Ninth, was transferred to Wilberforce University, a small black college in Ohio. At Wilberforce he served as professor of military science and tactics. "As long as he was stationed there, quietude prevailed among the white officers of the army, but one clear and sunny day [October 1, 1896]," the *Colored American* explained, he was assigned as a 1st lieutenant to the Seventh Cavalry. "A storm arose. What! the great Seventh, with its fighting record, the Seventh led by Custer at Little Big Horn, to be led by a Negro! The idea made the blood of every cavalryman freeze in his veins. It was awful to contemplate, and the regiment was actually threatened with desertions." Young was quickly transferred back to the Ninth, and he remained at Wilberforce.[28]

Although a number of blacks hoped that the new army would be integrated,[29] most were resigned to the fact that the white resistance encountered by Charles Young awaited any African American who sought to serve in the U.S. military. "There is an unmistakable aversion to close contact with the colored comrade," the *Colored American* declared.[30] If integration was out of question, then at least black Americans should receive the same opportunities as whites in segregated regiments. An editorial of the *Colored American* stated this demand with dignity and eloquence:

> We want for ourselves every right and privilege accorded to any other American citizen, and will be satisfied with nothing short of it. We are not more anxious to be shot at or killed than any other class, but the principle of military and civilian recognition is at stake, and we wish to be called on equality with our fellow-countrymen to bear the nation's burdens as well as to share her joys. . . . We want colored troops with colored officers. . . . We have the brains, the courage, and the strength. Give us the opportunity. . . . All we desire and all we can expect is an equal chance and fair play.[31]

However, the white press had a different definition of fair play. The *Washington Post* commented that a "policy which puts arms in the hands of the negroes . . . results in the artificial exaltation of an inferior race," and the *Times* (New Orleans) told blacks not to enlist "for their own sake."[32] The black press took note of this "mad determination" to prevent the enlistment of black volunteers.[33] "The Memphis *Commercial Appeal*," observed the *Colored American*, "is giving its dear little heart no end of uneasiness about what the Negro soldier will do 'when this cruel war is over.'" The *Commercial Appeal* claimed that "the colored soldier . . . has grown tyrannical in his dealings with white men. . . . [I]f any great number of Negroes are put into the army as soldiers it will have a demoralizing effect on them when they return. No doubt when they come back from fighting the battles of the country they will . . . be more or less disposed to arrogance."[34]

Some white Americans were less intransigent; and, as a matter of principle, they argued that blacks should be granted the privilege of fighting for the United States—in limited numbers. Others agreed for more practical reasons. "The African," explained the *St. Louis Globe*, "is immune from yellow fever."[35] Young blacks, the *Picayune* (New Orleans) warned, should not be allowed to stay at home while the South was stripped of its young white men.[36] In some states—particularly North Carolina, Illinois, and Kansas—concern for black votes was an important motivation. In other states—Alabama and especially Virginia—equally important was the sluggishness of white volunteers in filling the states' volunteer quotas. "The whites," the *Broad Ax* emphasized, "were not breaking their necks in falling over each other to enlist. It was then decided to permit the Negro to do so."[37]

Eight states accepted black volunteers, but these men were forced to serve in segregated units. Some ten thousand African Americans eventually entered the volunteer army. While some white volunteer regiments took part in the Cuban campaign, black volunteers left for the island only after the armistice had been signed on August 12, 1898.[38] Black volunteer units were allowed a full roster of black officers in only a few states, the most notable of which was North Carolina, the only southern state where the African American vote was still a significant force in politics. Some states permitted blacks to serve only as junior officers, while others allowed no black officers. The regular army maintained its standards—there would be no black officers in command of regular troops. Lt. Charles Young was raised to the rank of major and assigned to lead the Ninth Ohio (Colored) Volunteer Regiment. The four regiments of black regulars were sent to Cuba with the invading force—in segregated accommodations and with a full roster of white officers. They fought well, as even the white press acknowledged.[39] Six noncommissioned black officers were promoted to 2d lieutenant for gallantry in battle but were immediately transferred to volunteer regiments. Their new epaulets would last only as long as their new units did, and at war's end the men would have to either return to the regular army at their former rank or retire. "If there ever was a mockery on valor and patriotism it was in the promotion of these black heroes," observed the *Washington Bee*.[40]

The insult of white officers leading black regiments was felt keenly by the black press. And it was made more bitter still by the fact that many of the new white officers were former Confederates, or children of rebels. "Who are the white men that are being commissioned as officers to lead our troops to this war?" asked the *Colored American*. "Major General M. C. Butler of South Carolina . . . Major General Joe Wheeler of Alabama, Major General Fitzhugh Lee of Virginia. These men are ex-Confederates."[41] But while white northerners were marching "side by side, shoulder to shoulder with their late foes," overcoming the wounds of the past, "the colored brother . . . is unanimously and universally plainly told that his services are not desired. Not even to stop a bullet from a better (?) man."[42]

The *Colored American* and the *Washington Bee* scoffed at the southern states' obvious repugnance at the thought of enlisting black volunteers. "This amazing anxiety for 'Sambo's' health is entirely incomprehensible. Give us a chance."[43] They assailed the government's refusal to appoint black officers. "All the negro asks is a chance to show what he can do under the command of one his own soldiers," declared the *Washington Bee*.[44] The same newspaper even upbraided President McKinley—"does not . . . [your behavior] cause your cheeks to blush with shame?"[45] It also warned him that black Americans might abandon his administration: "we are tired of the [Republicans] patting the negro upon the shoulder and telling him he is 'a good negro.'"[46] Unlike the more cautious *Colored American*, the *Washington Bee* even intimated that African Americans might desert the flag:

> A man would be a very big fool to show patriotism for a government that says she does not want a people—not even to die in defence of a righteous cause—on account of color. . . . Have they [black volunteers] not been told that the unwashed rebels of the south are more preferable than they? Of the great number of colonels, generals, majors, captains, lieutenants etc. that have been appointed, how many who fought to destroy the union, and how many loyal blacks have been selected—who fought to uphold the government? . . . The Negro is willing and ready to serve his country when that country can serve and protect him.[47]

Black Americans stood between Scylla and Charybdis. If they failed to volunteer, they offered ammunition to those who "are striving to show that the martial spirit and sentiment of patriotism are absolutely wanting in our people" and that the black man "displays a dogged disposition to shirk the responsibility of citizenship in his indifference in the present war crisis." But these racists did not want "the colored soldier . . . except as plain hewers of wood and drawers of water or dirt fingers for fortifications. Herein lies the milk of the coconut." The *Washington Bee* argued that blacks should not enlist if they were going to be placed in humiliating circumstances—"when we go to war we want to go as men and not as servants, as citizens not as mere denizens." However, refusing to go to war unless these conditions were granted would only confirm the prejudices of their enemies who accused them of lack of patriotism and courage.[48] And so, the *Washington Bee* railed against the lack of black officers and, almost in the same breath, pleaded that more blacks be allowed to enlist.[49]

Washington's three white dailies responded in different ways to the complaints of the *Colored American* and the *Washington Bee*. The pro-administration *Evening Star* praised the bravery of the black soldiers on four occasions.[50] The Democratic *Times* was less generous: only on one occasion, shortly after the end of the war, did it mention the bravery of the black troops—and then only in order to contrast the soldiers' gallantry with their "deviltry and general intractability."[51] But when it came to the complaints voiced by the *Washington Bee* and the *Colored American*, the *Evening Star* and the *Times* followed an identical approach—they simply never mentioned them, just as they never referred to the two black newspapers of their city. Their response was utter and complete silence.

The Democratic *Washington Post*, on the other hand, acknowledged the complaints of the *Colored American* and the *Washington Bee* and was exas-

perated by them. Blasting "the frothing" of "self-appointed colored leaders,"
it warned,

> Nobody cares three straws whether they [the blacks] go into the army or stay
> out of it. Nobody wants them at all unless they are ready to obey orders and
> accept discipline. The war will go right along whether the colored warriors
> join the army or stay at home. . . . What our colored friends need is a little
> common sense, with a dash of modesty to make it palatable. We are well
> enough disposed regarding them, but we are getting just a trifle tired of their
> editors and spokesmen with their ridiculous bombast and their stupid airs.[52]

The *Colored American* and the *Washington Bee* were not chastened. "If
the *Post* ever loses an opportunity to insult and humiliate the colored people of the country, it is only when its editors are too busily engaged at the
moment to give us the vicious 'upper-cut' so pleasing to their sportive instincts."[53] Three days later the *Washington Post* retorted:

> We have very little time to waste on the negro newspapers and so-called lead-
> ers who do not approve of *The Post*. It is of absolutely no consequence to us
> whether they approve or disapprove. . . . These noisy complainants do not
> represent even their own race, excepting, perhaps, the impudent and trouble-
> some element of it. . . . This is the white man's country, which the white man
> intends to govern in its own way and for his own behoof.[54]

It was indeed the white man's country, the *Washington Bee* conceded, "and
a barbarous one at that. Citizens are murdered and lynched without judge or
jury, and because we demand recognition according to merit, we are told
that we are impudent and troublesome."[55] The *Colored American* commented with bitter irony:

> Here are some definitions drawn from the newest edition of the *Washington
> Post* lexicon, revised and especially adapted for the benefit of its colored
> readers:
>
>> "Sensible Negro": one who agrees with the Post's theory of the black
>> man's place in the social system. . . .
>> "A government of the people": one for the white people. . . .
>> "Enlightened code": recognition of the white man's natural and inher-
>> ent supremacy in all things, and divine right to rule the universe.[56]

While the *Colored American* and the *Washington Bee* crossed swords with
the *Washington Post*, black soldiers themselves traded blows with whites.

Rather than creating a sense of brotherhood between black and white
Americans, war with Spain increased racial tensions in the United States. "It
would seem," remarked the *Richmond Planet*, "that the war . . . would tend
to allay race prejudice and bring closer together the races in the South. It has
had an opposite tendency for the number of lynchings has been steadily on
the increase."[57] The reason for the increased violence against African Americans was simple: white Americans resented the sight of blacks with weapons—even (or perhaps especially) if the blacks were in the uniform of the

U.S. Army. Also black Americans with guns and in uniform had a disquiet-ing tendency to insist on their civil rights. Before the war the four black regiments of the regular army had been stationed in the distant western frontier. When the war began, black regiments, both regular and volunteer, gathered in the South, where most certainly they were not welcome. "The members of the Twenty-fifth infantry were so long in Montana that when they came in contact with the laws of Tennessee compelling the whites and Afro-Americans to ride in separate cars they strenuously objected, declaring that their uniforms entitled them to sit in any car on a train," explained the *Gazette*.[58] "The colored soldier must not permit himself to be betrayed into the assumption that he has changed or benefited his social condition by wearing a blue coat and carrying a gun," warned one Tennessee editor. "If he forgets himself, he will soon be reminded of his delinquency in a convincing manner."[59]

Incidents erupted between black soldiers and white civilians, and be-tween black and white soldiers. There were murders, beatings, and vandal-ism. Most of the victims were black; and, more often than not, white soldiers from the North sided with white southerners against blacks. Like their southern friends, white northerners resented the demands of African Ameri-cans in uniform and indulged in casual violence against the black popula-tion near the army camps where blacks were stationed. The old scars of the Civil War faded as white northerners sat around the canteen in military camps with white southerners.[60]

During the first two weeks of May, the four regiments of black regulars arrived at Tampa, Florida, from which they were to embark for Cuba. "The colored infantrymen . . . have made themselves very offensive to the people of the city," the *Tampa Morning Tribune* announced. "The men insist upon being treated as white men are treated and the citizen will not make any distinction between the colored troops and the colored citizens."[61] As a result, there were continuous clashes as the black soldiers often refused to submit to the color bar and as the whites—both civilian and military—were incensed by the impudence of the African American troops. On the night of June 6, the tension that had been steadily mounting for more than a month exploded. A group of white volunteers from an Ohio regiment "decided to have some fun." A two-year-old black child was snatched from his mother by one of the white soldiers. The child was held at arm's length with his head down while several soldiers fired their weapons as close as possible to him. "Presumably the winner was the soldier who sent a bullet through the sleeve of the boy's shirt."[62] The boy was then returned to his dazed mother. In response, black soldiers went on a rampage. "They stormed into the streets [of Tampa] firing their pistols indiscriminately, wrecking saloons and cafes which had refused to serve them, and forcing their way into white brothels. Apparently they clashed not only with white civilians but with white sol-diers." Finally, white troops from a Georgia volunteer unit were assigned to restore order, which they did with great relish. White soldiers from Michigan loudly expressed their regrets that the Georgians, not they, "had been chosen to 'get the niggers.'"[63]

The southern dailies were in an uproar about the savage behavior of the black troops. The *Colored American*, on the other hand, noted that

> The trouble between the negroes and whites at Tampa, Chattanooga, New Orleans and other points is due almost without exception to the fact that narrow-minded cads and shortsighted shopkeepers insisted upon making a difference in the treatment of United States soldiers, when the law did not recognize any. The black boys stood upon their rights, and the blame for the disorder rests wholly upon those who denied them what was legally theirs. Fair play would have prevented all the turmoil that has disgraced Uncle Sam's army in the South since the war began.[64]

The point was lost on the white press in both the North and South, which consistently assigned blame for these incidents to the African Americans. "The completely lawless conduct of these troops since they came to Florida is extremely discouraging to the idea of colored volunteer enlistments," droned the Washington *Times*. The *Washington Post* pontificated,

> We fear that the negro troops, and especially those which have colored men as commissioned officers, must be set down as a failure. . . . The experience of the past few months has shown us that the negro officer is impossible under any circumstances, and that the negro soldiers are, as a rule, discordant with our scheme of society and civilization. It is useless to ignore facts. This is a white man's country and the whites are not willing and cannot be compelled to accept the negro on equal terms in any relation of life.[65]

The end of the war brought no amelioration of relations between black and white Americans.

The armistice with Spain was signed on August 12, 1898. By October 1, when peace negotiations began in Paris, the November congressional campaign was well under way. The most important issue in the upcoming election was imperialism; but, in the few southern states where blacks retained some political rights, race became the crucial topic for political discussion. The concern for racial relations was paramount in North Carolina, the only southern state in which the Democrats were not in control and in which black officials were, as the New Orleans *Picayune* reported, "as plenty as blackberries."[66] In fact, African Americans in North Carolina comprised slightly more than one-third of the state's population, held less than seven percent of the seats in the state legislature, and occupied a limited (although impressive by southern standards) number of local offices.

North Carolina's leading Democratic newspaper, the *News and Observer*, boldly proclaimed, "the question has resolved itself into a simple one, 'shall the white man or the black man rule in North Carolina?'"[67] Issue after issue of the paper, which was edited by Josephus Daniels, spewed forth its message of hatred, inveighing against the arrogance, the crimes, and the physical appearance of "Mr. Nigger," with his "flipity-flop lips" and his "big white teeth."[68] The very participation of black men in the war was used in the indictment against them. North Carolina had been the only southern state to raise a regiment of black volunteers with a full roster of black officers — flagrant proof, the Democrats cried, of Negro domination. As the electoral campaign drew to a close, the *News* and *Observer* concluded, "there is but one solution of the problem . . . the white man proposes to rule, and he will rule. He will rule peaceably if he can, he will rule forcibly if he must."[69]

The Republican *New York Times*, reporting on the campaign in North Carolina, noted "the intense race feeling prevalent in that section." It blandly assured its readers that no violence was taking place and observed that whites were stockpiling weapons.[70] The *Washington Post* provided more extensive coverage. Its sympathy with the whites was explicit: at issue, the *Post* asserted, was "the integrity of the Caucasian race."[71] It reported that white violence was filling "the negroes' souls with fear."[72] The *Post* argued that "it has become necessary to teach the Southern Negroes that they cannot rule over the property and the destinies of the superior race."[73] The outcome — the reinvigoration of the white supremacy movement — was predetermined; only the means of its attainment were in doubt. "Whether the revolution will come to North Carolina through a baptism of blood no one can say, but that it will come seems absolutely certain. . . . The negro will be practically disfranchised, through constitutional amendment, and where this is not effective, the shotgun will stand beside the ballot box."[74]

The black press watched in horror. "Not in thirty years has the majesty of the law been so openly defied, or the rights of a people so ruthlessly trampled upon," the *Colored American* exclaimed in despair. It continued:

> The Governor of North Carolina can preserve order if he will only avail himself of the authority vested in his hands. . . . The President of the United States, notwithstanding the state sovereignty bugaboo, can step in and use his "good offices" with telling effect. The negroes of North Carolina and the nation are trying to sustain the Administration of Mr. McKinley. Will he not draw upon the strong arm of the federal power to sustain them?[75]

If the governor dared not intervene and the president remained silent, what then could be done to help the African American? A few days before the election, the *Colored American*, a loyal pillar of the Republican Party, noted dryly that "some oppressed races have used the torch for wrongs less shameful than the negroes are compelled to suffer in North Carolina."[76]

Could North Carolina's African Americans afford to fight back the attack against them? Neither the *Colored American* nor the *Washington Bee* had an answer. In addressing the "reign of terror in North Carolina," the Washington Bee lamented,

> The colored citizen of North Carolina is told if he . . . attempts to vote on Election Day, he will be killed. It is a question of conjecture with us whether it would be wise for the negro to repel these threats with armed force or

> whether it would be wise for him to remain away from the polls. If he goes to
> the polls, has he got sufficient force to protect himself? . . . Unless the negro of
> North Carolina is strong enough to meet any emergency, our advice to him is
> to remain away from the polls.[77]

The intimidation was successful: the great majority of African Americans
in North Carolina did not go to the polls thereby ensuring a Democratic
majority in the state's congressional delegation and their own political emasculation.

For many of North Carolina's white citizens the results of the election and
the worsening situation for the state's African American population were not
enough—blacks needed to be reminded that their situation was hopeless.
Where better for that lesson than Wilmington, the state's largest city, and the
place where African Americans enjoyed more influence than in any other
southern city? More than one-half of Wilmington's population was of African American descent. The mayor was white, but three of the ten aldermen
were black. The police chief and his five senior officers were white, but ten
of the twenty-six patrolmen were black. A number of Wilmington's African
Americans were successful lawyers, doctors, and craftsmen—professionals
who competed directly with their white counterparts. A racial incident was
overdue. The *New York Times* reported that in Wilmington on election day
"very few Negroes were seen standing about the corners, and the Negro
quarter was very quiet."[78] But, as the *Washington Post* noted, "many of the
more hot-headed white men are indignant that the day has been allowed to
pass without a clash of arms between the races . . . [Blacks needed] a severe
and bloody lesson."[79]

On November 10, two days after the election, a pogrom took place in
Wilmington, "Nineteen Negroes Shot to Death," announced the *New York
Times*.[80] "It was not a mob," a white eyewitness reported proudly. "It was a
gathering of white men who were determined to teach a lesson—a lesson
which should be practical, and contain no element of doubt."[81] Armed
whites hunted down African Americans with the assistance of local members of the North Carolina State Guard. "The negroes are thoroughly terror-
ized," the *New York Times* reported the following day. "Hundreds of them
have left the city, fleeing through the country in all directions tonight."[82] The
mob burned the offices of Wilmington's black newspaper, the *Daily Record*.[83] Many of the city's leading African Americans were deported along with
several whites who had "rendered themselves odious to the best element
of the community . . . [because of their] association with negro politics."
Among these white "leaders of turbulent negroes" whom Wilmington "has
vomited forth" were the mayor, Silas P. Wright, and the chief of police, John
R. Melton. The "good work" was accomplished "with fixed bayonets," and
many barely escaped lynching while boarding northbound trains "with
instructions to leave North Carolina and never return."[84]

The *News* and *Observer* bluntly established blame for the riot. "The
negroes are responsible for the precipitation of the race war," it announced

on November 11.[85] Two days later the Raleigh newspaper reflected on what had happened in the port town: "Unlike the French Revolution everything was done in Wilmington in due form and strictly in accordance with law. All those concerned in it were lovers of order and justice."[86] From pulpits throughout the state black preachers urged submission and white preachers sang praise to God. "This city . . . has been redeemed for civilization, redeemed for law and order, redeemed for decency and respectability," the *News and Observer* proclaimed.[87]

Surveying the ruins, the *Colored American* issued a solemn query: "Our people cannot honorably yield an inch of the ground now, after so much sacrifice, labor and bloodshed. . . . On the other hand, armed resistance, in our unprepared state, would avail us nothing but humiliation and defeat. . . . What, then, must we do to be saved?"[88] African Americans had few allies and even fewer choices. They could hope that the American people had a sense of justice and would not permit the violence against blacks to continue. They could also hope for renewed support from the President McKinley and the Republican-controlled Congress. But, as the *Colored American* challenged, "the white man's civilization is on trial. Will he be manly enough to choose the better part?"[89]

The *Colored American* and the *Washington Bee* did not ask the president to send troops to the South to uphold the rights of the African Americans. Instead, they proposed a more modest solution. The Fourteenth Amendment stated that if a state denied the right to vote to eligible citizens, the representation of that state would be reduced accordingly. "This means a reduction in the number of Southern congressmen, and the statute furnishes a legal and peaceful method of bringing it about," declared the *Colored American*.[90] Noting that "a great deal of fuss is being raised over the admission of Mr. [Brigham H.] Roberts of Utah to a seat in Congress, to which he has been honestly elected, the objection to him being that he has a plurality of wives," the newspaper argued, "we might have more faith in the sincerity of these moralists if they objected with equal fervor to the seating of a score of southern members whose seats were confessedly won by resort to the most shameful methods of fraud, bloodshed and outlawry. Why strain at a gnat and swallow a camel?"[91] The insult to America's white women by a polygamist congressman warranted more concern than the widespread violation of the rights of African Americans. "A man with three wives can consume more of the precious time of Congress than the cold-blooded murder of fifty or more American citizens who were refused the aid of the law in two or more states of the United States," mused the *Parsons Weekly Blade*. "Curious, isn't it? But this is America."[92]

The *New York Times* lamented the "the riotous proceedings in North and South Carolina,"[93] but it did so gently and with understanding. "We do not blame the whites of the South exclusively, . . . [or even] chiefly," it asserted.[94] There were so many extenuating circumstances, and far more important than apportioning blame was the building of a better future. "We like to think that as the Southern States grow in population, industry, and wealth the principles of orderly civic life and equality before the law will gain greater force." the *Times* continued.[95] Meanwhile, it warned that the only thing that the president could do to help the blacks was "to refrain from appointing any more colored men to Federal offices in the South."[96]

The black press, on the other hand, eagerly awaited McKinley's December 5 message to Congress with the hope that the president "will not fail to . . . recommend such action by Congress as will protect the citizens of the States from such tyranny, riot and assassination as were exhibited in North and South Carolina."[97] The message, however, proved to be another disappointment. "Our people . . . have been lynched, despoiled of property, denied justice in the courts, cheated at the ballot box, and outraged in innumerable ways," the *Colored American* observed. "Yet the Chief Executive . . . has no word of sympathy to offer—not a hint of regret or sorrow, not an appeal to his fellow countrymen to preserve the peace and honor the heritage of liberty bequeathed by our fathers."[98] McKinley said nothing, and he was not alone in his silence. "None of the other leaders of the republican party nor any of the prominent statesmen of the country have had anything to say in condemnation of the recent brutal exhibition in the Carolinas," proclaimed the *Gazette*.[99]

The president and white America were preoccupied with celebrating the end of the war and the return of harmony between white Americans, North and South.[100] A week after his message to Congress, McKinley left Washington to attend the Peace Jubilee in Atlanta. "Sectional lines no longer mar the map of the United States," he told the Georgia legislature.[101] "Under a hostile fire on a foreign soil, fighting in a common cause, the memory of old disagreements has faded into history." Southerners had responded promptly "to the call of the country, entrusted with the able leadership of men dear to them, who had marched with their fathers under another flag, now fighting under the old flag again."[102] McKinley's words, the *Evening Star* explained, "suggest that a long step has been taken toward the final closing of the breach between the sections which has been steadily narrowing year by year since the close of the war. The war with Spain did more than any previous event to bring the peoples of the two sections nearer together."[103]

In Atlanta, Montgomery, Selma, Savannah, and the other cities McKinley visited in his week-long tour of Georgia and Alabama, the people responded enthusiastically. The *New York Times* recorded several poignant moments. "One Confederate veteran, now a venerable legislator . . . buried his head in his arms and cried like a little child," as the President announced that the federal government would care for the graves of the Confederate dead.[104] Another Confederate veteran stood by the Confederate monument in Macon and "frantically waved a Confederate flag, while by his side was the son of the Colonel of one of Georgia's hardest fighting Confederate regiments, who was as vigorously waving the Stars and Stripes. When the president was abreast of them the two flags were brought to a salute side by side."[105] The *Colored American* noted that "today the name of McKinley is cheered to the echo, and he is hailed as the 'President of the whole people.' The Negro is studying the effect of this apparent 'era of good feeling' upon his own fortunes."[106] The answer was at hand; for as one African American newspaper had forewarned several weeks earlier, "The closer the south and north get as a result of the present war, the harder it will be for the Afro-American regardless of the part he plays in it."[107]

McKinley had traveled to Atlanta to encourage support for the most controversial provision of the peace treaty with Spain, the annexation of the Philippines by the United States. His rousing appeals — "who will haul . . . [the U.S. flag] down? Answer me, ye men of the South. Who is there in Dixie who will haul it down?"[108] — were appropriately matched by what the *Washington Post* called his "delicate tact . . . in dealing with the negro question."[109] The *News* and *Observer* recorded that "Mr. McKinley has come and gone and not a word has he said about the rights of the 'down-trodden' blacks."[110] This demonstrated, according to the *Washington Times*, "great good sense."[111]

In February 1899, the U.S. Senate moved to ratify the treaty with Spain, and the Filipinos began a war of independence to resist American conquest. At this time, white America was engaged in fierce debate: imperialists spoke of glory, commercial gain, duty, and the white man's burden; anti-imperialists spoke of America's democratic traditions, the costs of empire, and the burden of dealing with ten million savages. For African Americans, the backdrop of the debate was increased white violence against blacks at home. "Lynching Colored Men By the Wholesale," read a headline in the *Richmond Planet*. Meanwhile, the *Gazette* lamented that "there is not another country under the sun that is so absolutely neglectful of its colored citizens . . . not one where its children are so lawless and so heartless in its dealings with its black citizens."[112] A gruesome symbol of the growing white savagery against blacks was the lynching of Sam Hose, an African American who confessed to having killed a white man.

On April 23, 1899, Sam Hose was seized from his jail cell in Newnan, Georgia, by a mob of angry whites. For half an hour he was slowly mutilated. "While he pleaded pitifully for mercy and begged his tormentors to let him die," the men severed his ears, and then cut off his fingers one by one. Finally he was burned alive. "The torch was applied about 2:30, and at 3 o'clock the body of Sam Hose was limp and lifeless. . . . The body was not cut down. It was cut to pieces. The crowd fought for places about the smoldering tree, and with knives secured such pieces of his carcass as had not crumbled away." One special and two regular trains "carried nearly 4,000 people" to witness the burning or to visit the scene of the lynching.[113] "Special train for Newnan! All aboard for the burning!" the criers yelled.[114] The *New York Times* reported that "the excursionists returning . . . [were] loaded down [with souvenirs] . . . bones, pieces of flesh, and parts of the wood which was placed at the negro's feet."[115] The paper also noted that "one enthusiast procured a slice of the heart, which he took to Atlanta to present to the Governor."[116] Another three to four thousand spectators visited the scene of the lynching the following day.

In the days after the incident, the governor of Georgia blamed the blacks for the entire episode, and the U.S. attorney general hastened to declare that no federal law had been violated and that "the government would take no action whatever."[117] Following a series of lynchings in the summer of 1898, the *Colored American* had issued a challenging declaration:

> The attempt to acquit the government of all moral responsibility for the quin-
> tuple lynching in Arkansas is a contemptible plea in confession and avoid-
> ance. Technically, the theory of state rights, etc., may estop the federal powers
> from forcing a state to punish its murderers and lawbreakers, but there rests
> upon every nation a moral obligation to exhaust every resource, civil and
> military, to protect life and property within its borders. . . . If the organic law
> shields murder and rapine, the law is wrong, and should be modified or abol-
> ished.[118]

After the lynching of Sam Hose and in light of American involvement in the Philippines, the *Colored American* sarcastically suggested that "perhaps some members of the Georgia mob that burned Sam Hose might be in-duced to accept an assignment to carry civilization and Christianity to the heathenish Filipinos."[119]

It is not surprising that the *Colored American* and the *Washington Bee* were opposed to the annexation of the Philippines. Unlike the mainstream white press, they expressed concern for the rights of the Filipinos and admiration for their "stubbornness, bravery and prowess."[120] At a time when African Americans were being "butchered like hogs,"[121] robbed of the vote, and discriminated against in every sphere of life, it was impossible to deny that "there is some analogy between the struggle which is now going on among the colored people for constitutional liberty and that of a similar race in the Orient and hence a bond of sympathy naturally springs up."[122]

While white Americans rallied to British author Rudyard Kipling's call for an imperialist crusade, the *Colored American* remained skeptical, proclaim-ing that

> with all due respect for the alleged genius of one Rudyard Kipling, his latest
> conglomeration of rot about the "white man's burden" makes us very, very
> tired. It has ever been the dark races who have born the world's burdens both
> in the heat of the day and the travail of the night. The white man has never had
> a burden that was not self-imposed, sometimes through a temporary wave of
> indignation of charity, but more frequently through greed of gold and territory.
> Might has been made to pose for right and the weak and untutored people
> have had burdens forced upon them at the mouth of the cannon or point of the
> bayonet. The white man's burden is a myth. The black man's burden is a
> crushing, grinding reality. Let us have done with cant and hypocrisy.[123]

And so, African Americans opposed annexation; and, at times, they were hardly able to hide their contempt for and their rage at the lies, the insensitivity, and the injustice of the white race. At the same time black Americans were struggling not to appear unpatriotic and not to offend those on whose sufferance they depended. "We are none the less Americans when we say to our leaders: 'Go slow in this matter of expansion,'" pleaded the *Colored American.* "We are none the less loyal to our common country when we discountenance indiscriminate land-grabbing and the despoliation of weaker races."[124] While extolling "our magnificent government,"[125] the *Colored American* also complained that "a Negro was killed by a white man in Virginia this week. The murderer was fined $10. The press silent; the church dumb; the law impotent; the President indifferent!"[126] Ironically, as the black press observed, American troops were indeed needed, not in the Philippine conflict, but "to protect a larger class of American citizens on American soil, the boasted 'home of the free and the land of the brave.'"[127] Renowned African American clergyman Henry Turner dryly commented, "there's no place in this infernal country for manly Negroes." After making this statement, "he [Turner] strode across the platform shaking his massive head and incubating a sentence which he hurled at 'Old Glory,' saying of it the stars on you belong to the white man, the stripes to the Negro."[128]

Opposition in the African American press to the United States's annexation of the Philippines was short-lived. "Expansion is a fraud," the *Washington Bee* had thundered in February 1899.[129] Two months later, however, it pledged, "the colored people are willing and ready to do their part."[130] The *Washington Bee* was silent about its sudden conversion. The *Colored American,* which had engaged in a similar reversal a few weeks later, was more frank. "As is well known to our readers, the *Colored American* since the conclusion of the Spanish-American war, has not been enthusiastic for what is generally termed 'expansion.'" After much soul-searching, however, it had reached the conclusion that

> stripped of patriotic considerations, our racial sympathies would naturally be with the Filipinos. They are fighting manfully for what they conceive to be their best interests. But we cannot, for the sake of sentiment, turn our back upon our own country, to give aid and comfort to any people in arms against it. There can be no two opinions as to where the Afro-American's allegiance lies, when the parting of the ways is reached.[131]

White Americans could afford to be anti-imperialists, and they could afford to be accused of lack of patriotism; however, for black Americans the gamble was far more dangerous.

More important than the rights of the Filipinos and solidarity among nonwhites was the desperate eagerness of African Americans to be accepted at home. Despite all of the disappointments of the recent past, the opportunity to fight side by side with white soldiers and under their own officers in the Philippines seemed to be a crucial step toward citizenship. Yet, when it

PIERO GLEIJESES

soon appeared that black troops would not participate in the Philippine expedition, the *Colored American* reverted to its earlier position, stating that "we are glad no colored soldiers have so far been sent to assist in the subjugation of the spirited Filipinos. We hope none will be sent."[132] A few weeks later, when it became apparent that black regular troops would be sent to the Philippines, the *Colored American's* position changed again; and it pleaded, "give us officers of our own, and let all work together as one for the glory of the nation, since duty calls us to fight for the flag, wherever it waves."[133] The *Colored American's* conversion did not come without qualifications. "There can be but little or no heartfelt enthusiasm in the fight the black soldiers will put up against the Filipinos, . . . [but] as American citizens they can be depended upon to do their full duty, bravely and conscientiously."[134]

On September 17, 1899, the *Colored American* announced the good news that "the administration has realized that its failure to utilize the valor and experience of Negro soldiers in the Philippines was an unjust discrimination and a mistake. . . . An order for the organization of two colored [volunteer] regiments was issued by the War Department last Friday." Not only were black regular troops being sent to the Philippines, black volunteer soldiers would also be permitted to participate. All the senior officers of the regiments would be white, but the junior officers would be black.[135] Although this was not the ideal situation for which the *Colored American* had hoped, the editor reminded his readers that "it is step by step that a great people go forward—never by leaps."[136]

Just as the attitude of the *Colored American* and the *Washington Bee* toward the Philippine war shifted, so too did their attitude toward the McKinley administration. When the war against Spain began, both papers had been full of praise for the president. After the disastrous November elections, however, little of the enthusiasm remained. The *Colored American* declared that "Negroes who are not close personal friends of the President indict him . . . for his moral cowardice in failing to utter one word publicly in condemnation of the barbarities of the social degenerates of the South . . . for his failure to recognize and reward negroes who participated in the late war against Spain; and for refusing to appoint negro officers to command negro troops in that war."[137] Criticism of the president was accompanied by threats that African Americans would withdraw their support from the Republican Party. The Republican *Washington Bee*, pondering its future, insisted that "the *Bee* expects to be Republican if it is permitted to do so, but while that is true, it is not necessary for all the negroes to die the same death especially if it is to their detriment. The negro has been and is told that his government is powerless to protect him . . . The negro vote ought to divide, because it will be to his interest."[138] Threats soon gave way to praise as the *Colored American* and the *Washington Bee* swallowed their complaints, silenced their bitterness, and urged blacks to vote for the Republican Party and its magnanimous leader. "All things considered, the President has done exceedingly well toward the negro," the *Colored American* noted.[139]

It was a humiliating turnabout; but, as the *Washington Bee* asked, if the black man left the Republican Party, "where is he to go? Is he going to the men and party which are butchering him?"[140] And, if African Americans had no alternative but to remain with the Republican Party, could they afford to criticize the party and its leaders too harshly? Earlier in the year, the *Washington Bee* had declared that McKinley "will be nominated and if nominated he will be elected. Before the colored brother takes any hasty step he should first consider the cost and the final result."[141] The paper also cautiously observed that "We . . . are powerless without the aid of friends to better our political condition."[142]

President McKinley won reelection in 1900, as the African American voters—those who could still vote—overwhelmingly supported the Republican ticket. Black troops did fight in the Philippines, and they fought well. Meanwhile, the situation for African Americans in the South continued to deteriorate without interference from indifferent white Americans in the North. As one African American woman noted in 1904,

> The whole country seems tired of hearing about the black man's woes. . . . The wrongs of the Irish, of the Armenians, of the Roumanian and Russian Jews, of the exiles of Russia and of every other oppressed people upon the face of the globe, can arouse the sympathy and fire the indignation of the American public, while they seem to be all indifferent to the murderous assaults upon the negroes in the South.[143]

This indifference would prove to be resistant to change.

While a number of African American newspapers were more submissive and others were more outspoken, the *Washington Bee* and the *Colored American* represent the mainstream black press. The former appears to have been somewhat more aggressive than the latter; but, in fact, both papers zigzagged back and forth as they groped for a solution to an impossible and deteriorating situation. Time and again, they demonstrated themselves to be proud and servile, aggressive and submissive.[144]

It is a poignant story—the story of an oppressed people and how they dealt with their tormentors. It is a story that is repeated again and again in a great many countries and in the United States as well. In the 1960s Malcolm X could at least turn to the outside world, to the African countries in particular; it was of limited help, to be sure, but at least it relieved the sense of being desperately alone.[145] The disapproval of African countries and the opportunities that American racism might have offered to the Soviet Union did worry the United States government.[146] However, in the 1890s Africa lay in chains, and Europe was indifferent. The only hope for African Americans was to appeal to the conscience of white Americans. In October 1898 the *Washington Bee* proposed that "there is an American conscience. It needs only to be awakened to see its duty and to act."[147] At the end of the nineteenth century the American conscience was slumbering, and neither the *Washington Bee* nor the *Colored American* could awaken it.

NOTES

1. *Colored American* (Washington, D.C.), March 12, 1898.

2. *Washington Bee* (Washington, D.C.), January 8, 1898. There are no exact figures on the number of African American newspapers in the 1890s. For a discussion of the black press at the time, see Emma Lou Thornbrough, "American Negro Newspapers, 1880–1914," *Business History Review 50* (winter 1966): 467–490; L. M. Hershaw, "The Negro Press in America," *Charities and the Commons* 15 (October 1905): 66–68; Frederick G. Detweiler, *The Negro Press in the United States* (1922; College Park, Md.: McGrath Publishing Co., 1968), 12–77; Roland E. Wolseley, *The Black Press*, U.S.A. 2d ed. (Ames: Iowa State University Press, 1990), 38–74.

3. See especially Willard B. Gatewood Jr., *Black Americans and the White Man's Burden, 1898–1903* (Urbana: University of Illinois Press, 1975) and *"Smoked Yankees" and the Struggle for Empire: Letters from Negro Soldiers 1898–1902* (Fayetteville: University of Arkansas, 1987). See also, George P. Marks, ed., *The Black Press Views American Imperialism, 1898–1900* (New York: Arno Press, 1971).

4. *The Broad Ax* (Salt Lake City), arguably the most important African American Democratic newspaper, paid the *Colored American* a handsome compliment: "the *Colored American* has the best editorial staff of any of our race papers and it and its writers would be all right if they were not such intense republicans." Broad Ax, May 7, 1898.

5. James Bryce, "Thoughts on the Negro Problem," *North American Review* 153 (December 1891): 646.

6. Clarence H. Poe, "Suffrage Restrictions in the South: Its Causes and Consequences," *North American Review* 175 (October 1902): 543.

7. The device was so successful that it reduced African American participation about 30 percent in the 1888 presidential race to virtually nil in 1892. Bess Beatty, *A Revolution Gone Backward: The Black Response to National Politics, 1876–1896* (New York: Greenwood Press, 1987), 139; J. Morgan Kousser, *The Shaping of Southern Politics: Suffrage Restriction and the Establishment of the One-Party South, 1880–1910* (New Haven: Yale University Press, 1974), 144.

8. Edward L. Ayers, *The Promise of the New South: Life after Reconstruction* (New York: Oxford University Press, 1992), 156. Although usually associated with hanging, lynchings include any action in which a mob administers justice outside of the established court system.

9. John A. Hobson, "The Negro Problem in the United States," *The Nineteenth Century and After* 54 (October 1903): 587–588.

10. Ayers, *Promise of the New South*, 158.

11. Richard B. Sherman, *The Republican Party and Black America from McKinley to Hoover, 1896–1933* (Charlottesville: University Press of Virginia, 1973), 14.

12. Quoted in *Washington Bee*, October 15, 1898.

13. Beatty, *A Revolution Gone Backward*, 161, 171.

14. Quoted in Sherman, *Republican Party and Black America*, 7.

15. *Freeman* (Indianapolis), March 5, 1898.

16. *Outlook* (New York), March 5, 1898, 557–558.

17. *Broad Ax*, February 26, 1898.

18. *Literary Digest*, March 5, 1898, 273–274, quoting from the *Register* (Columbia, S.C.) and the *Post* (Charleston, S.C.).

19. *Freeman*, April 9, 1898; *Washington Bee*, April 16, 1898.

20. *Congressional Record*, 55th cong., 2d sess., 1898, 31, pt. 3: 2556.

21. *Colored American*, March 26, 1898.

22. *Colored American*, March 19, 1898.

23. *Colored American*, April 9, 1898.

24. *Washington Bee*, March 19, 1898.

25. Washington Bee, April 2, 1898.

26. Washington Bee, April 23, 1898.

27. See the Report of Adjutant General H.C. Corbin, *New York Times*, November 12, 1898. For discussions of African American participation in the United States military during this period, see Marvin Fletcher, *The Black Soldier and Officer in the United States Army, 1891–1917* (Columbia: University of Missouri Press, 1974), 61–118; John M. Carroll, ed., *The Black Military Experience in the American West* (New York: Liveright, 1971); Arlen L. Fowler, *The Black Infantry in the West, 1869–1891* (Westport, Conn.: Greenwood Publishing Group, 1971); William H. Leckie, *The Buffalo Soldiers: A Narrative of the Negro Cavalry in the West* (Norman: University of Oklahoma Press, 1967); Monroe Lee Billington, *New Mexico's Buffalo Soldiers, 1866–1900* (Niwot: University Press of Colorado, 1991).

28. *Colored American*, May 28, 1898. See also the *Gazette* (Cleveland), May 7, 1898; Abraham Chew, *A Biography of Colonel Charles Young* (Washington, D.C.: R. L. Pendelton, 1923), 13; Robert Ewell Greene, *Colonel Charles Young: Soldier and Diplomat* (Washington, D.C.: R. E. Greene, 1985), 22–42; William H. Powell, *List of Officers of the Army of the United States from 1779 to 1900* (New York: L. R. Hamersly and Company, 1900), 693.

29. *Parsons Weekly Blade* (Parsons, Kans.), April 23, 1898.

30. *Colored American*, May 14, 1898.

31. *Colored American*, May 28, 1898.

32. *Washington Post*, November 28, 1898. The quotation from the Times (New Orleans) appears in the *Richmond Planet* (Richmond, VA.), July 16, 1898.

33. *Gazette*, March 25, 1899.

34. *Colored American*, May 7, 1898.

35. Quoted in the *Parsons Weekly Blade*, April 16, 1898.

36. The quotation from the *Picayune* appears in *Literary Digest*, August 27, 1898, 248.

37. *Broad Ax*, July 22, 1899.

38. See Gatewood, *Black Americans*, 64–101. Graham A. Cosmas, *An Army for Empire: The United States Army in the Spanish-American War* (Columbia: University of Missouri Press, 1971), 131–137, estimates that by August 1898 the total strength of the U.S. Army was 275,000 men. This number includes more than 200,000 volunteers, of which between eight and ten thousand were African American.

39. On the performance of the Negro troops in the Cuban campaign, see Theophilus Gould Steward, *The Colored Regulars in the United States Army* (1904; New York: Arno Press, 1969), 102–106, 116–281; John H. Nankivell, *History of the Twenty-fifth Regiment United States Infantry, 1869–1926* (1927; New York: Negro Universities Press, 1969), 65–86, 195–198; William G. Muller, *The Twenty Fourth Infantry: Past and Present* (1923; Ft. Collins, Co.: Old Army Press, 1972), [unpaginated]; Hiram H. Thweatt, *What the Newspapers Say of the Negro Soldier in the Spanish-American War* (Thomasville, Ga.: n.p, n.d.); Francis Lewis, "Negro Army Regulars in the Spanish-American War: Smoked Yankees at Santiago de Cuba" (master's thesis, University of Texas at Austin, 1969), 16–65; Fletcher, *Black Soldier and Officer*, 35–47; David F. Trask, *The War with Spain in 1898* (New York: MacMillan, 1981), 221, 237, 247–248, 326.

40. *Washington Bee*, August 13, 1898. Only the *State Ledger* (Topeka), July 16, 1898, reported the promotions without any bitterness.

41. *Colored American*, June 4, 1898.

42. *Washington Bee*, May 14, 1898. Question mark appears in the original.

43. *Colored American*, May 14, 1898.

44. *Washington Bee*, May 7, 1898.

45. *Washington Bee*, June 25, 1898.

46. *Washington Bee*, August 13, 1898.

47. *Washington Bee*, May 28, 1898.

48. *Washington Bee*, June 18, 1898.

49. *Washington Bee*, July 23, 1898. All the newspapers in the survey were indignant except the *Freeman*, which warned that "an attempt to wring out concession at this juncture is simply suicidal." *Freeman*, May 28, 1898.

50. *Evening Star* (Washington, D.C.), August 3, 6, October 8, 24, 1898.

51. *Times* (Washington, D.C.), February 2, 1899.

52. *Washington Post*, May 26, 1898.

53. *Colored American*, June 4, 1898.

54. *Washington Post*, June 7, 1898.

55. *Washington Bee*, June 11, 1898.

56. *Colored American*, July 2, 1898.

57. *Richmond Planet*, July 2, 1898.

58. *Gazette*, April 30, 1898.

59. Quotation from the *Commercial Appeal* (Memphis) appears in the *Colored American*, May 7, 1898.

60. The best treatment of these incidents is a series of articles by Willard B. Gatewood: "Alabama's 'Negro Soldier Experiment,' 1898–1899," *Journal of Negro History* 57 (October 1972): esp. 345–351; "North Carolina's Negro Regiment in the Spanish-American War," *North Carolina Historical Review* 47 (October 1971): esp. 382–385; "Negro Troops in Florida, 1898," *Florida Historical Quarterly* 49 (July 1970): 1–15; "Indiana Negroes and the Spanish American War," *Indiana Magazine of History* 69 (1973): esp. 131–137. See also the letters of black soldiers in Gatewood, "*Smoked Yankees and the Struggle for Empire*," 101–178.

61. Quoted in Gatewood, "Negro Troops in Florida," 3.

62. *Gazette*, July 2, 1898.

63. Gatewood, "Negro Troops in Florida," 8, 10. "There is a good deal of feeling at Tampa between the white and colored soldier," a white volunteer from Arizona wrote home, "and a great deal of rough and tumble fighting has been the result, and a few negroes have been killed." A. D. Webb to the *Arizona Bulletin*, June 11, 1898, quoted in A. D. Webb, "Arizonans in the Spanish-American War," *Arizona Historical Review* 1 (January 1929): 55.

64. *Colored American*, August 20, 1898.

65. *Times* (Washington, D.C.), June 10, 1898; *Washington Post*, August 12, 1898.

66. *Picayune* quotation appears in *Literary Digest*, November 5, 1898, 540.

67. *News and Observer* (Raleigh), October 19, 1898.

68. *News and Observer*, October 25, 1898. Josephus Daniels acquired the *News and Observer* in 1894 and quickly transformed it into one of the South's most influential newspapers. Active in both state and national politics, Daniels served as secretary of the navy during both terms of Woodrow Wilson's presidency and was appointed U.S. ambassador to Mexico by President Franklin Delano Roosevelt. *Dictionary of North Carolina Biography*, s.v. "Daniels, Josephus."

69. *News and Observer*, November 6, 1898. On the 1898 election in North Carolina and its immediate aftermath, see especially, Helen G. Edmond's pioneering *The Negro and Fusion Politics in North Carolina, 1894–1901* (Chapel Hill: University of North Carolina Press, 1951), 136–177. See also, Jeffrey J. Crow, "Maverick Republican in the Old North State: The Governorship of Daniel L. Russell, 1897–1901" (Ph.D. diss., Duke University, 1974), 178–218; Robert Howard Wooley, "Race and Politics: The Evolution of the White Supremacy Campaign of 1898 in North Carolina" (Ph.D. diss., University of North Carolina, 1977); Jerome A. McDuffie, "Politics in Wilmington and New Hanover County, North Carolina, 1865–1900: The Genesis of a Race Riot" (Ph.D. diss., Kent State University, 1979), 515–815; H. Leon Prather Sr., *We Have Taken A City: Wilmington Racial Massacre and Coup of 1898* (Rutherford, N.J.: Fairleigh Dickinson University Press, 1984).

70. *New York Times*, October 25, 26, November 4,5 1898.

71. *Washington Post*, October 24, 1898.

72. *Washington Post*, November 1, 1898.

73. *Washington Post*, November 6, 1898.

74. *Washington Post*, November 7, 1898.

75. *Colored American*, November 5, 1898.

76. *Colored American*, November 5, 1898. Even the *Freeman* (Indianapolis), one of the most cautious of the newspapers in the survey, could not restrain its fury: "What has befallen the colored man in the South is fit for revolutions. No country on earth thus degrades a portion of its citizens." *Freeman*, November 5, 1898.

77. *Washington Bee*, November 5, 1898. The same issue also contained the recommendation, "Every colored voter in North Carolina should peaceably endeavor to cast one Republican ballot next Tuesday."

78. *New York Times*, November 9, 1898. A journalist who had covered the elections noted approvingly that "in the Wilmington district a Republican majority of 5,000 in 1896 gave place to a Democratic majority of 6,000 . . . No one for a moment supposes that this was the result of a free and untrammelled ballot; and a Democratic victory here, as in other parts of the state, was largely the result of the suppression of the Negro vote." Henry L. West, "The Race War in North Carolina," *Forum* 26 (January 1899): 590.

79. Washington Post, November 9, 1898.

80. *New York Times*, November 11, 1898. Estimates of the number of blacks killed run from a low of twenty to thirty to well over one hundred.

81. West, "Race War in North Carolina," 584.

82. *New York Times*, November 12, 1898.

83. Founded by Alex L. Manly in 1894, the *Weekly Record* proved so successful that it became a daily in 1897. Manly was in Philadelphia at the time of the riot and never returned to Wilmington. The *Daily Record* ceased publication after the destruction of its offices.

84. *News and Observer*, November 12, 1898.

85. *News and Observer*, November 11, 1898.

86. *News and Observer*, November 13, 1898.

87. *News and Observer*, November 15, 1898.

88. *Colored American*, December 3, 1898. For a summary of the reaction of eleven African American papers to the Wilmington riot, see the *Richmond Planet*, December 3, 1898. The Democratic *Broad Ax* (November 19, 1898) was as scathing in its condemnation of "the monstrous outrages which are now perpetrated upon us" in North Carolina as were the Republican papers and shared their despair. On November 12th the same newspaper had proclaimed that "We still believe that the negro would have been ten million times better off if the slave ships which brought him to these shores had sunk to the bottom of the sea while they were speeding from coast to coast, fanned by the wings of the holy ghost." *Broad Ax*, November 12, 1898.

89. *Colored American*, November 12, 1898.

90. *Colored American*, December 17, 1898.

91. Colored American, December 17, 1898.

92. *Parsons Weekly Blade*, December 10, 1898. On January 25, 1900, the U.S. House of Representatives refused to seat Roberts by a 268 to 50 vote. On the Roberts case, see *New York Times*, December 10, 1898; *Literary Digest*, December 10, 24, 1898, 682–683, 752–754; *Parsons Weekly Blade*, December 31, 1898; Davis Bitton, "The B. H. Roberts Case of 1898–1900," *Utah Historical Quarterly* 25 (January 1957): 27–46.

93. *New York Times*, November 13, 1898. While the worst violence was in North Carolina, South Carolina also celebrated the election results with a wave of lynchings. See *New York Times*, November 9, 11, 13, 1898; *Washington Post*, November 9–11, 15, 1898; *Evening Star*, November 17, 1898; Tom Henderson Wells, "The Phoenix Election Riot," *Phylon* 31 (spring 1970): 58–69; Bruce Lee Kleinschmidt, "The Phoenix Riot," *Furman Review* 5 (spring 1974): 27–31.

94. *New York Times*, November 22, 1898.

95. *New York Times*, November 13, 1898.

96. *New York Times*, November 18, 1898. The *Evening Star* followed a line largely similar to that of the *New York Times* in its reporting of the campaign in North Carolina, the election results, and the violence that occurred there and elsewhere in the South. The *Times* (Washington, D.C.), like the *Washington Post*, was more unabashed in its support of white violence.

97. *Washington Bee*, November 19, 1898.

98. *Colored American*, December 17, 1898. For a review of the reaction of twenty-two African American newspapers to McKinley's message, see *Richmond Planet*, December 17, 1898.

99. *Gazette*, December 10, 1898.

100. See especially, Richard Wood, "The South and Reunion, 1898," *Historian* 31 (May 1969): 415–430. See also, Nina Silber, "The Romance of Reunion: Northern Images of the South, 1865–1900" (Ph.D. diss., University of California at Berkeley, 1989), 333–397.

101. *New York Times*, December 15, 1898.

102. *New York Times*, December 16, 1898.

103. *Evening Star*, December 15, 1898.

104. *New York Times*, December 15, 1898.

105. *New York Times*, December 20, 1898.

106. *Colored American*, December 24, 1898.

107. *Gazette*, July 2, 1898.

108. *Washington Post*, December 16, 1898.

109. *Washington Post*, December 19, 1898.

110. *News and Observer*, December 20, 1898.

111. The *Times* (Washington, D.C.), December 19, 1898. The *Parsons Weekly Blade* observed that "It's a wonder the southern whites in Georgia didn't lynch a Negro just to show McKinley a freak of southern chivalry. No doubt he would have enjoyed such gay sport." *Parsons Weekly Blade*, December 31, 1898.

112. *Richmond Planet*, July 29, 1899; *Gazette*, February 11, 1899.

113. *New York Times*, April 24, 1899.

114. Quotation from the report of a white detective who had been hired by a group of African Americans from Chicago to investigate the incident. The report stated that the lynching had been advertised several hours in advance and that "a special train was engaged as an excursion train to take people to the burning.... After this special moved out, another was made up to accommodate the late comers and those who were at church." The report published in its entirety in the *Richmond Planet*, October 14, 1899.

115. *New York Times*, April 24, 1899.

116. *New York Times*, April 25, 1899.

117. *New York Times*, April 25, 1899. The same issue also contained other stories of violence against African Americans in Georgia. In one lynching the victim was strangled after having his ears cut off. Another black Georgian was stripped to his waist and received one hundred lashes. "His offense was the remark that the negroes should pay no attention to notices pinned on their doors to leave the country." There were also reports on "Race Troubles in Arkansas" and of blacks being attacked by a mob in Louisiana.

118. *Colored American*, August 20, 1898.

119. *Colored American*, April 1899. Not unreasonably, the *Gazette* argued that here was a relationship of cause and effect between African American participation in the war against Spain and increased savagery of southern lynchers: "It was repeatedly said by Afro-American volunteers, until a few months ago in camp in Georgia, that as soon as they were mustered out of the service the treatment of our people in that section of the country would be terrible. Their statements were only too true. Smarting under the check which the presence of these soldiers had upon them in various parts of the south, prejudiced white brutes ... lost no time in carrying out their nefarious crusade against our people ... the moment the Afro-American volunteers were mustered out." *Gazette*, April 29, 1899.

120. *Washington Bee*, March 11, 1899.

121. *Colored American*, March 18, 1899.

122. *Washington Bee*, March 11, 1899.

123. *Colored American*, March 18, 1899. The *Washington Bee* was no less firm: "The 'white man's burden' is his want of Christianity, his prejudice, his greed, his arrogance and false pride, and when they are removed the mythical burden will disappear as mist before the rising sun." *Washington Bee*, March 11, 1899. The *Parsons Weekly Blade* expressed the hope that whites would take their burden to the white savages "in a certain section of America, who lynch, shoot and burn at the stake innocent people." *Parsons Weekly Blade*, March 25, 1899.

124. *Colored American*, March 11, 1899.

125. *Colored American*, February 11, 1899.

126. *Colored American*, September 9, 1899.

127. *Colored American*, December 3, 1898.

128. *Colored American*, September 2, 1899.

129. *Washington Bee*, February 4, 1899.

130. *Washington Bee*, April 29, 1899.

131. *Colored American*, November 11, 1899.

132. *Colored American*, April 29, 1899.

133. Colored American, June 24, 1899. The first black troops arrived in the Philippines in July 1899.

134. *Colored American*, September 9, 1899.

135. *Colored American*, September 16, 1899. The two black volunteer regiments began arriving in Manila in January 1900.

136. *Colored American*, October 7, 1899. On African American participation in the Philippines expedition, the *Gazette* and the *Parsons Weekly Blade* followed the same tortured course as the *Colored American* and the *Washington Bee*. From the onset the *Freeman* and the *State Ledger* endorsed the administration's position that African Americans could not afford to be considered "half-hearted and cold" in their patriotism. *Freeman*, May 6, 1899.

137. *Colored American*, August 5, 1899.

138. *Washington Bee*, March 11, 1899.

139. *Colored American*, October 7, 1899.

140. *Washington Bee*, July 29, 1899.

141. *Washington Bee*, April 15, 1899.

142. *Washington Bee*, April 1, 1899.

143. Mary Church Terrell, "Lynching from a Negro's Point of View," *North American Review* 178 (June 1904): 868.

144. Of the newspapers in the survey only the *Richmond Planet* was more outspoken than the *Colored American* and the *Washington Bee*. It was also the only Republican paper in the survey that consistently opposed the annexation of the Philippines throughout 1899. See *Richmond Planet*, July 22, December 23, 1898. The *Freeman* and the *State Ledger*, on the other hand, were more submissive. The *Freeman* made its rationale clear when it stated that "for the race the questions are always as to the expediency and never as to the exact and even handed justice. Humiliation versus political and civil extermination is the just and correct summary of events as they stand today." *Freeman*, November 19, 1899. None of the other newspapers would have disagreed. In the end all agreed that humiliation was the only course available for African Americans. The Democratic *Broad Ax* was the most outspoken of the newspapers in its criticism of the Republican Party. Interestingly, its attitude toward the Democratic Party and William Jennings Bryan mirrored that of the *Colored American* and the *Washington Bee* toward the Republican Party and President McKinley.

145. See Malcolm X and Alex Haley, *The Autobiography of Malcolm X* (New York: Ballantine Books, 1973), 347–363; John Henrik Clarke, ed., *Malcolm X: The Man and His Times* (Trenton, N.J.: Africa World Press, 1990), 288–301, 335–342; Carlos Moore, *Castro, the Blacks, and Africa* (Los Angeles: Center for Afro-American Studies, Univer-

sity of California, 1988), 185–190. See also *Daily Nation* (Nairobi), July 11, 1964; *Egyptian Gazette* (Cairo), August 7, 17, 23, 25, 1964; *Dipanda* (Brazzaville), September 12, 1964; *Tanganyka Standard* (Dar es Salaam), October 13, 1964.

146. "I think you could make a barometric chart of how civil rights were going," a senior State Department official mused, "through the relationships you had with many Africans." See page 77 of Mennen Williams, "Oral History Interview," 1970, John F. Kennedy Library, Boston, Mass. Documents in the Kennedy Library (esp. National Security File, boxes 2 and 3) and the Mennen Williams Papers in the National Archives (esp. Subject File, box 16), Washington, D.C., show the concern of both the Kennedy and Johnson administrations about the impact on Africans of the civil rights situation in the United States. See also Piero Gleijeses, "'Flee! The White Giants Are Coming!' The United States, the Mercenaries, and the Congo, 1964–1965," *Diplomatic History* 18 (April 1994): 207–237.

147. *Washington Bee*, October 29, 1898.

PART FIVE

END-OF-THE-CENTURY
ARCHETYPES:
SYMBOLIC
CONSTRUCTIONS
IN
BLACK
MANHOOD
AND
MASCULINITY

SEVENTEEN

The Anatomy of Lynching

ROBYN WIEGMAN

> When Matt lowered his eyes he noticed the ribs had been caved in.
>
> The flesh was bruised and torn. [The birthmark] was just below [Willie's] navel, he thought. Then he gave a start: where it should have been was only a bloody mound of torn flesh and hair. Matt went weak. He felt as though he had been castrated himself. He thought he would fall when Clara stepped up beside him. Swiftly, he tried to push her back. . . . Then Clara was screaming. . . . Matt pushed [her] to go, feeling hot breath against the hand he held over her mouth.
>
> "Just remember that a car hit 'im, and you'll be all right," the patrolman said. "We don't allow no lynching round here no more."
>
> Matt felt Clara's fingers digging into his arm as his eyes flashed swiftly over the face of the towering patrolman, over the badge against the blue shirt, the fingers crooked in the belt above the gun butt. He swallowed hard . . . catching sight of Willie between the white men's legs.
>
> "I'll remember," he said bitterly, "he was hit by a car."

—RALPH ELLISON, "The Birthmark," in *New Masses*, July 2, 1940

Above all, lynching is about the law: both the towering patrolman who renarrates the body and sadistically claims it as sign of his own power, and the symbolic as law, the site of normativity and sanctioned desire, prohibition and taboo. In the circuit of relations that governs lynching in the United States, the law as legal discourse and disciplinary practice subtends the symbolic arena, marking out a topos of bodies and identities that gives order to generation, defines and circumscribes social and political behavior, and punishes transgression, from its wildest possibility to its most benign threat.

Operating according to a logic of borders—racial, sexual, national, psychological, biological, as well as gendered—lynching figures its victims as the
culturally abject, monstrosities of excess whose limp and hanging bodies
function as the specular assurance that the threat has not simply been
averted, but thoroughly negated, dehumanized, and rendered incapable of
return. The overdetermination of punishment in the lynching scenario
demonstrates its profoundly psychological function, reinforcing the asym-
metry of empowerment that initiates and sustains the disciplinary mechanism in all of its violent complexity. How we understand this complexity—
how we can approach the tableau of torture, dismemberment, and death
that shapes lynching's specifically racialized deployment—provides the locus around which this essay is organized and makes possible a theoretical
foray into the intersecting relations of race and sexual difference in nine-
teenth- and twentieth-century United States culture.

In particular, I focus on the sexual economy that underlies lynching's
emergence as a disciplinary practice for racial control at the end of the
nineteenth century, when the threat of ritualized death provided the means
for (re)articulating white masculine supremacy within the social and economic specificities of slavery's abolition. As I hope to show, the decommod-
ification of the African American body that accompanies the transformation
from chattel to citizenry is mediated through a complicated process of
sexualization and engendering: not only does lynching enact a grotesquely
symbolic—if not literal—sexual encounter between the white mob and its
victim, but the increasing utilization of castration as a preferred form of
mutilation for African American men demonstrates lynching's connection
to the sociosymbolic realm of sexual difference. In the disciplinary fusion of
castration with lynching, the mob severs the black male from the masculine,
interrupting the privilege of the phallus, and thereby reclaiming, through
the perversity of dismemberment, his (masculine) potentiality for citizenship.[1] While this imposition of feminization works to align the black male, at
the symbolic level of the body, with those still unenfranchised, it is significant that the narrative means for inciting and explaining the mob's violence
takes the form of an intense masculinization in the figure of the black male
as mythically endowed rapist. Through this double staging of gender—
where the hypermasculinized rapist must "become" the feminine through
ritualized castration—lynching inhabits and performs the border crossings
of race, sex, and sexual difference.

MARKING THE BODY

Readers familiar with nineteenth-century United States literature will no
doubt recognize that the epigraph from Ellison's exploration of the body
politic involved in relations between black and white men bears the same
title, "The Birthmark," as Nathaniel Hawthorne's 1843 allegory of sexual
difference. In each story, the figure of the birthmark establishes a system of

corporeal inscription that links the body to cultural hierarchies of power: Hawthorne's birthmark being the "crimson stain upon the snow" of the beautiful Georgiana, while Ellison's is the mark below the navel of a young black man, Willie.[2] Significantly, both marks evoke castration, Georgiana's "bloody hand" functioning as symbol of her feminine lack,[3] and Willie's mark, through its disappearance into the "bloody mound of torn flesh and hair," evincing his literal castration.[4] While the antebellum story depicts the white female body *as* sexual difference, Ellison's piece rearticulates the symbolics of gender and castration at the site of the black male body. Such a rearticulation is made possible by the shifting relations of race and sexual difference in the late nineteenth century, where Emancipation's theoretical effect—the black male's social sameness—is symbolically mediated by a disciplinary practice that literalizes his affinity to the feminine. A brief look at the intertextual connections between these two figurations of the birthmark offers an initial locus for tracing the highly sexual and gendered dimensions of difference that inhabit the anatomy of lynching.[5]

In Hawthorne's parable of sexual difference,[6] a man deeply committed to science marries a beautiful woman only to find that a small birthmark on her left cheek drives him mad. This "visible mark of earthly imperfection"[7] symbolized in his mind Georgiana's "liability to sin, sorrow, decay, and death,"[8] which aligns her, as emblem of the feminine, with materiality, the body, and the culturally abject. It evinces, in short, her castrated and castrating difference from the male. As the "frightful object"[9] that is the cause of Aylmer's "horror and disgust,"[10] the birthmark takes over his life, becoming, as Teresa de Lauretis might put it, the very ground of his representation, "the looking-glass held up to man."[11] But while Georgiana's imperfect image grants Aylmer the fantasy of his own unbounded power and sets him in struggle with "our great creative Mother,"[12] she remains throughout the story the objectified spectacle of his desire, forever tied, in Laura Mulvey's terms, "to her place as bearer of meaning, not maker of meaning."[13] This position of alienation and negation is so powerful, in fact, that we can hardly be surprised to learn that "not even Aylmer . . . hated [the birthmark] so much as she."[14] When the enigma represented by woman and linked to the secrets of the natural world seems finally overcome, when "the last crimson tint of the birthmark—that sole token of human imperfection—faded from her cheek," Georgiana exhales her last breath, leaving Aylmer with a dead but now perfect woman.[15]

In the project of restoring woman to perfection, Hawthorne's story serves as a paradigm for the relations of sexual difference that underlie nineteenth-century scientific discourses on the feminine, where cultural anxieties about (white) women's place in the emergent public sphere are mediated by returning her to the body and its ascribed inferiorities. Placed there, in the landscape of her anatomy, woman provides the nexus against which masculine *disembodiment* can be achieved: where the rationality of the mind surpasses, even as it appropriates, the physical limitations of the body. In deferring masculine castration by becoming its embodiment, in functioning as the displaced locus of mutation, loss, and death, the female body in Hawthorne's story shares more than a coincidental affinity to the castrated body of the black male in Ellison's piece written nearly a century later. For the literalization of castration pursues the logic of sexual difference from the seemingly self-contained realm of masculine and feminine to that of racial difference and its inscription of corporeal and social division. By depicting the black male within a symbolic system contingent on the discursivity of gender, Ellison's "The Birthmark" articulates the way lynching and castration stages the black male's relationship to masculine power itself.

Published the same year as Richard Wright's Native Son, Ellison's little-known story opens at the scene of an accident, as Matt and Clara prepare to identify a body that purportedly has been hit by a car. But their brother, Willie, has been beaten and lynched, his face so thoroughly disfigured they must seek his birthmark, located beneath the navel, for positive recognition. In searching for the mark, Matt discovers castration instead: "where it should have been was only a bloody mound of torn flesh and hair."[16] This discovery establishes the interplay between birthmark and penis that activates the narrative's symbolic structure, allowing us to read castration as the remedy for the symbolic birthmark—the penis—that "flaws" black men. Such a remedy becomes necessary in the social transformation from enslavement to freedom, where the measure of the African American's claim to citizenship is precisely his status as man—a status evinced by the penis, but ultimately rewarded in the symbolic exchange between penis and phallus. Castration circumvents this process of exchange, consigning the black male to the fragmented and decidedly feminized realm of the body. As in Faulkner's Light in August, castration literalizes the association of "womanshenegro" that binds together the racial, sexual, and gendered not only in Joe Christmas's psyche, but in the sociosymbolic of United States culture that both the novel and Ellison's story inhabit.[17]

But while the affinity between the castrating marks in Hawthorne's and Ellison's stories demonstrates the dynamic of sexual difference at work in each, such a reading can only partially account for the political and ideological investments underlying lynching and castration. Indeed, by ascribing the black male fully to the feminine, one runs the risk of reiterating the lynch scenario's cultural effect without further illuminating the historical and ideological mappings of race and sexual difference through which this effect has been achieved. For while United States culture has rather routinely posited the black male in relation to the feminine (as in the emasculated icons of nineteenth-century minstrelsy and their twentieth-century comic counterparts), race and sexual difference are not the same. If the phallic lack characteristic of the feminine must be physically and psychologically inscribed—thereby denying the black male the primary sign of power in patriarchal culture—then his threat to white masculine power arises are not simply from a perceived racial difference, but from the potential for gender sameness. Within the context of white supremacy, we must understand this threat of a masculine sameness as so terrifying that only the reassertion of a sexual and gendered difference can provide the necessary disavowal. It is this that lynching and castration offer in their ritualized deployment, functioning as both a refusal and a negation of the possibility of extending the privileges of patriarchy to the black man.

In Ellison's "The Birthmark," this refusal is graphically depicted in the story's final image of the body of the castrated black man lying, bloody and brutalized, "between the white men's legs."[18] For it is here that black male castration is figured in its relation to the power and privilege of white masculinity, and the body of the dismembered "other" takes its place as bearer of the white phallus's meaning, deprived of subjective boundaries, and thoroughly objectified and negated. Through the gendered positionalities of castration and its relation to the patriarchal symbolic, then, the conflict presented by the African American's masculine sameness is violently arbitrated in favor of the continued primacy of white masculine supremacy. In this way, the symbolic transposition of the birthmark from the stain of femininity in Hawthorne's tale to the threatening black phallus in Ellison's demonstrates not simply the powerful disciplinary function of race and sexual difference, but their historically contingent production.

BIRTH OF A NATION

The political effect of the lynch scenario presented by Ralph Ellison in his brief but evocative story relies on the reader's awareness of the broader cultural context of "race relations" in the late nineteenth and early twentieth centuries—a context in which the system of economic, social, and political organization was profoundly altered, as I have suggested, by the African American's emergence from slavery to citizenry. As a response to the ideological incommensurability between white supremacy and black enfranchisement, lynching marks the excess of discourses of race and rights, serving as a chief mechanism for defining relations of power in the postwar years. For the emancipation of five million slaves was neither a widespread cultural recognition of black humanity nor the proud achievement of the democratic ethos. As the late nineteenth century's turn toward the Ku Klux Klan and mob violence makes clear, the transformation from slavery to "freedom" was characterized by a rearticulation of cultural hierarchies in which terrorism provided the means for defining and securing the continuity of white supremacy.[19] The rise of black lynchings in the years following the war—10,000 by 1895, according to one source[20]—is indicative of a broader attitude in the United States toward African American entrance into the cultural order: greeted by a few as the manifestation of a liberal ideal, "freedom" was far from the reigning social reality.

For the *New Masses* reader in 1940, the narrative of dismemberment and murder, overseen by the figure of the law, marked the repetitiousness of white supremacist discipline that greeted the "free" black subject in the 1860s and continued to reiterate his or her secondary social position through-out the twentieth century, including the present day.[21] Both mainstream and alternative newspapers regularly ran stories documenting the scenes of vio-lence, often offering graphic detail of the practices of torture through which the entire African American population could be defined and policed as innately, if no longer legally, inferior.[22] Such accounts extended the func-tion of lynching as a mode of surveillance by reiterating its performative qualities, carving up the black citizen body in the specular recreation of the initial, dismembering scene. For Trudier Harris, who has studied the legacy of lynching for African American writers of the nineteenth and twentieth centuries, the imposition of a violent, bodily destruction works "to keep Blacks contained politically and socially during the years of Reconstruc-tion . . . convey[ing] to [them] that there was always someone watching over their shoulders ready to punish them for the slightest offense or the least deviation from acceptable lines of action."[23] What constituted "acceptable lines of action" for the newly emancipated slave depended, of course, on whose perspective was being articulated. In the conflict between a South deeply shocked by its lost hegemony and the slave's euphoric desire to grasp the rights and privileges of citizenry, the full panorama of racist violence emerges as the defining conditions of "America" (as ideological trope and national body) itself.

In this regard, we might understand the end of slavery as marking in fuller and more complex ways the birth of the nation, where one of the questions that divided the delegates at the Continental Congress in 1776 was finally settled in favor of a rhetorical and legal, though not altogether economic or political, equality. But as the rise of lynching in the postwar years indicates, this birth brings into crisis the definitional boundaries of nation implicit in the early constitutional documents: here, issues of generation, inheritance, and property rights are theoretically wrenched from their singular associa-tion with the white masculine and made available, at least in the abstract, to a new body of citizens. The effect of this transformation is the dissolution of a particular kind of patriarchal order, for while the slave system ensured a propertied relation between laborer and master, and discursively and legally bound the African American to the white father through the surname, Emancipation represents the literal and symbolic loss of the security of the white patronym and an attendant displacement of the primacy of the white male. The many documented reports of slaves changing their names in the first moments of their freedom—and the thematic value of naming itself in the African American cultural tradition—are indicative of the significance of the material and metaphorical eclipse of the white father's patronymic embrace.[24]

For the nonpropertied white male, the Civil War and Reconstruction represented important transformations in the historical articulation of a white underclass consciousness, offering on one hand the recognition of specific class-bound political interests, while often positing free men and women as competitors to their own economic survival. One of the most prominent national figures embodying this position was Lincoln's successor to the White House, Andrew Johnson. As Eric Foner discusses in his important reconsideration of the Reconstruction era, Johnson, having grown up in poverty himself, identified with the Southern yeomanry. "He seems to have assumed that the Confederacy's defeat had shattered the power of the 'slaveocracy' and made possible the political ascendancy of loyal white yeomen. The freedmen had no role to play in his vision of a reconstructed South."[25] Like other poor whites, Johnson saw slaves as complicit with their masters in maintaining economic and political power over nonslaveholding whites. In this scenario, Foner writes, "the most likely result of black enfranchisement would therefore be an alliance of blacks and planters, restoring the Slave Power's hegemony and effectively excluding the yeomanry from political power."[26] Johnson's inability to read the class interests of poor whites as aligned with the emergent black citizen—as in fact a multiracial underclass exploited by a feudalistic agrarian or developing free market system—demonstrates the contradiction between a class-conscious and white supremacist social vision. Such a contradiction contributed to the political fragmentation of the postwar years, producing violent reprisals toward the emancipated slave from the white yeoman as well as from the planter class.

In these reprisals for offenses more often imagined than real, lynching becomes a primary disciplinary tool, and it takes on over time a narrativizing context that both propels the white crowd to action and defines the methods of torture subsequently imposed. The narrative I refer to features the African American male in the role of mythically endowed rapist, with the white woman as the flower of civilization he intends to violently pluck, and the white male as the heroic interceptor who restores order by thwarting this black phallic insurgence.[27] But in the early decades of the nineteenth century, lynching does not function within this constellation of racial and sexual encodements. Instead, as Trudier Harris discusses, it is a component of the system of frontier justice, operating in lieu of a legally sanctioned trial and consisting of a variety of punishments—most often whippings—without the final denouement of death.[28] In fact, before 1840, writes James E. Cutler in his study of the history of lynching in the United States, "the verb lynch was occasionally used to include capital punishment, but . . . 'to lynch' had not then undergone a change in meaning and acquired the sense of 'to put to death' . . . It was not until a time subsequent to the Civil War that the verb lynch came to carry the idea of putting to death."[29] And it is not until that time as well that lynching becomes associated almost exclusively with acts of retribution against the legally free citizenry of African American subjects.[30]

The turn toward lynching as a racially coded practice owes its existence, as I have suggested, to the transformations attending Emancipation, from the threat to white economic security presented by the loss of a free labor force to the competitive inclusion of African Americans into the open market's laboring class. But the significance of lynching as coterminous with violence against African Americans in the Reconstruction era emerges as well from the historical configuration of citizenry as part of a broader economy of the body in United States culture. As feminist political theorists have discussed, the white male citizen of Enlightenment thought draws his particular suit of rights and privileges from the rhetorical disembodiment of the citizen as a social category, where in Lauren Berlant's words, "the generic 'person'" provides the abstraction necessary for replacing the historically located body with the discursivity of national identity.[31] As she explains: "The American subject is privileged to suppress the fact of his historical situation in the abstract 'person': but then, in return, the nation provides a kind of prophylaxis for the person, as it promises to protect his privileges and his local body in return for loyalty to the state. . . . The implicit whiteness and maleness of the original American citizen is thus itself protected by national identity."[32] In constituting the citizen through the value system of disembodied abstraction, the white male is "freed" from the corporeality that might otherwise impede his insertion into the larger body of national identity.

For the African American subject, on the other hand, it is precisely the imposition of an extreme corporeality that defines his or her distance from the privileged ranks of (potential or actual) citizenry. With the advent of Emancipation and its attendant loss of the slave system's marking of the African American body as property, lynching emerges to reclaim and reassert the centrality of black corporeality, deterring the now theoretically possible move toward citizenry and disembodied abstraction. Through the lynching scenario, "blackness" is cast as a subversive (and most often sexual) threat, an incontrovertible chaos whose challenge to the economic and social coherency of the nation can be psychologically, if not wholly politically, averted by corporeal abjection and death. That lynching becomes during Reconstruction and its aftermath an increasingly routine response to black attempts at education, personal and communal government, suffrage, and other indicators of cultural inclusion and equality attests to its powerful disciplinary function. As the most extreme deterritorialization of the body and its subjective boundaries, lynching guarantees the white mob's privilege of physical and psychic penetration, grants it a definitional authority over social space, and embodies the vigilant and violent system of surveillance that underwrites late nineteenth- and early twentieth-century negotiations over race and cultural power.

WHITE BEAUTY, BLACK BEAST

But why the charge of rape as the consolidating moment of lynching's justification? Why this sexualization of blackness as the precondition not only for mob action, but for lynching's broad cultural acceptance and appeal? The answer to this, like any accounting of the historical, is less apparent than the many contexts in which the evidence of lynching's sexualization appears.*

But if we begin where I have suggested, with the narrative of rape (and its culmination in lynching) translating the crisis of Emancipation from economic to sexual and gendered terms, we encounter a very powerful means through which not only black men but the entire black community could be psychologically and physically contained. Most important, we witness the way the rape narrative simultaneously recognizes and subverts the African American male's theoretical equality in the sexual as well as political and economic spheres. On a level less abstract, the rape mythos, as an overwhelmingly southern response to enfranchisement, also challenges the work of the Freedmen's Bureau, where the patriarchal logic of the dominant culture became the defining mechanism for organizing the newly freed slave: not only did the bureau appoint the husband as head of the household, assigning to him sole power to enter into contractual labor agreements for the entire family, but it fought for the allotment of land for every freed "male," while granting only unmarried women access to this domain.[33]

In these pronouncements—as in the routine gender segregation attending voting, jury duty, the holding of political and Republican party office—the official program of Reconstruction understood the freedom of black men to entail a "natural" judicial and social superiority over African American women. The nineteenth century's determination of public and private

---

*The rise of black lynchings in the late nineteenth century and the attendant articulation of the mythology of the black male as rapist demonstrates an increasing reliance on the discourse of sexual difference to negotiate race within the newly emergent economic structures of the twentieth century. This shift and its implications for reading gender and race emerge most fully in Richard Wright's *Native Son* (1940), our literature's most compelling story of the black man caught in the mythology of the rapist—that death, as Bigger Thomas says, "before death came" (Richard Wright, *Native Son* [1940, rpt. New York, 1966], p. 228). Revolving around the fated life of Bigger, his employment by a liberal white family, his accidental murder of their daughter, Mary, and his subsequent flight and trial, the novel demonstrates what Wright considers the definitive pattern of race relations in the United States. As he writes in "How 'Bigger' Was Born," "any Negro . . . knows that times without number he has heard of some Negro boy being picked up . . . and carted off to jail and charged with 'rape.' This thing happens so often that to my mind it had become a representative symbol of the Negro's uncertain position in America" (p. xxviii). In Wright's novel, such uncertainty is explicitly linked to masculinity and to the competitive dimensions of black male and white male relations.

The significance of masculinity for Wright's central character is apparent from the opening scene where Bigger's mother describes his failure: "We wouldn't have to live in this garbage dump if you had any manhood in you" (p. 12). Her words fill Bigger with shame and hatred, a deep alienating guilt repeatedly evoked throughout the text and

along strict gender lines thus provided a definitional structure through which social space and familial roles were shaped for a population no longer denied the right (and privilege) of maintaining family bonds.[34] But while the patriarchalization of the black family served to institutionalize it within the gender codes prevalent in white bourgeois ideology, thereby securing the black family to the formal dimensions of white social behavior, many whites were decidedly threatened by the definitional sameness accorded former slaves. The loss of one patriarchal organization of social life—that of sla-very—and its replacement by the seeming egalitarianism of a male-domi-nated black family, then, has the effect of broadening the competitive di-mensions of interracial masculine relations, especially as the black male's new property governance of black women threatens to extend to women of the dominant group as well.

It is in this climate that the mythology of the black male as rapist emerges, working the faultline of the slave's newly institutionalized masculinization by framing this masculinity as the bestial excess of an overly phallicized primitivity. In the contours of Western racial discourse, of course, the primi-tive sexual appetite associated with blackness is not a new articulation at the end of the nineteenth century, but its crafting in the highly stylized and overdetermined narrative structure of the rape mythos—along with the sheer frequency of its deployment—marks a particular historical configura-tion of the sexual and gendered in their relation to issues of race and nation. For while the slavery period in the United States often envisioned the Uncle

expressly linked to emasculation. When his mother visits him in prison at the novel's end and begs on her knees before Mrs. Dalton for Bigger's life, he is described as "para-lyzed with shame; he felt violated" (p. 280). This violation, this symbolic emasculation, functions as a central metaphor in the novel, defining the black man's status in a racist culture, which, as Wright says in his autobiography *Black Boy*, "could recognize but a part of a man" (Richard Wright, *Black Boy* [New York, 1945], p. 284). The partiality of masculinity serves to signify black alienation in United States society in general. As Bigger tells his friends: "Every time I think about it I feel like somebody's poking a red-hot iron down my throat. . . . We live here and they live there. . . . They got things we ain't. They do things and we can't. It's just like living in jail" (p. 23). In the figure of the red-hot iron, Wright casts Bigger's oppression in highly sexual and phallic terms, mark-ing segregation, racism, and poverty as the symbolic phalluses of white masculine power burning in Bigger's throat. "You ain't a man no more," Bigger finally says, "[White folks] . . . after you so hot and hard . . . they kill you before you die" (pp. 326–27). Equating being a "man" with access to freedom and power, Bigger posits the white world, so "hot and hard" against him, as castrating.

But importantly, this castration is also an inverted sexual encounter between black men and white men, as evinced in the elaborate scene of chase and capture that ac-companies the charge of rape against Bigger. Hiding on the roof of a building, Bigger is entrapped by white men wielding a fire hose, "the rushing stream jerked this way and that. . . . Then the water hit him. . . . He gasped, his mouth open. . . . The water left him;

Tom figure as the signification of the "positive good" of a system that protected and cared for its black "children," once emancipated, these children became virile men who wanted for themselves the ultimate symbol of white civilization: the white woman.[35] The transformation of the image of the black man from simple, docile Uncle Tom to violent sex offender characterizes the oppositional logic underwriting the representational structure of black male images in nineteenth- and twentieth-century United States culture, a logic in which the discourse of sexual difference—from feminized docility to hypermasculinized phallicity—comes to play a primary significatory role.[36]

South Carolina Senator Ben Tillman demonstrates this logic in his 1907 speech before Congress, when he argues for the abandonment of due process for blacks accused of sex crimes against white women:

> The white women of the South are in a state of siege. . . . Some lurking demon who has watched for the opportunity seizes her; she is choked or beaten into insensibility and ravished, her body prostituted, her purity destroyed, her chastity taken from her. . . . Shall men . . . demand for [the demon] the right to have a fair trial and be punished in the regular course of justice? So far as I am concerned he has put himself outside the pale of the law, human and divine. . . . Civilization peels off us . . . and we revert to the . . . impulses . . . to "kill! kill! kill!"[37]

In proposing mob retaliation against the defilers of white womanhood, Tillman assures his listeners that he does not hate blacks by recalling "the

---

he lay gasping, spent. . . . The icy water clutched again at his body like a giant hand; the chill of it squeezed him like the circling coils of a monstrous boa constrictor" (p. 251). The passage that depicts Bigger's subsequent conquest by this monstrous phallic image extends the horrific sexual encounter: "He wanted to hold on but could not. His body teetered on the edge; his legs dangled in the air. Then he was falling. He landed on the roof, on his face, in snow, dazed" (p. 252). Finally brought down by the monstrosity of white masculine desire for and hatred of the black man, Bigger loses consciousness, his strength gone as the violent parody of romantic coupling ends.

In capturing Bigger, the white men—nearly eight thousand searching the city—believe they have made the world safe again for white women. As the prosecutor, Buckley, says in his plea for the imposition of the death penalty: "The law is strong and gracious enough to allow all of us to sit here . . . and not tremble with fear that at this very moment some half-human black ape may be climbing through the windows of our homes to rape, murder, and burn our daughters! . . . Every decent white man in America ought to swoon with joy for the opportunity to crush with his heel the woolly head of this black lizard" (p. 373). While Bigger's murder of the white woman is accidental and the subsequent destruction of her body makes it impossible to garner physical evidence of sexual abuse, the central crime, as Buckley claims, "is *rape*" (p. 377). It is for the rape of Mary Dalton that Bigger must die, as his trespass of white masculine property makes him the symbol of all that the white world must protect itself from: an "infernal monster," a "treacherous beast" and "worthless ape" (p. 377).

negroes of the old slave days . . . the negroes who knew they were inferior and who never presumed to assert equality."[38] These blacks, with minds like "those of children," posed no sexual threat, as was witnessed, according to Tillman, by the fact that during the Civil War, with white men away fighting, "there if not of record a solitary instance of one white woman having been wronged" by the nearly 800,000 black men left on plantation land.[39] Only with Emancipation and the "return to barbarism" does rape follow; "the negro becomes a fiend in human form."[40]

As Tillman's rhetoric indicates, the white woman serves, in the ethos of nineteenth-century racialism, as a pivotal rhetorical figure for shaping the mythology of the black rapist. Using her emblem as the keeper of the purity of the race, white men cast themselves as protectors of civilization, reaffirming not only their role as social and familial "heads," but their paternal property rights as well. In this way, as Trudier Harris observes, the white male maintains a position of "superiority not only in assigning a place to his women, but especially in keeping black people, particularly black men, in the place he had assigned for them."[41] In this dual role, the mythology of the black male rapist simultaneously engineers race and gender hierarchies, masking the white male's own historical participation in "miscegenating" sexual activities and ensuring his disciplinary control over potential sexual — and, one must add, political — liaisons between black men and white women. Within the context of nineteenth-century abolitionist and feminist movements, the necessity for disrupting such potential bonds seems important indeed.

Given the intensity of the taboo against black men and white women, Bigger accepts Mary's death as a conscious act: "Though he had killed by accident, not once did he feel the need to tell himself that it had been an accident. He was black and he had been alone in a room where a white girl had been killed; therefore he had killed her" (p. 101). In accepting responsibility for Mary's death, Bigger sees himself not only as a refuting white masculine authority, but as gaining an advantage that had eluded him before: "The knowledge that he had killed a white girl they loved and regarded as their symbol of beauty made him feel the equal of them, like a man who had been somehow cheated, but had now evened the score" (p.155). Through his destruction of the objectified symbol of white patriarchal rule, Bigger claims his right to masculine selfhood; no longer does he need the knife or gun, traditional symbols of masculinity, that initially accompanied him to the Dalton home: "What his knife and gun had once meant to him, his knowledge of having secretly murdered Mary now meant" (p.141).

Bigger's acceptance of Mary's murder and his consequent sense of freedom are particularly meaningful when viewed in terms of an earlier and seemingly insignificant event in the novel. Before setting out for the Dalton home on the day of Mary's accidental death, Bigger gathers with friends at Doc's poolroom to discuss plans for robbing Blum's Delicatessen. While the men had pulled other "jobs," this was to be their first robbery of a white man. "For months they had talked of robbing Blum's, but had not been able to bring themselves to do it. They had the feeling that the robbing of Blum's would be a violation of ultimate taboo; it would be trespassing into territory

And yet, the central figuration of the white woman's sexuality in the rape mythos must be understood as a displacement of the deeper and more culturally complex relation between black men and white men and their claims to the patriarchal province of masculine power. As Harris writes, "The issue really boils down to one between white men and black men and the mythic conception the former have of the latter."[42] Such a mythic conception—in which, as Frantz Fanon says, "the Negro . . . has been fixated [at the genital]"[43]—works through the discourse of the biological, figuring blackness as the corporeal, and thereby equating the colonized laboring body with an extensive, uncontrollable sexuality. In reducing the black male to the body, and further to the penis itself, the psychic drama of masculinity as it is played out in the colonial scenario of United States culture hinges on the simultaneous desire and disavowal attending the black male's mythic phallic inscription. In *White Hero, Black Beast*, Paul Hoch reads this process of desire and disavowal as constitutive of the unconscious formation of white masculinity, where the overdetermination of the black male's mythic phalli-cism—as evinced in the proliferation of discourses proclaiming, describing, or denying it—represents "a projection of those aspects of [the white males's] *own* sexuality which society has made taboo."[44] Under such conditions, as Hoch writes, "abandon[ing] control over the bestial supermasculinity he has projected outward on to the black male would threaten the racist's control over his *own* repressed sexuality."[45]

Hoch draws this conclusion not simply from the Freudian psychoanalytic framework he employs, but from the context of the relationship between

---

where the full wrath of an alien white world would be turned loose upon them; in short, it would be a symbolic challenge of the white world's rule over them; a challenge which they yearned to make, but were afraid to" (pp. 17–18). The language here of "violation," "taboo," and "symbolic challenge" significantly scripts the robbing of Blum in the same terms as the mythic encounter between a black man and a white woman. This scene and a later one in which Bigger purposely argues with Gus as a way to avoid going through with the plan indicate the more fundamental conflict that lies at the heart of the mythology of the black male rapist: the struggle over social, political, and sexual power between black men and white men.

More important perhaps, the incident surrounding Blum clarifies the role of the white woman in the negotiation of power among men. While white women have been complicit in the lynching and burning of black men, at times using the charge of rape themselves in order to protect their positions in the racial hierarchy, the mythology of the black rapist sets them up as the displaced site of a masculine struggle, the embodi-ments of white masculine desire and hence the emblems of a thwarted masculinity for black men. Instead of robbing Blum or challenging Mr. Dalton, who makes his wealth from the overpriced rentals in the "Black Belt," Bigger lives out a drama crafted by the intersecting hierarchies of race and gender, a drama that raises the white woman to the pedestal only to make her bear the burden of the racist patriarchal structure by having her symbolize its hierarchical construction. This does not absolve the white woman from her complicity in maintaining racial oppression, though it does point to the

conquest and masculinity in Western cultures. Here, the nature of conquest
within the realm of the sexual underwrites the commodity status attached to
the female body, helping to produce, through the formation of the feminine
as masculine property, the contradictory logic of virgin/whore that subtends
"woman" in her various cultural guises. In the bifurcation of the feminine
into idealized and nonsexualized virginity on the one hand and defiled and
fully sexualized promiscuity on the other, the conquestatory narrative of
masculine sexuality is caught between a necessary restraint and a licensed
rein. But because conquest is preeminently motivated by the inaccessible,
by the taboos orchestrated around restraint, it is ultimately the defilement of
the feminine in its ideal state that activates the conquestatory dimensions of
"normative" masculine heterosexuality. For Hoch, this means that the phantasm of the black beast conquering the white goddess offers the most impressive demonstration of virility, as it is the greatest violation of the boundaries
of restraint. At a fundamental psychic level, he claims, the white male
"bitterly resents the black male for the greater opportunities for conquest
and defilement his debased standing apparently affords him."[46]

Such resentment literally engenders a complicated process of creation
and negation in which the white male invests the black male with definitive
masculine powers as the precondition for violently denying and withdraw-
ing such powers from him. In this regard, the white male creates the image

broader pattern in U.S. culture where differences between men are played out within a
highly charged configuration of gender.

Within this configuration, the role and status of the black women takes on a particular cultural negativity as she symbolizes the excess of white womanhood. In *Native Son*,
for instance, the raped and murdered body of Bessie Mears, Bigger's girlfriend, is
wheeled into the courtroom as graphic display of Bigger's violent criminality. As he puts
it, "Though he had killed a black girl and a white girl, he knew that it would be for the
death of the white girl that he would be punished. The black girl was merely 'evidence'"
(p. 307). But while Bigger recognized the asymmetrical value placed on black women
and white women, he nonetheless understands Bessie's murder within the same contex-
tual framework as that governing Mary's, finding both acts "the most meaningful things
that had ever happened to him. He was living, truly and deeply. . . . Never had his will
been so free" (p. 225). In tying Bessie to the symbolic act of the white woman's murder—
and in marking his violation of her as an equally cathartic trespass—Bigger redefines
rape itself: "Rape was not what one did to women. Rape was what one felt when one's
back was against a wall and one had to strike out, whether one wanted to or not. . . . It was
rape when he cried out in hate deep in his heart as he felt the strain of living day by day"
(p. 214). This displacement of the gendered dimensions of sexual violence casts the
mythology of the black male rapist as itself a cultural rape, one defined by the materiality
of black oppression. Such a transformation of the metaphorics of rape simultaneously
points to the gendered inscriptions of black male oppression, while crafting the African
American woman's death as the ricochet effect of the white woman's pedestaled superiority.

he must castrate, and it is precisely through the mythology of the black male as rapist that he effectively does this. In the process, the creation of a narrative of black male sexual excess simultaneously exposes and redirects the fear of castration from the white male to the black male body. And it is in the lynch scene that this transfer moves from the realm of the psychosexual to the material. Harris's descriptive account of the sexual undercurrent of lynching and castration is telling in this regard: "For the white males . . . there is a symbolic transfer of sexual power at the point of the executions. The black man is stripped of his prowess, but the very act of stripping brings symbolic power to the white man. His actions suggest that, subconsciously, he craves the very thing he is forced to destroy. Yet he destroys it as an indication of the political (sexual) power he has."[47] In this destruction of the phallic black beast, the white male reclaims the hypermasculinity that his own mythology of black sexual excess has denied him, finding in sexual violence the sexual pleasure necessary to uphold both his tenuous masculine and white racial identities.

In negating the black male's most visible claim to masculine power, Harris describes lynching as a "communal rape," a description that inscribes within the lynching and castration scene the relations of power and disempowerment at work in the disciplinary practice most associated with sexual difference: male sexual violence toward women.[48] Through the rape meta-

---

From a feminist perspective, there is something deeply disturbing about the novel's rearticulation of rape as "not what one did to women" and Bigger's subsequent insertion into the position of *sexual*—and not simply racial—victim. In the evacuation of the body of woman, particularly the black woman, from the terrain of sexual violence, Wright seems to hierarchicalize African American oppression of such a way that the thwarting of black masculinity, through literalized castration, outreaches and indeed negates the historical problem of the black woman's routinely violated sexuality. To find it necessary to deny the gendered dimensions of rape, then, to see only the black male as rape's social and sexual victim, serves not only to establish the black male's difference from the feminine, but to displace the category of woman altogether. (For a discussion of the role of black women in *Native Son*, see Trudier Harris, "Native Sons and Foreign Daughters," in *New Essays on "Native Son,"* ed. Keneth Kinnamon [New York, 1990], pp. 63–84.) In this way, the black woman is expelled beyond the narrative's critical gaze as Bigger becomes the universalized emblem of black oppression—a universalization clearly predicated on the framework of masculinity and differences among men.

But while Wright's method of foregrounding the masculine stakes at work in the rapist mythos is defined at the expense of black women, his novel refuses the more traditional structure of male bonding that Eve Kosofsky Sedgwick has defined, in which "the spectacle of the ruin of woman . . . is just the right lubricant for an adjustment of differentials of power [among men]" (Eve Kosofsky Sedgwick, *Between Men: English Literature and Male Homosocial Desire* [New York, 1985], p. 66). This we witness in the final moments of the novel, when Bigger makes a failed attempt to emerge from his alienation to connect with Jan, the white boyfriend of Mary Dalton. "Tell . . . Tell Mister

phor, the emasculation of the black male undertaken in lynching and castration emerges as the imposition of the binary figuration of gender, with the white male retaining hegemony over the entire field of masculine entitlements, while the black male is confined to the corporeal excess of a racial feminization. But as I have suggested throughout my discussion, and as my reading of *Native Son* in particular demonstrates, it is important to maintain the distinction between the imposition of feminization onto male bodies and the historical framework of the feminine as part and parcel of being born female. Such a distinction enables us to understand the force of the discourse of sexual difference as it constructs and contains hierarchical relations among men without negating the specific materiality of gender oppression that accompanies women's variously raced positions in United States culture. In other words, the imposition of feminization onto male and female bodies is not—politically, theoretically, or historically—the same.

But while castration may function as a means for enacting a gendered difference at the site of the black male body, it is also the case that such a practice of dismemberment enables a perverse level of physical intimacy between the white male aggressor and his captive ex-slave, pointing to an underlying obsession with sexual (as opposed to gender) sameness. Harris's report that "in some historical accounts, the lynchers were reputed to have divided pieces of the blacks man's genitals among themselves" allows us to envision the castration scene as more than the perverse sexual encounter

---

... Tell Jan hello" (p. 392), Bigger says to his lawyer, Boris Max, shifting as he does from the servile address of "Mister" to Jan's first name. But the contrast between this hesitant and rather hopeless attempt and the image of utopian masculine bonds offered earlier in the novel—"an image of a strong blinding sun sending hot rays down . . . in the midst of a vast crowd of men, white men and black men and all men, [with] the sun's rays melt[ing] away the many differences, the colors, the clothes, and [drawing] what was common and good upward toward the sun" (p. 335)—demonstrates the deep abyss of color and caste that will accompany the many Biggers to their graves.

In the seeming impossibility of the utopian image to extend to Bigger any hope within the narrative scenario of the black male as rapist, Wright's novel purposely counters the rhetoric of 1930s progressive politics (most obviously that of the Communist party) that offers the image of interracial male bonds as socially transgressive. Instead, his narrative marks the extremity of hatred and violence that ushers the black male into the patriarchal province of the masculine, that province where he is simultaneously endowed with masculine prowess and defiantly deprived of the ability to pursue sexual (as well as social) autonomy. But in exploring the complexities of the rape mythos, Wright cannot wend his way out of the ideological trap of gender that exerts so much power within the disciplinary practice of lynching and castration. Instead, he reiterates the binary inscriptions of sexual difference by positioning the black male's social freedom—as well as the critical reading of his victimization—as oppositional to women. As such, *Native Son* compelling and disturbingly captures Bigger in the definitional nexus of race, sexuality, and gender that Wright so defiantly sets out to explore.

offered by the rape metaphor.[49] In the image of white men embracing—with hate, fear, and a chilling form of empowered delight—the very penis they were so overdeterminedly driven to destroy, one encounters a sadistic enactment of the homoerotic, indeed its most extreme disavowal. As Eve Kosofsky Sedgwick has discussed in *Between Men*, the male bonding relations that characterize patriarchal structures are dependent in nineteenth- and twentieth-century Anglo-American cultures on the panic image of the homosexual, whose very visibility of same-sex desire provides the disciplinary terms for normalizing heterosexuality in its compulsory formation. From this perspective, we might understand the lynching scenario and its obsession with the sexual dismemberment of black men to mark the limit of the homosexual/heterosexual binary: that point at which the oppositional relation reveals its inherent and mutual dependence, and the heterosexuality of the black male "rapist" is transformed into a violently homoerotic exchange. "The homosociality of this world," Sedgwick writes in a discussion of the late Renaissance, which holds true for the history of Anglo and African men in the United States, "is not that of brotherhood, but of extreme, compulsory, and intensely volatile mastery and subordination."[50]

In such a volatile and sexually charged realm, the mythology of the black male as rapist functions to script the deeply disturbing transformation in United States racial relations in the late nineteenth century within the double registers of sexuality and gender, thereby granting to the white mob that captures and controls the black body the psychological power of arbitrating life and death. In choosing death—and accompanying it with the most extreme practices of corporeal abuse—whiteness enhances its significatory lack, filling the absence of meaning that defines it with the fully corporeal presence of a hated, feared, and now conquered blackness. The extremity of punishment in the lynching and castration scenario thus provides the necessary illusion of returning to the lost moment of complete mastery—a moment never actually "full," though yearned for, indeed frantically sought after, through the disciplinarity of random mob violence.

ANOTHER WILLIE

The enduring power of the black male rapist mythos is perhaps best witnessed in the contemporary era in the specter of Willie Horton, the convicted black male rapist used in George's Bush's 1988 presidential campaign to signify the potential danger of Democratic party control. Through the figure of Willie Horton, Bush challenged the toughness of his opponent, Michael Dukakis, whose penal reform program in Massachusetts reportedly was responsible for putting a rapist back on the streets. Bush's "get-tough" discourse, deployed here in the context of a test of masculine strength between white men, functioned to align racism with the broader and perhaps more nebulous fear of national decline—that fear so well orchestrated by

David Duke and other political spokesmen for white supremacy.[51] That
Bush had to quickly disaffiliate himself, in the 1992 presidential campaign,
from race-baiting in light of both Duke's tactics and his popular support
(which are not unconnected) is one of the more enriching ironies of contemporary politics. But it also points to the historically aphasic conundrum
in which we live: where the narrative scenario of black disempowerment
following Reconstruction can be eternally renewed as the fear-invoking
context for organizing various levels of white supremacist activity. In this
sense, the image offered by Ralph Ellison in "The Birthmark"—where the
body of that seemingly fictional Willie lies dismembered between white
male legs—occupies a symbolic range quite arresting in its historical diversity. For Bush, in fact, the representation of the black male as sexual threat
functioned as the phantasm of his own phallic potential, providing the
framework for escaping the limitations of corporeality, and thereby making
possible his ascension into the highest position the disembodied abstraction
of citizenry in the United States can offer.

Such a figuration of interracial male contestations has important implications for our understanding of the relationship between race and gender,
necessitating as it does a rearticulation of the assumption, as Mervat Hatem
writes, "that there is an automatic and natural patriarchal alliance among
men (of different classes and cultures) against women."[52] The history of
patriarchal organizations within the African American community—as well
as the definitional relation that reads race through the binary of gender—
points to the specificities of social and economic transformation and therefore cannot be assumed under a transhistorical model of masculine domination. In this regard, the equation of women with sexual difference that often
accompanies feminist theory's interrogations into the meaning of gender
within the social must necessarily be suspended in order to read the multiplicity of ways in which the discourse of a sexual difference has been, and
continues to be, deployed.[53] As the anatomy of lynching demonstrates, it is
precisely through the discourse of a sexual and sexualized difference that
racial hierarchies among men have been historically mediated in U.S.
culture—the threat posed by black men to white masculine hegemony
defined and recuperated by positioning that body as the site where gender
and race converge. In such processes of cultural production, all writing of
the black male body traverses the discursive terrain of race, sex, and gender.

NOTES

1. In focusing on black men in the lynch scenario, I am interested in the overlay of
sexual difference as witnessed in castration as the ultimate denouement of the mob's
violence. Such a focus, however, is not meant to suggest that black women were not
lynched, burned, and summarily mutilated in ways that would also speak to the race/
gender axis. As I will discuss later, the inscription of the black male as rapist, that "nec-

essary" narrativity that propels the white mob to violence, carries an inherent negation of the African American woman through the very absence of her significatory role in the psychosexual drama of masculinity that underwrites the lynching and castration of black men. But while black women may be absent from the cultural narrativity that defines and sanctions lynching, their intellectual and political work against mob violence during the late nineteenth and early twentieth centuries in particular was crucial to African American communal resistance on a broad scale. On this last note, see Hazel Carby, "'On the Threshold of Woman's Era': Lynching, Empire, and Sexuality in Black Feminist Theory," in *"Race," Writing, and Difference*, ed. Henry Louis Gates, Jr. (Chicago, 1986), pp. 301–16. On white women's antilynching struggle, see Jacquelyn Dowd Hall, *Revolt against Chivalry: Jessie Daniel Ames and the Women's Campaign against Lynching* (New York, 1979).

2. Nathaniel Hawthorne, "The Birthmark," in *The Scarlet Letter and Other Tales of the Puritans*, ed. Harry Levin (Boston, 1961), p. 369.

3. Ibid., p. 370.

4. In the final stages of revising this essay for publication, I encountered James R. McGovern's *Anatomy of a Lynching: The Killing of Claude Neal* (Baton Rouge, LA, 1982). While similarly interested in the practice of lynching, McGovern focuses on the specificities of the Neal case and his book is therefore more singularly historical and factual than my discussion here. But I think it significant—and certainly not coincidental—that the concept of anatomy figures centrally in his discussion as well, even as my analysis differs drastically in its deployment of both feminist and poststructuralist theoretical discourses.

5. Ralph Ellison, "The Birthmark," *New Masses* 36 (July 2, 1940), p. 16.

6. See also Judith Fetterley, *The Resisting Reader: A Feminist Approach to American Fiction* (Bloomington, IN, 1978), pp. 22–33, for a discussion of the story's tie to sexual difference.

7. Hawthorne, p. 369.

8. Ibid., p. 370.

9. Ibid., p. 371.

10. Ibid., p. 372.

11. Teresa de Lauretis, *Alice Doesn't: Feminism, Semiotics, Cinema* (Bloomington, IN, 1984), p. 15.

12. Hawthorne, p. 374.

13. Laura Mulvey, "Visual Pleasure and Narrative Cinema," in *Feminism and Film Theory*, ed. Constance Penley (New York, 1988), p. 58.

14. Hawthorne, p. 379.

15. Ibid., p. 386.

16. Ellison, p. 17.

17. William Faulkner, *Light in August* (New York, 1968), p. 147.

18. Ellison, p. 17.

19. On mob violence and the Ku Klux Klan, see National Association for the Advancement of Colored People, *Thirty Years of Lynching in the United States, 1889–1918* (New York, 1919); James E. Cutler, *Lynch-Law: An Investigation into the History of Lynching in the United States* (New York, 1905); Allen W. Trelease, *White terror: The Ku Klux Klan Conspiracy and Southern Reconstruction* (New York, 1971); Joel Williamson, *The Crucible of Race: Black-White Relations in the American South since Emancipation* (New York, 1984); and C. Vann Woodward, *The Strange Career of Jim Crow* (New York, 1957).

20. Ida B. Wells-Barnett, *On Lynchings: Southern Horrors; A Red Record; Mob Rule in New Orleans* (New York, 1969), p. 8. Much like statistics on rape, numerical accounts of lynching vary widely, most obviously because of the way the legal apparatus ignored violent crimes against African Americans. Trudier Harris, *Exorcising Blackness: Historical and Literary Lynching and Burning Rituals* (Bloomington, IN, 1984), for instance, cities 4,951 lynchings in the United States between 1882 and 1927, using figures provided by Cutler, who tends to rely on "official" statistics. Wells-Barnett's figure, on

the other hand, is an estimation that seeks to account for those violent acts not documented within the larger U.S. community. See also Dowd Hall.

21. As I write this in the aftershock of the April 1992 acquittals of the white Los Angeles police officers who beat a black male suspect, Rodney King, unconscious, it is apparent that the figuration of the law Ellison depicts in 1940 continues to function as the disciplinary mechanism for instantiating and perpetuating white supremacy. One might even venture to say that the decline of the lynch mob in the second half of the twentieth century has less to do with real advancements in white supremacy's abatement than with the incorporation of the mob's tenor and function within the legal and law enforcement systems themselves.

22. For discussion of various newspaper accounts of lynching, see Harris, *Exorcising Blackness*, pp. 1–19.

23. Ibid., p. 19.

24. The most famous name change, of course, is Malcolm Little's shift to X. On the significance of naming to the African American literary tradition, see especially Kimberly W. Benston, "I Yam What I Am: The Topos of Un(naming) in Afro-American Literature," in *Black Literature and Literary Theory*, ed. Henry Louis Gates, Jr. (New York, 1984), pp. 151–72; and Michael Cooke, "Naming, Being, and Black Experience," *Yale Review* 68 (1978): 167–86.

25. Eric Foner, *Reconstruction: America's Unfinished Revolution 1863–1877* (New York, 1988), p. 181.

26. Ibid.

27. D. W.Griffith's 1915 *The Birth of a Nation* is perhaps the classic example of the hysterical tie between the African American's social participation and the discourse of the black rapist. Here, in a film that literally transformed the technical achievements of American filmmaking, the glory and order of the Old South are contrasted with the devastation and ruin wrought by the Civil War and its aftermath. The picturesque racial harmony of the slave system gives way to massive black corruption, as the seemingly innate bestiality of the ex-slave wends its way to the surface. As blacks descend into laziness and drunkenness, they seize the polls and disenfranchise white citizens, before finally laying sexual claim to white women. In the film's finale, as Donald Bogle writes, "a group of stalwart, upright white males, wearing sheets and hoods, no less . . . [defend] white womanhood, white honor and white glory . . . restor[ing] to the South everything it has lost, including white supremacy. Thus we have the birth of a nation." See Donald Bogle, *Blacks in American Films and Television* (New York, 1988), p.20; Alan Casty, "The Films of D. W. Griffith: A Style for the Times," *Journal of Popular Film* 1, no. 2 (1972): 67–79; and Michael Rogin, "'The Sword Became a Flashing Vision': D. W. Griffith's *The Birth of a Nation*," *Representings* 9 (1985): 150–95.

28. See Harris, *Exorcising Blackness*, pp. 6–7.

29. Cutler, p. 116.

30. See also Dowd Hall, who writes that "the proportion of lynchings taking place in the South increased from 82% of the total [of execution] in the 1890s to 95% in the 1920s; over the same periods the proportion of lynch victims who were white decreased from 32% to 9%. Lynching had become virtually a Southern phenomenon and a racial one" (p.133).

31. Lauren Berlant, "National Brands/National Body: *Imitation of Life*," in *Comparative American Identities: Race, Sex, and Nationality in the Modern Text*, ed. Hortense Spillers (New York, 1991), p. 112.

32. Ibid., p. 113.

33. Foner, p. 87.

34. Because of this articulation of the public/private split in the postwar years—and its contrast to gendered relations within the slave community—Angela Davis, among others, has argued that "the salient theme emerging from domestic life in the slave quarters is one of sexual equality." See Angela Davis, *Women, Race, and Class* (New York, 1981), p. 18. Michele Wallace, *Black Macho and the Myth of the Superwoman* (New York, 1979), concurs with this, finding that through Emancipation, black men

were encouraged to adopt white patriarchal roles and practices. On the particular impact on black family structure in the transition from slavery to sharecropping, see Susan A. Mann, "Slavery, Sharecropping, and Sexual Inequality," in *Black Women in America: Social Science Perspectives*, ed. Micheline R. Malson, Elisabeth Mudimbe-Boyi, Jean F. O'Barr, and Mary Wyer (Chicago, 1990), pp. 133–58.

35. As Dowd Hall writes, "The ideology of racism reached a virulent crescendo, as the dominant image of blacks in the white mind shifted from inferior child to aggressive and dangerous animal" (p. 133).

36. On the Uncle Tom figure in Harriet Beecher Stowe's novel and its impact on rethinking race and gender in the nineteenth century, see Robyn Wiegman, "Toward a Political Economy of Race and Gender," *Bucknell Review* (Fall 1992).

37. Ben Tillman, "The Black Peril," in *Justice Denied: The Black Man in White America*, ed. William Chace and Peter Collier (New York, 1970), p. 182.

38. Ibid., p. 183.

39. Ibid., p.181, 184.

40. Ibid., p. 185.

41. Harris, *Exorcising Blackness*, p. 19.

42. Ibid.

43. Frantz Fanon, *Black Skin, White Masks* (New York, 1967), p. 165.

44. Paul Hoch, *White Hero, Black Beast: Racism, Sexism, and the Mask of Masculinity* (London, 1979), p. 54.

45. Ibid., p. 55.

46. Ibid.

47. Harris, *Exorcising Blackness*, p. 23.

48. Ibid.

49. Ibid.

50. Eve Kosofsky Sedgwick, *Between Men: English Literature and Male Homosocial Desire* (New York, 1985), p. 76.

51. See Nina Burleigh, "David Duke," Z *Magazine*, December 1991, pp. 47–51.

52. Mervat Hatem, "The Politics of Sexuality and Gender in Segregated Patriarchal Systems: The Case of Eighteenth- and Nineteenth-Century Egypt," *Feminist Studies* 12 (1986): 252.

53. For a more extended discussion of the way in which feminist film theory in particular has confined the meaning of sexual difference to the body of woman, see Robyn Wiegman, "Feminism, the *Boyz*, and Other Matters Regarding the Male," in *Screening the Male: Exploring Masculinities in Hollywood Cinema*, ed. Steven Cohan and Ina Rae Hark (New York, 1992).

EIGHTEEN

The Heroic Appeal of John Henry

BRETT WILLIAMS

Most compelling about John Henry's heroic legacy is its versatility in speaking to the vastly different needs of particular Americans in varied times, places, and life situations. Our sparse knowledge of the details of his life and of the purpose motivating his stand against the steam drill has made him most amenable to flights of creative fancy, as we make of John Henry almost whatever we wish. He has been a hero of several traditions in evolving community contexts: his spirit has been invoked by laborers and by railroad buffs as well as those passionately opposed to the railroad as an institution; he has symbolized evolving black consciousness and the celebration of southern culture. To appreciate John Henry's impact on American culture is to trace his life as hero in these several heroic traditions at the times when he has been appropriate to them. In this chapter, I explore each in turn and finally examine the possibility that he may be a universal hero, whose saga is best understood as a family tragedy. As we shall see, this last possibility may explain why John Henry's most powerful and lasting influence on American society has been through song.

Chapter 1 described the grim working conditions of Big Bend Tunnel, which most people believe to have been the source of the John Henry story. This story emerged as both a ballad whose authorship remains a mystery and in hammer songs, which almost certainly were composed, improvised, or adapted right in Big Bend. All of the earliest fragments of songs in the "Nine-Pound Hammer" complex (except the "Roll on Buddy" phrases) mention John Henry, which indicate that he was integral to the hammer motif from the very beginning.[1]

We can easily imagine why John Henry was a hero to the workers at Big Bend, especially when we recall the nature of their work, the role of music in that work, and the message of the John Henry hammer songs. The men at Big Bend were invisible, unsung laborers, toiling at some of the most grinding, unpleasant, dangerous jobs imaginable. Those who were steel drivers found that singing made that work tolerable by relieving the tedium and helping them find a rhythm by which to pace their strokes. John Henry might have been any one of hundreds of workers who died a gruesome, ugly death at the tunnel and experienced the most casual of burials. To speak of his death was to invite dismissal or harassment; to sing obliquely of him was to comment on both the hardships of the work and one's own determination not to suffer John Henry's fate, "This Nine-Pound Hammer, just a little too heavy for my size, for my size," may not summon up especially vivid images today, but for workers wielding hammers, it may have captured symbolically all that was arduous about their labor. "This old hammer, killed John Henry, But it won't kill me, it won't kill me," similarly invokes the hazards of work, but at the same time comments on an unmentionable death and avows the singers' determination not to suffer the same fate. It is a life affirming refrain in a tunnel filled with death. "Take this hammer, and carry it to the captain, tell him I'm gone, tell him I'm gone," is more fanciful, allowing singers to imagine that they could walk away from their work, leaving the captain to ponder the tool which spoke to the reasons why they would want to do so.

These hammer songs were very close to protest songs, although, like the John Henry ballad, they do not detail the grisly aspects of tunnel life; but they do evoke images that all workers in John Henry's situation could relate to. John Henry, in this community, was a very different hero from the one we think of today. Many of the workers may have been his intimates; some may have seen him die. They sing of him to dramatize their own pain, yet they call on his example as one they have no intention of following. He is much more a martyr than a leader.

Throughout the Reconstruction Era South—indeed, wherever there was rock to be driven—workers employed hammers. Laborers on canals, turnpikes, and dams, in tunnels, quarries, and mines also found music integral to their work; and like the men in Big Bend they shared the imagery evoked by songs of the deadly, heavy hammer. Because many of the black workers were itinerants, they probably carried the hammer songs to many job sites. Archie Green notes that railroad workers would have brought them into the mine, as they laid spurs into the coal-rich Allegheny Mountains or drove track into the mines for coal cars to travel on. In West Virginia, railroading and coal mining were always closely linked; her wealth of coal resources had been a major incentive for the C & O to build there. And the Nine-Pound Hammer songs have been significant pieces of the coal miners' repertoire for many years.[2] As underground workers, they had the most in common with the laborers at Big Bend; that the two sorts of jobs are quite similar is reflected in the fact that tunneling workers were often termed "miners."

However, the hammering motif had an appeal far beyond the tunnels and coal mines as it embodied the fears and hopes of hammering everywhere.

And the songs have endured, sung on chain gangs and in prisons at least into the 1960s, as long as laboring conditions were reminiscent of the primitive manual tasks of the late nineteenth century.

The ballad is more difficult to place in a laboring tradition because we do not know who composed it. It also may have emerged from Big Bend Tunnel, although such scholars as Barry and Cohen argue convincingly for the influence of white mountain narrative tradition.[3] Editors of folksong anthologies frequently classify the ballad as a workingman's song, and folklorists such as Archie Green see it as speaking to the needs of all workers.[4] Its message is quite different from the hammer songs; for in the ballad, as in many fictional accounts which elaborate it, John Henry is a hero to the displaced worker. He takes a stand against a machine which will take away his job and in doing so, he testifies to the ultimate dignity of humanity. In most versions of the ballad, this confrontation is not explicit, however, If the hammer songs comment obliquely on the horrors of underground work, the ballads avoid the issue altogether. Much is left unsaid, and we do not know if workers summon up the same images that popular storytellers and novelists do. Indeed, it is possible to argue, as does Roderick Nash, that the confrontation between man and machine transcends work altogether, that we should more appropriately see John Henry in a long line of folk heroes who, according to the time, controlled, spurned or befriended machines.[5]

But if the John Henry of balladry is problematic, his place in the hammer song tradition is irrefutable. Unlike would-be workers' heroes such as Joe Hill who may never have appealed broadly to those they sought to represent, or others such as Mother Jones whose following was more local and short-lived, John Henry through his life in work song had a universal appeal transcending the particular situation of Big Bend Tunnel. His life as a laborers' hero cannot be separated from his place in the songs which were rooted in communities of workers, guiding them in joining their work and providing relief by "underlining the truth that the individual worker did not suffer an individual fate."[6] Because he lived vividly through the communal process of making music in the workplace, and because he came to stand for the needs and fears of many in circumstances similar to his, John Henry may be our most authentic working people's hero.

Most often scholars and popular collectors have considered "John Henry" a railroad song, and the man a railroad hero. Objectively, this designation may seem inappropriate, as the man we can trace to Big Bend was an underground laborer under contract to a construction chief, rather than to the C & O itself. Hammer songs commemorating him must have carried all over the country by railroad workers, but often these workers performed other kinds of tasks as well, for the hammering theme was appropriate to many different jobs. The ballad barely mentions the railroad, and offers no details on railroading life or work, or John Henry's feelings about the institution. Most often the first stanza simply begins:

When John Henry was a little baby,
　Sittin' on his mama's knee
He said, 'The Big Bend Tunnel
　On the C & O Line
Is gonna be the death of me"

or with words to that effect. The reference is much more casual than in most songs we consider truly railroad songs, such as those celebrating Casey Jones and numerous other fatal wrecks; those praising the great trains such as the Wabash Cannonball or the Orange Blossom Special; others describing railroad work such as "I've Been Workin' on the Railroad," and "Brakeman's Blues"; or even those which summon the railroad as metaphor, including such gospel/blues pieces as "This Train is Bound for Glory." How, then, can we understand John Henry's heroic place in the railroading tradition?

Once again we must return to the period of John Henry's emergence. Today when we bother to think of trains at all, we are most likely to do so nostalgically—it is difficult to remember the passion with which Americans greeted them in the nineteenth century. The railroad was the quintessential machine, embodying, as Leo Marx has noted, all that was best and worst of the Industrial Revolution as it entered the pristine American landscape. The train dramatized the qualities of speed, power, smoke and noise which were to change our lives forever.[7] Railroads unified the continent, imported thousands of immigrants as laborers and homesteaders, revolutionized the distribution of agricultural and manufacturing goods, linked forsaken prairie towns to the economies of growing cities, and imposed on us the constraints of Standard Time. Even before America's first railroad (the Baltimore & Ohio) had begun to lay track, two songs celebrated that feat, hinting at a relationship between railroads and musicians which was to last well into the twentieth century.[8]

Railroad song, disregarding for the moment such big band pieces of the 1940s as "Chattanooga Choo Choo" and nostalgic contemporary works like "City of New Orleans," has stemmed almost exclusively from the black and white musicians of the South. It was first recorded commercially by the country and blues singers of the 1920s and 1930s. Setting their songs to the rhythms of the wheels on the tracks, reproducing with their instruments the sounds of the train (the harmonica as whistle, for example), these musicians captured much of the nineteenth century enthusiasm for railroading in a remarkable repertoire of song.

When we consider the role of railroading in southern small town life, this celebration of trains in southern expressive culture makes sense. While artists and writers saw them as harbingers of the industrial revolution, trains seem to have evoked a variety of other symbols for musicians of the south. They spoke of freedom and mobility, the departure or homecoming of loved ones, and restlessness or a longing to be home. Southern musicians captured, in short, many of the familiar sentiments inspired by riding on the train, awaiting its arrival and hearing it pass. Some pieces, such as the bluegrass band Seldom Scene's recent "On the Railroad Line" speak to all the affection and lore that might surround trains in a small town, as children befriended the regular engineers and laid pennies on the tracks to be miraculously flattened.[9]

But celebratory and friendly as railroad music may seem, this affection for trains if far from the whole story, especially during the years when Big Bend Tunnel was constructed. Popular enthusiasm for railroading may have peaked with the completion of the first transcontinental route in 1869, but in the 1870s many Americans grew to loathe and fear them. These years were the heyday of the great rail barons, who grew wealthy and powerful through often unconscionable acts of corruption and exploitation. Homesteaders had been lured to remote and desolate areas of the country by deceptive advertisements promising them they could grow rich there. Stockholders had lost small fortunes through owners' manipulation of railroad stocks. Farmers felt crushed by the monopolistic weight of railway companies in setting the prices and terms for shipping produce and stock. Finally the railroad workers, laboring long hours under hazardous conditions, with little pay and many arbitrary wage cuts, fueled a populist reaction against the institution which many had welcomed as one which would benefit all Americans.

Except perhaps for Chicago, West Virginia (more than any other place in the country) was a hotbed of antirailroad sentiments. We have seen how, even in tiny Hinton and Talcott, the Chesapeake & Ohio's overbearing presence created in the townspeople conflicting feelings of dependence and resentment. Almost all the residents owed their living to the railroad, but its high-handed politics, lackadaisical safety measures and hasty, shoddy construction of bridges, trestles and tunnels were bound to anger them.[10]

The C & O Railroad had opened up West Virginia's great lumber and coal resources for exploitation, but had behaved rather willfully in doing so. The railroad had swallowed up a number of small local lines in the process of consolidation and had then insisted on the same tax-exempt privileges granted its predecessors. When ordered by the Supreme Court to pay West Virginia several years' worth of back taxes, the railroad declared bankruptcy, dissolved, then reorganized itself—ownership intact—as the C & O *Railway*.[11]

Statewide resentment was evidenced by the popularity of the Grange, often a hotbed of railroad opposition, which organized its first lodge in 1873 and was active throughout the seventies and eighties in lobbying for regulatory legislation and promoting Populist political candidates. Also, our first nationwide strikes were initiated by West Virginia railroad men, angered by a slash in wages and harboring years of hostility due to the hazards encountered on their jobs. Before that time, the railway brotherhoods had been quiescent craft organizations whose main concerns were improved safety precautions and widows' insurance, which indicated how dangerous their work was. Norm Cohen notes that the pages of the early brotherhoods' journals often featured advertisements for artificial limbs (by such companies as the Veteran and Railroad Men's Artificial Limb Manufacturing Company) and "homiletic pieces about the tragic deaths and disfigurements of railroad employees."[12] Engineers and brakemen were more articulate, probably because they were less powerless, than the tunnel workers in voicing grievances about the hazards of their work; and the rapid mobilization of strikers in 1877 and again in 1893 testifies to a hostility toward their employers which transcended the immediate indignity of wage cuts.

Some of these sentiments did emerge in folksong, blatantly in such pieces as R. J. Harrison's "The Anti-Monopoly War Song," which begins: "Lo the car of Juggernaut, lo the ruin it had wrought." A more subtle manifestation of working people's concern was the trend in subjects for folksong: before the 1870s, most had treated the affairs of travelers; but during the 1870s, many of the Irish melodies commemorating construction tasks ("Drill ye Tarriers, Drill," for example) emerged—songs which, unlike the longer-lived hammer songs, were about work rather than to work by. In the 1880s, the many ballads celebrating heroic engineers and brakemen who lost their lives in legendary wrecks began to appear: some of the more familiar of these include: "The Wreck of the Old 97" and "Ben Dewberry's Final Run."[13] In part, this latter type of folksong still reflected an enthusiasm for railroading and in particular, the whole new cast of American heroic characters called forth by the often romanticized drama and danger of railroad work. Yet these songs also realistically reflect the concerns of the engineers and brakemen themselves, who must have known that during these years fatal wrecks actually occurred almost every day.

These legendary engineers lost their lives when their trains flew off the trestle, exploded from too much steam, or like Casey Jones', flew into the back of another train because the overzealous driver hoped to secure his reputation by meeting an approaching deadline. They constituted one of several heroic types inspired by American railroading. It is in this pantheon of heroes that we can best see folk hostility to the institution. The engineers are perhaps the least ambiguous of the lot; most are loyal railroaders, sometimes careless but always dedicated to their work. The songs and stories rarely blame their employers for their deaths which are more likely considered due to individual oversight or excessive enthusiasm for the job. They are true occupational heroes who embrace their work and their destinies. Occasionally, as seems to have been Casey Jones' fate on Tin Pan Alley, they become either comic or pathetic characters whose deaths are absurd; perhaps because they have linked their own egos too closely to the machines which they are supposed to control. Interestingly, all of the occupational heroes we associate with railroading were white, skilled laborers. The only exception is the black sleeping car porter Daddy Joe, who allegedly could make up two berths simultaneously, but seems to be a barely familiar character—even to lifelong sleeping car porters.[14]

Another heroic type is more accurately an antihero: in the outlaws who enjoyed extraordinary popularity, including commemoration in song, we can very clearly see Americans' growing hostility toward the rail barons. Probably the two best known are Jesse James, train robber of the 1870s and Railroad Bill, a black outlaw of the 1890s. Both were almost unfathomably admired, with Railroad Bill in particular transformed, probably mythically, into a sort of Robin Hood because he robbed the rich white railroaders and then shared his booty with poor blacks. The contrast between these outlaws and the loyal engineers seems clear enough and polarizes very well our contrasting sentiments toward railroading in the nineteenth century. John Henry's place in this heroic tradition, however, is quite ambiguous.

His very era probably makes John Henry a railroad hero, for his destiny was linked to the nation-building enterprise capturing the attention of most Americans during those years. That music was integral to the rhythms of railroad work and that itinerant railroad laborers carried his song to the farthest reaches of the country indelibly fixed him as a railroad man. Folk-song collectors probably found trackliners among the most accessible of workers singing at work, and may have been especially likely to term the song a railroad song. But the association has lasted: with the exception of Roark Bradford, every writer who has memorialized John Henry in fiction has portrayed him as a railroad man. Even the wide publicity of Bradford's work did not dislodge John Henry from an institutional role that novelists such as Harold Felton and John Oliver Killens, who recreated a compelling attraction between John Henry and the drama of railroad life, saw as a near sacred association.

Is John Henry an occupational hero like Casey Jones, or do we love him because he protests what railroading has come to mean, as did Railroad Bill? Through hammer songs, workers incorporated him into a medium of discreet and indirect protest but, again, the ballads are unclear. They do not speak to us of railroading, except to link John Henry's destiny to the C & O. I believe that this very ambiguity endears John Henry to both train buffs and those whose passions run the other way. He could be either kind of hero. He could care so much about his job that he would die to preserve it; like Casey Jones perhaps, his sense of self is tied too closely to his occupational prowess. On the other hand, in combating the steam drill he may be battling the machine as an abstraction, epitomized by the trains and the powerful images they evoke in bringing the industrial revolution to life. Or he may be protesting, not industrialization per se, but the railroad magnates' casual disregard for human life — be it a steel driver's whose duties are hazardous, or the worker's whose job is becoming obsolete, and who sees that no one will take responsibility for the problem of his obsolescence. There can be no answer to these questions, nor can we ever explain why John Henry would have wanted to preserve his right to such an unpleasant job as the one he held in Big Bend. It is the sparseness of John Henry's story that allows him to embody each individual's vision of railroading and of humanity.

Does it matter that he was black? Does he have a special heroic place in black culture? To understand John Henry as a hero to black Americans, we must trace the changing contexts of black experience in which heroes emerged.

Those who presented heroic possibilities to slaves were of two very different types. Slaves created a very sacred universe, not to escape the realities of the secular world, but rather to expand it. Through religion, slaves looked to Old Testament precedents which promised confrontation and deliverance in this world, not the next. The heroes celebrated in spirituals were men who took on a more powerful but overbearing authority and defeated it, thus liberating a people chosen by God as special. Old Testament heroes included little David (whose pretechnological victory, notes Lawrence Levine, is reminiscent of John Henry's), Moses and Joshua. Not only does this selection of heroes belie any notion that slaves looked forward to a better life only after death, but it also demonstrates that slaves had not internalized their masters' conception of them as less than human. They identified with the Israelites as a chosen people.[15]

Complementing these more sacred heroes in Afro-American culture under slavery was a more pragmatic figure, commonly referred to as the trickster and manifested in the forms of B'rer Rabbit and the slave John. Both operated in an amoral, arbitrary universe where the weak might defeat the strong through cunning and guile: John steals chickens from his master, when discovered cooking them claims they are possum, and when the master wants to share the possum, discourages him by relating how family members have spit into the pot to make the meat tender. When Wolf and Rabbit court the same woman, Rabbit hints to her that Wolf is only his riding horse. Responding to Wolf's demand that he go to the woman and set the story straight, Rabbit convinces him that he is too ill to travel unless Wolf will carry him on his back. Often the trickster (especially in animal form, for John suffers the real life constraints of slavery) is every bit as ruthless and merciless as his adversary. The trickster's victories can be seen as the victories of the slave; but even more importantly, the climate of the trickster tales recreated the everyday evil of slavery. While the sacred world of slaves helped to explain the present by drawing on the past to promise a better future, the world of the secular heroes offered guidelines to a practical morality for negotiating the senseless world of the plantation.[16]

With freedom Afro-Americans found these heroes increasingly inappropriate, and they turned to others who reflected the marginal, bicultural place of former slaves. In religion, gospel music replaced the old spirituals and Christ grew more important than the heroes of the Old Testament. The trickster, although he lasted many years in oral tradition, won fewer and fewer of his confrontations. As slaves, blacks had had little use for the individualist heroes of white culture—men like Davy Crockett—who grew to heroic, larger than life proportions when faced with a problem which required that they be more than an ordinary man. As free citizens, and in spite of continuing discrimination and segregation, blacks were bound to absorb some of the individualist ethos of mainstream white culture. It is in this climate that John Henry emerged.

Cunning and guile remained important as long as blacks were vulnerable to the greater power of whites, and trickster tales and heroes lasted well into this century. But other kinds of heroes gradually grew more important: slave ancestors who had directly confronted their masters, with much courage and at great personal risk, bad men/bandits who seemed to act out of a kind of nihilistic rage against white society—men like Railroad Bill, Stackolee and John Hardy—and those Levine labels moral hard men, strong self-contained heroes who for the most part acted within the rules of white society, but violated its preordained roles and stereotypes for blacks. Like the heroes of the Old Testament, these heroes met adversity through direct confrontation, but, reflecting the changing experience of black Americans, they operated on a secular level. Levine identifies four who emerged during Reconstruction and through the 1930s: John Henry, Jack Johnson, Shine, and Joe Louis.[17]

Johnson and Louis were verifiably real men, differing from one another in that Johnson's flashier life style and associations with white women were often interpreted as a deliberate flaunting of society's moral code. Louis was a quieter hero and easier for whites to accept as well. Similarly Shine and John Henry, both possibly mythical, differed in that Shine mocked white society by mercilessly swimming away from the Titanic and the remaining passengers who had not heeded his warnings that the ship would sink. What all share is a willingness to stand on their own, to confront the adversary on his own terms, and to demonstrate that individuals can succeed by relying on themselves alone. It is in this pantheon of heroes that some scholars argue John Henry belongs. He had undeniably been a hero to black Americans, who sang of him in the nineteenth century and knew of his prowess at least through the 1920s.[18] John Henry is less a hero to black Americans today, but understanding his contemporary fate requires a brief digression on his place in the evolution of black musical styles.

With freedom, black Americans gradually developed and recognized distinctive sacred and secular styles of music. Although as slaves they had punctuated their work with song, these work songs often incorporated religious themes. The expanded sacred world of slaves was one in which music, as well as other media of oral expression, was crucial to transmitting, sharing and recreating beliefs. But the demise of the sacred world after Emancipation meant that black music reflected more and more the marginal position of blacks in American society, incorporating purely secular themes and concerns.

As we have seen, wherever black laborers worked at tasks which were tedious or required a certain harmony of effort, they sang to relieve the boredom through lyrics which carried them beyond the present time, or to release hostility by graphically, realistically detailing the features of the task at hand. Work songs suffered a long, gradual decline with the changes in American labor wrought by urbanization and mechanization, surviving longest on the railroads and in prison settings.

The music which was to parallel John Henry's heroic career in black culture was the blues. The blues' roots lay in the same work songs which had so appropriately memorialized John Henry for black workers. Both musical styles rely on improvisation, and both are profoundly concerned with the troubles, the thoughts, the sentiments of the singers. The blues was originally a cultural product of rural black musicians of the nineteenth century who, after Emancipation, could travel through the South building a repertoire of song. Unlike work songs, it was refined by men at leisure, and unlike spirituals it became a music of pure self. Realistically portraying the experiences of the individual musician, its message is that a person's problems are significant. Not a music of self pity, blues songs often express pride, philosophical acceptance, even hope. A worldly musical style, blues themes rarely treat higher spiritual values or emotions. Often a song may be a specific response to a specific situation; through singing about that situation the singer appears to have achieved a kind of catharsis.

The blues was rooted in black history to the extent that it treated many of the themes more telegraphically expressed in work songs—problems with work or with women. Although often performed by an individual for an audience, it retained the communal spirit of the spirituals and work songs, in that the audience was generally a participatory one that responded to the singer's lyrics. The music remained communal as well in the musicians' evocation of themes with which the audience could identify; often the catharsis was one in which others shared.

Blues remained important to black historical experiences until the 1950s. The country blues of the Carolinas, Mississippi, and Texas, in which one man accompanied himself with a guitar, was succeeded by the classic blues of the 1920s and 1930s. The classic blues was characterized by female singers backed by piano or sometimes full orchestra, and was in turn succeeded by the even more sophisticated urban blues of Chicago, Memphis, and New York of the 1940s. The blues was integrally linked to the migration of southern blacks to northern cities, and its demise seems to have been an inevitable result of the pressures migrants suffered in urban contexts, as well as the aspirations that grew there. Many blacks came to see it as backward, as overly accommodative, as a tribute to all that was wrong with their lives in the old south. Its decline in popularity among blacks accompanied the civil rights movement, the ideology of soul, the rise of the more urban rhythm and blues style, and the more forthright and urbane soul music.[19]

John Henry's career traces the history of the blues. Because blues music relied so heavily on improvisation, it was not an especially appropriate medium for narrative ballads. The lyrical thread of a blues piece often involves a slow, tortuous opening in which a singer slowly works his way into the song through spoken narratives and fragments of tunes, carefully sets a mood, and then digresses frequently as the song progresses. Thus a blues song often takes on its shape and style in the course of the performance itself. In many situations, especially more relaxed settings in the rural south, a musician found it desirable to stretch out his songs as long as possible. Moreover, the subjective content of the blues makes it an unlikely medium for the celebration of folk heroes. As Paul Oliver puts it:

> Whilst the ballad singer projected on his heroes the successes that he could not believe could be his own, the blues singer considers his won ability to achieve them. The ballad hero of noble proportions had little relevance to modern life but the blues is realistic enough for the singer to declare his successes and failures with equal impartiality. Far from extolling the virtues of the folk hero, the blues singer is so brutally determined to deny them as to be markedly ungenerous toward the achievements of others even of his own race.[20]

Blues singers themselves were often heroes to other blacks, and the very nature of the medium indicates a problematic relationship to John Henry. That he was commemorated by blues singers at all testifies to the fact they shared a place in history: both arose from the turmoil of the industrializing south and the movement of blacks into a secular society in which they were still vulnerable and discriminated against. John Henry's ambiguous act seemed to speak to the hopes and fears of blacks at that time; and the sparseness of the ballad, which does allow for individual interpretation and flexibility, inspired a number of blues singers to include it in their repertoires.

John Henry's demise may also be rooted in the same circumstances which have led to the increasingly unpopularity of blues music among blacks. We know that as late as the 1920s, his was a familiar and respected name among blacks interviewed by Johnson and Chappell in many different parts of the country. Since then we have no evidence; for example, if we look to popular culture we find that he has most often been commemorated there by whites.

Although we cannot say for sure why John Henry became more an embarrassment than a hero to urban blacks, we can speculate that the roots of his decline lie in the dilemma of the urban situation. This situation varies by particular cities, but in those cities where circumstances of work and travel require black residents to interact in an urban milieu, they may find their southern heritage becomes something of a burden.

I base this claim on three years of research in a Washington, D.C., neighborhood, which is becoming increasingly multiethnic, international and multiclass, but whose core of residents are rural blacks from North Carolina. They have created in this neighborhood a community rooted in southern black lore, with a personalistic style much like that one expects to find in a very small town. Intimate, face to face relations characterize the life of the streets, the shops and the taverns; persons cement relationships by sharing the stories, the foods, the whiskeys, and the remedies of the rural South.

Yet this neighborhood, like many others in our cities, cannot exist as a self-contained community, for residents must commute long distances to work, to visit kin and friends, or for shopping and diversion. The urban rhythms are reflected in the life of the community as residents do not rely wholly on the rural south in constructing identities, but must testify to one another that they can successfully negotiate urban situations. In particular, mainstream popular culture intrudes in the worlds of music, fashion, and sports, as residents adopt, modify and ground popular styles to the smalltown southern world of the neighborhood. Traditional southern music has been displaced by popular urban forms such as disco, and those people who do not dress appropriately to the city are often termed "Bamas."[21]

I found this neighborhood a fruitful place to test the John Henry tradition, for in it residents selectively draw on, revise or abandon southern lore in constructing their community. In the neighborhood are almost a dozen men bearing the name "John Henry," most of them coming from families with many members also bearing that name. It seemed a likely place for his story to thrive. However, the very opposite is true. Those men named John Henry have no sense of being named for a hero—as has been true traditionally for black Americans, they feel that they were called after relatives with that name. Their older kin substantiate this feeling. In no case have I found a family in which the hero's story lives.

Interviewing others in the community, I have found only one older man who knows the story.[22] Most are familiar with the name's referent and may, for example, tease a man named "John Henry" by calling him "Steel Drivin' Man." Their knowledge of the tradition seems to go no further, however, with two exceptions: some children have learned the story in the District of Columbia public schools (which self-consciously transmit black history and culture to their students, ninety percent of whom are black), and one man (other than the elderly person just mentioned) knows the story from reading it in a magazine in his doctor's office a year ago. Although his brother is named John Henry, he had no inkling of the legend before then.

Those men named John Henry seem to consider the name a somewhat embarrassing allusion to the old-fashioned South rather than a reference to be proud of. All call themselves "John" in contexts outside the neighborhood, and most sign their names "John H. _____." Like blues music, the name is inappropriate to the urban situation.

Blues musicians today perform for largely white audiences, many of whom appreciate and can afford to celebrate its traditional folk qualities. I believe that in the urban situation, John Henry is experiencing the same fate. A new designer label, "John Henry," can be found today in Washington's finest stores; this is a classy, masculine brand somewhat reminiscent of L. L. Bean. Washington Bullets' basketball forward Mitch Kupchak, who is white, sometimes advertises this designer brand. A representative advertisement reads: "Action men appreciate the body-contoured comfort fit of tall John Henry shirts in *French poplin.* (emphasis is mine). . . . Solids, checks, stripes,

designer collars and the legendary John Henry tall fit . . . 6'10" Mitch
Kupchak . . . The Fashion Forward."[23] The John Henry design seems to sport
the same appeal as much of the back to nature paraphernalia of the last
decade. But the John Henry shirts are a far cry from the world of the Big
Bend Tunnel, and their appeal to fashion-conscious urban men at the same
time that the hero seems to have lost his clout for black men is telling. In
taking a stand against the machine, he also tried to resist an inevitably more
modern life; and he seems to have lost his appeal to those who must testify
that they can cope with it. Stripped of rebellious implications, he has entered the mainstream.

The crux of the matter is that, because of his legendary ambiguities, John
Henry personifies many diverse notions about who blacks are and what kind
of people they should be. We do not know what kind of person he was, but
we do know that certain of his most obvious attributes, his individualism and
his willingness to compete against a machine, seemed to be singularly
appropriate to a particular time and place. He probably could not have been
a hero to blacks before that time, and he has again become inappropriate in
the years since. John Henry is too vulnerable to misinterpretation, as the
various fictional portraits of him (often constructed by white authors) demonstrate. His story is easily twisted so that he symbolizes all the most demean-
ing white stereotypes of black Americans: dumb, brute strength, unrepressed
sexuality, retrograde Uncle Tomism, the comic naiveté of Amos and Andy.
Even the natural man motif, which to many of my informants evokes a still
valued set of characteristics embodying a "man who don't take *no* shit form
nobody," is easily distorted in mainstream culture to represent primitivism.
Thus, as he has moved out of the era which called him forth because it
needed him, and been subjected to both celebration and parody in a century
when his heroic act is ambiguous, John Henry seems to have become a less
potent figure for many black Americans.

The final heroic tradition to claim and memorialize John Henry has been
the expressive culture of the South—in particular, the world of southern
music. He seems to have appealed to southern white musicians almost
immediately for, as Norm Cohen notes, our earliest collected, printed and
recorded versions of the ballad are by whites.

The influence of mountain white narrative tradition on the shape of the
John Henry ballad has been discussed in Chapter 3, so I will recapitulate
only the major points here. In the first place, the very narrative strength of
the John Henry ballad is closer to white tradition; from what we know of the
nineteenth century black folksong, such structured ballads were rare. Further, stanzas from well known Anglo and Scottish ballads frequently intrude
into the John Henry sequence, most noticeable among these being the
"Who's gonna shoe your pretty little foot?" verse from "The Lass of Roch
Royal." We know that white folksingers actually sang the ballad because the
first reported stanzas (those of Bascom, Combs, Perrow and Lomax) came

from white singers. In part, this bias reflects the focus of early collectors who tended to concentrate their efforts among whites. That the ballad was truly a part of white mountain tradition is suggested by Bradley's report from Berea College in 1915.

The first broadside to emerge—that of Blankenship—was printed any-where between 1900 and 1920 and was surely of white authorship. And through the years, white hillbilly and country singers have recorded the ballad frequently, beginning with Fiddlin' John Carson's Okeh disc in 1924 and including hundreds since.[24]

It is easy to see how white singers might have learned the song, for often black and whites in the south lived and worked very closely, the music of each group coming from the sounds of the field, the railyard, the lumber camp and mine, as well as from the repertoires of family and friends and the music broadcast by commercial media. Southern blacks and whites shared a large common stock of folksong, including the ballads of Jesse James, Casey Jones, Railroad Bill, and Frankie and Johnnie, as well as John Henry.[25]

One can argue that a singer might find a ballad aesthetically pleasing without necessarily admiring its hero. Mulcahy argues that the song's sing-able tune and good lively story contribute equally to its phenomenal popu-larity.[26] Singers can make of the story and the man almost what they wish; the ballad is flexible enough to allow for several different emphases. Race is not an issue; the only way one knows from the song that John Henry is black is that he often speaks in dialect. Some of Johnson's and Chappell's informants in the 1920s, in fact, claimed that John Henry was a white man. So it is possible to argue that southern whites have enjoyed the ballad without necessarily honoring its hero as a black man.

On the other hand, one can imagine that he was a most appropriate hero for the late nineteenth century south. John Henry speaks to all the turmoil of industrialization; he captures all the anxieties of the time. The song, like the hero, grew from the meeting of Anglo-American ballad tradition and Afro-American worksongs in a labor-intensive integrated workplace unique to the southern experience. Thus, both speak to the southern cultural renaissance through which blacks and whites responded to a very different set of circum-stances. Perhaps this is why sometimes songs and often stories portray the steam drill salesman as a cool Yankee; the conflict becomes a confrontation between the impersonal North and the more humane South. John Henry speaks to the terrible bitterness dividing the two regions long after the Civil War had ended, and to the special humiliation and populist rage directed against northern capitalists who swallowed up the railroads and industries of the south, and reaped the benefits of her revitalization.

One might have expected John Henry to emerge as a true southern hero during the 1930s, a decade in which many Americans turned to the lore of their own regions as a source of patriotic pride. As far as I can tell, this did not happen.[27] Perhaps race relations were still too raw. However, in the last ten years, with the awakening of the New South, he has become a hero to southerners. In 1972, the Hillsdale-Talcott Ruritan Club erected his statue at the mouth of Big Bend. The grandson of his employer, also named W. R. Johnson, boasts a cast statuette of the hero on his desk at the Johnson Coal Company of Smithers, West Virginia. A 1966 issue of the journal the *Appalachian South* includes an anonymous article hailing John Henry as a hero who protested the same crass materialism "that grinds the poor and lays the mountains of a whole region waste by strip and sugar mining."[28] The author thus invokes John Henry to speak to contemporary concerns about the impact of industrialization. And finally, the John Henry Memorial Foundation's success testifies that John Henry can inspire those of very different ethnic backgrounds. He has at last become a local hero, preserved by nearly a century's worth of song, and celebrated through several additional media today.

These are the heroic traditions which have claimed John Henry: labor lore, the world of railroading, black culture, southern musical expression, and most recently, the New South. He has been appropriate and compelling to each in different ways and eras. Part of John Henry's appeal lies in his versatility at fitting the needs and goals of each; but to account for the phenomenal popularity of the John Henry ballad, American's most beloved folksong and medium through which most of us know John Henry, I believe that we must look beyond particular historical and cultural contexts. We must look to the universal message of the song.

"John Henry" has been transcribed, recorded, performed and rearranged countless times and with remarkable variety, so it may be fruitless to try to analyze its contents. Any attempt to do so will not do justice to its rich and appealing permutations in the hands of individual musicians and editors. With this caveat in mind, we can at least begin by considering what is *not* there. The ballad does not describe railroading or Big Bend Tunnel, it does not detail the conditions of work, it rarely (only once to my knowledge) elaborates on matters of race, and it does not report chronologically on an event. As Cohen notes, it is more like an editorial than a news article—it comments on an episode the listeners presumably already know about.[29] (It would be interesting to know how many listeners really do know the story, and if so, how? I suspect that many do not.)

Norm Coehn classified the ballad's elements as these five:

1. an infantile premonition,
2. preparation for the contest (including the challenge, a financial incentive, John Henry's request for hammers of a specific weight, and the like),
3. the contest itself (usually limited to such information as who stood where, how rapidly each contestant drove, John Henry's comments as the contest proceeded, and praise for John Henry's powerful strokes),
4. the hero's last words, death and burial
5. much editorializing on his woman (the clothes she work, her behavior at his funeral, sometimes her own steel-driving prowess).[30]

This classification seems accurate, but I am most struck by the ballad's fairly consistent frame. We first meet John Henry as a baby, sitting on the knee of either his mother or father or sometimes both, in sequence. As many other scholars have noted, he is a classic hero, born fully conscious of his fate, which he predicts from the lap of his parents and then stoically acts out. Although the middle of the song tells us nearly nothing of his workplace, it devotes a great deal of attention to his personal relationships: his wife or woman, or sometimes several women and his child, usually a son to whom he passes on the tragic burden. Often he addresses his last words to this child, and often he warns the boy that he too will die a steel-driving man. The ballad impresses us with a sense of an heroic legacy.

Thus, John Henry's infancy and death frame the ballad. He predicts his own death, does what he must and passes on the heroic burden to his son. The story is a family tragedy. It explores life and death and human purpose, generational continuity, parents and children, hopes and prophecies. It is this family context that gives John Henry his human dignity and complexity, renders his most profound statement, "A man ain't nothin' but a man," so proud and sad, and makes fictional parodies of him so often offensive. The song is a wonderful reaffirmation of the worth of a human life—a worker's in a workplace which denies it, a black man's in a context reminiscent of slavery, a southerner's during a time of bitter humiliation and drastic change —and, ultimately, of every ordinary person who through dignity and strength of will can be great. The ballad not only praises John Henry's courage and skill, but it also reminds us that the details of his personal life matter. Like all of us, he is a member of a family.

Anyone who has heard the John Henry ballad performed well can perhaps understand why his heroic life has been largely known through song and why, on the other hand, fictional efforts to pin down or elaborate the legend often do not quite work. The power of his appeal lies in the sketchiness of the story. The fluidity of the ballad, as well as the detail which it leaves to our imagination, allows individual musicians to interpret his heroic act in ways most appropriate to the moment. But even more importantly, the song's emphasis on John Henry's ordinary humanity enables the singer to stir us, though we may not be sure why, with profound empathy. That he combines heroic strength and courage with the simplest, commonest human emotions makes John Henry great.

NOTES

1. Norm Cohen, *Long Steel Rail*, pp. 575–76.
2. Archie Green, *Only a Miner*, p. 356.
3. Phillips Barry, "Reviews," pp. 24–26; Norm Cohen, *Long Steel Rail*, p. 70.
4. Archie Green, *Only a Miner*, p. 9.

5. Roderick Nash, "Machines and Americans," p. 104.

6. Lawrence Levine, *Black Culture and Black Consciousness*, p. 214.

7. For extensive discussion of this theme, see Leo Marx's *The Machine in the Garden*.

8. For discussion and texts of the B & O Songs, see Norm Cohen, *Long Steel Rail*, pp. 39–42.

9. See Lee Cooper, "Oral History and the Railroad: Examining Shifting Images of Transportation Technology through Popular Music, 1920–1980," as well as Norm Cohen's *Long Steel Rail* for excellent discussions of railroad songs' themes.

10. James H. Miller, *History of Summers County, West Virginia*, pp. 164, 181, 190.

11. Charles Henry Ambler, *History of West Virginia*, pp. 393, 398, 399; Miller, *History of Summers County*, pp. 175–76.

12. Cohen, *Long Steel Rail*, p. 53.

13. Ibid., pp. 39–55, offers a much expanded discussion of the trends in subjects of railroad songs.

14. Folklorist Jack Santino, who with his colleague Steve Zeitlin is interviewing many former sleeping car porters for a film on the Brotherhood of Sleeping Car Porters, communicated this information to me. Santino briefly discusses John Henry in his "The Folk Heroes of Occupational Groups."

15. Lawrence Levine devotes a whole chapter of his book *Black Culture and Black Consciousness* (pp. 3–55) to the sacred world of black slaves.

16. Again the best most recent discussion of trickster themes is Levine's *Black Culture and Black Consciousness*, pp. 90–133.

17. Ibid., pp. 367–420.

18. For a very different analysis, see Fred Weldon's "Negro Folktale Heroes," where he argues that John Henry, as more than a passive trickster, is unique among black heroes, but is not perceived racially.

19. In this brief discussion of blues music, I have relied heavily on Paul Oliver's *The Meaning of the Blues* and Eileen Southern's *The Music of Black Americans*. Michael Haralambos in *Right On: From Blues to Soul in Black America* convincingly discusses the demise of blues music in the city.

20. Oliver, *Meaning of the Blues*, p. 326.

21. For a more elaborate ethnography of this neighborhood, see Brett Williams, "The South in the City," *Journal of Popular Culture*, 16:2 Winter 1982.

22. See the Appendix for a telling interview with this man.

23. *Washington Post*, 1 November 1979, p. A29.

24. Norm Cohen reproduces Fiddlin' John Carson's text and tune on pp. 61–62 of *Long Steel Rail*.

25. Tony Russell, *Blacks, Whites, and Blues*, pp. 9, 10, 28.

26. Mary Lou Mulcahy, "John Henry," p. 9.

27. Although Bradford's novel and play appeared in the 1930s, as well as several tall tale collections, individual compositions and folksong anthologies, for the most part these were not self-consciously southern works. Nor was there a great surge in John Henry lore as in the 1960s. Of the Federal Writers' Project *American Guides*, dedicated to collecting and preserving local lore, none so much as mentions John Henry.

28. "Folk Heroes and Protest," *Appalachian South*, p. 26.

29. Cohen, *Long Steel Rail*, p. 72.

30. Ibid.

NINETEEN

Stack Lee: The Man, the Music, and the Myth

GEORGE M. EBERHART

The night was clear and the moon was yellow.
And the leaves came tumbling down.

—"Stagger Lee," words and music by
HAROLD LOGAN AND LLOYD PRICE, 1958

This stanza sets the scene for one of the most famous crimes in American
music, the murder of Billy Lyons by

that bad man, oh cruel Stack O' Lee
— "Stack O'Lee Blues,"
Mississippi John Hurt, 1928

. . . or Stacker Lee, or Stagger Lee, or Stagolee, depending on which of the
150 or so versions of the song you are listening to. And, like much of the story
itself, the words are partly true and partly mythical. The night was probably
clear (weather records are nonexistent); the moon, in First Quarter phase,
was only a very light yellow (Blunt; Minnaert 299); and if there were any
trees in the neighborhood their branches would have been bare. For Stack
Lee killed William Lyons in a saloon in downtown St. Louis on Christmas
night, 1895.

About eleven years ago, while examining St. Louis newspapers of the
1890s for another writing project, I discovered an intriguing headline:
"SHOT IN A SALOON. Drinks and Politics Get a Bullet in William Lyons'
Stomach." The murderer was Lee Shelton, "also known to the police as
'Stack' Lee," and subsequently known to jazz, rhythm and blues, and rock
music lovers as Stagger Lee or Stackerlee.

Curiously enough, when I turned to books on popular and folk music for
more details, I learned that the writers were uncertain when and where the
murder took place, and some even suspected that the crime was completely
mythical. Greil Marcus, in the third edition of his much respected cultural
history of rock music, *Mystery Train*, confesses that the origin of "Stagger
Lee remains a mystery," with the murder most frequently alleged to have

taken place in Memphis around the turn of the century (213). (Until 1994 there was even a restaurant in Memphis called "Stacker Lee's" [Koeppel]).

As often happens in human history, a tragically real event had been transformed into a mythical one, and this time there was a musical link tying the murder with the myth. But what made this particular murder so special? Why was it commemorated in a folk song?

Murders were not uncommon in that time and place. In fact, there were six others in St. Louis that same Christmas night. One newspaper editor complained:

> . . . bad as St. Louis is on every holiday, never before in its history did its record show so much crime on a single day as last Christmas. A local paper on Thursday stated: Up to 3 o'clock this morning there were eight violent affrays, a dozen serious cutting and shooting scrapes, two cases of poisoning, which may result in death, one death from delirium tremens. . . .
>
> Of the eight shooting and stabbing assaults, four have already resulted in murder, and of the four other cases, three will almost certainly prove fatal in the next few days. ("The Christmas of a Great City")

After a bit more research, other questions sprang to mind: Who wrote the music and the lyrics? How did the real Lee Shelton come to be an archetype for the "bad" black Stacker Lee who kills wantonly and mercilessly? Why was the incident forgotten? And, most intriguing, why did so many prominent individuals—including ten Missouri senators and representatives, the attorney who secured his conviction, the judge who sentenced him, and ten of the twelve jurors who found him guilty—write letters to the governor of Missouri asking for his release from prison?

In looking for the answers to these questions, I discovered a tale that sheds light on the history of the first postslavery generation of African Americans. It's also a reminder of how the consequences of one simple act can reverberate through the decades in music and myth.

The crime took place in a section of St. Louis then called the "bloody Third District," a predominantly African American neighborhood filled with saloons, small shops, cheap apartments, and music halls (Fig. 1). Many of its inhabitants worked on the Mississippi levee as roustabouts who unloaded bales of tobacco, sacks of wheat, and other goods from packet boats that came upriver from Southern plantations. After a hard day's work they went to saloons to drink, gamble, and talk politics. They were joined by others who worked as servants, day laborers, railroad porters, and teamsters (David 63–64, 71–74; "Snap Shots,"; Reedy, "I Have Often Wondered"). But the District was home to more than common laborers. As Rudi Blesh and Harriet Janis wrote:

> It was on Chestnut and Market Streets that the professional gamblers waxed prosperous; that the madams piled up the gold their girls earned from rich cattlemen, traveling businessmen, and the idle, moneyed local sports. The money got around: the dapper, foppish "macks" or "sweet-back men" in their

Stetson box-back coats, and St. Louis "flat" shoes got their gambling stakes from the girls. (39)

In those days the saloon was not just a place to get a drink—the saloonkeepers provided temporary room and board for roustabouts, and they served as word-of-mouth employment agents, loan brokers, and hosts for a variety of entertainments. Some saloons also became the headquarters for political clubs where both the older folk who were born in slavery and the younger, boisterous, and optimistic set who were born free could discuss their hopes for a better future and a stronger community (David 80–82).

Sometime before 10:00 P.M. on Wednesday, December 25, 1895, two black men approached one of these establishments, Bill Curtis's Elite Club at 11th and Morgan Streets. Their names were William Lyons and Henry Crump, and both were frequent visitors to this saloon, which also served as the headquarters of the Colored 400 Club (Wait, 4, 9; "Snap Shots"; *St. Louis Star Sayings* 29 Dec. 1895, qtd. in David, 186). Lyons mentioned to Crump, "You go in there where those bad niggers is you never get into trouble. I am liable to get into trouble. If you have got anything, give it to me." Crump then loaned Lyons his knife before they went inside (Withrow).

They both had been drinking before they came to Curtis's place, and Lyons was standing at the bar having a beer when another black man named Lee Shelton, whom everyone called "Stack Lee," entered the saloon (Fig. 2). Shelton asked, "Who's treating? and someone pointed toward the group of men around Lyons, who was leaning behind the saloon's heating stove. According to those who knew them, Shelton and Lyons were good friends, and by all accounts they entered into a sociable conversation. The room was crowded with about 25 people, most of them levee workers (Withrow; Wait 4–6, 9–10, 14; "Shot in Curtis' Place").

> Stackerlee and Billy Lyon was gamblin' one nite late
> Stackerlee fell seven, Billy Lyons he cotch eight.
> ("That Bad Man Stackerlee," Sullivan Rock, 1934)

No one knows what they were talking about, but they were probably not gambling. This activity was reserved for the back or upper rooms, and none of the witnesses mentioned it at the inquest ("At Curtis'"; "A Gambler Murdered"). The earliest newspaper accounts mentioned a quarrel over politics ("Shot in a Saloon"; "Shot in Curtis' Place"), and only one, seven months later, stated that they were shooting craps ("Stack Lee's Trial" 14 July).

Something sparked a disagreement, and Shelton and Lyons began to strike each other's hats. George McFaro, a laborer who lived in the neighborhood, testified that neither man looked drunk and it seemed as if they were just goofing around instead of fighting in anger (Wait 14).

> On an alley on a dark and drizzly night,
> Billy Lyons and Stack A Lee had one terrible fight,
> All about that John B. Stetson hat.
> ("Stack A Lee," Bob Dylan, 1993)

William Lyons wore a derby hat; if Stack Lee wore a Stetson hat (as most of the songs insist), all the accounts I have found failed to mention it. The Stetson, created by John B. Stetson in about 1850, was "a large hat with a broad brim for protection from the sun and rain, and it had a high crown" (Bousquet 19). It was certainly favored by well-dressed inhabitants of the district and is one of the commonest motifs of the ballad, becoming well established by 1911 (Odum).

Shelton then grabbed Lyons's derby and broke it. Lyons retaliated by snatching Shelton's hat. Shelton demanded it back at least three times, but Lyons refused, saying that Stack would have to pay him 75 cents for his crushed hat. Shelton said that six bits would buy a whole box of derbies, but he offered to pay for it later. Then Shelton pulled out his gun, a Smith and Wesson .44, and threatened to blow his friend's brains out unless he returned his hat. Lyons told him to go ahead, so Shelton smacked Lyons on the head with his revolver (Wait 2–3, 13–15, 17–18).

Stack Lee might have suspected that Lyons had some kind of weapon, since he warned Lyons to keep away from him. But Lyons stumbled forward and reached into his pocket as if for a knife, once against demanding money and saying, "You cock-eyed son-of-a-bitch, I am going to make you kill me" (Wait 18; Withrow).

By this time the saloon was clearing out quickly. The witnesses known to have been in the saloon at the time of the shooting were Henry Crump, 823 N. 8th St.; Thomas Edward Scott, of Rock Springs, Mo., a bewhiskered fellow tending bar; Frank Boyd, 917 N. 12th St. also tending bar: Leslie Stevenson, a farmer, 1008 Morgan St.; George G. McFaro, 1025 N. 9th St.; Arthur McCoy; Charley Mann; and James Butcher (Wait, Gould's 1895).

Shelton stepped back a pace or two and shot Billy Lyons once in the abdomen. Lyons fell back against the railing of the bar and staggered briefly, still clutching Stack's hat (Wait 18).

> Stackolee shot Billy, shot that poor boy so fast.
> The bullet went through poor Billy and it broke the bartender's glass.
> ("Stackolee," Paul Clayton, 1956)

No evidence exists for the bullet shattering the mirror behind the bar, although the bullet did pass completely through Lyons's body (Nietert). Lyons called for someone to hold him upright, but quickly slumped to the floor and let the hat roll free. "Give me my hat, nigger," Shelton said as he picked up his hat and walked coolly out of the saloon. Henry Crump and Arthur McCoy then took Lyons to a doctor, but not before Crump retrieved his knife from Lyons's pocket (Wait 7–8, 18–19; Withrow).

> [Policeman, a little scared of Stagalee:]
> "Stagalee, O Stagalee, I'm 'restin you just for fun,
> The officer jest wants you to identify your gun."
> ("Stagalee," Ella Scott Fisher, 1910)

Two police officers, Flanigan and Falvey, were sent to arrest Shelton. On the way, they ran into a woman who was carrying a note from Shelton to his girl friend. Suspecting that Shelton was hiding out at his girl's place, a "disreputable resort" at 513 S. Sixth Street in the red light district, they went there and found him in a room on the second floor with his friend Charley Mann, who had been at the saloon earlier. Stack Lee admitted to the shooting and went quietly with the policemen ("At Curtis'," Wait 10–12).

Officer Falvey later went back to the tenement on Sixth Street and retrieved Shelton's Smith and Wesson from the "woman of the house," who had hidden it in a bureau drawer. Falvey noted that "every chamber was full" (Wait 13).

Meanwhile, Lyons was admitted to the City Hospital partially conscious but unable to speak. The attending surgeon discovered that the bullet had gone through Lyons's colon, stomach, and kidney, fracturing a rib and causing severe internal bleeding. A perhaps hasty operation to remove the kidney was performed, but it was too late—William Lyons died at 4:00 A.M. on December 26 ("Sheldon's [*sic*] Victim Dies"; Sutter).

WHO WERE THESE PEOPLE?

Very little is certain about the backgrounds of either Stack Lee or Billy Lyons. As mentioned earlier, most commentators on the ballad in music books or folklore journals have been completely unaware of the true time and place of the murder. John and Alan Lomax, after conducting the world's first field recording of blues music in the deep South for the Library of Congress, thought the incident happened "probably in Memphis some thirty or forty years ago" (93). Francis Davis muses that it "is one of those instances in which it's difficult to say where fact ends and legend begins. You keep running into them in the blues—and only someone with no relish for mystery would have it any other way" (40–41).

Fortunately for music history, a doctoral student at Saint Louis University, the late John Russell David, discovered much of the true story in 1973 when he interviewed an elderly black St. Louisan named Edward A. McKinney. McKinney recalled visiting the St. Louis World's Fair in 1904 and remembered details about people and events in the African American community at the turn of the century. One of the people he remembered was Lee Shelton alias Stack Lee (David 15–16). After that it did not take David very long to track down the newspaper accounts of the murder.

One thing that has confused scholars over the years was the assumption that Lee was Stagolee's last name, not his first. This led some to connect Stack Lee with a famous riverboat captain, Samuel Stacker Lee, who was born in Dover, Tennessee, in 1847. When he was 15 or 16 years old, Lee enlisted as a private in Company A of McDonald's Battalion of the Tennessee Cavalry (Gen. Nathan Bedford Forrest's Old Tennessee Regiment).

Later stories embellished his Civil War adventures (Shields McIlwaine [199–200] has him as a dashing Cavalry captain with a black manservant), but the truth is that Private Samuel Stacker Lee was released from Federal custody at Gainesville, Alabama, on May 11, 1865, after Forrest's surrender.

Shortly afterwards, Lee's father, James Lee, Sr., established a fleet of riverboats called the Lee Line Steamers, which operated out of Memphis. Young Samuel helped with the family business and soon was appointed captain of the Lee Line's steamer *Pat Cleburne* in 1870. At the time of his death in 1890, he was vice president and part owner of the company with his brother, James Lee, Jr. (Buehler, "Stacker Lee").

In 1901, James Lee, Jr., launched a huge, new packet boat named in honor of his brother, the *Stacker Lee*. It was very expensive to build, earning it the nickname *Stack O'Dollars*. Its speed made it the envy of other river captains, who frequently challenged it to a race, but its great size and water displacement led to its downfall. It ran aground once, south of St. Louis near Kimmswick in 1903, and finally sank in 1916 after a similar mishap (Hereford; "Stacker Lee is Aground").

Mary Wheeler connected the two Stacker Lees in *Steamboatin' Days*:

> There seems to be no doubt that a rouster by the name of Stacker Lee really existed, but there are many conflicting stories about his life. Some of the Negroes say that his mother was for many years a chambermaid on the Lee boats; others will tell you that he was born while his mother was a cook on board the *Stacker Lee*. (100–01)

McIlwaine goes so far as to say that Stack Lee the killer was at one time a cabin boy on the Anchor Line based in St. Louis, a "short, black fellow . . . with a bad eye who was celebrated in the ballad, 'Stack-o-Lee,' or in the loose-mouthed, slow-drag version, 'Stagolee'" (200). McIlwaine names no informant for this factoid. On the other hand, remember that just before he was murdered Lyons called Shelton "cock-eyed" (Withrow).

What do we really know about Stack Lee? According to Lee Shelton's death certificate, he was born on March 15, 1865, the son of Nat Shelton. The Missouri State Penitentiary register book indicates that he was born in Texas. In 1897 he weighed 114 pounds and stood 5 feet 7-1/2 inches tall (somewhat on the short side for a legendary folk hero). He had two scars on his right cheek, two others on the back of his head, and one on his left shoulder blade. The index finger of his left hand was stiff. Although the scars and the stiff finger might have come about from a lifetime of fights and scrapes, they may also have been the result of hard labor on the levee. Interestingly enough, the register book also reveals that Shelton's left eye was crossed.

The many versions of the ballad focus primarily on the murder of Lyons, the trial, and Stack in prison, indicating only that one or the other (usually Stack Lee) was a bad man and a bully.

Stagolee was a bully man, an' ev'y body knowed,
When dey seed Stagolee comin', to give Stagolee de road.
O dat man, bad man Stagolee done come.
("Stagolee," in Odum, 1911)

The two bartenders at Curtis's saloon testified at the inquest that Shelton and Lyons visited the bar nearly every day. Frank Boyd, who had been working at the saloon for seven or eight months, had known both of them for 10 years, and Thomas E. Scott, who was helping tend bar in return for a room, had known Shelton "about 20 years or more ever since he a real small boy" (Wait 4, 9).

The only unquestionable entry in the St. Louis city directory is for the year 1887 when "Stack L. Shelton" is listed as a waiter living at the rear of 1314 Morgan Street. The other listings for a Lee Shelton that may refer to Stack are in the directories for 1888, 1892, 1894, 1897, where his occupation is respectively given as a teamster, laborer, driver and bartender (Gould's). Each entry provides a different address, but this would not be unusual for drifters or part-time laborers.

We know Stack's father, Nat or Nathan, was living in St. Louis as late as November 1902 because at that time an attorney had arranged for him to visit his son in the penitentiary:

> Mr. Nat Shelton of this City is going to Jefferson City some time this week for the purpose of seeing his son, Lee Shelton, now confined in the penitentiary, and for whose pardon a petition is now before your Excellency. Mr. Shelton desires to meet you [Governor Dockery], and if possible, give briefly his version of the facts of the case. (Drabelle, 17 Nov. 1902)

There are several Nathan or Nathaniel Sheltons scattered throughout the city directories, but my best estimate of his history is this: He arrived in St. Louis with his wife and son in the late 1870s, perhaps with many other African American "Exodusters" who were fleeing oppressive conditions in the South for the relative freedom of the West and North. In the 1880s he worked steadily as a coachman or teamster or porter for one of the railroad companies. In 1893 he was working as a bartender and by 1895 had saved up enough money to open his own saloon at 714 High Street with a partner, Isador Wagner. Success was short lived, however, and soon he went back to tending bar and railroad work. The last entry I could find in the city directory was for 1910 (Gould's, 1878–1880, 1882–1888, 1890–1891, 1893–1899, 1903–1908, 1910). It's unclear whether or not he outlived his son.

Stack was by all accounts very close to his mother. An early version of the ballad contains the line:

> I think he whispered "Mother," as he went by his home. —

and refers to "Little Lillie Sheldon" in another verse — the only time in the song's long history that Stack Lee's real last name occurs, though misspelled:

Little Lillie Sheldon, when she first heard the news,
She was sittin' on her bedside, just a-lacin' up her shoes. —
Everybody talk about Stackerlee!
("Stackerlee," in *Reedy's Mirror*, 1919)

When Shelton was in the city jail in the spring of 1896 awaiting his trial date, his mother fell ill and he talked the sheriff into granting him a visit. According to the *St. Louis Chronicle*, "two Deputy Sheriffs were sent out with him to see her. Shelton had a large day. He drank as often as he saw fit and spent some hours with his mistress. There was a howl from the press, as a matter of course, and Sheriff Troll punished one of the Deputies" ("Free Again").

Sometime in 1898 or 1899 Mrs. Shelton died. Edward McKinney told John Russell David that

> his mother took him to the funeral of Stack's mother at A.M.E. Zion Church on Morgan Street sometime before 1900. McKinney said that his mother and Stack's mother were both members of that church. He could not, however, recall what Stack's mother's name was, but had been told that she worked on board a Mississippi steamboat before coming to St. Louis. He recalled the funeral as a "thrilling experience" as Stack Lee was brought from Jefferson City for his mother's last rites. (David 174)

The evidence for a connection between Stack Lee and the Mississippi riverboats is intriguing. The nickname "Stack," if not directly linked to Captain Samuel Stacker Lee, is reminiscent of smokestacks and stacks of cotton bales. Even the variant name of "Stagger" Lee might refer to the way the roustabouts walked as they carried huge loads. Two former dockworkers demonstrated to Alan Lomax in 1978 how they used to rock the load to make it lighter: "staggering, playin with it and goin on" (*Land*, 154). Shelton may never have toted a bale in his entire life, but his mother could have given him the nickname based on her experience.

Much less is known about William Lyons's background. According to his death certificate, Lyons was born somewhere in Missouri in 1864. The City Hospital admission statement (mistakenly giving his name as Lee Stoge — in the confusion his name had been mixed up with Shelton's) lists his residence as 1309 Gay Street, his occupation as laborer, and the length of time he had been in St. Louis as eight years (Sutter). The city directories list a number of William Lyonses in the area, but none at that address, which is probably a mistake for 1329 Gay Street where Lyons lived with his step-brother (Gould's, 1880–1895).

The key fact of Lyons's life (and death) is that his sister Elizabeth was married to Henry Bridgewater, a prominent saloonkeeper and apparently a rival of Bill Curtis both commercially and politically. Lyons was buried in the Bridgewater plot in St. Peter's Cemetery.

One of the most vivid images of the Stack Lee ballad is the way in which Billy Lyons begs Stack to spare his life:

"Stagger Lee," cried Billy, "oh please don't take my life.
I got three little children, and a very sickly wife."
("Stagger Lee," Lloyd Price, 1958)

Lyons's death certificate classifies him as single. However, there is a persistent rumor of illegitimate children fathered by this man with such legendary family values.

THE MOB

Crowds jammed the sidewalk, far as you could see,
Tryin' to get a good look at tough Stackalee.

Over the cold, dead body Stackalee did bend,
Then he turned and faced those twelve jury men.

("Stackalee," Onah L. Spencer, 1941)

A revealing incident took place on the Friday after the murder. A mob of about 300 angry blacks gathered outside the coroner's office waiting for Lee Shelton to be taken to the city morgue to be sworn over Lyons's body.

When he appeared, escorted by two policemen, the crowd closed in and threatened to lynch him. The officers used their clubs freely but were nearly overpowered before reinforcements arrived with drawn revolvers. They opened a passageway and led a frightened Stack Lee to the morgue. The crowd grew larger and continued to cry for vengeance. Fearing for his life, Shelton begged the police not to take him back to the office for the inquest. However, a double squad of armed officers managed to get him there safely ("Wanted to Lynch Him"; "Help!").

During the inquest the mob pushed its way into the outside hallway, still making a nuisance of itself. After the coroner's jury returned a verdict of homicide, Coroner Walter J. Wait announced that Shelton would be held in custody pending an indictment on first-degree murder. This seemed to satisfy the crowd, which allowed itself to be dispersed by the police ("Coroner's Inquests"; *St. Louis Star Sayings* 29 Dec. 1895, qtd. in David 186–87).

Newspaper accounts of the episode identified the rowdies as members of the "Henry Bridgewater faction," while Lee Shelton was allied with the Colored 400 Club, a democratic organization that met at Bill Curtis's saloon ("Vendetta"; "Snap Shots"). Bridgewater was one of the wealthiest African Americans in the city, an expert billiards player, and a champion of community causes. It was at his saloon at 1309 Market Street that a club for black Republicans met to discuss social issues (David 75–77).

Understandably upset about the murder of his brother-in-law, Bridgewater did everything he could to ensure that Lee Shelton paid the full penalty for his crime. Even before the inquest he leaked a story to the newspapers and the coroner's office that Lyons had been killed because Stack Lee had sworn to avenge the murder of a friend in Bridgewater's saloon three years earlier.

Charles Wilson was Bridgewater's manager of gambling activities in September 1892 when he was fatally shot by a craps player who accused him of cheating. The gambler, who somehow escaped prosecution, was William Alexander Brown, Billy Lyons's stepbrother, who lived with him at 1329 Gay Street. The newspaper story implicated the 400 Club in the "vendetta" by identifying Shelton as its president ("A Gambler Murdered"; "Vendetta").

The charge was a serious one but, as it seems, groundless. The financial secretary of the 400 Club, J. C. Covington, wrote a letter to the *St. Louis Star Sayings* stating that all the allegations were false:

> . . . it only goes to show that some enemy or enemies of the Four Hundred is striving to place our club in a false light before the public or, perhaps, some festive reporter has drawn greatly upon his imagination and made a startling discovery of a mythical vendetta. . . . The Four Hundred was organized December 6, 1895, for the moral and physical culture of young colored men. We contemplate no acts of violence, and as law-abiding citizens and voters we stand ready and willing to protect the laws of our city, State and the United States. Our order was organized with Mr. Will Richmond as president, Robert Lee as secretary and Mr. Lee [Lee Shelton] as captain. It was asserted that Mr. Lee was president; but that is—as with other statements—utterly false. (*St. Louis Star Sayings* 29 Dec. 1895, qtd. in David 186–87)

The fact that Lyons and Shelton were considered friends also argues against premeditation. However, this charge of vendetta contains a clue to what the two might have been arguing about on the night of the murder. One of the newspaper reports said that the "shooting was an outgrowth of drink and a political argument" ("At Curtis'").

In the years following the Civil War, most African Americans with any political affiliation were Republicans, the party of Lincoln and emancipation. But at the end of Reconstruction in 1877 the Republicans were focusing less on social issues and more on tariffs, trusts, and currency. Some black supporters felt abandoned by the 1890s, when lynchings were frequent and poll taxes and unfair literacy tests prevented many from voting. Those who began to align themselves with the Democratic party as an alternative were seen as irresponsible by Republicans who still hoped their party would return to improving the quality of life for African Americans (Greene, Kremer, and Holland, 105–08).

Lee Shelton was a captain in a Democratic club; one newspaper even identified him as "a negro politician" ("Two Negroes Pardoned"). Another of John Russell David's informants who knew Stack Lee, Addison Burnett, called him a "damned Democrat—a worthless nigger who never did anything for the Negro people" (189). Fifty-three members of the black auxiliary of the white Jefferson Club, a Democratic fraternity that had helped elect Rolla Wells as mayor of St. Louis in 1901, signed a petition to the governor for Stack Lee's pardon in 1902 when more and more blacks were voting as Democrats (Rankin et al.; Wright, 53).

A factional rivalry explains the depth of feeling exhibited by the mob at the inquest. It may also have been one reason why this particular murder was commemorated in song.

THE TRIALS

The day after the inquest a warrant was sworn out against Lee Shelton for first-degree murder. It was issued at the request of the noted defense attorney (and Democrat) Nat Dryden (Fig. 3), who was "anxious to get his man out of the holdover and into jail" (*St. Louis Star Sayings* 29 Dec. 1895, qtd. in David 187; "For Murder"). Somehow in the previous 24 hours Stack or his friends had obtained Dryden's services in his defense.

Nathaniel C. Dryden was a graduate of Amherst College and had been practicing law in Missouri since 1871. He had a reputation both for eloquence in the courtroom and for a drinking habit that earned him a nickname as "the wickedest man in Missouri." He was also known as the attorney who had convicted the first white man ever hanged in Missouri for killing a black (Stewart 117). His associate Charles P. Johnson said of him:

> I think his power as an orator was his faculty of impressing a jury with the sincerity of his opinions, his capacity to accurately state all the facts and circumstances, as established by witnesses, together with his ability to logically connect them with a rational conclusion, which he usually substantiated by a very considerable power of rhetoric and pathetic and emotional appeal. ("The End of a Brilliant Man")

Unfortunately Dryden was also addicted to morphine, a habit that he was trying to quit about this time, along with alcohol. His practice had suffered because of these weaknesses and it was said that he often had to walk from home to his office to conceal from his children that he had no money for carfare. But recently he had regained some of his fame as a junior counsel for the defense in the prominent Arthur Duestrow murder trial ("Nathaniel Craig Dryden Dead"). He was not a bad choice for defending Stack Lee, even though he had just been involved in a bizarre scandal involving an infatuated shopgirl whose unsolicited love note forced Dryden to announce his recent secret second marriage. This caught his four daughters by his first wife by surprise; since they "possessed such a deep reverence for the memory of their departed mother," the girls had never been told ("Fled").

Shelton was bound over to a grand jury on January 3, 1896, by Judge David Murphy, who fixed his bond at $4,000 ("Lee Shelton Bound Over"). On February 12 the grand jury indicted him on a charge of first-degree murder ("Work of the January Grand Jury").

Shelton languished in the city jail until June 25, when he was released on a $3,000 bond guaranteed by a pawnbroker, Morris H. Smit. Attorneys Marshall F. McDonald for the state and Nat Dryden for the defense agreed to a reduced bond, "as the evidence was conflicting." The *St. Louis Chronicle* said that the large figure "caused comment" and alleged that Smit had taken $150 for the risk, which made the transaction seem somewhat shady ("Free Again"; "Shelton at Large"; "'Stack Lee' Gives Bond").

According to some of the ballad versions, Stack Lee's girlfriend raised the bail money by working overtime as a prostitute:

> Stack's gal went out to get some bond money
> For somebody to go his bail,
> She said, "There ain't a trick in this world that I wouldn't turn
> To get my Stack out of jail."
>   Oh, how she loved her Stack O'Lee.
> ("Stack O'Lee Blues," Cliff Edwards, 1928)

Recall that after the murder Stack Lee was found in a "disreputable resort" where his girlfriend worked, so it is possible that there is some truth to the matter. On the other hand, there may have been enough political support by the 400 Club to raise the money over a period of nearly seven months. The verse quoted above might have been written to show that Shelton was just a bad man who could only get out of jail through ill-gotten gains.

On Monday, July 13, 1896, Judge Thomas B. Harvey empaneled a jury in the Second Division of Criminal Court to try the case of the *State v Lee Shelton, alias Stack Lee*. Dryden was the defense attorney, and McDonald was engaged as special counsel for the state to assist C. Orrick Bishop, the assistant circuit attorney. Two days later, the trial began ("Stack Lee's Trial" 14 July).

The questioning of witnesses and the arguments by the state and the defense were completed by Friday afternoon. No trial transcripts appear to have survived, so we have no idea what logic or persuasive speeches Nat Dryden used. Judge Harvey spent 15 minutes instructing the jury that he expected them to return one of the following verdicts: murder in the first degree, murder in the second degree, manslaughter in the fourth degree, or acquittal ("'Stack' Lee Jury Out"). Morris Smit withdrew his bond while the jury deliberated and Shelton was forced to spend the night in jail ("Free Again").

The jury returned to the court at noon on Saturday and told Judge Harvey they could not agree on a verdict. Their last ballot stood at seven for murder in the second degree, two for manslaughter, and three for acquittal. It was said that Dryden had no hope of securing an acquittal, but was pleased with getting a hung jury. The jury was discharged and the judge scheduled the case for a retrial ("Shelton Jury Failed to Agree"; "Jury Couldn't Agree").

An early version of the song contained the following verse:

> Next Monday morning preliminary was tried —
> Don't be afraid, Stack, Nat Dryden's by your side.
> ("The Ballad of Stacker Lee," in *Reedy's Mirror*, 1919)

Shelton was again released from jail on July 20 after arranging with friends for Smit to resume the bond ("Free Again"). While waiting for his second trial he worked as a bartender and possibly managed a bar named the Modern Horseshoe Club (Gould's, 1897; "Two Negroes Pardoned").

Stack Lee's future definitely took a turn for the worse on August 25 when Nat Dryden died. He had admitted himself to the hospital a day earlier after first telling a friend that he was dying, this time for certain. His recent drinking bouts had worsened his rheumatism so that he occasionally had to use crutches, and his kidneys and heart were finally affected. He passed away at the age of 46 shortly before his doctors were to consult on a course of treatment. Lee Shelton's was the last murder case he tried ("Nathaniel Craig Dryden Dead"; "The End of a Brilliant Man").

On May 11, 1897, Shelton was again placed on trial, this time in St. Louis Circuit Court with Judge James E. Withrow (Fig. 4) presiding. Withrow was a three-year veteran of the Civil War and had fought with his Illinois regiment on many Southern battlefields, including Sherman's March to the Sea. He was admitted to the Missouri bar in 1868 and had served as circuit judge since 1888. The *Centennial History of Missouri* remarked that he was known for his "patient investigation of causes, his painstaking research, his fairness and courtesy" ("James Edgar Withrow").

Taking Nat Dryden's place for the defense was his friend and associate in the Duestrow case, Charles P. Johnson (Fig. 5), who was known as "Governor" Johnson since he had served as Lieutenant-Governor of Missouri in the 1870s. In 1862, as a member of the Missouri legislature, he had endorsed a bill that called for a state convention to consider unconditional and immediate emancipation (Stevens 3: 776).

Another prominent attorney was retained by Henry Bridgewater to serve as special counsel for the prosecution. C. Orrick Bishop (Fig. 6) had been the assistant circuit attorney at Stack Lee's first trial ("Lee Shelton's Second Trial"). The jurors' names in this trial are known: Andrew J. Bromwell, jury foreman, 2321 Albion Place, contracting agent for the B&O Southwestern Railway; Edgar M. Carr, 3012 Laclede Ave., a clerk at Drummond Tobacco Co.; Joseph Eike, 4124 Louisiana Ave., a carpenter; Oscar J. Goehner; Neal W. Hulser, 4144 Green Leaf Place, a janitor; Alexander J. Isch, 3813 Hartford, secretary and manager of the St. Louis Fuel Co.; Harry A. Kauffman, 4226–1/2 Easton Ave., a clerk at Samuel Cupples W.W. Co.; William Kirsch, 2557 Benton, a woodworker; Henry G. Manne; William G. Rust; Frederick E. Saettele, 4428 N. 2d, a clerk at Broderick & Bascom Rope Co.; John Siebke, 421 S. Garrison Ave., a painter.

One incident that occurred at noon during the trial on May 12 was given detailed treatment in the press. Bishop called Henry Crump, who had accompanied Lyons to the saloon on the night of the murder, as a witness for the prosecution. When Crump began to testify that Lyons had a knife with him and had drawn it just before Shelton shot him, Bishop jumped from his

seat. He interrupted Crump, saying that this conflicted with a signed statement Crump had made shortly after the murder when he had been interrogated by himself and William Zachritz, the circuit attorney at that time.
Governor Johnson objected to this, and Judge Withrow sent the jury from
the room while opposing counsel argued their points.

Bishop said that the prosecution had a perfect right to expect that a witness
would testify the same at the trial as at the examination. He was entrapped by
his own witness and he wanted to impeach him with his signed statement.

Johnson would have none of that line of reasoning. "The statement
should have no standing in any court," he said. "It was not made under oath.
The statement merely says the witness knows nothing about the case, and
counsel for the State has no right to plead surprise. The Circuit Attorney has
no right to take a man in his private office and obtain a written statement to
flaunt in his face, in case his testimony should vary at the trial. The witness
has a perfect right to say he knows nothing and he need not tell the truth, for
he's not under oath." Judge Withrow commented that if that were true,
morals were at a pretty low ebb.

Johnson then took his argument one step further, perhaps one step too far:
"We are not arguing morals," he said. "When it is possible for sneaking
detectives to pry around and obtain statements by fraud it is time for men to
be careful." He said this very angrily, at the same time folding a newspaper
tightly and shaking it in Bishop's face.

Bishop again jumped from his seat and advanced toward Johnson with
reddening face and clenched hands, bellowing, "What do you mean by your
insulting insinuation? Do you refer to myself or Judge Zachritz?" Johnson
replied that he was referring to detectives, not lawyers: "There is a sneaking,
cowardly way of 'sweating' or examining prisoners and witnesses outside of
courts. It is this system that I am complaining about."

Bishop retorted, "But it was Mr. Zachritz and myself who obtained the
statement, and not detectives. Your insinuation is a dishonorable one and
shows that you are diffident in manhood." He raised his arm and let it fall
with a loud smack on Johnson's arm. Several spectators rose to their feet and
a deputy sheriff called for silence. Johnson wheeled around and grabbed
Bishop by the wrist, saying: "There was nothing personal in my remark, but
if you are looking for a personal encounter, I will give it to you."

They stood glaring at each other for a full minute, then began to address
the court simultaneously, Johnson gesticulating constantly with his right
arm. "Governor," Bishop said, placing his hand on Johnson's arm, "keep
quiet a minute, please, I am addressing the court."

The sheriff, expecting a fistfight, moved toward the attorneys, but Judge
Withrow had heard enough. He called for order, overruled Johnson's objection, and spoke sternly to the defense attorney, advising him that "a man
should tell the truth under any circumstances." Henry Crump was not
allowed to testify any further ("Lawyers Try to Fight in Court"; "Came to
Blows"; "Lawyers Became Excited").

Arguments concluded the next day at 1:00 P.M. After two hours and three votes, the jury returned a verdict of murder in the second degree (Carr). The verdict was a compromise in consideration of Crump's conflicting testimony. The court set the punishment at 25 years in the Missouri State Penitentiary at Jefferson City. Johnson declared his intention to move for a new trial, but this motion was apparently never made or was perhaps denied ("Lee Shelton Gets Twenty-Five Years").

Stack Lee's future was sealed.

IN PRISON

Now the trial's come to an end, how the folks gave cheers;
Bad Stackalee was sent down to Jefferson pen for seventy-five years.

("Stackalee," Onah L. Spencer, 1941)

The Missouri State Penitentiary became Shelton's new home on October 7, 1897. At that time it was the largest institution of its kind in the United States and housed some 2,000 prisoners. At a cost of 11 cents per day per inmate, it was also the most efficient, especially as it allowed companies to set up small factories within its walls and charged them 50 cents per day per man to use convict labor for making shoes, clothing, twine, and other goods (Stout 20–21). At some point Shelton worked for the A. Preismeyer Shoe Company to earn some good behavior points (Guenther et al.)

Prison life was made harsher by the punishments inflicted in those days on inmates who broke the rules. Floggings with a steel-tipped leather strap were still administered (even though they had been officially abolished by Warden James L. Pace in 1894 [Stout 43]), and Stack was the recipient on three occasions: Five stripes for loafing in the yard (March 9, 1899), eight stripes for shooting craps (June 14, 1899), and ten stripes for stealing ham from the kitchen (July 16, 1902). On September 3, 1905, he was put in solidarity confinement for being out of his cell and crap shooting at night (Shelton, Description of Convict).

The state penitentiary had a long-standing practice of recommending for pardon two model convicts, one black and one white, every Fourth of July and Christmas. According to Stout, "the Governor himself would walk up to the men and present the precious documents granting clemency. The other convicts would stand and cheer the lucky two, and perhaps lament that they had not been chosen" (21).

Beginning in 1899 a very unusual series of petitions and requests for pardon or parole were sent to the Missouri governor's office on behalf of Lee Shelton. The first two sets of petitions went to Governor Lon V. Stephens, claiming

that the said Lee Shelton only acted in the fear of his own life, having come in contact with one William Lyons who was considered a dangerous man by all who knew him; that the said Lee Shelton has been sufficiently punished already. (Charles P. Johnson et al.)

One was signed by 139 residents of downtown and midtown St. Louis who were concerned for Stack's welfare. Some very interesting signatures are on this document: Thomas Turpin, well-known ragtime pianist, composer, and theater-owner; George N. Vashon, the first black graduate of Oberlin College and a noted jurist; his son, John B. Vashon, a teacher and principal in the St. Louis public schools; James Butcher, who was in the saloon at the time of the murder; Jim Ray, another wealthy saloonkeeper with a gun-slinging reputation; and C. C. Rankin, Jeff Covington, and Robert Lee, of the Colored 400 Club (Otey et al.).

The other petition was signed by 29 prominent citizens, among them Charles P. Johnson (Shelton's lawyer at the second trial), and attorneys James R. Claiborne and Robert H. Merryman. Most surprisingly, this petition was signed by ten of the twelve jurors at Shelton's second trial, with only Alexander Isch and Harry Kauffman absent. The jurors' names were bracketed to make sure that Governor Stephens took notice (Charles P. Johnson et al).

A letter to the governor from the jury foreman, Andrew J. Bromwell, dated November 25, 1899, was very revealing:

> I never have believed the verdict a just one, — did not think so at the time, and still of the opinion that a verdict of acquittal should have been given instead. Lyons the man who was killed was proven to be a very bad negro and was going at Shelton with his hand in his pockets in a threatening manner when the shot was fired. The charge was murder in the first degree. Some of the jury were for acquittal, others for conviction and the punishment for twenty five years was a compromise and never would have been agreed to except for the fact that I was suffering from a chronic case of eczema and simply could not hold out. I firmly believe that Shelton was fully justified for shooting Lyons under the circumstances, and it has been a question in my mind ever since the trial as to whether Lyons died from the effects of the shot, or from the operation by unskilled surgeons at the hospital. (Bromwell)

If the Shelton case were to be tried in 1997 instead of 1897, it would have mistrial written all over it. Suppression of relevant testimony, allegations of malpractice, political motivations for conviction, a juror who should have been excused for medical reasons — if the defendant had been a white man, the outcome would certainly have been different.

News of the petitions must have enraged Henry Bridgewater and his family. On December 21, 1899, his wife, Elizabeth (Billy Lyons's sister), wrote a letter to Governor Stephens begging him to ignore the petitions:

> I am the sister of William Lyons who was so brutally murdered by Lee Shelton, alias Stack Lee, and having heard that steps have been taken to have him pardoned . . . hope and pray that you will never agree to let a man who never worked a day or earned an honest dollar be turned out to meet us face to face.

As far as his character is concerned ask any old officer on the police force from Captain down to patrolman. Again as a sister I beg you not to turn a man like him on the community at large. If justice had been done he would have been hung. Just think he has not served half his term. (Bridgewater and Brown, 21 Dec. 1899)

The letter was also signed by Lyons's mother, Maria Brown. Governor Stephens did not grant Shelton a pardon. Elizabeth and Maria sent a nearly identical letter to Governor Alexander Dockery in 1901 when they heard that other requests for a pardon were in the works, and added:

. . . I have heard that the Warden of the Penitentiary is interceding in his behalf. . . . My brother had nothing to protect himself with, and this man shot him in cold blood. During Gov. Stephens' [*sic*] term they attempted to have him pardoned but I wrote to the Gov. and he refused to grant his pardon. (Bridgewater and Brown, 4 June 1901)

An impressive appeal was written by Judge Withrow on June 19, 1901 (Fig. 7). He presented Henry Crump's testimony that Lyons had a knife:

. . . The testimony of this witness (Crump) was in conflict (in some particulars) with a former voluntary statement made by him in the Circuit Attorney's Office, which was afterwards written out and signed by Crump. . . .

Having recently reviewed most of the evidence of the leading witnesses for the State, I am impressed with the fact that the punishment assessed by the jury was quite as severe as it should have been, under the circumstances. Lee Shelton has been incarcerated in the jail or penitentiary about six years for this offense. . . .

Under the circumstances I most respectfully join with numerous others, in recommending at least a commutation of his sentence.

It seems to me that an actual imprisonment of seven or eight years in this case would satisfy the ends of justice. (Withrow)

It's interesting to note that in the Stagger Lee myth, the judge has been transformed into a Judge Dread character who sternly hands out multiple sentences of 100 years—hardly the image of the conscientious Judge Withrow.

In November 1901 Governor Dockery also received a petition signed by ten Missouri senators and representatives on Shelton's behalf. The list included John P. Collins, State Senator, 31st District; William J. Schoenbach, State Senator, 33rd District; and John W. Drabelle, State Representative, 32nd District. The petition claimed that Shelton acted in self-defense and that Lyons was a "desperate character" (Collins et al). John W. Drabelle was the attorney who had coordinated the earlier petitions, and in 1902 he sent two letters to Governor Dockery, one repeating Judge Withrow's plea for clemency, and the other requesting that the governor meet with Nat Shelton, Stack's father (Drabelle, 24 June, 17 Nov. 1902).

In December 1902, 53 members of the Negro Jefferson Club, a revival of the 400 Club organized by Ed Butler, St. Louis's controversial Democratic ward boss and blacksmith, sent a petition. The names included Bill Curtis (the owner of the saloon), C. C. Rankin (president), George B. Jones (secretary), J. S. Shaffner (treasurer), William H. Field (African American political leader), and Ed Butler himself (Rankin, et al.).

Additional pleas for clemency were sent to Dockery and his successor, Governor Joseph Folk. Henry Bridgewater had died in April 1904 and his wife had ceased her lobbying (Bridgewater and Maguire), so there were no arguments countering the pleas.

One of the most revealing appeals was that written by James L. Dawson, the city jailer of St. Louis, on December 28, 1905. Dawson claimed that Lyons, not Shelton, was the bully, and unknowingly took up Elizabeth's Bridgewater's challenge to "ask any old officer on the police force" about Stack Lee:

> I wish to state that I served many years in this city on the police force in the locality where this crime was committed and know Lee and Lyons very well indeed as well as very many of their associates and friends.
>
> The locality in which Lee and Lyons lived and were most generally to be found was between Franklin and Washington Aves. and between 8th and 15th St. and at the time of the commission of this crime it was by no means a desirable location for even half decent people to live in and was the hang out of a low order of bawds, colored and white, also many crap shooters. Lee and Lyons both being well known and well recognized members by reason of their attention and activity in that very doubtful avocation.
>
> Their ivironments [sic] and avocation was bad indeed and their morals if possible were worse.
>
> The principal and only difference between the two men was in their temper and disposition to fight. If I recall correctly from memory Lee was no fighter while Lyons when not under the influence of liquor was very quiet indeed and at the time I believe he was related by marriage to Henry Bridgewater [sic], a prominent colored saloon keeper of some influence (now deceased) who was active in the prosecution of Lee for the crime.
>
> Lyons when under the influence of liquor which occurred occasionally was quarrelsome and at times dangerous. I recall a case which came under my observation a few years before this crime was committed.
>
> Wm. Curtis, col., at that time was and is still in the saloon business in this city. At the time referred to Curtis was proprietor of a colored saloon at no. 813 Morgan St. (on my beat). Curtis and Lyons who was under the influence of liquor at the time became engaged in a fight. Lyons had a long knife blade very sharp on *both* edges and tightly wound rags for a handle. With this he drove every one from the saloon except the proprietor Curtis who took refuge from Lyons behind a billiard table which stood in the center of the floor of a room in the rear of the bar room. As I entered the room I seized Lyons by the throat and with the assistance of Curtis I disarmed him and arrested him, having gained the pavement in front. I was obliged by reason of his violence to place the handle of the knife in my teeth and brought him to the Station three blocks distant, finally throwing him to the floor of the then Captain's (Kerrbler) office in the Station. Finally I wish to state that under the circumstance my first wish is that you may know as nearly as possible what type of men Lee and Lyons were. . . . (Dawson)

Another petition to Governor Folk was sent on June 6, 1906, by an African American attorney, R. J. Raymond, who had seen the governor in person the previous winter:

> The fight which resulted in the killing was a bar room brawl, and though I shall not attempt to justify the killing, I will say that Shelton then bore a pretty hard name, and the dead man though a hard character himself was of respectable family who had means. They employed special counsel to prosecute [C. Orrick Bishop] and have fought against any executive clemency ever since. I mentioned this fact to elicit your sympathy for this poor fellow who since his incarceration has been a model prisoner.

Raymond probably was not aware of Stack's transgressions in prison (Shelton, Description). Ironically, this letter was written just two months after the San Francisco earthquake, which the mythical Stackalee was said to have generated because a San Francisco bartender was slow in serving him a drink (Burt 202).

Meanwhile, back in prison Stack Lee had contracted tuberculosis in April 1909 (Hadley, 24 Nov. 1909). A letter to the new governor, Herbert S. Hadley, from the African American political leader William H. Field offered to get Shelton a job in the railroad yards where his health might benefit from being outside (Fields, 17 June 1909). Hadley also had received a recommendation from the prison contractors for whom Stack had worked (the Preismeyer Shoe Co.), who mentioned occasions when he had helped prison authorities "in detecting systematic theft" (Hadley, 24 Nov. 1909).

The last person to contact Governor Hadley about a pardon was partially repentant C. Orrick Bishop, who wrote that he had lost all track of the Bridgewater family who had employed him for the second trial and confessed that he would have been satisfied with a verdict of 10 years, not 25. He had recently visited Stack in prison, and "he impressed me pleasantly" (Bishop).

On November 25, Thanksgiving Day, 1909, after reviewing his file, Governor Hadley granted Lee Shelton a parole. The stipulation was that he break no further laws and go to work "at some honorable employment" (Hadley, 24 Nov. 1909).

Whether Stack went to work in the railroad yards is not known. The next time he made an appearance was on January 26, 1911, when he was arrested for robbery. He had broken into the home of Louis Akins at 4449 Lucky Street, beating him on the head with a revolver and breaking his skull. All he got was a meager $140 ("Two Negroes Pardoned").

This time there was no powerful Democratic organization to back him up and no excuse for his violence. On March 17 he was brought to court to answer a charge of robbery. Since this was a parole violation, there was no trial and he returned to the state penitentiary on May 7 to complete his original sentence.

But by January 1912 Shelton was in the last stages of tuberculosis. The prison physician, A. H. Myerdick, wrote that he "is getting pretty low and I fear he cannot live much longer. Is bed-fast practically all the time now, and extremely emaciated. Is in the last stages, one lung is solid and useless." His weight was down to 102 and he had lost 20 pounds in the previous six months.

Once again, in February 1912, Governor Hadley granted Shelton a parole, this time based solely on his terminal condition (Hadley, 8 Feb. 1912). Upon his return to St. Louis he was to report to his friend James D. Anderson, a junk dealer living at 104 Moore St. (Denton).

Shelton never left the prison hospital. He died at 4:35 A.M. on March 11, 1912, and was buried the following week in Greenwood Memorial Cemetery in St. Louis. No notice of death appeared in the St. Louis newspapers.

One odd fact is that Shelton's death certificate indicates he was married at the time of his death. This is either a mistake or else he got married while on parole, since he went to prison single in 1897.

To sum up, the evidence is overwhelming that Lee Shelton acted in self-defense and, because of the considerable influence wielded by Henry Bridgewater (and the altercation in the courtroom), this evidence was thrown out of court. The reasons for Bridgewater's antagonism were both personal and political: the dead Billy Lyons was his brother-in-law, and his killer Lee Shelton was a Democrat, a political adversary who seemed to be in conflict with the general well-being of African Americans in St. Louis and the United States at large.

While Lee Shelton was in prison, the "Stackolee" ballad was sung in St. Louis, up and down the Mississippi River, and throughout the South. One unexplored area is how this song came about and what effect it had on Stack Lee's trial and popular opinion.

THE MUSIC

The ballad that commemorated Stack's deed probably originated in St. Louis in 1896 or 1897. (A discography is given in Appendix A; for three examples of the ballad, see Appendix B.) Lee Shelton himself must have heard it, perhaps in the City Jail, or after he was released on bond. Charles Haffer, Jr., a levee-camp worker in the late 1890s, remembered singing it then, along with "Casey Jones," "Frankie and Albert," and "Bill Bailey." Will Stark, a sawmill worker and balladeer interviewed by Alan Lomax in the 1940s, first heard it in 1897 from a man who had learned it in the labor camps near St. Louis (interviews in Archive of Folk Song, qtd. by Levine 413; Lomax, Land, 202–03, 495). The ballad was popular throughout the South in the first decade of the 20th century, and by 1911 (the year before Stack died) two versions of it had been collected as an African American folk song by Howard Odum. Another early version was sent to John Lomax on February 9, 1910, by Miss Ella Scott Fisher, of San Angelo, Texas (Lomax and Lomax 93–96).

It seems likely that the lyrics were first written in the summer of 1896, shortly before or after the first trial. The ballad is fairly accurate up to that point, but no versions that I am aware of speak of two trials, conflicting evidence, conviction of second-degree murder, or parole. Only two versions accurately mention participants in the first trial, Nat Dryden (W.D.M.), and Judge Murphy (Robert Gordon papers, U of Oregon, 1927, qtd. by David 281–82). The latter is interesting because it confuses Judge David Murphy, who bound Shelton over to a grand jury, with Judge Thomas B. Harvey, who actually heard the case.

One possible candidate for the original lyricist is some unknown song-writer who was a member of the Henry Bridgewater faction. The verses almost unfailingly portray Stack Lee as a bad man who mercilessly cut down an innocent victim. The words seem designed to sway popular opinion and ensure Lee Shelton's conviction at a second trial:

Stagolee was a bully man, an' ev'y body knowed,
When dey seed Stagolee comin', to give Stagolee de road,
O dat man, bad man, Stagolee done come.
(Odum)

Stack O'Lee's on the warpath, and you better run,
'Cause Stack O'Lee is a bad man and he'll kill you just for fun.
He was my man, but he done you wrong.
(Ma Rainey version, 1927)

Stackolee was on the gallows, he got mad and cussed,
The judge said, "Maybe we better hang him fo' he kills one of us."
   Oh that bad Stackolee.
(Lomax, *Land*, 203)

On the other hand, there may have been a competing version of the ballad that favored Lee Shelton. A handful of verses in some of the earliest versions are sympathetic to Stack Lee:

Stack-o-lee was a good man,
One every body did love,
Everybody swore by Stack,
Just like the lovin' stars above.
Oh, that Stack—That Stack-o-lee.
(David 282)

It was in St. Louis on Pine Street,
That's exactly where it was at,
Stack up and shot himself a competin' colored man
On account of a dirty old Stetson hat.
And from then on they called him Hard Luck Stack O'Lee.
(Cliff Edwards version, 1928)

Stagolee cried to de jury an' to de judge: Please don't take my life,
I have only three little children an' one little lovin' wife,

> O dat man, bad man, Stagolee done come.
> (Odum)

Note in the last stanza that the words normally attributed to Billy Lyons when he is about to be killed are spoken by Stack Lee during his trial.

One individual who may have had something to do with the music was Bill Dooley, an African American lyricist with a knack for writing catchy tunes who flourished in St. Louis during the 1890s. Nathan Young was convinced that Dooley was responsible for the words to "Frankie and Johnnie." However, Dooley was content merely to sell his composition for ten cents a copy on the street, and his history died with him in Detroit in 1932 (*St. Louis Post-Dispatch* 17–18 Feb. 1942, qtd. in David 228).

The "Stackolee" music most probably originated as a ragtime composition. St. Louis in the 1890s was the center of a syncopated sound, even before the first ragtime sheet music appeared in 1897. Though ragtime's origins are both obscure and controversial (rag piano music may go all the way back to 1870s Philadelphia), St. Louis offered an ideal location for the fusion of African American song and dance with German American piano composition and marches that became ragtime (Berlin, *Ragtime*, 5–31; Jansen and Tichenor 1–27; David 260–70; Southern Young, *Guest*, 98–145).

The heart of St. Louis's popular song performances was the famous music hall and bordello at 212 S. Sixth Street, the Castle Club, run by Babe Conners (Fig. 8). It was the city's hottest night club and it periodically outraged the sensibilities of moralists like William Marion Reedy:

> The mohogany[sic]-colored proprietress and her coterie of saffron-hued cyprians make night hideous in their revels, and in the broad glare of the day display themselves at the windows of the three story mansion, known as Babe Connor's; and when the Southern Railway cars are taking their loads of working girls down town in the evening they must pass this brazen bagnio, with half-clad prostitutes displaying themselves at the open windows. (Reedy "There Is")

But the Castle Club played an important and now little-remembered role in the history of American music. As an obituary writer put it:

> Probably half of St. Louis knew her personally. The other half at least had heard of her dance hall and the music which emanated, if not originated, from that same concert-room. Originally is always praiseworthy, and it should be credited to the dead woman that many of the songs, the so-called "popular songs," which are sung to-day in the theaters all over the country, some of them going so far as the music halls of Europe and even played as up-to-date selections in the exclusive parlors and music-rooms of the United States, first were sung in "Babe" Connors's concert hall.
> The writer of these songs—he could hardly be called the composer—is not and never will be known. Indeed, the songs were never "written," nor "composed," . . . These songs, a tenfold more than the exponents who rendered them, made Babe Connor's place famous; the place was not notorious; it was not infamous; it was famous. ("'Babe' Connors")

Many famous songs, including "Ta-Ra-Ra-Boom-De-Ay," began as ribald versions at Connors's Castle Club, then were stolen later by white arrangers and cleaned up for popular sheet music. The headliner at the Castle Club was the very dark-complected singer from New Orleans, Mammy Lou, who was said to have been among the first to sing African American spirituals and field songs to white audiences and was one of the first to sing "Frankie and Johnny" at Babe Connors's club.

The celebrated Polish pianist Ignace Paderewski visited the Castle Club on a trip to St. Louis and met Babe Connors personally:

> After the formal and polite introductions—Babe Connors insisted on the most polished manners in her parlor—a dozen beauties danced to the music of a blind pianist, and Mammy Lou sang her raucous songs. Among them was "Ta-ra-ra-boom-de-ay." It was still unknown to the wide world, and it caught Paderewski's fancy. He went to the piano and asked her to sing it again and again. He learned that and a number of other songs from her; but "Ta-ra-ra-boom-de-ay" seemed the favorite. "That's going to be the theme of my new composition." In a season or two the song, like many others that originated with Mammy Lou, got into vaudeville by way of some manager who visited Babe's and became a sensation. (Johns 98)

Three clues link the "Stackolee" ballad to Babe Connors's Castle Club:

• The song has long been associated with "Frankie and Johnny" (based on another real-life incident that occurred in St. Louis), which definitely points to Mammy Lou and Babe Connors. At least two of the extant versions of "Stack O'Lee Blues," by Ma Rainey (1925) (Fig. 9) and Johnny Dodds (1938), employ the "Frankie and Johnny" melody to accompany the Stackolee lyrics.

• Before he opened his first saloon at 9 Targee Street in 1892, Tom Turpin played piano at the Castle Club. He was an energetic performer and an innovative composer of rags whose *Harlem Rag* (composed 1892; published 1897) was one of the earliest written specifically for piano (Berlin, *King*, 8, 47; Jasen and Tichenor 29–30). The year before he opened his soon-to-be-famous Rosebud Bar at 2220–2222 Market Street in 1900, he and his father ("Honest John" Turpin) were signers of a petition to release Lee Shelton from the penitentiary (Otey). An outspoken Republican on African American affairs whose brother was the first black man to hold public office in St. Louis ("Chas. H. Turpin"; Berlin, *King*, 194), Turpin would have had no political motivation for the Democratic Shelton's pardon (Jasen and Tichenor 28–29; Blesh and Janis 54–55). It's tempting to speculate that Turpin knew Shelton and had a hand in popularizing the ballad.

• Henry Bridgewater was close friends with Babe Connors and was instrumental in her conversion to Catholicism right before her death in 1899 (David 202; "A Notorious Woman"). This relationship alone points a suspicious finger at Bridgewater as a source for the ballad; his fulminations about "that bad man, Stack Lee" might well have inspired one of Babe's songwriters in 1896.

From its origins in ragtime the "Stackolee" ballad soon spread in two directions. Along one branch, the song reached urban centers like New Orleans and Chicago as a jazz tune, "Stack O'Lee Blues," which often was
rendered as an instrumental. The best extant version of the lyrics accompanying the jazz melody is that performed by Ukulele Ike (Cliff Edwards) in
1928 (see Appendix B). These lyrics can claim some precedence because
they are very similar to those half-remembered by Robert W. Gordon's 1927
informant who heard them sung by a "hillbilly sort of person" in 1913 or
1914 (David 281–82). Their treatment of Stack O'Lee is far from the absolute negativism found in other versions and the lighthearted way in which
Edwards sings the ballad brings to mind Babe Connors's music hall rather
than the Mississippi River roustabouts. Edwards was born in Hannibal,
Missouri, and performed in vaudeville shows in St. Louis at an early age,
which might explain his familiarity with the lyrics.

By the 1930s the lyrics were largely forgotten in jazz circles. Indeed, when
Cab Calloway attempted to sing the words to the same melody in 1931, it
was clear he had no idea what the song was about. Sidney Bechet was
apparently the last to record this tune in a jazz idiom in 1946, although it was
revived ten years later by Ken Colyer's Skiffle Group.

The other music branched in a second direction along the Mississippi
River and throughout the rural South as an African American folk ballad,
"Stagolee." This was the version heard in the levee camps and prison yards
in the late 1890s. The verses soon multiplied since, unlike jazz where the
melody is improvised, the words in this case were created or revised by
singers in many geographic areas to accommodate one or more standardized
tunes with a repeating chorus. The chorus was usually a variant of one of the
following verses:

> O dat man, bad man, Stagolee done come. (Odum)
> That bad, that bad man Stackalee. (Spaeth)
> When you lose your money, learn to lose. (Furry Lewis, 1927)
> Well it's cruel Stack O'Lee. (Long Cleve Reed, 1927)
> That bad man, oh cruel Stack O'Lee (Mississippi John Hurt, 1928)
> All about that John B. Stetson hat. (Frank Hutchinson, 1927)
> Everybody talk about Stackerlee! (Reedy, "Stackerlee")
> Stagolee, Lord, is surely dead. (John Bray, 1934)
> Wasn't he bad, he bad with a gun? (Vera Hall, 1937)

Although it was a black folk tune, the ballad was picked up by whites such as
Frank Hutchinson early on and copied by Doc Watson and Bob Dylan.
Woody Guthrie, Pete Seeger, and Paul Clayton were largely responsible for
keeping the ballad alive in recorded folk music until the early 1960s when
Mississippi John Hurt was rediscovered and played at the Newport Folk
Music Festivals. This version has been recorded by Jesse Fuller, Taj Mahal,
and Mickey Baker, among others.

The next major development came in 1950 when Dave Bartholomew recorded a New Orleans variant of the melody played on the piano by "Archi-

bald" (born Leon T. Gross), the last of the original New Orleans barrelhouse pianists. Archibald's version of "Stack-A-Lee" became an inspiration for the developing New Orleans rhythm and blues sound with its bouncing right-hand melody and insistent bass line. Dr. John commemorates Archibald's "Stack-A-Lee" in his own repertoire, and Marcus claims that "Dr. John can sing 'Stagger Lee' for half an hour without repeating a line" (218).

Archibald was also the inspiration for Lloyd Price's number-one hit in 1958, "Stagger Lee," which is the version most often covered by pop, rock, and rhythm and blues artists and which consequently introduced the Stack Lee legend to its widest audience ever. The opening stanza, credited to Harold Logan and Lloyd Price,

> The night was clear and the moon was yellow,
> And the leaves came tumbling down.

introduces a rollicking rhythm and blues melody with lyrics that at the time were too controversial to be played on Dick Clark's *American Bandstand* without being bowdlerized to remove the gambling and the murder itself (Marcus 218–19).

By 1971, Richard E. Buehler had catalogued 31 different versions of the lyrics (*Damn Near*), including some in the form of "toasts," or narrative declamations at one time performed nearly exclusively by African American prison inmates, but which now seem to have directly influenced gangsta rap (Jackson 43–55; Abrahams 123–36). As far as I know, rap music has ignored the Stacker Lee image, even though it is archetypically consonant; on the other hand, one of Abraham's toast versions has been covered recently by an alternative pop group from Australia, Nick Cave and the Bad Seeds (1996), which has caused some comment with its sexually explicit lyrics.

Another significant lyrical variant of the "Stacker Lee" ballad has revived the legend for a new generation in the 1970s and 1980s. The Grateful Dead's 1978 recording of "Stagger Lee" was an imaginative update of the storyline with a completely new melody. This time, the murder takes place 45 years later almost to the day:

> 1940, Xmas eve, with a full moon over town,
> Stagger Lee met Billy de Lion and he blew that poor boy down.
> Do you know what he shot him for? What do you make of that?
> 'Cause Billy de Lion threw the lucky dice—won Stagger Lee's Stetson hat.

Most young people these days when they hear about Stagger Lee will think of the Grateful Dead version, or possibly the two verses interpolated into the reggae-sounding "Wrong 'Em, Boyo" recorded by The Clash in 1979.

THE MYTH

The musical peregrinations of this simply story, from fact into folklore and from ragtime to reggae, demonstrate how well it resonates with both African

American and mainstream cultures. As soon as Stack Lee entered oral tradition he was transformed into the archetypal bad man, a figure to be feared
as well as respected, an antihero whose deeds are cheered vicariously but
who ultimately is brought down by the iron fist of the law. Though the legendary Stacker Lee's act was rash, explosive, and cruel, it could also be
viewed as a primeval cry in the wilderness by an emasculated class trapped
in a dystopia orchestrated by whites. As Levine writes,

> Coming from the depths of the society, representing the most oppressed and
> deprived strata, these bandits are manifestations of the feeling that, within the
> circumstances in which they operate, to assert any power at all is a triumph.
> (418)

Violence is necessary because life is not a craps game but a battleground.
The bad man knows what will happen if he is captured, but it doesn't
matter—he has already been sentenced, and prison walls are little different
from the barriers to success and self-esteem that he faces daily. While he is
still free he subsists on the juice of his enemies' fears and drinks from the
oppressor's cup.

The fact that Stackolee's victim, Billy Lyons, was also black must have
posed some problems of interpretation for folk singers and blues musicians
early on. The reason given for the killing is Lyons's theft, destruction, or
winning in a carps games of Stack's Stetson hat. Without his hat Stackolee is
stripped of his strength, like Sampson without his long hair or Popeye
without his spinach. Still, a hat is a replaceable commodity, unlike a man's
life, and murder "'Bout a five dollar Stetson hat" (Tom Bell version, 1937)
seemed an extreme overreaction. Perhaps this is why the devil was invoked
to explain Stack's behavior:

> Stagolee he went down to the devil,
> And he leaned up on his shelf.
> He said "Come out of here, Mr. Devil,
> I'm gonna rule hell by myself."

> Well, the devil called all his little imps around him,
> "Lord, let's climb up on the wall."
> He said, "Here's a bad man, Stagolee,
> And he's goin' to kill us all."
> ("Stagolee," Lonnie Robertson, 1936)

> And so when Stackalee growed up he got to be an awful rascal and rounder wit
> lots of triflin women and he staid drunk all the time. One dark night as he
> come staggerin down the road the devil popped up real sudden, like a grinnin
> jumpin jack. He carried Stackalee into the grave yahd and bought his soul. An
> that's how come Stack could go round doin things no other livin man could
> do. . . . (Botkin 122)

White society has God on its side, so Stackolee naturally chooses the demonic as a source of magical power and his Stetson hat becomes the focal point. No matter who messes with his hat, it's serious business:

You stold my magic Stetson; I'm gonna steal your life.
(Botkin 127–30)

A preternatural pact with the devil is central to Nathan Young's iconography, where Stackolee is the black Faust who "sold his mortal soul for a life of ease—women—songs—an' gambling" (*Guest* 130) (Fig. 10). Playwright Don Evans used the same theme in *The Trials and Tribulations of Staggerlee Booker T. Brown*, in which a reformed Stack has become a minister intent on breaking his devilish deal (Weeks). Stack's name possessed a magical power of its own when written on good luck charms, and these were prized in the South as late as the 1930s (Spencer).

In most versions of the ballad, however, Stackolee is bad on his own terms. As Marcus points out, his image permeates rock and blues music under other names and personas like Howlin' Wolf's "Back Door Man" and the Rolling Stones' "Midnight Rambler" (Marcus 67). Marsh and Bernard call "Stagger Lee" the most diabolical song of all time and list 15 other songs that "would be inconceivable without him," including "Cop Killer" by Body Count and "Mind of a Lunatic" by the Geto Boys (498–99).

John Roberts pinpointed the myth's popularity in today's culture:

Stackolee symbolizes the black urban male's idea of heroism. In one sense, he provides escape from the reality of urban existence, but his avenue of escape is never portrayed as ideal or even desirable. In another sense, he provides a realistic, though exaggerated, portrait of urban life as perceived by those who narrate his exploits. The oppressive system that gives rise to Stackolee is removed and the dangers that it imposes are less immediately threatening than the dangers that in fact exist in the urban ghetto environment. ("Stackolee" 190)

The original Stack Lee may have been a petty thief and gambler, but he was no murderer, much less the bloodthirsty, heartless bad man perpetuated in myth and music. After a century of vilification, it's time to separate Lee Shelton the man from Stackolee the myth and appreciate both man and myth on their own merits and demerits.

One hundred years of cultural accretion have mutated the myth of Stagger Lee into an icon much larger than the man. Henry Bridgewater managed to put Lee Shelton behind bars, but it's Stagger Lee's exploits that we sing about now. And those exploits are not less valid for being partially mythical—especially when we have some insight into the truth:

She had a common ordinary funeral,
She was planted right down by his side.
On the monument read this inscription:
"These riders rode their last ride."

And that is the story of the man called Stack O'Lee.
("Stack O'Lee Blues," Cliff Edwards, 1928)

APPENDICES

Appendix A is a chronological discography of all recordings, releases, and publications of the Stack Lee ballad that I have found relatively reliable information for. It is by no means comprehensive, but it does show how the song has evolved.

Appendix B provides examples of each of the primary varieties of lyrics: jazz, folksong, and New Orleans.

REFERENCES

Note: Correspondence and petitions regarding clemency for Lee Shelton are found at the Missouri State Archives under Record Group 5, Secretary of State, Commissions Division, Commutations of Sentence, Lee Shelton 1909, Box 3838 (22), No. 930; and 1912, Box 3589 (39), No. 1352.

Abrahams, Roger. *Deep Down in the Jungle: Negro Narratives from the Streets of Phila-delphia.* Chicago: Aldine, 1970.
All Music Guide Database. [Cited as AMG.] Available: Compuserve (GAllmusic). Producer: All Music Guide, Big Rapids, Mich. 1994–.
"At Curtis': Lyons Killed by Lee Sheldon over Politics." *St. Louis Chronicle* 26 Dec. 1895: 2.
"'Babe' Connors Has Passed Away." *St. Louis Republic* 5 Aug. 1899: 7.
Basinger, Julianne. "Storyteller Tells and Wails the Country Blues." *Durham* (NC) *Herald-Sun.* 25 Nov. 1994: C-11.
Berlin, Edward A. *King of Ragtime: Scott Joplin and His Era.* New York: Oxford UP, 1994.
——. *Ragtime: A Musical and Cultural History.* 1980. Berkeley: U of California P, 1984.
——. *Reflections and Research on Ragtime.* Brooklyn: Inst. for Studies in Amer. Music, 1987.
Bishop, C. Orrick. Letter to Governor Herbert S. Hadley. 9 Sept. 1909. Missouri State Archives.
"Bishop Was Abusive." *St. Louis Post-Dispatch* 14 May 1897:6.
Blesh, Rudi and Harriet Janis. *They All Played Ragtime.* New York: Knopf, 1950. Rev. ed. New York: Oak, 1971.
Blunt, Edmund M., ed. *Nautical Almanac and Astronomical Ephemeris.* Edinburgh: Edmund M. Blunt, 1895.
Botkin, Benjamin, ed. *Treasury of American Folklore.* New York: Crown, 1944.
Bousquet, Patrick. "The Hat of the West: John B. and His Stetson." *Western Horseman,* May 1993: 18–20.
Bradford, Roark. *John Henry.* New York: Harper, 1931.
Bridgewater, Eliza, and Maria Brown. Letter to Governor Alexander Dockery. 4 June 1901. Missouri State Archives.
——. Letter to Governor Lon V. Stephens. 21 Dec. 1899. Missouri State Archives.
Bridgewater, Henry, and C. Maguire, lot owners. St. Peter's Cemetery Record Book. Lot 289, section 5.

Bromwell, Andrew J. Letter to Governor Lon V. Stephens. 25 Nov. 1899. Missouri State Archives.

Brooks, Tilford. *America's Black Musical Heritage.* Englewood Cliffs: Prentice-Hall, 1984.

Brown, Cecil. *Coming Up Down Home: A Memoir of a Southern Childhood.* Hopewell: Ecco, 1993.

Buehler, Richard E. *Damn Near All I Know about Stacker Lee.* Unpublished ms. ca. 1971.

———. Personal communication. 4 Aug. 1987.

———. "Stacker Lee: A Partial Investigation into the Historicity of a Negro Murder Ballad." *Keystone Folklore Quarterly* Fall 1967: 187–91.

"Burial Permits." *St. Louis Chronicle* 28 Dec. 1895: 7.

"Burial Permits." *St. Louis Post-Dispatch* 28 Dec. 1895: 2.

Burt, Olive Woolley, ed. *American Murder Ballads and Their Stories.* New York: Oxford UP, 1958.

"Came to Blows." *St. Louis Star* 12 May 1897: 1.

Carr, Archibald. Certified copy of jury list, State of Missouri vs. Lee Shelton, Alias Stack Lee, 11 May 1897. Shows vote tallies. Signed 23 Oct. 1899.

"Chas. H. Turpin for Constable." *St. Louis Argus* 28 July 1922: 6.

"The Christmas of a Great City." *St. Louis Christian Advocate* 1 Jan. 1896: 1.

Collins, John P., et al. Petition to Governor Alexander Dockery for pardon of Lee Shelton, Nov. 1901, Missouri State Archives.

Corenthal, Michael G. *The Iconography of Recorded Sound, 1886–1986.* Milwaukee: Yesterday's Memories, 1986.

"Coroner's Inquests." *St. Louis Globe-Democrat* 28 Dec. 1895: 11.

Courlander, Harold. *Negro Folk Music, U.S.A.* New York: Columbia UP, 1963, 178–79.

Cowgill, James, John P. Gordon, and Elliott W. Major. Recommendation to Governor Herbert S. Hadley for commutation of sentence of Lee Shelton. 20 Jan. 1912. Missouri State Archives.

"Criminal Court Sentences." *St. Louis Globe-Democrat* 16 July 1896: 9.

Da Silva, Angela. *The St. Louis Attitude.* St. Louis: The author, 198–. Located in the Rare Books and Special Collections Division Pius XII Memorial Library, St. Louis University.

David, John Russel. *Tragedy in Ragtime: Black Folktales from St. Louis.* Diss. St. Louis U, 1976. Ann Arbor: UMI, 1976. 7622522.

Davis, Francis, *The History of the Blues: The Roots, the Music, the People; from Charley Patton to Robert Cray.* New York: Hyperion, 1995.

Dawson, James L. Letter to Governor Joseph Folk. 28 Dec. 1905. Missouri State Archives.

Denton, Charles A. Letter to James D. Anderson. 26 Jan. 1912. Missouri State Archives.

Dixon, R.M.W., and J. Goodrich. *Blues and Gospel Records, 1902–1943.* Chigwell: Storyville, 1982.

Docks, Les. *American Premium Record Guide, 1900–1965.* 4th ed. Florence Books Americana, 1992.

Dodd, David. *The Annotated "Stagger Lee": An Installment in The Annotated Grateful Dead Lyrics.* WWW site, Library, U of Colorado, Colorado Springs. Last revised, 29 July 1995. http://www.uccs.edu/~ddodd/stagger.html.

Dorson, Richard M. "Negro Tales." *Western Folklore* 13 (1954): 160–69.

Drabelle, John W. Letter to Governor Alexander Dockery. 24 June 1902. Missouri State Archives.

———. Letter to Governor Alexander Dockery. 17 Nov. 1902. Missouri State Archives.

"The End of a Brilliant Man: Nat Dryden's Death Brought Tears to Many Eyes." *St. Louis Post-Dispatch* 26 Aug. 1896: 6.

Fields, William Herbert. Letter to Governor Alexander Dockery. 3 Jan. 1905. Missouri State Archives.

———. Letter to Governor Herbert S. Hadley. 17 June 1909. Missouri State Archives.

Finger, Charles. *Frontier Ballads Heard and Gathered.* New York: Doubleday, Page, 1927.

"Fled: Mrs. Fannie Wood, Whom Col. Nat Dryden Dazzled." *St. Louis Chronicle* 30 Dec. 1895: 8.

Floyd, Samuel A., Jr. *The Power of Black Music: Interpreting Its History from Africa to the United States.* New York: Oxford UP, 1995.

"For Murder: 'Stack Lee' Now Being Tried by Judge Harvey." *St. Louis Chronicle* 13 July 1896: 6.

"For Murder in the First Degree." *St. Louis Post-Dispatch* 29 Dec. 1895: 15.

"Free Again Is Lee Shelton, the Murderer of Wm. Lyons: He Seems to Have an Unusually Strong Pull and Seems to Leave Jail Whenever He Pleases." *St. Louis Chronicle* 20 July 1896: 3.

Friedman, Albert B. *The Viking Book of Folk Ballads of the English-Speaking World.* New York: Viking, 1956.

"A Gambler Murdered: Charles Wilson, Manager of Bridgewater's Dive, Shot by a Patron." *St. Louis Globe-Democrat* 12 Sept. 1892: 9.

Gerould, Gordon Hall. *The Ballad of Tradition.* Oxford: Clarendon, 1932.

Gilbert, Douglas. *Lost Chords: The Diverting Story of American Popular Songs.* New York: Cooper Square, 1970.

Gillett, Charlie. *The Sound of the City: The Rise of Rock and Roll.* New York: Outerbridge & Dienstfrey, 1970.

Gordon, Robert W. "American Folksongs: Outlaw Ballads." *New York Times Magazine* June 5, 1927: 13, 19.

———. *Folk-Songs of America.* Washington, DC: National Service Bureau, 1938.

Gould's St. Louis Directory. St. Louis: Gould Directory Co. Volumes for 1876–1912.

Greene, Lorenzo J., Gary R. Kremer, and Antonio F. Holland. *Missouri's Black Heritage.* Rev. ed. Columbia: U of Missouri P, 1993.

Guenther, G.A., et al. Petition to Governor Alexander Dockery for pardon of Lee Shelton. Dec. 1904, Missouri State Archives.

Hadley, Herbert S. Commutation of sentence of Lee Shelton. 24 Nov. 1909. Commutations, vol. 2, p. 148. Commutation #1183, #2867. Missouri State Archives.

———. Commutation of sentence of Lee Shelton. 8 Feb. 1912. Commutation #1352, Box 445, Missouri State Archives.

Handy, W.C. *Father of the Blues: An Autobiography.* New York: Macmillian, 1941.

Hanousek, Ladislav, ed. *CD World Reference Guide: Popular Music Edition.* Milwaukee: CDI, 1994.

Harper, James. "Renewal of a Legend." *St. Petersburg* (FL) *Times.* Arts sec. 31. May 1987, 1E.

Harrison, Max, Charles Fox, and Eric Thacker. *The Essential Jazz Records, Vol. 1* Westport: Greenwood, 1984.

"'Help!' Cried Lee Shelton, the Slayer of William Lyons." *St. Louis Chronicle* 27 Dec. 1895: 3.

Hereford, Robert A. "Races That Were Races on the Mississippi." *St. Louis Globe-Democrat* 1 Feb. 1948.

Hughes, Langston, and Arna Bontemps, eds. *The Book of Negro Folklore.* New York: Dodd, Mead, 1958.

Jackson, Bruce, comp. *Get Your Ass in the Water and Swim Like Me: Narrative Poetry from Black Oral Tradition.* Cambridge: Harvard UP, 1974.

"James Edgar Withrow." In Walter B. Stevens, ed., *Centennial History of Missouri (The Center State): One Hundred Years in the Union, 1820–1921.* St. Louis: S.J. Clarke, 1921. Vol. 3: 202–05.

Jasen, David A., and Trebor Jay Tichenor. *Rags and Ragtime: A Musical History.* New York: Dover, 1978.

Jepsen, Jorgen Grunnet, ed. *Jazz Records, 1942–1965.* Holte, Denm.: Karl Emil Knudsen, 1966, 8 vols.

Johns, Orrick, *Time of Our Lives: The Story of My Father and Myself.* New York: Stackpole, 1937.

Johnson, Charles P., et al. Petition to Governor Lon V. Stephens for pardon of Lee Shelton. [Nov. 1899.] Missouri State Archives.

Johnson, J. Rosamond. *Rolling Along in Song: A Chronological Survey of American Negro Music.* New York: Viking, 1937.

"Jury Couldn't Agree: And Slayer Stack Lee Will Be Tried Again." *St. Louis Chronicle* 18 July 1896: 4.

Kiefer, Peter T., comp. *The Fred Waring Discography.* Westport: Greenwood, 1996.

Kinney, Michael. Letter to Governor Joseph Folk. 16 June 1906. Missouri State Archives.

Kinney, Thomas E. Letter to Governor Joseph Folk. 11 Dec. 1905. Missouri State Archives.

Koeppel, Fredric. "City Guide Is Kind To Memphis, Nashville." *Memphis Commercial Appeal* 8 May 1994: 1E.

Laird, Ross. *Tantalizing Tingles: A Discography of Early Ragtime, Jazz, and Novelty Syncopated Piano Recordings, 1889–1934.* Westport: Greenwood, 1995.

Lawless, Ray M. *Folksingers and Folksongs in America: A Handbook of Biography, Bibliography, and Discography.* New York: Duell, Sloan and Pearce, 1960.

"Lawyers Became Excited." *St. Louis Globe-Democrat* 13 May 1897: 9.

"Lawyers Try to Fight in Court." *St. Louis Post-Dispatch* 12 May 1897: 2.

Leach, MacEdward. *The Ballad Book.* New York: Harper, 1955.

Leadbitter, Mike and Neil Slaven. *Blues Records: January 1943 to December 1966.* New York: Oak, 1968.

"Lee Shelton Bound Over." *St. Louis Globe-Democrat* 4 Jan. 1896: 11.

"Lee Shelton Gets Twenty-Five Years." *St. Louis Globe-Democrat* 14 May 1897: 9.

"Lee Shelton Murder Trial." *St. Louis Post-Dispatch* 13 May 1897: 13.

"Lee Shelton's Second Trial." *St. Louis Globe-Democrat* 12 May 1897: 9.

Leonard, John W., ed. *The Book of St. Louisans: A Biographical Dictionary of Leading Living Men of the City of St. Louis.* St. Louis: St. Louis Republic, 1906.

Lester, Julius. *Black Folktales.* New York: Grove, 1970.

———. "Stagolee." *Sing Out!* 16 (Aug./Sept. 1966): 20–21.

Levine, Lawrence W. *Black Culture and Black Consciousness.* New York: Oxford UP, 1977.

Lewis, Gregory. "Down Home with Cecil Brown." *San Francisco Examiner Magazine* 27 Nov. 1994: M-7.

Library of Congress. *Check-List of Recorded Songs in the English Language in the Archive of American Folk Song to July 1940.* Washington, DC: LC Music Division, 1942.

———. *A List of American Folksongs Currently Available in Records.* Washington DC: LC Archive of American Folksong, 1953.

Lichtenstein, Grace, and Laura Dankner. *Musical Gumbo: The Music of New Orleans.* New York: Norton, 1993.

Lieb, Sandra. *Mother of the Blues: A Study of Ma Rainey.* Amherst: U of Massachusetts P, 1981.

Litchfield, Jack. *The Canadian Jazz Discography, 1916–1980.* U of Toronto P 1982.

Lomax, Alan. *The Folk Songs of North America.* Garden City: Doubleday, 1960.

———. *The Land Where the Blues Began.* New York: Pantheon, 1993.

Lomax, John A., and Alan Lomax. *American Ballads and Folk Songs.* New York: Macmillian, 1934.

Lyons, William. Death certificate. No. 3605. St. Louis: Missouri Bureau of Vital Statistics, Division of Health. Death: 25 Dec. 1895. Burial permit filed: 28 Dec. 1895. Signed Theo Gast, M.D.

M., W.D. "The Ballad of Stacker Lee: Washington, D.C., Jan. 7, 1919." *Reedy's Mirror* 17 Jan. 1919: 37.

McCardell, Roy L. *New York Morning Telegraph,* 22 Dec. 1918, qtd. by J.R. David.

McIlwaine, Shields. *Memphis Down in Dixie.* New York: Dutton, 1948.

Mackie, John. "Linden's Key for Blues Comes Fret by Fret." *Vancouver Sun* 17 Apr. 1993: F7.

Marcus, Greil. *Mystery Train: Images of America in Rock 'n' Roll Music.* 1975. 3d rev. ed. New York: Plume, 1990.

Marsh, Dave, and James Bernard. *The New Book of Rock Lists.* Rev. ed. New York: Fireside, 1994.

Mathes, J. Harvey. *The Old Guard Is Grey: Researches in the Annals of the Confederate Historical Association.* Memphis: Confederate Hist. Assn., 1897.

Minnaert, M. *The Nature of Light and Colour in the Open Air.* New York: Dover, 1954.

Missouri State Penitentiary, Jefferson City. *Register of Inmates.* Vol. 175. Lee Shelton, Alias Stack Lee. No. 12934/579/15087. 7 Oct. 1897.

Moore, L. Wayne. Personal Communications. Mar. 1995.

Myerdick, A.H. Letter to Chas. A. Denton. 20 Jan. 1912. Missouri State Archives.

"Nat Dryden's Talk." *St. Louis Chronicle* 2 Jan. 1896: 6.

"Nathaniel Craig Dryden Dead." *St. Louis Globe-Democrat* 26 Aug. 1896: 6.

Nietert, H.L. Post-mortem report. Coroner's Office of the City of St. Louis. 27 Dec. 1895.

"A Notorious Woman: 'Babe' Connors Will Be Buried by the Church." *St. Louis Post-Dispatch* 6 Aug. 1899: 5.

Odum, Howard W. "Folk-Song and Folk-Poetry as Found in the Secular Songs of the Southern Negroes." *Journal of American Folk-Lore* 24 (1911): 288–89.

——. and Guy B. Johnson. *The Negro and His Songs.* Chapel Hill: U of North Carolina P, 1925.

Oliver, Paul. *Songsters and Saints: Vocal Traditions on Race Records.* New York: Cambridge UP, 1984.

Osborne, Jerry. *Rock and Rock Record Albums Price Guide.* 5th ed. Phoenix: O'Sullivan Woodside, 1983.

Otey, Turner, et al. Petition to Governor Lon V. Stephens for pardon of Lee Shelton. [Nov. 1899.] Missouri State Archives.

Palmer, Robert. "The New Orleans Man Behind the 'Staggerlee' Sound." *New York Times* 17 Mar. 1987 Late City Final ed. Sec. C: 15.

Perry, Regenia A. *Free Within Ourselves: African-American Artists in the Collection of the National Museum of American Art.* Washington, DC: National Mus. of Amer. Art, 1992.

Rankin, C.C., et al. Petition to Governor Alexander Dockery for pardon of Lee Shelton. 8 Dec 1902. Missouri State Archives.

Raymond, R.J. Letter to Governor Joseph Folk. 6 June 1906. Missouri State Archives.

Reedy, William Marion. "I Have Often Wondered How all the Negroes . . . " *Reedy's Sunday Mirror* 16 Sept. 1894: 2.

——. "Stackerlee." *Reedy's Mirror* 3 Jan. 1919: 11.

——. "There Is a Noisome, Noxious Nuisance . . . " *Reedy's Sunday Mirror* 24 June 1894: 4.

Riis, Thomas L. *Just Before Jazz: Black Musical Theater in New York, 1890 to 1915.* Washington, DC: Smithsonian Inst. P, 1989.

Roberts, John W. *From Trickster to Badman: The Black Folk Hero in Slavery and Freedom.* Philadelphia: U of Pennsylvania P, 1989.

——. "Stackolee and the Development of a Black Heroic Idea." *Western Folklore* 42.3 (1983): 179–90.

Rose, Tricia. *Black Noise: Rap Music and Black Culture in Contemporary America.* Hanover: Wesleyan UP, 1994.

Rust, Brian, comp. *Jazz Records, 1897–1942.* 4th ed. New Rochelle: Arlington House, 1978.

——. *The Victor Master Book, Vol. 2 (1925–1936).* Stanhope: Walter C. Allen, 1970.

Scarborough, Dorothy. *On the Trail of the Negro Folk-Song*. Cambridge: Harvard UP, 1925.

Scott, Charles A. Letter to Governor Alexander Dockery. 20 Dec. 1904. Missouri State Archives.

Shaw, Arnold. *Honkers and Shouters: The Golden Years of Rhythm and Blues*. New York: Collier, 1978.

"Sheldon's Victim Dies." *St. Louis Globe-Democrat* 27 Dec. 1895: 9.

Shelton, Lee. Death certificate. No. 8668. Jefferson City: Missouri State Board of Health. Death: 11 Mar. 1912. Burial: 15 Mar. 1912. Signed A. H. Myerdick, M.D., and H.E. Evens, Missouri State Penitentiary.

Shelton Lee. Description of Convict, Missouri State Penitentiary. Registered no. 579. Missouri State Archives. Signed Matt W. Hall, Warden. 1897. Last entry, 1905.

"Shelton at Large." *St. Louis Chronicle* 25 June 1896: 7.

"Shelton Jury Failed to Agree." *St. Louis Globe-Democrat* 19 July 1896: 21.

Shook, Sidney. "Echoes on the River." *Midwest Folklore* 10 (Summer 1960): 73.

"Shot in a Saloon: Drinks and Politics Get a Bullet In Williams Lyons' Stomach." *St. Louis Post-Dispatch* 26 Dec. 1895: 4.

"Shot in Curtis' Place." *St. Louis Globe-Democrat* 26 Dec. 1895: 7.

Silvester, Peter. *A Left Hand Like God: The Story of Boogie-Woogie*. New York: Omnibus, 1990.

"Snap Shots of Daily Life on Lower Morgan Street." *St. Louis Post-Dispatch* 16 Aug. 1896: 18.

Southern, Eileen. "Afro-American Musical Materials." *The Black Perspective in Music* 1 (Spring 1973): 24–32.

Spaeth, Sigmund. *Weep Some More, My Lady*. Garden City: Doubleday, 1927.

Spencer, Onah. "Stackalee." *Direction* 4 (Summer 1941): 14–17.

"'Stack' Lee Gives Bond." *St. Louis Globe-Democrat* 26 June 1896: 7.

"'Stack' Lee Jury Out." *St. Louis Globe-Democrat* 18 July 1896: 8.

"Stack Lee's Trial." *St. Louis Globe-Democrat* 14 July 1896: 12.

"Stack Lee's Trial: The Murderer's Fate Will Be Settled Friday." *St. Louis Chronicle* 16 July 1896: 1.

"Stacker Lee Is Aground at Kimmswick: Lee Line Boat Is Supposed to Have Got Out of the Channel of the Swollen Mississippi." *St. Louis Post-Dispatch* 8 Apr. 1903: 1.

Stevens, Walter B. *St. Louis: History of the Fourth City, 1763–1909*. 4 vols. Chicago: S.J. Clarke, 1909.

Stewart, A.J.D. *The History of the Bench and Bar of Missouri*. St. Louis: Legal, 1898.

Stewart-Baxter, Derrick. *Ma Rainey and the Classic Blues Singers*. New York: Stein and Day, 1970.

Stout, Laurie A. *Somewhere in Time: A 160 Year History of Missouri Corrections*. Jefferson City: Missouri Dept. of Corrections, 1991.

Sutter, Otto. Hospital admission statement. St. Louis City Hospital. 26 Dec. 1895.

The Trial of the Lonesome Pine. Film. Dir. Henry Hathaway. Singer: Al "Fuzzy" Knight. Paramount, 1936.

"Two Negroes Pardoned Are in Cells Again: Lee Shelton, Alias Stack Lee." *St. Louis Post-Dispatch* 17 Mar. 1911: 6.

Umphred, Neal. *Goldmine's Price Guide to Collectible Record Albums*. Iola: Krause, 1989.

"Vendetta: William Lyons Belonged to the Bridgewater Faction." *St. Louis Chronicle* 27 Dec. 1895: 3.

Wait, Walter J. *Inquest Held at the Coroner's Office, City of St. Louis, on the 27th Day of December, 1895, at 1 o'clock P.M., on the Body of William Lyons (col'd) by W.J. Wait, M.D., Coroner*. No. 738. Coroner's Office of the City of St. Louis.

"Wanted to Lynch Him: Excited Mob Stormed the Morgue While Murderer Lee Was There." *St. Louis Post-Dispatch* 27 Dec. 1895: 9.

Weeks, Jerome. "Feisty Fun: Jubilee Theatre Cast Puts Comic Twist on Faust Legend." *Dallas Morning News* 31 Jan. 1994: Overnight sec., 25A.

Wheeler, Mary. *Roustabout Songs: A Collection of Ohio River Valley Songs*. New York: Remick Music Corp., 1939.

——. *Steamboatin' Days: Folk Songs of the River Packet Era*. Baton Rouge: Louisiana State UP, 1944.

Withrow, James E. Letter to Governor Alexander Dockery. 19 June 1901. Missouri State Archives.

"Work of the January Grand Jury." *St. Louis Globe-Democrat* 13 Feb. 1896: 12.

Wright, John A. *Discovering African-American St. Louis: A Guide to Historic Sites*. St. Louis: Missouri Hist. Soc. P, 1994.

Young, Nathan B. [Amanuensis "Notebook"]. *A Guest of Honor: A Re-creation — 1999 A.D.; Scott Joplin's 'White-Black' Magic Years in Texarkana, Sedalia, Chicago & St. Louis, 1868–1908*. St. Louis: Warren H. Green, 1986.

——. *"Madam Babe": St. Louis' Golden Bordello Idyllic*. Unpublished ms. 1982. Located in the Rare Books and Special Collections Division of Pius XII Memorial Library, St. Louis University.

——. *Transgressions, Death Legends & Music of Bad Man Stackolee*. Unpublished ms. 1982. Located in the Rare Books and Special Collections Division of Pius XII Memorial Library, St. Louis University.

APPENDIX A

Partial Discography

Date	Rec.	Rel.	Pub.	Title	Performer	Place	Album	Label	Source
1897				Stackolee	Will Stark	St. Louis			Levine 413; Lomax, Land, 202-203
1897				Stagolee	Charles Haffer, Jr.	Miss.			Lomax, Land, 495
early 1900s				Stagolee		Miss., La., Tenn.			Odum
early 1900s				Stagolee Done Kill Dat Bully		Georgia			Odum
1910, Jan. 26			x	Stagalee	Ella Scott Fisher	San Angelo, Tex.			Lomax & Lomax 93-96
1914			x	Stack-o-lee	"hill-billy"	The West			David 281-82
1918, Dec. 22			x	Everybody Talk About Stackerlee		New York			McCardell
1919, Jan. 3			x	Stackerlee	D'Arcy Fanning	Muskogee, Okla.			Reedy, "Stackerlee"
1919, Jan. 17			x	Ballad of Stacker Lee		St. Louis			W.D.M.
1923, Oct. 16	x			Stack O'Lee Blues	Fred Waring Orchestra	Camden, N.J.		Victor 19189-A; M-28665-5	Kiefer
1923, Oct 18	x			Stack O'Lee Blues	Frank Westphal & His Orchestra	Chicago		Columbia 32-D; 81315-2	Rust, Jazz

Date	Rec.	Rel.	Pub.	Title	Performer	Place	Album	Label	Source
1923, Dec.			x	Stackerlee	H. A. Shannon	Asheville, N.C.			David 277-78
1924, May 14	x			Stack O'Lee Blues	Herb Wiedoeft's Cinderella Roof Orch.	Los Angeles		Brunswick 2660; A-95	Rust *Jazz*
1925, Dec.	x			Stack O'Lee Blues	Ma Rainey w/Joe Smith, cor; Charlie Green, tb; Buster Bailey, cl; Coleman Hawkins, bsx; Fletcher Henderson, p; Charlie Dixon, bjo	New York	Ma Rainey's Black Bottom	Paramount 12357; 2376-2; Sig 908; Jazz Collector L-73; Jazz 5001; Yazoo 1071; King Jazz KJ-182 FS; Milestone MCD-47021-2	Lieb; Stewart-Baxter; Dixon; AMG
1926?	x			Stack O' Lee Blues	Sol Hoopii's Novelty Trio		Masters of the Hawaiian Guitar, vol 1	Columbia 797-D-2; Rounder 1024	Dodd; AMG
1926?	x			Stack-O-Lee Blues	King, Queen & Jack		Hawaiian Guitar Hot Shots	Yazoo L-1055	
1927, Jan.			x	Stackalee	S.J. Duffield	Lodi, Calif.			David 278-81; Spaeth
1927, Jan. 31	x			Stack O'Lee Blues	Evelyn Thompson	New York		Vocalion 1083; E-4502	Rust, *Jazz*
1927, March 16	x			Stack O'Lee Blues	Jack Linx and His (Birmingham) Society Serenaders	Atlanta		80547-A-B-C: Harrison LP-M: Mx-W80547-C	Rust, *Jazz*: Moore
1927, May	x			Original Stack O'Lee Blues	Long Cleve Reed and The Down-Home Boys	Chicago	Country blues: The First Generation; The Songster Tradition, 1927-1935	Black Patti 8030; Matchbox MSE 20l; Document 5045	L. C. *Check-List*: Dodd

Date		Title	Artist	Location	Album	Catalog	Reference
1927, June 5	x	Stackolee [composite]	Robert W. Gordon	New York			Gordon, "American"; Gordon, Folk-Songs 44-45; Friedman 381-82
1927, Oct. 9	x	Billy Lyons and Stack O'Lee	Furry Lewis	Chicago	Listen to Our Story; Furry Lewis: Complete Works (1927-1929)	Vocalion 1132; C-1244/45; Brunswick 80092; Brunswick BL 59001; Document DOCD 5004	L.C. Check-List AMG
1927	x	Stackallee, or Staggerlee	Frank Hutchinson		Anthology of American Folk Music, vol. 1: Ballads	Okeh W80-359A; Okeh 45106; Folkways FP251	L.C. List: Dodd
1927	x	Stack O'Lee Blues	The Washingtonians			Velvet Tone 1601-V	Dodd
1928, Jan. 9	x	Stack O'Lee Blues	Duke Ellington and the Washingtonians	New York	Hot frm Harlem	14589-3; Harlem 601-H; World Records SHB58; Columbia C2K-46177	Harrison; AMG
1928, Mar. 12	x	Stack O'Lee Blues	Sam Ku West Harmony Boys	Oakland, Calif.		Victor 42078-2	Rust, Victor
1928, Mar 21	x	Stack O'Lee Blues	Sam Ku West Harmony Boys	Oakland, Calif.		Victor 42078-5	Rust, Victor
1928, Apr. 18	x	Stack O'Lee Blues	Fred Waring's Pennsylvanians	New York	Fred Waring Memorial Album	Victor 21508-A; M-28665-12; Stash ST-126	Rust, Jazz: Kiefer

Date	Rec.	Rel.	Pub.	Title	Performer	Place	Album	Label	Source
1928, May 3 or 8	x			Original Stack O'Lee Blues	Boyd Senter and His Senterpedes w/Mickey Bloom, Jimmy Dorsey, Charlie Butterfield, Jack Russell, Eddie Lang	New York	Solos and Senterpedes, 1927-1928	Okeh 4115; Harlequin HQ-2044; Vocalion 3105; Clarion 5054-C; Parlophone R-501; PMC-7133; Diva 6044-G; Columbia M-37; Velvet Tone 7070-V; MX-400647 B; Harlequin HQ 2044	Harrison; Moore; Rust, Jazz; Dodd
1928, July 25	x			Stack O'Lee Part 1; Stack O'Lee Part 2	Ukulele Ike [Cliff Edwards]	New York	I'm a Bear in a Lady's Boudoir	Columbia 1551-D; Columbia 1820-D; Clarion 5449-C; Harlem 1408-H; VT 2509-V; Yazoo L-1047	Rust, Jazz
1928, Dec. 28	x			Stack O'Lee Blues	Mississippi John Hurt	New York	Mississippi Blues; Transition, 1926-1937; 1928 Sessions; Greatest Songsters; The Story of the Blues	Okeh 8654; 401481-B; Columbia G-30008; Origin Jazz Library 17; Yazoo 1065; Document 5003; Vanguard VSD7-9248	LC, Check-List Dodd; AMG; Marcus; Umphred
1931, Nov. 16?18?	X			Stack O'Lee Blues	Cab Calloway	New York	Cab Calloway and His Orchestra, 1931-1932	Banner 32278; Romeo 1794; Oriole 2421; Melotone 91278; Perfect 15572; MX-11018-1-2; Jazum 29; Classics 526	Rust, Jazz; Moore

Date			Title	Performer	Location	Catalog	Source
1932, June 2	x		Stack O'Lee Blues, Parts 1, 2	Carson Robinson and His Pioneers	London	Decca F-3026; GB-4541/2-2	Rust, Jazz
1933, June 28	x		Stagolee	unidentified girl	Normal, Tex.	LC CYL-(24)-4	Dixon
1933, July 11	x		Stackolee	Ivy Joe White (?)	Wiergate, Tex.	LC CYL-8	Lomax & Lomax; LC, Check-List
1933, Aug. 15	x		Stagolee	black convict	Nashville, Tenn.	LC 180-A-1	Dixon
1933–1934?		x	That Bad Man Stackerlee	Sullivan Rock	New Orleans		David 283-85
1934, Aug. 1	x		Jim Stack O'Lee Blues	Lucille Bogan; w/Walter Roland, p	New York	ARC 15512	LC, Check-List
1934, Sept. 27	x		Stagolee	Blind Pete and Partner	Little Rock	LC 239-A-2	LC, Check-List
1934, Oct.	x		Stagolee	Albert Jackson	Atmore, Ala.	LC 231-A1	LC, Check-List
1934, Oct.	x		Stagolee	black convict	Gould, Ark.	LC 245-A1	LC, Check-List
1934, Oct. 17	x		Stagolee	John (Big Nig) Bray	Morgan City (?), Ala	LC 1853-A-2	LC, Check-List
1934, Nov.	x		Stackerlee	Foy Gant [Grant?]	Austin, Tex.	LC 61-A2	LC, Check-List
1935?	x		Stack O'Lee	Ray Noble	Ray Noble and His American Jazz Dance Orchestra	Jazz Archives JA-22	Dodd
1935, Oct. 28	x		Stagolee	Mrs. George A. Webb [= Ella Scott Fisher?]	San Angelo, Tex.	LC 577-B	LC, Check-List

Date	Rec.	Rel.	Pub.	Title	Performer	Place	Album	Label	Source
1930s?	x			Stackolee	Ed Haley		Parkersburg Landing Sound Recording	Rounder LP	OCLC search
1936		x		Stack O'Lee Blues	Al "Fuzzy" Knight		Trail of the Lonesome Pine [film]		Moore
1936, Apr.	x			Stagolee	Lonnie Robertson	Parchman, Miss.		LC 733-A	Dixon
1936, May 3	x			Stagolee	Roscoe McLean	Raiford, Fla.		LC 694-B-2	LC, Check-List
1936, May 4	x			Stagolee	Buena Flynn [Flint?]	Raiford, Fla.		LC700-A-2; LC 699-A-2?	LC, Check-List; Dixon
1937			x	Stagolee					Johnson
1937, July 23	x			Stagolee	Tom Bell	Livingston, Ala.		LC 1326-B-1	LC, Check-List
1937, July 23	x			Stagolee	Vera Hall	Livingston, Ala.		LC 1323-B	LC, Check-List
1937, July 24	x			Stagolee	Blind Jesse Harris	Livingston, Ala		LC 1328-B	LC, Check-List
1937, Oct.	x			Stagolee	Bert Martin	Manchester, KY		LC 1479-B-1	LC, Check-List
1938, Jan. 21	x			Stack O'Lee Blues	Johnny Dodds and His Chicago Boys	New York	Jazz Heritage Series, v. 55	Decca 1676; Vocalion S-207; 63193-A; MCA 510-106	Rust, Victor, Dodd
1940, Oct. 19	x			Stagolee	Lucius Curtis w/Willie Ford, guitar	Natchez, Miss.		LC 40027/3; B-2; Matchbox SDM 230	LC, Check-List

Date		Title	Performer	Location	Recording	Catalog	Source
1941, Jan. 4	x	Stagolee	Woody Guthrie	Washington, DC		LC AFS 4491-A-2; Legacy Int=l CD 345	
1941, summer	x	Stackalee					Spencer; Botkin; Hughes & Bontemps 359-61
1942, July 20	x	Stagolee	David "Honeyboy" Edwards	Clarksdale, Miss.	Delta Bluesman	LC 6610-B-4; Earwig 4922-CD; Indigo IGOCD-2003	LC, Check-List; AMG
1942, Aug. 9	x	Stackerlee	Will Stark	Clarksdale, Miss.		LC 6652-B-3	Lomax 202-204, Dixon
1944	x	Stacker Lee					Wheeler, Steamboatin'
1946	x	Stackerlee	Bama	Parchman, Miss.	Negro Prison Songs from the Mississippi State Penitentiary; Blues in the Mississippi Night; Murderer's Home	Mississippi Trad. TLP 1020; Rykodisc RCD-90155; Tradition 1020	Lomax 280-81; AMG
1946, Feb. 12	x	Old Stack O'Lee Blues	Sidney Bechet, cl sop; Albert Nichols, cl; Art Hodes, p; PopsFoster, b	New York	Sidney Bechet Jazz Classics, vol. 2; The Best of Sidney Bechet; Complete Blue Note Recordings	Blue Note LP 1202; Blue Note CDP 7243-8-28891-2-0 Mosaic MD 4-110; Blue Note B2-28891	Harrison; Jepsen; AMG
1950	x	Stagolee	Vera Hall Ward	Ala.	Negro Folk Music of Alabama	Folkways	Courlander

Date	Rec.	Rel.	Pub.	Title	Performer	Place	Album	Label	Source
1950, Mar. 23	x			Stack-A-Lee, Parts 1 and 2	Archibald, w/Dave Bartholomew's Band	New Orleans	Complete New Orleans Sessions, 1950-1952; The Genius of Dave Bartholomew	Imperial 5068, 5358, 5563; IM 164, 165; Krazy Kat 7409; EMI 0777-7-80184-21	Leadbitter & Slaven Marcus
1951, Jan.		x		Stack-O-Lee	Tennessee Ernie Ford		16 Tons of Boogie	Capitol 1349-B; Rhino R2-70975	AMG
1952		x		Stackolee	Sonny Terry			LC AFM 106	Leadbitter & Slaven
1954		x		Stagolee	Cisco Houston		Hard Traveling	Folkways FA 2042; FP42	Dodd
1954, July			x	Stagolee	John Blackamore				Dorson
1956	x			Stagolee	Woody Guthrie		Chain Gang Songs, vol. 1; Bound for Glory	Stimson SLP 7; Folkways FP 78/1; Smithsonian/ Folkways 02481	LC, List, Dodd
1956, May		x		Stackolee	Paul Clayton	New York	Bloody Ballads	Riverside RLP 12-615	Lawless
1956, May 25	x			Stack-O-Lee Blues	Ken Colyer's Skiffle Group	London		Decca DR 22016; Flo 772	Jepsen
1957?		X		Return of Stagolee	Titus Turner			King 45-5186	Dodd
1958			x	Stagolee	Pete Seeger		American Favorite Ballads, Vol. 2	Folkways FA 2321	Lawless

Date			Title	Performer	Location	Album	Catalog	Reference
1958	x		Stackalee					Burt 202
1958	x		Stackolee		Harlem version			Hughes & Bontemps 631-38
1958, Jan. 19		x	Stagolee (Stackolee)	Jesse Fuller	San Francisco	Jazz, Folk Songs, Spirituals, & Blues	Good Time Jazz 12031; Original Blues Classics 2530-564-2	Leadbitter & Slaven AMG
1958, Feb. 4		x	Stack-O-Lee	Champion Jack Dupree and His Combo	New York	Blues from the Gutter	Atlantic LP 8019; Atlantic 82434-2	Leadbitter & Slaven AMG
1958, Dec.	x		Stagger Lee	Lloyd Price		Personality Plus; Mr. Personality Revisited	Speciality SP2156; ABC-Paramount 9972; Charly CRB 1052	Shaw; Marcus
1958, Dec.	x		Stagger Lee [modified]	Lloyd Price		Rock'N'Soul		Shaw, Marcus
1959		x	Stagolee [toast]		Philadelphia			Abrahams
1959	x		Stack & Billy	Fats Domino		Let's Play Fats Domino	Imperial LP-9065	Dodd; Osborne
1960s	x		Stack-A-Lee	Johnny Otis	Los Angeles	Great Rhythm and Blues Oldies, Vol. 3.	Blues Spectrum BS 103	Osborne
1960s	x		The Great Stack-A-Lee	Johnny Otis		Snatch and the Poontangs	Snatch 101	

Date	Rec.	Rel.	Pub.	Title	Performer	Place	Album	Label	Source
1960	x			Stagolee	Robert Pete Williams, Matthew Hogman and Maxey	Angola, La.	Angola Prisoner's Blues	Louisiana Folklore Society LFS A-3; Arhoolie 2011	AMG
1960	x			Stagolee	Clarence Edwards	Baton Rouge		Storyville SLP1 29	Leadbitter & Slaven
1960, Aug. 9	x			Stagolee	Buster Pickens	Houston		Heritage HLP 1008?	Leadbitter & Slaven
1961		x		Stack o Lee	Tex Johnson		Gunfighter Ballads	Promenade 2239	Dodd
1961, Jan.	x			Stack Alee	Memphis Slim, w/Muddy Waters	New York	Broken Soul blues; Chicago Blues Masters, Vol. 1; Muddy Waters and Memphis Slim	UAS 6137; Capitol CDP 7243 & 29375 2 4	Dodd; Osborne
1962?		x		Stagger Lee	Neil Sedaka		Come See About Me	MCA 5466	AMG
1962		x		Stackerlee	New Lost City Ramblers		New Lost City Ramblers, v.4	Folkways FA 2399	
1962		x		Stagger Lee	Dion and The Belmonts		Lovers Who Wander	Ace CH163; Laurie LLP-2012	AMG; Osborne
1962		x		Stagger Lee	Dave Van Ronk		Folksinger, Inside Dave Van Ronk	Prestige INT-13056; Prestige PRS-7716; Fantasy 24710	AMG: Umphred

Date		Title	Artist	Location	Album	Label	Source
1962, Jan. 12	x	Stackolee	Curtis Jones	Chicago	Lonesome Bedroom Blues	Delmar DL-605	Jepsen; Osborne
1963	x	Stackolee	The Journeymen		New Directions in Folk Music; Capitol Collectors Series	Capitol ST-1951; Capitol C2-98536	AMG; Umphred
1963?	x	Stagolee [extended]	Mississippi John Hurt		Monday Morning Blues; Avalon Blues; The Immortal; Mississippi John Hurt	Flyright 553; Flyright CD06; Vanguard VMD 79248; Rebel 1068; Vanguard 73103	
1963	x	Stagolee	Mississippi John Hurt	Newport, R. I.	Evening Concerts; Newport Folk Festival 1963	VanguardAMG VCD-77002	
1963, Mar.	x	Stagger Lee	Big Joe Williams		Blues for 9 Strings	Prestige Bluesville BV-1056	AMG; Osborne
1963, Sept. 20	x	Stagger Lee	The Isley Brothers		Famous Isley Brothers; Complete UA Sessions	UA 638; UAS 6313; UA CDP-7-95203-2	Marcus, Osborne
1964	x	Stack-O-Lee	Woody Guthrie		One of a Kind	Pair 1294	AMG
1964	x	Stackerlee	Alice Stuart		All the Good Times	Arhoolie F 4002	Dodd
1964, July 25	x	Stagolee	Mississippi John Hurt	Newport, R. I.	Blues at Newport	Vanguard VRS 9145 Vanguard 115	Leadbitter & Slaven

Date	Rec.	Rel.	Pub.	Title	Performer	Place	Album	Label	Source
1965			x	Stagolee	Julius Lester		Julius Lester Accompanying Himself on the Guitar	Vanguard VRS 9199	Lester, Black 116-17; Lester, "Stagolee"; Dodd
1965		x		Stagger Lee	Shirley Ellis		The Name Game	Congress CGS-3003 MCA 20452	AMG
1965, May		x		Stackerlee	Tom Rush		Blue/Songs/Ballads	Prestige PRS-7374; Fantasy FCD-24709-2	AMG; Osborne
1965, Oct. 26	x			Stagolee	Jesse Fuller	London		Fontana TL 5313	Leadbitter & Slaven
1966		x		Stagger Lee	Dave "Baby" Cortez		Tweetie Pie	Roulette SR 25315	Osborne
1966, Sept.		x		Stagger Lee	The Righteous Brothers		Go Ahead and Cry	Verve V-65004	AMG
1967		x		Stagger Lee	Tim Hardin		This Is Tim Hardin	Atco SD-33210	AMG
1967, Aug.		x		Stagger Lee	James Brown		Cold Sweat	King KS-1020; Javelin HADCD-164	AMG, Hanousek
1967, Oct. 12		x		Stagger Lee	Wilson Pickett		I'm in Love	Atlantic 2448; Rhino 72218-2	
1968?	x			Stagger Lee & Billy	Ike and Tina Turner		b-side of "Can't Change a Breakup"; Greatest Hits	EMI; Curb D2-77332	AMG

Year			Artist	Title	Album	Catalog	Source
1969	x		Taj Mahal	Stagger Lee	Giant Step/De Ole Folks at Home	CBS GP-18; Columbia CG-18	AMG
1970s	x		The Green Mountain Boys	Stagolee	The Green Mountain Boys	Green Mountain GMS 1053	Dodd
1970s		x	Doug Sahm	Stagger Lee	Doug Sahm Live	Bear Tracks BTCD 943401	AMG: Hanousek
1970	x		Wilbert Harrison	Stagger Lee	Let's Work Together; Kansas City: His Legendary Golden Classics	Sue 8801; Collectables COL-CD-5294	Marcus
1971	x		The Quintet	Stagger Lee	Future Tense	USA 5514	AMG
1971?		x	Jerry Lee Lewis	Stagger Lee	Killer; The Mercury Years, Vol. 2 (1969-1972)	Mercury 836938	AMG
1971, May		x	Doc Watson and Merle Watson	Stack O'Lee (Stack-A-Lee)	Ballads from Deep Gap	Vanguard VSD 6576	AMG
1971, Aug.	x		Tommy Roe	Stagger Lee	Greatest Hits	ABC 11307; MCA 1519	
1972	x		Dr. John	Stack-A-Lee	Dr. John's Gumbo	ATCO SD-36-7006; Alligator AL 3901	AMG; Osborne
1972	x		Freddy Weller	Stagger Lee	Promised Land	CBS 64643	AMG
1973		x	Fats Domino	Stagger Lee	Live at Montreux	Atlantic 50107	AMG

Date	Rec.	Rel.	Pub.	Title	Performer	Place	Album	Label	Source
1974		x		Stagger Lee	Terry Melcher		Terry Melcher	Reprise 2185	AMG
1974, Apr. 4	x			Stag-O-Lee	Professor Longhair	Bogalusa, La.	Rock'N'Roll Gumbo	Dancing Cat DD-3006-2	AMG
1975		x		Stagger Lee	P. J. Proby	Somewhere		Liberty LST-7406; Sunset 50404	AMG; Osborne
1976		x		Stackolee [toast]	Bruce Jackson		Get Your Ass in the Water and Swim Like Me!	Rounder 2014	Jackson; Marcus
1977		x		Stack O Lee	Roy Book Binder		Ragtime Millionaire	Yellow Bee 5BG-2023	Dodd
1977		x		Stagger Lee	Downchild Blues Band	Toronto	So Far	Adelphi 4116; Posterity PT 13004	Litchfield; Osborne
1977		x		Stack O'Lee	Mickey Baker		Blues & Jazz Guitar	Kicking Mule 142	AMG
1978	x			Stagger Lee	Professor Longhair		Live on the Queen Mary	Harvest 4086; One Way 56855; Harvest SW-11790	AMG; Osborne
1978	x			Stagger Lee	Professor Longhair	New Orleans	Last Mardi Gras	Atlantic SD-2-4001; Rhino 4001	AMG
1978, Nov. 15		x		Stagger Lee	The Grateful Dead	San Francisco	Shakedown Street	Arista AL-4198; ARCD 8228-2	AMG
1979		x		Wrong 'Em Boyo	The Clash	Wessex Studios	London Calling	Epic 36328	Marcus

Year	Song title	Artist	Album	Location	Label / Catalog	Source	
1980	Stagger Lee	Neil Diamond	September Morn		Columbia 36121	AMG; Hanousek	x
1980, July	Stagger Lee	Southside Johnny and the Asbury Jukes	Reach Up and Touch the Sky—Live		Mercury 826285; SRM 1-8602; Polygram 826285-2	AMG; Osborne; Hanousek	x
1982?	Stacker Lee	Bertha Wenzel and Bill Small	Folk Songs of the River		Century Custom Recording Service 20074	Dodd	x
1983	Stack-A-Lee	Dr. John	On a Mardi Gras Day	London	Great Southern 11024	AMG	x
1986	Stack O'Lee	Merle Travis	Rough, Rowdy and Blue		CMH-C-6262	Dodd	x
1986	Staggerlee	John Cephas and Phil Wiggins	Dog Days of August		Flying Fish FF-9034	AMG	x
1991	Stackerlee	Tom Paley	Old Tom Moore and More		Global Village C 309	Dodd	x
1991	Stagger Lee	Zim Zemarel and His Orchestra	Big Band Swing		Vanguard 246; Hindsight HCD-246	AMG	x
1991, Sept.	Stagger Lee	Threadgill Troubadors	Threadgill's Super Session	Austin, Tex.	Watermelon 1013	AMG	x
1992	Stack O'Lee	Mickey Baker	Blues, Jazz & Rock Guitar	London	Shanachie 97019	AMG	x
1992	Stack o Lee Aloha	Bob Brozman	A Truckload of Blues		Rounder 3119	Dodd	x

Date	Rec.	Pub.	Rel.	Title	Performer	Place	Album	Label	Source
1992, Mar.			x	Stagger Lee	Tim and Mollie O'Brien	Westminister, Colo.	Remember Me	Sugar Hill 3804	AMG
1992, July 31	x			Stagger Lee	Willie and The Poor Boys	Halmstad, Sweden	Tear It Up Live	Blind Pig 5012	AMG; Hanousek
1993			x	Stagger Lee	Professor Longhair		Big Chief	Rhino 71446-2	AMG
1993			x	Richard Lee	Colin Linden	Toronto	South at Eight, North at Nine	Deluge 3004	Mackie; Hanousek
1993			x	Stagger Lee	The Fabulous Thunderbirds		Wrap It Up	Sony Music Special Products A24202	AMG
1993, Oct.			x	Stack A Lee	Bob Dylan		World Gone Wrong	Columbia CK 57590	AMG
1994			x	Stagger Lee	Huey Lewis & The News	San Rafael, Calif.	Four Chords and Several Years Ago	Elektra 61500-2	AMG
1994			x	More About John Henry	Tom T. Hall		Great Country Hits	SPM 5029	AMG
1994, Mar. 30			x	Stagger Lee	Sleepy LaBeef	Hanson, Mass.	Strange Things Happening	Rounder CD-3129	AMG
1995			x	Stagger Lee	Mike Russo		Mike Russo	Arhoolie 4003	
1996			x	Stagger Lee	Nick Cave and the Bad Seeds	Melbourne, Australia	Murder Ballads	Reprise 9 46195-2	
1996			x	The Unrepentant	Steve Earle	Nashville	I Feel Alright	Warner 9 46201-2	

APPENDIX B: THE PRIMARY VERSIONS OF THE BALLAD

The jazz version, recorded by Ukulele Ike (Cliff Edwards), July 25, 1928:

Stack O'Lee Blues

Listen folks, I'm gonna tell you
A story you've never heard.
It's all about a high-yellow colored man,
There's truth in every word.
I'm talkin' about the man called Stack O'Lee.

It was in St. Louis on Pine Street,
That's exactly where it was at,
Stack up and shot himself a competin' colored man
On account of a dirty old Stetson hat.
And from then on they called him Hard Luck Stack O'Lee

The sheriff came up and said, "Hello, Stack,
Let's have a little talk."
Then he threw the handcuffs onto Stack
And said, "Come on, buddy, let's walk."
Down to the jailhouse they took poor Stack O'Lee.

Stack's gal went out to get some bond money
For somebody to go his bail,
She said, "There ain't a trick in this world that I wouldn't turn
To get my Stack out of jail."
Oh, how she loved her Stack O'Lee.

Next mornin' down in the courtroom
The judge sat down on the bench,
The first one to occupy the witness stand
Was old Stack O's sweet-lovin' wench.
She said, "I'm gonna argue with the jury for Stack O'Lee."

The judge got up and called the sentence,
His eyes was filled with tears.
He said, "I'm gonna be good to you this time, Stack,
I'm only gonna give you 69 years.
You got plenty of time now, Stack O'Lee."

They told him, "Don't ever sharpen your razor,
Brother, don't shave your face,
Don't ever ask anybody the hour of the day
'Cause you ain't goin' no place.
You're in here from now on, Stack O'Lee."

This song is just about half through.
To get it all here I've tried.
You better stop your machine, turn your record over,
And play the other side.
And you'll hear some more of the song called "Stack O'Lee."

Stack O's gal was a good gal,
Most everybody knows,

She said, "I've gotta go and get myself a lot of bucks
To buy Stack some new prison clothes.
In a way I must provide for Stack O'Lee."

But one mornin' she began to moan,
Great God, how she cried.
She got a letter from the jailhouse,
Said, "Lady, your Stack has died.
He just up and kicked the bucket, did Stack O'Lee."

She went out and got a big rubber-tired hearse,
She got a little old lonesome hack,
Took him to the graveyard,
And laid him right down on his back.
And then they kicked a lot of dirt on the face of Stack O'Lee.

A man standin' by said, "Last night while I was sleepin',
I had myself an awful dream.
If you got some tar, I got some Stenman lamps,
I'll show you just how to cook with steam.
I might as well hop right along with Stack O'Lee."

But finally, one might say eventually,
Stack O'Lee's gal died,
The last thing she said was that she wanted to be
Buried right by his side.
She said, "I wants my body to cool with Stack O'Lee."

She had a common, ordinary funeral,
She was planted right down by his side.
On the monument read this inscription:
"These riders rode their last ride."
And that is the story of the man called Stack O'Lee.

The folksong version, a composite from several texts collected by Robert W. Gordon, printed in the *New York Times Magazine*, June 5, 1927:

Stackolee

Now what you all know about this?
An' what you all know about that?
They say Stack killed Ole Billy Lyons
'Bout a damned old Stetson hat!
Oh, poor, poor Stackolee!

It was on a dark
And cold stormy night
That Billy Lyons and Stackolee
They had that awful fight.
That bad, that bad man Stackolee!

"Oh, Stackolee, oh, Stackolee,
Please spare my life!
For I have got two babies,
And a darling little wife!"
That bad, that bad man Stackolee!

"I care not for your babies
Nor your darling little wife;
You done ruint my Stetson hat,
An' I'm bound to have your life."
That bad, that bad man Stackolee!

It was no Stetson hat,
He didn't have a good excuse;
They say he killed Ole Billy Lyons
'Cause he gave his gal abuse,
Oh, poor, poor Stackolee!

Stacko's wench was a good girl,
She was as true as steel;
She said, "I'll stand by you, Stack,
On you I'm never goin' to squeal!"
Down at the trial of Stackolee.

The judge put on the black cap,
His voice was stern and cold;
"I sentences you to be hanged.
The Lord have mercy on your soul!"
That bad, that bad man Stackolee!

He had a rubber-tired hearse,
A lot of rubber-tired hacks;
Took old Stackolee to the cemetery
Never to bring him back.
Oh, poor, poor Stackolee!

The New Orleans version, words and music by Harold Logan and Lloyd
Price, December 1958:

Stagger Lee

The night was clear and the moon was yellow,
And the leaves came tumbling down.

I was standing on the corner
When I heard my bulldog bark,
He was barking at the two men
Who were gambling in the dark.

It was Stagger Lee and Billy,
Two men who gamble late,
Stagger Lee threw seven,
Billy swore that he threw eight.

Stagger Lee told Billy,
"I can't let you go with that,
You have won all my money
And my brand new Stetson hat."

Stagger Lee went home,
And he got his forty-four,
Said, "I'm going to the barroom
Just to pay that debt I owe."

Stagger Lee went to the barroom,
And he stood across the barroom door.
Said, "Now nobody move,"
And he pulled his forty-four.

"Stagger Lee," cried Billy,
"Oh please don't take my life.
I got three children,
And a very sickly wife."

Stagger Lee shot Billy,
Oh, he shot that poor boy so bad,
Till the bullet came through Billy,
And it broke the bartender's glass.

TWENTY

Where Honor Is Due: Frederick Douglass as Representative Black Man

WILSON J. MOSES

Frederick Douglass may or may not have been the greatest African American abolitionist and orator of the 19th Century, but he was certainly the most accomplished master of self-projection. His autobiographical writings demonstrate the genius with which he seized and manipulated mainstream American symbols and values. By appropriating the Euro-American myth of the self-made man, Douglass guaranteed that his struggle would be canonized, not only within an African American tradition, but within the traditions of the mainstream as well. He manipulated the rhetoric of Anglo-Saxon manhood as skillfully as did any of his white contemporaries, including such master manipulators as Abraham Lincoln, Ralph Waldo Emerson, and Phineas T. Barnum. I mention Douglass along with these wily exemplars of American showmanship, not because I want to drag out embarrassing cliches about making heroes more human, but in order to address the truly monumental nature of Douglass's accomplishments. Douglass, like Lincoln, Emerson, and Barnum, was abundantly endowed with the spiderish craft and foxlike cunning that are often marks of self-made men.

Douglass, like his bluff contemporary Walt Whitman, made his living by the art of self-celebration, a skill that has always figured in the strategies of American literary figures. He sang his song of himself, through four main versions of his autobiography, creating himself as a mythic figure and racial icon.[1] The result is that even scholars and historians who may be relatively unfamiliar with other black American personalities of the 19th Century are acquainted with the major events of Douglass's life, or at least with his version of them. He was born into slavery in 1818, escaped to the North in 1838 and, with amazing rapidity, by 1840 was well on the way to establishing himself as the principal black abolitionist in the United States. Among his

accomplishments, Douglass served as a newspaper editor, Civil War re-
cruiter, president of the Freedman's Bank, minister to Haiti, recorder of
deeds, and Marshall of the District of Columbia. In the final analysis, he was
a man of great dignity, principle, and courage, but he was also a showman,
and he made his living mainly by cultivating the myth of Frederick Douglass.

When he attempted to function as a businessman or politician, he sometimes waded in beyond his depth, and thus he was embarrassed by the failure
of the Freedman's Bank, shortly after he assumed its presidency. His tenure
as minister to Haiti, was troubled from the beginning. As he made preparations to assume the post, he found that he could not get first-class accommodations by railroad or steamboat going south. Special arrangements were
made for him to travel on a U.S. naval vessel, the *Kearsarge*, which moved
some to comment that not every black American found it possible so to avoid
the indignities of Jim Crow travel. Douglass was constantly pressured by the
State Department and the American business community to deal with the
Haitians in an imperious and insulting manner. This, to his credit, he would
not do. Black people everywhere identified passionately with Haiti, the
world's first sovereign black republic, and Douglass could not allow himself
to be seen as a puppet for American racist expansionism. As part of his duties,
he attempted to negotiate for a military base at Môle St. Nicholas, but his
respect for Haitian sovereignty led to his being accused of incompetency by
those whose interests he refused to slavishly serve. When his efforts were
unsuccessful, whites rebuked him as an inept representative of American
interests.

But even Douglass's setbacks were somehow transmuted into victories by
the alchemy of a brilliant personality and the fact that black America has
always had a desperate need for heroes. Nonetheless, it must be admitted
that many aspects of Douglass's life and writings are controversial. No serious historian can ignore the problem of self-serving selectivity that lies
behind the veil of homely modesty that he assumes in his autobiographical
writings. The task of every biographer of Frederick Douglass has been to fill
in some of the discreet omissions in Douglass's skillful work of self-promotion. Historians and literary scholars are increasingly aware of the craft with
which Douglass manipulated audiences and readers, and they have recently
provided us with considerable information that Douglass did not see fit to
reveal. Many of these matters were discussed in the first full-length biography of Douglass, published by Benjamin Quarles in 1948.[2] More recent
biographers have built on Quarles' work, giving us a portrait that is admi-
rable and believable; nonetheless, in far too many instances, Douglass has
been allowed to dictate the terms of his own biography.[3]

Because even the best biographies of Douglass have been appendices to
his own brilliant autobiographical writings, the point is often forgotten that
Douglass was not a gigantic abnormality in black American history, but in
many ways a typical black American man of the class and region he represented. In typical American fashion, Douglass sought in his writings to dem-

onstrate his individuality, along with his individualism. The very self-reliance and independence that he stressed in his autobiographies represented
conformity to the American type of the self-made man. Thus, Douglass was,
to use Emerson's phrase, a representative man. Much of the present-day
biographical and literary treatment of Douglass makes him appear to be
exceptional. For his own part, Douglass at times stressed the Emersonian
dictum that the great man is often great because he is representative, not
because he is exceptional. Self-reliance, for him as for Emerson, often
existed in the paradox of blending one's ego into larger "transcendental"
forces, of believing that what is true of one's self is true of others. Douglass's
concept of self-reliance, like Emerson's, was grounded in the principle or
universality rather than difference. Douglass was, as I hope to show pres-
ently, not only a representative man, but a representative *black* man.

On the other hand, there were ways in which he was not representative.
Douglass seemed, at times, to be less attuned to the cultural sentiments of
black Americans and to their political struggles than were some other black
men among his contemporaries. Among black-power advocates, he is celebrated as a prophet of self-determination. They celebrate his founding of
The North Star, an independent newspaper, and it is with relish that they
recall his rallying cry "We must be our own representatives!" But Douglass
could change positions dramatically on black-power-related issues. He did at
times champion black institutions, and then on other occasions he denounced them as self-segregating. Douglass's ideology was thoroughly in-
consistent, usually opportunistic, and always self-serving. I suspect that if
Douglass were alive today, he would be as uncontrollable as ever, and that
his often shifting ideology would be now, as it was then, often unacceptable
to liberals and conservatives alike.

Douglass represented a class of free black males who were literate in
English, influenced by Christianity, and afflicted with a sometimes unconscious Anglophilism.[4] Mary Helen Washington and Valerie Smith remind
us that he was obsessed with attempts to emulate and compete with white
males in terms of the values of assertive masculinity.[5] Nonetheless, the
recent interpretation by James McFeely depicts Douglass in ways specifically
adapted to liberal ideologies on the 1980s.[6] A case in point is Douglass's
relationship to the women's movement. He did indeed commendably support women's suffrage, but this support was at times less than lukewarm.
Douglass gave black male suffrage a much higher priority than white female
suffrage, even when his feminist friends became exasperated with him.
While on the one hand he got along well with white liberal women, and
even married one of them, he was not afraid to confront them when he felt
their interests to be in conflict with his as a black male.

Today there is endless discussion of Douglass's private life and his friendships with women, both black and white, for we now know much more
about his personal affairs than did his earlier biographers. Douglass had a
commanding personality; he was strikingly handsome and stood over six feet

tall; he was athletic and he possessed an intense sexual attractiveness. I believe that a great deal of what he accomplished was a result of his magnetic virility. As Mary Helen Washington has observed, he largely owed his escape from slavery to a black woman, Anna Murray, who became his first wife. One historian has speculated, probably accurately, that Anna was pregnant with their first child, Rosetta, before the couple left the South. It is impossible not to be curious about the early sexual development of Douglass, who later portrayed himself as a puritanical feminist, an image that was so useful to him in his dealings with his New England abolitionist contemporaries. Was it really possible for a heterosexual black male to grow up in a slave society without being affected by the earthy values of plantation sexuality? Douglass's autobiography is silent on such matters, unlike that of his 18th-Century predecessor, Benjamin Franklin, who admits to sexual adventurism during youth.

In recent years, black feminists have become increasingly critical of Douglass's treatment of his first wife. Anna Douglass was a dutiful help mate to her husband; she was a hard worker and a thrifty housewife. A portion of Douglass's financial success has been attributed to her able administration of his domestic finances, but she was not up to the management of a newspaper and she apparently never learned to read. Furthermore, it does not seem that she provided Douglass with much in the way of intellectual companionship; for this, he often went outside his home. The women were usually white, and his friendship in later years with the young journalist Ida B. Wells is the best-known intellectual friendship he is known to have developed with a black woman. It is interesting to note in this regard that Wells frequently separated herself ideologically from other black women leaders. That uncompromising militancy that earned her the hostility of the leadership of the National Association of Colored Women apparently endeared her to Douglass, while isolating her from the likes of Mary Church Terrell and Margaret Murray Washington. Ida B. Wells was, significantly, one of the few black women who did *not* resent his second marriage at the age of sixty-six (after Anna's death) to Helen Pitts, a forty-six-year-old white woman.

Douglass's ambivalent feelings toward Sojourner Truth are seldom discussed. Sojourner was a dynamic black woman abolitionist who once caused him public annoyance by responding to his declamations with the question, "Frederick, is God dead?" This was a matter of some embarrassment, since Douglass was more than once plagued by charges of irreligiosity. Sojourner Truth, on the other hand, was closely associated with the strident religiosity of the day and was much more closely related to proletarian evangelical Christianity than was the transcendental Douglass, with his increasing pretensions to gentility. Late in life, Douglass dealt with Truth rather ungenerously, when he compared her speaking style to the ungainly dialect of a minstrel show, implying that her language was "grotesque" and only quoted in order to belittle and degrade black people generally.[7]

Douglass's relationships with white women generated controversy as early as 1849, when he paraded down Broadway in New York with the two Englishwomen, Julia and Eliza Griffiths—one on each arm. Julia eventually moved in with the Douglass family to assist with the operation of *The North Star,* and within a year she had brought it from the brink of ruin to a sound financial footing. Rumor was rife in the abolitionist community that the relationship between Douglass and Miss Griffiths had led to difficulties in the Douglass household. Apparently the relationship was purely a matter of business and political sympathy. Douglass's relationship with Ottilla Assing, a German reformer, is still the subject of speculation. William McFeely is convinced that the friendship did indeed have a sexual dimension, although he cannot document his contention. It has, however, long been known that Assing left Douglass a substantial inheritance after her suicide in 1884. McFeely implies that the suicide was a result of hearing the news of Douglass's second marriage to Helen Pitts.[8]

Douglass's relationships with white women were not without troubles of another sort. In 1865, he was angered by what Waldo Martin has called the "blatant racism" of Elizabeth Cady Stanton.[9] Stanton was incensed by the denial of women's voting rights and protested that this denial placed white women on a level "classed with idiots, lunatics, and Negroes." This statement, and others that were even more offensive, would seem to indicate that Stanton saw black people as inferior to white women. Douglass took exception to being classed with idiots and lunatics, but the friendship apparently endured, and Stanton was a well-wisher at the time of Douglass's second marriage.

It is not difficult to understand why Douglass played up to white feminists after the demise of the abolitionist movement, for in them he found a receptive audience for his writings and speeches. Within this view, his marriage to a white feminist was not only an affair of the heart, but a significant political move. Black men and women were not well positioned to help him maintain public visibility once the abolitionist movement had run its course; the women's rights movement, headed by white women, still offered him a forum. Another way of seeing it was that in his first marriage he made an alliance with a free black woman who could assist him in his flight to freedom, whereas in his second marriage he cemented ties with his new audience, which was largely composed of white feminists.

In an 1884 letter to Elizabeth Cady Stanton, Douglass argued the naturalness of his marriage to a white woman, saying that his closest personal friends for the preceding forty years had been white.[10] It was true enough that many of his friends had been white women, with whom he interacted in the abolitionist and women's movements. It was equally true that many of his strongest supporters and most intimate associates had been black during those forty years. Had Douglass forgotten his involvement in business with Martin Delany or in politics with the black convention movement? Had he forgotten that he had married Helen Pitts in the Fifteenth Street Presbyterian Church, and that the ceremony had been conducted by its black pastor, Rev. Francis J. Grimké, a black man with whom he had much in common? Like Douglass, Grimké was the offspring of a wealthy white planter and a slave mother. Archibald Grimké, Frank's brother, had married a white woman in 1879.

Like other black male leaders of his generation, including the Grimké brothers, William Wells Brown, and John Mercer Langston, Douglass had a complex set of feelings regarding his identity as the son of a white man. There have been interesting speculations, of late, as to whether Douglass actually knew and loved his white father.[11] In one version of his autobiography, Douglass reports the rumor that his master was his father. In another version, he does not repeat the rumor, but instead describes the boyhood memory of his master leading him about by the hand, and treating him affectionately and calling him "his little Indian boy." The late Allison Davis, a distinguished black American psychologist at the University of Chicago, opined that Douglass did in fact know his white father, and that he spent his entire life attempting to win the love of his rejecting parent. Davis also made much of what he saw as a father-son relationship between Douglass and his white patron, William Lloyd Garrison.[12]

There can be no doubt that Douglass had great respect for Garrison, the contentious and courageous white abolitionists, who strongly influenced his ideology in the early years after his escape from slavery. As a Garrisonian, Douglass often shared the platform with Charles Lennox Remond, who until that time had been the foremost of Garrison's black supporters. But Douglass soon supplanted Remond as the premier black antislavery lecturer. Then, over the next several years, Douglass went through the painful process of separating himself from the Garrisonian position. Perhaps as a result of contact with Samuel Ringgold Ward, who rejected some Garrison positions, Douglass eventually began to challenge Garrison himself. In a move that occasioned much bitterness, he moved out on his own to become a newspaper editor, and to champion the view that the Constitution was not a proslavery compact, but a living document that could be used effectively in the crusade against slavery.

Douglass's complaints against the white abolitionists had a foundation on a personal level as well. On his first trip to England in 1845, Douglass was forced to travel with the officious and condescending James Buffum, a white American, who doled out Douglass's traveling expenses. One contemporary observed in Buffum "an enormous degree of love, affection," which he attributed to a "feminine" element in Buffum's manner "that Douglass does not respect."[13] But what truly enraged Douglass, we can be certain, was the idea that he could not be trusted to handle his own financial affairs. Douglass was also offended by the insistence of some white abolitionists that he deliver his speeches in plantation dialect. Plantation dialect was not Douglass's preferred style of discourse. He was proud of his standard English and he had acquired it before leaving the South, since he had spent some of his time on the plantation in the "big house." Furthermore, he was committed to expanding the content of his lectures to include not only his personal reminiscences, but also his developing philosophy of human rights. In the second edition of his autobiography, he expressed his resentment of those white abolitionists who wanted him to confine himself to descriptions of his personal victimization.

But Douglass's break with Garrison arose from philosophical issues as well as personality conflicts. In large part, his changing attitude had to do with the influences of other black men, often occurring in conventions of black men. In his autobiography, he does in fact speak of the importance of these conventions. Douglass admits to bonding with black men before his escape from slavery and describes these friendships with vivid detail. He shares with us the affectionate recollection of studying the Bible with Father Lawson, the pious preacher. He recalls with gratitude how Sandy Jenkins assisted him after his beating by Covey and of how he gave him the magic root that helped him finally to resist him. And, in his autobiography, he credits the influences of other black men with whom he interacted after his escape from slavery.

In a chapter of his autobiography of 1892 entitled "Honor to whom Honor is Due," Douglass acknowledged several black men who were rivals and who clearly possessed intellects and rhetorical skills of their own. Douglass, to his credit, did pay tribute to Samuel Ringgold Ward, whom he acknowledged as the greatest black orator of the day. Ward probably had a hand in persuading Douglass away from the sterile and narrow Garrisonian interpretation of the Constitution, since it was during a debate with Ward that Douglass was forced to analyze the logic of the Garrisonian position. Ward presented him with the position putatively held by the majority of black people—that the Constitution could bear interpretation as an antislavery document.[14]

William Wells Brown, another black abolitionist, reports an interesting story concerning Douglass and Ward. Douglass was once interrupted on the podium by a heckler who asserted that Douglass's oratorical ability was due to his white ancestry. It happened that Ward, a tall and robust man of unadulterated African ancestry, was in the audience and rose to acquit himself in such a manner as to impress some in the audience that he was certainly on a par with Douglass.

Douglass's relationship with Martin Delany was also significant. When in 1848, over the objections of Garrison, Douglass founded his newspaper *The North Star*, it was with Delany as coeditor, but Douglass soon fell out with Delany over a number of issues, most important among them being the issue of black pride. "I thank God for making me a man simply," said Douglass, "but Delany always thanks him for making him a '*black* man.'"[15] Douglass considered Delany a racial chauvinist and an extremist. Delany did in fact show a great interest in Africa and in the prospects of founding a national homeland for the black race, a position that Douglass could not endorse. He once said that, if he were inclined to go to Africa, he would unhesitatingly enroll under Delany's leadership, but Douglass had no interest either in going or in supporting the movement. Delany's position implied that American slavery would not be abolished until a powerful and independent black republic was founded in Africa, and thus placed much emphasis and effort on achieving that end. Douglass relied on more immediate and direct means to abolitionism, based on moral persuasion and political agitation within the United States.

Douglass, of course, was proven correct when the Civil War eventually led to universal emancipation and black citizenship, but the war also delivered a serious personal affront to his ego. We know that Douglass and Delany each had meetings with Abraham Lincoln, seeking to obtain commissions in the United States Army during the Civil War.[16] To Douglass's eternal chagrin, Delany was commissioned a major, while Douglass was ignored and left to brood throughout the great crusade like some black Achilles.

Douglass also had several run-ins with Henry Highland Garnet, who like Delany favored African emigration. Douglass's refusal to endorse Henry Highland Garnet's call for slave insurrection at the Convention of 1843 receives scant attention in heroic treatments of Douglass's life. Garnet was a formidable opponent and Douglass took him seriously enough during the 1850s to attack this position in *Frederick Douglass Monthly*.

Douglass's hostility to the black congressman John Mercer Langston is one of the more intriguing puzzles in the lives of the two men. Their backgrounds as favored slaves of mixed background were similar, but similarity of background does not necessarily provide a basis for political friendships. In 1850, when Douglass was thirty-three and Langston twenty-one, the two had traveled together on an Eastern speaking tour. But, by 1853, Langston was accusing Douglass of using his newspaper primarily as a means of self-promotion. The journal reported the most trivial of events in the East, he wrote, but "Men of the West cannot be noticed . . . [T]he *North Star*, edited by Frederick Douglass, is not the organ of the colored people."[17] A not altogether friendly rivalry persisted for many years. Langston advised against making Douglass president of the Freedman's Bank, recognizing correctly that the presidency would prove "difficult, trying and disappointing."[18] Douglass's embarrassment might have been avoided were it not for the egotism that Langston had long noted in him.

We seldom hear of Douglass's sometimes uneasy relationship with Alexander Crummell (1819–98), the American-born and educated son of a West African captive, and prominent spokesman of the back-to-Africa movement. Douglass had accused Crummell of abandonment during the 1850s at a time when he himself was being accused of dereliction by the nationalist emigrationists. Crummell, after several years' residence in England attending Cambridge University and lecturing for the abolitionist cause, had migrated to Liberia, West Africa, and dedicated himself to the building of a black republic. In 1855, Douglass called on him in the name of black unity to renounce the "agreeable duty" that anyone could perform, and to return to the United States to perform the "disagreeable duty" of abolitionist struggle.[19] This spirit of accusation was consistent in the writings of Douglass when addressing Crummell, Garnet, Delany, and other black nationalists. Douglass maintained his confrontational stance long after the constitutional abolition of slavery and the decline of nationalist versus abolitionist controversy. In 1885, he challenged the position that Crummell took during a speech at Storer College, where Crummell had argued that black American leaders must stop dwelling on slavery and focus their attention on "new ideas and new aims for a new era." Douglass vociferously objected, saying that we should forever hold slavery in mind. Douglass and Crummell also disagreed over the need for black social institutions. Douglass considered them harmful, while Crummell insisted that they would remain a necessity of life for many years to come.

Douglass is not entirely to blame for the silence of his biographers on his involvement with other black men. I do not believe that it is Douglass's fault that in the final analysis his status was giganticized until he came to be seen as the only great black man of the 19th Century. Part of the reason is that many of Douglass's rivals were too black, and there has been a tendency to downplay the significance of 19th-Century black-power advocates in favor of the integrationist, assimilationist Douglass.

But if Douglass could accuse some black figures of being too black, he could accuse others of not being black enough: thus, his attacks on the memory of Alexander Dumas, during his trip to Paris in 1886, when he wrote to friends:

> So we have nothing to thank Dumas for. Victor Hugo, the white man, could speak for us, but this brilliant colored man who could have let down sheets of fire upon the heads of tyrants and carried freedom to his enslaved people, had no word in behalf [of] liberty or the enslaved. I have not yet seen his statue here in Paris. I shall go to see it as it is an acknowledgment of the genius of a colored man, but not because I honor the character of the man himself.[20]

But if Douglass felt entitled to criticize Dumas for not speaking out on the issue of black slavery, Douglass himself had been criticized for failing to support African nationalism. True enough, he showed an interest in the African background of black folk and what he saw as their "ethnological" tie to ancient Egypt, but this should not be interpreted as support for 19th-Century black nationalism or the African Civilization movement of the day.[21] Douglass was unlike Edward Wilmot Blyden, who saw in the Egyptian heritage the basis for the future greatness of an African state. Douglass's pilgrimage to Egypt in 1887 and his writings on the claims of the American Negro to a noble Nilotic past were clearly aimed at proving that black Americans were fit for biological assimilation in America.

Douglass noted with bitter humor that many persons who would have had no objection to his marrying a person darker than himself and the color of his mother were shocked by his marriage to a person lighter than himself and the color of his father.[22] He wrote to Oliver Johnson, making the point that his second wife resembled him more closely in physiognomy than did his first.[23] In his 1886 essay "The Future of the Colored Race," he said it was "only prejudice against the Negro which calls everyone, however nearly connected with the white race, and however remotely connected with the Negro race, a Negro. The motive is not a desire to elevate the Negro, but to humiliate and degrade those of mixed blood; not a desire to bring the Negro up but to cast the mulatto and the quadroon down."[24] Douglass, in short, denied that mulattos, like himself, were truly Negroes.

Intermarriage and race mixing have never been among the spiritual strivings of the majority of African Americans, but for Douglass racial amalgamation was the ultimate goal. He was thus, in at least one respect, not a representative man. Moreover, he was not a race man, for although he remained true to the goal of racial equality in America, he repudiated any special feelings of racial pride, saying,

> Our color is the gift of the Almighty. We should neither be proud of it nor ashamed of it. . . .I have seen myself charged with a lack of race pride. I am not ashamed of that charge. I have no apology or vindication to offer. If fifty years of uncompromising devotion to the cause of the colored man in this country does not vindicate me, I am content to live without vindication. . . . When a colored man is charged with a want of race pride, he may well ask, What race? for a large percentage of the colored race are related in some degree to more than one race. But the whole assumption of race pride is ridiculous.[25]

The historian William McFeely and the conservative columnist George Will have praised Frederick Douglass for his repudiation of reverse racism. Are we to assume then that Americans, black or white, have come to endorse Douglass's advocacy of a "color blind society" based on the biological amalgamation and cultural absorption of African Americans? That was the message of Frederick Douglass, but does this embody the spirit of black America? What does it mean to be a hero? What does it mean to have the shaggy-headed leonine portrait of Frederick Douglass staring down at us from the bulletin boards of schoolrooms across America during Black History Month?

My answer to the first question is that black Americans have always rejected Douglass's vision of America, and that neither black nor white Americans are committed to the eradication of racial distinctions in American life. While the spirit of black folk in the United States is clearly democratic and egalitarian, it is also essentially one of racial self-determination and ethnic pride. Douglass believed that the concept of ethnic pride and black unity was a mistake. He felt that it was actually unsafe for black people to stand together as a separate entity. We should beware the danger of isolating ourselves. We should not attempt to be "a nation within a nation." Rightly or wrongly, the spirit of black folk runs counter to such talk. There may be some exceptions, but these are rare and remarkable. The essential separatism of the black American people is to be seen in its marriage patterns. Marriage outside the race is uncommon and will probably continue to be so for the foreseeable future. Douglass ultimately renounced not only marital separatism, but all forms of racial unity and ethnic pride. Douglass offered the example of his own social adjustment, not only as a statement of personal preference, but as a proposed solution to the race problem in America.

If Frederick Douglass represents the spirit of black folk, then, he certainly represents it in all of its complexities, ambivalences, and contradictions. Who is to say whether the genius of self-promotion that characterized Douglass was more attributable to African American exuberance or to a typically American showmanship and flimflammery? Like many black leaders of the present day, and many American leaders throughout our history, Douglass made an industry of himself. When compared with other black men of the 19th Century, Douglass was in no way a giant among dwarfs, but certainly he managed to stamp his name on an era much more effectively than did Martin Delany or John Mercer Langston. And the great irony of Douglass's sainthood is that he openly violated some of the most sacred canons of African American political culture. At the peak of his power and influence, Douglass scoffed at the idea of black unity, opposed the idea of separate black institutions, and sometimes denied the need for any concept of racial pride. And yet he continued to participate in black institutions, took pride in black accomplishments, and exploited his status as a black spokesman.

Since Douglass seems to have attained an unassailable position in the pantheon of heroes we dutifully trot out every year for black history month, it is appropriate for us to ask what we really mean when we speak of an African American hero. Academic politicians will never find it necessary to ask the question, of course; for them it will be adequate simply to say that black people need heroes. After all, doesn't everyone need heroes? Hero worshippers are seldom committed to accurate reporting of what great men and women have thought and said. Analytical reflection on their writings is neither desired nor tolerated. Hero worshippers are looking for paper dolls that they can call their own, pasteboard silhouettes who can be clothed in the ideological garb of passing fancies.

Perhaps much of the continuing popularity of Frederick Douglass may be attributed to the facility with which he can be adapted to the conveniences of any hour. Douglass's aphoristic pontifications may be conveniently invoked on almost every occasion in this age of the "sound bite," and his ideologically malleable pronouncements may be rationalized with Emersonian blandness, as we recall the facile observation that "Consistency is the hobgoblin of small minds." Douglass may be claimed by nationalists like Molefi K. Asante as a symbol of militant black messianism or by George Will as a representative of some vaguely imagined and yet-to-be-glimpsed color-blind society. Perhaps one reason for our continuing fascination with Douglass is the amorphous quality of his symbolism. He seems to encompass the continuing ambivalence of black men in America with respect to many issues, including separatism, integration, Afrocentrism, Eurocentrism, and male-female relationships. He is, perhaps, a more representative black man than even he realized, and perhaps more typical than he suspected of those other 19th-Century black men to whom he paid cursory and fleeting tribute in his autobiographical writings.

NOTES

1. Frederick Douglass, *Narrative of the Life of Frederick* (Boston: At the Antislavery Office, 1845); *My Bondage and My Freedom* (1855; rept. New York: Arno, 1969); and *The Life and Times of Frederick Douglass* (1892; rept. London: Collier, 1962). The possibility that Douglass may have collaborated with Otilla Assing on the German translation of *My Bondage and My Freedom* is suggested by the treatment of their relationship in William S. McFeely, *Frederick Douglass* (New York: Norton, 1991), pp. 184–86.

2. Benjamin Quarles, *Frederick Douglass* (Washington, D.C.: Association for the Study of Negro Life and History, 1948).

3. Dickson J. Preston was the first scholar to address the contradictions in the autobiography of Douglass. See Preston, *Frederick Douglass: The Maryland Years* (Baltimore: Johns Hopkins University Press, 1980). Preston's work inspired the psychological analysis of Allison Davis in *Leadership, Love and Aggression* (New York: Harcourt Brace Jovanovich, 1983). Henry Louis Gates in *Figures in Black: Words, Signs, and the Racial Self* (New York: Oxford University Press, 1987), correctly observes that "Preston has given us in his major biography a more three dimensional, more human Frederick Douglass than has any other biographer" (p. 114).

4. See the chapter "Political Nationalism and Cultural Assimilation," in Wilson J. Moses, *The Golden Age of Black Nationalism* (1978; rept. New York: Oxford University Press, 1988), pp. 15–31.

5. Mary Helen Washington quotes Valery Smith in Mary Helen Washington, ed., *Invented Lives: Narratives of Black Women, 1860–1960* (Garden City, N.Y.: Doubleday, 1987).

6. McFeely, *Frederick Douglass.*

7. Frederick Douglass, *The Life and Writings of Frederick Douglass*, ed., Philip S. Foner, 4 vols. (New York: International, 1950–55), vol. 4, p. 507.

8. McFeely, *Frederick Douglass*, pp. 185, 321–22.

9. Waldo Martin, *The Mind of Frederick Douglass* (Chapel Hill: University of North Carolina Press, 1984), p. 158.

10. Frederick Douglass to Elizabeth Cady Stanton, May 30, 1884, *Life and Writings*, vol. 4, p. 410.

11. Allison Davis, *Leadership, Love and Aggression* (New York: Harcourt Brace Jovanovich, 1983), pp. 17–101.

12. Davis, *Leadership, Love and Aggression*, p. 58. However, Davis interestingly sees Garrison as having confused and complex feelings toward Douglass, who, Davis suggests, played dual roles as both dominant and subordinate male figure in Garrison's unconscious thinking (p. 69).

13. Quoted in McFeely, *Frederick Douglass*, p. 121.

14. Robert C. Dick, *Black Protest: Issues and Tactics* (Westport, Conn.: Greenwood, 1974), p. 62.

15. Frederick Douglass quoted in William J. Simmons, *Men or Mark* (Cleveland: George M. Rewell, 1887), p. 1007.

16. For Douglass' meeting with the President, see David Brion Davis' review of William McFeely, *Frederick Douglass*, "The White World of Frederick Douglass," *The*

New York Review of Books, May 16, 1991, pp. 12–15. Delany told his biographer of a meeting with Abraham Lincoln. See Frank A. Rollin, *Life and Public Services of Martin R. Delany* (Boston: Lee and Shepard, 1868). Victor Ullman, in support of Delany's claim that he obtained an interview, cites a note to Secretary of War Stanton, in Lincoln's handwriting, but Ullman's idiosyncratic avoidance of footnotes makes the claim difficult to trace, and in any case the note simply reads: "Do not fail to have an interview with this most extraordinary and intelligent black man. A. Lincoln." See Victor Ullman, *Martin A. Delany The Beginnings of Black Nationalism* (Boston: Beacon, 1971), p. 294.

17. William Cheek and Aimee Lee Cheek, *John Mercer Langston and the Fight for Black Freedom, 1929–65* (Urbana: University of Illinois Press), pp. 154, 159.

18. Douglass, *Life and Writings,* vol. 4, p. 87.

19. Douglass, *Life and Writings,* vol. 2, p. 361.

20. The profound importance of Alexander Dumas's novel, *Georges, or the Planter of the Isle of France,* was brought to my attention by Prof. John Wright, who conducted a seminar at the W. E. B. Du Bois Institute on the subject of Dumas's racial consciousness during March, 1991.

21. Frederick Douglass, "African Civilization Society," *Douglass Monthly* (February, 1859): 19–20, is a response to the challenge of Henry Highland Garnet to defend himself with respect to African interest.

22. Douglass, *Life and Times.* This is a reprint of the revised edition of 1892 with a new introduction by Rayford W. Logan, pp. 14–24. For Douglass's defense of his marriage, see p. 534.

23. Frederick Douglass to Oliver Johnson, *Life and Writings,* vol.4, p. 427.

24. Frederick Douglass, "The Future of the Colored Race," *North American Review,* reprinted in Howard Brotz, ed., *Negro Social and Political Thought, 1850–1920: Representative Texts* (New York: Basic, 1966), pp. 316–17.

25. Frederick Douglass, "The Nation's Problem," a speech delivered before the Bethel Literary and Historical Society in Washington, D.C., April 16, 1889; this was originally published as a pamphlet (Washington, D.C., 1889). It is reprinted in Brotz, *Negro Social and Political Thought,* pp. 316–17.

SOURCES

Arnesen, Eric. "'Like Banquo's Ghosts, It Will Not Down': The Race Question and the American Railroad Brotherhoods, 1880–1920." *American Historical Review* 99.5 (December 1994): 1601–1633.

Eberhart, George M. "Stack Lee: The Man, the Music, and the Myth." *Popular Music and Society* 20.1 (Spring 1996): 1–69.

Fletcher, Marvin E. "The Black Bicycle Corps." *Arizona and the West* 16.3 (Autumn 1974): 219–233.

Gleijeses, Piero. "African Americans and the War against Spain." *The North Carolina Historical Review* 73.2 (April 1996): 184–214.

Hardwick, Kevin R. "Your Old Father Abe Lincoln Is Dead and Damned": Black Soldiers and the Memphis Race Riot of 1866." *Journal of Social History* 27.1 (Fall 1993): 109–128.

Hine, William C. "Black Politicians in Reconstruction Charleston, South Carolina: A Collective Study." *The Journal of Southern History* 49.4 (November 1983): 555–584.

Howard, Vicki. "The Courtship Letters of an African American Couple: Race, Gender, Class, and the Cult of True Womanhood." *Southwestern Historical Quarterly* 100.1 (July 1996): 64–80.

Kremer, Gary R. "For Justice and a Fee: James Milton Turner and the Cherokee Freedmen." *The Chronicles of Oklahoma* 58.4 (Winter 1980–1981): 376–391.

Kuyk, Betty M. "The African Derivation of Black Fraternal Orders in the United States." *Comparative Studies in Society and History* 25.4 (October 1983): 559–592.

Lichtenstein, Alex. "'A Constant Struggle between Interest and Humanity': Convict Labor in the Coal Mines of the New South." *Labor's Heritage* 7.2 (Fall 1995): 62–77.

Lowe, Richard. "The Freedmen's Bureau and Local Black Leadership." *The Journal of American History* (December 1993): 989–998.

Marable, Manning. "The Politics of Black Land Tenure, 1877–1915." *Labor History* 53.1 (January 1979): 143–152.

Moses, Wilson J. "Where Honor Is Due: Frederick Douglass as Representative Black Man." *Prospects* Vol. 17 (1993): 177–189.

Oldfield, J. R. "A High and Honorable Calling: Black Lawyers in South Carolina, 1868–1915." *Journal of American Studies* 23.3 (1989): 395–406.

Porter, Kenneth W. "Negro Labor in the Western Cattle Industry, 1866–1900." *Labor History* 10.3 (Summer 1969): 346–374.

Rousey, Dennis C. "Black Policemen in New Orleans during Reconstruction." *The Historian* 49.2 (February 1987): 223–243.

Savitt, Todd L. "Entering a White Profession: Black Physicians in the New South, 1880–1920." *Bulletin of the History of Medicine* 61.4 (Winter 1987): 507–540.

Wiegman, Robyn. "The Anatomy of Lynching." *Journal of the History of Sexuality* 3.3 (January 1993): 445–467.

Wiggins, David K. "Peter Jackson and the Elusive Heavyweight Championship: A Black Athlete's Struggle against the Late Nineteenth Century Color-Line." *Journal of Sport History* 12.2 (Summer 1985): 143–168.

Williams, Brett. "The Heroic Appeal of John Henry." In *John Henry: A Bio-Bibliography*, 110–126. Westport, Conn.: Greenwood Press, 1983.

SELECTED BIBLIOGRAPHY

Abbott, Richard H. "Massachusetts and the Recruitment of Southern Negroes." *Civil War History* 14.3 (1968): 197–210.

Adeleke, Tunde. "Black Biography in the Service of a Revolution: Martin R. Delany in Afro-American Historiography." *Biography: An Interdisciplinary Quarterly* 17.3 (1994): 248–267.

Akpan, M. B. "Alexander Crummell and His African 'Race-Work': An Assessment of His Contributions in Liberia to Africa's 'Redemption,' 1853–1873." *Historical Magazine of the Protestant Episcopal Church* 45.2 (1976): 177–200.

Allen, Ray. "African-American Sacred Quartet Singing in New York City." *New York Folklore* 14.3–4 (1988): 7–22.

Anderson, Jervis. "Black Heavies." *American Scholar* 47 (1978): 387–395.

Andrews, David. "The Fact(s) of Michael Jordan's Blackness: Excavating a Floating Racial Signifier." *Sociology of Sport Journal* 13.2 (1996): 125–158.

Bailey, Anne J. "A Texas Cavalry Raid: Reaction to Black Soldiers and Contrabands." *Civil War History* 35.2 (1989): 138–152.

Bailey, Ben E. "Music in the Life of a Free Black Man of Natchez." *Black Perspective in Music* 13.1 (1992): 3–12.

Banat, Gabriel. "Le Chevalier de Saint-Georges, Man of Music and Gentleman-at-Arms: The Life and Times of an Eighteenth-Century Prodigy." *Black Music Research Journal* 10.2 (1990): 177–212.

Barbour, George. "Early Black Flyers of Western Pennsylvania, 1906–1945." *Western Pennsylvania Historical Magazine* 69.2 (1986): 95–119.

Barr, Alwyn. "Black Legislators of Reconstruction Texas." *Civil War History* 32.4 (1986): 340–352.

Bartlett, Andrew. "Cecil Taylor, Identity Energy, and the Avant-Garde African American Body." *Perspectives of New Music* 33 (Summer 1995): 275–293.

Beaver, Harold. "Run, Nigger, Run: Adventures of Huckleberry Finn as a Fugitive Slave Narrative." *Journal of American Studies* 8.3 (1974): 339–361.

Belz, Herman. "Law, Politics, and Race in the Struggle for Equal Pay during the Civil War." *Civil War History* 22.3 (1976): 197–213.

Benedetto, Robert. "The Presbyterian Mission Press in Central Africa, 1890–1922." *Presbyterian History* 68.1 (1990): 55–69.

Berenson, William; Kirk Elifson; and Tandy Tollerson. "Preachers in Politics: A Study of Political Activism among the Black Ministry." *Journal of Black Studies* 6.4 (1976): 373–392.

Bergeron, Arthur W., Jr. "Free Men of Color in Grey." *Civil War History* 32.3 (1986): 247–255.

Bigsby, C. "The Divided Mind of James Baldwin." *Journal of American Studies* 13.3 (1979): 325–342.

Biles, Roger. "Robert R. Church, Jr. of Memphis: Black Republican Leader in the Age of Democratic Ascendency, 1928–1940." *Tennessee Historical Quarterly* 42.4 (1983): 362–382.

Bisher, Catherine. "Black Builders in Antebellum North Carolina." *North Carolina Historical Review* 6`.4 (1984): 423–461.

Blackett, R. "Fugitive Slaves in Britain: The Odyssey of William and Ellen Craft." *Journal of American Studies* 12.1 (1978): 41–62.

———. "William G. Allen: The Forgotten Professor." *Civil War History* 24.1 (1980): 39–52.

Blankenship, Kim. "Bringing Gender and Race In: U.S. Employment Discrimination Policy." *Gender and Society* 7.2 (1993): 205–226.

Bogle, Lorie. "On Our Way to the Promised Land: Black Migration from Arkansas to Oklahoma,1889–1893." *Chronicles of Oklahoma* 72.2 (1994): 160–177.

Boyd, Richard. "Violence and Sacrificial Displacement in Harriet Beecher Stowe's *Dred.*" *Arizona Quarterly* 50.2 (1994): 51–72.

Boyer, Horace Clarence. "Charles Albert Tindley: Progenitor of Black-American Gospel Music." *Black Perspective in Music* 11.2 (1983): 103–132.

Bruce, Dickson D., Jr. "Ancient Africa and the Early Black American Historians, 1883–1915." *American Quarterly* 36.5 (1984): 684–699.

———. "National Identity and African-American Colonization, 1773–1817." *Historian* 58.1 (1995): 15–28.

Bynum, Marjorie. "Thomas Washington Talley: A Pathmaker in African-American Folklore." *Tennessee Folklore Society Bulletin* 57.4 (1996): 154–165.

———. "Violence, Revolution, and the Cost of Freedom: John Brown and W.E.B. DuBois." *Boundary 2* 17.1 (1990): 304–330.

Campbell, Finley C. "Prophet of the Storm: Richard Wright and the Radical Tradition." *Phylon* 38.1 (1977): 9–23.

Campbell, Randolph B. "The Burden of Local Black Leadership during Reconstruction: A Research Note." *Civil War History* 39.2 (1993): 148–153.

Captain, Gwendolyn. "Enter Ladies and Gentlemen of Color: Gender, Sport, and the Ideal of African American Manhood and Womanhood during the Late Nineteenth and Early Twentieth Centuries." *Journal of Sport History* 18.1 (1991): 81–102.

Carney, Judith. "From Hands to Tutors: African Expertise in the South Carolina Rice Economy." *Agricultural History* 67.3 (1993): 1–30.

Carter, Marva Griffin. "In Retrospect: Roland Hayes–Expressor of the Soul in Song (1887–1977)." *Black Perspective in Music* 5.2 (1977): 188–220.

Cartwright, Joseph. "Black Legislators in Tennessee in the 1880's: A Case Study in Black Political Leadership." *Tennessee Historical Quarterly* 32.3 (1973): 265–284.

Cato, John David. "James Herman Robinson: Crossroads Africa and American Idealism, 1958–1972." *American Presbyterians* 68.2 (1990): 99–108.

Cecelski, David. "The Hidden World of Mullet Camps: African-American Architecture on the North Carolina Coast." *North Carolina Historical Review* 70.1 (1993): 1–13.

———. "The Shores of Freedom: The Maritime Underground Railroad in North Carolina, 1800–1861." *North Carolina Historical Review* 71.2 (1994): 175–206.

Cheatham, Wallace McClain. "Black Male Singers at the Metropolitan Opera." *Black Perspective in Music* 16.1 (1988): 4–19.

Cheek, William F. "John Mercer Langston: Black Protest Leader and Abolitionist." *Civil War History* 16.2 (1970): 101–120.

Chenier, Robert. "Moses Fleetwood Walker: Ohio's Own 'Jackie Robinson.'" *Northwest Ohio Quarterly* 65.1 (1993–94): 34–49.

Chenoweth, Lawrence. "The Rhetoric of Hope and Despair: A Study of the Jimi Hendrix Experience and the Jefferson Airplane." *American Quarterly* 23.1 (1971): 25–45.

Childs, John. "Concepts of Culture in Afro-Political Thought, 1890–1920." *Social Text* 2.1 (1981): 28–34.

Christian, Garna. "The Ordeal and the Prize: The 24th Infantry and Camp MacArthur." *Military Affairs* 50.2 (1986): 65–70.

Cimbala, Paul A. "Fortunate Bondsmen: Black 'Musicians' and their Role as an Antebellum Southern Plantation Slave Elite." *Southern Studies* 18.3 (1979): 291–303.

Cimprich, John, and Mainfort, Robert C., Jr., eds. "Fort Pillow Revisited: New Evidence about an Old Controversy." *Civil War History* 28.4 (1982): 293–306.

Clark, James. "Civil Rights Leader Harry T. Moore and the Ku Klux Klan in Florida." *Florida Historical Quarterly* 73.2 (1994): 164–183.

Clegg, Claude. "'A Splendid Type of Colored American': Charles Young and the Reorganization of the Liberian Frontier Force." *International Journal of African Historical Studies* 29.1 (1996): 47–70.

Clifton, James. "The Rice Driver: His Role in Slave Management." *South Carolina Historical Magazine* 82.4 (1981): 331–353.

Cooper, Arnold. "Booker T. Washington and William J. Edwards of Snow Hill Institute, 1893–1915." *Alabama Review* 40.2 (1987): 111–132.

Cosgrove, Stuart. "The Zoot-Suit and Style Warfare." *History Workshop* 18 (1984): 77–91.

Cripps, Thomas, and David Culbert. "The Negro Soldier (1944): Film Propaganda in Black and White." *American Quarterly* 31.5 (1979): 616–640.

Cummins, Roger. "'Lily-White' Juries on Trial: The Civil Rights Defense of Jesse Hollins." *Chronicles of Oklahoma* 63.2 (1985): 166–185.

Dailey, Maceo C. "Booker T. Washington and the Afro-American Realty Company." *Review of Black Political Economy* 8.2 (1978): 202–210.

Dalfiume, Richard. "The 'Forgotten Years' of the Negro Revolution." *Journal of American History* 55.1 (1968): 90–106.

Dann, Martin. "Black Populism: A Study of the Colored Farmers' Alliance through 1891." *Journal of Ethnic Studies* 2.3 (1974): 58–75.

Deburg, William. "Elite Slave Behaviour during the Civil War: Black Drivers and Foremen in Historiographical Perspective." *Southern Studies* 16.3 (1977): 253–269.

De Genova, Nick. "Gangster Rap and Nihilism in Black: Some Questions of Life and Death." *Social Text* 43 (1995): 89–132.

Dennis, Ruth E. "Social Stress and Mortality among Nonwhite Males." *Phylon* 38.3 (1977): 315–328.

Dibble, Ernest F. "Slave Rentals to the Military: Pensacola and the Gulf Coast." *Civil War History* 23.2 (1977): 101–113.

Dole, Carol. "The Return of the Father in Spielberg's *The Color Purple*." *Literature/Film Quarterly* 24.1 (1996): 12–16.

Douglas, Robert. "From Blues to Protest/Assertiveness: the Art of Romaire Bearden and John Coltrane." *International Review of African American Art* 8.2 (1988): 28–43.

———. "Black Males and Television: New Images versus Old Stereotypes." *Western Journal of Black Studies* 11.2 (1987): 69–73.

Early, Gerald. "The Black Intellectual and the Sport of Prizefighting." *Kenyon Review* 10.3 (1988): 102–117.

Eberhart, George M. "Stack Lee: The Man, the Music, and the Myth." *Popular Music and Society* 20.1 (1996): 1–69.

Erenberg, Lewis. "News from the Great Wide World: Duke Ellington, Count Basie, and Black Popular Music,1927–1943." *Prospects* 18 (1993): 483–506.

Evans, Robert, and Helen Evans. "Coping: Stressors and Depression among Middle Class African American Men." *Western Journal of Black Studies* 19.3 (1995): 211–217.

Farley, Foster. "The South Carolina Negro in the American Revolution,1775–1783." *South Carolina Historical Magazine* 79.2 (1978): 75–86.

Faust, Drew. "'Trying to Do a Man's Business': Slavery, Violence and Gender in the American Civil War." *Gender and History* 4.2 (1992): 197–214.

Feldman, Glenn. "Lynching in Alabama, 1889–1921." *Alabama Review* 48.2 (1995): 114–141.

Fenn, Elizabeth. "'A Perfect Equality Seemed to Reign': Slave Society and Jonkonnu." *North Carolina Historical Review* 65.2 (1988): 127–153.

Filene, Benjamin. "'Our Singing Country': John and Alan Lomax, Leadbelly, and the Construction of an American Past." *American Quarterly* 43.4 (1991): 602–624.

Finkle, Lee. "The Conservative Aims of Militant Rhetoric: Black Protest during World War II." *Journal of American History* 60.3 (1973): 693–713.

Fletcher, Marvin E. "The Black Bicycle Corps." *Arizona and the West* 16.3 (1974): 219–232.

———. "The Black Volunteers in the Spanish-American War." *Military Affairs* 38.2 (1974): 48–53.

Flusche, Michael. "On the Color Line: Charles Waddell Chesnutt." *North Carolina Historical Review* 53.1 (1976): 1–24.

Franklin, Clyde W. "Black Male–White Male Perceptual Conflict." *Western Journal of Black Studies* 6.1 (1982): 2–9.

———. "Conceptual and Logical Issues in Theory and Research Related to Black Masculinity." *Western Journal of Black Studies* 10.4 (1986): 161–166.

Freeman, Richard B. "The Relation of Criminal Activity to Black Youth Employment." *Review of Black Political Economy* 16.1/2 (1987): 99–108.

Fryer, Paul H. "Brown-Eyed Handsome Man: Chuck Berry and the Blues Tradition." *Phylon* 42.1 (1981): 60–72.

Gabbard, Krin. "Signifyin(g) the Phallus: *Mo' Better Blues* and the Representations of the Jazz Trumpet." *Cinema Journal* 32.1 (1992): 43–62.

Gaines, Kevin. "Assimilationist Minstrelsy as Racial Uplift Ideology: James D. Corrother's Literary Quest for Black Leadership." *American Quarterly* 45.3 (1993): 341–369.

Gaston, John C. "The Destruction of the Young Black Male: The Impact of Popular Culture and Organized Sports." *Journal of Black Studies* 16.4 (1986): 369–384.

Gatewood, Willard B., Jr. "Black Americans and the Boer War,1899–1902." *South Atlantic Quarterly* 75.2 (1976): 226–244.

———. "John Francis Cook, Antebellum Black Presbyterian." *American Presbyterians* 67.3 (1989): 221–230.

———. "'To Be Truly Free': Louis Sheridan and the Colonization of Liberia." *Civil War History* 29.4 (1983): 332–348.

Geary, Lynette G. "Jules Bledsoe: The Original 'Ol' Man River.'" *Black Perspective in Music* 17.1–2 (1989): 27–54.

Genovese, Eugene D. "Black Plantation Preachers in the Slave South." *Southern Studies* 2.3/4 (1991): 203–229.

Gibson, Donald B. "Strategies and Revisions of Self Representation in Booker T. Washington's Autobiographies." *American Quarterly* 45.3 (1993): 370–393.

Gill, Glenda E. "Careerist and Casualty: The Rise and Fall of Canada Lee." *Freedomways* 21.1 (1981): 15–27.

Gilman, Stuart. "Black Rebellion in the 1960's: Between Non-violence and Black Power." *Ethnicity* 8.4 (1981): 452–475.

Gilmore, Al-Tony. "The Myth, Legend, and Folklore of Joe Louis: The Impression of Sport on Society." *South Atlantic Quarterly* 82.3 (1983): 257–268.

Gleijeses, Piero. "African Americans and the War against Spain." *North Carolina Historical Review* 73.2 (1996): 184–214.

Gough, Robert. "Black Men and the Early New Jersey Militia." *New Jersey History* 88.4 (1970): 227–238.

Gower, Calvin W. "Edgar G. Brown, a Civil Rights Advocate in Franklin D. Roosevelt's 'Black Cabinet.'" *Western Journal of Black Studies* 8.2 (1984): 111–119.

Griffin, Joseph. "Calling, Naming, and Coming of Age in Ernest Gaines' 'A Gathering of Old Men.'" *Names* 40.2 (1992): 89–98.

Grim, Valerie. "Black Participation in the Farmers Home Administration and Agricultural Stabilization and Conservation Service,1964–1990." *Agricultural History* 70.2 (1996): 320–336.

Gross, Seymour. "History, Politics and Literature: The Myth of Nat Turner." *American Quarterly* 23.4 (1971): 487–518.

Grothaus, Larry. "'The Inevitable Mr. Gaines': The Long Struggle to Desegregate the University of Missouri, 1936–1950." *Arizona and the West* 26 (1984): 21–42.

Haller, Mark. "Policy Gambling, Entertainment, and the Emergence of Black Politics: Chicago from 1900–1940." *Journal of Social History* 24.4 (1991): 719–739.

Hardin, John A. "Green Pinckney Russell of Kentucky Normal and Industrial Institute for Colored Persons." *Journal of Black Studies* 25.5 (1995): 610–621.

Hardwick, Kevin. "'Your Old Father Abe Lincoln is Dead and Damned': Black Soldiers and the Memphis Race Riot of 1886." *Journal of Social History* 27.1 (1993): 109–128.

Harris, Robert, Jr. "Charleston's Free Afro-American Elite: The Brown Fellowship Society and the Humane Brotherhood." *South Carolina Historical Magazine* 82.4 (1981): 289–310.

Hartnett, Stephen. "Cultural Postmodernism and Bobby McFerrin: A Case Study of Musical Production as the Composition of Spectacle." *Cultural Critique* 16 (1990): 61–85.

Hay, Fred. "The Sacred/Profane Dialectic in Delta Blues: The Life and Lyrics of Sonny Boy Williamson." *Phylon* 48.4 (1987): 317–327

Hayles, Robert, and Ronald Perry. "Racial Equality in the American Naval Justice System: An Analysis of Incarceration Differentials." *Ethnic and Racial Studies* 4.1 (1981): 44–55.

Hine, Darlene Clark. "Carter G. Woodson, White Philanthropy and Negro Historiography." *History Teacher* 19.3 (1986): 405–425.

Hine, William C. "Black Politicians in Reconstruction Charleston, South Carolina: A Collective Study." *Journal of Southern History* 49.4 (1983): 555–584.

Hodes, Martha. "The Sexualization of Reconstruction Politics: White women and Black Men in the South after the Civil War." *Journal of the History of Sexuality* 3.3 (1993): 402–417.

Holland, Antonio,F. "Education over Politics: Nathan B. Young at Florida A&M College,1901–1923." *Agricultural History* 65.2 (1991): 131–148.

Holmlund, Christine. "Visible Difference and Flex Appeal: the Body, Sex, Sexuality, and Race in the Pumping Iron Films." *Cinema Journal* 28.4 (1989): 39–51.

Horton, James. "Freedom's Yoke: Gender Conventions among Antebellum Free Blacks." *Feminist Studies* 12.1 (1986): 50–76.

Horton, James Oliver, and Lois E. Horton. "Race and Class." *American Quarterly* 35.1–2 (1983): 155–168.

Howard, Vicki. "The Courtship Letters of an African American Couple: Race, Gender, Class, and the Cult of True Womanhood." *Southwestern Historical Quarterly* 100.1 (1996): 64–80.

Howland, Jacob. "Black Boy: A Story of Soul-Making and a Quest for the Real." *Phylon* 47.2 (1986): 117–127.

Hunter, Andrea, and James Davis. "Constructing Gender: An Exploration of Afro-American Men's Conceptions of Manhood." *Gender and Society* 6.3 (1992): 464–479.

Hyatt, Marshall. "'The Political Ned Negro': Neval Thomas, Civil Rights Ideologue." *Western Journal of Black Studies* 13.2 (1989): 92–102.

Inscoe, John. "Generation and Gender as Reflected in Carolina Slave Naming Practices: A Challenge to the Gutman Thesis." *South Carolina Historical Magazine* 94.4 (1993): 252–263.

Jackson, Kathryn. "LeRoi Jones and the New Black Writers of the Sixties." *Freedomways* 9.3 (1969): 232–247.

Jackson, Walter. "Between Socialism and Nationalism: The Young E. Franklin Frazier." *Reconstruction* 1.3 (1991): 124–134.

James, Portia. "Hubert H. Harrison and the New Negro Movement." *Western Journal of Black Studies* 13.2 (1989): 82–91.

Janken, Kenneth. "African-American Intellectuals Confront the 'Silent South': The *What the Negro Wants* Controversy." *North Carolina Historical Review* 70.2 (1993): 153–179.

JanMohamed, Abdul R. "Negating the Negation as a Form of Affirmation in Minority Discourse: The Construction of Richard Wright as Subject." *Cultural Critique: The Nature and Context of Minority Discourse* 2.7 (1987): 245–267.

Japtok, Martin. "Between 'Race' as Construct and 'Race' as Essence: The Autobiography of an Ex-Coloured Man." *Southern Literary Journal* 28.2 (1996): 33–47.

Jezierski, John. "Photographing the Lumber Boom: The Goodridge Brothers of Saginaw, Michigan (1863–1922)." *Michigan History* 64.6 (1980): 28–33.

Johnson, Charles. "The Army, the Negro and the Civilian Conservation Corps, 1933–1942." *Military Affairs* 36.3 (1972): 82–88.

Johnson, Victoria. "Polyphony and Cultural Expression: Interpreting Musical Traditions in *Do the Right Thing*." *Film Quarterly* 47.2 (1993–94): 18–29.

Jones, George. "The Black Hessians: Negroes Recruited by the Hessians in South Carolina and Other Colonies." *South Carolina Historical Magazine* 83.4 (1982): 287–302.

Jordan, William. "'The Damnable Dilemma': African-American Accommodation and Protest during World War I." *Journal of American History* 81.4 (1995): 1562–1590.

Judy, R. A. T. "On the Question of Nigga Authenticity." *Boundary 2* 21.3 (1994): 211–230.

Kahn, Robert M. "The Political Ideology of Martin Delany." *Journal of Black Studies* 14.4 (1984): 415–440.

Kelley, Robin. "'Comrades, Praise Gawd for Lenin and Them!': Ideology and Culture among Black Communists in Alabama, 1930–1935." *Science and Society* 52.1 (1988): 58–82.

King, Samantha. "The Politics of the Body and the Body Politic: Magic Johnson and the Ideology of Aids." *Sociology of Sport Journal* 10.3 (1993): 270–285.

Kremer, Gary R. "For Justice and a Fee: James Milton Turner and the Cherokee Freedmen." *Chronicles of Oklahoma* 58.41 (1980–81): 376–391.

Kuyk, Betty M. "The African Derivation of Black Fraternal Orders in the United States." *Comparative Studies in Society and History* 25.4 (1943): 559–592.

Lacey, Barbara E. "Visual Images of Blacks in Early American Imprints." *William and Mary Quarterly* 53.1 (1996): 137–180.

Lanning, Michael Lee. "Reconstruction and the Indian Wars." In Lanning, *The African-American Soldier: From Crispus Attucks to Colin Powell*, 62–81, 295–296. New Jersey: Carol publishing Group. 1997.

Larson, Tom. "The Effect of Discrimination and Segregation on Black Male Migration." *Review of Black Political Economy* 20.3 (1992): 53–74.

Lehman, Cynthia. "The Social and Political Views of Charles Chesnutt: Reflections on His Major Works." *Journal of Black Studies* 26.3 (1996): 275–286.

Levesque, George A. "Boston's Black Brahmin: Dr. John S. Rock." *Civil War History* 26.4 (1980): 326–346.

Lewis, Ronald. "Race and the United Mine Workers' Union in Tennessee: Selected Letters of William R. Riley, 1842–1845." *Tennessee Historical Quarterly* 36.4 (1977): 524–536.

Lichtenstein, Alex. "'A Constant Struggle between Interest and Humanity': Convict Labor in the Coal Mines of the New South." *Labor's Heritage* 7.2 (1995): 64–77.

Lindfors, Bernth. "'Nothing extenuate, nor set down aught in malice': New Biographical Information on Ira Aldridge." *African American Review* 28.3 (1994): 457–472.

Lindroth, Colette. "Spike Lee and the American Tradition." *Literature/Film Quarterly* 24.1 (1996): 26–30.

Littlefield, Daniel F., and Patricia Washington McGraw. "The Arkansas Freeman, 1869–1870–: Birth of the Black Press in Arkansas." *Phylon* 40.1 (1979): 75–85.

Lively, Adam. "Continuity and Radicalism in American Black Nationalist Thought, 1914–1929." *Journal of American Studies* 18.2 (1984): 207–236.

Logan, Frenise. "Black and Republican: Vicissitudes of a Minority Twice Over in the North Carolina House Of Representatives, 1876–1877." *North Carolina Historical Review* 61.3 (1984): 310–346.

MacMaster, Richard. "Henry Highland Garnet and the African Civilization Society." *Journal of Presbyterian History* 48.1 (1970): 95–112.

Mahiri, Jabari. "African American Males and Learning: What Discourse in Sports Offers Schooling." *Anthropology and Education* 25.3 (1994): 364–375.

Maloney, Thomas. "Degrees of Inequality: The Advance of Black Male Workers in the Northern Meat Packing and Steel Industries before World War II." *Social Science History* 19.1 (1995): 30–62.

Marable, Manning. "The Politics of Black Land Tenure." *Agricultural History* 53.1 (1979): 142–152.

Massood, Paula. "Mapping the Hood: The Genealogy of City Space in *Boyz N the Hood* and *Menace II Society*." *Cinema Journal* 35.2 (1996): 85–97.

Matthews, John M. "Jefferson Franklin Long: The Public Career of Georgia's First Black Congressman." *Phylon* 42.2 (1981): 145–156.

Mayberry, B. D. "The Tuskegee Movable School: A Unique Contribution to National and International Agriculture and Rural Development." *Agricultural History* 65.2 (1991): 85–104.

McCallum, Brenda. "Songs of Work and Songs of Worship: Sanctifying Black Unionism in the Southern City of Steel." *New York Folklore* 14.1–2 (1988): 9–33.

McGuire, Philip. "Judge William H. Hastie and Army Recruitment, 1940–1942." *Military Affairs* 42.2 (1978): 75–79.

McLean-Meyinese, Patricia, and Adell Brown, Jr. "Survival Strategies of Successful Black Farmers." *Review of Black Political Economy* 22.4 (1994): 73–82.

McMillen, Neil. "Perry W. Howard, Boss of Black-and-Tan Republicanism in Mississippi, 1924–1960." *Journal of Southern History* 48.2 (1982): 205–224.

McTighe, Michael. "Jesse Jackson and the Dilemmas of a Prophet in Politics." *Journal of Church and State* 32.3 (1989): 585–607.

Meier, August. "Benjamin Quarles and the Historiography of Black America." *Civil War History* 26.2 (1980): 101–116.

Miller, Ivor. "Night Train: The Power That Man Made." *New York Folklore* 17.1–2 (1991): 21–43.

Miller, Laura, and Charles Moskos. "Humanitarians or Warriors? Race, Gender, and Combat Status in Operation Restore Hope." *Armed Forces and Society* 21.4 (1995): 615–637.

Moore, Moses N. "Righteousness Exalts a Nation: Black Clergymen, Reform, and New School Presbyterianism." *American Presbyterians* 70.4 (1992): 222–238.

Mootry, Maria K. "J. Saunders Redding: A Case Study of the Black Intellectual." *Western Journal of Black Studies* 7.2 (1983): 62–67.

Mormino, Gary. "GI Joe Meets Jim Crow: Racial Violence and Reform in World War II Florida." *Florida Historical Quarterly* 73.1 (1994): 23–42.

Moses, Wilson. "Where Honor Is Due: Frederick Douglass as Representative Black Man." *Prospects* 17 (1993): 177–189.

Moses, Yolanda T. "Laurence Foster, a Black Anthropologist: His Life and Work." *Western Journal of Black Studies* 7.1 (1983): 36–42.

Nadell, James. "*Boyz n the Hood*: A Colonial Analysis." *Journal of Black Studies* 25.4 (1995): 447–463.

Naison, Mark. "Black Agrarian Radicalism in the Great Depression: The Threads of a Lost Tradition." *Journal of Ethnic Studies* (1973): 47–65.

Nelson, Bruce. "Organized Labor and the Struggle for Black Equality in Mobile during World War II." *Journal of American History* 80.3 (1993): 952–988.

Newton, Merlin Owen. "Rosco Jones and the Alabama Judicial Establishment." *Alabama Review* 48.2 (1995): 83–95.

Oja, Carol J. "'New Music' and the 'New Negro': The Background of William Grant Still's Afro-American Symphony." *Black Music Research Journal* 12.2 (1992): 145–170.

Oldfield, J. R. "A High and Honorable Calling: Black Lawyers in South Carolina,1868–1915." *Journal of American Studies* 23.3 (1989): 395–406.

Outland, Robert. "Slavery, Work, and the Geography of the North Carolina Naval Stores Industry,1835–1860." *Journal of Southern History* 62.1 (1996): 27–56.

Palmer, Annette. "The Politics of Race and War: Black American Soldiers in the Caribbean Theatre during the Second World War." *Military Affairs* 47.2 (1983): 59–62.

Park, Marlene. "Lynching and Antilynching: Art and Politics in the 1930's." *Prospects* 18 (1993): 311–365.

Patrick-Stamp, Leslie. "Numbers That Are Not New: African Americans in the Country's First Prison." *Pennsylvania Magazine* 119.1/2 (1995): 95–128.

Philips, Paul. "The Interracial Impact of Marshall Keeble, Black Evangelist, 1878–1968." *Tennessee Historical Quarterly* 36.1 (1977): 62–74.

Piliawsky, Monte. "The Impact of Black Mayors on the Black Community: The Case of New Orleans' Earnest Morial." *Review of Black Political Economy* 13.4 (1985): 5–24.

Pitre, Mergione. "The Economic Philosophy of Martin L. King, Jr." *Review of Black Political Economy* 9.2 (1979): 191–198.

Poe, William. "Lott Cary: Man of Purchased Freedom." *Church History* 39.1 (1970): 49–61.

Porter, Kenneth W. "Negro Labor in the Western Cattle Industry, 1866–1900." *Labor History* 10.3 (1969): 345–374.

Price, Hollis F., Jr. "The Cost of Male Subemployment in the Black Community." *Review of Black Political Economy* 6.2 (1976): 213–224.

Raboteau, Albert J. "Fire in the Bones: African-American Christianity and Autobiographical Reflection." *America* 170.18 (1994): 4–9.

Rachleff, Marshall, ed. "Economic Self Interest versus Racial Control: Mobile's Protest against the Jailing of Black Seamen." *Civil War History* 25.1 (1979): 84–88.

Ransby, Barbara, and Tracye Matthews. "Black Popular Culture and the Transcendence of Patriarchal Illusions." *Race and Class* 35.1 (1993): 57–68.

Redkey, Edwin S. "Black Chaplains in the Union Army." *Civil War History* 33.4 (1987): 331–350.

Reed, Merl. "The FEPC, the Black Worker, and the Southern Shipyards." *South Atlantic Quarterly* 74.4 (1975): 446–467.

Reich, Steven. "Soldiers of Democracy: Black Texans and the Fight for Citizenship, 1917–1921." *Journal of American History* 82.4 (1996): 1478–1385.

Richardson, Joe M. "'Labor Is Rest to Me Here in This the Lord's Vineyard': Hardy Mobley, Black Missionary during Reconstruction." *Southern Studies* 22.1 (1983): 5–20.

Riggs, Gayle D., and Lynn Dwyer. "Salary Discrimination by Black Males? Evidence from an Historically Black University." *American Journal of Economics and Sociology* 54.2 (1995): 231–238.

Riis, Thomas L. "Bob Cole: His Life and Legacy to Black Musical Theatre." *Black Perspective in Music* 13.2 (1985): 135–150.

Riss, Arthur. "Racial Essentialism and Family Values in *Uncle Tom's Cabin*." *American Quarterly* 46.4 (1994): 513–544.

Roberts, Randy. "Galveston's Jack Johnson: Flourishing in the Dark." *Southwestern Historical Quarterly* 87.1 (1983): 36–56.

Roberts, Rita. "Patriotism and Political Criticism: The Evolution of Political Consciousness in the Mind of a Black Revolutionary Soldier." *Eighteenth-Century Studies* 27.4 (1994): 569–614.

Rousey, Dennis C. "Black Policemen in New Orleans during Reconstruction." *Historian* 49.2 (1987): 223–243.

———. "Yellow Fever and Black Policemen in Memphis: A Post-Reconstruction Anomaly." *Journal of Southern History* 51.3 (1985): 357–374.

Rout, Leslie. "Some Post-war Developments in Jazz." *Midcontinent American Studies Journal* 9.2 (1968): 27–50.

Rubin Sarah, Ann. "Reflections on the Death of Emmett Till." *Southern Cultures* 2.1 (1996): 45–66

Rushdy, Ashraf. "The Properties of Desire: Forms of Slave Identity in Charles Johnson's *Middle Passage*." *Arizona Quarterly* 50.2 (1994): 72–108

Saillant, John. "The Black Body Erotic and the Republican Body Politic, 1790–1820." *Journal of the History of Sexuality* 5.3 (1995): 403–428.

Savitt, Todd L. "Entering a White Profession: Black Physicians in the New South, 1880–1920." *Bulletin of the History of Medicine* 61.4 (1987): 507–540.

Schubert, Frank. "The Suggs Affray: The Black Cavalry in the Johnson County War." *Western Historical Quarterly* 4.1 (1973): 57–68.

Schweninger, Loren. "James Rapier and the Negro Labor Movement, 1869–1872." *Alabama Review* 28.3 (1975): 185–201.

———. "John Carruthers Stanly and the Anomaly of Black Slaveholding." *North Carolina Historical Review* 67.2 (1990): 159–192.

———. "A Vanishing Breed: Black Farm Owners in the South, 1651–1982." *Agricultural History* 63.3 (1989): 41–61.

Shelden, Randall. "From Slave to Caste Society: Penal Changes in Tennessee, 1830–1915." *Tennessee Historical Quarterly* 38.4 (1979): 463–478.

Shepperson, George. "The Afro-American Contribution to African Studies." *Journal of American Studies* 8.3 (December 1974): 281–301.

Sherer, Robert G., Jr. "John William Beverly: Alabama's First Negro Historian." *Alabama Review* 26.3 (July 1973): 194–208.

Sitkoff, Harvard. "Racial Militancy and Interracial Violence in the Second World War." *Journal of American History* 58.3 (1971): 661–681.

Skinner, Robert. "The Black Man in the Literature of Labor." *Labor's Heritage* 1.3 (1989): 51–66.

Skotnes, Andor. "'Buy Where You Can Work': Boycotting for Jobs in African-American Baltimore, 1933–1934." *Journal of Social History* 27.4 (1994): 734–761.

Slotkin, Richard. "Narratives of Negro Crime in New England, 1675–1800." *American Quarterly* 25.1 (1973): 3–31.

Slovenz, Madeline. "'Rock the House': The Aesthetic Dimensions of Rap Music in New York City." *New York Folklore* 14.3–4 (1988): 151–163.

Smith, David. "Amiri Baraka and the Black Arts of Black Art." *Boundary 2* 15.1–2 (1986–87): 235–254.

Smith, Eric. "'Asking for Justice and Fair Play': African American State Legislators and Civil Rights in Early Twentieth-Century Pennsylvania." *Pennsylvania History* 63.2 (1996): 169–203.

Smith, Ronald. "The Paul Robeson–Jackie Robinson Saga and a Political Collision." *Journal of Sport History* 6.2 (1979): 5–27.

Smith, Thomas G. "Outside the Pale: The Exclusion of Blacks from the National Football League, 1934–1946." *Journal of Sport History* 15.3 (1988): 255–281.

Smith, Timothy. "Slavery and Theology: The Emergence of Black Christian Consciousness in Nineteenth-Century America." *Church History* 41.4 (December 1972): 497–512.

Sommers, Richard J. "The Dutch Gap Affair: Military Atrocities and Rights of Negro Soldiers." *Civil War History* 21.1 (1975): 51–64.

Southern, Eileen. "In Retrospect: Letters from W. C. Handy to William Grant Still." *Black Perspective in Music* 7.2 (1979): 197–235.

———. "In Retrospect: Letters from W. C. Handy to William Grant Still. Part 2." *Black Perspective in Music* 8.1 (1980): 63–119.

Spillers, Hortense. "The Crisis of the Negro Intellectual." *Boundary* 2 21.3 (1994): 64–116.

Staples, Robert. "Black Manhood in the 1970's: A Critical Look Back." *Black Scholar* 12.3 (1981): 2–9.

Stone, Albert E. "After Black Boy and Dusk of Dawn: Patterns in Recent Black Autobiography." *Phylon* 39.1 (1978): 18–34.

———. "The Return of Nat Turner in Sixties America." *Prospects* 12 (1987): 223–253.

Storhoff, Gary. "Reflections of Identity in *A Soldier's Story*." *Literature/Film Quarterly* 19.1 (1991): 21–26.

Swift, David E. "Black Presbyterian Attacks on Racism: Samuel Cornish, Theodore Wright and Their Contemporaries." *Presbyterian History* 51.4 (1973): 433–470.

Tausky, Curt, and William J. Wilson. "Work Attachment among Black Men." *Phylon* 32.1 (1971): 23–30.

TeSelle, Eugene. "The Nashville Institute and Roger Williams University: Benevolence, Paternalism, and Black Consciousness,1867–1910." *Tennessee Historical Quarterly* 41.4 (1982): 360–379.

Thorp, Daniel. "Chattel with a Soul: The Autobiography of a Moravian Slave." *Pennsylvania Magazine* 112.3 (1988): 433–451.

Trotman, C. James. "Matthew Anderson: Black Pastor, Churchman, and Social Reformer." *American Presbyterians* 66.1 (1988): 11–21.

Tyler, Bruce. "Black Jive and White Repression." *Journal of Ethnic Studies* 16.4 (1989): 31–66.

"'A Very Stern Discipline': An Interview with Ralph Ellison." *Harper's* (March 1967): 76–95.

Wade-Lewis, Margaret. "Lorenzo Dow Turner: Pioneer African-American Linguist." *Black Scholar* 21.4 (1991): 10–24.

Watson, Charles. "Portrayals of the Black and the Idea of Progress: Simms and Douglass." *Southern Studies* 20.4 (1981): 339–350.

Weeks, Louis. "Racism, World War I and the Christian Life: Francis J. Grimke in the Nation's Capital." *Journal of Presbyterian History* 51.4 (1973): 471–488.

Westwood, Howard C. "Captive Black Union Soldiers in Charleston–What to Do?" *Civil War History* 28.1 (1982): 28–44.

———. "The Cause and Consequence of a Union Black Soldier's Mutiny and Execution." *Civil War History* 31.3 (1985): 222–236.

———. "Mr. Smalls: A Slave No More." *Times* 25.3 (1986): 20–23, 28–31.

Whatley, Warren. "African-American Strikebreaking from the Civil War to the New Deal." *Social Science History* 17.4 (1993).

White, Frances. "Africa on My Mind: Gender, Counter Discourse and African-American Nationalism." *Journal of Women's History* 2.1 (1990): 73–97.

Whitman, Stephen. "Industrial Slavery at the Margin: The Maryland Chemical Works." *Journal of Southern History* 59.1 (1993): 31–62.

Wiegman, Robyn. "The Anatomy of Lynching." *Journal of the History of Sexuality* 3.3 (1993): 445–467.

Wiggins, David K. "'The Future of College Athletics Is at Stake': Black Athletes and Racial Turmoil on Three Predominantly White University Campuses, 1968–1972." *Journal of Sport History* 15.3 (1988): 204–333.

———. "'Great Speed but Little Stamina': The Historical Debate over Black Athletic Superiority." *Journal of Sport History* 16.2 (1989): 158–185.

———. "Peter Jackson and the Elusive Heavyweight Championship: A Black Athlete's Struggle against the Late Nineteenth Century Color-Line." *Journal of Sport History* 12.2 (1985): 143–168.

———. "Wendell Smith, the Pittsburgh *Courier-Journal* and the Campaign to Include Blacks in Organized Baseball,1933–1945." *Journal of Sport History* 10.2 (1983): 5–29.

Williams, Brett. "The Heroic Appeal of John Henry." In *John Henry: A Bibliography*, 110–126. Connecticut: Greenwood Press, 1983.

Williams, Donald R. "Job Characteristics and the Labor Force Participation Behavior of Black and White Male Youth." *Review of Black Political Economy* 18.2 (1989): 5–24.

Williams, Nudie. "The African Lion: George Napier Perkins, Lawyer, Politician, Editor." *Chronicles of Oklahoma* 70.4 (1992–93): 450–465.

———. "Black Men Who Wore the Star." *Chronicles of Oklahoma* 59.1 (1981): 83–90.

———. "The Black Press in Oklahoma: The Formative Years, 1889–1907." *Chronicles of Oklahoma* 61.3 (1983): 308–319.

———. "United States vs. Bass Reeves: Black Lawman on Trial." *Chronicles of Oklahoma* 68.2 (1990): 154–167.

Wilson, Dale. "Recipe for Failure: Major General Edward M. Almond and Preparation of the U.S. 2d Infantry Division for Combat in World War II." *Journal of Military History* 56.3 (1992): 473–479.

Wright, Beverly. "Ideological Change and Black Identity during Civil Rights Movements." *Western Journal of Black Studies* 5.3 (1981): 186–198.

Wright, George C. "The Billy Club and the Ballot: Police Intimidation of Blacks in Louisville, Kentucky, 1880–1930." *Southern Studies* 23.1 (1984): 20–41.

Wright, W. D. "The Thought and Leadership of Kelly Miller." *Phylon* 39.2 (1978): 180–191.

Wyatt-Brown, Bertram. "The Mask of Obedience: Male Slave Psychology in the Old South." *American Historical Review* 93 (1988): 1228–1252.

Wynes, Charles. "William Henry Heard: Politician, Diplomat, A.M.E. Churchman." *Southern Studies* 20.4 (1981): 384–393.

INDEX

EARNESTINE JENKINS is Assistant Professor of Art History in the Department of Art at the University of Memphis. She has published articles that have appeared in numerous books and journals, including *Milestones in Black American History* and *Aspects of Ethiopian Art*.

DARLENE CLARK HINE is John A. Hannah Professor of History at Michigan State University. She is co-editor of *Crossing Boundaries: Comparative History of Black People in Diaspora* and *More Than Chattel: Black Women and Slavery in the Americas*, co-author of *A Shining Thread of Hope: The History of Black Women in America*, and author of *Hine Sight: Black Women and the Reconstruction of American History*.